Mapping the Nation

Mapping the Nation

An Anthology of Indian Poetry in English, 1870–1920

Edited and with a Critical Introduction by
Sheshalatha Reddy

ANTHEM PRESS
LONDON · NEW YORK · DELHI

Anthem Press
An imprint of Wimbledon Publishing Company
www.anthempress.com

This edition first published in UK and USA 2013
by ANTHEM PRESS
75–76 Blackfriars Road, London SE1 8HA, UK
or PO Box 9779, London SW19 7ZG, UK
and
244 Madison Ave. #116, New York, NY 10016, USA

First published in hardback by Anthem Press in 2012

Introduction, editorial matter and selection © Sheshalatha Reddy 2013
The moral right of the authors has been asserted.

Cover image: "Bhārat patākā series – wealth segregatively concentrating | poverty entropically increasing," oil on canvas, 10 × 18 inches
© 2001 Kakoli Mitra; all rights reserved

All rights reserved. Without limiting the rights under copyright reserved above, no part of this publication may be reproduced, stored or introduced into a retrieval system, or transmitted, in any form or by any means (electronic, mechanical, photocopying, recording or otherwise), without the prior written permission of both the copyright owner and the above publisher of this book.

British Library Cataloguing-in-Publication Data
A catalogue record for this book is available from the British Library.

Library of Congress Cataloging-in-Publication Data
The Library of Congress has cataloged the hardcover edition as follows:
Mapping the nation : an anthology of Indian poetry in English, 1870–1920 / edited and with a critical introduction by Sheshalatha Reddy. – 1st ed.
p. cm.
Includes bibliographical references and index.
ISBN 978-0-85728-441-9 (hardback : alk. paper)
1. Indic poetry (English)–19th century. 2. Indic poetry (English)–20th century. I. Reddy, Sheshalatha.
PR9495.6.M37 2012
821'.8–dc23
2012009595

ISBN-13: 978 1 78308 044 1 (Pbk)
ISBN-10: 1 78308 044 2 (Pbk)

This title is also available as an ebook.

Contents

Acknowledgments	xv
Note on Transcription and Transliteration	xvii
Note on Abbreviations	xvii
Critical Introduction	xix

EAST

1. Shoshee Chunder Dutt ... 1
   A Vision of Sumeru, and Other Poems (Calcutta: 1878) ... 2
   - Address to the Ganges ... 2
   - My Native Land ... 6
   - Sonnets—India ... 9

2. Greece Chunder Dutt ... 10
   Cherry Stones (Calcutta: 1879) ... 10
   - XXVII. Sonnet (The Nepali Peasant) ... 10
   - XXX. Sonnet (Near Goa) ... 11
   - XLVII. Sonnet (1858) ... 12
   - LIV. Sonnet (Sacoontala) ... 12

3. Joteendro Mohun Tagore ... 13
   Flights of Fancy in Prose and Verse (Calcutta: 1881) ... 13
   - The Rajpootnee's Song ... 13
   - Sonnet to the Kokil ... 14
   - Song ... 15
   - The Dewallee, or The Feast of Light ... 16
   - Moonlight on the River ... 17
   - Sonnet to India ... 17
   - The Hindu Widow's Lament ... 18

4. Avadh Behari Lall ... 19
   The Irish Home Rule Bill, a poetical pamphlet (Calcutta: 1893) ... 19
   - The Irish Home Rule Bill, a poetical pamphlet ... 19
   Behar, and other poems (Calcutta: 1898) ... 24
   - An Epistle to the Right Hon'ble Alfred Lord Tennyson, Poet-Laureate, England ... 24

5. Romesh Chunder Dutt ... 26
   Reminiscences of a Workman's Life (Calcutta: 1896) ... 27
   - The Exile ... 27
   - Home ... 28
   - Lines on India ... 29
   - Lines on Ireland ... 30
   - Autumn-Night in a Bengal Rice-Field ... 32

6.	Lala Prasanna Kumar Dey	39
	Indian Bouquet (Calcutta: 1906)	39
	– War	39
	– Svami Vivekananda at Chicago	40
7.	A. S. H. Hussain	41
	Loyal Leaves (Calcutta: 1911)	42
	– Ode for her Imperial Majesty Queen Victoria's Golden Jubilee	42
	The Voice of Islam and other poems (Calcutta: 1914)	47
	– The Voice of Islam	47
8.	Charu Chandra Bose	60
	A Voice from Bengal: Welcome Address to Their Majesties Landed in India (Calcutta: 1912)	61
	– Welcome Address to Their Majesties landed in India	61
9.	Nanikram Vasanmal Thadani	62
	The Triumph of Delhi and Other Poems (Calcutta: 1916)	62
	– The Triumph of Delhi	62
10.	Ram Sharma	74
	The Poetical Works of Ram Sharma (Calcutta: 1919)	75
	– Song of the Indian Conservative	75
	– An Old Indian Melody	76
	– The Song of the Tirhoot Planters	77
	– The Anglo-Indian War-Cry, or Bluster *in Excelsis*	78
	– India's Vindication of Lord Ripon and her Farewell	80
	– Ode on the Meeting of the Congress at Allahabad on the 26th December 1888	85
	– India to Britain	89
	– To Indian Patriots	89
	– Bande Mataram	90

WEST

1.	Behramji Merwanji Malabari	93
	The Indian Muse in English Garb (Bombay: 1876)	94
	– "The dream of my youth" H. R. H. the Prince of Wales	94
	– The Stages of a Hindu Female Life	95
	– To the Missionaries of Faith	98
	– Time of Famine	100
	– The British Character	101
	– A Protest	102
2.	Cowasji Nowrosji Vesuvala	104
	Courting the Muse: being a Collection of Poems (Bombay: 1879)	105
	– True Indian Opinion, or Native Croakers	105
	– Sonnet: Bombay Harbour	130

3.	Aurobindo Ghose	130
	Songs to Myrtilla and other poems (Baroda: 1895)	131
	– O Coil, Coil	131
	– Charles Stewart Parnell	132
	– Lines on Ireland	132
	– Saraswati with the Lotus	136
4.	S. D. Saklatvala	136
	An Appeal for Peace, some verses (Bombay: 1910)	137
	– [Excerpts]	
5.	C. R. Doraswami Naidu	141
	Heart Buds, poems (Ahmedabad: 1914)	142
	– Foreword	142
	– To the Motherland	144
	– The Taj Mahal – Agra	148
	– To K. V. M., A Vision – Young India	148
6.	Jamasp Phiroze Dastur	150
	The Temple of Justice [a poem in praise of justice] (Bombay: 1916)	150
	– The Temple of Justice	150
7.	Rustam B. Paymaster	153
	Navroziana, or The Dawn of a New Era: Being Poems on Mr. Dadabhai Naoroji and Other Friends of India, with "The Voice of the East on the Great War" (Bombay: 1917)	153
	– Mr. Dadabhai Naoroji, An Ode of Welcome	153
	– Mr. Dadabhai Naoroji, On His 79th Birthday	155
	– Dadabhai Naoroji	158
	– The Late Hon. Mr. G. K. Gokhale, C. I. E.	159
	– Lord Hardinge	160
	– The Secret of a Successful Rule	165
	– The Parsi New Year's Day	166

NORTH

1.	Babu S. C. Dutt [Shoshee Chunder Dutt]	167
	Last Moments of Pratapa (Lahore: 1893)	168
	– Last Moments of Pratapa	168
2.	Bipin Bihari Bose	172
	Congress Songs and Ballads (Lucknow: 1899)	173
	– "Mother and Mother-Country are more estimable than Heaven itself"	173
	– The Congress-man's Confession	175

3. Sir Mian Muhammad Shafi   180
    Poems (Lahore: 1907)   181
    – To a Chinar-Tree   181
    – The Sirinagar Flood and the Dal Lake   182
    – On Entering the Kashmere Valley   185
    – On the Occasion of Queen Victoria's Diamond Jubilee   185
    – To Delhi   186
    – The Rise and Fall of Islam   187
    – To India!   191
    – "To my mother"   191

4. Tej Shankar Kochak [a "Georgian Brahmin"]   192
    *Oriental Welcome to Their Most Gracious Majesties the
    King-Emperor and the Queen-Empress* (Cawnpore: 1911)   193
    – [Excerpts]

5. Sushila Harkishen Lal   196
    Stray Thoughts (Lahore: 1918)   196
    – Dreams   196

SOUTH

1. R. Sivasankara Pandiya   199
    The Empress of India and Other Poems (Madras: 1888)   200
    – Empress of India and Indian Poets   200
    – The University of Madras   202

2. Krupabai Satthianadhan   203
    Miscellaneous Writings of Krupabai Satthianadhan (Madras: 1896)   203
    – Recollections of Childhood   203
    – Social Intercourse between Europeans and Natives   205

3. M.V. Venkatasubba Aiyar   206
    Ventures in Verse (Madras: 1899)   206
    – To the Land of My Birth   206
    – Sonnets, I. Faith   207
    – Ravana's Doom   207

4. M. Dinakara   212
    *A Ballad of the Boer War…in Celebration of the Prowess
    of the British Army* (Ramnad: 1902)   213
    – The Gathering   213
    – How Great Britain was Regenerated and Became 'Greater Britain'   214
    – A Tribute to the Gallant Boers, Who Fought, and Fell,
      for their Country   217

5.	Chilkur C. S. Narsimha Row	217
	The Poetical Works of Chilkur C. S. Nar Simha Row (Ellore: 1911)	218
	– The Greatest Need of India	218
	– Madras or Rome, where's thy home?	220
	– Vande Mataram	221
	– The grand old man of India	222
	– India	225
6.	C. Lakshminarayana Aiyer	233
	Poems (Tinnevelly: 1914)	233
	– To the Lord Bhupalaswami, Srivaikuntam	233
	– To His Gracious Majesty George V Emperor of India	233
	– Coronation Song	234
	– The New Year, 1912	234
7.	P. Seshadri	236
	Bilhana: An Indian Romance, Adapted from Sanskrit (Madras: 1914)	237
	– Bilhana	237
	Sonnets (Madras: 1914)	255
	– Toru Dutt	255
	– The Marquis of Ripon	255
	– Victoria	256
	– Romesh Chunder Dutt	256
	Champak Leaves (Madras: 1919, originally published 1915)	257
	– The Sacrifice	257
	– Jahangir and the Little Children	257
	– Widowed	258
	– Queen Tissarakshita's Jealousy	258
	– Lali and Majnun	259
	– Indumathi's Death	260
	– A Sister's Wail	260
	– The Exile	261
	– The Rani of Ganore	262
	– Anakarli	262
8.	Ardeshir Framji Khabardar	263
	The Silken Tassel (Madras: 1918)	264
	– An Indian Funeral Song	264
	– To India	264
	– The Patriot	265
9.	Rabindranath Tagore	266
	The Gift of the Poet Laureate of India to National Education Week, 1918 (Adyar: 1918)	266

10.	Harindranath Chattopadhyay	267
	The Feast of Youth (Madras: 1918)	268
	– The Hour of Rest	268
	– Sufi Worship	269
	The Coloured Garden (Madras: 1919)	269
	– The Coloured Country	269
	– Pride	270
	– A Sad Thing	271
11.	Aurobindo Ghose	271
	Baji Prabhou, a poem (Pondicherry: 1922, originally published 1909)	272
	– Baji Prabhou	272
12.	Nizamat Jung	284
	Poems (Hyderabad: 1954)	285
	– Ode, The Awakening of the East	285
	– The Imperial Coronation at Delhi	287
	– India to England, 1914	291
	– On the admission of Indians to the British Army	292
	– In Memoriam	293

ABROAD

1.	Govin Chunder Dutt, et al.	295
	The Dutt Family Album (London: 1870)	296
	– Home	296
	– Lines (Written while on a Visit to Kalighat)	297
	– Vizagapatam	299
	– Madras	300
2.	Toru Dutt	302
	Ancient Ballads and Legends of Hindustan (London: 1882)	302
	– Savitri	302
	– Sîta	328
3.	Hamid Ali Khan	329
	A Farewell to London: The Story of the Slave and the Nose-Ring (London: 1885, 2nd ed.)	329
	– A Farewell to London	329
	– The Slave and the Nose-Ring	332
4.	Dejen L. Roy	339
	The Lyrics of Ind (London: 1886)	340
	– The Land of the Sun	340
	– The Island	341

5.	Greece Chunder Dutt	342
	Cherry Blossoms (London: 1887)	342
	– The Soonderbuns	342
	– The Neem Tree	345
	– In the Bush	346
	– The Taj Mahal	348
	– On the Day of Lord Ripon's Departure from Calcutta	349
	– Sita	350
6.	T. (Pillai) Ramakrishna	351
	Tales of Ind, and Other Poems (London: 1896, 2nd ed.)	352
	– Lord Tennyson	352
	– Seeta and Rama, A Tale of the Indian Famine	352
7.	Manmohan Ghose	357
	Love Songs and Elegies (London: 1898)	357
	– The Exile	357
	Songs of Love and Death (Oxford: 1926)	362
	– London	362
	– Home-Thoughts	362
	– Song of Britannia	363
	– On the Centenary of the Presidency College	366
8.	Romesh Chunder Dutt	368
	Ramayana: the Epic of Rama, Prince of India, Condensed into English Verse, trans. (London: 1899)	369
	– Recital of the Ramayana	369
9.	Hary Sing Gour	371
	Stepping Westward and Other Poems (London: 1890)	371
	– Stepping Westward, or Emigrants to the West	371
10.	Sarojini Naidu	377
	The Golden Threshold (London: 1905)	377
	– To India	377
	– Nightfall in the City of Hyderabad	378
	– Ode to H. H. The Nizam of Hyderabad	378
	The Broken Wing: Songs of Love, Death & Destiny, 1915–1916 (London: 1917)	380
	– Awake!	380
	– The Gift of India	381

11.	Roby Datta	381
	Echoes from East and West (Cambridge: 1909)	382
	– The Grief of Ravan	382
	– The Fair Martyrs	387
	– The Sworn Hero	388
	– Piyadasi	389
	– On Tibet	390
	– To Britain	391
12.	Hasan Shahid Suhrawardy	392
	Faded Leaves, a collection of poems (London: 1910)	392
	– Dedication	392
	– The Indian Maid's Lament	393
	– Swinburne	394
13.	Rabindranath Tagore	394
	Gardener, trans. by author (London: 1913)	395
	– [Excerpts]	
	Fruit-Gathering, trans. by author (London: 1916)	395
	– [Excerpts]	
14.	Peshoton Sorabji Goolbai Dubash	398
	Rationalistic and Other Poems (London: 1917)	398
	– Britannia and Mother Hind	398
15.	Śrî Ânanda Āchārya	412
	Snow-birds (London: 1919)	412
	– LXXXII. Ode on the Rishis, the Dārsanikas, and the Sannyāsins of India	412

APPENDICES

1. Indian Poets on their Poetry — 415
    a. "Preface" by Behramji Merwanji Malabari, from *The Indian Muse in English Garb* (Bombay: 1876) — 415
    b. "Prefaces" and "Appendix" by Hamid Ali Khan, from *A Farewell to London: The Story of the Slave and the Nose-Ring* (London: 1885, 2nd ed.) — 417
    c. "Translator's Epilogue" by Romesh Chunder Dutt, from *Maha-Bharata: Epic of the Bharatas, Condensed into English Verse* (London: 1898) — 421
    d. "Preface" by Avadh Behari Lall, from *Behar, and other poems* (Calcutta: 1898) — 429
    e. "Preface" by Roby Datta, from *Echoes from East and West* (Cambridge: 1909) — 431

2. British Poets/Critics on Indian Poets 433
   a. "Introductory Memoir" by Edmund Gosse for Toru Dutt's
      Ancient Ballads and Legends of Hindustan (London: 1882) 433
   b. "Introduction" by Arthur Symons for Sarojini Naidu's
      The Golden Threshold (London: 1905) 439
   c. "Introductory Memoir" by Laurence Binyon for Manmohan
      Ghose's *Songs of Love and Death* (Oxford: 1926) 443
   d. "Introduction" by W. B. Yeats for Rabindranath Tagore's
      Gitanjali (London: 1912) 448

3. "Preface," "Introduction" and poems from *A Garland of Ceylon Verse,
   1837–1897* (Columbo: 1897), edited and with an introduction and
   notes by Isaac Tambyah 452

Bibliography 459
Index of Titles 464
Index of Authors 467

Acknowledgments

I would like to thank Yopie Prins, Martha Vicinus, Lucy Hartley, and Christy Merrill for their encouragement and invaluable advice, especially during the initial stages of this project. The collections at the Library of Congress in Washington DC, the British Library in London, and at the National Library in Kolkata are truly astounding and I am grateful for the help, guidance, and patience of the staff and librarians of all three institutions, especially G. Kumarappa of the National Library. Although I never had the good fortune to correspond with or meet her, I want to acknowledge the late Irene Joshi, former librarian at the University of Washington. Her masterful and comprehensive bibliographies, especially of pre-independence poetry in India, have been an invaluable resource in culling material for this anthology. It is through her work in the archives, that this anthology can exist.

A summer faculty fellowship granted by the University of Mary Washington enabled me to undertake a portion of the further archival work necessary to complete this project. My colleagues in the English, Linguistics, and Communication Department at the University of Mary Washington, including Antonio Barrenechea, Claudia Emerson, Paul Fallon, Chris Foss, James Harding, Terry Kennedy, Ben LaBreche, Janie Lee, Eric Lorentzen, Maya Mathur, Marie McAllister, Tim O'Donnell, Judith Parker, Anand Rao, Colin Rafferty, Gary Richards, Mary Rigsby, Warren Rochelle, Mara Scanlon, Constance Smith, Danny Tweedy, Steve Watkins, and Zach Whalen are gratefully acknowledged for their always warm support and encouragement.

I am thankful for the guidance of Janka Romero and Tej P. S. Sood of Anthem Press for guiding this project into publication as well as the anonymous reviewers for their comments. I am also grateful to Rob Reddick and the editorial team at Anthem for their much-needed attention to detail in the final stages of the manuscript process.

And, finally, I would also like to thank my friends and fellow researchers Ji-Hyae Park, Alice Weinreb, Elspeth Healey, Lauren LaFauci, Rebecca Smith, Olivera Jokic, Emil Kerenji and Kakoli Mitra, especially for her art which graces the cover of this volume. My debt to my family is too deep to fathom so I am aware I only glide across the surface in acknowledging my sister Veena, Smitha and Alex, Varun and Christy, Vidya and Sujay, Madhu and Namitha and Rohan and Kushi, and all my family in India, especially my aunt and uncle, Suma and Rajana Reddy, whose presence upon my arrival in Calcutta for my first research trip so many years ago meant so much and the Doshi family, who generously welcomed me into their home and their lives. This anthology is dedicated to my parents, Vanamala and S. N. Srinivasa Reddy.

I would like to offer my thanks to Mr. Rashid Suhrawardy for permission to reprint the poems of Hasan Shahid Suhrawardy from *Faded Leaves* (London: J. M. Baxter & Co., 1910).

Every effort has been made to trace holders of copyright material. The editor would be grateful to hear from any such holders who have not been contacted.

Note on Transcription and Transliteration

With the exception of a few cases, I have always included the first edition, or date of original publication, of each poet's work. Annotations to the poems included in the original text have been reproduced in the footnotes of this anthology and placed in brackets with a brief indication of who has written the annotation: either the author [Poet's Note] or occasionally, the editor [Editor's Note]. All other annotations are my own.

In order to remain as faithful as possible to the original publication in transcribing these poems, I have kept the original spelling and punctuation of the texts. I have also kept the poet's own designation and spelling of their name, usually anglicized, as it appears in their work.

In my own editorializing in the critical introduction, chapter and biographical introductions, and annotations, all words or terms in italics are either "foreign" words from the Sanskrit, Bengali, Persian, Arabic, French, etc. or titles of other works. I have not included diacritical marks for foreign words. All proper names, whatever their origin, are not placed in italics. All geographical locations both manmade and natural – such as towns, cities, regions, mountains, lakes – are referred to by their common designation under colonial rule. Thus the three presidency towns of Chennai, Kolkata, and Mumbai are referred to as Madras, Calcutta, and Bombay. When I do refer to a location as it is now known in the twenty-first century, I refer to it as "modern-day" – for example, the "modern-day state of Karnataka."

Note on Abbreviations

OED   *Oxford English Dictionary*, 2nd ed., http://www.dictionary.oed.com/ (accessed 19 June 2010).

ArchNet *ArchNet: Islamic Architecture Community*, http://archnet.org/library/sites (accessed 19 June 2010).

Critical Introduction

Mapping "India"

What *was* "India" in the nineteenth and early twentieth centuries prior to "its" official recognition as a nation-state in August 1947 at the moment of independence? The spatial and temporal markers defining any nation-state as a geographical and historical entity and as an ideological construct are in a constant process of redefinition. Benedict Anderson argues in his seminal study on nationalism, *Imagined Communities* that all nations in the modern era are constituted by the fiction that their identities have long been established even as they are in perpetual negotiation.[1] As Sandra Bermann notes, work by Anderson as well as Timothy Brennan, Partha Chatterjee, Neil Lazarus, Bruce Robbins, Edward Said, Gayatri Chakravorty Spivak, Gauri Viswanathan, Robert J. C. Young and others has shown "that nationhood is better described as a never-ending, conflictual process driven by changing cultural practices… a 'nation' need not be synonymous with a 'state.'"[2] In other words, even though the modern era has been defined by the constitution of the nation-state, national practices can exist without the support of the state.

Before independence, the difficulty in defining "India" was not only an anxiety voiced by the colonizers in their perpetual need to catalogue, classify, and document the other,[3] but one also explored by those who identified themselves as "Indian." The extent and variety of the geographical space that constituted Great Britain's Indian empire, the British Raj, magnified this anxiety. The Raj included what are now the nation-states of India (including the Andaman Islands, used by the British as a penal colony during the nineteenth century)[4] as well as Pakistan, Bangladesh, and Burma (modern-day Myanmar). Ceylon (modern-day Sri Lanka), Nepal, Bhutan, and the Maldives entered into separate agreements with the British government. This wide swathe of territory is now delineated by the term "South Asia," which also sometimes additionally includes Afghanistan and Iran. Following both partition in 1947 when Pakistan and India emerged, bloody and bruised, as separate nation-states and the Bangladesh Liberation War of 1971 when Bangladesh declared its independence from Pakistan, the subcontinent has become an amalgamation of nation-states. Yet from 1870 to 1920, under British colonialism, the poets included in this anthology largely identified themselves as "Indian" and pledged allegiance both to "India" and the British Empire. Thus, I include poets from regions now officially beyond the borders of the modern nation-state of India to illustrate the way in which the physical and imaginative borders of national belonging are redrawn over time.

---

1 Benedict Anderson, *Imagined Communities*, rev. ed. (New York: Verso, 2000).
2 Sandra Bermann and Michael Wood, eds, *Nation, Language, and the Ethics of Translation* (Princeton: Princeton University Press, 2005), 3.
3 See Mathew Edney, *Mapping an Empire: the Geographical Construction of British India, 1765–1843* (Chicago: University of Chicago Press, 1990), 2. Edney writes of British East India Company rule: "the geographers created and defined the spatial image of the Company's empire. The maps came to define the empire itself, to give it territorial integrity and its basic existence. The empire exists because it can be mapped; the meaning of empire is inscribed into each map."
4 Certain regions of the subcontinent were under the control of nominally independent princely states, which entered into separate treaties with the British government Barbara N. Ramusack, *The Indian Princes and Their States* (Cambridge: Cambridge University Press, 2004).

Indianness was rehearsed explicitly and implicitly by elites in a variety of literature including poetry, novels, newspaper articles, political pamphlets, magazine columns, diaries, essays, histories, and economic and sociological tracts in a time of empire. These material artifacts, which exist for us in the archives now in varying states of preservation and impending obsolescence, give material existence to an Indian history, or pre-history (if "India" only comes into existence on the birthdate of its independence). *Mapping the Nation: An Anthology of Indian Poetry in English, 1870–1920* focuses specifically on the imagining of India in poetry written in English by those who identified themselves as Indians from what was once Britain's Indian empire during a 50-year period, which witnessed both the height of British imperial rhetoric[5] as well as the beginning of Indian nationalism. As Manu Goswami has argued, "from the moment of its emergence in the 1870s, nationalist discourse both presupposed an already given national space and sought to institute a spatial coincidence between the imagined nation's history, culture, people, and economy. The reconfiguration of colonial space as national space in the late nineteenth century represented a radical socio-epistemological break from received conceptions of historicity, space, political subjectivity, and sovereignty."[6] This nation, as Goswami and other scholars such as Romilia Thapar and Gyan Prakash have shown, was (and continues to be) often defined as Hindu. Yet a number of poets who identified as Muslim, Parsi, Christian, and Hindu resisted and questioned this exclusion of other religious groups from the historical narrative of "India" in and through their poetry as evidenced in this anthology.

Numerous scholars have produced rich and complex studies of literary production in English from Bengal. Calcutta, as the seat of East India Company rule and later British Empire administration for several decades, is extraordinarily rich in English-language literature produced as a result of this contact zone. But such a focus on the Bengali Renaissance of the nineteenth and early twentieth centuries has somewhat obscured cultural production from other regions of India. In contrast, this anthology "maps" India both as an idea within the poetry and as the actual location in which the poetry was produced and circulated and so includes poetry published in various geographical nodal points on the subcontinent (in what are now the nation-states of India, Pakistan, and Bangladesh) as well as in the imperial metropole of Great Britain, London, where many English-language poets from India traveled, studied, and hoped to be published. After all, while "[a]n international border is rigorous…literary borders are porous, ill-defined, and overlapping."[7] The poetry included in this anthology defines

---

5 See John MacKenzie, *Propaganda and Empire* (Manchester: Manchester University Press, 1984), 3–5. MacKenzie notes that "[r]everence for the monarchy developed only from the late 1870s, and when it did it was closely bound up with the monarch's imperial role," which was formalized in 1877 when Queen Victoria was declared Empress of India. During this period, the monarch's new role as empress came to be seen as an opportunity for both "commercial exploitation" and spectacle since "imperialism made spectacular theatre, with the monarchy its gorgeously opulent centerpiece."

6 Manu Goswami, *Producing India: from Colonial Economy to National Space* (Chicago: University of Chicago Press, 2004), 7.

7 Arvind Krishna Mehrotra, "Editor's Preface" in *A History of Indian Literature in English*, ed. Arvind Krishna Mehrotra (London: Hurst and Company, 2003), xx.

India in a number of ways: against Britain in loyalty and/or critique; in "exile" in or memory of England; through a reconstructed past, whether Oriental or regional; through satirical or earnest commentaries upon contemporary politics; through descriptions of the subcontinent's landscape and scenery; through depictions of the subcontinent's various inhabitants, their customs, cultures, and religions; and through odes to British and Indian literary figures and politicians. In other words, the diversity of India's imagining by her poets corresponded only to the diversity of her inhabitants and geography.

I divide the table of contents according to broadly based geographical areas, which I designate by the headings East, West, South, North and Abroad. These areas correspond to the British-administered presidencies of Calcutta, Bombay, and Madras and the imperial capital of Delhi (which was anointed as capital only in 1912 when it was moved from Calcutta) as well as the "center" of these imperial "outposts," London. These cities of imperial power witnessed the establishment, both in support of and in reaction to such power, of various political, social, economic, and cultural institutions, including publishing houses and printing presses, all marked by varying degrees of prestige and profit. The section headings East, West, North, South, and Abroad simultaneously acknowledge the influence and power of the three presidencies of Calcutta, Bombay, and Madras as well as of Delhi and London even while resisting complete identification with these cities and thus with the imperial enterprise – in part by including the vast array of materials published in the surrounding regions of each of these urban areas.

I place poets within sections based on the original region of publication of the work included rather than on the poet's birthplace or place of regional identification. Some poets, such as Aurobindo Ghose and Rabindranath Tagore for example, appear in two sections since their included works were published in two different regions. I have organized poets according to region of publication for three reasons. First, the poets studied here are by no means bound by their region of birth or settlement since their affiliations were often multiple: to regions in which they worked, studied, or visited; to caste or socio-economic class; to religious and/or ethnic groups; to educational status; to profession; to family lineage; to gender; to nation; to the British. Second, organizing writers in this way emphasizes the material processes of publication, circulation, and consumption since the region of printing was often where the work would have been most heavily, or even exclusively, distributed and read. And third, such a grouping illustrates the rich variety of poetry published around the subcontinent and the way in which this poetry can be read as a material manifestation of the idea or place known as "India" and how that idea may have taken on subtle nuances of meaning in different parts of the subcontinent. While critical works focusing on particular regions are crucial in understanding the cultural, historical, social, economic, and political conditions of those regions, studying the works of various regions in conjunction with one another can lay bare larger concerns, which during the 50-year period under consideration here are also often the concerns of an incipient nation.

Within each section heading, poets are arranged in chronological order based on the date of publication of the work included. In those cases in which excerpts from more than one collection by a poet are included in a single section, the poet is placed in the chronology relative to the other poets in that section in order of the publication date of their earliest work. Thus, the dates included in the table of contents are not the usual biographical dates but the dates of publication of the first (and often only) edition of their work, emphasizing each text's publication history both in space as well as time. This ordering also highlights the shifts in generic forms, themes, and motifs that occurred during the late nineteenth and early twentieth centuries as a nationalist ideology gained hold and gained ground.

Actual figures are difficult to come by but through rhetorical clues provided by the introductions, prefaces, reviews in newspapers and periodicals, and intertextual references, we can ascertain that this poetry circulated to varying extents on the subcontinent and abroad. Circulation – the mediation between production and consumption – is negotiated in part through the reviews published in newspapers and reprinted in later editions of the work or in different works by the same author (that is, if the work is taken up for review by the press and if the author is fortunate enough to have second editions of this work or first editions of other works published) and in part through the work itself. Authors and editors guide how readers *read* through prefaces, prologues, afterwords, and footnotes, which are sometimes written in response to critiques or interpretations of that author's work.[8] These commentaries raise several interesting issues, including for example: how does the author, editor, or reviewer/commentator of the work situate that work? These authorial/editorial framings, intrusions, and digressions are as important as the actual poem itself insofar as they mediate entry into, acceptance by, and promotion of the poet and his/her work within the literary establishment and so a selection of these are included in the appendix of this anthology. Both the appendix "Indian Poets on Their Poetry" as well as "British Poets/Critics on Indian Poets" are actually prefaces, introductions, and epilogues included *within* the volumes themselves. Thus, these two appendices are meant to be read in tandem, as parallel discussions on Indian poetry in English: the first allows readers a glimpse into the way poets framed their poetry to their audiences while the second allows readers a glimpse into the way British poets and critics (who were often asked by Indian poets and their publishers to introduce the volume to add some cachet, especially to Western audiences) framed this poetry. The third appendix showcases "native" poetry included in an early anthology of English-language poetry from the island of Ceylon (modern-day Sri Lanka). Although many of these poets express sentiments, including praise for Queen Victoria and subtle critiques of Empire, similar to those expressed by poets from the subcontinent, the Ceylonese poets' descriptions of their landscape and their allusions to specifically Ceylonese regions, events, and people points to subtle differences in their colonial situation and their own national imagining.

English in India

To some influential literary critics and poets in England, English-language poets in India during this time were expected to write only on "Indian" subjects or themes. As he recounts in his preface to the Indian politician and English-language poet Sarojini Naidu's collection *The Golden Threshold* (1905), Edmund Gosse had (in)famously advised her to discard some early poems that he perceived as too "English": they were "skillful in form,

---

8 See Gerard Genette, *Paratexts: Thresholds of Interpretation*, trans. Jane E. Levin (Cambridge: Cambridge University Press, 1997). Genette makes similar claims when he writes that the authorial preface that accompanies and, indeed, introduces the first edition of a work, has two functions including "*to get the book read* and *to get the book read properly*" (emphasis in original, 197).

correct in grammar and blameless in sentiment" but were "Western in feeling and in imagery."⁹ He instead instructed Naidu to write about something recognizably "Indian," to give "some revelation of the heart of India" and "set her poems firmly among the mountains, the gardens, the temples" and be "a genuine poet of the Deccan."¹⁰ Gosse's advice is admiringly quoted and elaborated upon two decades later by Gwendoline Goodwin, editor of the *Anthology of Modern Indian Poetry* (1927): "The Indian poet of to-day is torn, like the Indian painter, between admiration for Western models and a desire to mould himself thereon, and an inherent Indian tradition that runs in his veins and will not be denied... We of the West do not want from the East poetic edifices built upon a foundation of Yeats and Shelley and Walt Whitman. We want genuine Taj Mahals and Juma Masjids,¹¹ cameos of rural sweetness and the hopes of faithful hearts."¹² Goodwin's dictum captures the contradiction Indian poets writing in English during the nineteenth and early twentieth centuries faced: acceptance by the literary establishments of England and English literary culture was contingent upon the performance of an essentialism, the "tradition that runs in his [the poet's] veins," that entailed such acceptance. It also highlights the long and fraught engagement of Indians writing in English with the British Empire and the latter's role in disseminating this literature.

Official British presence dates to the East India Company's first charter, which was signed by Queen Elizabeth I in 1600, for exclusive rights to trade in the East Indies. The East India Company gradually gained control over the subcontinent after a series of wars with other trading companies, including those owned by the Dutch, French, and Portuguese, and with existing rulers on the subcontinent, both Mughal and Hindu. Company forces successfully defeated the Portuguese at Surat in 1612, prompting the Mughal emperor Jahangir (1569–1627) to grant trading concessions to the Company. The Company staged three wars against the French in the Carnatic (the Coromandel Coast and its outlying regions in southern India) from 1746 to 1761, quelling any French imperial ambitions. The decisive victory of the East India Company in the Battle of Plassey in 1757 gave it control over Bengal, which would become the seat of its holdings, and signaled the beginning of the steady expansion of Company control over the subcontinent. Through a series of wars fought against the Muslim rulers of Mysore (1767–1769), the Maratha Empire (1775–1818), and the Sikhs for control of the Punjab (1845–1849), as well as various diplomatic negotiations and treaties with other rulers, the Company reigned over almost the entire subcontinent by the time of the Indian Uprising in 1857. States that had not been annexed by the Company retained only nominal control of their respective regions.

Over the course of the eighteenth century and into the next, the Company transformed itself from a commercial enterprise to a state presence protected by its military and defined in part by its desire for territorial sovereignty. This desire was justified through a belief in the civilizing mission of British presence and rule. The rhetoric of "progress" – and related ideas of improvement, development, evolution, and education – frequently

---

9 Edmund Gosse, "Introduction," in Sarojini Naidu, *The Bird of Time: Songs of Life, Death, and the Spring* (London: William Heinemann, 1912), 4.
10 Ibid., 5.
11 Juma Masjid, or the Jama Masjid, of Delhi is the largest mosque in India and was constructed in the seventeenth century by the Mughal emperor, Shah Jahan.
12 Gwendoline Goodwin, *Anthology of Modern Indian Poetry* (London: John Murray, 1927), 9–10.

appears in nineteenth-century texts on empire and was crucial in justifying Company rule overseas. Thomas Babington Macaulay famously contended that the history of England is the history of progress,[13] an ideology imposed upon Britain's colonies by utilitarians such as Jeremy Bentham, James Mill, and J. S. Mill.[14] Such progress was thought to manifest itself in education[15] as famously argued by Macaulay himself in his "Minute on Indian Education" (1835), which promoted the teaching of the English language through English literature, a policy recommendation formally adopted by the governor-general William Bentinck.

In his "Minute," Macaulay endorses an "Anglicist" view of instruction that calls for the education of Indians through English literature rather than through literatures in Sanskrit and the vernaculars, or an "Orientalist" view of instruction. Poetry in the vernaculars and classical languages in India under colonial rule was ideologically burdened as a lesser, feminine, irrational, and thus "native" form of literature by Occidentalists even while it was studied and promoted by Orientalists such as William Jones and Max Müller (the latter frequently and favorably mentioned by the Indian-English press). Yet this poetry – whether oral or written – also occupied a traditionally elite status in Hindu and Muslim high literary cultures. Macaulay believed an English-language education necessary for the maintenance and progress of empire insofar as it created a class of "native" intermediaries between the British rulers and the Indian populace: "We must at present do our best to form a class who may be interpreters between us and the millions whom we govern; a class of persons, Indian in blood and color, but English in taste, in opinions, in morals, and in intellect."[16] Although Macaulay saw all Indians as intellectually, morally, and culturally inferior, he believed a class of Indians who would act as both cultural and linguistic intermediaries for the British in India could exist. This class would not only interpret Indians to the British but the British to Indians. According to Macaulay, English instruction not only drives the native's progress from barbarity to civilization,[17] but also is used increasingly around the world in commerce and government and thus has a defined use-value.[18]

---

13 See Thomas Babington Macaulay, *The History of England* (1848–1861).
14 See Eric Stokes, *The English Utilitarians and India*, 2nd ed. (Delhi: Oxford University Press, 1989) and Martin I. Moir, Douglas M. Peers, and Lynn Zastoupil, eds, *J.S. Mill's Encounter with India* (Toronto: University of Toronto Press, 1999).
15 See Robert Watson Frazer, *A Literary History of India* (New York: Charles Scribner's Sons, 1898). Frazer comments that though it is "difficult...to discriminate in how far the British rule in India has worked towards implanting new ideals destined to advance the moral and intellectual condition of the people" (386), literature from the period can serve as "[t]he surest evidence," though certainly not incontrovertible, of this supposed advance (387). Frazer continually questions the ability of Indians to flourish morally and intellectually in the absence of British rule, indirectly alluding to the rising threat of Indian nationalist movements.
16 Thomas Babington Macaulay, "Minute on Indian Education," in *Selected Writings*, ed. John Clive and Thomas Pinney (Chicago: University of Chicago Press, 1972), 249.
17 Macaulay, "Minute on Indian Education," 241–2. Macaulay assumes the inherently moral qualities of the English language and, by extension, all literature written in English. Russia, uneasily straddling the boundaries of Oriental and Western, stands as an example of a country which has successfully "progressed" through the influence of Western language and literature: "The languages of Western Europe civilized Russia. I cannot doubt that they will do for the Hindoo what they have done for the Tartar."
18 See Macaulay, "Minute on Indian Education," 242.

English was not only a practical tool for Macaulay, it was also a proselytizing one. He claims that since the home government employed a policy of "tolerance" in religious matters, English literature must shoulder the responsibility of inculcating the ethical values of the West in the "native." By claiming that the English language is inherently superior in "recording facts" and "investigating general principles," Macaulay posits a scientific, rational, and moral superiority for its literature.[19]

As Gauri Viswanathan outlines in *Masks of Conquest: Literary Study and British Rule* (1989), English literature was used to civilize and control a population. Viswanthanan claims that while nineteenth-century Evangelists saw literary education as the moral force which would regenerate "an innately depraved self," utilitarians saw such instruction as "providing the means for the exercise of reason, moral will, and critical understanding."[20] English literature masked the economic and political exploitation it helped justify.[21] Ruth Vanita has pointed out that the ideologies, including revolution and freedom, espoused by some British Romantic poets, ensured it would not have a prominent place in early curricula on the subcontinent. In fact, "the English literature texts in Hindu College in the 1820s were Gay's fables, Pope's version of the *Aeneid, Paradise Lost* and one of Shakespeare's tragedies. By the mid-nineteenth century the syllabi in government and mission schools occasionally included Wordsworth. Other writers included were the overtly Christian Cowper, Goldsmith, Southey, Young, Campbell, Otway, while the bulk of the syllabi was still occupied by the Augustans such as Pope, Johnson, Addison."[22] According to N. Krishnaswamy and Lalitha Krishnaswamy, "[t]he standard fare" in the purportedly secular government curriculum included "[p]oetical selections (Goldsmith, Gray, Addison and Shakespeare), Milton's *Paradise Lost* (the first four books), Pope's *Iliad by Homer*, Shakespeare's *Hamlet, Othello* and *Macbeth*, Addison's *Essays*, Johnson's *Lives of the Poets*, Goldsmith's *History of England*, Bacon's *Essays*, and prose readers prepared by Macaulay when he was President of the Committee."[23] Missionaries such as the Scottish Alexander Duff modified this curriculum to include overtly religious texts such as "the Bible, Paley's *Nature Theology*, Plato's *Dialogues*, Bunyan's *Pilgrim's Progress*, and Milton's *Paradise Lost* but excluded Addison, Johnson and Pope" with the express purpose of attracting upper-caste Hindus and Muslims to missionary education and Christianity.[24] It was exactly those Indians aspiring to the middle-classes, often through employment in the civil service, who would be most concerned with acquiring the cultural capital that a study, and even production, of English-language literature would allow.

Of course, most educational initiatives were focused on instructing young Indian men. The history of Indian women's education in English on the subcontinent runs on a parallel, and often more bumpy, track. Radha Kumar notes that the first schools for girls were started by English and American missionaries in the 1810s for economically

---

19 Ibid.
20 Gauri Viswanathan, *Masks of Conquest: Literary Study and British Rule in India* (New York: Columbia University Press, 1989), 19.
21 Ibid., 20.
22 Ruth Vanita, "Gandhi's Tiger: Multilingual Elites, the Battle for Minds, and English Romantic Literature in Colonial India," *Postcolonial Studies* 5.1 (2002): 104.
23 N. Krishnaswamy and Lalitha Krishnaswamy, *The Story of English in India* (New Delhi: Foundation Books Pvt. Ltd, 2006), 43.
24 Ibid.

underprivileged girls. By the mid-1800s, "women's education had become an issue which was campaigned for by unorthodox Hindus, Brahmos, and radical students in Bengal, especially Calcutta. Fears of the evangelical intentions of missionary schools were aired at the same time as Brahmo and Hindu schools for girls were opened in Bengal, and were partly responsible for their opening." In contrast to the earlier missionary schools, "these new schools catered to girls of the upper castes."[25] By the turn of the twentieth century, a number of women such as the poet and politician Sarojini Naidu; India's first female barrister Cornelia Sorabji; the social reformer, writer and editor Kamala Satthianadhan; English-born Theosophist Annie Besant; and the women's groups and publications in which they were involved or supported, vociferously advocated for increased female (and often English-language) education as well as suffrage as crucial in shaping the proper Indian middle-class woman as a reader (if not necessarily a writer) of English-language texts.

The history of English-language publications produced on the subcontinent is a fascinating one. Printing presses were first brought to the subcontinent in the sixteenth century by Christian missionaries to Goa. Presses were later brought into Bombay in 1674, Madras in 1772, and Calcutta in 1779. These areas would become imperial administrative centers, or presidencies, and thus centers of English-language writing and publishing in India although Calcutta, as the center of Company administration, especially flourished as a producer of English-language texts during the late eighteenth and early nineteenth centuries. The first English-language newspaper to achieve mass printing and distribution was the *Bengal Gazette* published in 1780 by James Hicky in Serampore. The Bengali reformer Raja Rammohun Roy produced the first Indian newspapers in the early 1820s including *Sambad Kaumidi* in Bengali, *Mirat ul Akhbar* in Persian, and the *Brahmunical Magazine* in English.[26] The first known English-language text published by an Indian was *The Travels of Dean Mahomet, a native of Patna in Bengal, through several parts of India, while in the service of the Honourable the East India Company* (1794). A soldier in the service of the East India Company, the Muslim Dean Mahomet published his epistolary travelogue after emigrating to Cork, Ireland in 1784.[27]

The increasingly widespread employment of mass print technologies during the nineteenth century in India, as in Britain, radically altered reading habits and practices. Priya Joshi writes of the publications produced in the three presidencies of Madras, Calcutta, and Bombay that "educational titles formed over half the total published output, followed by government and commercial printing. Over half the literary titles published in Indian presses were works of poetry; approximately a third were works of fiction; and less than a sixth were dramatic works, often translated or adapted from the ancient epics, the Mahabharata and the Ramayana."[28] Reading became a much more accessible venture that, in the words of Tanika Sarkar, "penetrated into all sorts of times and spaces within

---

25 Radha Kumar, *The History of Doing: An Illustrated Account of Movements for Women's Rights and Feminism in India 1800–1990* (New Delhi: Kali for Women, 1993), 14.

26 G. N. S. Raghavan, *The Press in India: a New History* (New Delhi: Gyan Publishing House, 1994), 2–10.

27 See Dean Mahomet, *The Travels of Dean Mahomet: An Eighteenth-Century Journey through India*, ed. Michael Herbert Fisher (Berkeley: University of California, 1997).

28 Priya Joshi, *In Another Country: Colonialism, Culture, and the English Novel in India* (New York: Columbia University Press, 2002), 145.

everyday life by its sheer portability."²⁹ Yet literacy was still severely limited relative to the total population on the subcontinent: only 6 percent was literate in any language and only 1 percent was literate in English by 1911.³⁰ The turn of the century did witness a steady increase in the numbers of students studying English "from 298,000 in 1887 to 505,000 in 1907" and usually in the presidency towns of Calcutta, Madras, and Bombay since English allowed Indians access to employment in the civil service.³¹

This anthology showcases a mere sampling of English-language poetry published in Bombay, Madras, Calcutta, Delhi, London, and in other regions around the subcontinent. Some of this poetry was originally published in the periodical press, as the authors note in prefaces or notes to their collections, before being included in pamphlets or books by that author. Poetry was also self-published by poets at small, usually local, printing presses. The earliest English-language poetry by Indians seems to have circulated in Bengal at the beginning of the nineteenth century when the first institutions of English-medium education began appearing on the subcontinent, especially with the founding of Hindu College (now known as Presidency College) in Calcutta in 1817 through the efforts of the Bengali social reformer Rammohan Roy, the Scotsman David Hare, and others. It is here that Henry Louis Vivian Derozio, often considered the first Indian-English poet, taught from either 1826 or 1828 (there seems to be some disparity on the date in the critical literature on Derozio) until 1831. He was forced to resign after protests that he was supposedly "corrupting" the Indian youth by teaching them to question the traditions, rituals, and ideologies of their Hindu upbringing, thereby angering the Hindu orthodoxy of Calcutta.

K. R. Ramachandran Nair establishes Derozio's primacy in *Three Indo-Anglian Poets* (1987), a study of Derozio and the two most famous female Indian-English poets of the nineteenth century, Toru Dutt, and Sarojini Naidu: "The history of Indo-Anglian poetry begins with Henry Louis Vivian Derozio."³² Nair argues that despite an Indo-Portuguese father and English mother and thus having "had very little Indian blood in him," Derozio was wholly Indian nonetheless since "he was born and brought up in India, he taught Indian students in an Indian college and was inspired by Indian themes and sentiments in his poetry."³³ Nair establishes Derozio's nationality through the latter's place of birth, upbringing, friends, professional affiliations, and the "themes and sentiments" of his poetry.³⁴ Indeed, while Derozio's mixed blood allows Nair to categorize Derozio as Indian *despite* his race, it also led both nineteenth- and early-twentieth-century critics to identify him through the category of race, as something *other than* white. Nair's elaborate justification for including Derozio in the canon of Indian-English poetry indicates the contentious definition of "Indianness" itself. In a nation

---

29 Tanika Sarkar, *Hindu Wife, Hindu Nation: Community, Religion, and Cultural Nationalism* (London: Hurst and Company, 2001), 28.
30 Sarkar, "'Middle-Class' Consciousness and Patriotic Literature in South Asia," in *A Companion to Postcolonial Studies*, ed. Henry Schwarz and Sangeeta Ray (Oxford: Wiley-Blackwell, 2002), 252.
31 Ibid.
32 K. R. Ramachandran Nair, *Three Indo-Anglian Poets* (New Delhi: Sterling Publishers Private Limited, 1987), 19.
33 Ibid., 19.
34 Ibid.

marked by the heterogeneity of its inhabitants in language, religion, region, ethnicity, and which, as a state that only officially came into existence in 1947, over a century after Derozio's death in 1825, who or what was "Indian" was necessarily historically contingent and in a process of constant negotiation.

The mid-century marked a crucial moment for the growing presence of English-language institutions on the subcontinent. Three "modern" universities in Bombay, Calcutta, and Madras were established by then viceroy-general, Lord Canning, in 1857: Calcutta was incorporated on 24 January, Bombay on 18 July, and Madras on 5 September. These three institutions of higher education were the first to issue degrees but did not initially serve as places of instruction themselves. Modeled after the University of London system, students would complete coursework at the numerous affiliated colleges before presenting themselves for examinations administered by these three major universities. Punjab University was incorporated in 1883 (prior to this it was known as the Punjab University College and could only confer titles, not degrees). The University of Allahabad was incorporated in 1887.[35] Only after the Indian Education Act of 1904, implemented under Viceroy Curzon, did the original three universities of Bombay, Calcutta, and Madras join Punjab and Allahabad as teaching institutions by forming academic departments and beginning instruction, mainly in English.

The mid-century marked a crucial moment for British imperial history and Indian colonial history as well. Beginning in May 1857 and lasting until June 1858, a widespread uprising by Indian sepoys, or soldiers serving in the British army, in the northern part of India shook the British Empire to its core. Rhetorical constructions and reconstructions of this event, termed the "Sepoy Mutiny" in British colonial discourse, shaped the relationship of power and rule between colonizer and colonized for decades to come.[36] Indeed, the uprising – deemed India's first war of independence by nationalists – continues to inform the Indian national imaginary as seen in the Bollywood film *The Rising: The Ballad of Mangal Pandey* (2005), which further mythologizes the purported sepoy leader of the revolts, Mangal Pandey. The Indian-American blog title *Sepia Mutiny* cleverly appropriates the derogatory term for this failed rebellion to indicate racial difference through the technology of early photography.[37]

---

35 *Encyclopedia Britannica*, 11th ed., s.v. "Universities."
36 Indeed, nineteenth-century British imperial discourses which construct this event as sudden and unexpected, ignored the history of resistance prior to 1857. See Clare Anderson, *The Indian Uprising of 1857–8: Prisons, Prisoners, and Rebellion* (London: Anthem Press, 2007), 12: "Historians accept that the mutiny-rebellion was not the unique and unprecedented event contemporaries often spoke of, but party of what [historian C. A.] Bayly has described as endemic armed revolt across early colonial India. Landholders and landlords, tenants and peasants, itinerant communities, religious and caste-based groups, villagers, city dwellers, and townspeople were all involved in the instigation of periodic disputes, riots, and rebellions during the first half of the nineteenth century. Each episode can be traced, however indirectly, to a Company policy which sought to increase revenue and monopolize political authority."
37 *Sepia Mutiny*, http://www.sepiamutiny.com/sepia/faq.php (accessed 23 December 2010). As they write of their name in the FAQs section, "It's a pun that combines the name of the first widespread rebellion against the British Raj with sepia, an ink associated with photography that is described as a 'shade of brown with a tinge of red.'"

In 1858, the uprising was brutally crushed by the British imperial forces following a year-long siege at Lucknow and then Delhi, which resulted in the exile to Burma of the last Mughal emperor, the Bahadur Shah Zafar, who ruled (in name only) from Delhi's Red Fort. Administration of India was transferred from the East India Company to the British Crown despite the protests of many including J. S. Mill, the commissioner of correspondence at India House, London. Mill, like the previous generation of utilitarians, including his father James Mill, saw India as a testing ground for their theories of efficient government administration. The rhetoric of progress informs Mill's "Memorandum of the Improvements in the Administration of India during the Last Thirty Years" (1858), a work of propaganda endorsing the continuance of Company rule in India. The "perpetual striving towards improvement" supposedly characterizing the Company's presence indicates a constant effort towards some always near but never fully reached goal that nonetheless invests the government with its reason for being, its "vital principle,"[38] and self-justification. Thus, it is not only the material conditions of the natives which have been and are being improved (as Mill details in the body of his "Memorandum") but also the natives themselves – though these natives are still "a people most difficult to be understood and, still more difficult to be improved."[39] Despite Mill's pleas, India became a Crown colony under parliamentary control, governed in England by the secretary of state for India and in India by the viceroy of India.

The 1880s were shaped by a rabid jingoism in British imperialist discourses even as Indians began advocating for limited self-governance through the establishment of the Indian National Congress in 1885. The partition of Bengal in 1905 into the Muslim-dominated East and the Hindu-dominated West further contributed to the rhetoric of communalism,[40] aggravated by the British encouragement of the All-India Muslim League in 1907 as well as the relocation of the capital of the British Raj from Calcutta to New Delhi in 1911.

During the early part of the twentieth century Indian soldiers participated in unprecedented numbers in World War I and Indian material resources were further depleted for the war effort: "the War affected Indian life through massive recruitments, heavy taxes and war loans, and a very sharp rise in prices, and may be directly related to the two-fold extension of the national movement – towards considerable sections of the peasantry and towards business groups – which manifested itself immediately afterwards under Gandhi."[41] Although the numerous international conflicts of the late nineteenth and early twentieth centuries (including the Boer Wars, the European imperial Scramble for Africa, the Boxer

---

38 John Stuart Mill, "Memorandum of the Improvements in the Administration of India during the Last Thirty Years," in *Writings on India*, ed. John M. Robson, Martin Moir, and Zawahir Moir (Toronto: University of Toronto Press, 1990), 155.
39 Ibid.
40 See Gyanendra Pandey, *The Construction of Communalism in Colonial North India* (Delhi: Oxford University Press, 1990) for a nuanced exploration of the colonialist and nationalist constructions of communalism.
41 Sumit Sarkar, *Modern India: 1885–1947*, 2nd ed. (London: Macmillan, 1989), 168. Sarkar goes on to note that "[t]he Indian army was expanded to 1.2 million, and thousands of Indians were sent off to die in a totally alien cause in campaigns which were often grossly mismanaged" (169).

Rebellion, the "Great Game" played by Russia and Britain for control of Central Asia, and so on) led to the publication of anti-war verse such as S. D. Saklatvala's *An Appeal for Peace, some verses* (1910) and Lala Prasanna Kumar Dey's "War" in *Indian Bouquet* (1906), the role of Indian troops during World War I also occasioned a great deal of poetry by Indians about the forced expenditure of life. Poets such as Sarojini Naidu detailed the sacrifice of Indian mothers, whose sons' corpses littered "the blood-brown meadows of Flanders and France" in her poem "The Gift of India," which was first recited at a meeting of the Hyderabad Ladies' War Relief Association in 1915 and later included in Naidu's last, and most explicitly nationalist, collection *The Broken Wing* (1917).

The year 1920 signals the end date of publication for the poetry included in this anthology insofar as it also signals the end of an era: the recent experience of World War I and events such as the Amritsar Massacre of 1919 occasioned an increased vociferousness and intensity in the Indian independence movement as well as the beginnings of change in Indian-English poetic forms as well as the ideologies surrounding those forms. In addition, Indian-English poetry, though always only one of many forms of Indian-English textual production during the nineteenth and early twentieth centuries and while still produced and circulated in great numbers after World War I, was now forced to compete with the rise of the Indian-English realist novel and novelists such as Mulk Raj Anand, R. K. Narayan, and Raja Rao beginning in the 1930s, for prestige and readership.

Indian Poetry in English

Much Indian-English poetry during the long nineteenth century was published in newspapers and magazines and so was subject to the contingencies of newspaper publishing, which was by nature immediate, topical, and ephemeral. Poetry occupied an accepted place in nineteenth-century newspapers that is foreign to us in the twenty-first century. Many newspapers published various genres of poetry including odes, satires, lyrics, and verse dramas, as well as essays on English poets as varied as Shakespeare, Milton, Shelley, Tennyson, and Ebenezer Elliot (author of the *Corn Law Rhymes* (1831)), Toru Dutt, and Tagore. Whereas all English poets and some of the more popular Anglo-Indian poets, such as Kipling, Edwin Arnold, and Alfred Lyall, published in these newspapers are reprinted from English or Anglo-Indian publications and periodicals, most of the original poetry, proportionately far less than the reprints, is penned almost entirely by Indians or by lesser-known Anglo-Indians. The poems authored especially for Indian-English newspapers took on a variety of topics including love, domesticity, nature, and religion. Explicitly political poems usually addressed topical issues such as Irish Home Rule, taxation, imperial jingoism, and included odes to or satires of various imperial figures. A great deal of Orientalist poetry, whether "translated" or "inspired," was also published by Britons, Anglo-Indians, and Indians. The types of poetry included in these newspapers was mandated, in part, by the limited access these Indian-English newspaper editors had to English-language publications, periodicals as well as poetry, and may have played a small part in the newspapers' commitment to Indian poets and lesser-known Anglo-Indian poets. Although this anthology does not include any poetry published *only* in periodicals due to space constraints, many of the poems included in this anthology were often published in newspapers and magazines before or after their inclusion in single-author volumes.

Newspapers often featured poetry that was political in content despite an often draconian regulatory system.[42] The Indian-English newspapers zealously monitored the various laws by which the native press, which included the vernacular as well as the English-language presses, lived or died. Although the Marquis of Hastings, under the East India Company's Rule, abolished censorship in 1819, the Bengal Regulations Acts of the 1820s instituted mandatory licensing for papers produced in its territories.[43] Sir Charles Metcalfe repealed these acts in 1835. After the 1857 Revolt and subsequent fears of further Indian uprisings, Lord Canning instituted the Gagging Act, which was remarkable for the intensity of its repressive measures: requiring all printing presses to be licensed with the government; prohibiting any newspaper from criticizing the government in Britain or in India or inciting unrest, resistance to the government, or criticism of its policies or laws; and applying its regulations equally to European and Indian publications. It was soon repealed. The Press and Registration of Books Act of 1867 established a registration system for all printed materials in order to allow the government to keep track of newspapers and printing presses.[44] The Vernacular Press Act was aimed at newspapers written in the vernaculars and "thereby privileg[ed] the English-medium press not subject to the Act."[45] Based on the Irish Coercion Act, the Vernacular Press Act allowed the government to punish and suppress potentially seditious writing. After the partition of Bengal in 1905 and as British rule became less accommodating to Indian interests and Indians themselves increasingly critical of continued imperial rule, the British instituted the Newspapers (Incitement to Offences) Act of 1908 empowering Magistrates to seize a press if convinced that it contained material that could incite sedition or violence.

Yet poets persevered in writing and publishing highly charged political poetry in often creative ways. The Indian-English newspapers, often self-acting as appointed representatives of the Indian masses, directly addressed their critiques of Anglo-Indian imperial governance to a supposedly sympathetic, and distant, English audience. Ram Sharma, the pseudonym of Nabokissen Ghose, published innumerable poems first in *Mookerjee's Magazine* and later in *Reis & Rayyet*, both edited by Babu Sambhu Chunder Mookerjee, that were serious and satirical but almost always politically topical. For example, Ram Sharma's piece "India's Gleam of Hope," included in his collected poems, the *Poetical Works of Ram Sharma* (1919), reads:

> In every Government, though terrors reign,
> Though tyrant kings or tyrant laws restrain,
> How small, of all that human hearts endure,

---

42 See Uma Dasgupta, *Rise of an Indian Public: Impact of Official Policy, 1870–1880* (Calcutta: RDDHI, 1977). Since the newspapers made little, if any, profit, contributors were often unpaid and wrote at the urging of the editors or for the sake of publication (17).

43 Aled Jones, *Powers of the Press: Newspapers, Power and the Public in Nineteenth-Century England* (Aldershot: Scolar Press, 1996), 24–5.

44 See R. C. S. Sarkar, *The Press in India* (New Delhi: S. Chand & Company Ltd, 1984). Sarkar discusses the development of a "free press" ideology enshrined in the post-independence Indian constitution.

45 Julie Codell, "Introduction: the Nineteenth-Century News from India," *Victorian Periodicals Review* 37.2 (Summer 2004): 111.

> That part which laws or kings can cause or cure;
> Still to ourselves in every place consigned,
> Our own felicity we make or find.

Sharma's entire poem, which is composed of a quote from the eighteenth-century English poet Oliver Goldsmith's "The Traveller," illustrates how English culture was used against England by invoking, even if not inciting, rebellion as a form of resistance.

British poetry and poets exerted a profound influence both biographically and aesthetically on Indians' own textual production in English during the nineteenth and early twentieth centuries. The English Romantic belief in the poet as legislator of the world[46] was especially apparent in Indian-English poetry of the early to late nineteenth century. For the Bombay poet and editor of the *Indian Spectator*, Behramji Malabari, who also established and wrote for the *Indian Spectator*, an Indian-English weekly, British Romantic poetry was both the standard and the ideal as Malabari admits in the preface of his 1876 collection, *The Indian Muse in English Garb*: "Many of the British poets, Shakespeare, Byron, Shelley, Burns, Wordsworth, Keats and Campbell in particular have long become his [Malabari's] household gods." These poets, of whom Shakespeare is the only non-Romantic in the canon, are worthy of Malabari's worship as well as his emulation. Implicit in such homage is the supposed confidence that he too can write verse like his heroes.[47]

For the Bengali poet Toru Dutt, the favorable reviews of her first book of poems, a translation of French sonnets into English, prompted her to compare herself to two famous Romantic English poetesses in a letter to her friend, Mary Martin: "You see I have become quite a public character, like L. E. L. or Mrs. Hemans!"[48] The Madrassi poet T. Ramakrishna Pillai dedicated the first edition of his book of poems, *Tales of Ind*, to Tennyson and included an ode to the poet laureate of Great Britain and the British Empire in the second edition (and, indeed, periodical reviews of his work frequently compared it to Tennyson's *Idylls of the King*). The Hyderabad-based poet Sarojini Naidu was influenced by her association with the Rhymer's Circle during her sojourn in England from 1895–98 and her friend, the Symbolist poet Arthur Symons, would write an introduction to her first volume of poetry. The poetry and life of Elizabeth Barrett Browning was featured in a number of essays by Indian women in the periodical, *The Indian Ladies Magazine* (1901–1938), over the course of its run.

Not only English poets, but English poetic forms, such as the sonnet, ode, and ballad, exerted a profound influence on Indian-English poets, who recast and modified these genres as they saw fit. In choosing to use a particular form, at a specific historical moment, Indian-English poets drew from a particular set of literary traditions and generic conventions, all buttressed by particular ideologies, which were then relied upon, resisted, and/or reformulated.

The sonnet is a familiar form in poetic collections from the period under study here. In his anthology *This Strange Adventure* (1947), Fredoon Kabraji notes of the form: "As to how much regard Indians have paid to the forms of English poetry may be seen

---

46 See Percy Bysshe Shelley's "A Defense of Poetry" (written in 1821 and first published posthumously in 1840).
47 Behramji Merwanji Malabari, *The Indian Muse in English Garb* (Bombay: "Reporters" Press by Merwanjee Nowrojee Daboo, 1876), 4.
48 Harihar Das, *Life and Letters of Toru Dutt* (Oxford: Oxford University Press, 1921), 178.

from the preponderance of sonnets they have written. Even where the thought has been undistinguished, the discipline in expression has been loyally maintained."[49] Although both statements are questionable, there is no doubt that the sonnet was popular among Indian-English poets. Nizamat Jung's *Sonnets and other poems* (1913) and *Love's Withered Wreath* (1914) are explorations of the form. His collected poems include memorial sonnets to the Nizam Mir Mahbub Ali Khan, the Muslim prince of Hyderabad, and Mohandas Gandhi. P. Seshadri was a gifted practitioner of the sonnet form as seen in a number of poetic collections, most especially in *Sonnets* (1914).

The frequent use of the ballad form is especially interesting considering its ideological place in English literary history and the adaptation and transformation of that ideology in Indian-English literary history. In English literary tradition, two sources of tension manifest themselves regarding the origin and continuance of the ballad as a literary genre. On the one hand, a tension exists between the status of the ballad in medieval and Renaissance literature as the popular and populist oral medium of the rural "masses," in the ephemeral form of the folk ballad, or the commercial and written medium of the urban "masses," in the material form of the broadside.[50] On the other hand, a tension exists between this earlier version of the ballad (which, whether rural or urban posits the ballad as of the people), and the eighteenth-century literary construction of the ballad as a literary form, the recovered oral "artifact" of a supposedly national folk literature that implicitly glorifies feudalism.[51] In her long poem "Savitri" (1882), which draws from a Vedic tale, Toru Dutt utilizes the ballad, which, with its standard, or at least roughly standardized, meter and rhyme-scheme, is a form marked as English, to accommodate something else entirely, a tale marked as Indian. The English nationalism implicit in nineteenth-century British uses of the form becomes complicated by imperialism and other instantiations of nationalism when taken up by Indian colonial subjects.

Odes to Mother India (or *Bharat Mata*) as well as odes to various political figures such as the Parsi intellectual and nationalist leader Dadabhai Naoroji, the "Grand Old Man of India," Queen Victoria and other royals, Prime Minister Gladstone, and the various viceroys and officials of the British Raj were standard fare for most Indian-English poets. For example, Sukhendu Bikash Roy's *A Poem on the Coronation of Their Majesties King George V and Queen Mary as Emperor and Empress of India* (1911) sings its praises of British royalty. Sarojini Naidu's famous poem "Awake!", which was recited at the meeting of the Indian National Congress in 1915 and published in *The Broken Wing* (1915–16), structures itself as both an ode to Mother India as well as a call to arms to her loving, worshipful children. Naidu's poem posits a slumbering nation that must be roused and revitalized by her subjects, by Indians.

Yet the concerns of Indians' poetry in English are nonetheless unique to its specific historical, geographical and cultural contexts, including the presence of indigenous poetic traditions both regional as well as "classical." The authoritative Sanskrit renderings of the

---

49 Fredoon Kabraji, ed., *This Strange Adventure: An anthology of poems in English by Indians* (London: New India Pub. Co., 1946), 9.
50 Alan Bold, *The Ballad* (New York: Methuen, 1979), 66.
51 Susan Stewart, *Crimes of Writing: Problems in the Containment of Representation* (New York: Oxford University Press, 1991), 105.

Hindu "epics," the *Mahabharata* and the *Ramayana*, came to be conceptualized as national productions by nineteenth-century Indians. This was accomplished in part through an extended comparison, made by both European Orientalist scholars as well as Indian elites themselves, to the ancient Greek epics, the *Odyssey* and the *Iliad*, and based on a construction of the ancient Sanskrit versions of the epic as definitive (though innumerous regional and generic variations of these tales exist and continue to be produced). The English-language translations of the *Mahabharata* (1898) and the *Ramayana* (1899) of Romesh Chunder Dutt came to be seen as authoritative translations of the authoritative textual tellings of the Indian epics in part due to the status of the author himself as a well-respected scholar and politician, and in part by his claiming the status of "condensations" and "translations," or narratively and historically accurate renderings, of the originals. For Dutt, faithfulness to the originals is accomplished in part through an attention to the regular metrical form of the Sanskrit meter, the *sloka*, which marks out the nation in verse.

Roby Datta's preface to his collection *Echoes from East and West* (Cambridge 1909) includes a fascinating discussion of rendering the "accuracy" of meter in translation that echoes that of Romesh Chunder Dutt. Datta claims his translations from ancient Greek, Latin, Pali, and Sanskrit consist of

> rendering the sense of the original in my own manner and in a metrical form something like that of the original; while all the rest show what I call the process of translation, that is, rendering the original in the order of its words and in its exactly equivalent metrical form as far as it is in keeping with the true genius of the English language. In a few cases the process of translation has been more or less that of modernization. The essential thing in these processes, which I have always tried to keep in view, is to fall into the inspiration of the original poet before attempting a rendering. Next, with regard to the prosody, I may say that most of the poems are in recognized English or Anglicised metrical forms, but there are a few poems written in Hexameters, Elegaics, Alliterative Verse, Assonant Verse, and Unrimed Verse...[52]

This anthology includes original as well as translated poetry, though recent critical work in translation studies has shown how translations are never faithful transcriptions from one language to another, but are themselves original renderings. The English-language translations by Indians under colonialism also allow some insight into the ways that the act of translation itself (the selection of texts, meters, words) was implicated within the asymmetrical power dynamics of imperial structures, both in co-optation by and resistance to those structures.[53]

Like classical Sanskrit poetry, classical Persian and Urdu poetry provided a source of inspiration and material for many Indian poets – both in its "original," by poets such as Zeb-un-Nisa, Kabir, Rumi, and Ghalib, and as filtered through Orientalist discourse. Many Indian-English poets such as Sarojini Naidu, who was heavily influenced by the

---

52 Roby Datta, *Echoes from East and West, to which are added stray notes of mine own* (Cambridge: Galloway and Porter, 1909), ix.

53 See Tejaswari Niranjana, *Siting Translation: History, Post-Structuralism, and the Colonial Context* (Berkeley: University of California Press, 1992) and Lawrence Venuti, ed., *The Translation Studies Reader* (London: Routledge, 2000) for example.

Muslim royal court of the Nizam of Hyderabad, drew from the tropes of Urdu verse. Naidu as well as poets such as Hamid Ali Khan and A. S. H. Hussain experimented with the *ghazal* – a form structured by a *aa ba ca da* etc. rhyme scheme, traditionally addressed to masculine objects of desire (in expressions of earthly or divine love), often written to be sung, and incorporating the poet's own name towards the end of the poem.

The influence of Persian and Urdu literary traditions were in large part a byproduct of the Mughal incursions onto the subcontinent beginning with Babur, founder of the Mughal dynasty, in the sixteenth century (though Muslim invasions had occurred for centuries preceding). In nineteenth century (Hindu) nationalist discourse, Mughal rule was often cast as a benighted period in Indian history, a characterization that sometimes served as a coded allusion to British imperial rule. In this rendering, India's glorious ancient past was disrupted by Mughal invasion, which plunged her into a darkness from which she was only now beginning to awaken.[54] For example, Nanikram Vasanmal Thadani's "The Triumph of Delhi" alludes to Delhi's "triumph" over a series of Muslim invasions and Aurobindo Ghose's long poem, *Biju Prabhou* details the efforts of the poem's eponymous leader, a lieutenant under Shivaji, founder of the Maratha Empire after successfully staging a number of victories over the declining Mughal Empire and various Rajput forces. Muslim poets, on the other hand, often cast the Mughal Empire as a period of intellectual, cultural, and religious flourishing. Although most, if not all, Indian poets of the period cast the nation as currently inhabiting a period of degeneration, slumber, and/or despair, many of the Muslim poets included here, including A. S. H. Hussain and Nizmat Jung, believed that *British rule* would allow India to flourish once again through the enlightened influence of the West.

Since many of Indian-English poets took historical subjects or anticipated that Western readers would be unfamiliar with terminology drawn from cultural practices or linguistic traditions (including classical languages such as Persian, Urdu, and Sanskrit as well as the vernaculars) from the subcontinent, they often included annotations within their texts to inform and guide their readers. In *Oriental Welcome to the Most Gracious Majesties, the King-Emperor and the Queen-Empress* (Cawnpore: 1911), Tej Shankar Kochak presents his readers with a somewhat extreme, though charmingly informative, example of this tendency. His annotation of any word or allusion that might be met with confusion or ignorance on the part of the reader has ensured that almost one-fourth of his volume of verse consists of footnotes annotating that verse. Poets also included annotations in order to elaborate upon an issue about which they felt particularly passionate. The Bombay-based, Parsi poet and civil servant Cowasji Nowrosji Vesuvala includes an annotation, several paragraphs long, for a phrase included in verse XXVII of his long poem "True Indian Opinion, or Native Croakers." This annotation details the various perfidies, especially "crushing taxation," meted out by the Government of India and Indians' lack of redress.

As with any literary tradition, some Indian-English poetry is exceptionally good, much is enjoyable, and some is simply unreadable. For example, in his *Indian National Odes with*

---

54 See Romila Thapar, "Interpretations of Ancient Indian History." *History and Theory* 7.3 (1968): 318–35 and Gyan Prakash, "Writing Post-Orientalist Histories of the Third World: Perspectives from Indian Historiography," *Comparative Studies in Society and History* 32.2 (April 1990): 383–408.

an *Apology of Poesy* (1906), J. Mangiah writes in his "Prologue: An Apology of Poesy" these lines justifying his poetic practice:

> I have as great a right to be,
> A singer as one right that has,
> Of Indian life of heroes great,
> Because it was my lot to hear.
> Should there be aught in Indian life,
> That should please man of right research...[55]

While the poet's proclamation of his "right to be,/ A singer" inspires sympathy, his verse falls rather infelicitously upon the ear. Yet despite his difficulties with meter and diction in English, Mangiah also published *To Gurukul* (1911) and *Select Poems* (1935). Another metrically "challenged" collection includes *Songs with Native Tunes of Different Sorts and Dances* (1864) by Babu Ramkinoo Dutt (billed as a "retired medical officer on pension"), who also self-published *Manipure Tragedy: Composed in Rhyming Form* (1893). One collection, Methasing Tiloksing Advani's collection *My Gems* (1910), is riddled with grammatical and typographical errors and the difficulty in ascertaining one category of error from the other speaks to the crucial role editors play in any publication. Although none of the works just listed are included in this anthology, they bring attention to the fact that the form and content of a poem embeds that poem within and shows that poem to be a product of a specific set of institutional (social, economic, political, and cultural) relationships and that some works and authors benefit to a greater degree from the advice, prestige, support, privilege, and capital of regional or global networks than others. As the talented Behramji Malabari angrily though somewhat obliquely asserts in the preface to his collection *The Indian Muse in English Garb* (1876), "[t]hough aware of the necessity of an Englishman to examine the proof-sheets, the author has even that satisfaction denied him"[56] forcing the author "to be his own scribe and proof-reader."[57] This comment offers some insight into the publication of Indian works in English and Indian reaction to perceptions of English neglect and/or superiority.

Distinctions by Anglo-Indians (Britons living and working in India) between the supposedly standard English of the metropole and the (substandard) English spoken and/or written on the subcontinent by "natives" frequently disparaged the latter and made such "Baboo English" (the derogatory term for the English, often seen as native mimicry, spoken by Indians) an object of ridicule. Such ridicule, which was part of a heavily racialized (and racist) discourse, not only magnified the unease some English-speaking and writing Indians felt working in the language of the colonizer but fueled the anger of educated Indians. For example, in an article entitled "Anglo-Indian Criticism," which appeared in an 1886 issue of the Calcutta-based, English-language newspaper *Reis & Rayyet*, the anonymous Indian author critiques a presumably Anglo-Indian writer of the Anglo-Indian periodical, the *Pioneer*, for his snide comments on "Baboo English":

> [I]t has no mercy for the poor Indians who are constrained by political necessity to use the English language as the medium of communication in the whole external

---

55 J. Mangiah, *Indian National Odes with an Apology of Poesy* (Madras: Ananda Steam Press, 1906), 15.
56 Malabari, 4–5.
57 Ibid., 5.

commerce of life. A little reflection – a little recollection of the inaptitude of foreigners nearer home and the same race, like the Germans for instance – a little introspection and candid acknowledgement of the everyday blunders in French committed by educated Englishmen – might lead to more moderation and perhaps more sympathy too for the difficulties – the almost insurmountable obstacles of aliens in the Antipodes in mastering the mysteries of the pure well of English undefiled.[58]

English has been made a "political necessity" due to the power exerted by Britons in "the whole external commerce of life" so that the political and economic imperatives for the use of English seem inseparable. The writer notes the contradiction in Anglo-Indian attitudes towards Indians: Anglo-Indians excuse "foreigners" such as Germans for their linguistic "blunders" and readily commit their own when speaking French but are intolerably cruel when considering the "blunders" of those "aliens in the Antipodes," who, due to their distance from England, have greater difficulty in "mastering the mysteries of the pure well of English undefiled." In a further irony, the writer himself seems to have mastered "the pure well of English" enough to inject a heavy dose of sarcasm into his critique.

The literary use of English thus caused a great deal of anxiety, sometimes performed in the prefaces to their works, in the poets of the nineteenth and early twentieth centuries. In the preface to the second edition of his work, *A Farewell to London, and the Story of the Slave and the Nose-Ring* (1885), the poet Hamid Ali Khan excuses clothing the Indian tale about the slave and the nose-ring in his poor "English poetic garb": "If I have unconsciously offended against English idiom, or used an inappropriate word, or inaccurate expression, or written an intolerably bad line – for these and similar shortcomings I trust to the generosity and forgiveness of my English readers."[59] The early nineteenth-century Indian-English poet Henry Louis Vivian Derozio, who is often assigned a position of primacy, both as the origin of Indian poetry in English and as one of the most critically celebrated practitioners of said literature, also prefaced his first volume, *Poems* (1827), with apologies for his work's "imperfections":

> Though fearful of the inutility of general apologies, yet the Author feels that the circumstances under which his work appears before the Public require some explanations.
>
> Born, and educated in India, and at the age of eighteen, he ventures to present himself as a candidate for poetic fame; and begs leave to premise, that only a few hours gained from laborious daily occupations have been devoted to these poetical efforts.
>
> The publication of a work of this nature in India is not a frequent occurrence; and the Author trusts that a simple reference to the facts which he has laid before the Public will prove a sufficient plea for the imperfections of his little work.[60]

---

58 Anonymous, "Baboo English," *Reis & Rayyet*, 2 October 1886, 474.
59 Hamid Ali Khan, *A Farewell to London: The Story of the Slave and the Nose-Ring*, 2nd ed. (London: W. Whiteley, 1885), xii–xiii.
60 Henry Louis Vivian Derozio, *Poems* (Calcutta: H. L. V. Derozio, 1827).

Following a literary convention of the period, Derozio's third-person reference to himself as author both implicates him in and distances him from the publication of these poems. By claiming that "only a few hours gained" away from his professional labors have been spent in writing poetry, Derozio attempts to forestall any possible critiques of his work. By noting the infrequency of "[t]he publication of a work of this nature in India," Derozio highlights the supposed difference of " a work of this nature" from most other work published in India and, as implied in this statement, marks the commonality of his work with works published elsewhere, as in England.

Indeed, the poets included in this anthology often self-consciously located themselves within a literary tradition of other Indian-English as well as British and even global writers. For example, Roby Datta translates Michael Madhusudhan Dutt's Bengali poem, *Meghnadbadh Kayva*, or *The Slaying of Meghanada* (1861),[61] thereby including the earlier poet as part of the "Eastern" canon, as well as works from the Greek, Latin, among other languages as part of the "Western" canon. In doing so, he places himself somewhat uneasily in both – neither a poet of the vernaculars nor solely an English-language poet, he is something else, something new.

Such anxieties regarding an Indian-English writer's "place" within existing literary traditions continues even to this day. In a more recent *Boston Review* essay entitled "The Cult of Authenticity"(2000), the Indian-English novelist Vikram Chandra counteracts criticisms regarding Indian writing in English, which include charges of pandering to Western audiences through the Orientalist depiction and annotation of issues, events, and allusions particular to India. He claims this "censorious rhetoric about correct Indianness… lays claim not only to a very high moral ground but also a deep, essential connection to a "real" Indianness. Despite all their demurrals about not essentializing Indianness, and their ritual genuflections in the direction of Bhabha and Spivak, the practitioners of this rhetoric inevitably claim that they are able to identify a "Real India," and so are able to identify which art, and which artists, are properly Indian." The object of this scathing rebuttal is Meenakshi Mukherjee (indeed many of his counter-attacks seem personal – a response to her brief remarks on his work) and her essay "The Anxiety of Indianness." This public battle between author and critic illustrates that Indian writing in English continues to be controversial in large part because it continues to beg the still unanswered question of what constitutes "Indianness."[62]

Indian English?

Designating Indian poetry in English is a necessarily fraught endeavor. Discussions on how to name such literature are inextricably intertwined with discussions on what constitutes said literature. During the early part of the twentieth century, "Anglo-Indian" was used to categorize a whole range of fiction produced on the subcontinent including fiction by the British in India as well as by Indians and those characterized as "Eurasians" (or mixed-race Indians). In his 1934 monograph, *A Survey of Anglo-Indian Fiction*,

---

61 For a excellent translation of the epic see Michael Madhusudhan Datta, *The Slaying of Meghanada, A Ramayana from Colonial Bengal*, trans. Clinton B. Seely (Oxford: Oxford University Press, 2004).
62 Vikram Chandra, "The Cult of Authenticity," *Boston Review*, February/March 2000. http://bostonreview.net/BR25.1/chandra.html (accessed 10 June 2010).

Bhupal Singh writes: "The phrase 'Anglo-Indian fiction' may be used in a broad or narrow sense. Broadly speaking it includes any novel dealing with India which is written in English. Strictly speaking it means fiction mainly describing the life of Englishmen in India. In a still narrower sense it may be taken to mean novels dealing with the life of Eurasians."[63] In *The Moving Finger: Anthology of Essays in Literary and Aesthetic Criticism by Indian Writers* (1945), the editor V. N. Bhushan uses the term Indo-English to refer to any original literature and criticism written in India in English or any English-language text (usually canonical and British) since "[n]ext only to poetry, criticism is the most extensive activity of the Indo-English writers."[64] In one of her earliest monographs, *Twice Born Fiction* (1971), Meenakshi Mukherjee claims that only in the 1930s and 1940s had there been a serious systematic attempt to place Indian-English literature in context and evaluate it. While early criticism used the term "Anglo-Indian" to discuss all works in English about India, only with the publication of the works, *Indo-Anglian Literature* (1943) and *The Indian Contribution to English Literature* (1945), by K. R. Srinivasa Iyengar, did "Indian writing in English by Indians began slowly to be recognized as a distinct entity, different in nature from the writings of Flora Annie Steele or Meadows Taylor or Rudyard Kipling," those British living in and/or writing about colonial India.[65]

In *Indo-Anglian Literature* (1943), Iyengar carefully delineated the rubric by which such a literature should be known: "I have used the compound 'Indo-Anglian' in preference to 'Anglo-Indian' and 'Indo-English.' The term 'Anglo-Indian' should be used only with reference to the writings of Englishmen in India or on subjects relating to India. 'Indo-English' is a suitable alternative to 'Indo-Anglian,' but the latter is more widely used in India."[66] Two years later, he published *Indian Contribution to English Literature* (1945), which expanded upon the first book and his favored term, "Indo-Anglian": "More recently, especially during the past two decades, 'Indo-Anglian' has acquired considerable currency. Further the term can be conveniently used as an adjective and as a noun…"[67] In his most famous work *Indian Writing in English* (1962; editions were reissued in 1973 and 1983), Iyengar writes: "Indian writing in English (not in English alone, but *all* Indian writing) is greatly influenced by writing in England, and we have had our own 'Romantics', 'Victorians', 'Georgians', and 'modernists'. But in its own way Indo-Anglian literature too has contributed to the common pool of world writing in English."[68] Though Iyengar claims the influence of British literature on Indian-English literature by forcibly mapping the historical periodization of the former onto the latter, he also claims for Indian-English literature a status of its own, separate from British literature though part of "world writing in English."[69]

---

63 Bhupal Singh, *A Survey of Anglo-Indian Fiction* (Oxford: Oxford University Press, 1934), 1.
64 V. N. Bhushan, ed., *The Moving Finger: Anthology of Essays in Literary and Aesthetic Criticism by Indian Writers* (Bombay: Padma Publications, 1945), xvii.
65 Meenakshi Mukherjee, *The Twice Born Fiction: Themes and Techniques of the Indian Novel in English* (New Delhi: Heinemann, 1971) 9–10.
66 K. R. Srinivasa Iyengar, *Indo-Anglian Literature* (Bombay: P.E.N. All-India Centre, 1943), ix.
67 K. R. Srinivasa Iyengar, *The Indian Contribution to English Literature* (Bombay: Karnatak Publishing House, 1945), ii.
68 K. R. Srinivasa Iyengar, *Indian Writing in English* (New York: Asia Publishing House, 1962), 5.
69 Ibid., 5.

Until the 1970s, with the publication of Mukherjee's *Twice Born Fiction* (1971), the preferred term seemed to be "Indo-Anglian." However, critics like Mukherjee began to evince some unease with that designation: "There is a persistent feeling that it is infelicitous even though it has been in circulation for some time and may be on the point of being confirmed for future use. Alternatives like *Indian-English* literature or even *India-English* literature have been suggested. Whatever term is finally chosen to refer to Indian writing in English, either by fiat or by usage, it will take some time for it to gain currency."[70] This confusion in terminology has persisted to the present day. Josna Rege, for example, parses out these various terms in the preface to her book *Colonial Karma* (2004): "Indian literature written in English has variously been called Anglo-Indian, Indo-Anglian, and Indo-English. Although it has been a matter of some controversy whether Indian literature in English can be considered Indian literature, it has been accepted as such by the Sahitya Akademi, India's national literary body, which has officially adopted the term "Indian English literature" in order to make clear that it is part of Indian literature."[71] Rege continues: "The term "Anglo-Indian," which was also used to denote British colonial officials in India, is now taken to refer to literature about India by British writers, set or written in the colonial period. "Indo-Anglian" was coined to distinguish literature in English by Indian writers, since it had formerly been subsumed under Anglo-Indian literature. 'Indo-English' has been suggested to describe English translations of literature originally written in an Indian language."[72] Such official recognition by the Sahitya Akademi bestows a certain cultural cachet and respectability onto this literature that only a well-regarded institution, with its concomitant status and support, can bestow. Indeed, by the year 2000, in her collection of essay *The Perishable Empire*, Mukherjee uses the term "Indian-English" without comment.[73] More recently the critic Eunice de Souza has used the designation "Indian Poetry in English" in her anthology *Early Indian Poetry in English, an Anthology 1829–1947* (2005)[74] while "anglophone" literature is used by Priyamvada Gopal in *The Indian English Novel* (2009).[75]

Nineteenth- and early twentieth-century Indian-English poetry has occupied a curious position in studies of Indian literature, in postcolonial studies, and in nineteenth-century studies. This early poetry, especially when juxtaposed against the globally circulated, critically acclaimed, and commercially successful novels (including works by Salman Rushdie, Kiran Desai, Vikram Chandra, etc.) of the late twentieth and early twenty-first centuries, continues to be seen as naïve, imitative, and inauthentic. Such a view, part of colonial discourse and Indian critique then, and even now still deeply ingrained in our understanding of this literature, stems in part

---

70 Mukherjee, *The Twice Born Fiction*, 14–15.
71 Josna E. Rege, *Colonial Karma: Self, Action, and Nation in the Indian English Novel* (New York: Palgrave Macmillan, 2004), xiii.
72 Ibid., xiii.
73 Meenakshi Mukherjee, *The Perishable Empire: Essays on Indian Writing in English* (New Delhi: Oxford University Press, 2000).
74 Eunice de Souza, ed., *Early Indian Poetry in English, an Anthology: 1829–1947* (New Delhi: Oxford University Press, 2005).
75 Priyamvada Gopal, *The Indian English Novel: Nation, History, and Narration* (Oxford: Oxford University Press, 2009).

from the politically charged conception, by both the colonizer then and Indians now, of early uses of English as native mimicry of the colonizer.

Many critics of Indian-English literature, like H. M. Williams, V. N. Bhushan, and Amaranatha Jha trace the tradition of Indian writing in English to Thomas Babington Macaulay's "Minute on Indian Education" (1835). More recent devaluations of nineteenth-century Indian-English literature may stem from unease with the relative privilege of Indian-English writers, those educated in British institutions, of the time. Presumably it was these writers that were Macaulay's mimic men: apologists for colonial rule both in their ideology as well as in their imitation of British literature and literary standards, which also marked them as supposedly unoriginal and inauthentic in their writing. Yet, as evident in the poetry itself, many, if not most, of these writers critically engaged with the ideology of colonial rule in and through their writing, which may have drawn in part from a genuine regard for British literary culture but which did not necessarily entail a naïve imitation of that culture or an uncritical promotion of British imperialism.

Indians writing in English during the long-nineteenth century engaged in a fundamentally political act insofar as the teaching and learning of English – whether used to advance or resist existing power structures, ideologies, and cultural constructs – immediately located the writer relative to British rule and presence. Aijaz Ahmad makes the crucial point that the metropolitan language in India was English since it was "the chief cultural and communicational instrument for the centralization of the bourgeois state in the colonial period." British colonial administrators and, later, Indian nationalists all believed that a central language was needed to unify the heterogeneity of India.[76]

This anthology does not argue for the primacy of the English language in colonial India but for its placement as one among many languages circulating on the subcontinent. The English language contributed to a small but significant portion of the literature produced in India during the nineteenth and early twentieth centuries and was thus ineluctably intertwined with this "nation['s]" culture. English, the language of the colonizer, of British administration, power, and control, was also the language used by an emerging Indian elite and, as more than amply demonstrated in the prefaces to the books and pamphlets of poetry published during the time, in the articles on "Baboo English," and in the constant reference to British literary sources that peppered the Indian-English newspapers and periodicals, was always already fraught with emotional as well as political, social, economic, and cultural valences. "Indian English" can be read as both a place and a language – as the unique form of English spoken by Indians as well as an English shaped by and adapted to its use on the subcontinent.

As the language of the colonizer and metropolitan Indian elite during the early to mid-nineteenth century, the language was a flash point for an emerging, or perhaps solidifying, national consciousness. In the introduction to a collection of essays by various critics in *A History of Indian Literature in English* (2003), Arvind Krishna Mehrotra claims that the stances taken against the use of English in Indian literature before independence arose from feelings of nationalism or "pride" in one's regional language.[77] Mehrotra discusses

---

76 Aijaz Ahmad, *In Theory: Classes, Nations, Literatures* (New York: Verso, 1992), 74.
77 Mehrotra, "Introduction," 11. See also Sumathi Ramaswamy, *Passions of the Tongue: Language Devotion in Tamil India, 1891–1970* (Berkeley: University of California Press, 1997) for a discussion of language debates in South India, especially around Tamil.

the rancorous debates over language in the twentieth century when "Hindi, Sanskrit-blest, purged of Urdu elements, and 'written in Devanagari script'" was made the official language of Indian in the constitution.[78] The language debates again materialized in the early 1960s though this time between northern states, which saw Hindi not just as another regional language but as a pan-Indian one, and southern states, which preferred English to the unwelcome imposition of Hindi.[79]

Mehrotra goes further in arguing that "a striking feature of Indian literature in English is that there have been no schools, literary movements, or even regional groups within it. Its history is scattered, discontinuous, and transnational. It is made up of individual writers who appear to be *sui generis*."[80] Claiming that Indian-English literature transcends region, community, and any grounding in the institutions in which literature is produced, circulated, and consumed does not take into account the complexities of Indian-English literature as an ideologically determined and determining act and as a material object. Indian writers in English relied and continue to rely upon networks of support (in the case of contemporary Indian-English novelists, this support comes in the form of publishing houses willing to support globally profitable authors). This last point is crucial — many, if not most, who wrote in English in the nineteenth and twentieth centuries did belong to the metropolitan elite. However, despite the relative privilege of these writers, whose privilege nonetheless varied greatly with each individual, it does not therefore follow that these writers were grounded in similar subject positions, were informed by similar ideologies, or did not use English to both support and critique the imperial government.

In studies of nineteenth-century colonial literature, the novel occupies a higher status than poetry and any other form of writing. Priya Joshi writes of the novel: "Though frequently regarded as a tool for inspiring assent and anglicization among colonial subjects in the nineteenth century, the novel, as we will see, paradoxically emerged in India as one of the most effective vehicles for voicing anticolonial and nationalist claims in the late-nineteenth and early-twentieth centuries."[81] As a genre that came into existence on the subcontinent only after and as a result of British colonial and commercial presence, the novel was supposedly also "initially outside the immediate sphere of the colonial state apparatus, whose emphasis on literature in the educational curriculum was primarily conveyed by English poetry, with essays and drama following."[82] Even though this genre played a much lesser role "in the ideology of rule," Indians were still avid consumers of British novels.[83] For Joshi, novels occupy a privileged space *outside* of colonial rule while poetry, which she sees as intimately implicated "in the ideology of rule," does not.[84]

Timothy Brennan similarly writes: "It was the *novel* that historically accompanied the rise of nations by objectifying the 'one, yet many' of national life, and by mimicking the structure of the nation, a clearly bordered jumble of languages and styles. Socially, the novel joined the newspaper as the major vehicle of the national print media, helping

---

78 Mehrotra, "Introduction," 12.
79 Ibid., 14.
80 Ibid., 26.
81 Joshi, *In Another Country*, xvii.
82 Ibid., 17.
83 Ibid.
84 Ibid.

to standardize language, encourage literacy, and remove mutual incomprehensibility. Its manner of presentation allowed people to imagine the special community that was the nation."[85] In other words, according to Brennan, the novel "objectif[ied] the nation's *composite* nature: a hotch potch [sic] of the ostensibly separate 'levels of style' corresponding to class; a jumble of poetry, drama, newspaper report, memoir, and speech; a mixture of the jargons of race and ethnicity."[86] The novel thus occupies a special place in nation-building – following Benedict Anderson, it allows communities to imagine themselves into existence. Yet Brennan qualifies the power of the novel by noting that in the twentieth century, "under conditions of illiteracy and shortages, and given simply the leisure-time necessary for reading one, the novel has been an elitist and minority form in developing countries when compared to poem, song, television, and film."[87]

Indeed, most critics of Indian-English literature often posit an evolution of said literature in both its style, from naivety to sophistication, as well as its form, from early ephemera to journalism to imitative verse to, finally, novels. Even the most famous critic of Indian-English literature, K. R. Srinivasa Iyengar, sees early work in English as less sophisticated and cruder than later work in his survey, *Indo-Anglian Literature* (1943), when he traces the "development" of English in India over the centuries. Iyengar claims that during the early part of the nineteenth century,

> the newly educated Indian grew more and more into an absurd copy of his Western contemporary... The educated community evolved into a superior caste apart and speedily lost touch with the masses. The false culture – false because it was in disharmony with normal Indian categories of experience – learned at school and college made Indian youths hanker after the thrills of urban life and finally made them incredible anachronisms in their own once happy homes. A new generation conversed and corresponded in English. "Indianisms" and "Babuisms" were the order of the day. Is it any wonder that no healthy literary growth was possible on such uncongenial soil?[88]

This last comment on the supposed mangled English of Indians, whose solipsisms were often referred to as "Babuisms" or "Baboo English," draws from a long line of Anglo-Indian critique of English as discussed earlier. According to Iyengar, although Indians initially found it difficult to master English idiom for composition, they "quickly mastered the intricacies of the English language and made it a fit vehicle for the communication of ideas. Poetic composition was not possible – as yet; but letters, memoranda, monographs, and translations in English appeared in due course. Presently, Indians boldly ventured into the domain of English journalism; they published political and economic pamphlets, partial portraits of men of importance, even occasional skits and short stories."[89] For Iyengar, poetic production was a stage in development made possible only by and after the journalistic endeavors of Indians writing in English, their

---

85 Timothy Brennan, "The National Longing for Form" in *Nation and Narration*, ed. Homi Bhabha (New York: Routledge, 1990), 49.
86 Ibid., 51.
87 Ibid., 56.
88 Iyengar, *Indo-Anglian Literature*, 6.
89 Ibid., 7.

publication of pamphlets, and so on. Indeed, the composition of poetry preceded that of novel writing. Such a line of reasoning establishes a problematic narrative of literary evolution. It also occludes the fact that India-English poetry not only began appearing in the early nineteenth century, at the very latest, according to the historical records but also that it cannot be separated from other forms of print. Indeed, Indian-English poetry often appeared in newspapers, magazines, in speeches, as pamphlets, as well as in book form throughout the nineteenth century and beyond.

The poetry of the later part of the twentieth century takes on the sheen of modernity and thus gains literary value through an association with difficulty and experimentation. In *Indo-Anglian Literature, 1800–1979: A Survey*, H. M. Williams argues that "[t]he history of Indo-Anglian literature is broadly speaking a development from poetry to prose and from romantic idealization to various kinds of realism and symbolism."[90] He locates the prevalence of poetry in English by Indians during the nineteenth century within a broadly defined Indian literary tradition: "It is easy to explain the prevalence of poetry over other genres such as prose fiction at this period. Indian languages had a long poetic tradition; and so there was an abundance of poetry available in the vernaculars. The great Indian epics were written in Sanskrit verse and translated into vernacular poetry... Thus poetry appeared as the 'natural' medium of expression."[91] For Williams, only during the interwar period, with its consolidation of nationalist movements that brought about a corresponding political urgency, did realism became a more "natural" medium for these Indian writers in English.[92] He privileges Indian-English realist novels written during the advent of European modernism as more thoroughly "modern." By claiming that "[t]he history of Indo-Anglian literature is broadly speaking a development from poetry to prose and from romantic idealization to various kinds of realism and symbolism"[93] as many critics of Indian-English literature do, Williams implicitly devalues nineteenth-century poetry. This poetry was and still often is seen as artificial, superficial, and imitative of English verse, as for example in the critical reception of the poet Sarojini Naidu.

In contrast, in her extended discussion of the familial poetic production that makes *The Dutt Family Album* a unique historical and poetic document, the critic Rosinka Chaudhuri offers a nuanced reading of early to mid-nineteenth-century Indian-English poetry from Bengal during the years 1827 to 1875:

> This minor poetic tradition was a site, however unlikely, for the emergence of a modern Indian identity. An attempt is made here to retrieve a whole body of neglected nineteenth-century writing, neglected primarily because it is poetry, and because this sort of 'derivative' poetry, especially, gets very little attention in this context as it is unable to correspond to the protocols of the kind of native/colonized/indigenous writing that the academy expects and looks for. As these poets

---

90 H. M. Williams, *Indo-Anglian Literature, 1800–1979: A Survey* (Bombay: Orient Longman, 1976), 3.
91 Ibid., 3–4.
92 See Williams, *Indo-Anglian Literature, 1800–1979*, 4. Williams writes: "Indo-Anglian fiction waited an impetus from outside literature in the shape of the nationalist movement that gained great potency after World War I – to which could be added the social-revolutionary tendencies that became urgent and pervasive at that time (between 1920 and 1940)."
93 Ibid., 3.

were the first members of a newly formed Indian middle class to express themselves in literary terms inherited from an education in English, they constitute a necessary and unignorable part of any history of colonial India and its literatures.[94]

Indian-English poetry that imitated English Romantic and Victorian verse but that simultaneously idealized an ancient or medieval India is termed by Chaudhuri as "Orientalist verse" insofar as it drew from "discourse generated by the Orientalist project."[95] She links Orientalism — and part of Orientalism's project as the "recovery," translation, study, and annotating of ancient texts including the *Vedas*, the Sanskrit epics, and so on — to growing Indian concerns with historiography.[96] Chaudhuri also convincingly posits a connection between "Orientalist verse" by Indians and incipient Indian nationalism since only during the nineteenth century did there develop any "conception of Indian heritage or culture in an autonomous sense as was now available in a systemized way through Oriental scholarship."[97] According to Chaudhuri, although Orientalist poetry by Indians was not concerned with realist representation and so is "remarkably alike in subject matter, form and expression, evoking few particularities or complexities of place or of individual experience," the language of this genre gave early Indian poets a vocabulary to speak *about* India.[98]

A number of anthologies featuring Indian poetry in English from the nineteenth and early twentieth centuries have been published over the last century including *India in Song: Eastern Themes in English Verse by British and Indian Poets* (1918) edited by Theodore Douglas Dunn, *Anthology of Modern Indian Poetry* (1927) edited by Gwendoline Goodwin, *The Peacock Lute* (1945) edited by V. N. Bhushan, *This Strange Adventure: An Anthology of Poems in English by Indians, 1828–1946* (1947) edited by Fredoon Kabraji, *Modern Indian Poetry in English: An Anthology and a Credo* (1969) edited by P. Lal, *The Golden Treasury of Indo-Anglian Poetry 1828–1965* (1970) edited by V. K. Gokak, *Indian Poetry in English* (1993) edited by Makarand Paranjape, *Early Indian Poetry in English, an Anthology: 1829–1947* (2005) edited by Eunice de Souza, and *Anglophone Poetry in Colonial India, 1780–1913* (2011) edited by Mary Ellis Gibson.

The anthologies focusing on post-independence verse have taken an interesting attitude to verse published before World War II. For example, in *The Bloodaxe Book of Contemporary Indian Poets* (2005), the anthology's editor, the poet Jeet Thayil, writes that until the publication of the poet Nissim Ezekiel's first volume of poetry, *A Time to Change*, in 1952 "Indian poetry in English was a 19th-century product that survived well into the 20th. A backward glance over the 150 years before Ezekiel turns up only four figures of

---

94 Rosinka Chaudhuri, *Gentlemen Poets in Colonial Bengal: Emergent Nationalism and the Orientalist Project* (Calcutta: Seagull Books, 2002), 3.
95 Ibid.
96 See Chaudhuri, *Gentlemen Poets in Colonial Bengal*, 162. Such a past was also a narrowly constructed vision of a Sanskrit Hindu India — a reconstruction that Chaudhuri glosses over as insignificant since it supposedly coexisted with "a tolerance and appreciation of their [the poets'] Islamic heritage." Yet such a self-conscious reconstitution, often unquestioningly accepted by Hindu writers, proved to be a problematic model for other Indian writers who identified as Muslim, Christian, Parsi, Sikh, or anything else.
97 Ibid., 6.
98 Ibid.

note in English three of them are Bengali, all of them Calcutta-based: Tagore, Toru Dutt, Michael Madhusudan Dutt (no relation) and Henry Louis Vivian Derozio."[99] Thayil, and many other anthologists of post-independence poetry such as Arvind Krishna Mehrotra in *The Oxford Anthology of Twelve Modern Indian Poets* (1992), not only categorically dismiss any poetry which does not meet standards of "modernist complexity" but ignore the wealth of poetic production prior to this period.

This anthology aims to counteract such assumptions regarding Indian-English poetry of the late nineteenth and early twentieth centuries as naïve or imitative by showing that such critical assessments miss the point. Indian-English poetry from the period 1870–1920 acts as a window onto a particular historical and cultural moment. Its formal innovations, radical politics, and "sophistication" are more interesting when they are read against its perhaps more common formal conservatism and political moderation since both represent a fascinating engagement with the politics of form and a form of politics.

The Indian English Novel, Priyamvada Gopal's survey of Indian-English novels from the nineteenth century to the present, offers one of the most nuanced considerations of both English-language fiction and poetry from India: "Not all forms of anglophone writing are, however, equally prolific or visible. While English-language poetry has had a steady if relatively muted presence, it is one that has generally been eclipsed by the vibrancy and popularity of verse and lyric traditions in other Indian languages that have an oral rather than strictly literary presence. Here, as with drama, the 'Indian scene' contrasts with regions such as the Caribbean or parts of West Africa."[100] She later argues that due to their conditions of production as arising under and in response to British imperialism and written in an initially foreign tongue, the Indian novel is intimately, though not intrinsically, bound with the history of the nation. Gopal qualifies: "The conditions of its emergence – out of the colonial encounter, addressing itself to empire rather than a specific region or community – meant that the anglophone novel in the subcontinent returned repeated to a self-reflexive question: 'What is India(n)?'"[101] This question was one that threaded itself through the writing of Indian-English poetry as well.

Theorists of nation explicitly often argue for or implicitly posit the conflation of nation and culture – itself an ambiguous and shifting concept. This culture is often predicated on literacy and writing. Benedict Anderson has famously argued that nation came into being through the products and processes of print-capitalism. According to Anderson, print-languages allowed for the development of national consciousness in three ways: first, it created a community of those who used a particular language defined against those who did not; second, it fixed language and

---

99 Jeet Thayil, ed. *The Bloodaxe Book of Contemporary Indian Poets* (Tarset: Bloodaxe Books, 2008). See also Rajeev S. Patke, *Postcolonial Poetry in English* (Oxford: Oxford University Press, 2006), 59. Patke similarly claims that "Indian poetry in English began in a spirit of imitation that took more than a century to shed" and goes on to mention Derozio, Toru Dutt, Naidu, Aurobindo Ghose, and Tagore. He also valorizes post-independence poetry: "[a] contemporary tone was introduced into Indian poetry in English by Nissim Ezekiel (1925–2004) and Dom Moraes (1938–2004). Each published a book of poems from London in 1952… Their range was comparable to the work of the Movement poets in 1950s Britain."
100 Priyamvada Gopal, *The Indian English Novel: Nation, History, and Narration* (Oxford: Oxford University Press, 2009), 3.
101 Ibid., 6.

allowed that language the aura of antiquity; and, third, certain dialects were closer to the print-form of a language and thus legitimated.[102] Anderson's narrative of nation is thus predicated on the historical "development" of culture. This culture is based in part on language, which he notes is characterized as "primordial" even when "known to be modern" and which uniquely intimate "a special kind of contemporaneous community…above all in the form of poetry and songs" as in the case of the national anthem when "people wholly unknown to each other utter the same verses to the same melody" creating "[t]he image: unisonance."[103] The consolidation of a community through culture, in particular through poetry and poetic song, ultimately depends on the ubiquity and commonality of the language in question. But what happens when the language, in this case English, is only one of many linguistic traditions in India, when it is a language of privilege based on access to education, and when its status as a "national" language cannot be separated from its status as an imperial one?

The imagining of nation, in which one's community was no longer one's immediate locality but the multiple and often geographically far-flung localities of a geographical landmass, all of which were re-imagined as local because Indian, can be seen in Rabindranath Tagore's anthem for India, "Bharata-Vidhata" (or "Jana Gana Mana"). This song, composed in a Sanskritized Bengali, was first sung at the annual meeting of the Indian National Conference in 1911 and "translated" by Tagore into English in 1919. The first verse was adopted by the newly constituted Indian Republic as its official national anthem in 1950:

> Thou art the ruler of the minds of all people,
> Thou Dispenser of India's destiny.
> Thy name rouses the hearts of the Punjab, Sindh, Gujarat and Maratha, of Dravida,
>   Orissa, and Bengal;
> It echoes in the hills of the Vindhyas and Himalayas,
> mingles in the music of Jumna and Ganges
> and is chanted by the waves of the Indian Sea.
> They pray for thy blessing and sing thy praise,
> Thou dispenser of India's destiny.
> Victory, Victory, Victory to thee.[104]

Tagore deploys the poem to catalogue various regions in India including Punjab, Sind, Gujarat, Maratha, Dravidia, Orissa, Bengal, the Himalayas, the Ganges, and the Indian Ocean; south India is here confined to the overarching term "Dravidia." In the second stanza, the poem goes on to enumerate the variety of religions (including Hindus, Buddhists, Sikhs, Jains, Parsis, Muslims, and Christians) contained within the geographic space of India in an effort to represent all "types" of Indians — in other words, to represent all *of* India in its parts *to* India as a whole in a construction that Sumathi Ramaswamy terms "good colonial sociology and geography."[105]

---

102 Anderson, *Imagined Communities*, 44–5.
103 Ibid., 145.
104 Sumathi Ramaswamy, *The Goddess and the Nation: Mapping Mother India* (Durham, NC: Duke University Press, 2010), 140. Ramaswamy also presents a fascinating discussion of Tagore's poem in the context of verse usually addressed to a feminized "Mother" India.
105 Ibid., 141.

Yet, despite the focus of this anthology on national imagining, it is crucial, as Aijaz Ahmad's *In Theory* cautions, not to read all literatures of the "third world" as allegories of the nation. Though his critique applies specifically to postcolonial literatures, we should nevertheless remain aware of his contention that, "[i]f we replace the idea of the 'nation' with that larger, less restrictive idea of 'collectivity,' and if we start thinking of that process of allegorization not in nationalistic terms but simply as a relation between private and public, personal and communal, then it also becomes possible to see that allegorization is by no means specific to the so-called Third World."[106]

Excavating the Archives and (De)Forming the Canon

Another way of reading the poetry included in this anthology is as a minor literature, now largely existing in the margins of the canons of Anglophone poetry and, at the time of its production, occupying a secondary status as the cultural productions of the colonized. According to Deleuze and Guatarri, "minor" literature can subvert existing structures insofar as this literature articulates and maintains alternate perspectives and is defined by its innate politicization and revolutionary potential. What they identify as minor literature "doesn't come from a minor language; it is rather that which a minority constructs within a major language."[107] For Deleuze and Guattari, minor literature is not aesthetically marginalized but rather politically subversive literature that exists both within and against the dominant language and culture of, most importantly, any oppressive state: "minor no longer designates specific literatures but the revolutionary conditions for every literature within the heart of what is called great (or established) literature."[108] This literature is not imitative of or concerned with the major literature of the dominant group and exists effectively outside it. Deleuze and Guattari celebrate minor literature's supposedly marginal status even as they seemingly acknowledge this very marginality as endowing such literature with a certain cultural and academic cachet. The poets included here are situated in a similarly difficult position of marginality but they do not possess the renegade status of a modernist writer such as Kafka, Deleuze and Guattari's exemplar of "a minor literature." The Indian-English poetry presented here is not inherently revolutionary or subversive since its very presence speaks to the hegemonic power of imperial structures of education and rule. These works' implication within such structures negates any valorization of their minority status as subversive. This literature does, however, comment upon and deal with the imperial government and in this way conceptualizes or determines national ones.

Yet the very term minor literature in most usages connotes lesser or secondary status. Thus it is in complicated ways a value judgment upon the way these works and, by extension, these poets, were, and perhaps still are, evaluated. Even as he acknowledges the importance of Deleuze and Guattari's work, Vijay Mishra contends in his monograph on Indian diasporic literature that even the term "minor" is problematic, in its implication that it is peripheral to a major literature, thereby reaffirming the importance of the center: "Minorities are, however, very much part of the centre; they are not erratic and

---

106 Ahmad, *In Theory*, 110.
107 Gilles Deleuze and Félix Guattari, *Kafka: Toward a Minor Literature* (Minneapolis: University of Minnesota Press, 1986), 16.
108 Ibid., 18.

unassimilable groups somehow extraneous to the nation; they are indeed part of the national imaginary with their own legitimate perspective."[109] Granted, some of these "minor" poetic texts have not been completely occluded from literary studies insofar as they have been read, discussed, and critically evaluated by Indian academics such as Meenakshi Mukherjee, Eunice de Souza, and Susie Tharu, yet they are minor regarding their place in the archives and in the canons. This literature is not part of the regular curriculum of English departments either in the United States, Britain or India and so can be considered minor regarding their position in the Western academy and in the canons of "world" literature.

Canonization is ineluctably intertwined with higher education and the university. As John Guillory contends, aesthetic representation in the university does not lead to political representation in the liberal pluralist sense and the unquestioned rallying for the inclusion of authors in the "canon" bypasses the importance of the structural constitution of literature as *access* to social, economic, political capital such as education in the university.[110] Authors, such as Sarojini Naidu, Toru Dutt, Henry Derozio, and Michael Madhusudhan Dutt, who are recognized within literary criticism or discussion of English literature are continually reified *as* minor authors despite their ironically "major" status in this particular field of literary production. Those authors or texts completely absent from the university and the literary marketplace are included in this anthology not only to introduce them to a new readership but also to point to the perils of canonization, in which inclusion is based in part on the ability of a work or artist to situate himself within certain discourses, cultures, and traditions. In other words, canonicity depends upon the ability of the work or artist to produce cultural capital within an existing system of aesthetic *and* economic value (for publishing houses, advertisers, printers, editors, authors). It also depends in part on the artist's ability to garner social capital, to situate themself in existing networks of social relations.

At the time of their publication, these poetic works were clearly not intended for mass consumption by an Indian audience due to the very nature of their endeavor as works composed in English. Yet the rather surprising number of self-published works of poetry illustrates the determination of writers to circulate their works, to release their words into the world. And the extent of these works' reassessment and preservation into the twenty-first century as "Art" and as part of an archive depends on the support of institutions (libraries, publishing houses, governments, universities, and so on).

The term "archive" is a rather complex and heterogeneous one. It can encompass both a collection of documents housed, stored, collated, collected by an institution that the scholar will then approach and sift through or the documents the scholar themself locates, takes interest in, and gathers. It can signify both a set of literal objects (most often in paper) and a theoretical, methodological, epistemological, and emotional construct (one can actually becomes possessed by the compulsion to retrieve, to know, perhaps to recreate). In his discussion of the public archive and its relationship to the nation-state, Achille Mbembe writes that the archive "is fundamentally a matter of discrimination and of

---

109 Vijay Mishra, *The Literature of the Indian Diaspora* (New York: Routledge, 2007), 61.
110 John Guillory, *Cultural Capital: The Problem of Literary Canon Formation* (Chicago: University of Chicago Press, 1993).

selection, which, in the end, results in the granting of a privileged status to certain written documents, and the refusal of that same status to others, thereby judged 'unarchivable.' The archive is, therefore, not a piece of data, but a status."[111] In other words, the collection and cataloguing of certain materials by institutions of the state endows those materials with importance and ensures that our understanding of the past is shaped by those materials. Mbembe begins his piece by noting: "The term 'archives' first refers to a building, a symbol of a public institution, which is one of the organs of a constituted state. However, by 'archives' is also understood a collection of documents – normally written documents – kept in this building. There cannot therefore be a definition of 'archives' that does not encompass both the building itself and the documents stored there."[112] Most of the poetry included in this anthology is housed either in the British Library in London or National Library in Kolkata, illustrating the importance and power of these state institutions of both the former colonizer and the "new" nation in cataloguing their intertwined cultural history. Yet, as a human endeavor, the archive – both that of the state and that of the individual scholar – is also marked by unpredictability, circumstance, and happenstance. As Carolyn Stedman observes, the archivist uses their materials to construct a history or narrative: "Our understanding of all sorts of plot – fictional plots and social plots – our understanding of *how things happened* indeed, is bound up with this understanding: that there is a sequence, event, movement; things fall away, are abandoned, get lost. Something emerges, which is a story."[113] The selective archive of Indian-English poetry presented in this collection creates a particular narrative, tells a structured story of English-language literature and literary history in India during a 50-year period.

Any anthology, no matter how carefully considered and edited, no matter how thoroughly researched, will always be "incomplete." Sources will remain buried in various collections and libraries or lost forever. Any anthology relies on a necessary exclusion – not necessarily meant to be exclusivity – as a way of managing and presenting an otherwise seemingly haphazard set of documents. The limits of the anthology, as conceived by the anthologizer, ultimately shapes the reader's understanding of the type of literature the anthology purports to collect, define, and present. In some cases, the anthology may be the first introduction to an unfamiliar (or even familiar) category of literature for a reader and thus serves to shape conceptions of what constitutes that category of literature, or even "literature" itself.

Thus, anthologies may form and deform canons; but, most significantly, they allow us to consider the process of canon formation itself. This anthology does not propose to insert texts into any existing canon of English-language literature since, as Neelam Srivastava has pointed out, canon (de)formation "carries within it the dangers of essentializing differences and of instituting new forms of marginalization. The anthology of South Asian writing runs the risk of becoming "representative" of something called Indian literature, and in an even more obfuscatory move, of something called India."[114] The poetry selections

---

111 Achille Mbembe, "The Power of the Archive and its Limits," trans. Judith Inggs in *Refiguring the Archive*, ed. Carolyn Hamilton et al. (Cape Town: David Philip Publishers, 2002), 20.
112 Ibid., 19.
113 Carolyn Stedman, *Dust: The Archive and Cultural History* (New Brunswick, NJ: Rutgers University Press, 2001), 166.
114 Neelam Srivastava, "Anthologizing the nation: Literature anthologies and the idea of India," *Journal of Postcolonial Writing* 46.2 (May 2010), 153.

presented here do not represent the "India" but do allow a glimpse into the way poets imagined a "India," or even what it meant to be an "Indian," in their verse. This anthology not only hopes readers will enjoy the poetry selections presented here as literary texts in and of themselves but also hopes to encourage readers to read critically, to understand how and why these texts have remained unread for so long. As Srivastava goes on to argue, anthologies can reveals the processes of canonization: "Anthologies are (literally) textbook examples of how processes of canonization might work. However, unlike the syllabus, the anthology lays bare its own criteria of selection and arrangement, through the introductions and framing statements of the editors. It is, in more than one sense, a meta-genre, in that it incorporates a self-reflexive element within its structure. This is why it is a useful form to study for those researching the processes of canonization in contemporary South Asian writing, and the evolution of a notion of literary value inhering to its production."[115] Anthologies "teach" students, a young generation of readers and writers, about literature but also about history, politics, economics and their attendant ideological formations. One of the purposes of *Mapping the Nation* in particular has been to question accepted canons of English literature and notions of literary culture by illustrating the variety of Anglophone productions, in particular Indian-English productions, during the period 1870–1920.

---

115 Ibid.

East

Eastern India encompasses the Calcutta presidency and its various outlying districts including the modern-day states of West Bengal, Orissa, Bihar, and Assam as well as Bangladesh (once East Bengal) and Nepal. The 1905 partition of Bengal produced a corresponding psychic split that can be seen in some of the later poetry, which can also be said to have become increasingly nationalist after this point. As the center of imperial administration until 1911, when it was announced that the capital of the British Raj would be relocated to Delhi, Calcutta (now Kolkata) was home of the first English-medium college, Hindu College, established in 1817. Founded by the Bengali social reformer Ram Mohan Roy, the Scottish watchmaker and philanthropist David Hare and Radhakanta Deb, the college changed its name to Presidency College in 1855. Calcutta was also the birthplace of the "Bengali Renaissance," which began with the social reform movements of Ram Mohan Roy among others and which produced innumerable Bengali and English-language poets, novelists, dramatists, essayists and journalists during the nineteenth century. Music, dance, theater and the visual arts were also "revived" during this period. Indeed, the man usually credited as the first Indian-English poet, Henry Louis Vivian Derozio, was a product of early nineteenth-century Calcutta's intellectual and social fervor. The Dutt family, which produced generations of English-language poets, figures prominently in this section.

Shoshee Chunder Dutt

Another member of the famous Dutt family of Calcutta, Shoshee Chunder Dutt (1824–1885) attended Hindu College and worked as a civil servant, justice of the peace and writer. Like many other Indian-English writers, he worked in a variety of genres. His publications include collections of poetry such as *Miscellaneous Verses* (1848), *A Vision of Sumeru, and other poems* (1878), *Works of Shoshee Chunder Dutt* (1885) and *Last Moments of Pratapa* (1893), poems from which are included in the "North" section, as well as novels such as *The Young Zemindár, his erratic wanderings and eventual return...* (1883) and the hodge-podge *Bengaliana: A Dish of Rice and Curry, and other Indigestible Ingredients* (1880), which includes an account of life as a civil servant and a tale of the 1857 Indian Uprising. His ethnographic work, *A Wild Tribes of India* (1882), was published under the pseudonym Horatio Bickerstaffe Rowney. Accompanying the *Vision of Sumeru* is a photograph of the author, who notes in an "Advertisement" to his volume: "Most of the poems in this volume were originally published in India, and have been out of print for several years. In bringing out a new edition of them the author has preferred to get the book printed in England. The course followed may not be approvable on other grounds: what was held passable in India will, perhaps, not be tolerated in Britain; but the author being solely responsible for the error, will have no one to blame for the consequences but himself."

A Vision of Sumeru,[1] and Other Poems (Calcutta: 1878)[2]

Address to the Ganges

I.

The waves are dashing proudly down,
    Along thy sounding shore;
Lashing, will all the storm of power,
The craggy base of mountain tower,
    Of mosque, and pagod[3] hoar,
That darkly o'er thy waters frown;
As if their moody spirits' sway
Could hush thy wild and boist'rous play!

II.

But reckless yet of gloomy eye,
    As heedless too of smile,
Through various climes, with regal sweep,
Rolls on thy current dark and deep;
    Nor ever stoops to wile
The blooming fruits and flow'rets shy,
That lightly bend to reach thy wave,
    Their beauteous breasts therein to lave.

III.

Unconscious roll the surges down,
    But not unconscious thou,
Dread spirit of the roaring flood!
For ages worshipp'd as a god,
    And worshipp'd even now –
Worshipp'd, and not by serf or clown;
For sages of the mightiest fame
Have paid their homage to thy name.

---

1 Mount Mêru, or Sumeru: abode of Brahma and the lesser divinities; thought to be historically located in Kashmir. It is also a part of Buddhist cosmology.
2 Shoshee Chunder Dutt, *A Vision of Sumeru, and Other Poems* (Calcutta: Thacker, Spink, 1878).
3 *Pagod*, or *pagoda*: tiered tower.

IV.

Canst thou forget the glorious past?
    When, might as a god,
With hands and heart unfetter'd yet,
And eyes with slavish tears unwet,
    Each sable warrior trod
Thy sacred shore; before the blast
Of Moslem conquest hurried by;
Ere yet the Mogul spear was nigh.[4]

V.

Thine was the glory's brightest ray
    When the land with glory teem'd;
The fairest wreath the poet won,
The praise of every daring done,
    On thee reflected beam'd:
When glory's light had pass'd away
Thine were India's wrongs and pain,
Despite that brow of proud disdain.

VI.

O'er crumbled thrones thy waters glide,
    Through scenes of blood and woe;
And crown and kingdom, might and sway,
The victor's and the poet's bay,
    Ignobly sweep below.
Sole remnant of our ancient pride,
Thy waves survive the wreck of time,
And wanton free, as in their prime.

---

4 The Mughal Empire of the subcontinent was founded in 1526 with the defeat of the Delhi Sultanate by Babur (a descendent of Timur). It was greatly expanded by Akbar in the late sixteenth century and by Aurangzeb in the late seventeenth century. After the latter's death in 1707, a series of weak rulers led to a decline in the fortunes of the empire until its end in 1857 as a result of the Indian Uprising (or "Sepoy Mutiny"). The last Mughal emperor, Bahadur Shah Zafar, was deposed by the British and sent into exile in Burma.

VII.

Behold, alas! all round how drear,
    How mangled, and how torn!
Where are the damsels proud and gay,
Where warriors in their dread array,
    In freedom's temple born?
Can heroes sleep? Can patriots fear?
Or is the spark for ever gone
That lights the soul from sire to son?

VIII.

'Tis gone, aye gone, for ever gone –
    E'en like a midnight dream!
And with it, on the whirlwind blast,
Our fame and honour too have past,
    And glory's latest beam;
But thou unheeding roll'st alone,
Still proud of thy untarnish'd name,
As if untouch'd by India's shame.

IX.

I gaze upon thy current strong
    Beneath the blaze of day;
What conjured visions throng my sight,
Of war and carnage, death and flight!
    Thy waters to the Bay
In purple eddies sweep along,
And Freedom shrieking leaves her shrine,
Alas! no longer now divine.

X.

'Twas here the savage Tártár[5] stood,
    And toss'd his brand and spear;
The ripples of thy sacred stream
Reflected back his sabre's gleam,
    While quaked with dastard fear
The children of a haughtier blood,
No longer now a haughty race,
Their own, their sires', their land's disgrace.

---

5 Tatars, or tatars: members of an ethnic group compromising nomadic tribes from Central Asia. Dutt seems to use the term to refer to the invading Mughals, and especially the Mughal emperor Babur (1483–1530), who founded the Mughal dynasty after successfully attacking the Delhi Sultanate. Babur was said to have directly descended from the Tatar rulers Genghis Khan and his successor, Tamerlane the Great.

XI.

The Suttee's[6] slow but willing feet
    Ascended here the pyre;
Anxious for a happy lot,
Her fears, her tortures all forgot,
    She clasp'd the kindling fire —
Expecting soon her lord to greet
In ether's emerald realms above,
Beneath the beams of light and love.

XII.

On yonder bank the mother stood,
    Her baby on her breast!
A madd'ning horror thrill'd her frame,
Adown her cheeks the tear-drops came;
    Hush, baby, hust to rest!
Sleep, baby, sleep beneath the flood!
Her pleasing burthen sinking smiled;
In vain the mother call'd her child.

XIII.

But why recount our woes and shame?
    Upon thy sacred shore
Be mine to dream of glories past,
To grieve those glories could not last,
    And muse on days of yore!
For ever harp on former fame,
Remembering still those spirits brave
Who sleep beneath thy boist'rous wave.

XIV.

Roll, Gungá, roll in thy pride,
    Thy hallow'd groves among!
Glorious art thou in every mood,
Thou boast of India's widowhood,
    Thou theme of every song!
Blent with the murmurs of thy tide
The records of far ages lie,
And live, for thou canst never die.

---

6 *Suttee*, or *sati*: Brahmin widow who sacrificed herself on her husband's funeral pyre. A number of movements by British and Indian social reformers during the nineteenth century sought to abolish the practice of *sati*; the issue was a fraught one in contemporary discourse.

My Native Land

I.

My native land, I love thee still!
There's beauty yet upon thy lonely shore;
   And not a tree, and not a rill,
   But can my soul with rapture thrill,
      Though glory dwells no more.

II.

My fallen country! on thy brow
The ruthless tyrants have engraved thy shame,
   And laid thy haughty grandeur low;
   Yet even thus, and even so,
      I love to lisp thy name.

III.

What though those temples now are lone
Where guardian angels long did dwell;
   What though from brooks that sadly run,
   The naiads are for ever gone –
      Gone with their sounding shell!

IV.

And haunted shades and laurel bowers
Resound not now the minstrel's fiery law,
   And e'en though deck'd with orient flowers,
   They ne'er recall those witching hours,
      For ever past away:

V.

My heart yet may not cease to burn
For thy sweet woodlands, and thy sunny shore;
   Though oft unconscious it will turn,
   Unconscious sigh, unconscious yearn
      For glorious days of yore!

VI.

Those days of mythic tale and song,
When dusky warriors, in their martial pride,[7]
   Strode thy sea-beat shores along,
   While with their fame the valleys rung,
        And turn'd the foe aside.

VII.

Then sparkled woman's brilliant eye,
And heaved her heart, and panted to enslave;
   And beauteous veils and flow'rets shy,
   In vain to hide those charms did try
        That flash'd to woo the brave.

VIII.

My fallen country! where abide
Thy envied splendor, and thy glory now?
   The Páthán's and the Mogul's pride,[8]
   Spread desolation far and wide,
        And stain'd thy sinless brow.

IX.

In freedom's shrine, the slave alone
Now dwells — a lasting monument of thy shame!
   The mighty and the brave are gone;
   Thy hallow'd triumphs overthrown —
        The trophies of their fame!

X.

But still the sun his noon-tide ray
Darts proudly on thy mountains towering round;
   And heedless winds with streamlets play,
   As slow they murmur on their way,
        Through th' lovely, classic ground.

---

7 A reference to the tales recounted in the *Vedas* and the ancient Hindu epics, the *Ramayana* and the *Mahabharata*.

8 Pathans, or Pashtuns: Pashto-speaking people from parts of modern-day southeast Afghanistan and northwest Pakistan. Many Pashtuns migrated to other parts of the subcontinent, including Gujurat, Rajasthan and Punjab, to serve as soldiers under the Mughal Empire, especially in patrolling the North-West Frontier.

XI.

And human naiads love to roam
Where reckless sweep thy regal rivers bold;
By temple, and by shatter'd dome,
Of gods the consecrated home,
　　The hallow'd shrines of old!

XII.

And beauty's eye retains its fire,
What though its lightnings flash not for the brave;
And beauteous bosoms yet aspire,
With passion strong and warm desire,
　　To wake the crouching slave.

XIII.

My country! fallen as thou art,
My soul can never cease to heave for thee:
I feel the dagger's edge, the dart
That rankles in thy widow'd heart,
　　Thy woeful destiny!

XIV.

I cannot choose but love thee yet;
And, while I rove thy fragrant meads along,
I only wish I could forget
That thy sun hath for ever set,
　　Sweet land of love and song![9]

---

9 [Poet's Note: The following beautiful stanza was added, to a presentation copy of the poem, by the late Rev. J. H. Parker:
"Nay, not *for ever* set thy sun;
Truth's brighter, holier sun shall rise to shine: —
　See, even now, the dawn begun,
　A glorious course thou yet may'st run,
　Beneath the beamings of that 'Sun
　　Of Righteousness' Divine."]

Sonnets—India

I.

What buried ages mingle in my dreams,
And what visions wild of dread sublimity,
While slowly pacing by thy lordly streams,
I muse, "Niobe of nations!"[10] on thee.
The page of history unveiléd seems,
And virtue's brightest triumphs there I see;
The victor's laurel, and the patriot's crown,
And Science' trophies piled aspiring high —
Braving the tempest's darkest, gloomiest frown,
And, almost impious, reaching to the sky!
A giddy throb my wondering pulses own,
And, lost in admiration, mute I gaze
On scenes whose memory, as ages fly,
Catch holier sympathy, and brighter blaze.

II.

My dreams dispell'd, in vain I seek around
The faintest semblance of those visions fair;
All-grasping Glory sits apart discrown'd,
Her monuments swept, or melted in the air!
Her children's hands with fetters mean are bound
And none, alas! to loose those fetters dare;
And Science, stooping from her condor flight,
Now grovels low in dark, Cimmerian[11] gloom!
The victor's path is lost in rayless night,
The patriot's crown lies buried in the tomb.
Each nobler virtue now has found its grave,
And hideous sins thy hallow'd bosom stain;
At freedom's altar whines the recreant slave,
And servile hugs the despot's loathsome chain!

---

10 In Greek mythology, Niobe was punished for her hubris by both Apollo, who killed her sons, and Artemis, who killed her daughters. Niobe fled and was turned to stone thought she continued to weep as a rock cliff on Mt. Sipylus.
11 Cimmerians: tribe which lived in a land of perpetual darkness at the edge of the world in Greek mythology.

III.

And shall I to the future turn my gaze?
The future is a sealéd book to man,
And none so high presumes his sight to raise;
God's mystic secrets who shall dare to scan!
But sure it is no mighty sin to dream;
I dreamt a dream of strange and wild delight,
Freedom's pure shrine once more illumed did seem,
The clouds has pass'd beneath the morning light;
On beauty's cheek I mark'd the tear-drops dry,
And sighs and groans for ever fled the land;
Science again aspiréd to the sky,
And patriot valour watch'd the smiling strand:
A dream! A dream! Why should a dream it be?
Land of my fathers! canst thou ne'er be free?

Greece Chunder Dutt

A member of the famous Dutt family, Greece Chunder Dutt, brother to Govin Chunder Dutt and uncle to Toru Dutt, was an accomplished poet in his own right. His first single-author volume of poetry, *Cherry Stones* (1879), was followed by *Cherry Blossoms* (1887). (Poems from *Cherry Stones* are included in the "East" section.) Many of the fifty-six sonnets and "Miscellaneous Pieces" republished in *Cherry Blossoms* were also published in *Cherry Stones* although Dutt includes a number of newer poems in this second collection. One poem in particular, "In the Bush," is a fascinating and unusual piece that seems to take as its subject the experience of the Indian exile in South Africa.

Cherry Stones (Calcutta: 1879)[12]

XXVII. Sonnet
The Nepali Peasant[13]

Nursed with the eagle's blood, afar from men,
   A simple hind, the hardy mountaineer
   Lives on wild herbs and waters sparkling clear
And chestnuts gathered in the bosky glen;

---

12 Greece Chunder Dutt, *Cherry Stones* (Calcutta: P. S. D'Rozario, 1879).
13 Nepal was never formally part of the British Empire but entered into treaties with the British, which exerted a great deal of control over this supposedly independent state.

Yet he is happy as the lonely wren
> Warbling by fits her hymns of lofty cheer,
> At shut of eve on Kanchun's[14] summit drear,
Hid in her nest from blasts and human ken,
Nor lacks he patriot zeal to keep his land
> Of snow and fog and chasms yawning wide,
From foreign insult, – witness that bold hand
> Of England's sons, who, vainly struggling, died –
Urged to the contest by the rash command
> Of careless rulers – by Gillespie's side.[15]

XXX. Sonnet
Near Goa[16]

I love this churchyard by the voiceful sea,
> With its low wall, its heaps of mouldered stone
> Its shattered urns, its effigies o'erthrown,
Its velvet turf, its gloomy banyan tree,
Its timid bats that flit mysteriously
> Like ghosts at nightfall, and its bell whose tone
> Reminds the pilgrim as he plods alone,
That Time glides onward to Eternity:
For here they rest, whose patient fortitude,
> Delivered Xavier from the heathen's hand,[17]
Who fought with Albuquerque the pirates rude,[18]
> Of wild Socotra,[19] girt with surf and sand,
Who watched the needle undepressed by fear,
In stedfast Gama's bark,[20] when rocks loomed near.

---

14 Kanchun, or Kanchung: one of the faces of Mount Everest.
15 Major Rollo Gillespie (1766–1814): soldier who led a contingent of British troops during the Gurkha War (also known as the Anglo–Nepalese War), which raged from 1814–1816. He was killed in battle.
16 Goa: located on the west coast of India. Now a popular tourist destination, Goa was a Portuguese colony from 1510 until 1961, when it was annexed by India after a successful campaign by Indian forces against Portugal for control of the territory.
17 Saint Francis Xavier (1506–1552): Spanish missionary who traveled throughout South and East Asia (including Japan). He spent some time in Goa and was instrumental in founding the Society of Jesus.
18 Afonso de Albuquerque (1453–1515): Portuguese nobleman who sought to gain control of all maritime trade routes with the East under the Portuguese king Manuel. He and his squadron conquered Goa in 1510.
19 Socotra, or Soqotra: small archipelago of four islands in the Indian Ocean.
20 Vasco da Gama (1460?–1524): Portuguese explorer sent by King John III to rule as viceroy over the Portuguese possessions on the subcontinent, including Goa, where he died.

XLVII. Sonnet
1858

While ruthless wars around our cities roll,[21]
    And marts re-echo the wild cry of fear,
    Far from all noise by Teesta's[22] current clear,
Oh for the maple dish and beechen bowl!
The hermit's life, from childhood, was the goal
    Of all my thoughts, – but now the joys severe
    Of the lone cell, hemmed in by mountains drear,
With double power attract my longing soul.
How sweet, while moonlight silvers wood and lawn,
    To 'sleep with upward face,' or pipe at ease;
Or to cull simples ere the meek-eyed dawn
    Hath edged with burning gold the green-robed trees;
Or yet to rove in valleys far withdrawn,
    Cheered by the linnet's song and whispering breeze.

LIV. Sonnet
Sacoontala[23]

To him who plods with weary steps and slow,
    Through her antique tomes, how fresh these pages seem!
    Not fresher in the wilderness the gleam
Of the cool fountain, round which the date palms grow,
And purple stonecrops in rich masses glow,
    To the worn pilgrim, when the noonday beam
    Smites with relentless rage, the jaded team
Of camels that he leads, with head bent low: –
He reads, and summoned by the verse appear,
    The lovely hermitage, and garden small,

---

21 This is most likely a reference to the 1857 Indian Uprising (or "Sepoy Mutiny") a resistance movement now commonly cast by nationalist historians as the first Indian war of independence.
22 Teesta, or Tista: river which flows through what is now the Indian state of Sikkim and forms the border between Sikkim and West Bengal.
23 The story of Sacoontala, or Shakuntala, is told as a digression within the "main" plot of the *Mahabharata*. King Dushyanta encounters Shakuntala in the forest, falls in love with and marries her. Before leaving to attend to affairs of state, the king bestows upon his wife a ring as a token of his affection and promises he will return for her. Due to a curse, the king forgets his wife, who bears his child. A fisherman finds Shakuntala's ring and brings it to the king who is then reminded of his wife. King Dushyanta searches the forest for his long-lost love and is finally reunited with wife and child after many years.

Smooth lawns, that slope down to the brooklet clear,
    Bright plots of yellow corn 'mid forests tall,
And peerless maids, in robes of bark that bear
The osier[24] basket, heaped with fruitage rare.

Joteendro Mohun Tagore

Joteendro Mohun Tagore (1831–1908), a member of the famous Tagore family of Bengal, was an important patron of theater and music along with his brother, Saurindra Mohan Tagore, who published *A Few Specimens of Indian Songs* (1879), a collection of traditional songs set to music. Born into a wealthy family of landowners, Joteendro Mohun Tagore was educated at Hindu College. He was famous for commissioning Tagore Castle, modeled on English castles. Bestowed various official titles by the Imperial government for services rendered to the Empire, Tagore was known by the end of his life as "the Maharaja Sir Jotindro Mohan Tagore Bahadur."

Flights of Fancy in Prose and Verse (Calcutta: 1881)[25]

The Rajpootnee's Song[26]
On the Occasion of the Festival of Camdev[27]

I.

Sweet Spring is now ended – the Summer wind blows,
So weave we the chaplet of *Champac* and Rose,
Chameli and *Magra* in garlands we twine,
For this is the Feast of the *Kandurva* divine.[28]

---

24 Osier: species of willow; the branches of which are used in basket work (adj. "osier" *OED*).
25 Joteendro Mohun Tagore, *Flights of Fancy in Prose and Verse* (Calcutta: Sourindro Mohun Tagore, 1881).
26 Rajpoots, or Rajputs: thought to be mostly members of the Kshetriya, or warrior, caste but their status varied widely. These landowning, patrilineal clans ruled central and northern India from around the tenth century, when they began to gain political power, until the collapse of the Mughal Empire, with which they made settlements, at the end of the eighteenth century. After independence in 1947, the Rajput states were merged to form the state of Rajasthan. Known as soldiers, the Rajputs were celebrated for their military prowess and heavily recruited by the British East India Company and later the British Empire. They are often depicted in highly romanticized terms in Orientalist literature.
27 [Poet's Note: The Hindu Cupid.] Kamadeva: Hindu god of love.
28 *Champac*, or *champak*: evergreen tree with fragrant orange-yellow flowers. *Chameli* and *magra*, or *mogra*: fragrant jasmine flowers native to Southeast and South Asia. Kandurva, or Kandarva, or Gandharva: race of male demigods associated with nature and music in Hinduism.

II.

God of the bright bow! we hail thee with joy,
Mays't though add to our peace, and our sorrows destroy,
Thou who canst fill creation with mirth,
Thou who has power o'er heaven and earth.

III.

Glory to *Cam*! – thou the loveliest still,
Thou who e'en sage minds with raptures can fill;
Though of sweet flowers thine arrows be made,
Even great *Shiva* their power hath obeyed.[29]

IV.

We are but women, by nature made weak,
'Tis therefore thus humbly thy favour we seek;
Grant us this boon, that our lov'd lords may never
Regard us unkindly, but love us for ever.

V.

Then, oh Ruler of hearts! sincerely shall we,
Each year, with fresh spirits, pay homage to thee;
Only grant us this boon, which thus humbly we crave,
And with songs shall we honour the Feast of *Camdev*.

Sonnet to the Kokil[30]

Melodious *Kokil*! – warbler of the wood!
Whose song can melt into a milder mood
    E'en winter stern; – we welcome thy return;
For thou dost usher in delightful Spring,
    Who smiling scatters from her plenteous urn
Fresh flowers and leaves, and in her train doth bring
    Celestial Joys – a glorious band who roam

---

29 Shiva: one of the major Hindu deities and often represented as one aspect of the Trimurti, which also included Vishnu and Brahma. Shiva is able to destroy and thus transform. In some versions of the tale, Shiva was disturbed from his meditation by Kamadev's arrow, which incites him to make love to his wife, Parvati.

30 *Kokil*, also known as the *coil, koil, koel, koyal*, or *kokila*: bird famed for its melodious calls; often termed the Indian cuckoo.

'Midst fields and plains. Sweet bird, thy songs invite
      The timid loving maidens from their home
To meet fond lovers by the pale moon's light
      In bliss supreme, to chase dull care away.
Thrice happy bird! for these we love thee well,
Oh! may'st thou ever in these green groves dwell,
      And tune thy lays of love all night and day.

Song
Radha's Anxiety for the Absence of Krishna

I.

Where roves the youth whose beaming eye
      My maiden heart hath stole?
He cometh not, the night is nigh,
      Ah! what shall cheer my soul.

II.

Perchance some other nymph, whose lot
      Is happier than my own,
Doth now engross my lover's thought
      While thus I weep alone.

III.

Ha! was that his sweet flute which sent
      That charming silver sound? –
It was the gale that sighing went
      And all is still around.

IV.

O! haste thee, love, why thus delay?
      The twilight gloom doth lour,
The evening star shall guide thy way,
      O! haste thee to my bower.

The Dewallee, or The Feast of Light[31]

I.

The sun hath sunk down on the Ganges' broad stream,
And faded and gone is the evening's last beam;
Grey twilight fast yields to the darkness of night,
And flowerets and fields are enshrouded from sight.

II.

But lo! the fair city illumin'd and bright
Shines 'mid the darkness – an ocean of light,
And seems a dear dream, or an image adored
From the depths of Oblivion divinely restored.

III.

On the *Ghauts*[32] and the mansions, a thousand lamps shine
And gleams thro' the palm-grove the half reveal'd shrine,
On *Gunga's*[33] calm breast, all, in splendour pourtray'd –
    A land of the Faery, by magic displayed.

IV.

On the River's smooth bosom, maids graceful and fair
Are launching their love-lamps with tenderest care;
And are swayed, or with fear, or with hope's ardent glow,
As flick'ring like fire-flies, the barks onward flow.

V.

Here pray'rs and devotions their blessings impart,
There music and poetry enrapture the heart;
O! ne'er was there yet a more beautiful sight
Than this city thus holding its gay "feast of light."

---

31 Dewallee, or Diwali: festival of lights that occurs sometime between October and November. It is celebrated in Hinduism, Jainism and Sikhism and associated with a variety of tales. In some versions, the festival celebrates the return of King Rama to his kingdom in Ayodhya after his long exile and his defeat of the demon-king Lord Ravana.
32 *Ghauts*, or *ghats*: series of steps leading down to a body of water (such as the Ganges, for example) or a path leading down from a mountain (n. "ghats" *OED*).
33 Gunga: Ganges River.

Moonlight on the River

The silv'ry moon, in majesty serene,
Enthronéd sits. Beneath, the Ganges spreads
Its breast, – a sheet immense of crystalline,
Where heaven's ethereal dome, begemmed with stars,
Is mirrored, – "beautiful exceedingly!"
Along the verdant banks the stately palms
Their lengthened shadows fling; the mangoe tree,
Its leaves with silver tipp'd, a chequered shade
Extends; while oft some silken plot of ground,
Enamelled o'er with flowers of orient hue,
Laughs gaily on the sight. In tranquil flow
The stream rolls on, unruffled with a wave,
Like infancy's sweet thoughts – so pure, so calm!
That not a rippling sound is heard against
The vessel's sides. The winds, now weary grown
With wafting fragrance from the nectar'd cup
Of each fresh opening flower, have sunk to rest,
Nor aught else stirs; except at intervals,
In melting cadence from some far off tree,
Is heard the *Kokil*[34] singing to his mate;
Or, oftener yet, the cricket's piercing chirp
That makes the silence doubly felt. 'Tis now
That Contemplation reigns supreme;
'Tis now that Nature with her Maker holds
Communion deep. A spell there is in such
A time as this that leads the pensive soul
To tender mem'ries of the blissful past!

Sonnet to India

Land of my fathers! once for learning famed,
In whose green groves the Muses loved to sport,
Whose luckless children once sweet freedom claimed,
Whose friendship foreign nations once did court,
For ever Liberty hath left thy shore,
Thy ancient prowess is now past and gone;
Thy former glory that so brightly shone,
Now dim'd, like star-light gleams but warms no more; –

---

34 *Kokil*, also known as the *coil*, *koil*, *koel*, *koyal*, or *kokila*: bird famed for its melodious calls; often termed the Indian cuckoo.

But still my heart with fondness clings to thee,
Although no more that soul within thee shines,
As fondly round a leafless, withered tree
The grateful creeper still its tendril twines;
For though for ever hath thy bright sun set,
My own, my NATIVE LAND, I love thee yet.

The Hindu Widow's Lament [35]

I.

Ah! when shall these my sufferings end
    My solitary grief?
Ah! when from all these sorrows deep
    Shall I have found relief?
Thus early am I doomed to know
    A widow's lot severe;
This world is now a blank to me,
    A lonely desert drear.

II.

With penance and with fastings I
    A widow's virtue keep,
And when I think upon my lot,
    With heavy heart I weep.
Alas! the time when fortune smiled,
    How little then I thought,
Such endless grief and pangs severe
    Should ever be my lot!

III.

My mother loved me dearly once,
    But now she weeps to see
My features wild and widow'd stated,
    But speaks no word to me;
And when upon her lap I lie,
    My head she presses slow,
And as she fondly plaits my hair,
    Her tears unbidden flow.

---

35 Upper-caste Brahmin women in certain regions such as Bengal were considered social outcastes once they became widows. They were forced to wear white, abstain from all bodily ornamentation and severely restrict their diet.

IV.

How sweetly do my youthful friends
　　The bliss of wedlock share,
While I, a wretched girl, am doomed
　　To pine in lonely care;
Kind KRISHNA, do receive the pray'rs
　　Of a poor widow'd wife;
And if my tears can move thee, Lord,
　　O rid me of my life!

Avadh Behari Lall

Avadh Behari Lall was from the area now known as Bihar. It can be inferred from the prefaces to his collections, which were published in remarkably quick succession (all spaced about one year apart), that he was very young, only in his twenties, when he published most of his poetry. His volumes include *The Irish Home Rule Bill, a Poetical Pamphlet* (1893), *Behar, and Other Poems* (1898), *An Elegy on the Late Right Hon'ble William Ewart Gladstone, M.P.* (1898), *An Ode on the Coronation Durbar at Delhi* (1903) and *A Poem on the Coronation of Their Majesties King George V and Queen Mary as Emperor and Empress of India* (1911). His poetry, most of it political in nature, evinces a complicated admixture of both loyalty towards and eviscerating critique of the British government. Although he offers the usual paeans to British rulers, his long poems on the Irish Home Rule bill and on Gladstone illustrate his sympathies with Ireland's efforts to gain a measure of autonomy under the British Empire.

The Irish Home Rule Bill, a poetical pamphlet (Calcutta: 1893)[36]

The Irish Home Rule Bill, a poetical pamphlet[37]

Must Erin[38] still bleed; must sororicide
Be Albion's[39] great shame, glory, and pride;
Must centuries of misrule be still backed
By further misrule – must Freedom be packed;

36　Avadh Behari Lall, *The Irish Home Rule Bill, a poetical pamphlet* (Calcutta: I. C. Bose & Co., 1893).
37　In 1893, Gladstone sponsored the second Home Rule bill (the first Home Rule bill failed to pass through Parliament in 1886). This Home Rule bill, which called for limited self-government such as an Irish parliament, was passed by the House of Commons but vetoed by the House of Lords.
38　Erin: Ireland.
39　Albion: England.

Must Englishmen, while making nations free,
Make their own cousins slaves of Liberty;
Must subject-races consolations find
In being oppressed by their mightier kind;
Must Irish hearts, by th' Englishmen purloined
Through miscalled Union,[40] still be kept disjoined;
Must Erin's records one long tale present
Of th' English oppressions cont'nuedly lent;
Must Irish leaders be great rebels called,
Threatened and "shadowed," imprisoned and mauled;
Must Patriots' efforts still remain uncrowned,
And Erin show herself but in chains bound;
Must Lord North's follies sure succession find
In politicians *true*, of Balfour's[41] mind;
'Must ancient failings be examples made,'
And Tories[42] insist on th' oppressing trade;
Must Conservatives th' Ulster men[43] befool,
And preach that Erin's strength lies in sword-rule;
Must England's name be with distrust severe
Held to the world for her great tyr'nnies *here*;
Must no angel-saint – induce fair St. George[44]
To set his brother St. Patrick[45] at large;
Must still the hated Union, by bribes gained,
Be by co-ercion Bills or fraud maintained:[46]
Must the "Enlightened" men in freaks delight
Of great oppressions, legalized by might;
Must faction-mongers, rank-seceders, breed
Obstructions great, and justice' paths impede;
Must the reformed Nineteenth Century see

---

40 The 1801 Act of Union was a legislative agreement uniting Great Britain (England, Scotland and Wales) and Ireland under the name of the United Kingdom of Great Britain and Ireland.
41 Arthur Balfour (1848–1930): British Conservative politician who acted as chief secretary of Ireland from 1887 to 1891 and prime minister of Great Britain from 1902 to 1906. He presided over the end of the Boer War and took a firm position against Irish Home Rule. Balfour was referred to by Irish Nationalists as "Bloody Balfour" due to his ruthless enforcement of the Irish Coercion Act.
42 Tories: members of the British Conservative Party.
43 Ulster: an ancient kingdom and geographical region of northern Ireland, comprising nine counties spread across what are now Northern Ireland and the Republic of Ireland. By the late nineteenth century, the region was divided (often along religious lines) between those supporting Irish Home Rule (usually Catholics) and those opposing Irish Home Rule (usually Protestants).
44 St. George: patron saint of England.
45 St. Patrick: patron saint of Ireland.
46 The Acts of Coercion were emergency laws passed by the British government in Ireland between the eighteenth to early twentieth centuries to "maintain" law and order by suspending habeas corpus, imposing restrictions on the press and imposing martial law.

Shamefaced violations and great mockery
Of princ'ples of const'tutional liberty;
Must misled statesmen others now mislead,
And lend no gracious ear to Erin's need;
Must English ground *bear* Demonstrations foul
Where statesmen preach the justice of misrule;
Must Patriots' Leagues by cruel laws be dissolved,
And the great Home Rule Question live unsolved;
Must Irish liberty be but a name,
And none allowed to burn with a true patriot's flame;
Must Parnell's dreams be no real'ties now,
Though the great dreamer is himself but low;
Must great Gladstone[47] in vain to hearts appeal,
Known for great mercies, for Ireland's great weal;
Most "Joe" and "Cecil" and the Unionist train
Still find short success 'gainst the Grand Old Man;[48]
Must Albion's justice still so tardy be
As not t' allow her Sister liberty;
Must Home Rule Act be still a dream of yore,
When the great Premier is come to the fore;
Must th' Em'rald Isle, Hibernia,[49] known so long,
Be quite effaced or sunk, or live but in old song?
    See now great Gladstone's come with all the weight
Of long experience, Erin t' elevate
Full sixty years in Parliaments he has sit;
With wisdom sharpened his sagacious wit;
With Truth and Justice as his watch-words ruled,
The good encouraged and the turb'lent cooled;
Has taken part in Reform Bills, and made
His own and England's name wonder and dread
Of all nations: nay, the world can't show,
Midst all her sons that in politics glow,
A name equal in sageness to the Man who's now
England's great-honoured Premier the fourth time,[50]
Though old yet vigorous, though grey yet sublime.
May thou great man (around whose name so shine
The glory's halo that 'tis held divine,
Whom Fame has giv'n so much of her applause
That she can hardly louder cheer her cause,)

---

47 William Ewart Gladstone (1809–1898): served several terms as Liberal prime minister of Great Britain (1868–1874; 1880–1885; 1886; 1892–1894). His actions in protection of Irish tenants and his support of Irish Home Rule as well as his appointment of Lord Ripon as viceroy of India in 1880 won him the support of Indians. He was known as a great orator as well.
48 Grand Old Man: William Ewart Gladstone.
49 Em'rald, or Emerald Isle and Hibernia are both names for Ireland.
50 "Premier the fourth time": Gladstone.

Thy last great case with justice's fire plead,
And in thy best worthiest effort succeed!
May all the pow'r which wisdom t' eloquence lends,
The fiery speech to which ev'ry one bends,
Britannia's angels backing thee in need,
With triumph crown thy great masterly deed!
To thy laurel-leaves, still green in thine age,
Add one greener leaf more, thy last desire t' assuage;
With one bright ray illumine all the past
Pages of Irish Clio,[51] dark to the last;
May a great Nation's grat'tude be thy prize,
And thy last joy to see the sunken rise;
"Ireland's Redeemer" be thy future name,
A greater boast than her "Liberator's" fame![52]

O Liberty! the nation's great idol,
The joy and aim of all, of ev'ry life the soul,
The countries or th' individuals without which
Think living but a burden or an itch,
Long-banished from thine own Hibernian shore,
The Em'rald Isle, long praised and sung of yore,
Come to thy Ierne, to live with her e'er more.
In thy loved Gladstone thy great champion find,
To wipe thy tears with a true heart inclined —
Will not one's brothers' woes rouse symp'thy in one's mind?
Throw a veil of Oblivion o'er thy past,
And think thy wrongs and sorrows will no longer last.
Ye Spirits of the great departed Sons
Of misshaped Erin, now arise at once;
Through your Country's Ben'factor your cause plead
And bless that his be most successful lead!
Through 'Welsh by marriage, Englishman by birth,
Scotch by descent,' he's the Man of whole Earth;
And Ireland finds in his heart's inmost core
A cherished place, confiding and secure.
That Liberty — for whom O'Neils have bled,
For whom Patriots have been to Tyburn led;[53]

---

51 Clio: Muse of History in Greek mythology.
52 "The Liberator" was the title given to Daniel O'Connell (1775–1847), the Irish political leader who campaigned for Catholic emancipation (a successful bid to allow Catholics to sit in Parliament) and the repeal of the Act of Union.
53 Tyburn: village in the English county of Middlesex, now the Hyde Park neighborhood; infamous location of a gallows where criminals and political dissidents were executed from 1196 to 1783. Tyburn Convent, a Catholic convent, is dedicated to the memory of the Catholic martyrs executed there.

Whose cause Flood the orator, with mighty force,
Pleaded to English audience — deaf of course;
For whom mod'rate Curran in vain did try,[54]
And dashful Emmet did on gallows die;
'Gainst whom Min'sters have e'en to bribing stooped,
And by illusive hopes th'ignoble duped;
To whom wise Grattan did his life devote[55]
(The man who didn't sell his patriotic vote);
For whom O'Connell's name (short though success)
Does oppressed Ireland with gratitude bless,
Calling him her "Liberator," and no less;
For whom Dillons, O'Connors, and O'Briens,[56]
Have played th'unfortunate heroes of great chequered scenes;
For whom good Shaws, Textons, Davitts,[57] have been
Imprisoned, for their having patriotic mien;
For not gaining whom, her last Leader lies
With a broken heart, midst Ireland's loud cries;
'Gainst whom hoarse solemn compacts have been made
With a glorious aim — men's rights to invade;
For whom old Gladstone, with loft a front,
Stands nobly firm erect — Oh! stoop he can't! —
Will be from her long stupor soon restored,
The one Goddess long sought to be adored!
On subjects' love, an Empire's solid base,
A structure built, hoar Time can't it efface;
And Britain's glory and strength will consist
(Not in bringing more nations to the list
Of her subject-races but) in good sway,
In respecting the rights of those who her obey.

---

54 John Curran (1750–1817): Protestant Irish lawyer and statesman who fought for Catholic emancipation and defended the leaders of the United Irishmen in their treason trial after the 1798 Rebellion.

55 Henry Grattan (1746–1820): Irish lawyer and statesman who also worked for Catholic emancipation.

56 John Dillon (1814–1866) and William O'Brien (1803–1864): leading members of the group Young Ireland, which advocated force in repealing the Act of Union, and who spearheaded the failed Young Ireland Rebellion of 1848. O'Connor might refer to Arthur O'Connor (1763–1852), who joined the United Irishmen as a youth and was arrested and imprisoned in 1798 before finally being released in 1802.

57 William Shaw (1823–1895): Irish politician, member of Parliament in the House of Commons, a founder of the Irish Home Rule movement and chairman of the Home Rule Party until his deposition by Charles Stewart Parnell in 1880. Michael Davitt (1846–1906): Irish politician, member of the revolutionary Fenian Brotherhood (a secret society which sought political and economic freedom from Great Britain) and founder of the Land League. The Land League, founded in 1879, organized against absentee landlords and promoted fair rent and fixed tenure for tenants among other things.

When a distinguished Countryman of mine,
To back the Irish Cause, does freely join
The members of the present Parliament,
A right to Ind by Central Finsbury lent,[58]
A grace of England's Radical element,
Why will not another Indian try to speak
For his fellow-subjects' good, though his voice be weak?
Though unheard be my words, my heart's sincere
As wishing to Ierne[59] true good cheer.
May Grand Old Man's attempt, noble and wise,
To heal the old sores and to stop just cries,
Be a *fait accompli!*[60] Erin the free,
Remember, Sing, "Gladstone and Liberty!"

Behar, and other poems (Calcutta: 1898)[61]

An Epistle to the Right Hon'ble Alfred Lord Tennyson, Poet-Laureate, England
Dated Gya, the 22nd July, 1892[62]

I.

The Sun shines on all things or good or bad;
    And you might have, our Poets' laurelled King!
In long experience which you sure have had
    In your eighty years, seen (to say nothing
Of poets' gradual strides in verse-making,)
    Verses of all kinds — even the "prose-verse,"
Or "prose run mad" of some weak brains' rhyming:
    Now a much youngster poetaster worse,
A simple scribbler — who, artless, does dare rehearse,

---

58 Central Finsbury, or Finsbury Central: parliamentary constituency created in 1885 and located in North London. Finsbury elected the first MP of Indian descent, Dadabhai Naoroji, in 1892.
59 Ierne: Ireland.
60 *Fait accompli*: accomplished fact.
61 Avadh Behari Lall, *Behar, and other poems* (Calcutta: Avadh Behari Lall, 1898).
62 Odes to Tennyson and other public figures, both poetic and imperial, were commonly published by Indian-English poets. Poetry was often sent by Indians to various British poets and men-of-letters in hope of recognition and publication in England.

II.

In simple strain, the long and glorious Rule
    Of fifty years of our great Sovereign,[63]
And also in low tone (being in no school
    Of Poesy taught laws how to maintain
The dignity of verse,) describe in plain
    And unaffected words the season prime
Of his own country — begs with a heart fain
    To greet the great Lord Tennyson sublime,
    The great acknowledged Fount of Poesy of his time,

III.

With verses these and two books herewith sent,
    Himself half-convinced that all are worthless.
But, thou great Poet! Lend me a moment
    Of thy precious time and but deign to bless
My lines with a glance: 'twill be happiness
    Supreme to me if in one place thou find
One single verse that may seem to possess
    A thought high-flying or a sense refined;
    Oh! then, my Lord! 'twill be a solace to my mind.

IV.

Or else think these attempts a school-boy's fun,
    Like many doggrels [sic] that you must have seen,
Destined in Time's great course no race to run,
    And to be hidden 'neath Oblivion's screen.
But 'tis custom, illustrious Lord! I ween
    For the good old verses to teach the young,
To find a joy in lines e'en when they mean
    Almost nothing; to rectify the wrong,
    To help the rising spirit and t'inflame the tongue.

V.

So let me hope — it is a pleasing thought —
    That though un-English I'm by birth and race,
The English Poets' King (for so you ought
    To be styled justly,) does read, nay does bless,

---

63 Tennyson acted as poet laureate of Great Britain from 1850 to 1892; Queen Victoria ruled from 1837 to 1901.

The English rhymes of one who may be less
    E'en than a rhymester bad. One spark is fire,
And stim'lus is almost itself success:
    So if you think my hopes worth to inspire,
    One good word from your Lordship is all I desire.

VI.

An under-graduate I, who long ago,
    (Some eight years have past since,) ill-health compelled,
Gave up at early age my studies; so,
    Though oft I have, with books, communion held,
My knowledge is but too confined, unswelled.
    For my own amusement's sake my soul I fix
Upon verse-making — not by gold impelled.
    "Practice makes perfect," bids me in heart mix
    Some hope with much despair — I am but twenty-six.

VII.

The mellow judgment of the mellow years —
    Ready to give the praise where justly due,
To prune the faults when such the need appear,
    Or to encourage and shew the path true —
Is the great boon this Epistle craves of you.
    In Gya town, in Province of Bengal,
Lives ever praying, with pray'rs ever new,
    For your health, happ'ness, and prosper'ty all,
    Your Lordship's servant true, Avadh Behari Lall.

Romesh Chunder Dutt

The Bengali poet, novelist, historian, economist, and civil servant was a widely respected figure in late nineteenth-century India. A member of the famous Dutt family of Calcutta, which included his cousin Toru Dutt, Romesh Chunder Dutt (1848–1909) published works in a variety of genres in both his native Bengali and in English: a travelogue entitled *Three Years in Europe* (1872); political and economic treatises such as *Bengal Peasantry* (1875), *England and India* (1897), *A History of Civilization in Ancient India, based on Sanscrit Literature* (1893), *Famines in India* (1900), *Economic History of India (1757–1857)* (1902, 1904); four historical novels entitled *Banga Bijeta*, *Madhabi Kankan*, *Rajput Jiban Sandhya* and *Maharastra Prabhat*; two social novels entitled *Samaj* (1885) and *Sangsar* (1893); and books of original poetry and poetic translations including *Lays of Ancient India: Selections from Indian Poetry Rendered into English Verse* (1894) and *Reminiscences of a Workman's Life* (1896). He famously published two English-language translations of the authoritative Sanskrit versions of the

Hindu epics, the *Maha-Bharata: Epic of the Bharatas, Condensed into English Verse* (1898) and the *Ramayana: the Epic of Rama, Prince of India, Condensed into English Verse* (1899). (The "Translator's Epilogue" to his rendering of the *Mahabharata* is included in the Appendix.) Like many later twentieth-century nationalists, Dutt was a product of imperial rule; but he was also a supporter of rising nationalist movements at the end of the nineteenth century as evidenced in works critical of British imperial policy. Educated in Calcutta as well as at University College and the Middle Temple, London, Dutt worked as an Indian Civil Service officer from 1871 to 1897. He returned to University College, London, to act as lecturer in Indian history from 1898 to 1904. The poems below are from his only collection of original English-language poetry.

Reminiscences of a Workman's Life (Calcutta: 1896)[64]

The Exile

1

It is the sunny April, —
    My native skies are blue;
My native fields are painted fresh
    In nature's fairest hue;
It is the season of the year
    When life the sweetest seems,
When brightens Age's cheerless face,
    And Youth is lost in dreams!

2

It is the sunny April, —
    But what is that to me?
An exile from my father's home,
    A wanderer o'er the sea!
Ten thousand waves around me rage,
    And roar in wanton glee,
The sea wind soundeth in my ear
    A boisterous melody!

3

It is the sunny April, —
    The April of my life!
Ambition sounds her bugle wild,
    It is the time for strife.

---

64 Romesh Chunder Dutt, *Reminiscences of a Workman's Life* (Calcutta: Elm Press, 1896).

Away each timid, pensive thought,
    Ye treach'rous drops away,
I'll follow that soul-maddening tune,
    O! lead me where it may!

Home

1

I stand upon the airy deck,
    And gaze upon the wide wide sea,
Yon distant hills a purple speck,
    Yon sea-fowls swimming merrily,
But in whatever realms I roam,
My heart still yearns for thee, my Home.

2

I've been among the spicy trees
    Of Ceylon's[65] most enchanted land,
I've been where beat the eternal seas
    'Gainst Aden's[66] barren rocks and sand!
But in whatever realms I roam,
My heart still yearns for thee, my Home.

3

I've been where Pompey's[67] lofty spire
    Since thousand years hath braved the sky,
I've trod the floor where, − souls of fire, −
    The knights of St. John buried lie.[68]
But in whatever realms I roam,
My heart still yearns for thee, my Home.

4

In foreign climes when wandering lone
    Still shall I mourn thy countless woes,
The Rhine, the Thames, the dark blue Rhone
    Will call to mind where Ganga flows.
For in whatever realms I roam,
My heart still yearns for thee, my Home.

---

65 Ceylon: modern-day Sri Lanka.
66 Aden: seaport city in what is now Yemen. The Gulf of Aden is located in the Arabian Sea.
67 Pompei: the "lost" city near modern-day Naples.
68 Knights of St. John: order of the Catholic Church.

Lines on India

1

'Twas once great Ganga! on thy shore
    I silent stood one even tide,
Thy rushing waters ran before,
    Frowning, dashing in their pride,
And foaming down unchained and free,
And reckless in their boisterous glee.

2

I heard thy sea-like solemn roar,
    I marked thy billows fierce and free,
I deemed the land thou rollest o'er
    Must be the land of liberty.
Alas! the soil thy waters lave
Has been for aye fair Freedom's grave!

3

Is this the land of ancient pride
    Where Freedom lived, where heroes bled,
Ask of these regions vast and wide
    From billowy sea to mountains dread!
Hark every spot in India wide
Doth tell a tale of ancient pride!

4

Hark, every pass and every hill
    Recalls the days of liberty!
Hark, how from every peak and rill,
    From echoing vales, from woods and lea,
Awakes one voice of maddening glee,
The thrilling voice of liberty!

5

In vain! in vain! the stirring voice
    No echo finds in haunts of men,
From peopled marts no sounds arise,
    No hamlets answer back again.
What silent all! No sound, no breath!
A nation sleeps — the sleep of death!

6

The children of a godlike race
    Sleep senseless of their glorious past,
Or void of strength and manly grace
    They tremble at each passing blast,
Unconscious of their ancient name,
Unmindful of their father's fame!

7

Enough! Enough! What boots it then
    To sing of days now passed away,
In halting verse why call again
    The glories which have had their day? —
Because I cannot e'er forget
My ancient country once was great.

8

Remembrance sweet! — mine be it then
    To muse on days when brightest shone
Thy light among the haunts of men,
    Thy glories bright as Eastern Sun!
Thy strength of thought, thy Manhood's power!
Thy wealth of song, thy Beauty's dower!

Lines on Ireland[69]

I

Sweet Erin![70] on thy emerald hills
    I've strolled, light-hearted as thy roe,
And on thy lakes and silver rills
    Have rowed my light and swift canoe.
Bewitching vales and woodland streams!
As fair, as wild as childhood's dreams!

---

69 Ireland was frequently invoked by Indian poets in sympathetic and even empathetic tones. Indians saw in the Irish a similar plight of oppression under British imperial rule and a concomitant desire for home rule. Ironically, however, the Irish played an important role in Britain's colonial project as civil servants and administrators as demonstrated in M. L. Brillman, "A Crucial Administrative Interlude: Sir Antony's MacDonnell's Return to Ireland, 1902–1904," *New Hibernia Review* 9.2 (Summer 2005): 65–83.

70 Erin: Ireland.

2

I've been Avoca![71] where in glee
    Thy limpid waters roll along,
And where vain beats th' eternal sea
    Against the Giant's pillars strong,
And where Dunluce's castled rock
For ages stands the ocean's shock.[72]

3

I've stood where stands the man of steel
    Who safe a virgin fortress held,
And seems to guard her fortunes still!
    Sweet Auburn![73] seem thy classic fields.
And slept where mid romantic hills
Sleep fair Killarney's[74] lakes and rills!

4

Sweet isle! oft by thy ruined fanes[75]
    I've thought of thy inglorious time,
Thy poverty, thy woes, thy pains![76]
    I've thought too of another clime,
Far far across the billow's roar,
Like thee distressed, – alas as poor!

5

The Irish heart, that owns no lord,
    Still beats it not for Freedom's cause?
And gleams not still the Irish sword
    The soldier for his country draws?
Alas! the sword rusts on the wall,
The heart but weeps on Ireland's fall!

---

71 Avoca: small town in County Wicklow, Ireland.
72 Dunluce castle is a medieval castle in Northern Ireland and is accessible via a bridge from the mainland.
73 Auburn: small town in Westmeath, Ireland.
74 Killarney: town in southwestern Ireland.
75 Fane: temple (n. "fane" OED).
76 "Thy pains": reference to the Great Famine of the 1840s as well as subsequent political battles with England over taxation, tenant's rights and Irish Home Rule.

6

And glows not bright the patriot's ire
    In every Irish bosom still?
And wakes not still the note of fire, –
    From Erin's harp the maddening peal?
Hide patriot! Hide thy blush of shame,
For ever hushed the harp of flame!

7

And must this emerald isle for aye
    Remain in endless penury?
And mourn the night that knows no day
    This home of patriots bold and free?
Queen of a thousand ocean wave!
Land of the Shamroc [sic] and the brave!

8

Rend Future! rend thy misty veil,
    A glorious day is still to shine,
And as in the antique days this isle,
    Shall be once more the dearest shrine
Of freedom born in skies above,
Of truth and valour and of love!

Autumn-Night in a Bengal Rice-Field

I

Far and near, the moonbeams fall
On the rice, luxuriant, tall,
Bounteous nature's richest scene, –
Endless sea of waving green!
Fed with rains still more and more,
Rivers, flooding bank and shore,
Spread for miles the corn-field o'er,
Oft a fathom deep or more.
But the *Amon* higher grown
Glances in the autumn moon.
Far as the eye can reach, the scene
Is on sea of waving green,
Yon dark line of deeper hue
Is a village in our view,
Pass the island village by,
Stretches still the *Amon* sea.

2

'Tis evening now, my boat goes on
Still rustling through the green *Amon*,
On either side they bending gently,
Leave a way as reverently.
No sound is on the earth or sky,
Save of my boat that rustles by.
Save of some boatman's distant cry
In evening stillness faintly heard.
Save note of some wild lonesome bird,
That on the plants had built her nest,
And nestled there in quiet rest.
She sees the intruding boat and flies,
And flapping upwards fills the skies
With clamours 'gainst intruding men,
Disturbers of her nightly reign.

3

'Tis eve, now glides my boat all gently,
On the waters silently,
I stretch myself the bark upon
And gaze upon the bright full moon.
O! Autumn's moon is clear and bright,
And sheds a dazzling flood of light,
I gaze, and think, and gaze again,
And pensive fancies fill my brain.
The mellow stillness of the scene,
The moonbeams sleeping on the green,
The dark line of the hazy shore,
The drip from the suspended oar,
Like music in my ear soft stealing,
Fill my heart with tender feeling!
Ah! tender thoughts of days gone by,
When hope was high and blood was young,
When love was new and friendship strong,
And when there were, who are no more,
And joys there were that now are o'er!
They wake a long forgotten sight,
With tear unbidden fill my eye!

4

But soft! I hear a distant song,
And sound of boatmen's dashing oar,
And in an instant see before
Some boats that swiftly pass along.
The merry tillers of this place,

Await a goodly harvest yield,
And with no work at home or field,
With gladsome heart they hold a race!
And loud they sing some stirring song,
Composed by some unlettered bard,
And all their oars plied quick and hard
Keep time to their tempestuous song!
For their's a life of joy and sorrow,
Without a care or thought of morrow.
Their Zemindars are rich and great,[77]
And paddy-lenders hard as fate!
The tillers have no thought of saving,
Borrowing live all twelve-month round,
And when the Autumn floods come round
Hold their *bách* and merry-making!

5

I'd merrily lead a boatman's life, –
Ah! censure not a poet's dream, –
Their joys and woes a mingled stream,
Their artless converse, simple life,
Are dear to me. Then would I row
My little fish-boat to and fro,
Then would I toil, and sing the while,
From morning's glow till evening's smile,
And when my work and toil was o'er,
Would hasten to my cottage door.
For there, my love, my village fair,
The gentle partner of my care,
She would my daily meals prepare,
And wait beside the cottage door,
With throbbing heart and anxious thought,
To view the far benighted boat,
To meet her loving spouse though poor.
And he would part her locks so gently,
And kiss her fears away so gently,
And gaze upon the moon on high,
And then upon her sparkling eye,
And eager kiss those lips so dear,
And gently kiss away her fear.
For those two meek and bashful eyes,
For that true heart, – a poor man's prize, –
The poet gladly would be poor,
In poverty range the wide world o'er!

---

77 *Zemindars*, or *zamindars*: wealthy landowners in British India responsible for collecting and paying taxes to the British for land under their jurisdiction (n. "zamindar" *OED*).

6

For sooth, a boatman's life I'd lead,
A life of sweet content in need,
And where yon topes of mango tree
Disclose long vistas to the eye,
And clumps of arched bamboo green
Create a cool and fairy scene,
And humble huts beneath yon tree
Bespeak content in poverty,
There, there mid scenes of sweet repose,
With summer breeze its music lending,
And shade and sunshine sweetly blending,
Mid scenes of mingled joy and woes,
Content to toil the live-long day,
I'd work and sing my life away.
Where mango branches spread above,
And *Kokil*[78] sings eternal love,
I'd lay me on the bright green grass,
In toil and rest my hours would pass.
All nature mute; − the birds on high,
The beasts upon the grassy lea, −
All nature mute except the dove,
Soft cooing from some mango grove,
That stretching over acres wide,
Would shed deep gloom in bright noontide.
What sweetness in thy gently song
Resounding through the bush and lea,
The bamboo grove, the mango tree,
Its mellow sweetness would prolong!
Dwells in thy eye what tender love,
What winning art in every move,
What grace and beauty in each action,
What gentle thoughts of sweet affection
Dwell in thy little fluttering heart,
Thou bird of love and winsome art!
And simple hearted village men,
With lusty limbs and open mien,
And gentle, bashful village girls,
With down-cast eyes and raven curls,
And healthy limbs, and rounded arms,
And gentle face and sable charms,
Would meet their fond familiar friend,
And tales of joys and woes would blend,

---

78 *Kokil*, also known as the *coil, koil, koel, koyal,* or *kokila*: bird famed for its melodious calls; often termed the Indian cuckoo.

Smile o'er the prospects of the year,
And for their sorrows claim a tear.
Dearer to me such converse kind
Than polished arts and talk refined,
Where midst the honied words, I feel
The heart, the heart, is wanting still.

7

But truce. What sounds my ear assail,
At midnight hour what voice of wail?[79]
Upon the islet village standing,
Upon the waters eager bending
Her locks dishevelled on the air,
Her arms extended, bosom bare,
Oppressed with woe, oppressed with fears,
A very Niobe[80] in tears,
Why, with repeated shrieks of pain,
Doth she disturb night's silent reign?
She's heard, — her father old and grey
Has mid the waters lost his way,
Drowned where 'tis ten feet deep or more,
Not long ago, not far from shore.
What pain, what woes more cruel prove
Than death of those we fondly love?

8

Speed, speed my boatmen swiftly on
Like lightning through the tall *Amon!*
The boat flies bounding o'er the wave,
Perchance the man we still may save.
But long before we reached the goal,
A braver heart, a kinder soul,
Had jumped into the midnight wave,
And saved the old man from his grave.
"Old man! the hair upon thy head
Is gray" 'twas thus to him I said,
"Thy eyes have lost their wonted glow,
Thy frame is feeble, steps all slow,
Why in this midnight's feeble ray
Did'st venture lone this watery way?"

---

79 [Poet's Note: The story narrated in the succeeding verses is founded on fact.]
80 In Greek myth, Niobe was punished for her hubris by Apollo, who killed her sons, and Artemis, who killed her daughters. Niobe fled and was turned to stone though she continued to weep as a rock cliff on Mt. Sipylus.

9

"Sire!" 'twas thus to me he said,
"The hair is grey upon my head,
My eyes have lost their wonted glow,
My frame is feeble, steps all slow,
Yet in this midnight's feeble ray,
Still must I cross this watery way.
My boy, — great Alla[81] bless his soul!
My boy, — the darling of my soul,
For years wide fertile acres held,
And paid his rent and ploughed his field,
And reaped his harvest, gentle boy,
And filled my aged heart with joy.
But Alla give and takes away,
And each hath his ordained day,
The arrow sped, — I only grieve,
It struck not me my boy to save."
The old man slowly bent his head,
And fast and thick the tear-drops sped.
I silent marked the old man's grief,
It gave his swelling heart relief.

10

"My daughter, my remaining joy,
The wife of my departed boy,
Wept day and night, yet toiled in grief,
To give my old age some relief.
She milked the cow, she spun the thread,
For work to distant places sped,
From morning's smile till evening's glow
She ceaseless toiled and toiled in woe,
And still as eve returning came,
Her placid, drooping face the same,
I saw her toiling still in grief,
To give my old age some relief.
But this unwonted ceaseless toil,
And grief as ceaseless all the while,
Did break her heart, — oh! she is gone, —
Great Alla, let thy will be done!

---

81 Alla, or Allah: God in Islam.

11

"My story need I further say?
It is a tale of every day.
My neighbour saw me rich and poor,
With bribes he sought the richman's door.
Our *Gomashta*,[82] a faithless man,
Transferred to him by fields of *dhan*,[83]
Which we have tilled this hundred year
And I must wander, – where, oh where!
A week is gone, a week is come,
From village I to village roam,
Perchance a few more weeks will come
Before I cease to weep and roam.
My hut is down, my things are sold,
Gone is my son, so true and brave,
My heart is weary, I am old,
Great Alla! speed me to my grave."

12

Enough, old man, thy simple tale
Doth smite this heart, as with a flail.
What throes of woe what deep-felt pain,
What bitter tears that unseen start,
What silent anguish of the heart,
Even at this hour pollute night's reign!
Ah, dreams of rural bliss are vain
And life hath trouble life hath pain!
Then toil, it is the will of Heaven,
And labour all thy mortal span,
For rest unto us is not given,
Still toil and help thy brother man!
When next thou sailest o'er life's calm sea
'Neath moon-beams of prosperity,
Thy work remember, – 'tis to save
The old man in the midnight wave!
And thou! proud man of wealth and power,
When maddened in thy prosperous hour,
Thou liftst thy hand to smite and quell,
Be calm and stretch thy hand to save,
Think of the maiden's midnight wail,
Think of the old man in the wave!

---

82 *Gomastha*: Indian agent employed by the British East India Company to compel artisans to sign bonds to deliver goods to the Company.
83 *Dhan*: rice plant.

Lala Prasanna Kumar Dey

Dey's slim volume of verse chronicles the many wars of the early twentieth century, especially the recently fought Second Anglo–Boer War, and, in doing so, showcases the increasingly global scope of politics. Little is known of Dey except that, as he claims on his volume, he was headmaster of Jubilee High School.

Indian Bouquet (Calcutta: 1906)[84]

War

Repugnant sound infernal! why,
I'm sick of it; from Transvaal first,[85]
Then Afric's western coast,[86] and next
From China comes this sound accursed.[87]
Is world gone mad and Doom's day night,
Or why such murd'rous thirst for blood?
Why all on a sudden the battle rage?
Why bathes the earth in purple flood?
Did Christ or Buddha ever dream,
Their followers thus would slight their word,
And welcome him abhorred of hell,
To reign on earth supreme as lord,
When, "slapped on the left thy right cheek turn,"
The former said in meekness true,
And, "meanest life destroy ye not,"
The latter taught to world anew?
The mandate now to nations all
On earth, to go about and meet
Unloading maxims each to each
Not hearts, doth come, and all submit;
And war, war, war, this hideous cry
 From south and east, and erelong shall
 From west, the ear of man oppress,

---

84 Lala Prasanna Kumar Dey, *Indian Bouquet* (Calcutta: n. p., 1906).
85 The Second Anglo–Boer War between Britain and the Boer republics was fought from 1899 to 1902. The war resulted in a humiliating defeat for the British.
86 The general Scramble for Africa began in the 1880s and continued until World War I and refers to the aggressive expansionist struggle between Britain, Germany, Italy, France, Belgium, Portugal, and Spain for territory on the African continent.
87 Boxer Rebellion (1898–1901): Chinese uprising against European imperialist expansion.

And vulture, fox, and crow revel;
And air with bloody grains surfeit,
Shall breed around diseases fell,
And land, all white with human bones,
Proclaim the hideous hand of hell?
A Budha [sic], Christ, or Chaitanya[88]
Despatch, O God, to earth again,
To teach man how to love in deed,
And work the end of Satan's reign.

Svami Vivekananda at Chicago[89]

Indeed he is great, "that prince of man," that son
Of Ind, Vivekanand; his name shall live
Eterne, his deeds as deeds endure of Paul,[90]
Of Sankar great,[91] a Pyramid sublime,
Defying all the frowns of jealous Time.
A Hindu, yet who can dare oppose
His will to Chicago at once to sail?[92]
He goes away, nor minds the threats of fools
Who vaunting say, "We oust thee if thou go."
The "orange monk," with turban red and green,
And Cassock belted, falling down the knee,
And face clean shaven, lands in India west.[93]
From east and west here all have come as he
Invited: all the master minds of earth
They spake, and he too stood to speak in turn: –
A splendid sight! His figure fine and bold,
And chiselled lips, and face square cut, and teeth

---

88 Chaitanya (1486–1534): Hindu saint and social reformer in eastern India.
89 Svami, or Swami, Vivekananda (1863–1902): chief disciple of Sri Ramakrishna. Born into a Brahmin family in Calcutta, Vivekananda became a Hindu spiritual leader after his guru's death. He famously spoke about Hinduism, in particular the philosophies of Vedanta and Yoga, at the Parliament of the World's Religions in Chicago in 1893.
90 Paul: Apostle in the Judeo-Christian tradition.
91 "Sankar great": Shankara was an eighth-century philosopher and theologian whose commentaries on various ancient religious texts have made him the most important teacher of Advaita Vedanta.
92 During the nineteenth century, crossing the ocean was seen as a taboo by orthodox, high-caste Hindus who believed it violated caste strictures. Vivekananda received much criticism from orthodox Brahmins for his journey.
93 Vivekananda's usual dress included an orange robe for which he was introduced as the "Orange-monk" by the president of the Parliament of the World's Religions in Chicago.

As white as milk, and eyes exceeding bright:
He stood — the cynosure of all around;
A host of audience, great surprised to see
A heathen preacher, for their ear had oft
Before, against the sons of Ind condemned
Been poisoned by the words of fools hare-brained,
Who thoughtless seem to think and heartless feel.
The Svami spake, — his words' majestic flow,
By logic valved, their blindness off did sweep;
They saw the light of truth and owned him great;
And wonder-wrapt they cried, "Can pagan soil
Of Ind such brilliant gems produce?" — aye can:
Not one but hundreds such and better still,
Unnoticed live and move, while many a Price
And puny Jones[94] attract the jaundiced gaze
Of men diseased by outland prejudice,
Who thoughtless take both good and bad as bad.

A. S. H. Hussain

A. S. H. Hussain, or Alkadari Syed Hasib Hussain, seems to have published only one work of poetry. It has been difficult to locate biographical information on Hussain that is not provided by the author himself in this volume, which includes a foldout of a "Genealogical tree showing the descent of the 'Author' from the great Arabian Prophet and his connections with the other ancient, noble and loyal families of Bengal." A starred notation at the bottom of the foldout states: "The author is the first in the family who learnt English and accepted Govt. Service. All his ancestors were spiritual leaders with a few exceptions." Hussain's "Prefatory Note" to his collection *Loyal Leaves* praises British governance even as it tries to sidestep the usual (Hindu) nationalist rhetoric that posited the British incursion as relieving the dark period brought about by Mughal rule. For the Muslim Hussain, British rule brought an end to a state of warfare perpetuated by Europeans *other than* the British. As he writes in this "Prefatory Note":

> Let us go back to History. Prior to its final conquest by the English, India had, for well nigh a thousand years, been a perpetual battle-field, and acknowledged no single ruler until the paramount power of England was established. During the four hundred years immediateley preceding that time, it was the prize for which many European nations struggled, and, indeed, dreams of an Indian Empire had allured some of the greatest European nations. To the Portuguese, for instance, India seemed a second Peru where diadems might be torn from the brows of princes, while to the French it was a theatre for lucrative intrigue in which splendid reputations might be won.

---

94 "while many a Price/ And puny Jones": generic English names.

The triumph of British arms quelled all disturbances and restored to India such unbroken peace as she had not known since the days immediately preceding the invasion of Alexander. And there cannot be the shadow of a doubt that it has been the constant endeavour of our British rulers to enable to the country to realize fully the blessings of peace. They have done so much for our good that from the baldest recital of their doings one is at a loss to make out how so much could have been achieved...

The above, though but a brief – all too brief – summary of what England has done for India, makes it abundantly clear that the British Government exists for the benefit of every Indian race. Our highest and most paramount duty, therefore, is to the State – a duty before which all our petty jealousies and narrow class-interests must cheerfully give way – a free flow of loyalty and devotion to the British Raj. And, in seeking the good of the Government, every man will be but working for his own good.

Loyal Leaves (Calcutta: 1911)[95]

Ode for her Imperial Majesty Queen Victoria's Golden Jubilee[96]

1

Most Gracious Queen, the brightest and the best,
Thy fifty years have shed a glorious light,
Which visiting the darkest nooks of earth,
Dispelled the gloom that spread o'er human sight.

2

Thy reign has been the reign of justice pure
Whose sunshine reached the high as well as low,
Whose brightest light illumes the poorest cot
And beacon-like does the safe pathway show.

3

Thy life has been as pure as ether pure,
Sweet as the rose's pleasant odour is,
And tender as the lambkin's gentle heart,
Delightful as refreshing morning's breeze.

---

95 A. S. H. Hussain, *Loyal Leaves* (Calcutta: S. M. Hossain, 1911).
96 [Poet's Note: This and the poems that follow have been reprinted from the author's previous work entitled *Priceless Pearls* as well as from another publication by him. The concluding poem is, however, a new one.] Queen Victoria's Golden Jubilee in 1887 celebrated her fiftieth year of rule and was marked by elaborately staged celebrations in Great Britain and its colonies. British and Indian-English poets marked this moment by writing numerous odes on the occasion and to the queen-empress.

4

Fair, spotless Queen, in deepest reverence held;
Hearts are thy throne, thy weapon human love,
Well hast thou founded thy bright empire here,
And spread thy gentle rule as by a dove.

5

The soul of innocence and love art thou,
The pleasing picture of a blessed life,
The person of a truly Christian soul:
May God preserve thee safe from human strife!

6

Thy foes malicious many a time did aim
At thy sweet, chaste and amiable life;
But virtue did thee shield, and chastity
Defend thee from the en'my's fatal knife.

7

Art speaks to Science of thy noble grace,
And Music breathes thy praise in melody,
And Commerce opes her heart in welcome true
For keeping all in pleasant harmony.

8

Thy glorious reign has wonders great achieved,
Has changed to flower-gardens jungles drear
Where ruled the king of beasts, with wolf and fox;
Lo! now thy subject's humble homes appear.

9

Deserts are human habitations now;
Such are the glorious triumphs of thy reign.
Thank God, dear Mother-Queen,[97] for godly grace
On thee; for no success shall make thee vain.

---

[97] Victoria was known as the "Queen-Mother," an image which she carefully cultivated for the public. See Margaret Homans, *Royal Representations: Queen Victoria and British Culture, 1837–1876* (Chicago: University of Chicago Press, 1998) for further information.

10

Like all thy daughters India claims thy love;
Although she is afar from thee, yet near
She should be to thy heart; for she is poor,
To thee her poverty must make her dear.

11

Eager she longs to see her Mother-Queen,
For mother's heart must bleed to see her poor;
She will embrace her daughter dear and say
"Poor India all thy sufferings are now o'er.

12

I see it truly now, my daughter dear,
That thou art really such as poets say.
I now will try my best to make thee rich,
Like all my daughters thou too shalt be gay.

13

Long, long neglected have my children been,
Now must I make them such as they deserve;
They are a loyal race – my grandsons dear.
Them like a true grandmother must I serve."

14

So come to his far land, Victoria blest,
And see thy Ind once fabulously rich,
A land of misery, prey to ruin fell,
Now cast by Penury in her darkest ditch.[98]

15

Be not dismayed at Russia's vaunted march;
For Indians must their hearts' blood gladly shed
To save thee from the grasp of the White Bear,[99]
If only thou dost give them timely aid.

---

98 India was often cast in nineteenth-century discourse as once inhabiting an ideal state of learning, wealth and culture in ancient times. This ideal period usually was seen as having been disrupted by the dark period of Mughal rule. In Hussain's poetic history, however, the period of India's decline was not caused by Muslim rule but by the rapaciousness of continental Europe. British rule thus saved India from plundering by the other European nations.

99 "White Bear": Russia. Russia had designs on British possessions in India and the Middle East, beginning with Afghanistan. The "Great Game" was a strategic rivalry between the two powers for supremacy in Central Asia over the course of the nineteenth century.

16

Let Russia hatch her plans and hideous schemes,
The Afghan furnace-heats will them destroy,
And Russia's boasted march would be a dream –
A nightmare wild, instead of dreams of joy.

17

Perchance the Afghans fail or thee betray,
And court the country of the Polar bear,
Our Indian heroes to a man would fight
And Victory's fruit with Albion's children share.

18

Once more would Moslem sabres gleam on fields,
While swords of Islam would from scabbards leap;
And Rajput war-note, with the Sikh war-cry,[100]
Would strike to en'mies' hearts a terror deep.

19

Even, weak Bengal would contribute her share
To save thee, Empress dear, from fatal foe.
She is with intellect and culture armed,
And with these weapons to the field must go.

20

The Indian Moslems are a loyal race,
They have the lion's heart, though they are poor.[101]
Prithee neglect them not, our Empress dear,
For they thy rule in Ind would make secure.

21

If thou neglectest them and let'st them lie
With Poverty, within her chilling clasp,
No doubt destruction's fruit will be their lot,
But who will save thee from thy en'my's grasp?

---

100 The Rajputs are members of the warrior caste in northern and central India and were recruited and celebrated by the British East India Company and later the British Empire for their military prowess. The Sikhs are an ethnic-social-religious group founded by the teachings of Guru Nanak in the Punjab region during the early sixteenth century and are known for their skills as warriors.
101 The author himself was an Indian Muslim.

22

No race alone can make thy rule secure;
The sunshine of our aid is needful too
'Twill animation add and vital life
To Hindoo aid — to Christian help, 'tis true.

23

A Moslem hero young, a lion bold
His Highness is — the braze Nizam most true,
He will his heart's last life-drop gladly shed
And will in thy foes' blood his sword imbrue.

24

Cherish this hero, nourish his domain,
Lend him whate'er he wants to fight for thee,
This noble youngling foster, nurse and feed;
His vigour's outburst will on Russia be.

25

Had I a Byron's pen, a Gladstone's voice,[102]
I might have pictured to my country's eyes
The blood-red picture of dark Horror's reign
The rule of despot Czars and their allies.

26

Thou dost not choke our voice, our Empress dear,
Thou dost not smother free-thought's babes at all,
Enjoy we our Religion's soothing balm,
And with thy fetters thou dost not gall.

27

For whom shall India fight if not for thee?
For whom shall Indians shed their precious blood?
For whom shall Moslems, Hindoos, Parsees, Jews.
Pour out their fountain's costly ruddy flood?

---

102 William Ewart Gladstone (1809–1898): served several terms as Liberal prime minister of Great Britain (1868–1874; 1880–1885; 1886; 1892–1894). His actions in protection of Irish tenants and his support of Irish Home Rule as well as his appointment of Lord Ripon as viceroy of India in 1880 won him the support of Indians. He was known as a great orator as well.

28

> For thee! But only let us pray thee, Queen,
> The crime of colour banish from this land;
> Then Ind were blest indeed, will have no fear;
> United thus her children safely stand.

The Voice of Islam and other poems (Calcutta: 1914)[103]

The Voice of Islam
Part I.

> Let Hist'ry's Muse her page unroll,
>   And point us to the distant past;
> We'll ponder o'er the flight of Time
>   Our eyes along its vista cast.
>
> Before great Alexander's day[104]
>   India had known nor strife nor sword;
> And here that ancient reign of peace
>   The rule of England hath restored.
>
> Well nigh upon a thousand years
>   Before the British wielded sway
> This land had been a battlefield
>   The weaker for the strong to prey.
>
> And then for twice two hundred years,
>   The nations of the distant west
> To found an empire here assayed,
>   By dreams of eastern power possessed.

---

103 A. S. H. Hussain, *The Voice of Islam and other poems* (Calcutta: B. M. Dutt, 1914). Hussain writes the following in his "Prefatory Note" to this work: "The booklet is a poem in three distinct parts. In the first part, the author brings the reader face to face with the much-raised, much-debated, now-set-at-rest question as to how far India has been [sic] benefited by the British rule by attempting a presentation of India passing through different stages…The last two parts form an appeal of Islam to her adherents… [The poet] reminds his co-religionists of the glory and the sunny days and palmy days which once were theirs, of the vast worldwide and miracle working Moslemdom… He has reconciled the two seemingly incompatible, seemingly antepodal [sic] virtues, loyalty and patriotism, implicit and unquestioning devotion to the British Throne and national consciousness."

104 Alexander the Great (356–323 BCE): king of Macedonia and eventual emperor of a vast territory spanning the Mediterranean to the South Asian subcontinent (including the Persian Empire).

Proud Portugal to snatch the gems
    From brows of orient princes came;[105]
Fair France foresaw in flowery Ind
    A fitting field for warlike fame.[106]

Then triumph of the British arms
    Bid rivalry and discord cease,
To our war-wearied country grave
    The priceless heritage of peace.

No pen may dare enumerate,
    Nor grateful heart may fully say,
How much for all hath England done
    What blessings showered on our way.

And Peace had led Prosperity
    A captive in her radiant train;
Secure are now our hearths and homes,
    No robber-hordes molest again.

While Thuggee and infanticide[107]
    And cruel practices have ceased,
'Mid other benefits we find
    Comforts at every step increased.

Injustice, crime, and lawlessness,
    Repressed have been with iron hand,
With courts of law and equity
    Established now throughout the land.

Learning her ample page unfolds
    Holding aloft the torch of Truth;
While schools rise up on every side
    To nurse the ardent minds of youth.

---

105 The Portuguese Empire in India was established in the beginning of the sixteenth century with the appointment of the first viceroy of India. Portuguese possessions included territories on the western coast of the subcontinent, including Goa and Bombay, as well as parts of the modern-day state of Kerala.

106 French expeditions to India date to the early seventeenth century. French possessions included territories on the eastern coast of the subcontinent including Pondicherry.

107 In British imperial discourse, *thuggees* took on an almost mythical status as menacing native figures, members of the "cult of Kali." They were infamous for supposedly committing armed robbery and assault on unsuspecting travelers in colonial India.

Material blessings too are ours,
    Pest-haunted jungles disappear,
Waste-lands reclaimed, sweet wells spring up;
    Canals bring streams of water clear.

With breath of steam, the iron steed
    Goes rushing through the smiling land,
Harbours, and mills and factories
    Are seen around on every hand.

When fever grips this human frame
    And wasting sickness overpowers,
The hospitals invite our stay
    Till health and strength once more are ours.

Hostels and Post and Telegraph,
    The village-bank, the delv'd mine,
Roads, famine-works, the daily Press
    To cheer the people's lot combine.

Though want and mis'ry still exist
    (The poor with us will ever be)
We know what measures have been wrought
    To stem the tide of poverty.

The Pilgrim-Fathers left their homes,
    The future's unknown perils braved,
And midst the prairies of the West
    "Freedom to worship God" they craved.

Such liberty we need not seek
    'Tis ours indeed. Our rulers kind
To all the privilege allow
    To worship God as they're inclined.

Along with mercy justice finds
    In England's heart the largest place;
How fairly she the balance holds
    'Twixt class and class 'midst race and race?

Then fling aside all jealousies
    'Tween class and class (these must give way)
And for the interests of the State
    Let each of his best essay.

The State our noblest powers demands,
  Devotion, love and loyalty
While working for the good of state
  Each working for his own will be

Then surely it behooves us all
  Moslems, Hindus – whate'er we be
To pray the Lord of all to grant
  To Britain's rule, stability.

For England's ceaseless weal we pray
  That unconfined her sway may be,
Still Empress of both East and West,
  Still mistress over land and sea!

To visit us our Emperor King
  Came with his royal consort fair
And from his Indian subjects met
  A loyal welcome everywhere.[108]

Tho' far Britain's sea girt isle
  Such mem'ries cannot all depart,
Our hearts are *his*, as Indians all
  Are dear unto his kingly heart.

Of noble sire noble son
  May his reign further blessings bring,
Long, long, may he the sceptre sway
  O'er loving hearts – God save the King!

Part II.[109]

1.

In days of yore I was the queen
  Of learning, wisdom and of art
And with the strength of knowledge I
  Long swayed Humanity's great heart.

---

108 King George V and Queen Mary visited India in 1911 for the Delhi Durbar, where they were declared emperor and empress of India.
109 The speaker of Part II is Islam.

2.

My fountain then was free to all,
    Even Europe drank its water pure,
And from the Age's darkness dire
    Received a healthy lasting cure.

3.

My milky stream of learning sweet
    To Afric's arid bosom flowed,
And Afric's swarthy children drank
    This flood and with great glory glowed.

4.

Poor Asia's darkness I dispelled;
    Though Age has done his work on me
My silvery steps I hope will roam
    Over Columbia's bosom free.

5.

For centuries my word was law
    To sunny land of flow'ry Spain;
I banished all her mental gloom,
    And made her free with all my main.

6.

Ah! Spain forlorn, how dark thy land
    No more the crescent sheds its light,
Did it not grow into full moon?
    But now 'tis hid in endless night.

7.

I preached the one and only God;
    Humanity men from me learned
And foll'wing glad by voice sublime
    Grand glory's glare they greatly earned.

8.

With lightning, thunder too I spoke,
    And made them feel my power's weight;
Cheerful they wore my thraldom's chain,
    For I was kind to them though great.

9.

My ancient children me obeyed,
    And heard my words with ear's sincere
They were thus victory's brightest gems
    To me than all the earth more dear.

10.

My children had their palmy days!
    And godly sons their crimson dawns
And nursed by freedom's fairest hands
    They bounded o'er the fields as fawns.

11.

But ye are my degenerate sons;
    For ye have wrought my dark disgrace,
Hence from my sacred presence pure!
    I wish not now to see your face.

12.

Remember what your fathers were;
    They changed the aspect of the earth;
And held the torch of Learning bright
    Which ushered a new Era's birth.

13.

Slumber no more, dear Moslems hear,
    And give attentive heed to me;
Know Life is work and work is praise,
    'Tis work alone that sets us free.

14.

If ye have eyes, mark well my sons
    What Japan is and what she was;
Once in the shade, unknown to fame;
    The Japs have now their Victory's share.

15.

The Japs indulge in pleasant dreams,
    Sons do your duty, play your part!
And "heart within and God o'er head"
    Fight out your ways with manly heart.

16

'Tis Education which has made
    The Japanese what they are now;
If progress be, indeed your dream
    To better be, then take a vow.

17.

Do not give way to jealousy;
    For others reap their labour's fruit.
Hard work and application strong,
    Are opulence and honour's root.

18.

Rise children and well revive
    Your social and your public life:
And strong in manhood, high in soul,
    Arm yourselves for the coming strife.

19.

Lose not your heart, my children dear!
    A lustrous star is gleaming high
To shed its light upon your head
    In an unclouded Western sky.

20.

Do ye not know what star that is?
    That star is England's high desire,
To make you now what you were once;
    To make your present status higher.

21.

Place all your hopes in England now;
    For she alone can show the way;
On England's warmest bosom dear,
    Your sleepless, restless heads now lay.

22.

Do you not know what England is?
    The home of freedom she is sure,
And the asylum for the weak
    And for the sick she is a cure.

23.

Fair Albion's[110] name a synonym
    For justice, strength and for fair play
The injured nations look to her
    For help when they are in dismay.

24.

The avenger of wrongs she is
    She is the champion of the weak.
Her strength colossal does protect
    The helpless, and withal she's meek.

25.

"Read and you will know" recollect,
    And well remember duty's call,
Do nothing else but learn and read;
    For that will save you from your fall.

26.

Let Learning be your guiding star,
    And Education be your dream,
Drink deep the sacred water pure
    Of Learning's life-reviving stream.

27.

Indulge no more in silken sloth,
    Let not that life-destroying worm
Have the small place within your heart;
    There she will lay destruction's germ.

28.

Let not that canker Pride have room
    Within your heart the throne of God,
Fall follows pride as you must know
    And ruin is God's chastising rod.

29.

Moslems, you are but brothers all;
    For you are all my children dear,
Then hear my words and me obey,
    Be to your brothers e'er sincere.

---

110 Albion: England.

30.

Crescent and Cross the same aim have,[111]
    The elevation of mankind,
They should e'er work with harmony
    And themselves to each other bind.

31.

Untied ye shall live and die
    Like those sweet birds that fly together
Linked by a golden ring and hook
    With feather always touching feather.

Part III.[112]

1.

My children dear! beware, beware
    Of weakness which means death, indeed,
Know strength is Life, and freedom sure,
    And weakness does destruction breed.

2.

Rise Ind'ans rise! with might to fight
    For England's flag, for England's cause:
'Gainst treach'rous foe, and thankless horde
    For ever shut your loyal doors.

3.

Remember Moslems! what I say,
    Be faithful loyal subjects dear,
Fight for your king if need there be,
    Be to your sovereign e'er sincere.

4.

Gird up your loins, unsheathe your swords,
    And boldly fight for Albion dear,
When Albion needs thy help, indeed,
    Give it to her with hearts sincere.

---

111 "Crescent and Cross": symbols of Islam and Christianity respectively.
112 The speaker of Part III is Islam.

5.

You must for Albion sacrifice
    All things that are to you most dear,
You must by England stand, and fight
    With all her foes both far and near.

6.

To loyal and to faithful ken
    Their king, indeed, is all in all,
Their lives are bound up with his life,
    With him they rise, with him they fall.

7.

The greatest statesman of the day,
    Lord Hardinge[113] is, indeed, by far.
The greatest soldier of the time,
    Earl Kitchener[114] surely, keen in war.

8.

The peoples of this loyal Ind,
    The Princes of this faithful land,
Must guided be by Hardinge great
    Whose trait's conciliation grand.

9.

Rise children dear! and arm yourselves
    With powers and a conscience clear,
And strong in faith and great in soul,
    For Life's great battles ye prepare.

10.

These are the hardest days, my sons!
    And if ye long for victory sure;
Bring all your forces to the field,
    And for a glorious End endure.

---

113 Charles Hardinge (1858–1944): viceroy of India from 1910 to 1916. During Hardinge's tenure, the capital of British India was moved from Calcutta to Delhi in 1912. He was seen in a more favorable light by his subjects than was one of his predecessors, Lord Curzon (viceroy from 1898–1905), due to his reversal of the partition of Bengal, his criticism of the government's anti-Indian immigration policies in South Africa and his respect for Gandhi. Nonetheless, several assassination attempts were made upon Hardinge's life while he was in office.

114 Horatio Herbert Kitchener (1850–1916): British field marshal whose military conquest of the Sudan, role in the Boer War, position as commander-in-chief, India and appointment as secretary for war during World War I earned him acclaim and recognition in Britain.

11.

Meet troubles and all hardships great,
      Brave dangers with a fearless heart,
And suffer for the End sublime
      All pains however great their smart.

12.

Remember what your fathers were,
      And how they fought Life's battles great
What led to their success in life,
      And how they lorded o'er hard Fate.

13.

What's allotted can't be blotted
      This is a truth which ye avoid,
Work, work, for work is worship sure,
      And never get with work annoyed.

14.

Let Dangers show their threatening eyes,
      Let storms arise and tempests roll,
Let mountain-waves your life-barque toss,
      Be not dismayed, ye mind your goal.

15.

Let lives of men of glorious ends
      Be land-marks for your own career.
Like Moslems of the ancient days,
      Sincerely work and persevere.

16.

Let Perseverance guide your course;
      Though starless it may seem to be.
There is an end to everything,
      And as such to your poverty.

17.

The longest lanes have turnings sure,
      The darkest nights have mornings bright
And soon behind a cloudy sky
      The Hea'ens present a glorious sight.

18.

Your sky is overcast with cloud,
    The cloud is herald of a sun
Whose sunny light will life infuse
    Into your organs, dreamt by none.

19.

This glorious sun of radiant ray
    Will such a brilliant lustre shed;
As never human ken beheld;
    As will restore to life the dead.

20.

Do ye not know what sun is this?
    This sun is zeal and true desire
To make ye now what ye were once
    To make your present status higher.

21.

My children dear! the sun adore;
    For this will set from bondage free
Yourselves who are wrapt in a cloud
    Of penury and poverty.

22.

If you resolve to better be
    No earthly pow'r can put you down.
Your resolution strongly formed
    No adverse Force can on ye frown.

23.

To Moslems all I do appeal
    In Honour's and in good Faith's name
To cast off from them silken sloth
    Which leads to sure and certain shame.

24.

A word to my rich Hindoo friends
    I have neighbour's right to say,
Let them their poorer brothers help
    In Education's sacred way.

25.

With wealth which from their fountain flows
    Like showers from a rainy sky.
Let them perform the nobler work
    Of giving education high.

26.

God gave them wealth to serve and end,
    This end is sure a glorious one;
Then let them with their opulence
    Affliction's just demand not shun.

27.

If ye have mind, my sons! to thrive,
    From nature calm your lessons draw.
Like Nature's trees and plants be still,
    And be resolved like Nature's Law.

28.

If ye have eyes mark well, my sons!
    How Nature bears the sun and storm,
And how withal she prospers great:
    With her majestic, fairy form.

29

She yields herself to Tempest's dash,
    With patience, she receives its shock,
And laughs and smiles a hearty smile
    Like a firm adamantine rock.

30.

Know, Patience lives, Impatience dies,
    And "cowards die before their death"
Be patient, firm, like Nature bold
    Breathe boldness like dame Nature's breath.

31.

Defy all Storm's and Tempest's frown.
    Like sailors brave work on and toil.
The destined shore is close at hand,
    One bound, one leap and there's the soil.

32.

Whom do I warn, to whom I speak?
    To stone, to rock, to plants or trees?
Or do I throw these wisdom's grains
    Upon the cold and careless breeze.

33.

Why no response, Ah where are they?
    And where are ye? my children dear
With filial ardour run and come
    To meet your mother warm and sincere.

34.

Let me imprint my kiss on you,
    Let me embrace you to my heart,
Let me with love maternal pure
    My ardent fire to you impart.

35.

Receive these sacred precepts, sons!
    "And heart within and God o'er head,"
Fight out your ways with manly soul,
    And leave this world with honour fed.

FINIS

Panda Hakim aina sowab ast o mahza khair
    Frkhunda bakhat anka ba samaa reza shaneed.

Charu Chandra Bose

There is no biographical information available on Charu Chandra Bose although, as the title proclaims, the speaker considers himself a "voice from Bengal," most likely Calcutta where this text was published. This small pamphlet of verse is cleverly presented in the form of an invitation to board a ship, presumably the same ship that brought King George V and Queen Mary, who were declared emperor and empress of India at the 1911 Delhi Durbar, to India.

A Voice from Bengal: Welcome Address to Their
Majesties Landed in India (Calcutta: 1912)[115]

Welcome Address to Their Majesties landed in India
Voice from Bengal

Chorus

1.

Sound trumpet, sound aloud,
Their Majesties' arrival to Hind,[116]
Sound thy sonorous voice about,
To Heaven above and the wind.

2.

Our Gracious Emperor with his Queen
To our Indian soil has come,
Our devotion prompt us greet them well,
Bid them a loyal welcome.

3.

Raise all flags on tops of houses
Decorated with flowers and leaves;
Let Ladies sound their conchs[117] within,
Signs of joy and Bliss.

4.

Hark minstrels! tune thy notes,
In harmony sing thy song,
That they sound well in their Majesties' ears
Passing the way along.

5.

Ask Muezzins[118] call to prayer
And Priests in Temples abound,
'Long live our Emperor and Empress'
Every throat shall it sound.

---

115 Charu Chandra Bose, *A Voice from Bengal: Welcome Address to Their Majesties Landed in India* (Calcutta: The Herald Printing Works, 1912).
116 Hind: Hindustan, or India.
117 Conches: shells of mollusks used as instruments of call in Hindu temples (n. "conch" *OED*).
118 *Muezzin*: Muslim public crier who calls the regular hours of prayer from the minaret or roof of a mosque (n. "muezzin" *OED*).

6.

> Victoria's grandson to us is dear
> A Royalty in sovereign ties,
> Victoria's grandson is our own,
> Most sacred in our eyes.

Nanikram Vasanmal Thadani

Nanikram Vasanmal Thadani (1890–1956) graduated as a barrister and published a number of works throughout his life including *The Triumph of Delhi and Other Poems* (1916), *Krishna's Flute, and other poems* (1916), *Asoka, and other poems* (1921), *The Garden of the East* (1932) as well as *Ghandi: the Man of Destiny, a Passion Play* (1930). He was among the first to introduce blank verse to Sindhi literature in his translation of the Sanskrit *Bhagavad Gita* into the Sindhi, *Srīmada Bhaġvatu gītā: Sindhi salokan men* (1923). Echoing (Hindu) nationalist rhetoric, which posited that India was only just recovering from a dark period of Mughal rule, Thadani's poem "chronicles" this time with particular attention to Delhi, a region that was beset by attacks from various groups over the centuries.

The Triumph of Delhi and Other Poems (Calcutta: 1916)[119]

The Triumph of Delhi[120]

I.

> Awake, oh mighty Goddess of the heart
> From thy enchained slumbers and to me
> Who know not aught of this ethereal art
> Save in meek silence and humility

---

[119] Nanikram Vasanmal Thadani, *The Triumph of Delhi and Other Poems* (Calcutta: Rai M. C. Sarkar Bahadur, 1916).

[120] The last few centuries of Delhi's history have been intimately linked to the history of the Mughal Empire and that of the British Empire. The Mughal Empire of the subcontinent was founded in 1526 with the defeat of the Delhi Sultanate by Babur (a descendent of Timur) and ended in 1857 as a result of the Indian Uprising (or "Sepoy Mutiny") when the last Mughal emperor, Bahadur Shah Zafar, who "ruled" from Delhi's Red Fort, was deposed by the British and sent into exile in Burma. The British announced that the capital of the British Raj would be shifted from Calcutta to Delhi at the Delhi Durbar of 1911, held to commemorate the coronation of King George V and Queen Mary as emperor and empress of India. The "triumph" of Thadani's poem may refer to the shift of control of Delhi from the Mughal Empire to the British.

With folded hands to watch and worship thee,
Oh speak sweet mother. Long hath been thy sleep,
And countless years to vast Eternity
Have rolled their weary length since thou didst keep
Thine eyes so firmly closed in deathlike stillness deep.

II.

For ages hath thy harp of wondrous notes
Been hanging silent to the passing wind;
And still no joy-awakening music floats
To the enraptured soul and ravished mind,
As in the past, when thou hadst not resigned
To sleep thy aerial kingdom. Rise again,
And re-assume they powers, and unbind
The spell of years, and in thy glory reign
Until the end of Time, and rule the hearts of men.

III.

O'er snowy Kailas[121] was thy music heard
By holy sages in their daily prayer,
And mingling with their matins deeply stirred
The kindled soul to joy beyond compare,
And thrilled the waves, the mountain, and the air,
With its ethereal echo; and below,
Where Ganga passes through this land so fair,
And woven trees in verdant forests grow,
Thy strains to meditative ears were wont to flow.

IV.

But now thy heart is silent, and no sound
Doth swell the listening bosom: – all is still;
E'en as the soul of midnight, when around,
The glowing stars their dreamy dews distil,
And earth of deepest slumbers hath her fill.
Yes, all is hushed, and not a breath doth rise,
Or echo whisper, save when hoarse and chill,
The wind awakens on the darkened skies,
And wailing o'er thy idle harp in sorrow dies.

---

121 Mount Kailas: peak in the Himalayas in what is now Tibet. It is known as the abode of the Hindu god, Shiva.

V.

Hushed is thy voice, and gone those happy days,
Wherein were moulded India's mighty men;
And now the ancient past of wondrous ways
Seems but the vision of some viewless reign —
A fairy land we may not see again.
Gone are the heroes of that Golden Age,
And buried are their sword and broken pen,
That once could awe, enrapture, and assuage,
As when the warrior ruled, the poet, and the sage.

VI.

Oh India, mother of the good and great,
Who made thy past a picture, wherein we
In morning hues the glory of thy state,
And all that makes thy name immortal, see,
Where art thou now, and who are born of thee?
Where is that mighty power which more than steel
Could lead thy sons to gates of victory?
And where the mind and heart to think and feel,
And where the soul eternal secrets to reveal?

VII.

But lonely ruined piles now stand to view
To mark the site where once great kingdoms lay;
The earth has taken what she deemed her due,
And heaven withheld the living light of day
From them, and darkness swallowed them away.
How slowly raised, how soon they disappeared!
Ah! Indra, hast thou lost thy might and sway,[122]
And what thyself to India's heart endeared,
Unnoticed now and old, unhonoured, and unfeared —

VIII.

That all those princely mansions are no more?
No more is heard that golden triumph's peal,
Nor seen those happy visions as of yore,
Which to the heart of sages did reveal

---

122 Indra: Hindu god of thunder and rain. In the *Vedas*, the religious scriptures predating the Hindu epics, Indra is described as the ruler of the gods but was later supplanted in importance by the Trimurti (which is composed of the gods Brahma, Vishnu and Shiva).

What only they can ever know and feel?
Alas for thee, oh reckless, ruthless Time,
What stores of anguish doth thy grave conceal,
What marble halls have mouldered into lime,
And what remains on earth of all her glorious prime!

IX.

They are no more — their very names have gone
And vanished in the haze of many years;
And yet perchance, in silence gazing on
This fallen fabric as it now appears,
Some heart may weep and say with flowing tears,
"Oh here they lived, and there they ceased to be,
Those mighty ones whose memory endears
Thy dust, oh India, to Eternity,
And makes thy earth an altar where to worship thee."

X.

They are no more — the body perisheth;
Their names are gone — they are but as the wind;
Their pride hath vanished — 'tis a bubble breath;
And buried kingdoms but the jest unkind
Of passing death, when earth is undermined.
All these are mortal, but there is a soul
In the vast Universe which unconfined
In aught of these, remains a changeless whole,
The eternal lord of life, though years to ages roll.

XI.

The noble deeds of virtue, truth, and love,
And service meek, and selfless sacrifice,
Survive the fall of kingdoms, and above
The ruined mass of sunken cities rise.
The good and brave, the holy, pure, and wise,
Have life immortal, though no monument
In history or in marble glorifies
Their sacred name. On earth they came and went,
But in the heart of man for ever live content.

XII.

So do thou wake again. With eager eyes
The myriad souls of India gaze on thee;
Her ancient heroes, and her sages wise,
And those who are, and those who yet will be,

Watching thy balmy bosom anxiously.
For a new hope is once again now born
In the vast regions of Eternity;
And unto thee is given to adorn
With an ethereal name this Infant of the Morn.

XIII.

And with thy fairy words, as with a charm,
Show to the earth anew her glories past
Of golden light. And now with hopes more warm,
The trembling eyes of all are on thee cast
To see if thou wilt gaze on them at last.
And now they smile to see thee move, and shake
Their heart with joy to hear thee breathing fast;
That whisper doth a wondrous music make,
Restoring life: – Awake, Saraswati, awake.[123]

XIV.

It is the hour of morn, and in the east
The maiden eye of dawn doth meekly shine;
And balmy breezes play upon her breast,
And round her musky hair and heart entwine,
And breathe upon her tender lips, and thine.
But still the birds are silent, for the Spring
Hath yet not heard thy melody divine;
And voiceless in their homes are slumbering,
Till wakened by thy music: – Oh arise, and sing.

XV.

In sweetest strains of India's happy days,
When duty born of love did reign supreme,
And wedded unto wisdom and its ways
Upheld the land from end to end extreme.
And gloriously did truth and honour beam,
And manhood dauntless in the cause of right;
And deeds of service flowed into the stream
Of sacrifice, and chastity's pure white
Enrobed the life of all, and deep was its delight.

---

123 Saraswati: Hindu goddess of learning and knowledge.

XVI.

And red-eyed lust, ambition's restless pace,
The biting glance of sneaking jealousy,
And gnawing hatred, anger's fiery face,
And blood-born murder, and its grim ally,
Revenge, with iron heart and stony eye,
Unseen in ancient India, were unknown;
Nor was there unjust war's iniquity,
That burns to ashes all it breathes upon,
And spares nor widowed wives nor orphan babies lone.

XVII.

But sweet was life upon this mortal earth,
And all of love was holy, pure, and true,
As notes of music full of tender mirth,
Or on the roses balmy drops of dew.
No roaring tempest rushed, no hot winds blew
Of foul disease, or famine gaunt and bare;
But simple were men's ways, their wants but few,
And calm their thoughts of meditative prayer,
And harmony of peace was vocal everywhere.

XVIII.

The royal father sat upon his throne,
Amidst a pomp which glory wins from love;
His subjects were as children of his own,
And did in duty and affection prove
What filial fondness did their bosoms move,
And lived as brothers born in unity.
And he for justice, truth, and mercy strove,
The mighty ruler of this family
Of happy hearth and home, a nation great and free.

XIX.

And holy Brahmans sat within his hall,
And sages versed in wisdom by his side,
And statesmen calm and cautious at his call,
On whose great foresight and experience wide,
And an unclouded judgment, he relied.
And might warriors of a noble birth,
With dauntless valour, and unsullied pride,
Stood ready to defend their native earth,
To conquer, or to die, when honour bade them forth.

XX.

No father for his boy did weep and mourn,
Nor for her husband wailed the widowed bride,
When he was gone and never would return,
To cheer his age, or press her heaving side.
But mothers blessed their sons, and bravely tried
To soothe their sorrow, though their hearts did ache;
And wives suppressed their owe, nor vainly sighed,
When parting grief did their fond bosoms break,
And those beloved went out to die for duty's sake.

XXI.

The honest merchant busy at his trade;
The patient farmer labouring in his field;
And the meek servant silently obeyed
His master's will in smile or word revealed.
And then no woeful wretch for aid appealed,
For all with as one soul in harmony,
Did lead a life of love, and help and shield
The young, and poor, and old, and unasked and free,
With an untiring zeal and selfless sympathy.

XXII.

And golden harvests glowed with plenteous corn,
And blessed the land with Nature's bounteous store;
And maiden flowers lifted to the morn
Their virgin veil, and bridal garments wore.
For every heart was happy to the core,
And mighty Indra smiled that joy to see;
And vernal showers and summer rain did pour
Into the bosom of the earth, and free
His purest, choicest winds to nurse her tenderly.

XXIII.

And then the world entire was blithe and gay,
And lightly danced along her paths on high;
A golden crown adorned the brows of day,
And bright and lovely was the night to spy,
With beaming jewels on the ear and eye.
And waters laughed and leaped in merriment,
And gazed enraptured on the waking sky;
And dewdrops kissed the moon, and softly bent
To cast one melting glance at her so innocent.

XXIV.

And Nature's Deities in notes sublime,
And an ethereal voice, did sweetly sing;
The Spirit of the past and future Time,
His bride, Life, did in rainbow garments bring,
And played with Death the melodies of Spring.
For every orb in Space, around, above,
Was vocal with a soul-enravishing
And heavenly harmony of Light and Love,
And with a joy divine the Universe did move.

XXV.

The gentle pupil at his master's feet,
Upon the book of Nature bent his eye;
And with a father's love the sage did treat
His new-got son, and gave him patiently
The eternal wisdom of the earth and sky.
His heart was pure and simple, and believed
With open faith and meek humility
The truths of life his watchful mind received,
And with his soul and body consonantly heaved.

XXVI.

And all her secrets Nature did unfold
To her own darling, as a mother kind;
And from his eyes the veil of darkness rolled,
And he beheld the wonders of her mind;
And learnt the language of the wave and wind,
And o'er the earth at pleasure would he roam;
Nor in these narrow paths his gaze confined,
But mused on fire's bright essence, and his home
In the ethereal regions of the starry dome.

XXVII.

Aye, he was pure and simple, and the birds
Would bend the boughs to hear him, when alone
He sang beside a fountain, and his words
Of thrilling music, sweeter than their own,
Arose in language unto them well known.
And the beasts marked the magic of his eyes,
And felt a subtle influence upon
Their softened nature, and in glad surprise
With new emotions did their gentle bosoms rise.

XXVIII.

The dove would fly to him in meek delight,
Or dance about him in a fairy ring;
And from his hand, the swan as snowy white,
Receive the bread which daily would he bring
To feed upon the lake so fair a thing.
And at his feet in rainbow robes arrayed,
The peacock stood and gazed as if a king;
And the green parrot laughed in joy and said
In human notes, "Behold", and shook its little head.

XXIX.

Through field or forest wild, the gentle fawn
Would follow him with beaming eyes and face;
And o'er the mountain, or the open lawn,
Remain or roam beside him with a grace
Of tender softness or an aerial pace.
The light-limbed ape would watch him from behind
With grinning looks, of mischief, or grimace,
Yet curb the antics of its restless mind,
And eat upon his knee the fruit that it could find.

XXX.

The hungry lion did he meet unharmed;
Nor frowned at him the tiger furiously;
And happy was the serpent as though charmed
By the strange music of his steps, when he
Did pass by it, and danced in ecstasy.
For he was Nature's own beloved child,
And when they saw his native purity,
Their heart was hushed with all its passions wild,
And low to him they bowed as creatures meek and mild.

XXXI.

How happy was this life of innocence,
When earth was sweet as heaven, and delight
As pure and deep as love, and as intense
As musky breezes that in joy unite,
And kiss the new-born roses red and white.
How wondrous calm, and how divinely fair,
And blessed, as the soul-entrancing flight
Of that ethereal music rich and rare,
Which angels pour in song in ecstasy of prayer!

XXXII.

And so he grew with knowledge deep imbued,
And wisdom, pure as rays of morning light;
With eyes of truth the Universe he viewed,
Its glorious splendour and essential might.
And Life in all its shades and beauties bright
Was the vast ocean of his study deep;
And often in the silence of the night,
When earth reposes in the arms of sleep,
His mind would wake and with his soul communion keep.

XXXIII.

Now see him as a man in newer life,
Enraptured by the music of her soul,
Who linked to him for ever as his wife,
Hath made the twain but one harmonious whole.
The Spring of Youth her charms doth all unroll,
And in heir musky bosom joy inspire;
Their blissful union hath attained its goal,
And with a rosy smile to bless his sire,
Behold the sweet-eyed babe, in Nature's own attire.

XXXIV.

How bright his home where bounteous Lakshmi smiled,
And silver light of peace did play around;
And lisping tongue and prattle of a child,
And all its tender calls an audience found,
Sweet as the rippling music of the sound
That fondly whispers in the fountain's ear;
And heart to heart was in affection bound;
Allied in joy and sorrow, hope and fear,
In trustful arms of love that longing eyes endear.

XXXV.

His task was in each lowly office done,
Whereon its dove-like wings contentment spread,
With gentle words that charmed, and smiles that won,
And sweet simplicity of heart inbred.
Nor lacked the manly virtues of the head —
A purpose firm, unwavering strength of will,
A dauntless mind which nought on earth may dread,
And patience slowly climbing up the hill
To gain its mountain end, with calmness, labour, and skill.

XXXVI.

A statesman in the castle's gilded hall,
A warrior on the battle-field would be;
And bravely answered every duty's call,
In paths of death, or floral victory.
At home, a husband, son, and father he,
And in the daily walks of life, a man –
A humble servant of Humanity:
To lift the lowly, ever in the van,
And out to them his heart in joy and sorrow ran.

XXXVII.

And so the days move on: – the life's incline
Descends along the paths of youthful hope,
Through azure rays that bathe in warm sunshine,
To cooler shades of evening, and the slope
Of hoary age; and newer regions ope
Before him on the threshold of the night;
And he beholds the starry kingdoms cope
This mortal earth, and their celestial light
Point to eternal realms of wondrous glory bright.

XXXVIII.

His tasks not all completed, he resigns
His active duties to a younger race;
And Nature's lonely calmness and confines
Are now his sylvan home and resting place,
Where all is silent, and no bustling trace
Of life is seen. And in that lowly haunt,
Where lie a hermit's bowl and roving mace,
Is heard the cadence of a solemn chant,
That bids the soul awake, and earthly cares avaunt.

XXXIX.

He sleeps but lightly on a bed of grass,
And leaves and fruits compose his fixéd fare:
In watchful vigil many a night doth pass,
And many a day in fasting and in prayer.
Within, he bends the wayward mind, and there,
Sees truths unknown to mortals dark and dense;
And in the silence of his heart, the air
Is charged with music strange, he knows not whence,
But fills his soul with joy to feel its eloquence.

XL.

And in a world of glory now revealed,
He sees a mighty power on every side,
Whose various forms in splendid beauty yield
The wealth of Life with all its wonders wide,
Where One is all, and all in One abide.
Himself, a crystal drop in a vast ocean
That heaves its breast where earth and air confide
Their secrets of a life of ceaseless motion
To ears of peaceful calm and eyes of deep devotion.

XLI.

Under the shade of an o'er-spreading tree,
In robes of Nature meet the anchorites;
And high discourses on Eternity,
And secrets dark of Death's mysterious rites,
And boundless Grace that equally invites
The great and small, and Love that purifies,
Uplift the soul, and waken deep delights,
And teach new truths whose memory never dies,
Of Life beyond this land and narrow seas and skies.

XLII.

And regions of eternal Light unseen,
Unending bliss, ethereal ecstasy,
Ineffable beatitude serene,
And everlasting immortality,
The visioned heart beholds with glory's eye.
No shadow's cast by darkness in that Clime,
But in one garb both night and morning vie
To illuminate those purple paths sublime,
In infinite Space, and far beyond the realms of Time.

XLIII.

Fire kindleth fire, and light with Light is mingled,
And life in Love receives its sacrament;
The enraptured soul her own Mate hath out-singled,
And flaming with her wings of glory, rent
The cage wherein her leaden days were spent.
Afar she flies to brighter realms than this,
How sweet, how pure, and oh how innocent —
And with the sinless ones entranced in bliss,
Beholds the Light of Life, that will be, was, and is!

Ram Sharma

Ram Sharma (1837–1918) was the pseudonym of Nabokissen Ghose, a well-known and well-published poet who wrote for *Mookerjee's Magazine* and later *Reis & Rayyet*, both Calcutta-based English-language periodicals founded and edited by Sambhu Mookerjee, an eminent Calcutta businessman and man-of-letters who felt deeply about English-language poetry and often supported the works of Indian-English poets. Sharma's work was mostly published in these two periodicals and was usually politically topical and highly satirical, especially towards the British. In contrast, Sharma's independently published volumes of poetry were often structured as lengthy spiritual mediations. These independent collections include *The Last Day: A Poem* (1886) and *Shiva Ratri, Bhagabat Gita and Miscellaneous Poems* (1903). His periodical poetry was collected and published after his death in 1919 by Debendra Chandra Mullick, who writes:

> It is no small gratification to me that I have been the instrument of rescuing from oblivion the poetical works of perhaps the greatest poet of India writing in English Verse by giving them a permanent shape. I cannot say I have been able to collect all his poems, for the poet in his ascetic indifference never cared to keep copies of his works. Embracing a period of more than half a century and scattered over the pages of different newspapers and periodicals it was indeed hard work to collect them. Perhaps the next edition will be fuller, the reader in the meantime must be satisfied with what he gets. But most of his important works have been included in the book. I have given notes, for without them it is impossible for the ordinary reader, particularly Englishmen, to fully understand and appreciate the poet's works. They are not copious, but enough for the purpose of making the meaning sufficiently clear. It is not for me to make a detailed criticism of his works; that will be done by competent critics. What their verdict will be, is unknown, but the notes will largely facilitate a correct and proper understanding…

The Poetical Works of Ram Sharma (Calcutta: 1919)[124]

Song of the Indian Conservative[125]

I'm a tory[126] by instinct all true,
  Nay, prove me aught else if you can;
I give even the Devil his due,
  Let him take, then, his "liberal man!"

'Tis the hour of tory reaction,
  Down with liberalism, my boys;
Down – down with the humbug, – the faction,
  That so deafens the ear with its noise.

Liberalism's a sham and a snare,
  'Tis moonshine and gammon and *jhoot*;[127]
For your "liberal man's" only care
  Is for chances of plunder and loot!

Yes, plunder and blunder still mark
  His career, be he statesman or scribe;
And whether they whine or they bark,
  Never trust the "liberal" tribe.

All their talk is but nonsense and stuff,
  Come, honest conservatives, come!
Away with proud Argyll and Duff,
  Let's have Salisbury or Derby *ekdum*.[128]

---

124 Ram Sharma, *The Poetical Works of Ram Sharma*, ed. Debendra Chandra Mullick (Calcutta: P. N. Mallick, 1919).
125 The poem seems to satirize the Indian mimic man, the promoter of conservative English values and discourses regarding India's lack of civilization, against his own (and his people's) better interests.
126 Tory: used colloquially, indicates attachment to old-fashioned policies; used disparagingly, refers to a conservative in economic and political issues; one who is bigoted and opposed to reform (n., adj. "Tory" *OED*).
127 [Editor's Note: False.] *Jhoot*: ridiculous nonsense suited to deceive only simple persons; misleading or nonsensical talk (n. "jhoot" *OED*).
128 [Editor's Note: At once.] George Campbell, Duke of Argyll (1823–1900) and Robert Duff (1835–1895): Liberal Party politicians. Robert Cecil, Marquess of Salisbury (1830–1903): Conservative Party politician who served as prime minister. Edward Stanley, Earl of Derby (1826–1893): Conservative Party politician who served as secretary of foreign affairs.

Three cheers for brave Dizzie,[129] my lads,
    Let his genius have full and fair play;
Turn out all the "liberal" pads,
    Let honest conservatives away.

Our first parents by Satan were sold
    In a serpent's guise, – shining and bright;
He has changed now his tactics, I find,
    And deceives as a "liberal" wight![130]

I am a tory by instinct all true, –
    Nay, prove me aught else if you can;
I give even the Devil his due,
    Let him take, then, his "liberal man!"

An Old Indian Melody

The stranger now revels and reigns in the halls,
    Where once thou in pride and glory hadst moved,
And the voice of the alien is heard on the walls,
    Whence floated the banner thy children so loved.

Thou drudgest as hand-maid, where, humbly of yore,
    Proud monarchs and heroes had courted thy grace;
And the brow, that for ages, a diadem wore,
    Now bends in observance to vain mushrooms in place.

Fickle Fortune to thee is sternly unkind
    Not a gleam of sweet hope, nor a glimmer of joy,
Illumes for a moment the gloom of thy mind
    While lurid marsh flames lure but thee to destroy.

Untouched is thy lyre, which the world loved to hear,
    And silent thy voice, which once thrilled with this song;
While the heart-breaking music that falls on the ear
    Is the clang of the chains that thou draggest along.

---

129 "Dizzie," or Dizzy: mocking nickname for Benjamin Disraeli (1804–1881), who was a leading member of the Conservative Party for decades and served as prime minister for two terms.
130 Wight: living being in general; a creature (n. "wight" *OED*).

Like a tree gay with amaranths fragrant and bright,
  Thy person in beauty and loveliness shone!
But as looks the same tree, when 'tis withered by blight,
  Too mournful art thou with thy glories now gone.

Neglected thy garments — dishevelled thy hair —
  Thy ornaments carelessly strewn on the floor,
Thou sittest like "Grief" fondly nursing her care, —
  The dead hopes of the past that may waken no more.

In streams from thy eyes thy tears carelessly fall.
  Fine words have no balm for thy sorrows and cares;
  Perchance, this reflection pains thee above all,
That thy fetters are love-gifts of Freedom's proud heirs.

Thy children, once famed for their science and art,
  And for marvellous works they had done,
Now languish forlorn, in deep anguish of the heart,
  'Mid scenes where their fathers great triumphs had won.

Arise hapless Ind, my loved country arise
  No longer bewail this deplorable state
See, Hope's iris lonely gleams in the skies
  Now strive to redress all the rigours of Fate.

If Britons to God and their pledges be true,
  And knock off the fetters that cause thee such pain,
Swaraj[131] will be thine from Himadri[132] to the main,
  And dazzle the world with its splendour again?

The Song of the Tirhoot Planters[133]

  The famine's o'er — our task is one,
    Let us back to our vats again!
  The season for our dye is come —
    For sweating toil in sun and rain.

---

131 [Editor's Note: Self-government.]
132 [Editor's Note: The Himalayas.]
133 Tirhoot: located in the Bengal presidency, in what is now northwest Bihar. The area of northwest and southwest Bihar as well as what is now Bengal state was the site of a devastating famine from 1873 to 1874. The loss in crops was aggravated by the forcible payment of revenue by peasants to landlords. See Christopher V. Hill, "Philosophy and Reality in Riparian South Asia: British Famine Policy and Migration in Colonial North India," *Modern Asian Studies* 25, no. 2 (May 1991): 263–79 for a discussion of this famine.

The Famine was a jolly thing,
    A jolly thing and nice and dear;
The nicest, dearest famine, lads,
    In India known for many a year!

A God-send, friends, it was to us;
    While millions starv'd all through Tirhoot,
We fatten'd on the stricken land,
    And – bless Reach Hard! – had our loot!

Some people say, it was a myth,
    A humbug, and that sort of thing;
But mock or real, take our word,
    It gave most freely like a king!

Let's drink its health in well-fill'd cups,
    In well-fill'd cups of ruddy wine;
Oh crown its brow with loving hands,
    Crown it with myrtle wreaths and vine!

But dearest friends are doom'd to part:
    Heigh ho! It break our heart to bid
Adieu to one that well has prov'd
    A saving Angel in our need!

The Anglo-Indian War-Cry, or Bluster in Excelsis[134]

I

Wake, Britons! from your slumbers wake!
    A miscreant band of recreant Whites
Have sworn forth from you and yours to take
    Your Magna Charta, Bill of Rights![135]
Our fathers fought and won this land,
    By Right of Sword we hold it still;
Who dare restrain our mighty hand?
    Who dare resist our sovereign will?

---

134 "*in Excelsis*": in the highest degree.
135 The Magna Carta (1215) was an English legal charter requiring King John of England to guarantee some rights to a limited group of men, thereby limiting his own power as sovereign. The English Bill of Rights (1689) enumerated the rights of certain subjects under the monarch, including prohibiting the monarch from suspending laws or levying taxes without the consent of Parliament and guaranteeing liberties such as freedom of debate in Parliament and freedom from cruel and unusual punishments. Both texts are considered key documents in the British "constitution."

II

  The Indians are our conquer'd Slaves, —
    Shall we, the Victors, stand their sway?
  Did we cross the ocean-waves,
    These Helots[136] base to serve — obey?
  They hate us all — they must, — the race
    Is blacken'd deep with every crime;
  Will ye your wives and daughters place
    Beneath them for a moment's time?

III

  Was it for this that Havelock fought?[137]
    That Peel and Neil their lives laid down?[138]
  From yonder plain, on such mean thought,
    See, see our marble heroes frown!
  Ye shades of Hampden and of Pym,[139]
    Of Barons bold of Runnymede,[140]
  Who tyrants quell'd with courage grim,
    Speed to our rescue! swiftly speed!

IV

  By all that's sacred, Britons, swear!
    Ye, who fair Freedom prize so high,
  Swear to stand firm, — the worst to dare,
    To fight for hearth and home, or die!
  Hark to the thunders from the Press!
    Hark to the cry from districts far!
  Our free-born rights, — nor more nor less, —
    It must be *that*, or bloody War!

---

136 After Sparta conquered neighboring Messenia in 640–620 BCE, the Messenians became state-sponsored slaves, or serfs, known as Helots.
137 Henry Havelock (1795–1857): British commander during the Indian Uprising (or "Sepoy Mutiny") of 1857.
138 Sir Robert Peel (1788–1850): British Conservative Party politician who served as chief secretary in Ireland from 1812 to 1818 and as prime minister from 1841 to 1846. He was responsible for creating the modern British police force, whose members came to be known as Peelers or Bobbies.
139 Henry Brand, Viscount Hampden (1814–1892): British Liberal Party politician who served as Speaker of the House of Commons. John Pym (1583?–1643): prominent member of the English Parliament from 1621 to 1643 and critic of the monarchy. He sought to balance the power of the Crown against that of Parliament.
140 King John most likely sealed the Magna Carta at Runnymeade, which is located in present day Surrey, England.

V

On, Britons, on! The Flag unfurl
    That stream'd in darkest Stuart days![141]
Hurl! from their seats the tyrants hurl!
    And deck your brows with crown of bays!
Down — down with Ripon and his crew![142]
    Hiss — hiss that traitor Ilbert's name![143]
They're recreants all-with souls untrue!
    Not England's sons, but England's shame!

India's Vindication of Lord Ripon and her Farewell

Up, brothers, up! behold in yonder skies
    The glorious sun-down in the crimson west!
Thus noble Ripon — gen'rous, just and wise —
    Goes to his island-home from toil to rest.

His reign has been poor India's halcyon day,
    A sun-look piercing through the deepest gloom,
A radiant morn all redolent of May,
    Ay, Hope's own resurrection for the tomb!

Or not the hero's Fame, the Lily red
    That grows on crimson stream of blood he sought;
His purer, loftier aim has been to shed
    The life and light that cheers the People's lot.

---

141 The Stuart family took over the throne of England in 1603 after the death of the last Tudor monarch, Queen Elizabeth I. The Stuart dynasty presided over the English Civil War (1629–1651) and the Restoration (1660).

142 Lord Ripon (1827–1909): viceroy of India from 1880 to 1884 under then British prime minister William Gladstone. Ripon was a proponent of the Ilbert Bill (which would have allowed Indian judges to preside over cases involving Europeans) and limited self-government. He was often referred to reverently in Indian-English political discourses during the nineteenth century as a figure sympathetic to Indians and as a proponent for reform within the British Raj.

143 The Ilbert Bill proposed allowing Indian judges to preside over trials concerning Anglo-Indians. The possibility that Anglo-Indians could be tried and convicted by Indian judges aroused the ire of the Anglo-Indian community. This in turn elicited a strong reaction from Indians who resented such inequality before the law since Indians were often tried by white judges but whites refused to be tried by Indian judges.

His guide's the law revealed on Sinai's height,
        The sermon on the Mount his fount of love
And the Great book has taught his hopes aright,
        To seek for glory but in realms of above![144]

The bonds of Love, like silk though soft and light,
        Are stronger yet than adamantine chain,
And more than bayonet or sword of might
        Potent t'attach men to a foreign reign.

Fetters can shackle limbs, but not men's hearts,
        Coercion is the tyrant's poor resource;
For Loyalty is born of loving arts,
        Of gen'rous sympathy, and Moral Force.

Arms may restrain awhile the stubborn breast,
        May force allegiance from reluctant land:
Empires thus raised, on weak foundations rest,
        Like houses built by children on the sand!

But Love, confined to no one race or clan,
        And Justice, emulous of Heaven's own, –
Holding the balance ev'n 'tween man and man, –
        These are the rock of pow'r, of earthly throne.

And these, O Ripon! are thy title just
        To the land's love and lasting gratitude;
For true to duty and thy sacred Trust
        Thy ceaseless care has been this country's good.

Shame on the lying tongues which falsely say,
        That England's hold on India's heart has been
Weakened beneath this virtuous ruler's sway, –
        So just to all, so faithful to his Queen!

They call him weak! because he has not thrust
        All he could wish down their reluctant throat,
Because he has been firmly, strictly just
        In all he ever did, or spoke or wrote!

---

144 Mount Sinai: where the Ten Commandments were given to Moses by God in the Judeo-Christian tradition.

Weak — weak indeed! he who at Duty's call
    Spurned Faction's threats, lies, slanders, and did stake
Position, influence, and power — all —
    And that the world holds dear, for conscience' sake![145]

Weak — weak indeed! the Christian hero bold
    Who, from rav'nous pack, like shepherd good
And vigilant, hath saved the helpless fold,
    And still beneath the strong and feeble stood![146]

Mark! how they yell and chafe and strain their necks
    To rush, with furious violence, on him —
The man who, of all men, imposed the checks
    So needful to restrain each savage grim!

There are who blame him for great lust of fame,
    Unblushing preachers of repressive force!
If to serve God and Man deserves the blame,
    He shares it with Hare, Howard, Wilberforce![147]

Misguided fools! as fragrance in the rose,
    Sweetness in the honey, nectar in the palm;
So Man's love in God's love inheres and grows,
    Humanity's elixir, — healing balm!

And fame, unsought, attends such hallowed Love,
    As Life attends the Universal Space;
Or as the songsters from the sylvan grove
    Attend fair Usha[148] when she shows her face.

An adult'rous class clamour for a sign!
    But will they, can they see? the purblind band!
Behold! propitious to his rule benign,
    With health and plenty Heav'n hath blest the land!

---

145 A reference to Ripon's rather embattled position as viceroy, especially in his support of the controversial Ilbert Bill, which would allow Indian judges to preside over cases involving Europeans and which was therefore bitterly and rancorously opposed by the Anglo-Indian community in India.

146 Ripon is often presented in Indian-English poetry as a Christian leader or shepherd of his flock.

147 David Hare (1775–1842): Scottish watchmaker, philanthropist and reformer who lived in India and founded a number of educational institutions, including Hindu College of Calcutta. John Howard (1726–1790): British prison reformer who advocated for more humane conditions for prisoners and also acted as high sheriff of Bedfordshire from 1773 to 1790. William Wilberforce (1759–1833): British statesmen who took a leading role in the movement to abolish the slave trade.

148 [Editor's Note: Dawn.] Usha: Hindu goddess of the dawn.

Apart from thousand nameless acts of grace,
    The kindly charities of life unbought,
It has been Ripon's glory to efface
    From Statute Book the law which shackled Thought.

A liberated Press![149] Then view his plan
    Of Local Self-Government![150] Measures twain
That make the Patriot feel himself a man,
    And raise up India's drooping head again!

These are his triumphs! these the talisman
    Which Indian Union silently has wrought,
Making the Hindu, Parsi, Mussulman,
    All one in feeling, interest, and thought!

Are not these great achievements, golden deeds
    That should in golden characters be writ?
The prescient husbandman hath sown the seeds,
    And these will grow in grace in season fit.

Will the acorn, which doth in its tiny shell,
    The stately monarch of the forest hold,
Will it, as by a juggler's magic spell,
    Before its time the giant oak unfold?

Wait, brothers, wait! Oh nurse the seeds with care,
    Still-still the soil prepare, manure, refine;
Time will change them to goodly plants and rare,
    The Tree of Life to nations in decline![151]

---

149 Although the Marquis of Hastings, under the East India Company's rule, abolished censorship in 1819, the Bengal Regulations Acts of the 1820s instituted mandatory licensing for papers produced in its territories. Sir Charles Metcalfe repealed these Acts in 1835. After the 1857 Indian Uprising (or "Sepoy Mutiny") and the fears of native uprising that it induced in the British regulatory mechanisms, however, Lord Canning instituted the Gagging Act, which required all printing presses to be licensed with the government; prohibited any newspaper from criticizing the government in Britain or in India or to incite unrest, resistance to the government, or criticism of its policies or laws; and applied its regulations equally to European and Indian publications. It was soon repealed. The Press and Registration of Books Act of 1867 established a registration system for all printed materials in order to allow the government to keep track of newspapers and printing presses.

150 Ripon forwarded proposals for local self-government by introducing an election system into the local boards. Although this plan was not fully implemented due to opposition from Anglo-Indians, it did open these boards to participation through newly introduced elective methods even while maintaining the formerly used nomination process.

151 "Tree of Life": appears as a figure in numerous belief systems including Hinduism (the banyan tree and the bo tree) and Buddhism (the bo tree).

The Muse of History will fondly dwell
    On the bright record which embalms his fame;
When selfish rowdies at his name who yell,
    Will have sunk to Nothingness whence they came.

She does not build her verdict on the views
    Of class or clique or buzz of idle moth;
The People's voice is echoed by the Muse,
    All else she spurns as frowzy, worthless froth.

See, India, though long unto marble grown,
    Like fair Ahulya's[152] vivified again! —
She breathes — she weeps — no longer now a stone —
    At touch of kindness thrilling heart and brain!

In tears, dear Mother! in a flood of tears!
    Flow on, ye precious dews of surcharged breast!
Ye best express her grief profound and fears,
    At loss of him who gave her strength'ning rest,

The Ages have not seen such stirring sight;
    A Continent with one pulsation moving; —
One heart — one mind — one soul ablaze with light
    Of glowing passion for one loved and loving.

O England! what thy sword could ne'er achieve,
    That Ripon's gen'rous rule has gently done!
The Millions here have motive now to live,
    And closer cleave unto Victoria's throne!

The greatest conqu'ror he of modern Ind, —
    Mightier than Mahmood, Nadir, Tamerlane,[153]
Who built their pow'r on woes of human kind,
    On ravished land, and desecrated fane!

---

152 In the ancient Hindu epic, the *Ramayana*, Ahulya, or Ahalya, is created by the god Brahma as the most beautiful woman in the world. She is married to the ascetic and abstinent sage Gautama. The god Indra, who cannot control his desire for Ahalya, disguises himself as her husband and seduces her. The real Gautama curses Indra and his wife, whom he turns to stone. Years later during a visit to the hermitage, the hero of the epic, Rama, unwittingly redeems Ahalya after his feet touch her stone form. Ahalya regains her human form as a result of this touch.

153 Mahmood, or Mahmud of Ghazni (971–1030 CE): ruler of an Islamic dynasty centered in the Afghan city of Ghazni and led a series of invasions into India. Nadir Shah (1688–1747) won a series of battles against the Afghans and eventually became shah of Iran in 1736; he invaded Mughal India, including Delhi and Lahore and was known for his brilliant methods of conquest and rule. Tamerlane the Great (1336–1405): Mongol ruler who succeeded Genghis Khan as ruler of Central Asia and expanded his empire into Western and South Asia.

Not his triumphs of that robber band!
    He's conquered hearts, the living are his slain;
The Olive branch of Peace his flaming brand,
    And Justice, Mercy, Love, his warrior train!

Up, brothers, up! your grateful homage pay
    To him whose rule benign will shortly cease;
Pour out your glowing hearts in thrilling lay,
    Make the present one Carnival of Peace!

O twine his brow with wreaths that will not fade,
    Such wreaths as never warriors' temples bound, –
By fond affection's loving fingers made: –
    With such be Ripon by the Empire crowned!

And, now, Farewell! e'en though it breaks the heart
    To say the word; still fare thee well, once more!
And think, O think, – all kindly as thou art, –
    Of us who love thee, honour, and adore!

May God, thy God and ours, our common God,
    Bless thee with health and strength, and evening calm!
And when thy mortal part's placed 'neath the sod,
    Be thine the Coveted White Robe and Palm![154]

Ode on the Meeting of the Congress at Allahabad on the 26th December 1888[155]

Wake, Harp of India, from thy slumber long!
    Pour forth thy richest melodies once more,
    In varied cadence, such as thrilled of yore
The Aryan soul,[156] responsive to thy song!
Oh for the skill of earlier minstrel band

---

154 Revelations 7:9 (King James version).
155 The Indian National Congress (INC) held its first meeting in 1885. The INC, which included delegates from various regions throughout the subcontinent, met at the end of every year to address political and economic issues. The INC eventually split into two factions: the Extremists, the more radical members of Congress who pressed for greater freedoms from the imperial government and the Moderates, who professed loyalty to Britain and wanted greater autonomy within a colonial framework.
156 Orientalists famously "traced" Indian, especially northern Indian, descent to the Aryans and proclaimed an Indo-European commonality. In Orientalist, and later, Indian nationalist discourses, northern Indians were thought to be of Aryan origin and thus genealogically related to Europeans while southern Indians were thought to have descended from the Dravidian race.

To fling thy harmonies around the land!
      Venturous over-much
      The magic strings I touch
      With feeble, falt'ring hand,
Hoping, perchance, these rugged numbers may
Call forth some nobler strain — some loftier lay,
In memory of this happy, blessed day!

For, Lo! where ancient Pryag[157] proudly stands,
      Laved by the waters of two sacred streams,
      Realising the patriots fondest dreams
The Pilgrim Fathers meet from many lands!
Theirs is the forward spirit of the age,
      That bids the nations onward roll;
And public zeal still ruled by counsel sage;
      And equal love to lord and thrall.
      A confluence of waters graces!
Bold hearts all loyal to Victoria's throne!
England's creation and her pride alone!
Rich harvest of the seed her loving care hath sown!

They come! they come! Apostles true of Peace,
      Tied each to each by sympathy profound!
      Oh clear the mists that Ign'rance spreads around,
And bid the lying tongue of Slander cease!
Alas! was one reform e'er wrought on earth, —
      One precious right or boon secured to man,
When Malice did not spit her venom forth
      Upon the gallant souls that led the van?
See! Bureaucracy, with a servile band
      Of placemen hoar, the nations Movement thwart;
But Self's the only chord they understand
      Of the deep organ of the human heart.
"Beware," they cry, "of these our foes, beware!
      Suppress them, crush them, sweep them all away!
Come weal or woe, it must be still our care
      To hold uncheck'd our arbitrary sway!"
Yes, perish India! perish every man
Who seeks the Indian polity to scan,
And harmonize all interests on a loyal plan!

They come! they come! from India's farthest ends
      They come, from north and south, from east and west, —

---

157 [Editor's Note: Modern Allahabad.]

>   The flower of the land — its wisest — best,
> The Crown's true liegemen, th' Empire's staunchest friends!
>
>   Oh! not in mid'night's gloomy hour,
>   Like baleful ghosts, about they flit;
>   Or traitor-like in ruined tow'r,
>   In secret conclave grim they sit!
>   Ah no! in perfect blaze
>   Of day, before the gaze
> Of all the world, the land's own chosen meet, —
> Ev'n in the shadow of Power's castled seat, —
> To aid her, strength her with counsels wise and fit!
>
> They come! they come! from sylvan bower and hall,
>   From bar and counter, temple, mosque, and mart —
>   Of diff'rent cults and creeds, but one in heart —
> To celebrate New India's festival!
> See! Moslem, Hindu, Parsi, Christian, Jain,
> Walk hand in hand, linked in fraternal chain;
> The Trident, Crescent and the Cross combine[158]
> To act harmonious on a common line: —
>   Our country's weal through England's grace,
>   And perfect loyalty to both
>   The ruling and the subject race,
>   To Crown and People, Man and Truth!
>   How sweetly blend red, white and blue,
>   The three creeds' sacred, mystic hue!
>   How meetly at this season when
>   Jesus was born to save all men!
> Flow, Aryan Hearts, from Himachal[159] to sea,
> In streams of Joy, for Indian Unity
> Sprung from th' ashes of tribal, creed-born Jealousy!
>
> They come! they come! with music's blythest strain,
>   O brothers greet the Amphictyons[160] of the land
>   Greet them with loving heart and lavish hand!
> Greet them from house and street, from field and fane!
>   Away! Away!
>   With flowers strew their way!

---

158 "The Trident, Crescent and the Cross": symbols of Hinduism, Islam and Christianity respectively.
159 Himachal: snowy mountain region in what is now the state of Himachal Pradesh and which borders Jammu and Kashmir in the north.
160 *Amphictyons*: deputies from the various states of ancient Greece to a congress, council or assembly (n. "amphictyon" *OED*).

Crown them, crown them one and all,
With heart's own coronal!
  They come! they come!
While the reaper is reaping
  The bounty of earth;
And the rustic's heart leaping
  With joy and with mirth,
As, bound in sheaves, the golden corn
Leaves the field for the peasant's barn;
And the palm grove and mangoe tope
Ring with the song of joy and hope –
  Harvest-home! harvest-home!
Fitly the Congress meets 'mid scenes so bright!
May Heaven guide its counsels all aright,
And India shine once more with her pristine light!

'Twas said by Olney's bard and sage –
"We have no slaves at home – then why abroad?"[161]
Is England's sceptre, then a tyrant's rod?
No! we repel the charge with honest rage!
Still, England! there are rivets in our chain,
Which, thou wilt own, had better not remain;
Remove them; and make it thy duteous care
To mete thy weaker Sister measure fair.
Give us a wider verge to frame our laws,
  A fairer share in our domestic rule;
And oh! with Roman loftiness of soul,
  Fit us to guard the Empire and her cause!
   Rule Britannia! India rise!
   By methods just, and measures wise!
Like yon untied streams that nought can part,
Let us onward move – two nations, one in heart!
Breathes there the Briton, free from racial hate,
Who'll taunt the Congress still with Phaeton's fate,[162]
As seeking, not to help, but guide the car of State?

---

161 The bard of Olney is William Cowper (1731–1800) and the quote is from his anti-slavery poem, "The Task" (1784).

162 Phaeton: son of the sun god Helios in Greek mythology. Phaeton drives the sun chariot too close to the earth, threatening to incinerate it. To prevent this occurrence, Zeus kills Phaeton with his thunderbolt and the dead Phaeton falls to earth and into the river.

India to Britain

Britons! to your professions now be true!
       If selflessly ye seek my lasting good,
       Stand fast to me! for rightly understood,
My cause and yours, in sooth are same though few
Seem willing yet to realize this view
       In deeds, bespeaking that calm mental mood,
       Which sees in mine and England's sisterhood,
My right to claim from [her] a sister's due.
Blest heirs of Freedom! act as freemen should!
       Some of her blessings on my sons bestow;
And thus secure my endless gratitude.
       And one more wreath of glory for your brow!
Oh spread those blessings through this Empire wide,
And let my sons march onward by your side!

To Indian Patriots

On, on ye men of India, fearless on!
       Your cause is just; your ways and methods right;
       Press on! Nor heed the deep'ning shades of night,
Which shall disperse before the rosy dawn!
Rely on your own efforts, firmly, now!
       With vision clear, and vain illusions gone —
       Still true and loyal to Britannia's throne —
Work for the common weal with lifted brow!
Foster home industries with jealous care!
       Your vast resources far and wide expand,
       And make an Eden of this glorious land.
Whose golden fruitage all alike shall share!
Now, put, ye friends, your shoulders to the wheel
And serve your Motherland with ceaseless zeal!
Yes, self-reliance is a pow'r, indeed —
       Aladdin's wond'rous lamp and magic ring,
       Whose genii most readily would bring
Their happy owner all that he might need!
Cherish it, then, with loving heart and hand:
       'Twill soon revive your drooping energies —
       Enable you to brave inclement skies —
And drive grim Famine from your native land.
On, on, ye friends, avoiding feud and strife!
       Hindu, Moslem, by your actions prove,
       That he are brethren, knit in bonds of love,

Striving, with Moral strength for light and life!
O God! when will arise that glorious morn,
Which shall redress the wrongs that Ind has borne!
Brush Politics aside, if but, to please
   The lordlings here! Eschew all signs and show
   Which rudely interfere with their repose,
And meekly yield to Kismet's stern decrees!
Begone! servile thoughts, offspring of dastard Fear!
   Swadeshi, still Swadeshi things produce![163]
   Swadeshi goods still largely, widely use!
And go on prospering more and more each year!
Let Opulence her ample hoards employ
   To save the land from drought, disease, and flood
   With roads and drains, canals and stores of food,
Filling the peasant's home with mirth and joy.
   The gen'rous flame will more and more inspire
   Your dauntless breasts with quenchless patriot fire!

Bande Mataram[164]
(Translation of the famous song of "Bande Mataram" by Bankim Chandra Chatterjee)

Mother, to thee I bow!
   Rich with fine streams and fruits art thou!
Cool breezes, cornfields green are thine,
      Mother mine!

The silver, thrilling moonlight night;
   Gay groves with blooms and flowers bedight;
Sweet smiles, mellifluous speech, are thine,
   Giver of bliss and boons benign,
      Mother mine!

---

163 "Swadeshi goods": home-manufactured goods, or goods produced by Indians and for Indians. *Swadeshi* was a central tenet of the Indian independence movement to break the economic stranglehold of British imperial rule.

164 *Bande Mataram*, or *Vande Mataram*: loosely translated as "hail mother." This phrase was a rallying cry for Indian nationalists. This poem was originally included in the novel *Anandamath* (1882) by the famous Bengali novelist Bankim Chandra.

With many million ardent throats
Singing thy praise with swelling notes
　　With many million sturdy hands,
Ready to smite thy foes with sharpen'd bands;
　　　How art thou weak, when these are mine,
　　　　　　　　　　　Mother mine!

　　Yes, might immense is thine!
From throngs on throngs of ruthless foes,
　　From perils dire and whelming woes,
Defender and deliverer thou!
　　To thee I bow!
　　　　　　　　　　　Mother mine!

Wisdom and Righteousness thou art!
　　Thou sovereign spirit of the heart!
　　　　　　　　And vital Air within!

Thou givest vigour to the arm,
　　And to the breast devotion warm;
In every home, in every shrine,
　　The image all adore is thine,
　　　　　　　　　　　Mother mine!

Thou ten-armed Durga, whom fell demons fear!
　　Thou lotus-ranging Lakshmi ever dear!
　　　Goddess of arts, bright Saraswati thou![165]
　　　　　　　　　　　To thee I bow!

　　To thee I bow!
O Fortune's Pow'r divine!
　　Faultlessly fair,
　　Beyond compare,
Rich with fine streams and fruits art thou
　　　　　　　　　　　Mother mine!

　　Mother, to thee I bow!
With robe of green, devoid of guile,
　　With grace adorn'd and lovely smile.
Earth ever bounteous, thou!
　　Nourisher, Cherisher benign,
　　　　　　　　　　　Mother mine!

165　Durga: Hindu goddess who represents the Supreme Being and is known as the Divine Mother. She is a popular figure of worship in the Bengal region and is often depicted with ten arms. Lakshmi: Hindu goddess of wealth and prosperity. Saraswati: Hindu goddess of learning and knowledge.

West

Western India encompasses the Bombay presidency and its various outlying districts including the modern-day day states of Maharashtra, Gujarat, and Goa, which is included in this section despite its rule by Portugal during the late nineteenth and early twentieth centuries. Portugal made the first Western European incursion into this region, capturing Bombay in 1534. It retained control of Goa despite eventually losing most of its territory, including Bombay (now Mumbai), to the British Empire in the seventeenth century as part of the dowry presented to King Charles II at his marriage to Catherine of Braganza. The nineteenth-century "creation" of Bombay from a collection of seven swampy islands into a single island-city through modern advances in British engineering cemented Bombay's pre-eminence as a port city. The mid-nineteenth century witnessed the opening of the first railway, connecting Bombay to Thana, on the subcontinent. Bombay was home to a relatively large, educated and successful Parsi population. Many of the poets, including Jamasp Phiroze Dastur, Behramji Merwanji Malabari, Rustam B. Paymaster, S. D. Saklatvala, and Cowasji Nowrosji Vesuvala, reprinted here identified themselves as Parsis. Bombay produced a number of English-language essayists and novelists as well.

Behramji Merwanji Malabari

Behramji Merwanji Malabari (1853–1912) was a prominent Parsi social reformer, ethnographer, journalist and poet. He edited the Bombay-based periodical *The Indian Spectator* from 1880 until 1901 when he sold the newspaper. He re-purchased the newspaper in the early 1900s (the exact date is unclear) and the newspaper continued under his guidance until his death in 1912. Malabari was also the founder and first editor of the periodical *East and West* (1901–1921). Although *Indian Muse in English Garb* (1876) was his only collection of English-language poetry, Malabari also published several books including *Gujarat and the Gujuratis* (1884), *An Appeal from the Daughters of India* (1890) and *The Indian Eye on English Life* (1893). Dayaram Gidumal's admiring biography of Malabari's early years, *The Life and Life-Work of Behramji M. Malabari* (1888) notes Malabari's tireless campaigning for such "progressive" causes as the Age of Consent Act, which was passed by the British government in 1891 and raised the age of consent for Indian girls from ten to twelve years of age. Sympathetic to what he viewed as the progressive practices and ideas of Christian missionaries, Malabari was critical of the supposedly more conservative beliefs of the Hindu orthodoxy, especially in relation to women. His self-conception as a poet in English is movingly elaborated upon in his preface to *Indian Muse in English Garb* (included in the "Appendix" section).

The Indian Muse in English Garb (Bombay: 1876)[1]

"The dream of my youth" H. R. H. the Prince of Wales[2]

I dreamt a grateful dream,
Nor heavy nor uncouth,
When life's unsettl'd stream
Scarce met the waves of youth.

I dreamt a cradle high,
With rich surroundings free;
Its head protected by
Th' etherial canopy.

Its noble pillars bright
Were pure and solid gold;
Their straight and soaring height
Spoke majesty untold.

Its graceful form, the frame,
To stately cedar ow'd;
And stones of deathless flame,
Were on its sides bestow'd.

And from the China worm
It took its silk supply;
And faithful she and firm,
Did naught for use deny.

Its folds were fill'd anon,
With breaths of fragrance choice;
Whose soothing power won
My soul to lasting joys.

The portraits round it cast,
Were splendid tho' grotesque;
In effect, they surpast
The quaint and picturesque!

---

1 Behramji Merwanji Malabari, *The Indian Muse in English Garb* (Bombay: "Reporters" Press by Merwanjee Nowrojee Daboo, 1876).
2 Edward VII (1841–1910): Prince of Wales until the death of his mother, Queen Victoria in 1901 when he assumed the throne, inheriting the rule of an empire.

And from the land of dreams,
My roving mind tho' turn'd;
But still my mem'ry's gleams,
In all their freshness burn'd.

I woke, and strange to see,
Unlike such scenes surmis'd,
In all fidelity,
My dream was realiz'd![3]

The cradle is the land
Of glorious Hindustan,[4]
Whose sketches midst I stand,
Though now a full-grown man!

And all the sights I saw,
No empty-shadows were;
Then undefin'd and raw,
They now with motion stir!

This wondrous land is mine,
And all its fertile banks;
For this Thy gift divine,
O Lord! I give Thee thanks.

The Stages of a Hindu Female Life

In Kachh[5] I saw the light of Heav'n: a sad and dreary day
The first of my existence was, from welcome far away.
My baby-mother paid too dear, for one who could not bail
Her sad devoted life, from ills that motherhood assail.
Her infant years had trac'd their course thro' sad and harrowing scenes,
And fresh afflictions greeted her, before she reach'd her teens.
Long ere the light of womanhood upon her soul had dawn'd,
Her hopeful life was basely to precarious future pawn'd.

---

3 [Poet's Note: Yes realized and perhaps more than realized. But I wonder if less august personages see *their* dreams come true: for human nature, it must be owned, is sadly given to dreaming. I, for instance, sometimes dream that we are to have, in God's good time, a certain little Prince of the Blood Royal as our own Emperor, to live in the midst of us, and have an *Indian* parliament with *Indian* Legislative and Executive Officers. But then it is *my* dream!]
4 Hindustan: India.
5 [Poet's Note: Once the hot-bed of the frightful social crime, female infanticide.]

A dry and lack-love man of four and fifty was her spouse,
And she of tender ten, when urg'd, she took the nuptial vows!
A self-imposèd duty taught her visions to conjure,
In whose delusive lull, she sold her heart to lust impure.
Now all the mock solemnities and heartless pageants o'er,
The spell-bound spirit starts with fear th' excitement hid before.
Scarce wean'd from happy infancy, her dream of life undreamt,
From all contaminating thoughts, her mind was yet exempt
Awe-struck and mute, foul custom's prey, she strove to face the change;
But nature ever faithful, self from self could not enstrange.
And love, of his approach her soul had hardly yet appriz'd,
When bitter duty, through her wife's estate, she realiz'd.
Those hallow'd extacies and joys, divinely sanctified,
Which heart to heart unite, were to this hapless pair denied.
Those sanction'd sweets that render life deserving of a trial,
Of these, the ill-match'd lives had e'er to take a cold denial.

★   ★   ★   ★

Time shook his magic wand and smooth'd the serious gap of age,
Th' unhappy girl now felt advancing towards maternal stage.
And proud and fond my sire caress'd his strangely wedded ward,
And breath'd a selfish pray'r to Heav'en his coming heir to guard!
And tho' my martyr-mother cross'd the stage with crucial throes,
The frightful task upon her did the stamp of death impose.
Though God in mercy did not like her weckèd life to save,
To soothe my selfish sire, reclaim'd me from a fleshy grave.
More dead than live the mourning friends in pity carried me,
To him who anxious stood to take his dead love's legacy.
My sire gave a mingl'd look of grief and joy intense,
And then his pent up feelings with a burst unhing'd his sense.
For days and nights he raving pass'd a fearful struggle through,
Till soft the 'peace of hope' crept up his troubl'd mental view.
But soon the tide of time effac'd each vestige of his pain;
His loss he now made light of, as he gloated on his gain.
His love to her he lost, was but a means to end devis'd;
What reck'd he for the means, now that his end was realiz'd?
Thus early doom'd was I, to lose the tenderest of kin;
Unconscious of the ruin I wrought, so strangely usher'd in!
the joy a first-born e'er creates in fond maternal heart –
The welcome glimpse of hope, at which her pulses swifter start –
The shrinking glance with which she meets the husband's fondest gaze –
The boundless faith in future which her mortal fears allays –
The smile triumphant which her look in chasten'd love arrays –
While with the gift instinct, her lord's anxiety she repays –
These soft emotions which her life to anguish reconcile,
Such anguish as no joys but those of motherhood beguile –

These thrills, my mother felt not, nor that glad triumphant glance
Adorn'd her face, now wrapt in pale repose of deadly trance.
And thus, a stranger's breast retain'd in me the passing breath;
And for a world of woes, reserv'd me, from a happy death.
My infant years sped in bliss serene, that knew no bound;
For both the parents' love and care, I in my sire found.
But thro' a female heir, his hope of Swarg,[6] he said, was scant;
So urg'd by fate, a stranger now he let his girl supplant!
And with the remnant of his age, as if, to temporize,
He launch'd himself, once more, upon a martial enterprize!
Though turn'd of three score six, he brought a second baby bride,
In age and size and female grace, a pigmy at my side!
For youth and health spontaneous had in me their charms combin'd,
And there I stood in Asian bloom most gorgeous and refin'd.
Now conscious of the fact, at once, my sire took alarm.
And studiously he sought, he said, 'to keep me out of harm!'
A sickly boy of twelve he found to take me off his hand,
As guardian of my honour and as husband to command!
My soul at first revolted at a union so uncouth –
I long'd to live in answ'ring love, impell'd by sangine youth.
But false I could not be to him, whose fault I saw was none;
So with a trust in time, on-self, a victory I won.
And time was true as e'er, and soon my soul felt want supplied;
And flush'd with mellow manhood, stood my lord in manhood's pride!
My melted soul in music waves, towards him began to flow;
For Love's the steward faithful of true happiness below.
And he, my lord, my patience long, as if to recompense,
Ador'd me with a passion, oh! so lasting, so intense!
Thus soul in soul dissolv'd, we drank our fill of wedded joy;
Our lives a live-long rapture which e'en sameness could not cloy!
But short-liv'd was the raptur'd dream, now loathsome for its glare;
It vanish'd, leaving to my sight, its shadow pale and bare.
Secure in nuptial calm, when least the shoals of life I fear'd,
My love was wreck'd upon a rock which sudden there appear'd
Content not with my sire's love, his young unhappy spouse,
Had e'er so long been trifling with my husband's sacred vows!
To keep me off my guard he play'd so cleverly his role,
That ere my doubts found being, he with guilt had stain'd his soul.
One windy night, a hideous cry my fitful slumbers broke;
And quick my father dragg'd me out of bed before I woke.
His wither'd frame was writhing sore, in passion's agony:
His eyes exhal'd the sparks subdued of sated jealousy.

---

6 [Poet's Note: The place where the Hindu's soul finds final rest.]

He pointed at his room, wherein, I rush'd with bodings rife:
I saw my hapless spouse beside my father's second wife!
Too true my doubts; that night he was the lawless woman's guest;
And dreadful was the fate that reach'd this violent incest!
My sire had, in a frenzied fit, supris'd the guilty pair;
And with a vengeful blade despatch'd my husband then and there!
The siren he reserv'd for fate proportionately fell;
But ere he could the threat perform he saw the murd'rer's cell!
Though great the wrong he bore, the world *his* outrage could not bear:
And ere a month elaps'd, he had his victim's fate to share
An orphan and a widow! oh what thrills that thought inspires!
Made orphan by a husband's hand, and widow by a sire's!

To the Missionaries of Faith[7]

Ye harbingers of love divine!
Inheritors of grace!
Bestow your efforts to refine
The fallen Indian race.

Once wanton Darkness here prevail'd,
In callous hearts and small;
And empty Learning naught avail'd,
But strengthen'd mental thrall

The haze of hesitating Doubt
Eclips'd the sun of Faith;
The soul her vital fare without,
Once liv'd in moral Death.

---

7 [Poet's Note: It hardly seems to be in the nature of things that Christianity can gain on the subtle Indian intellect. As a race, we have little emotion or impulse in a matter like this; and thus what is readily accepted by the more exquisitely nerved European, as the direct outcome of revelation, with us, sinks into a burst of pure fanaticism. *Faith*, which precedes and supersedes *thought* with the devout Christian, and which as been, from time to time, working magically on the most sublime intellects of the West, seldom actuates the heart of the proud Asiatic who strives to purchase salvation with work, and never stoops to accept it as alms, as it assuredly would be, if *faith* were to be his only merit. Still, it must be borne in mind, that all human work falls short in this, as in every other case. But I am drifting into speculations infinitely above my powers. I have only to add here, that missionary influence, in all other respects, has been the making of India; for more than half of the spiritual and mental blessings we at present enjoy, are through the noble efforts of these children of God.]

For future weal, the soul's relief,
Was left no solid scope;
The cankerworm of Unbelief
When sapp'd the tree of Hope.

The spring of Charity refus'd
Its life-breathing supply;
For giant Selfishness then us'd
Its fountain shoal and dry.

From sire to son, foul Error's heirs,
Our lives undeck'd remain'd;
That lamp of Love which Death out-stares,
In darkness wax'd and wan'd.

And thus midst sound apparent health,
A mighty system wheel'd;
The core Corruption gnaw'd by stealth,
The body kept conceal'd.

Till, at catholic Love's behest,
And Sympathy's appeal,
Ye brought the unction of the West,
Our souls diseas'd to heal.

Midst thoughts incredulous and free,
With Superstitions rife,
Ye taught the blest economy
Of spiritual life.

The burst of light your advent grac'd
That flash'd on callous hearts,
Dispell'd their Doubt, and thus replac'd
In pristine glow their parts.

And Faith, emerging from the cloud,
An ample glory shed;
Oh may it its recipients proud
To life eternal wed!

The empty fountain of Good-will,
Replenish'd and alive,
Yields living waters, to the fill
To drink, and Death survive.

A verdant bow'r of Hope appears,
Before the human view;
The troubl'd soul no longer fears
A wither'd avenue.

Oh may the Lord, His heralds gift
With martyr-strength and grace!
Away may scepticism drift,
At Persuasion's caress!

May all foretaste eternity,
The joys which it presents;
May God in us erected see
'His Mercy's monuments'!

Time of Famine[8]

The Lord sits erect on His high throne of grace;
And wrath righteous starts, in red flames, from His face.
A nation's neglect of His awful commands
Results in the ruin of the once happy land.
The scenes that the eye once with smiles did salute,
Bereft of their charms, wear a dark mourning suite.
The tall verdant trees that once whisper'd to Heav'n
Their thanks for the glorious inheritance giv'n,
Now bankrupt and bare, from their dwellings depart,
In nakedness vile to the cold venal mart.
The fields of their glory, no longer, can boast;
The wind for their plight doth them far and wide post.
The faint vegetation lies breathless and dry;
And some quarters it begs of the hot frowning sky.
The rich soil is turn'd to a desert of dirt;
And lives in its bosom lie cold and inert.
The Lord's heated breath all fresh waters have dried;
The land of its annual rain is denied.
The poison'd air carries diseases throughout;
Its effects discomfit hearts tender and stout.

---

8 Malabari seems to lay some of the blame for the famines on the "heathen" beliefs of the people. His collection was published during a time of devastating famine (1876–1878) in the Deccan region of southern India, part of the Madras presidency. Famine also affected Orissa in 1866. Northwest and southwest Bihar as well as what is now Bengal state was the site of a famine from 1873 to 1874.

The farmer runs wild, while his looks interpret
The fact that the foul reign of famine has set.
For weeks now he waits for his once daily pelf;
And prays to his gods, more inane than himself!

The British Character[9]

Brave Isle![10] what rugged life is thine,
E'er rocking on Oceania's breast!
And yet thy sons and daughters shine,
The pride and charm of modern West!
How proudly true, how nobly fair
The children that belong to Thee!
Where Work is lov'd and Wisdom rare;
Where Learning spread her canopy.
Where Indolence, a vice is held;
Where Caste and Custom never thrive;
Where Freedom, by deep Faith impell'd,
Keeps Thought and Action e'er alive!
By nature true, they're prompt and bold,
While rock'd in cradle, country-proud;
The widow's stay, the orphan's hold,
The tyrant's constant foes avow'd!
To them the Main's no mistery [sic];
Their minds have reached the Firmament.
Them mighty Mounts teach history;
And Sand and Stone a life present!
They care to live, they dare to die,
They live to learn; and last they leave
Their works, that Nature's ire defy;
They work, and in their might believe!

---

9 [Poet's Note: 1870.]
10 "Brave Isle": Great Britain.

A Protest[11]

Does not a foreign and invidious rack,
Out here in India, break poor Labour's back?
Is not our Skill, adorn'd with sterling worth,
Condemn'd unseen, because of *Indian* birth?
Does not Conceit our conscious Strength deride?
And call it Weakness, with unblushing pride?
But right of Conquest is not stinted still:
Our lives are forfeit at the stranger's will!
We heard, erewhile, of Fuller masterful:
How well he knows his heathen slaves to rule!
Is Rámá idle? Kicks and cuffs must cure
That heinous crime, which law can ne'er endure!
One day the Saheb, in his lordly style,
Some orders issues to the syce[12] senile.
Now sick of spleen, the syce o'er-sleeps the hour,
And puts his carcass in vex'd Virtue's pow'r.
The household stands in mute unbroken awe,
As he drags the culprit from his bed of straw.
In breathless rage, hot kicks he lays about,
Till footsore nature can no more hold out.
Then shakes that frame of dry disjointed bones
And flings him ruthless, midst his bitter groans!
The victim reels, each limb in mortal siege,
From reckless force, to 'scape fresh sacrilege.
'What? run when punish'd?, the Saheb's[13] heard to yell';
'Is that the way, my righteous wrath to quell?'
'I'll teach ye manners'; and with murd'rous breath,
'The wretch he chases to a certain death!
Plump drops the syce! but the lord relents,
A friendly swoon his instant death prevents!
The timid wife – her woman's soul astir,
Against this conduct breathes a faint demur.
'For the Lord's love, my dear, some doctor search,'

---

11 [Poet's Note: Mr. Fuller's apologists might not relish these lines; but they would do well to reflect whether the learned Vakeel was under any circumstances justified in behaving as he did. It is one thing to sympathize with an awkwardly-placed friend; and another to hold him up as a mirror of manliness, simply because he happened to have animal strength enough to kick a poor bed-rid Bengali out of existence!] This is an interesting commentary on an actual case involving an Anglo-Indian's maltreatment of his Indian servant.

12 *Syce*, or *sais*: servant employed to attend to horses as a groom or follow carriages and mounted horseman on foot (n. "sais" *OED*).

13 *Saheb*, or *sahib*: respectful term of address placed after a man's name. In colonial India, it was often used by "natives" to address Englishmen or Europeans (n. "sahib" *OED*).

'Oh h – g the Lord! will you now got to Church?'
A man of church, each Sabbath he attends
The house of God, and there in prayer bends!
The mild divine his flock to love exhorts –
Such love as e'en all scorn and hatred courts.
Then charm'd with th' audience all-absorbèd gaze,
His soul's glad tribute on the altar lays.
His pious lips a grateful pray'r absorbs:
And the tear of peace steals down his agèd orbs.
What kens the guileless sire, of our hero's sin?
His warm responses straight of friendship win!
Long kneels he there, the grace of Heav'n to seek,
For all the errors of the bygone week!
Then light of heart, he homeward wends his way,
In *peace* and *love* to spend the blessèd day!
But now his guilt, its effects dread unfolds,
And the lifeless syce, his trembling lord beholds!
The court assembles, where strange lights they glean –
The syce was suff'ring from a *ruptur'd spleen*!
All deeply weigh'd, the court impartial says,
That *two pounds* English can such lives purchase!
Thus died the syce, to splenic mem'ry link'd,
And the world sang praises, as His Worship wink'd!
A soul despatch'd, in nudeness and in woe,
To glooms eternal, in the shades below!
Rash Guilt, excus'd by pamper'd Prejudice,
Erewhile goes free, and thanks the law remiss.
But fix'd as fate, and quick as crime conceiv'd,
Alights fair Justice, in her heart aggriev'd.
At first she falters; but a herald brave,
With words of welcome, doth her advent pave.
His Daniel's soul,[14] thro' birth and breed has worn,
A range unbounded and a godly turn.
Thus walks the maid of sempiternal youth,
'Tween Christian candour and celestial truth.
Hail virgin goddess! Heav'n-affianc'd bride
Of British Honor, Britain's noblest pride!
Faith's glorious first-born! in all fairness giv'n,
To lend the righteous firmer hold on Heav'n!
Hail beauteous pow'r! long-ancestor'd maid!
Whom Perse[15] and Israel pristine homage paid!
Whom Greece and Rome and hoary Egypt knew!

---

14 Daniel: figure of law in the Judeo-Christian tradition.
15 Perse: Persia.

And from whose presence, Ind her splendour drew!
Hail proud Justitia![16] stern, unerring grace!
Thou ancient heirloom of the Aryan race!
Best friend to Order and to spirit free,
All hail thou soul of sacred majesty!!
So Justice came; and to the world proclaim'd,
That black or white, she was for either fram'd –
That Law has meaning of no stinted breadth;
That death it hates, tho' 'tis a heathen's death.
The syce is dead: beyond all troubles hurl'd,
Of a sad existence in a weary world!
How feels his lord? Has he the sight forgot,
Of death and anguish, by his passion wrought?
Do not pale fancies and grim shadows wan,
His vision haunting, scare the inner man?
Does not he weep, what time two pleading eyes
Remind the tyrant of th' expiring syce?
Does not he tremble, midst his safest joys,
When hush'd he hears the faint imploring voice?
Be that his scourge! enough, if in is breast,
He feels his guilt – the guilt of heartless haste.
To Heav'n he's false; and false to nature most,
If of this guilt, he makes a wanton boast!

Cowasji Nowrosji Vesuvala

Little biographical information is available for Vesuvala. The rhetorical clues given in the poet's introduction and footnotes indicate that he was a Bombay native, a Parsi, fairly young (only in his mid-twenties) and worked as a civil servant at the time he published *Courting the Muse*. This volume seems to be his only work. The title of the collection indicates romance – the courtship of lovers – but also brings to mind images of a court, both royal and legal. Such an allusion to institutions of governance is apt since, as indicated in the longest poem of the collection, entitled "True Indian Opinion, or Native Croakers," Vesuvala is intimately invested in imperial politics. Published before the founding of the Indian National Congress in 1885, the poem focuses on the British imperial civil service, which was staffed, especially at its lower levels, by Indians. Vesuvala, like many other clerks within the British imperial bureaucracy, bitterly resented the lack of opportunities for advancement due to his race. However, in this long poem Vesuvala takes the unusual step of also claiming that the East India Company's rule was more just and equitable than current British imperial rule.

---

16 Justitia: Justice.

Courting the Muse: being a Collection of Poems
(Bombay: 1879; printed at the Industrial Press, Fort)[17]

True Indian Opinion, or Native Croakers

(In the following stanzas I have endeavoured as much as possible to relate the existing discontent and widespread opinion about the present English administration of India. It is but manifest to every civilian, commissioner or traveler, and the unanimous, but far from cheering tone of the Native Press in general at a critical stage of British Politics, when wars and dissolution loom in the horizon, may well serve as a warning to future ministers and Indian administrators. It is incumbent on me to add that the tone and utterances here given to many native sentiments, however vague, must be attributed to the novel-reading rising generation of India, and not to the author himself.)

I.

O Dizzy, Dizzy you are a great bore,[18]
    A fool, a cheat, a Jew, cunning, unwise,
Ruling the state like Mogul kings of yore,
    With imperial edicts and vain surmise,
Turning a free and generous race to soar
    On eagle pinions ranging to'ard the skies,
And like the Eagle in the end prostrate
Our English sons, and make us desolate.

II.

Such are the sanguine cries of righteous Whigs,
    Who in their time a blunder ne'er commit,
But, like the pious sons of God, intrigues
    Heap on, as holiest on their forehead writ!
So rival candidates call brothers prigs,
    Though self-same blots and virtues intermeet!
Such is God's framework in human beings shown, –
Laud but yourself, while others fools are grown!

---

17 Cowasji Nowrosji Vesuvala, *Courting the Muse: being a Collection of Poems* (Bombay: Gopal Narayen, 1879).
18 "Dizzy" is a mocking nickname for Benjamin Disraeli (1804–1881), who was a leading member of the Conservative Party for decades and acted as prime minister for two terms. Disraeli, the first British prime minister of Jewish origin (he later converted to Anglicism), was often subject to anti-Semitic comments and attacks both in Britain and abroad.

III.

Far be it from me, thy patriot breast
        To scar, Gladstone! thou England's sacred tower,
Whereon reclining calm in peaceful rest
        Hangs Freedom's crest, effulgent, full of power;
Once that awful form, bold, majestic, blest,
        Time's withering hand to dust shall embower, –
And hateful tyranny's unbridled scope
Shall rage o'er all the land, blasting ev'ry hope.

IV.

But should the Muse essay to charm the throng
        By recriminations silly, unjust?
Let Dizzy steer the ship, and 'tis not long
        To public voice he will resign the trust;
Then take thy turn to rate him sharply, strong.
        And ask account of every leak or burst
Thou find'st, and if the nation's voice consent,
Be thou our Captain on reform intent.

V.

'Tis moderation that the world accredits
        With sense, in all things earthly, good or evil;
And with precision if you weigh its merits
        In your mind's scale, you wont [sic] find room to cavil
At this my maxim, though man scarce inherits
        This virtue, or having, ne'er had its civil
Influence felt throughout his life; at least
You'll own Gladys should keep it in his fist.[19]

VI.

For when wise ones the modest paths would shun,
        And lead their horse in jungle, brake or bush,
Giving wild impulse every headlong run,
        Instructed foremost all to kick and push;
Some wicked wag against his will out done,
        And twinging smart under the horseman's lash,
Would murmur soft with gestures quaint and funk,
"Well, gentlemen – I know the seignor's drunk."[20]

---

19 Gladys seems to refer to Gladstone. William Ewart Gladstone (1809–1898) served several terms as Liberal prime minister of Great Britain (1868–1874; 1880–1885; 1886; 1892–1894). His actions in protection of Irish tenants and his support of Irish Home Rule as well as his appointment of Lord Ripon as viceroy of India in 1880 won him the support of Indians.

20 *Seignor*, or *seigneur*: feudal lord or landed gentry (n. "seigneur" *OED*).

VII.

Such carping spirit leads to scenes of woe,
    And changes friends to foes, the nation grieves;
While rival empires laugh and try to throw
    Out fire an oil, and thus the blaze conceives
An awful form, spreading from top to toe
    Of the great country, till firmness relieves
And throws cold water at the issuing heat,
Cooling John's head with icy lotion sweet.

VIII.

Such rows are very common at the 'Change,[21]
    In London, the resort of wealth and fashion –
Where men nev'r cheat, but purses sharp estrange,
    So honourable is their intention;
While women sleep for pennies at the Grange,
    So damn'd to shame is their wicked passion;
If Indians for a moral place you seek,
I recommend you London, safe for a week.

IX.

There see the Prince with hundred paramours,
    There find the Duke a lovely girl entrancing,
There Marquis old with Baronet encounters,
    And fights with zeal for beauteous Emma Chanson;
There Lord John Lust but freely endeavours[22]
    To seduce my Lady at waltz or dancing;
There find pure maids and wives become unchaste,
Simply because they have that awkward taste.

X.

There fraud is practis'd on unlimited scale,
    There men and women butcher for your money,
There cheats and rogues are honest to a nail,
    There females plenty as flies o'er honey;
There lords are vicious, ladies brusque and hale,
    Though seem as lean as a miser's pony;
There all that's wicked, all that's worse abound,
Clergy, laity all are scoundrels found.

---

21 Change: London Exchange, or stock market.
22 "Emma Chanson" and "Lord John Lust" seem to be Vesuvala's satirical names for the English aristocracy.

XI.

There Devil's great and God is all unknown,
        There Virtue's hiss'd and Truth has little sway
There Modesty's but feign'd, and Vice alone
        Shines out all foremost in glitt'ring array;
There men and women adulteries atone
        And sins confess, so awkward to essay,
Before the Bishop's purest, reverend gown –
Well – no – if used when throwing Lucy down!

XII.

There Queen Victoria – no! Dame Fashion reigns,
        And bows all London 'fore its royal court;
There Premier Dizzy's chang'd and Mammon deigns
        To sway his golden rod at Fame's resort,
Not Justice; there Simplicity's power wanes
        Before Etiquette's sterner, prouder port;
There wives and daughters but do as they please,
For all are such and therefore none can tease.

XIII.

With them to lead your wife is 'Etiquette,'
        To press her, kiss her is no shameful sight;
Embrace her, and the husband bids a bet
        Your conduct is so charming, sweet, polite;
In short Etiquette's the phrase to dead set
        All outside sneers which envious fools indite [sic];
At the same time hiding the grossest evils
Of society's wildest, blackest devils.

XIV.

Ye boasters of a prouder name, – ye whites,
        English, Scottish, Irish, whate'er your race,
Are ye not brethren to those British kites
        Of who I am speaking? Are ye not face
To face those very men whose hist'ry cites
        Such direst, grievous, social disgrace?
Why then you frighten India's sable sons,
When seeds of infamy linger in your loins?

XV.

And ye, hypocrite missionaries, that range
    Our groves and lanes in Jesus' holy guise,
Why not pack up, and Bombay's air exchange
    For London's cool and misty frosty skies,
To check their sins who God's pure love estrange,
    Dipp'd in foulest pools of debaucherous vice?
Go here and preach salvation to the throng,
Your brothers, castemen, kinsmen all go wrong.

XVI.

'Tis not to boast that natives are all right,
    That I take up this subject, hackney'd, stale,
But show that Whites are just the same in spite
    Of all their bant'rings, pride and selfish tale;
They walk in India, ev'n the plebiscite,
    Like giants marching o'er the Elburz vale.[23]
Even their very feet disdain to tread
A slavish ground, where natives slaves are bred!

XVII.

Well, well, no matter; they are conquerors,
    And Whites can do what none on earth can do;
They are but privileged marauders,
    They'll loot if they like whole India thro'.
Have ye not read of Scottish Highlanders
    In Scott's novels, so pleasing, strict and true,[24]
Where Highland robber pilfer without show,
And kick the ladd'r that upwards did them throw.

XVIII.

But never mind: you but generous grow,
    And show their brightest, gleaming, silvery side,
Arts, sciences, freedom from their channels flow,
    And peace and discipline but softly glide,

---

23 The Eburz, or Alborz: mountain range in northern Iran.
24 Sir Walter Scott (1771–1832): famous Scottish novelist and poet whose historical works such as *Ivanhoe* and *The Lady of the Lake* cast the Scottish highlanders and way of life in a romantic light.

Where once were tumults, anarchy aglow.
    Allow them also their Education's pride,
For were I not accord them this small bit,
    This silly *ottawa-rima* had ne'er been writ.[25]

XIX.

There are some fools who question, 'cause we write,
    The government, why our mouths do not they gag,
Or else these native boys will turn downright
    The whole nation, which themselves would fag,
And bring discredit on the English might!
    Fools, real fools are they; why do they brag
The foremost place as theirs in this vast world,
When likely they are headlong to be hurl'd?

XX.

But men are men, and English selfish are,
    Proud for their lot, despising all beneath,
And never budging inch where interests jar,
    As stirring little were to them a death.
When needy, mild and flatt'ring as sekar
    In the huntsman's clutches; but once they breathe
And pass but out the door – "I don't know sir
Who you are at all, nor ev'r did confer."

XXI.

O English, Scottish, Irish whites, that haunt
    Our Indi[26] soil and cling to it like leeches,
Remember, ere our humbleness you taunt,
    That most of you when come had no whole breeches!
But thanks to India and your needy want,
    That native money made you lords and teaches, –
Nay taught – your ingrate self more pranks to play
With native sons and keep them back away.

---

25 Vesuvala's poem is in *ottava rima*. The Italian *ottava rima*'s hendecasyllables, which Vesuvala often strays from, are structured by an *abababcc* rhyme scheme. It was developed as the dominant form of Italian narrative verse in the fifteenth century and was used by English Renaissance poets such as Sidney, Spenser, and Milton.

26 Indi: Indian.

XXII.

What have I written your own annals show,
    Your English books, periodicals are at hand
From which I cull, and try at random throw
    A bit to you, what writers of your band
Opine for you, our morals and your go.
    I do not write of mine own, dear friend;
You know I hope to take a London fare
Some day, only to note what ways get there.

XXIII.

Ye brother writers of the "Coming K" –
    Who picture coming king so horrid vicious, –
Or in the Siliad Bob Lowe's face betray –
    Or copy Byron in that epic precious,
Don Juan, mildly transposing D and J – [27]
    Ye brother writers of these poems factious,
Would you not see worth while our wrongs to paint,
And take our thanks, though humble and though faint.

XIV.

And best and foremost of philanthropic throng,
    Faucett! that name to our hearts so endear'd,
Well merit'st thou our India's choicest song,
    Who for reform, redress our hearts so cheer'd.
Excuse if humbler strains thy praise prolong,
    For worth like thine a monument had rear'd, –
But thine own country sucks what we possess,
A sum of twenty crores,[28] upwards not less.

XXV.

And every year this twenty crores! a sum
    To buy a kingdom! ye natives attest,
Ye ministers attend; for when o'ercome
    By poverty's sharpest pangs, by tax opprest,
And one more famine makes them torpid, numb,
    Her sons know well the thing to do at best,
For there is temper mild, but once if fir'd,
It leaves no middling range to be desir'd.

---

27 Byron's *Don Juan*, an epic poem written between the years 1819–1824, was published in installments.
28 *Crore*: measure of ten million; a unit of measurement still widely used on the subcontinent.

XXVI.

'Tis well the Government knows this placid fact,
    The Government know their people discontented;
They know that taxes hard press all the sect,
    Though servile parliaments half-half consented;
They know their justice keeps but guilt intact,
    And honest men instead are freely pented;
They know all these, yet gladly vaunt their fame,
Have they not humane feelings, sense nor shame?

XXVII.

O boast not aids of armies to suppress
    But those whose money gave them food and drink!
In causes just, patriotic redress,
    A soldier's fire to lowest pitch does sink.
While God's avenging hand would vict'ry bless
    To those alone, who join'd in single link,
Their country's truer, juster claims defend,
And ask but subjects' rights, not slaves that bend.[29]

---

29 [Poet's Note: It may be questioned what grievances and what rights these natives desire to have redressed and upheld? Here the Baboos of Bengal, the Madrasses of the Southern Presidency and the Hindoos of Bombay, though only differing in trivial details, boldly and unanimously speak out. The crushing taxation the people of India are subjected to by Municipalities, Local Funds, Public Works, Presidency Governments and lastly, the Supreme Government of India, compared with their meager resources; the enhancement of these taxes year by year when depression predominates in all branches of trade and industry, rather than their diminution and gradual abolition; the exacting nature of Government revenue officials pinching every pie from the resourceless taxpayer to propitiate Government and to apply for increase in pay; general favourtism shown to Indian Treasure on account of their enormous salaries; the enjoyment of religious ministration by the European Civil population at the expense of the native taxpayer; the selfish bar set up against intending civil servants from India by reducing their maximum age for admission to nineteen, – all these are some of their prominent grievances.

The extension of electoral franchise to India for Parliament, as it is enjoyed by Scotland and Ireland; the increase in the age of intending civil servants and modification of their salaries and the laws that regulate the same, as may be suited to the present times; the widest employment of learned natives in the Government higher offices, as was the policy of Todarmul, the minister of Akbar; the reduction of the magnificent salaries now drawn by Europeans, from His Excellency the Viceroy down to the deputy Collector and Magistrate; the currency of India to be paramount in all pensions, bonuses and allowances, and in all payments of contracts in England; the abolition of the Royal Engineering College at Cooper's Hill; the majority of the natives of the country being essential in all legislative councils of the Viceroy and the Governors of presidencies, – all these are some of the prominent rights they demand.

Since the above was on paper since April last, the Government of India have circulated an order to employ natives in the civil service without any competitive examination. Doubtful and treacherous as was their hope, so doubtful and treacherous is this order. Since the accession of Lord Lytton to office, it had been more than once reported by the papers that the noble

XXVIII.

Do you remember those eventful days,
>When Grenville's taxes ruin'd your English name
In far America?[30] the mutineer's craze
>That blots our Indian soil with deeds of shame?[31]
'Tis your own folly, Englishmen, which plays
>Such pranks severe, detracts your lucid fame,
And brings discredit on your noble nation,
So modest, pleasing, just in estimation.

XXIX.

Poor India! "thou art a devoted deer,"
>Beset on all thy sides by English hounds,
Who'll suck thy blood as long as they are near,
>And leave thee bankrupt till thy soul rebounds
And pleads for self; or consciences grow clear,
>Or hunter's bugle mercy's notes resounds;
Once England sav'd thee, who shall save thee next
From its wild government, taxing, vexing, vext.

Lord had been contemplating a serious change, so that a liberal and an adequate system for the employment of natives in Government service may be regulated. As observed above, the hope has proved treacherous. While recognizing the necessity, for sake of economy, of employing the natives, it has been ruled that one native to seven Europeans may only be provided for from next year! Again, the natives will not be admitted into the following services... It will now be easy to the simplest observer that, only forced by natives in India and liberals at home, the Government have been obliged to publish and give out to the world, merely to check and appease the indignant but just cries of their political opponents, this sham resolution.

One thing is certain. This new resolution will stimulate favouritism more than ever. Sons of rich and influential natives, no matter that their minds be as hollow as the reed and their experience as multifarious as that of a Cockney, will be thrust in unreservedly. Cry how you will, money and influence shall make the mare to run.

Adhering loyally to the Queen and the English, discarding military terrorism of Germany as oppressive and detesting Russia's slavish Imperialism, the natives of India shall always be grateful to that country which has been the means of raising them, by liberal education and freedom in speech and thought, to the noble standard of an enlightened subject. Many rights have already been conferred, and they hope that what they candidly profess to be necessary may candidly be considered.]

30 George Grenville (1712–1770): British Whig statesman who acted as prime minister during the imposition of the infamous Stamp Act of 1765 on the American colonies. This act, which required that most printed materials be produced on stamped paper in an effort to increase tax revenue, invoked a great deal of resistance to the law and was one of many grievances that led to the American Revolution.

31 The 1857 Indian Rebellion, while considered the first battle for Indian independence by Indian nationalists, was termed the "Sepoy Mutiny" by the British imperialists who viewed it as an act of sedition. A contingent of soldiers rose up in protest against the British army administrators; the protest spread across northern India and claimed thousands of lives on both sides.

XXX.

We know that Ind is govern'd for England's self,
    We know English for India's sake are proud;
We know that England fatt'ns on Indian pelf,
    Or interests' cry had not been rais'd so loud;
We know your good intentions, like Sir Guelph,[32]
    Who looted wealth under humanity's shroud.
We know, all know and all the powers above,
That you us hate and hating plead your love.

XXXI.

That's the 'unkindest cut of all' – that bites
    And rankles in our warmest hearts; we feel
Degrad'd by those who eat our salt; like mites
    On cheese, they proudly fare on sumptuous meal
An eat our own, yet thanklessly it smites
    On our heart their hate, – lo! their martial zeal,
With blood they fought their road to regal sway!
"No body ask'd you Sir" for that, we say.

XXXII.

Time was when Moguls rul'd the land with rigour,
    And satrap[33] princes sway'd with tyrant hand,
When Bheels[34] for wealth our houses did beleaguer,
    And ruffian kings had lives at their command.
But now the English reign with awful vigour,
    And wave with force their stately iron wand!
Let none presume their sacred rites to hiss,
But all, like Soldan's slaves,[35] their shoes should kiss!

XXXIII.

Oh! how we wish once more your sov'reign sway,
    John Company![36] when all was happiness,
And nothing marr'd our calm and sober way!
    When all was cheap and plenty; no distress

---

32 Sir Guelph may refer to Queen's Victoria's husband, Albert, Prince of Wales, who was a descendent of the House of Guelph, a German royal dynasty.

33 *Satrap*: governor of a province in ancient Persia; a subordinate ruler or official, often suggesting tyranny or ostentation (n. "satrap" *OED*).

34 Bheels, or Bhils: tribal, or *adivasi*, group spread out over the western part of the subcontinent. They were often cast as bandits in colonial discourse.

35 *Soldan*: Muslim ruler; the supreme ruler of one of the great Muslim powers of the Middle Ages; the Sultan of Egypt (n. "soldan" *OED*).

36 John Company: East India Company, which was granted its initial charter on the subcontinent by the British government in the early seventeenth century.

Of taxes or oppressive tyranny's day
        Had dawn'd, but gold and silver in excess
Abound'd, for Ind was healthy, wealthy, wise,
And every thing was desirably nice.

XXXIV.

For then did triumph beam in every eye,
        And friendship bound each subject's kindly heart,
And rul'd and rulers mingled as the fry
        Under one Naiad's[37] sway; so part by part
Harmonious feelings grew a tender tie,
        And India flourish'd as a golden mart,
Where wealth from various centres then o'erflow'd,
And native features like the metal glow'd.

XXXV.

Then simple justice gain'd desired end,
        Without its present complicated rules;
Then hosts of boyish civilians fleec'd no land,
        Collectors, Commissioners, oppression's tools;
No farmers groan'd as now, ambition fann'd
        No country fools to pass with forg'd capsules
Each rubbish heap as cotton finest grown; –
At last for wealth from humbler state o'er thrown.

XXXVI.

No lavish charges burden'd then the state,
        Not thousands were the order of those days;
No separate plans Europeans procreate,
        Or "more for whites" was not the ruler's craze.
Not choicest bits assign'd at highest rate
        To them alone, as modern India pays, –
Ev'n to idiots – with horses, garden, hansom,
Clear two thousand every, every mensam!

XXXVII.

Time was when one for five departments work'd,
        When wise experienc'd heads alone had chance,
When busy, jolly, talking, never shirk'd
        Each his duty for gaming, ball or dance;

---

37 *Naiad*: nymph presiding over fresh-water bodies, such as streams and brooks, in ancient Greek mythology.

When no disdain for natives o'er had lurk'd
        In their kind hearts, but one vast field immense
Was open unto all for all to till,
With honest manly bosoms, energetic will.

XXXVIII.

But these are chang'd and Empress' banner furls
        O'er yon proud castles, turrets, moats in ruin!
See, see! how wreathed with light but ruddy laurels
        It waves and beckons ocean's mighty queen!
See, see once more! how deck'd with diamonds, pearls,
        The horizon greets and dims its starry scene!
O were it shining, bright and light as seems,
Who dares not bless it basking in its beams?

XXXIX.

Woe worth the day that Nana's host inflam'd,
        And rous'd the sleeping million's fiery roar!
Woe worth the day that native loyalty sham'd
        And cast a slur on India's loyal shore!
Woe worth the day when natives, fed and tam'd,
        Rose 'gainst their masters with murd'rous furore!
Oh who can paint that scene of vilest butchery,
That took its root in native Raja's cutchery?[38]

XXXX.

Like Scottish firecross, at the signal giv'n,
        Whole Cawnpore burst, and troops their heads all turn'd
To where their foremost might should have been striv'n,
        To defend; while onward, as firecross burn'd,
Whole cities, villages to desperation driv'n,
        Began to flock, for freedom's spirit yearn'd –
Poor souls! not knowing (bribes so made them blind,)
But what they do or why they're so inclined.[39]

---

38 *Cutchery*: hall or chamber of audience and thus a court of administration used for business (n. "cutchery" *OED*).

39 The Siege of Cawnpore (or Kanpur) was a central episode during the 1857 Indian Uprising. Indian soldiers, led by Nana Sahib, besieged the British garrison at Cawnpore, brutally murdering dozens of British men, women and children. "Cawnpore" then became a rallying cry and justification for British soldiers sent to remorselessly suppress the rebellion and punish the mutineers.

XXXXI.

From the far North to Bengal's river land,
        And up the Vindhuya's snaky mountain heights,[40]
There rose a cry of woe your hearts would rend,
        Of wives, children, husbands murder'd outright
Without a tinge of pity; who can bend
        A bow – even infirm and weak – to fight
Were there, with English caffirs[41] so accurst –
Thus term'd were they who fed them, cloth'd and nurst!

XXXXII.

And every street was strew'd with English heads,
        Which ere now this but talk'd complacent mild;
And barracks all were empty of the cads
        Who just long cheer'd their gloomy walls, now wild.
While Captains, Col'nels suffer'd from the raids
        Of the mad mob, who corpse on corpses pil'd,
And hack'd and harass'd the bloody bodies so,
O God! why did not thou but pierce them thro'?

XXXXIII.

Here Pathans[42] ravish'd maids, daughters, wives
        In view of fathers, husbands, sons and all;
And then with spears they took their tender lives,
        So cruel, reckless of their coming fall;
There cradle babes were cut with sharpen'd knives,
        And infant youths in vain for mercy bawl.
Alas for them! each, each was upwards thrown
And swung on spear's gleaming blade and blown!

XXXXIV.

Round the wide world the tumult's news was flash'd,
        And England started from her placid dream,
While India hop'd completely to be thrash'd,
        And natives rag'd against the mutinous team.

---

40 The Vindhuya, or Vindhya, Range: chain of hills in the central Indian subcontinent that form the boundary between north and south.

41 *Caffirs* or *kaffirs*: non-Muslims; the term is sometimes used to refer to infidels (n., adj. "káffir" *OED*).

42 The Pathans, or Pashtuns: Pashto-speaking people from parts of modern-day southeast Afghanistan and northwest Pakistan. Many Pashtuns migrated to other parts of the subcontinent, including Gujurat, Rajasthan, and Punjab, to serve as soldiers under the Mughal Empire, especially in patrolling the North-West Frontier.

The English fled the land afraid, and dash'd
    In ships and native homes, with wrath a-gleam;
The country round was so distrait and hideous,
That each his neighbour doubted to be factious.

XXXXV.

But now the factious spirit's died away,
    As Victoria's assum'd direct control,[43]
Who drove insurgent bands in disarray
    And put to death the rebels on the pole.
And with her reign have also fled away
    Contentment, happiness, cheap plenty role
Of Company's simpler, healthier power,
When every one was Raja in his bower.

XXXXVI.

Oh for those palmy days once more to cheer
    Our present feeble hearts, our poorer lot,
So that once more our dry shorn veins appear
    Ruddy, bloody, strong, vigorous and hot.
How gladly would we bless, respect, revere
    Those our increasing poverty 'd check, so fraught
With danger and distress, and find a cure
To make us happy, themselves assure.

XXXXVII.

Vain, very vain, are hopes of thy redress,
    Land of the mighty, land of luscious fruits,
Land of diamonds, pearls and gaudiness,
    Land of the Brahmins and their mean pursuits;
Land whence hundred empires had their ingress,
    Whence hundred thrones set their enchanted roots;
Land of witchcraft, magic, sorcerer's charms,
So strange, so horrid, all the world alarms!

---

43 The 1857 Indian Uprising, termed the "Sepoy Mutiny" by the imperial government and later seen as the first Indian war of independence by Indian nationalists, marked the end of East India Company rule and the transfer of its lands to the British Crown.

XXXXVIII.

India! land of mountains, rivers, towers,
    Domes, cupolas, musjids that gorgeous rise,[44]
And show their origin as Mussul's dowers
    When they but made thee bride; land of clear skies
Whose golden hue thy sable womb enflowers,
    Whence pours mild rain thy parch'd fields to rejoice;
Land of thousand godheads, grotesque, rude,
Land of pagans, idols many headed, nude.

XXXXIX.

Land where cold and heat bear alternate sway
    Where tempests, earthquakes hundreds yearly sweep;
Where seasons change, or humid, warms or gray,
    And ice and snow constant Himalayas steep;
Where birds of sorts brisk chirrup on the spray,
    Or palms, cedars, babuls[45] gay o'erleap;
Where sweetest, rarest fruits and flowers abound,
And greenest, choicest herbage press the ground.

L.

Land of Rajput warriors and Goorkhas slim,
    Land of Sikhs, Pathans and Afgans furious,
Land of timid Hindoos and Musuls grim,
    Land of scheming Baboos, Purbhoos spurious;
Land of tall Sindhis, Marattas short and trim,
    And swordsmen Hyderabadees supercilious;
Land of Ghati Deccaneers, Madrasses black,
And Koli fishermen's poor scrupulous pack.[46]

LI.

Our Parsees are but foreigners in fact,
    Like English, Dutch, Portuguese, Chinese sort;[47]
Again they are a handful, smaller sect,
    Compar'd with all the hundred tribes that port

---

44 *Cupolas*: rounded vaults or domes forming the roof of any building or part of a building (n. "cupolas" *OED*). Musjids, or masjids: mosques.

45 *Babul*: thorny mimosa, common in parts of India (n. "babul" *OED*).

46 Vesuvala lists groups by geographic region, "ethnicity" and religion and also includes the term "Baboos," or Babus, normally a term of respect but used derogatively by Anglo-Indians to refer to Indians who were educated in English and/or worked for the imperial bureaucracy.

47 Vesuvala was a Parsi. Parsis descended from a group of Zoroastrians from Iran who, migrated to India in the tenth century due to religious persecution.

In thy vast harbour; though endow'd with tact
        And business ways, theirs is a narrow court, –
The narrowest in the world's exhibition
Of religious, sectarian, characteristic nation.

LII.

Besides, observe they are one single whole
        In this vast world; other tribes, other nations,
Like English, Hindoos, Mussuls have a hole,
        A seam, a sort of gap in their nations
Of their own religion; but Parsees' soul
        Is their own religion; of God's creations,
The purest, best conforming to humanity
Is their one single creed of originality.

LIII.

O rob'd in purest white, with sceptre crown'd,
        And angels hov'ring round to do commands,
The music breathing sweetest, softest sound,
        And fireball gleaming, dancing in thy hands,
Come, come Zoraster! bless this mortal ground
        Whereon thy humble flock its body bends,
And asks a boon, (forgive its humble tone),
To live in peace and die without a groan!

LIV.

And Thou! Highest Essence, Sublime, Unknown,
        Whose ruddy chariot full of rainbow tints,
Ever present, ever driven, a throne
        Immortal, ranging o'er earth and heaven's prints,
And circling, binding wide each zone to zone,
        Extending far to planets, star-like flints, –
O give us power – assist our meagre sect,
To think, speak, act as virtue, truth direct.

LV.

How noble are these words! Earth, Heaven, Paradise
        Are mingled in those sounds! We think us proud
To share ministration which all analyse,
        But none find fault with! by oppression bow'd,
Though driven from Irán, our fathers wise
        Relinquished ne'er their creed; so may the crowd
Despise, contemn or foreign missions jeer,
Parsees don't care a pin for all they sneer!

LVI.

Let Christians proud their superiority boast,
      Let fanatic Mahomedans indulge in gups,
Let Hindoos worship idols at the most,
      Or Jews enshrine but golden silver cups;
Let Buddhist bigots their religion toast,
      Or Chinese heathens claim to be the ups,
We care not: ours was the first empire on earth,
Whence Freedom, Arts, Philosophy had their birth.

LVII.

Ah bless'd Iran! thy days were number'd o'er
      When great Secander[48] first thy soil did pace!
Was there no Rustum[49] ready at thy call
      To take the haughty Greeks in war's embrace?
Was there no Gave, Godrej or reverend Zal[50]
      To guide thy kingdom, stop his bloody chase?
Alas! alas! thy luxury pav'd the way
Which armies, warriors could but weak essay.

LVIII.

Ah blessed spot! can we forget thy clime,
      Salubrious, modest, fertile, pleasant, cold,
Rich in resources, flowers, mankind sublime,
      Seat of the world's forefathers and their fold!
Seat of the First on earth, whom aged Time
      Alone doth know! seat of godly grace where roll'd
Primeval, long ere Hist'ry could recite,
The Persian banner in it awful might!

---

48 Secander, or Sikander, Shah Sur: ruler in the Pashtun Sur dynasty. He reigned as sultan of Delhi after overthrowing Ibrahim Shah Sur and was unseated by the Mughal emperor, Humayun, in 1555.
49 In Zoroastrianism, the adventures of the warrior Rustum are described in the *Shah Namah* (*Book of Kings*), a chronicle of the history of the Persian Empire and its great kings, written by the poet Firdausi in 976–1010 AD.
50 "Gave, Godrej or reverend Zal": leaders described in the *Shah Namah* (*Book of Kings*).

LIX.

Ages pass'd since the Greeks were foremost hight,
  When Jason golden fleece from Cyprus fetch'd,[51]
And Macedonians in chivalrous fight
  Thy hardy sons and mountaineers o'ermatch'd;[52]
Triumphant borne, with Victory's plumes bedight,
  Once Rome again thy waving ensign snatch'd;[53]
At last Mahomed's caffir tribes accurst
Burst the strong chains, that bound us to thee first![54]

LX.

Without a home, outcast, championless, lorn,
  Wretched, poverty-stricken, what would have been
Our lot, had Ind forbid and defiance sworn
  To enter weary pilgrims on her green?
Why sure to distant coasts had blown our horn,
  Where cannibals mayhap had hemm'd us in;
At least we Bombay had not seen, I guess,
Some fifty thousand, likely more or less.[55]

LXI.

Digression is a sin, all poets said,
  Yet all the musing throng however humble, –
From Homer downwards to the modern maid
  And wife who, invoking Fashion, mumble
Some silly lines to show they're perfect made,
  The more, in Cupid's snares the sooner tumble, –
All, all poets, you know, have far digress'd,
And verging back in turn came out refresh'd.

---

51 In Greek myth, Jason, whose uncle, King Pelias, usurps the throne, embarks on a sea voyage with his crew, the Argonauts, to find the magical fleece of the golden ram in order to reclaim his birthright.

52 During the fourth century BCE, the Macedonians under King Philip II (father of Alexander the Great) conquered the Greek city-states. Alexander the Great (356–323 BCE) was the king of Macedonia and eventual emperor of a vast territory spanning the Mediterranean to the South Asian subcontinent (including the Persian Empire).

53 The Roman Empire conquered the Greek peninsula during the second century BCE.

54 Vesuvala seems to be referring to Mughal rule on the subcontinent. The Mughal Empire of the subcontinent was founded in 1526 with the defeat of the Delhi Sultanate by Babur (a descendent of Timur) and ended in 1857 as a result of the Indian Uprising (or "Sepoy Mutiny") when the last Mughal emperor, Bahadur Shah Zafar, who "ruled" from Delhi's Red Fort, was deposed by the British and sent into exile in Burma.

55 Vesuvala recounts the story of Parsi emigration from Iran to India.

LXII.

For bathing in the Muse's Helicon[56]
    May veer from south to north, east west at pleasure;
And every plunge would bring you safely on
    A heap of pearls, to poets choicest treasure;
Of course undue exertion nerves would slacken,
    And blunt the mind with too furious a pressure,
That you're confus'd, not knowing how to act,
What leave aside, what precious to select.

LXIII.

O Tennyson, Arnold, Swinburne who 'dorn
    Our England's clime with poet's sacred name,
Excuse, if one by birth a Parsee born,
    Your noble muse so humbly dare inflame.
Excuse a modest youth, a boy forlorn,
    Who from his lowly cot his songs proclaim.
Excuse his first attempt, his trembling muse –
Perhaps from Ind the first that public woos.

LXIV.

O teach your nation – give but India due,
    No more complaining voice from her shall hear;
Give her natives justice in every clue,
    Nor hard oppress who already burden'd are.
Oh think to lighten loads, and strength imbue
    In their shorn limbs which life could scarcely bear;
Oh teach them, teach the English India's good,
Not selfish interests' search or brutish mood.

LXV.

How mild and gentle, guileless, obliging
    Is that Young Men's Christian Association![57]
Every week some subject moralizing
    For native's sake with calm deliberation;
With true Christian spirit intermingling,
    Without dignity's crude consideration!
Were India bless'd throughout with sons like these,
O England! thy Government were truly bliss!

---

56 Helicon: mountain in Boeotia in ancient Greece; sacred site of the Muses in Greek mythology (n. "helicon" *OED*).

57 The YMCA began establishing centers in various urban centers on the subcontinent during the mid-nineteenth century.

LXVI.

But errors creep and plausibility sounds
        With weaker force their arguments' domain;
And canst thou show that India free abounds
        With zealous, genuine converts to thy fane?
Ah dear Park! on what assuring grounds
        You bas'd the world's conversion in the main
To Jesus' flock and Scriptures' garbled text,
When your own millions disapprove it next.[58]

LXVII.

What if Franciscan cannibals were tam'd
        By Christianity? wild, reckless, devoid,
They never knew their God, but Him asham'd
        Who them created; hence morality shed
Its genial influence, intellect reclaim'd,
        And Christianity the poor victims decoy'd.
As well as Hindoo'sm had with ensnaring arts
Entic'd their sect with mirrors, knives or darts.

LXVIII.

What if Koli fishers, Madrasses black,
        And Hindus, Purbhus, Baboos join'd your flock?
These all have no religion, and they lack
        In that pure creed, without which there's a balk
In their way to society's tumultuous pack.
        Again the first are poor, ignorant stock
Who never reason; why then all shouldn't hail
That calling shore whence blows a social gale?[59]

LXIX.

Besides they never think of good or bad,
        So long their worldly interest proceed;
They don't inspect the thesis or their head,
        Before they launch their souls in Christian creed.

---

58 [Poet's Note: 'Are Christian Missions a failure?' was the subject of a lecture delivered by the Revd. Mr. Park of America.]

59 [Poet's Note: Idolatrous or Pantheistic doctrines do not constitute a pure or an intelligent religion.]

Many for madam, some for service mad,
    Pour souls! perverting father's holy seed!
O Conder![60] we all know how such recommendation
Ensures prompt service on G. I. P. station.[61]

LXX.

Again, the strongest plea that acts with force
    Against yourself, is that slow reversion
Of your own castemen to the ancient course
    Of true, reveal'd original religion;
The Theosophists among us,[62] who endorse
    The Braminical doctrines are, in addition
To hundreds more of sages learned, wise,
A sign that shows which was they tumult flies.[63]

LXXI.

Know that aft'r all the Parsee's sacred creed
    Shall shine out triumphant, foremost at the end,
And theologians, doctors shall give the lead
    To its just codes and mark'd assistance lend;
Its scriptures are an epitome indeed
    Of philosophy, medicine at hand,
And the best laws for health and sanitation,
The two ingredients that make life complacent.

LXXII.

O doom'd to wildest government, tyrannic laws,
    And gagging edicts that our voice suppress,
In vain dost thou the Parliament engross,
    Which can't afford relief or wrongs redress.
In vain do liberals attempt thy cause
    With power combin'd and vigour limitless, –
The conservatives are so merciless freezy,
The servile foolish slaves of Benjam Dizzy![64]

---

60 Vesuvala seems to refer here to Josiah Conder (1789–1855) who was a poet, bookseller, Protestant Nonconformist and well-known composer of hymns.
61 G. I. P.: acronym for Great Indian Peninsular, a railway company serving Bombay.
62 Theosophy: religious doctrine founded by Madame Helena Blavatsky and Colonel H. S. Olcott in the United States in 1885. Blavatsky and Olcott came to India in 1879 where they founded the periodical, *The Theosophist*, that year and toured the subcontinent lecturing and attracting followers.
63 [Poet's Note: There are in England, nay in Europe, many thousands who discard altogether the Christian doctrine. An instance of their growing apathy towards their own religion is the cremation of their dead, now being so general amongst them.]
64 "Benjam Dizzy": mocking reference to Benjamin Disraeli (1804–1881), who was a leading member of the Conservative Party for decades and acted as prime minister for two terms.

LXXIII.

Ye shades of Puritans! attend and see
    The Parliament once your sacred rights upheld!
Ye shades of Puritans! where e'er ye be,
    Stretch forth your eyes to where you once rebell'd,
And gain'd for country, selves, that monarchy
    Of constitutional government, impell'd
By worthier motives of subjects' sacred rights,
And tyrant kings who wage on ceaseless fights.

LXXIV.

See from on high your successors betray
    Their sense of sober judgment, righteous zeal;
See from on high how far from truth they stray,
    And conservatives are dumb slaves by will;
How party spirit mingles in the fray
    And right and justice, truth in vain appeal.
See how ministers sell our India's cause
For votes of Manchester, party applause![65]

LXXV.

'Tis throughout admitted by all mankind,
    Of whatever sect or nationality,
To succour those who're poor, leaderless, blind,
    Or those who could not speak for want of polity;
Perhaps the modern sort M. P.s[66] don't mind
    "The harebrain'd chatter of outside frivolity; – "
Or why, ye Parliamentarians of Britain,
You shut your gates to India's poorer kitten?

LXXVI.

O feel not, take not this our censure just,
    Ye liberal bands, that toil'd for India's good;
In your cool heads and sober counsels trust
    Implicit put our India's rising brood;
Full well aware are thy you try to oust
    The grasping, warlike conservative mood
From out the whole empire; we wish success,
And next expect our burden'd clime's redress.

---

65 During the nineteenth century, Manchester became a industrialist hub and center for textile manufacturing for export to the colonies.
66 M. P.: acronym for a British member of Parliament.

LXXVII.

Perhaps your lib'ral sway had tended far
    Ere now, if Gladstone sudden had n't resign'd;[67]
Perhaps none dar'd impeach or sought to mar,
    If boldly, fearlessly to work inclined;
Perhaps majority had retriev'd your star,
    Or subtler tactics, policies combin'd;
Perhaps you were in too great a hurry,
And resignation put you all in flurry.

LXXVIII.

Perhaps the nation's temper was for war,
    Perhaps their spirits yearn'd for rate's increase;
Perhaps they long'd for poverty at their door,
    Too long a time of luxury could but tease;
Perhaps they wish'd the Turks to steer ashore
    At their expense, from Bankruptcy to Ease;
Perhaps they thought Russians all are duffers,
And Zulus mere mercenary wafers.

LXXIX.

Perhaps for Cyprian Goddess[68] their wom'n yearn'd
    To look as beauteous, fairylike as she;
Perhaps their maids from Roman poets learn'd
    The arts and pranks of prostitution free;
Perhaps for stalwart Afghans hearts, eyes burn'd
    In place of present lords of weak degree;
Perhaps they thought their host of maiden spinsters
Would better wed the warlike Zulu bachelors!

LXXX.

Perhaps tinsel, bragging government's their taste,
    Instead of solid, frank, unwavering zeal;
Perhaps Gladstone's moderation ill could last,
    When Jingoes rose in arms at Mars' appeal.[69]

---

67 This statement most likely refers Gladstone's resignation as leader of the Liberal Party in 1874 after an electoral defeat.
68 Cyprian Goddess: Aphrodite, the Greek goddess of love.
69 Jingo: "nickname for those who supported and lauded the policy of Lord Beaconsfield in sending a British fleet into Turkish waters to resist the advance of Russia in 1878; hence, one who brags of his country's preparedness for fight, and generally advocates or favors a bellicose policy in dealing with foreign powers; a blustering or blatant 'patriot'; a Chauvinist" (n., adj. "jingo" *OED*). Mars: god of war in Roman mythology.

Perhaps at Dizzy's call, whole regions vast
    They thought to lay at England's noble will;
Making the Queen Shansha-Banu[70] o'er world,
With Premier Dizzy's Beacons-flag unfurl'd!

LXXXI.

Whate'er it be: the conservative now
    Range o'er the land by people's voice elect,
And canst thou, Benjamin! this juncture show,
    Their trust they gave to thee is all intact?
Ah nation deceiv'd, rise from slumbers low,
    And ask account of guardians of your sect,
Why in such needless wars the country launch,
And saddle India's overburden'd haunch?

LXXXII.

Why, why should present ministers engrasp
    At as much country bord'ring on their way?
Why, why annex'd Transvaal[71] and rag'd the wasp,
    The furious Zulu king of Delagoa Bay?[72]
Why, why provok'd the Afghan war so crass,
    Instead of safely guarding what they may?
Why, why for shame they boast their nation's gain,
When hundreds, thousands every day are slain?

LXXXIII.

Why frighten Russia and your fright betray,
    By sending troops to Malta, some few score?[73]
Instead of weaving, in their toils you play,
    And costs and charges reach to lacs and crore.[74]
No rectification of boundaries we pray,
    But cost of Afghan war we ask you for –
Yours is wildest policy ever known,
Scheming, secret, unfortunate, madgone.

---

70 Vesuvala seems to coin this term to designate satirically the queen as "strong woman" of the world.
71 Britain annexed the Transvaal in 1877; the Dutch Boers of the Transvaal saw this as an act of aggression.
72 The African slave trade had been based in Delagoa Bay (now known as Maputo Bay) on the southeastern coast, which was in Zulu territory. The 1870s witnessed a number of border disputes between the Boers in the Transvaal region and the Zulus, resulting in the British invasion into Zulu territory, under the rule of Zulu king Cetshwayo, in 1878. The Anglo–Zulu War ended in the loss of independence for the Zulu nation.
73 Malta was made a British colony in 1814. In 1877, Russia invaded Turkey and Britain sent Indian troops to Malta to shore up defenses, resulting in fears of a possible Anglo–Russian War.
74 *Lakh*: measure of one hundred thousand. *Crore*: measure of ten million. Both units of measurement are still widely used on the subcontinent.

LXXXIV.

Shame, shame to thee, Northcote![75] presumptious fool,
    Why tellest thou a lie ignoble, base,
That Ind is willing under Lytton's rule
    To pay the cost of minister's mad gone-ways?[76]
That Ind is prosp'rous, thriving, growing cool,
    When depression, discontent are all ablaze?
Sit thou down quiet silent on thy chair,
Rather than blab forth or untruth declare.[77]

LXXXV.

How well becomes thy comrades each to deck
    With titles, earldoms, laces, pearls and garters!
Not so had Gladstone twin'd round his own neck
    Such wreaths, proclaiming fame like Holi Carters;[78]
No title, lordship, K. G. C. B.[79] pack
    Haunts his staid name, or fame immortal barters;
Though dukes and lordlings plenty did make,
Himself the lord of all, Gladstone's sweet sake.

---

75 Henry Northcote (1846–1911): Conservative Party member. He served as governor of Bombay from 1899–1903.
76 Robert Bulwer-Lytton (1831–1991): English diplomat and poet. He served as viceroy of India from 1876–1880 during the Great Famine in South India, which was aggravated by British policies. See Mike Davis, *Late Victorian Holocausts: El Niño Famines and the Making of the Third World* (New York: Verso, 2001) for a brilliant analysis of these policies.
77 [Poet's Note: It was in the session of 1878, on the motion of Mr. Whitbread condemning the Afghan War, when Lord Hartington denounced in strong terms the viceroyalty of Lord Lytton, that Sir Stafford stated that the people of India had never been more content under any other viceroyalty than his; and at a later stage of the session, on the question of the cost of this war, Sir Stafford stated that the Indians were willing to defray it wholly, – a statement totally false and misleading as the above, and hence the House had the good sense to laugh it out. The people of India are wholly averse to the Afghan War and the policy that dictated it.]
78 [Poet's Note: The Purbhoos of Bombay generally organise masquerade processions in carts on the Holi-festival, dressing as Lords, Kings and Queens - something akin to a petty Lord Mayor's show.]
79 K. G. C. B.: acronym for Knight of the Grand Cross of the Order of Bath, a British order of chivalry.

Sonnet: Bombay Harbour

Rise, rise my Ocean-queen! with bolder view
Magnificent. Each steeple, spire and tower
Is rob'd with beams of that immortal flower,
That took its root since ages past and flew
The world's existence; whose ethereal hue
Bedims bright nature's noblest lightning power!
How with majestic front the ship Renfrew[80]
Lords o'er the sea! How towering in grandeur,
While screws, gunboats, merchants, all sorts adorn,
Far as the eye can reach, thee, ocean-born
Bombay! No sight, no fleet so fair appears
As that which meets thy charm'd Apollo's[81] gaze,
European, American, Orient race.

Aurobindo Ghose

Aurobindo Ghose (1872–1950) was brother of the poet Manmohan Ghose and a famous nationalist, yogi and poet. Born in Calcutta and educated in England for many years, he returned to India in 1893 to work for the Maharaja of Baroda where he published his earliest poems. He also worked as a professor of English and vice-principal at Baroda College and as principal of National College in Calcutta. As a radical nationalist politician, he was vociferous in his critiques both of British imperialism and the Indian National Congress, which he felt was too moderate and too accommodating to imperial rule. Although Ghose was gradually turning towards spirituality, it was not until 1910, after a series of encounters with the British imperial government (including being placed on trial for a bombing), that he completely abandoned politics for spirituality. He journeyed to Pondicherry where he established an ashram. Sri Aurobindo, as he came to be known, published consistently in the second half of his life including spiritual tracts such as *Essays on the Gita* (1922) and *The Life Divine* (1939–40), and his most well-regarded poetic work, *Savitri: A Legend and a Symbol* (1950). The early poems reprinted below allow readers a glimpse of a younger Ghose.

---

80 *Baron of Renfrew*: large ship built in 1825.
81 Apollo: son of Zeus and Leto and the god of music, poetry, light and prophecy in Greek mythology.

Songs to Myrtilla and other poems (Baroda: 1895)[82]

Publisher's Note.
These early poems of Aurobindo Ghose, all except five written between his eighteenth and twentieth years (1890–92), were printed for private circulation at Baroda in 1895 and are now first given to the general public.

O Coil, Coil[83]

O coil, honied envoy of the spring,
Cease thy too happy voice, grief's record, cease:
For I recall that day of vernal trees,
The soft asoca's[84] bloom, the laden winds
And green felicity of leaves, the hush,
The sense of nature living in the woods.
Only the river rippled, only hummed
The languid murmuring bee, far-borne and slow,
Emparadised in odours, only used
The ringdove his divine, heart-moving speech;
But sweetest to my pleased and singing heart
Thy voice, O coïl, in the peepul tree.[85]

O me! for pleasure turned to bitterest tears!
O me! for the swift joy, too great to live,
That only bloomed one hour! O wondrous day,
That crowned the bliss of those delicious years.
The vernal[86] radiance of my lover's lips
Was shut like a red rose upon my mouth,
His voice was richer than the murmuring leaves,
His love around me than the summer air.
Five hours entangled in the coil's cry
Lay my beloved twixt my happy breasts.
O voice of tears! O sweetness uttering death!
O lost ere yet that happy cry was still!

---

82 Aurobindo Ghose, *Songs to Myrtilla and other poems* (Baroda: Laxmi Villa Printing Press, 1895).
83 *Coil*, also known as the *koil, koel, koyal, kokil,* or *kokila*: bird famed for its melodious calls; often termed the Indian cuckoo.
84 *Asoca,* or *ashoka*: small evergreen flowering tree; the flowers, which grow in bunches, are fragrant and usually flame colored.
85 *Peepul,* or *peepal*: fig tree, thought to be sacred (n. "peepal" *OED*).
86 Vernal: to appear or occur during the spring (adj. "vernal" *OED*).

O tireless voice of spring! Again I lie
In odorous gloom of trees; unseen and near
The windlark gurgles in the golden leaves,
The woodworm spins in shrillness on the bough:
Thou by the waters wailing to thy love,
O chocrobacque![87] have comfort, since to thee
The dawn brings sweetest recompense of tears
And she thou lovest hears thy pain. But I
Am desolate in the heart of fruitful months,
Am widowed in the sight of happy things,
Uttering my moan to the unhoused winds,
O coïl, coïl, to the winds and thee.

Charles Stewart Parnell[88]
1891

O pale and guiding light, now star unsphered,
Deliverer lately hailed, since by our lords
Most feared, most hated, hated because feared,
Who smot'st them with an edge surpassing swords!
Thou too wert then a child of tragic earth,
Since vainly filled thy luminous doom of birth.

Lines on Ireland
1896

After six hundred years did Fate intend
Her perfect perseverance thus should end?
So many years she strove, so many years,
Enduring toil, enduring bitter tears,
She waged religious war, with sword and song
Insurgent against Fate and numbers, strong
To inflict as to sustain; her weak estate
Could not conceal the goddess in her gait;

---

87 There is no translation available for this word.
88 Charles Stewart Parnell (1846–1891): Irish politician and leader. An active opponent against Irish land laws, he was elected president of the National Land League in 1879 and became undisputed leader of the Irish nationalist movement. A personal scandal helped bring down his political career and reputation as a nationalist hero; he died shortly thereafter.

Goddess in her mood. Therefore that light was she
In whom races of weaker destiny
Their beauteous image of rebellion saw;
Treason could not unnerve, violence o'erawe –
A mirror to enslaved nations, never
O'ercome, though in the field defeated ever.
O mutability of human merit!
How changed, how fallen from her ancient spirit!
She that was Ireland, Ireland now no more,
In beggar's weeds behold at England's door
Neglected sues or at the best returned
With hollow promise, happy if not spurned
Perforce, she that had yesterday disdained
Less than her mighty purpose to have gained.
Had few short change of seasons puissance then,
O nurse and mother of heroic men,
Thy genius to outwear, thy strength well-placed
And old traditionary courage, waste
Thy vehement nature? Nay, not time, but thou
These ancient praises strov'st to disavow.
For 'tis not foreign force, nor weight of wars,
Nor treason, nor surprise, nor opposite stars,
Not all these have enslaved nor can, whate'er
Vulgar opinion bruit, nor years impair,
Ruin discourage, nor disease abate
A nation. Men are fathers of their fate;
They dig the prison, they the crown command.
Yet thine own self a little understand,
Unhappy country, and be wise at length.
An outward weakness doing deeds of strength
Amazed the nations, but a power within
Directed, life effective spirit unseen
Behind the mask of trivial forms, a source
And fund of tranquil and collected force.
This was the sense that made thee royal, blessed
With sanction from on high and that impressed
Which could thyself transfigure and infuse
Thine action with such pride as kings do use.
But thou to thine own self disloyal, hast
Renounced the help divine turning thy past
To idle legends and fierce tales of blood,
Mere violent wrath with no proposed good.
Therefore effective wisdom, skill to bend
All human things to one predestined end
Renounce thee. Honest purpose, labour true,
These dwell not with the self-appointed crew

Who, having conquered by death's aid, abuse
The public ear, – for seldom men refuse
Credence, when mediocrity multiplied
Equals itself with genius – fools! whose pride
Absurd the gods permit a little space
To please their souls with laughter, then replace
In the loud limbo of futilities.
How fallen art thou being ruled by these!
Ignoble hearts, courageous to effect
Their country's ruin; such the heavens reject
For their high agencies and leave exempt
Of force, mere mouths and vessels of contempt.
They of thy famous past and nature real
Uncareful, have denied thy rich ideal
For private gains, the burden would not brook
Of that sustaining genius, when it took
A form of visible power, since it demanded
All meaner passions for its sake disbanded.
As once against the loud Euphratic host
The lax Ionians of the Asian coast
Drew out their numbers,[89] but no long enduring
Rigorous hard-hearted toil to the alluring
Cool shadow of the olives green withdrew;
Freedom's preparators though well they knew
Labour exact, discipline, pains well nerved
In the severe unpitying sun; yet swerved
From their ordeal; Ireland so deceiving
The world's great hope, her temples large relieving
Of the too heavy laurel, rather chose
Misery, civil battle, triumphant foes
Than rational order and divine control.
Therefore her brighter fate and nobler soul
Glasnevin[90] with that hardly-honoured bier
Received. But the immortal mind austere,
By man rejected, of eternal praise
Has won its meed and sits with heavenly bays,
Not variable breath of favour, crowned
On high. And grieves it not, spirit renowned.
Mortal ingratitude though now forgiven,
Grieves it not, even on the hills of heaven,
After so many mighty toils, defeats

---

89 At the end of the fifth century BCE, the Ionian cities of Asia Minor unsuccessfully rebelled against the Persian Empire. The five-year revolt, which lasted from 499 to 494 BCE, is thought to have begun the Greco-Persian wars.
90 Charles Stewart Parnell was buried in the Glasnevin Cemetary in Dublin, Ireland in 1891.

So many, cold repulse and vernal heats
Of hope, iron endurance throned apart
In lonely strength within thy godlike heart,
Obloquy faced, health lost, the goal nigh won,
To see at last thy strenuous work undone?
So falls it ever when a race condemned
To strict and lasting bondage, have contemned
Their great deliverer, self and ease preferring
To labour's crown, by their own vileness erring.
Thus the uncounselled Israelites of old,
Binding their mightiest, for their own ease sold,
Who else had won them glorious liberty
To his Philistian foes, as thine did thee.[91]
Thou likewise, had thy puissant soul endured
Within its ruined house to stay immured,
With parallel disaster and o'erthrow
Hadst daunted and their conjured strength laid low.
But time was adverse. Thus too Heracles[92]
In exile closed by the Olynthian seas,
Not seeing Thebes nor Dirce any more,
His friendless eyelids on an alien shore.
Yet not unbidden of heaven the men renowned
Have laboured, though no fruit apparent crowned
Nor praise contemporary touched with leaf
Of civic favour, who for joy or grief
To throned injustice never bowed the head.
They triumph from the houses of the dead.
Thou too, high spirit, mighty genius, glass
Of patriots, into others' deeds shalt pass
With force and tranquil fortitude thy dower,
An inspiration and a fount of power.
Nor to thy country only nor thy day
Art thou a name and a possession, stay
Of loftiest natures, but where'er and when
In time's full ripeness and the date of men
Alien oppression maddened has the wise, –
For ever thus preparing Nemesis[93]

---

91 Philistines: group of people of Aegean origin who settled on the coast of Palestine during the twelfth century BCE around the time of the arrival of the Israelites.
92 Heracles: son of the ancient Greek god Zeus and Alcmene. Zeus's wife, Hera, drove Heracles mad. In his insanity, Heracles, who was known for his tremendous strength, killed his children. After regaining his sanity, the grief-stricken Heracles exiled himself from Thebes until he completed a series of feats in repentance. The reference to Dirce is unclear.
93 Nemesis: goddess of retribution or vengeance in ancient Greek myth (n. "nemesis" OED).

In ruling nations unjust power has borne
Insolence, injustice, madness, outrage, scorn,
Its natural children, then, by high disdain
And brave example pushed to meet their pain,
The pupils of thy greatness shall appear,
Souls regal to the mould divine most near,
And reign, or rise on throne-intending wings,
Making thee father to a line of kings.

Saraswati with the Lotus [94]
(Bankim Chandra Chatterji. Obiit 1894)

Thy tears fall fast, O mother, on its bloom,
O white-armed mother, like honey fall thy tears;
Yet even their sweetness can no more relume
The golden light, the fragrance heaven rears,
The fragrance and the light for ever shed
Upon his lips immortal who is dead.

S. D. Saklatvala[95]

S. D. Saklatvala, or Shapurji D. Saklatvala (1874–1936), was a Parsi politician dedicated to the labor struggle. A member of the famous Tata family, he worked for his uncle's firm, Tata Industries, for a number of years until resigning to become involved in leftist politics in England where he relocated in 1905. He was elected to the British parliament as a member of the National Labour Party for North Battersea in 1922 and was elected to represent the same constituency as a member of the Communist Party from 1924 to 1929. Also the author of *India in the Labour World* (1921) and *Is India Different?* (1927), *An Appeal for Peace* is Saklatvala's only poetic work. Unfortunately forgotten by his biographers, this long poem echoes the ideals evinced in his life's work. Although "Dedicated with Love to my Country India with earnest hopes that Peace may long continue in India under the British Rule," the poem is critical of the imperial greed which leads to war. Written, as the author notes, after the second Peace Conference at The Hague in 1907, the noble

---

94 Saraswati, the Hindu goddess of learning and knowledge, is often depicted seated on a lotus flower.

95 For further biographical information see Panchanan Saha, *Shapurji Saklatvala: A Short Biography* (Delhi: People's Publishing House, 1970), which includes appendices of speeches made by Saklatvala on the labor movement and against British imperialism, and Mike Squires, *Saklatvala: A Political Biography* (London: Lawrence & Wishart, 1990).

sentiments advanced in the somewhat awkward meter characterizing this work evince an idealistic worldview. Saklatvala writes in his "Explanation" preceding the poem:

> For a long time past I have wondered why there has not existed a poem setting forth the benefits of Peace in general and celebrating great events in the history of Peace which could rank with the grand epics of ancient or modern times – the great martial songs of the world which have contributed not a little towards the martial spirit of many a nation. Why should there not be a grand poem – after the style of an epic so as to impress the people with its grandeur – which could tell us of the achievements of Peace and so imbue us with a desire for Peace …
>
> As regards the form which the verses should take, I searched for a model best suited to the idea, and I am glad to say I owe it to a country-man of mine – the late Mr. Romesh Chandar Dut [Romesh Chunder Dutt] in his English translations of the great Hindu Epics – that I got the right model. I have, however, selected a different metre which in my opinion is best suited for the purpose…
>
> As regards the subject-matter itself there is a distinct tendency now to look on war as the survival of an antiquated custom which hampers the progress of true civilization. Men have awakened to the fact that disputes which are always bound to arise can be settled by other means than war – that moral and intellectual force can be made as influential in deciding quarrels as the physical. And here I cannot help mentioning the brave little band of Indians in the Transvaal who are striving daily to the world the superiority of the moral force as against the physical, the superiority of the mind over the body…
>
> In conclusion I only fitly dedicate this poem to my country – India – which is just passing through turbulent times, which, I doubt not in the least, will soon be put an end to by the combined efforts of an awakened People that need wise restraint and of a benign Government that has so long proved a true friend to Humanity and to Peace, and whose high statesmanship might be fully relied on to be equal to the task of adjusting their time-worn policies to the present needs of the country.

Only the first two parts of this seven-part poem are reprinted below.

An Appeal for Peace, some verses (Bombay: 1910)[96]

An Appeal for Peace

I.

From times of yore we've heard in song, achievements on the battle-ground
Each nation has its songs of war, that do with tales of blood abound.

Men ne'er have ceased their direful song, the deeds of doughty arms to tell,
How did a brother kill his brother, and how his fellow-creatures fell.

---

96 S. D. Saklatvala, *An Appeal for Peaces, some verses* (Bombay: Times Press, 1910).

And how in ancient times the javelin, so deftly thrust against the breast,
And how the spear of later age, did give the foe eternal rest.

Or how the modern cannon's roar loud thundered and destruction played,
What way the vessels of the sea down sank with precious lives unsaved.

The Kalewala of the Fins,[97] that doth of antique heroes sing
Who brave and glorious fought and died, still with their praises countries ring.

Romantic India has its song, of God-like Chiefs and Giants tall,
The men who fought the battles brave, their war-like array and their fall.

Three thousand years have nearly rolled the mighty chiefs since perished,
Whom sweetly sang Valmiki and the ancient Ramayana cherished.[98]

But still more antique is the song so sweetly sung from age to age,
Tradition's Treasure, lore of Bharata's[99] wars e'er handed from sage to sage!

All Royal bards and minstrels, in Greece of old so fair and free
E'er chanted forth heroic lay from Iliad and Odyssey.

Since when men have never tired, Achilles praising and Hector fierce,
And all the horrors and the fears, woes unnumbered and streams of tears.

And if we turn to learned Rome, the war-like deeds of heroes old
Which number thousands killed and torn, so proudly sung by poets bold.

Heroic Caesar brave in war, whose exploits formed unholy theme
Of prose and verse where savage deeds of cruel murder chiefly gleam.

Proud Persia none the less thy joy in the war and war-like deed
Wild Chief and Hero, fierce and keen, with theme thy learned poets feed.

Firdusi sage of world-wide fame, who sang of battles bravely waged
Where men did fight forgetting Death, and tribe 'gainst tribe fiercely raged.

---

97 *Kalewala*: Finnish national epic, which was probably composed at various times by various authors. Oral fragments were collected and systematically arranged and published during the nineteenth century.

98 Valmiki: poet-sage who is usually thought to have authored the "original," authoritative version of the Hindu epic, the *Ramayana* around 300 BCE. He also appears as a character within the narrative of the *Ramayana* itself.

99 Bharata: India.

Sweet Sha-Nameh[100] of olden kings that sings a father's piteous moan
Unknowingly who slays his son, and rends the Heavens with his groan.

The holy Crusaders then did fight; fanatic zeal great murder wrought
And rang the Heavens with their cry, each slaying with religious thought.

II.

We then turn to better ages, but do better things prevail?
The battle-arms are deadlier far, and all the greater is our wail!

For who can fitly sing the woes that terrible French Revolution made,
No life was then inviolate, and to Revenge men homage paid.

Uprose the dint of savage cry "War to the Castle – Peace to the Cottage"
Destruction scatt'ring far and wide, and leaving Crime as heritage.

Then rose above this dint of war, Napoleon silent fiercely stern,
Determined to divide mankind, and Fortune's wheel himself to turn.

With pride and pomp of war beset, proved himself the scourge of men,
On War and ruination bent – and nothing could retard him then.

As if the Ocean's swelling wave, he onward ran and sweeping all
He dashed himself 'gainst Rock of Fate, involving others in his fall!

All men may praise his valiant deeds and raise the hero to the sky,
But had he fought for Peace not Gain, his glory would the Fates defy.

Not less a war was sooner heard, with folly waged against blind fate –
Light-hearted French with pride of war, were sure of vict'ry soon or late.

They thus fought 'gainst Germanic host, unmatched in cunning art of war
And in their pride they fell alas! and lost their land and still much more.

Europa's wars are great and many, and who can count the millions spent,
The millions spent on active wars and the craze for armament!

And Oh! The sum of human woes, that all victorious wars entail,
Human wrongs and human suff'ring, beside the loss of life prevail.

---

100 *Sha-Nameh*, or *Shah-nameh*: translated as the *Book of Kings*; an epic account of Persian "national" history by the Persian poet Firdusi (c. 940–1020 AD) and was presented to his patron, the sultan Mahmud.

E'en mighty England rises up, secure and safe from enemies,
By greed of Empire led she fights, unequal war on peasant wages.

Ah! Peaceful England carries death into the simpler Boer home,
To war incited Boers fight, and make the Britons fret and foam.[101]

Amazed and dazed the world looks on, thy Boer vainly fights and dies;
At last with over-powering strength, old England's vet'ran chiefs arise.

And soon the gay victorious day, when banner rose above the trees
When joyous British flags of pride all fluttered in the Afric Breeze!

But see the parents weep and sigh, all crying for their slaughtered son;
The mourning wives lamenting die – all for the cruel action done!

And poets of the distant date will sing of war the Russians made,
On Mikado's troops alert and gay, and tell about the hundreds dead[102]

Much worse the wars the Orient fought – their frenzied fights more brutal still,
That counted thousands vainly killed, at bidding of a despot's will.

With crude but fatal arms they killed, without remorse they butchered all,
Knew not the cause that led them on, and blindly marched to downward fall.

Unlike their brethren of the west, plead not for "cause" which makes them fight –
Led on by lust of war they fight, with hopes of gain but not for "right."

Each soldier was with passions burnt, with brutal force to kill or die –
His was to do each murd'rous act – his was to stab but know not why!

The King waged war on his subjects own; and now the people killed the King,
The war was here, and the war was there, and murder was the common thing.

Each powerful despot had his way, he cared not for his subject's groan
Till another rose more powerful still, with brutal might to crush his throne!

And India own beloved land – in all the turmoil had thy share,
Thou hadst no Peace for ages past, each victor knew thy beauty rare!

---

101 Boers: descendents of the Dutch colonist settlers in South Africa. The First Anglo–Boer War was fought between Britain and the Boer republics from 1880 to 1881 while the Second Boer War was fought from 1899 to 1902. This last war resulted in a humiliating defeat for the British.
102 Mikado: term for the emperor of Japan in Europe. The Russo–Japanese War (1904–1905) grew out of conflicting claims to Manchuria and Korea and resulted in Japan's victory and the humiliating defeat of Russia.

An everlasting prey so rich, but poorer with each stab of knife,
Thy fate was by each victor sealed, or settled by internal strife.

Thy ancient wealth and glory gone, with tyrants marching through thy land,
Unknown to thee was Peace or Rest, till Peace thou hadst at England's hand.

And may this Peace be long thy own, with freedom-loving England's reign
For Peace alone will prosper thee and get thee back thy ancient fame!

Then think, ye noble sons of Hind,[103] and keep from acts of cruelty
Then think, ye England fair and free, and lead us to our destiny.

And let united India bend to path of peaceful progress still,
And let true England build her Empire on a loyal nation's will.

And may then India long preserve and guided be in peaceful paths
May Morleys wise and Mintos just make happy our homes and hearths![104]

C. R. Doraswami Naidu

As indicated on the title page, this collection, which ran an initial print run of 1,000 copies and sold for 1 rupee, was self-published "by the author C. R. Doraswami Naidu, B.A. of Bangalore, during his sojourn at Ahmedabad." No other information is available about the author though the "Addresses to Young India" included at the end of the volume seem to have been delivered as lectures to students and indicate that Doraswami may have worked as an educator. The titles of these addresses range from "An Oration on the Culture of Manhood and Character" to "The Function of Poetry."

---

103 Hind: India.
104 John Morley, secretary of state for India (1905–1914) and Lord Minto, viceroy of India (1905–1910) introduced reforms, embodied in the Indian Councils Act (1909), to allow the admission of Indians into various administrative and legislative councils. While some Indian moderates welcomed these reforms, which were introduced to placate Indians angry over the 1905 partitioning of Bengal, most nationalists, including many members of the Indian National Congress, viewed it as overly cautious. Many Hindus also resented the act's provision for a separate electorate for Muslims.

Heart Buds, poems (Ahmedabad: 1914)[105]

Foreword

In launching forth this barge of mine,
Upon the vast Atlantic brine,
Alone and friendless with my muse,
In search of Hope and faith, I cruise.
I trust its fate to mercy's wave,
For it was built my faith to save,
I stranded was beside this isle,
In haste I made it in this style;
A simple shallop[106] in its face,
It took for building twenty days!

Ye gales that mighty Titans shake
Upon my shallop pity take;
Yon stormy ocean shoreward breaks,
In billows foaming with their flakes;
My canoe trembles tossed amain,
It struggles with the waves in vain.

I have a fancy for the sea,
I wish to build a ship for me.
And if the promise of my art,
Doth promise give of better sort,
If time and tide, do favours brings,
My India's fame I live to sing,
If breathing time, these tempests give,
The seeds of truth, to sow, I live,
If Mammon saves my faith and trust,
A Mighty Vessel build I must.

Then shall I brave the stormy seas,
My banners waving in the breeze,
From India shall I take some rare
And mystic thoughts to Europe's fair!

---

105 C. R. Doraswami Naidu, *Heart Buds, poems* (Ahmedabad: C. R. Doraswami Naidu, 1914).
106 Shallop: either a light sailboat used mostly for coastal fishing or a large heavy boat usually with two masts.

To Europe lost in seeking self
In fleeting shades of power and pelf;
To Greece the ancient, classic home
Where freedom lost in dreams did roam,
Where Athens, Thebes their shadows cast
As fables of a dreamy past;
Whose dreamy dotage gave its way
To Roman Eagle's sweeping sway –
Italia! Thou land of great
And mighty Caesar's mighty fate,
Thy legions sleep in snowy graves,
Thy conquests left thy sons as slaves,
Till from thy plough a hero rose,
A Master-mind defied thy foes!

Britannia, my Island blest,
Thy Britons broaden East and West!
Thy Union Jack is waving free,
On Continent and Colony!

I have a fancy for the sea,
I wish to build a ship for me.
O how I wish to sail thy seas,
My banners waving in the breeze.
Great Chaucer guide me from the gales,
The Fairy Prince unfurl my sails,
The Soul of Avon[107] pilot me,
The Epic-Soldier rudder be,
My keel be planned on Wordsworth's lines,
My rafts as Tennyson designs,
If Byron comes again to be,
Bereft of passion, tempered free,
And Keats sings through his "Grecian Urn,"
And Shelley doth from 's ramblings turn,
How shall I brave the stormy seas,
My banners waving in the breeze!
O England! How I hope to be,
The Hope of Indian Minstrelsy,
A worthy cargo shall I bring,
When I shall India's glory sing!

---

107 "Soul of Avon": Shakespeare.

To the Motherland

My native land, my native shores,
    Where dewy morning dawns,
Where many a torrent proudly roars,
    To court the smiling lawns.

Thy sacred feet are washed by waves,
    Whom Kanya's rock divides –
Kumary kneeling proudly braves,
    The meeting of the tides.[108]

Thy summer belts are set with palms
    For milky nuts renowned;
Thy limpid currents sing the psalms
    Of life in sweetness drowned.

Beneath thy shades of plantain groves
    Whose banners swell the breeze,
Thy rural beauty madly roves
    To kiss the bridal trees.

Thy ancient homes of pilgrimage,
    Thy citadels of fame,
Thy great Himalayas, grey with age,
    Thy mightiness proclaim!

Thy womanhood, a noble band
    Of world's immortal gems,
Thy dames to virtue wedded stand,
    Heroic diadems.

Thy meadow blossoms bloom to greet
    The maids of Travancore,[109]
Thy mountains, fragrance, rich and sweet,
    On Kashmir beauties pour;

Their slender forms like creepers seem
    To grow in beauty's groves,
And on their cheeks the apples dream
    And violet on their brows.

---

108 Kanyakumari: town in what is now Tamil Nadu, India at the southernmost tip of the peninsula where the Arabian Sea, the Bay of Bengal, and the Indian Ocean meet. It is also the site of a famous temple of Kanya Devi, an avatar of the goddess Parvati (wife of the god Shiva). As a virgin (*kumari*) goddess, she is said to manifest her divine female spirit in young girls.
109 Travancore: princely state in southern India in the modern-day state of Kerala.

Thy Heart, a garden full of flowers,
    Thou Hope of dreamy youth,
Thy music melting into showers
    Of Universal Truth;

Where laughing waters leaping go
    Revolving cataracts,
Where northern winds commanding blow,
    Defying human acts.

Where Phoebus[110] kneels at Nandy's[111] feet
    On Kailas'[112] crystal floor,
Eternal snows evolve the heat
    Of hoary Vedic lore.[113]

My garden-forests, ocean streams
    My snow-clad mountain slopes,
My world's record of mystic dreams,
    My fairy land of hopes!

My happy Kashmir's lovely vales,
    My Paradise on earth,
Where apple gardens blush in dales,
    Of beauty taken birth.

My wild Mahratta Ghats of yore,[114]
    My Malwa's mellow plains,[115]
My marble rocks of Jubbulpore,[116]
    And Vindhyas rugged chains.

---

110 Phoebus: alternative name for Apollo, the god of music and light; radiant, bright, or shining (n. "Phoebus" *OED*).
111 Nandy, or Nandi: bull upon which the Hindu god Shiva rides; the gatekeeper for Shiva and his wife Parvati.
112 Mount Kailas: a peak in the Himalayas in what is now Tibet; known as the abode of the Hindu god, Shiva.
113 *Vedas*: ancient Hindu Sanskrit scriptures revealed by the gods and predating the composition of the Hindu epics.
114 Mahratta Ghats, or Western Ghats: mountain range on the western side of India. It runs north to south along the western edge of the Deccan Plateau. Over half of the range is located in the modern-day southern state of Karnataka. During the seventeenth century, the Marathas conquered much of this area and even challenged the territory held by the powerful Mughals.
115 Malwa Plateau: region in north-central India located mainly in the modern-day state of Madhya Pradesh.
116 Jubbulpore, or Jabalpur: city in the modern-day state of Madhya Pradesh. Jabalpur was a district in the Central Province region of British India.

My Amarnath in caves of snow
    With flags of silver pines,[117]
My Ganges glassing in thy flow
    My Kashi's golden shrines.[118]

My Mysore Home,[119] my land of gold,
    My groves of Chandan trees,[120]
Of emerald hills and vales untold,
    Where Champaks[121] scent the breeze.

My golden Bengal, glorious land
    Of genius full in bloom,
Whose spirit wakes in sweet command
    Religion from its tomb!

Thy singers soaring high above,
    Entrance thy hopeful race;
Thy damsels send their darts of love
    Their heroes' deeds embrace.

Thy music flows in full-brimmed flood,
    Delighting thirsty souls,
Thy canvas glows with living blood
    Which chivalry extols.

Thy voice of thunder, lightning charged,
    With love of truth resounds,
Thy voice of freedom, faith enlarged,
    In one pulsation bounds.

Historic Gujerat, slowly freed
    From custom's iron cage,
Renowned for Krishna's ancient creed,
    And holy hermitage.[122]

---

117 Amarnath caves: located in the modern-day northern state of Jammu and Kashmir and dedicated to the god Shiva.
118 Kashi: Benares, or Varanasi; a holy city located on the banks of the Ganges River in the modern-day state of Uttar Pradesh and considered a pilgrimage site for Hindus.
119 Mysore: center of a kingdom in southern India; part of the modern-day southern state of Karnataka.
120 *Chandan*: sandalwood trees. Mysore is especially known for producing this fragrant wood.
121 *Champak*: evergreen tree with fragrant orange-yellow flowers.
122 Gujarat: now a state in India; once ruled by a succession of Hindu dynasties before being conquered by the Mughals, who were replaced by the Marathas until British rule displaced the direct power of that empire. Dwarka, located in Gujarat, is said to have been the home of the Hindu god Krishna.

Thy pulse of rising trade is felt
    Thro' rolling clouds that make
Thy great metropolis, the belt
    Of industry awake!

Heroic Punjab, land of deeds,
    Recorded with the blood,
Of martyrdom whose mem'ry feeds
    The nation-feeding flood.[123]

Thou altar oft where India's crown
    The victor-hordes received,
My Thermopylae[124] of renown,
    My gates of hopes deceived.

My India whom I love to see
    Advancing with the times,
In league with all humanity
    In tune with vedic chimes,

Thou art a gem in Britain's Crown,
    Resplendent with thy love,
Thy Kohinoor of great renown,
    Shines on our Sovereign's brow![125]

O Britain! Land of liberty,
    Heroic mother that breeds
The heroes of humanity
    And nation-making creeds,

Thy Parliament of Justice is
    Our Parliament of Hopes,
Our genius fed in freedom's breeze
    In search of freedom gropes!

My India, how I love to see,
    Advancing with the times,
In love with all humanity,
    In tune with freedom's chimes!

---

123 The Punjab region is known as the home of the Sikhs, an ethnic-social-religious group founded by the teachings of Guru Nanak during the early sixteenth century and known for their skills as warriors.

124 The Battle of Thermopylae of 480 BCE was fought between an alliance of Greek city-states and an invading Persian army. The outnumbered Greeks were able to ward off the Persians until the latter finally achieved victory after discovering a hidden path.

125 The Kohinoor diamond belonged to various rulers in India (Hindu, Mughal, Afghan, Sikh, etc.). Seized by the British East India Company, it became part of the British Crown Jewels.

The Taj Mahal – Agra[126]

The Taj, the Taj, my soul's delight,
A world's refuge, a wondrous dome,
A fairy dome of frozen light,
And love's enamoured crystal home!
Behold in weary summer nights
When Jumna's[127] stream with sapphires shine,
And sweet the radiant moon invites
The devotees of truth divine,
The shadow of her beauty sleeps,
And in that beauty sleeps the love
That drowned in sorrow ever weeps,
Bedewing Jumna's anguished brow,
Whose rippling breast in sorrow turns;
Where sunbeams lingering sleepy day,
The silver moon within her burns
That love in death forgets her sway.
Pause, stranger, pause, and see the fate
Of human love for fleeting breath,
The circle moves from state to state,
Of endless waves of life and death.
Love blesseth him on whom it breathes,
To Shah Jahan it gave her sway,
And crowning him with amaranth wreathes,
It frozen dreams where Mumtaz lay!

To K. V. M.
A Vision – Young India

Slow and steady courts the sun, blushing west with burnished gold,
Slow the far off lands are wakened, into streaming radiance rolled;
Soft the world is bathed in breezes, filled with fragrance worship yields,
Nature wears her bridal robes, in rolling seas and emerald fields.
Life is ever full of glory, life is constant in its change,
Life is not the breath of folly, lost in doubt or seeming strange;
Life is rich with mines of wisdom, life is fed by love supreme,
Life is action, radiant mercy, 'life is not an idle dream'!

---

126 The famous Taj Mahal in Agra is a mausoleum complex commissioned by the Mughal emperor Shah Jahan (1592–1666) to commemorate his favorite wife, Arjumand Banu Begum, who died in 1631 ("Taj Mahal" *ArchNet*).
127 Jumna, or Yamuma: tributary of the Ganges River that passes through Delhi.

In the dream of coming glory, in the haze of rushing lights,
I, an infant dreamer saw the shining nations scale the heights –
Saw them march in earnest zeal to where their Master silent stood,
Hoist their flags of love and glory, preach the law of brotherhood!
Rose the moon of ancient wisdom, flooding all the spotless skies,
With her light of winning glories, rousing life in billows rise –
Great and glorious was her gospel flashing from her learning's shrines,
India claimed her brilliant jewels from her ancient wisdom's mines.
Flashing sword and fiery canon, flung her arts to dust and shame,
Till the growth of ancient knowledge went out like a flickering flame,
And the songs of early poets, hushed in silence lay asleep
Covered in ashes lay her wisdom, vedic love lay buried deep.
India loiters far away, her tender feet are wet with gore, –
Vedic India, far renowned for her ancient vedic lore – [128]
"Fallen India" thought the Master, "Great in deeds of Love shall rise,"
"India, India" rang the heavens, "India, World's Immortal Prize."
India in her summer heat of ceaseless warfare fainted lay,
Till the clouds of enterprise came marshalled in their proud array;
Freedom laden breezes sent them, from the far Atlantic seas,
Till the showers of their wisdom, wooed the woeful land to peace,
Faith in God and valour in them, made the Merchant-Kings to hold,
Even balance in a land where race and creed in madness rolled.
Thunder-belted heroes came, with lightning in their cartridge-rolls,
Nailed the lands to iron-girders and the skies to magic poles,
Slow their steaming six-wheeled boiler, carried culture through the land,
Well their magic magnet needles held their language in command.
   I then dreamt another dream, a dream of happy days to dawn,
India growing young and healthy, England's diadem brightly shone.
Then the Master's earnest wishes beat their thunder in my soul,
Then the lightning-flash of wisdom, lit the passage of my goal.
   There I see a happy vision, lifting me to altitudes
Of a higher world of knowledge where the future wistful broods,
Sphinx like, radiant gleams the vision, floating on Eternity,
Poising on the wings of time and breathing out humanity.
On her face the riddle of life in silence hangs, the worlds to shake,
And her lips in silence kiss the music of the soul to wake.
There before this mighty vision radiating love abright,
Like a speck of dust I floated, on the rippling waves of light.

---

128 *Vedas*: ancient Hindu Sanskrit scriptures revealed by the gods and predating the composition of the Hindu epics.

Jamasp Phiroze Dastur

Very little information is available on the author other than that he was a Parsi barrister from Bombay as he writes in his only published work, *The Temple of Justice*. This long poem on the nature of justice allows a glimpse into imperial governance from an Indian perspective.

The Temple of Justice [a poem in praise of justice] (Bombay: 1916)[129]

The Temple of Justice[130]

Behold the splendour of the stately pile,
Whose column, arch, and frieze, of Gothic style,
Look out upon a fascinating view,
When sea and sky are bathed in golden hue,
When faint with toil, the sun's departing ray,
Sinks on the ruffled bosom of the Bay,
That hems the crescent beach with silver frill,
From fair Colaba's[131] strand to Malabar Hill,[132]
And, leaping proudly o'er its vain confines,
Spreads the white foam on swamps of Marine Lines.[133]

    Ensconced above the tumult of the brine,
Here Justice sits serene. It is her shrine.
She sits, with folded eyes and balanced hand,
To weigh the merits of the motley band,
That to her open temple daily throng
To pour their doleful tales of woe and wrong.

---

129 Jamasp Phiroza Dastur, *The Temple of Justice [a poem in praise of justice]* (Bombay: J. P. Dastur, 1916).
130 The Temple of Justice here most likely refers to the Bombay High Court, which was chartered by the British in 1862 and built in a Gothic revival style.
131 Colaba, or Kolaba: district in southern Bombay.
132 Malabar Hill: located in southern Bombay; now an affluent residential area.
133 Marine Lines: area in southern Bombay; it takes it name from the soldiers stationed there during the nineteenth century.

And seven priests[134] around the altar stand
To guard it from profaning tongue and hand,
And, with unceasing effort, daily strive,
To keep the flame and fragrance still alive.
Above them all, the Prelate[135] erudite,
Of ship-wrecked worshippers the beacon light.
Each clad in sable stole and snowy bands;
Each with the even balance in his hands;
Each at his lectern with his load of books,
Listens to the cause with pensive looks.

The lesser clergy, lo! a blust'ring crowd.
With wagging tongues and din of voices loud,
And tedious brawl, and disquisitions vain,
And crafty quibble o'er expressions plain,
Confuse the Judge, and twist and strain the laws,
To suit the needs of their despairing cause.
The tickled client pays a heavy fee
To watch such clever feat of jugglery.

Behind these, yet another crowd you see;
The satellites – a dumb fraternity.
The hack of all, but praised or thanked by none;
The dupe, the drudge, the scape-goat, all in one.
Awaiting meekly, with suspense and fears,
The Taxing Master's devastating shears;
A weapon with two edges, made to strike,
The helpless sheep and shearer both alike.

And yonder stand the anxious multitude,
Of varied type and trait, of varied mood.
The Khoja youth,[136] whose knowledge is confined
To wasting wealth his father left behind.
The Marwari[137] who has not paid a groat,
Yet holds the bogus promissory note.
The wily merchant, who so long defies

---

134 The seven priests seem to refer to the seven judges on the bench. Although the letters patent of the Bombay High Court authorized 15 judges, the court began and continued work with only seven judges until the end of World War I.
135 Prelate: person having superiority or authority (n. "prelate" OED).
136 Khojas: ethno-religious community in modern-day India and Pakistan; they descend from a Hindu caste which converted to Islam.
137 Marwaris: Hindus of varying castes originally from Rajasthan; many settled in various parts of India and adopted some local customs. They are usually employed as entrepreneurs and traders.

His partner's widow, and her claim denies,
And flings at her the fabricated book
To prove the loss in trade he undertook.
The wretched cuckold seeking to divorce
His fallen wife, for sinful intercourse.
The greenhorns, who so gaily institute
The ruinous administration suit.
The slim Director there, who spreads the snares
To trap unwary folk who take his shares.
The men who on their neighbour's land encroach,
Or speculate in cotton ginned at Broach,[138]
And, armed with legal subterfuges arch,
Await the fateful twenty-fifth of March.
The Cutchi Memon,[139] whom quaint custom mocks,
And constitutes a legal paradox.
For, though a Moslem while he draws his breath,
He changes to a Hindu on his death.
He follows the Koran until he dies,
When, lo! the Mitakshara[140] law applies.

    The Beadle[141] ushers all these, one by one,
And bids them truth to tell and lies to shun.
As each relates his set and varnished tale,
In haze of lies he tries the truth to veil.
And for a moment Daniel[142] looks askance,
To search the truth with penetrating glance.
He marks the lips that hide, the eyes that speak,
And from each shrug and nod the signs that leak.
At last, with tranquil brow and looks composed,
He passes judgment, and the Court is closed.
And Daniel rises midst applauding strains,
And in the Temple, solemn silence reigns.

---

138 Broach, or Bharuch: located in the northern part of Bombay. It was known under colonialism for its cotton mills.

139 Cutchi Memon, or Kutchi Memon: ethnic and religious group that traces its roots to the Kutch region and identifies as Muslim. There was a great deal of debate among British imperial administrators whether they were to be classified as subjects under "Hindu" or "Mahomedan" law.

140 *Mitakshara*: Hindu legal commentary dating to the twelfth century and concerned with laws of inheritance.

141 Beadle: crier or usher of a law court; one who executes the mandates of authority and keeps order in a court (n. "beadle" *OED*).

142 Daniel: figure of wise judgment in Judeo-Christian theology.

Rustam B. Paymaster

Rustam B. Paymaster (d. 1943) published a number of works including *The Voice of the East on the Great War* (1916), *Poems on Dadabhai Naoroji* (1925), *Navroziana, or The Dawn of a New Era* (1917) and *Life of Dr. William Wordsworth* (1927), which includes his views on political, social and educational reforms. An ardent admirer of the great Parsi politician and Indian nationalist, Dadabhai Naoroji (1825–1917), Paymaster, also a Parsi, wrote a number of poems about and dedicated to his hero. As an advertisement slip included in *Navroziana* notes: "Out of the net sale proceeds of the Navroziana Rs. 500 will be invested in Government Securities, the interest of which will be utilized in awarding a medal every year in memory of Mr. Dadabhai Naoroji to a student, male or female, for general proficiency. Out of the sale proceeds of the first series of the *Voice of the East on the Great War* the author sent within two months of its publication Rs. 550 to the Women's Branch of the Bombay War and Relief Fund, besides sending 48 copies of the book to the Great War sale." Paymaster's poetry celebrates empire and the benefits accrued to the Parsi community under the British Raj. But it also constructs loyalty to the British as coexisting with Indian nationalist feeling. Of particular interest is Naoroji's response, published in a footnote to one of Paymaster's poems, to the poet's somewhat fawning verse.

Navroziana, or The Dawn of a New Era: Being Poems on Mr. Dadabhai Naoroji and Other Friends of India, with "The Voice of the East on the Great War" (2nd series) (Bombay: 1917)[143]

Mr. Dadabhai Naoroji,[144]
An Ode of Welcome

> No sceptred monarch now the shore doth grace,
> No Archduke grand of famous Austrian race,
> No Czar with proud in ruddy mantle fine,
> No Prince of Wales, of Royal British line,
> No crowned potentate of Western shore,

---

143 Rustam B. Paymaster, *Navroziana, or The Dawn of a New Era: Being Poems on Mr. Dadabhai Naoroji and Other Friends of India, with "The Voice of the East on the Great War"*, foreword by Sir Narayen G. Chandavarkar (Bombay: R. B. Paymaster, 1917).

144 Dadabhai Naoroji (1825–1917): a Parsi and one of the most respected leaders of the Indian nationalist movement. After teaching at Elphinstone College in Bombay for several years, he moved to England in 1855 to become a partner in the first Indian company in London. In London, he advocated for India through organizations such as the London India Society and was elected Liberal MP for Finsbury Central in northern London in 1892. He served as president of the Indian National Congress three times in 1886, 1893, and 1906 and famously critiqued Britain for its "drain of wealth" of India in his monograph *Poverty and Un-British Rule in India*.

No Viceroy-Elect, nor King, nor Emperor
But simple, modest soul of sterling worth,
With vantage none of rank, or wealth or birth –
Unique in millions full two-fifty two –
We greet, with national rejoicing true,
Spontaneous joy, sincere, as ne'er did stir
The heart of woman, child or man, before.

Hail! Hero, Hail! Thrice welcome King uncrown'd!
Hail India's son to Indian home now bound!
Hail bloodless Victor, Hail thou valiant knight!
Hail sturdy Champion of Truth, Justice, Right!

Who fought his country's fight with earnest zeal,
With one pure aim, one mind, midst woe and weal,
Who lived in exile from his native home,
Full thirty years did like Ulysses roam
In foreign land, to advance his country's Cause,
Unmindful both of scorn and of applause,
Alone, untended, unbefriended [sic], bold,
Thou country's guardian, friend, and seer old!
Just like a lambkin gathered long set free,
When first it sees its dam is filled with glee
Her whom it life and light and being owes –
Such pure delight from thy compatriots flows
To see once more in flesh and blood the sage
Who manfully did Duty's battles wage
His health, his life, his substance did devote,
And serve his country in bleak climes remote,
With single aim traversed the tract of sand
By constant efforts reached the Promised land!

What dire rebuffs, repulses trials stood,
In country's sacred cause, for millions' good,
O Dadabhai! O selfless, stainless soul!
O earnest patriot, to reach thy goal!

And won thy way to the historic House
Of Commons, didst the British Nation rouse,
Teach them to India justice fair to deal
And break for aye of cold neglect the seal?

A Nation's hope, its pride dost thou now bear
O Siam[145]! Bestow thy blessed load with care,
A Caesar's fortune, sooth dost thou set down –
India's true Hero with immortal crown!

What though God in his wisdom called thy son,
Are not the crores[146] of Ind thy sons, Great One?
Is not thy grief their grief, thy joy their joy.
Thy pain a nation's pain, O Dadabhoy?

A people's prayers warm on thee attend,
A nation's eyes to watch thy deeds now bend,
Hail! Hero, Hail! Thrice welcome King uncrown'd!
Hail India's son to Indian home now bound!

Mr. Dadabhai Naoroji, On His 79th Birthday
4th September 1903

Alone,[147] unfriended, unattended, bold,
Full fifty years ago he left our shores
For far-off Britain's free and favoured land,
To fight our cause and Justice to secure
To multi-coloured millions of his race,
Redress their long-felt wrongs, their rights protect,
By force of Reason, Persuasion's pow'r,

---

145 [Poet's Note: The Steamer that brought Mr. Dadabhai to India.]
146 *Crore*: measure of ten million; a unit of measurement still widely used on the subcontinent.
147 [Poet's Note: The following is a copy of an autograph letter received by the writer from Mr. Dadabhai Naoroji in which with characteristic humility he remarks that he did not go to England alone, unfriended &c. It need hardly be said that Mr. Dadabhai Naoroji

"Alone, unfriended, unattended, bold
Full fifty years ago left our shores....
..........*To fight our Cause*"

though he may have also gone, as we all know, as a partner in a business firm.
Washington House, 72, Anerlep Park, London, S.E., 7th October 1903

Dear Rustom,
Your poem has elicited a response from an English friend. I send you a copy of it, which I think will please you. You will be at liberty to make any use of it. While I am writing this letter I may just as well inform you that your first line is not accurate.
 I did not come here fifty years ago - "Alone, unfriended, unattended.
 I came here as a partner in the firm of Cama & Co. the very first Indian firm in this country, and a large firm too.

To show what fabled wealth of India meant,
How vanished her "barbaric pearl and gold",
Who shook her great pagoda tree of yore,
To prove her storied riches all were myth,
Delusion, snare, aye, mischief-working cant;
How poor, in truth, she was, how starved her sons –
The brown-skinned children of her suffering soil,
Accursed by dreadful droughts and famines dire,
When angry Nature did put on her frown;
How her own sons from service were debarred,
While posts fell freely to the heav'n-born race.
    Ev'n in his darkest hour of blank despair,
With lamp of Hope and inward light his guide,
And Faith in righteousness of his just Cause,
With Patience, Courage as his watchwords sole,
And India's needs and wants his battle-cry,
His banner proud of Truth, to Heav'n he raised,

    There were two other partners with me Mr. Mancherjee Cama and Mr. K. R. Cama and I represented in the firm here the Bombay firm of Messrs. Cursetjee Nosserwanjee Cama & Co. If Mr. Clarke's Poem is printed on your side, send me copies. With kind regards

Yours truly,
Dadabhai Naoroji

The following is the poem referred to by Mr. Dadabhai Naoroji: –

But now; the valiant Parsee does not stand
Alone, unheeded in a foreign land;
Friends he has made, not one, not two, but more,
Nay, he can count them by the fifty score.
A man who 'as lived beyond the allotted span,
Who 'as striven his best to serve his fellow man
Has found such welcome on Great Britain's shore,
No Englishman could even wish for more.
We speak of British pluck, endurance, fame;
What man has earned a more endearing name?
A torch he has lighted for the Indian's guide,
While Anglo fellow-subjects rally to his side.
In Eighteen-ninety-two he won such fame,
Which oped the doors of Parliament to India's claim
For three short years he strove with all his might,
Pleading for justice, honesty and right.
And now in Nineteen-three he stands again,
And asks North Lambeth to endorse his claim.
And when the fight is o'er, all hope to see,
Dadabhai Naoroji, India's Pride, M.P.

G. W. Clarke]

And gallant rushed, midst rivals' packed phalanx,
With fainting, aching soul and bleeding heart,
And waged full Seven Years his holy War,
Until he triumph gained and victory!
He knocked and knocked persistent at the gate;
And suffrage won of Central Finsbury,[148]
And made his honoured way to Parliament, –
The refuge last of every injured race,
Where Freedom's battles proud are daily won.
Behold! A wonder of the age! that he,
A 'dark' man proved the champion of the ruling race.
      Ah! Patriots by hundreds come and go
On India's barren plain, but he, alone,
Of thirty crores, unflinching foremost stood,
T' advance his country's long-neglected cause,
The fierce fight to brave and bear the brunt
Of scorn, rebuke, derision, obloquy –
Fore runners of success in emprise great.
No tinsel glory craved, no hollow fame,
Nor lagged behind, nor courage lost, nor swerved
From sacred Duty's strait and cheerless path.
His course, like Argos',[149] hourly watched by all,
Approval's silent, grateful voice invoked
From Com'rin's point[150] to Kinchinganga's height![151]
Brave son of Ind! her bulwark and her strength!
Collyrium of her eyes![152] Her soothing balm!
What hope inspired, what ambition moved.
Thy modest soul, that thou, without demur,
Didst all at once thyself expatriate
From country of thy birth, from Mother Ind?
Didst tear thyself away from consort's side,
Dissever from thy friends and kith and kin,
And seas and oceans plough and mountains climb,
And plunge thyself unto the battle-field,
And single-handed lead thy vast crusades,

---

148 Central Finsbury, or Finsbury Central: parliamentary constituency created in 1885 and located in North London. It elected the first member of Parliament of Indian descent, Dadabhai Naoroji, in 1892.
149 In the *Odyssey*, Argos is Odysseus's faithful dog and awaits his master's return.
150 Cape Comorin (now known as Kanyakumari): located in what is now Tamil Nadu, India at the southernmost tip of the peninsula where the Arabian Sea, the Bay of Bengal and the Indian Ocean meet.
151 Kinchinganga, or Kinchinjunga: mountain in the Himalayas on the border between Nepal and China.
152 Collyrium: medicated preparation for the eyes; an eyewash (n. "collyrium" OED).

Like heroes brave of Achaemenian times?[153]
Thou didst devote thy life, to Duty's call
And ruthlessly did crush thy noble self
For India's sake, O exile self-condemned?
O pilgrim blest! O wandering minstrel bold
From home, from friends, from kindred, self-expelled"!

Could one from life's appointed portion spare
Some years and add them to thy hoary age,
Then Parsi, Sikh, Bengali, Madrasi,
Maratha, Sindhi, Rajput, all alike,[154]
Would each with th' other vie and gladly lay
At thy blest feet an offering of his life,
And round thy sacred brow with zeal would twine
Together strung, like pearls, with heart and soul,
In such high reverence they hold thy worth!
Let India now unite and humbly pray
To Him that grants just prayer and desire, –
The bounteous Lord of all that's pure and good,
That thou unto St. Stephens be returned, – [155]
The glorious scene of Freedom's struggles bold;
God grant thee further lease of useful years,
To serve thy country and promote its good,
O'er Empire vast thy sacred gospel spread,
And east and west its teaching loud proclaim!

Dadabhai Naoroji

True son of Ind! Your life's great mission was
Your country's pristine glory to restore,
For which all ease and comfort you foreswore,
Nor sought mere hollow praise nor vain applause,
But ceaseless served her long-neglected Cause,
In her defence Truth's shining armour wore,
And drew the flashing sword of Justice pure,
Unceasing till death brought the final pause,
To India's youth a newer faith you taught,

---

153   Achaemenians: ancient Iranian dynasty that ruled from 559–330 BCE.
154   Paymaster uses the phrase "Parsi, Sikh, Bengali, Madrasi, / Maratha, Sindhi, Rajput" to designate the various regional, ethnic and religious communities on the subcontinent.
155   St. Stephen's Chapel was built in the fourteenth century. Although a large portion was destroyed in the 1834 fire, what remained was incorporated into the new Palace of Westminster, which houses the debating chambers of both houses of Parliament.

To their young minds a healthy creed you brought,
Showed them the path of fearless sacrifice,
Of selfless love that sought no earthly price,
For decades seven their boundless love you won,
India has not yet borne a nobler son!

The Late Hon. Mr. G. K. Gokhale, C. I. E.[156]

All India doth with grief disconsolate,
Now mourn and weep a loss so deep, so great, –
The loss of Gokhale, noble Champion, bold,
Who did fair India's sacred Cause uphold,
To mother Ind himself did dedicate,
And for loved India his life immolate,
Who sacrificed himself and all he had
A hundred battles single-handed led,
In all whose moments, waking or in a dream,
His country and her cause were e'er supreme,
Who wise and well did guide her destinies,
Neglecting comfort and forsaking ease.
For her, by night and day, with zeal he burned,
To her, as to a sacred altar turned.
The high-souled patriot, who the bar hath crost,
Stood up for Right and Truth at every cost.
In council-halls with his radiant face did shine,
That with great eloquence did nerve combine.
Who Knighthood did like empty honour treat,
In work and worth his best reward did meet.
Like an example of life nobly lived,
By selfless love a deathless name achieved.
Just as a candle, in pure, stainless white,
Stands straight and lonely on a cold dark night,
Nor cares for outward glory, nor for praise,
But sweetly casts its own transcendent rays,
Of light and warmth and life on all around,
Without a bluster, or an empty sound,
And melts and sheds its modest smiling tears,

---

156 Gopal Krishna Gokhale (1866–1915): educator, leading figure in the Indian independence movement and a member of the Indian National Congress. He led the moderate faction of the party in Congress. In 1905, he founded the "Servants of India Society," which was established to train Indians in social justice work such as increasing literacy and helping the underprivileged.

And all about with quiet gladness cheers, –
Intent to bless by its own mellow light,
Its lustre, showing all things pure and bright,
Wastes its own body, finally expires,
To blissful death as a great prize aspires,
So Gokhale by his eloquence divine,
In Council chamber did so sweetly shine,
Glad for all India to extinguish self,
Disdained aggrandizement and power and pelf,
To serve us well his like did consecrate,
And for the general good self annihilate,
With patience laboured to dispel the dark,
By Education's clear and heavenly spark.
With ardour, cool and calm, defeat he bore,
The more the strength consumed he shone the more.
True son of Ind! Patriot great and good!
All opposition thou hast bravely stood.
By Conscience led, hast well they Duty done,
In public life the proudest laurels won.
Where'er thou wert, to Ind thou turn'dst thy face,
Nor else but Ind did e'er thy thoughts embrace
Erased thyself, thou hat upraised thy race,
Didst bring it honour, but thyself efface.
Drink, evermore in full serenity,
The nectar sweet of immortality!

Lord Hardinge[157]

I.

Five years of noble strenuous work in Ind
Are crowned to-day with Victory's Laurels green.
You doff your fav'rite armour with just pride,
Midst Indians' deep and lasting gratitude.
You've borne the heat and burden of the fight,
And bravely met all troubles unperturbed.
Firm like a rock all storms and winds withstood,
And great in suffering as in action proved.

---

157 Charles Hardinge (1858–1944): acted as viceroy of India from 1910 to 1916. During his tenure, the capital of British India was moved from Calcutta to Delhi in 1912. He was seen in a more favorable light by his subjects than was one of his predecessors, Lord Curzon (viceroy from 1898–1905) due to his reversal of the partition of Bengal, his criticism of the government's anti-Indian immigration policies in South Africa and his respect for Gandhi. Nonetheless, several assassination attempts were made upon him while he was in office.

II.

Time was when "Nabob" Viceroys ruled the land,[158]
Whom oft did Sun-dried bureaucrats surround,
Who humoured and cajoled them e'er so long
And taught them to repress our noble rage.
But times are changed, now Viceroy true is he,
Who works and feels the most for India's weal;
Who studies night and day her wants and needs,
And treats her as a partner in the realm.

III.

Such was Lord Hardinge, honoured Viceroy great,
Whose policy was laid on liberal lines.
How wisely he the "People's Viceroy" proved,
And gained the nation's grateful blessings true.
By his courageous sympathetic acts
He leaves the country happier than he found,
His name endearing every hearth and home
Will always cherish with a reverent mind.

IV.

A Trinity the Indians worship now –
Three Empire-builders great of foresight keen –
Our Clement Canning, Righteous Ripon, just,[159]
And Hardinge Sympathetic, High-soul'd, kind;
The Greatest Viceroys known these decades five,
Who loved the people and were in return
Loved with a ten-fold love and reverence,
As benefactors of the struggling race.

---

158 *Nabob*, or *nawab*: provincial governor under the Mughal Empire in India; the term was appropriated by Anglo-Indians to refer to anyone who had made a fortune in the "Orient." Paymaster's use of this title to describe the viceroys of India serves as a searing critique of colonial officials who governed India according to the dictates of their own personal and financial gain.

159 Lord Ripon (1827–1909): viceroy of India from 1880 to 1884 under then British prime minister William Gladstone. Ripon was a proponent of the Ilbert Bill (which would have allowed Indian judges to preside over cases involving Europeans) and limited self-government. He was often referred to reverently in Indian-English political discourses during the nineteenth century as a figure sympathetic to Indians and as a proponent for reform within the British Raj.

V.

How bravely you soon aft the outrage mean,
At Delhi, where the great Durbar[160] was held,
Expressed your faith, unfaltering and firm,
In that same liberal policy of love
That erstwhile guided all your noble acts.
How proud we are, your generous faith in us,
Reposed so long, by noble instinct moved,
Remains to-day unshaken as before!

VI.

You ruled us through the heart with mildest curb,
With breadth of vision, justice, tack and above;
You made us citizens of Empire vast,
Removed the foul, invidious bar that lay,
Like lead, on all the struggling sentiment
And aspirations of the country's sons;
Displayed great qualities of statesmanship,
As liberal-minded ruler of the land.

VII.

Broad sympathy, the secret of your rule,
Lay at the root of your just policy,
It was the measure of all righteous acts, –
The healing balm applied, with marvellous skill,
To all our festering sores and wounds and pain.
You rested not the rule on conquering sword,
Nor hasty proved to smell sulphurous smoke,
Or danger-scent where danger there was none.

VIII.

Fair England needs no sharpened sword to win
Her multi-coloured subjects to her side.
She wants nor arms nor ammunition, too,
To keep in check her crores[161] of swarthy sons.
You gave us in the Empire our due place,
By sympathy a myriad hearts thus won;
The welfare of the Indians was your care,
It first and foremost stood in all you did.

---

160 Hardinge was the first viceroy to host a British sovereign at an Indian Durbar. King George V (1865–1936) was crowned in 1910 after the death of his father, King Edward VII. He was the only English sovereign to be present at a Durbar, in this case the Delhi Durbar of December, 1911 where he was crowned with the Imperial Crown of India, created for this occasion.

161 *Crore*: measure of ten million; a unit of measurement still widely used on the subcontinent.

IX.

From Duty's path you ne'er retraced your steps,
But always forward placed your cherished goal.
By six years' blessed rule o'er us you've earned
A glorious name to shine in Indian skies.
In your own land now higher guerdon waits
For you, O statesman, worthy of your fame!
True to your country and your blessed King,
You've ruled the land with priceless sympathy.

X.

Amidst afflictions great of heart and home,
Your high and lofty sense of Duty gleamed.
That kept you at your post with firm resolve,
A cruel fate cut off in manhood's prime
Your son, your hope, and your own consort dear,
At whose sweet touch did vanish all your cares.
Whose words of comfort breathed in angel tones
Eternal happiness and boundless joy.

XI.

Say, ardent champion of the Indian race!
What more we should admire – your insight keen
In problems great you faced with courage rare,
Or faith unshaken in the common weal?
Your sympathy that felt what we did feel,
That healed our bleeding sores, assuaged our pains,
Or zeal to serve the land at any cost,
And once for all its rightful place secure?

XII.

O advocate of aspirations just!
Inspirer of new hopes, new sentiments
So eager and prepared to face the storm
Of conflict and of scorn with dignity.
Far-sighted mariner! you steered with care
The bark of State through troublous waters high,
Through rage of scowling storms and growling winds
To safe and certain destination marked.

XIII.

Ah! you have proved a faithful messenger,
Whom Providence had sent, in anxious times,
To lull the storm and hush the furious winds
And teach those higher truths of peace and love.
Thy fame, O avatar of sweet Sympathy!
Will sure resound, with that of British rule,
From Himalayas to Rameshvaram,[162]
Across long centuries in our history!

XIV.

Dear, dear to you were all your Indians here;
With parent's care you kept them near your sight,
How close were to your heart the Indian crores,
You carried whom in your warm bosom's fold.
The kindly waters of your sympathy
Have reared a plant so fretful and so sweet;
The key of deep-felt sympathy has oped
The hearts of India's ever-grateful sons!

XV.

You lit the land you loved by inward light,
And with a statesman's eye you looked ahead
Uplifted us from our once fallen state,
Our status raised, new India did create,
And found your dream fulfilled to leave the land
A trusty friend and not dependent mere –
With worthy rank amongst the colonies!

XVI.

You were the first to send our troops to fight
On far-off Europe's blood-stained battle-fields,
How proud to find the Indian forces march
Through Marseilles in the panoply of war,[163]
With heaving breast to take their honoured place,
Beside King George's British soldier's brave,
And gain a just rank in the Empire vast
As equal partner in its weal and woe.

---

162 Rameshvaram: town in the modern-day southern state of Tamil Nadu.
163 Hardinge oversaw the deployment of Indian troops in the British armed forces during World War I.

The Secret of a Successful Rule

"I have trusted India, I have believed in India, I have hoped with India, I have feared with India, I have wept with India, I have rejoiced with India, and in a word, I have identified myself with India. India's response has been a wonderful revelation to me and sometimes I feel as if she had in return confided her very heart to my keeping."
– (Lord Hardinge on the eve of his retirement from India.)

O! grateful Indians, let me now declare
My views to you entrusted to my care.
How well I've trusted Ind thro' thick and thin,
Believed in her, with faith to love akin.
With her I've hoped, and feared with her as well,
On varying fortunes one could scarce foretell.
I've wept with Ind, all sorrow hers I knew,
Rejoiced with her in her rejoicing true.
She, in return, did make my sorrows hers,
Dispelled my grief and made its cloud disperse.
Aye, in a word, I made her cause my own,
Her life, my life, her comfort mine I've known.
My heart-strings bound with hers as if from birth –
My land of hope, my paradise on earth!
I knew not my existence save in her
I drew not breath save with her own to stir
To her with thread of gold myself did bind
In her did I my true salvation find.
The kind response she 'as made so cheerfully,
What wondrous revelation 'twas to me!
I've seen with pride, how grateful, in return,
For me, ev'n now, her weeping soul doth burn,
Confiding full her inmost heart to me,
Unasked, ungrudging and unstintingly
How I have ruled her time alone can tell,
But sympathy hath won her heart full well.
There is the key, in it the secret lies,
Of my success, my guerdon and my prize?

The Parsi New Year's Day[164]

Hail! Morning of the new-born hopeful year,
Bring tidings of great victory and cheer,
Success to British arms, th' Allies great Cause,[165]
A glorious peace, and joy for Nations' laws
In Western Ind by strength of grace divine,
The Parsis now in public spirit shine.
Since the advent of the British here in Ind,
Zoroastrians[166] deep to them attached you'll find,
Firm with the British rule our fate is sealed,
On it our highest hopes we always build. –
A thrice-blest rule, ordained by Providence,
For India's needed slow, but sure, advance, –
A happy rule, where Righteousness governs,
Where Faith and Freedom's taper constant burns;
Where valour true and martial glory shine,
And truth and right with manliness combine;
Where wolf and lamb at one same fountain drink
And high and low their differences sink.
Where salmon and the whale still sleep in peace,
In waters of the Empire's circling seas;
Where undisturbed do we our faith preserve,
Our ancient customs and our rites observe.
With thee, O Britain! Parsis stand or fall,
To thee, in thy sore need, we give our all,
Thy strength our strength, thy honour is our pride,
Our fullest trust and hope in thee confide!

---

164 Parsis: Indian followers of the Iranian prophet Zoroaster, are said to have descended from Persian Zoroastrians who emigrated to India to escape religious persecution. The exact date of emigration is unknown (sometime before the tenth century). Usually known as educated and successful businesspeople, they were famously loyal to the British Empire.
165 "Allies": reference to the Allied Powers during World War I.
166 Zoroastrians: followers of the prophet Zoroaster and descend from Iran.

North

North India encompasses Delhi and its various outlying districts including the modern-day states of Himachal Pradesh, Punjab, Jammu and Kashmir, Rajasthan, Uttar Pradesh and Madhya Pradesh as well as Pakistan. For the purposes of this anthology, Pakistan is considered a site of "Indian" poetic production prior to partition in 1947. Due to its importance as center of trade and commerce, Delhi has had a long history of conquest by various groups, including the Mughals and the British, and became a symbol of India's subjection for many Indian-English poets. Yet as a contact zone, Delhi was the home of a rich and varied culture, which was manifest not only in its poetry but in its renowned Mughal architecture. This architectural beauty made it an object of reverie for a number of poets, such as Mian Muhammad Shafi, who wrote proudly of his city's Islamic influences and heritage. Delhi was placed under the control of the British Crown after the unsuccessful Indian Uprising (or "Sepoy Mutiny" as it was termed by the British) of 1857 and the infamous "Siege of Delhi." The last Mughal emperor, Bahadur Shah Zafar, was deposed by the British and sent into exile in Burma. In 1911, the British imperial government announced that Delhi would become the new capital of the Raj and the 1920s and 1930s saw the architectural development of New Delhi. Though not as prolific as the other regions in its production of Indian-English poetry during the period under consideration in this anthology, this region nevertheless witnessed the publication of several fascinating volumes of poetry.

Babu S. C. Dutt [Shoshee Chunder Dutt]

Another member of the famous Dutt family of Calcutta, Shoshee Chunder Dutt (1824–1885) attended Hindu College and worked as a civil servant, justice of the peace, and writer. Like many other Indian-English writers, he worked in a variety of genres and published works of poetry such as *Miscellaneous Verses* (1848), *A Vision of Sumeru, and other poems* (1878), *Works of Shoshee Chunder Dutt* (1885) and *Last Moments of Pratapa* (1893), poems from which are included in the "North" section, as well as novels such as *The Young Zemindár, his erratic wanderings and eventual return...* (1883) and the hodge-podge *Bengaliana: A Dish of Rice and Curry, and other Indigestible Ingredients* (1880), which includes an account of life as a civil servant and a tale of the 1857 Indian Uprising. His ethnographic work, *The Wild Tribes of India* (1882), was published under the pseudonym Horatio Bickerstaffe Rowney. The poem printed below, which seems to have been originally published eight years earlier in Dutt's collected works, was published later as an eight-page pamphlet of verse.

Last Moments of Pratapa (Lahore: 1893)[1]

Last Moments of Pratapa[2]

I.

He cannot and he will not yield,
  Though every gorge and glen
Is crowded now by desperate foes,
  And fled his craven men.

II.

He will not bow his haughty head,
  His royal 'scutcheon[3] stain;
His friends are few, his hopes are lost,
  Yet he would fight again!

III.

Misfortunes crowd upon his path
  And clouds the sky deform,
But, stubborn still and unappall'd,
  He yields not to the storm.

IV.

The traitor wretches taunt him now,
  He deigns them no reply;
His big heart mourns his country's doom,
  But scorns the hireling's eye.

---

1 Babu S. C. [Shoshee Chunder] Dutt, *Last Moments of Pratapa* (Lahore: Arorbans Press, 1893).
2 [Poet's Note: *Vide* Tod's *Rájasthán*, chap. xi. Annals of Mewár.] James Tod's *Annals and antiquities of Rajast'han, or the central and western Rajpoot states of India* was first published in two volumes between 1829 and 1832 and was reprinted in Madras in 1873, Calcutta in 1884 and London in 1914. This work, which purports to describe the geography of Rajasthan and sketch out a history of the Rajput clans and their customs, spends most of its time recounting major historical events surrounding the clans and their rule. The work captured the imagination of Indians at the time in its romantic portrayal of Rajasthan. Pratapa Rudra, who ruled from 1289–1323, was the last ruler of the Kakitiya dynasty in the eastern Deccan. This poem re-imagines his fateful stand against the sultan of Delhi (Richard M. Eaton, *A Social History of the Deccan, 1300–1761: Eight Indian Lives* (Cambridge: Cambridge University Press, 2005), 9–11).
3 Escutcheon: shield or shield-shaped surface depicting a coat of arms; an ornamental plate (n. "escutcheon" *OED*).

V.

Though on the naked sward[4] he lies
    He covets not their shame;
With pride he counts his sufferings o'er,
    His deeds of deathless fame!

VI.

The tiger's den, the leopards's home,
    The panther's awful lair,
He sought them 'neath the angry sky,
    A covert shade to share.

VII.

And on the rocks his queen reposed
    While darksome fell the shower,
Unbending still the Kshetriya's[5] soul
    Defied great Akbar's[6] power.

VIII.

The wolves they whined before his path,
    Behind the shout arose –
A vaunting shout of warlike glee –
    The shout of gathering foes!

IX.

But still he held his purpose high,
    Nor paused his daring soul,
And fiercer burn'd the flame within,
    And burn'd without control.

---

4 Sward: grassy surface of land (n. "sward" *OED*).
5 Kshetriya, or Kshatriya: traditionally, the warrior caste in the Hindu caste system.
6 Akbar (1542–1605): considered one of the great leaders of the Mughal Empire, Akbar ruled from 1556 until his death. He expanded the reach of the empire over the subcontinent to include almost all of northern India, reformed the central administration system and instituted a more efficient tax-collection process. His tolerance and sympathy towards other religions, illustrated in part by his inclusion of a number of Hindus in the imperial bureaucracy and allowing Hindu territories within the empire a measure of autonomy, ensured the loyalty of many non-Muslims.

X.

And fiercer did the fighting rage
    On blasted heath and moor,
And many a valiant deed was done
    On Chumbul's[7] lonely shore.

XI.

In every pass, in every glen,
    In every widow'd vale,
With weeping eyes his children trace
    His valour's bloody tale.

XII.

And moated walls, and mountains cairns,
    And caverns dark and grim,
Which witness'd oft his struggles fierce,
    Now loudly speak of him.

XIII

But life can bear no more, his race –
    His glorious race is run
He sinks with every honour crown'd –
    So sinks the setting sun!

XIV.

But O! the Moslem's feet accurst
    Are on his native plain,
The crescent-standard flouts the sky,
    And will it flout in vain?

XV.

That thought lies heavy on his heart;
    When he for aye is gone,
Shall then the Káffirs[8] proud assume
    The Kshetriya's stainless throne?

---

7 Chumbul, or Chambal: river that runs through Rajasthan in northern India.
8 *Káffirs*: peoples inhabiting the Hindu Kush mountains of northeast Afghanistan. Also a term used by Muslims to mean a non-Muslim or infidel. Dutt turns the term upside-down to refer to the "infidel" Muslims (n., adj., "káffir" *OED*).

XVI.

And trampled 'neath their iron sway
    Must hoary elders bend,
No arm to guide the Rájpoots'[9] pride,
    Their honour to defend?

XVII.

His lofty heart is heaving now,
    His eyes are fill'd with tears;
O could he but repeat once more
    His toil of bygone years!

XVIII.

His son, brave Umru, stands beside
    The dying warrior's bed,
An heir of all his father's worth,
    In danger nursed and bred.

XIX.

He marks his father's heaving breast,
    He marks his weeping eye:
"Speak, father, what thy bosom grieves?
    And whence thy agony?"

XX.

The hero's eyes are closing now,
    He draws his darling near,
And strains him to his aching heart,
    And vents his boding fear.

XXI.

"Now swear, my boy, upon thy sword
    Thy country to defend,
And swear that ne'er in homage mean,
    Thy royal knees shall bend.

---

9 Rajpoots, or Rajputs: thought to be mostly members of the Kshetriya, or warrior, caste but their status varied widely. These landowning, patrilineal clans ruled central and northern India from around the tenth century, when they began to gain political power, until the collapse of the Mughal Empire, with which they made settlements, at the end of the eighteenth century. After independence in 1947, the Rajput states were merged to form the state of Rajasthan. Known as soldiers, the Rajputs were celebrated for their military prowess and heavily recruited by the British East India Company and later the British Empire. They are often depicted in highly romanticized terms in Orientalist literature.

> XXII.
>
> "Eternal conflict thou must wage –
> Such as thy sire begun –
> To crush the haughty Moslem power,
> Or be thyself undone.
>
> XXIII.
>
> "Then will my soul sleep sound in peace,
> This troubled spirit-rest:" –
> He closer drew his weeping child,
> And clasp'd him to his breast.
>
> XXIV.
>
> And in that warm embrace the boy
> Eternal warfare swore;
> The father smiling closed his eyes,
> And then spake never more.

Bipin Bihari Bose

Bipin Bihari Bose's *Congress Songs and Ballads* (1899) was published "[i]n aid of the Congress Committee's Funds" for the Indian National Congress. The January 1900 issue of the Indian-English Bombay-based newspaper the *Indian Spectator* included a review of *Congress Songs and Ballads*. The review, heavily laced with irony, commends the poet's "zeal" but evinces skepticism regarding whether these poetic labors "brought in much to the Congress' coffers." The reviewer continues: "Verily, as Renan has observed, the Oriental does not understand irony. We can not, however, afford to be ironical at the expense of a fellow-countryman, and one, in particular, who is fired with such generous and patriotic ideas of nationality and progress as Mr. Bipin Behari Bose. Even to the mechanisms of versification Mr. Bose does not appear to have paid much attention. Of course, when a poet "lisps in numbers, because the numbers come," or "does but sing, because he must, and pipes but as the linnets sing," an occasional lapse from the rules of prosody might not attract attention." The reviewer objects to the "number of extraordinary liberties with accent and scansion" in poems such as "To the delegates proceeding to the Tenth National Congress at Madras, 1894" and claims "the reader might be pardoned for wishing with all his heart that the writer had accompanied the delegates to Madras instead of remaining behind to write such verses.[10] Despite their literary shortcomings, Bose's poems evince a sincere support for the efforts of the "nationalist" Congress and a desire to sponsor its mission and be sponsored by its members.

---

10 Anonymous, "Review," *Indian Spectator*, 14 January 1900, 29.

Congress Songs and Ballads (Lucknow: 1899)[11]

"Mother and Mother-Country are more estimable than Heaven itself"

1

Friends, sing the song, sweet Congress[12] song,
    Patriots, as march we on,
The darkness clears, and light appears,
    We've slept and slept too long!

2

The interminable night is o'er,
    Gives way to glorious dawn,
The blazing sun of Western lore
    The veil of mists has drawn.

3

Rise and see,[13] you have eyes to see,
    Dear Countrymen and all,
And anxious hear, with willing ear,
    Your Mother-India's call.

4

She old and poor, so reverent more,
    With sufferings all pale,
With entreating eye she looks on you,
    O heed her woeful tale.

5

With age tho' hoar, and fallen far,
    New hope yet lights her mien,
New life, born of a joyous faith,
    Now courses thro' her frame.

---

11 Bipin Bihari Bose, *Congress Songs and Ballads* (Lucknow, India: Sukh Sambad Press, 1901).
12 The Indian National Congress (INC), established in 1885, sought to bring the voices of Indians to bear on the affairs of Empire. It included delegates from various regions throughout the subcontinent and met at the end of every year.
13 The tropes of rising, awakening and seeing are tropes in poetry about India during this period. Indians were often called upon to bring India out of her long slumber, which represented a dark period between her ancient glorious past and a possibly glorious future as repeated in stanza 5 of this poem.

6

Oh stand and bless, with united voice,
    The Great Empress and Queen,[14]
Whose glorious reign of weal untold
    Has shed on us its sheen.

7

The source of light and life and hope
    How well her rule doth prove,
The Sovereign of a loving people,
    She bids us on to move.

8

England, dear home of every virtue,
    Sweet nurse to Liberty.
The Mother of many nations, true,
    Thou kind to us must be.

9

The noble fires that burn in us,
    Thy teachings' gift they are,
O should'st thou make a Tantalus[15] –
    To rouse them and then mar?

10

The path of Duty is one and straight,
    Leading us to the goal,
Brothers unite, leave selfish spite,
    And serve the country whole.

11

To croaking fools their folly leave, –
    Their canting puerile rant,
To your noble mission steadfast cleave,
    And sprouts devoutly plant.

---

14 "The Great Empress and Queen": Queen Victoria (1819–1901), who ruled as queen from 1837–1901 and empress of India from 1877–1901.
15 Tantalus: son of Zeus in Greek mythology. Tantalus is variously depicted as stealing the nectar of the gods for humankind, revealing the secrets of the gods to mortals, or killing and serving his son Pelops to the gods. He was punished by Zeus, who left food and water just out of reach (thus tantalizing him with their presence).

12

The word is gone – 'tis Will Supreme,
    The harvest will be great;
The peace and love reigning serene
    Augur your bett'ring fate.

13

All that's futile, man's malice puts
    To retard pure Progress,
'Tis Dispensation of the Age –
    We hie to the Congress.

14

'Tis come this time, lo, nearer home,
    To rouse, to mould, to raise,
All dull inertia 'side well flung,
    We hie to the Congress.

The Congress-man's Confession

1

I am a Congress-man – I own,
    The Truth I follow fast,
The Truth by reason's light ashown
    Which doth through ages last!

2

The Truth by dear experience bought,
    And dearer to my heart,
The Truth which history hath me taught,
    Oh, how can with it part?

3

Though Anti-congress brothers whine
    In darkness and in spite,
The lustre of the truth divine
    In wisdom's rays is bright;

4

The Truth which man never forgets
    Tho' in sloth sunk deeper far;
Kind Heaven 'gainst a hundred lets
    Still moveth for the Car;

5

The Truth[16] which England hath us taught
    Thro' her noble sons and great;
The laboured lessons by them brought, –
    You want to dissipate!

6

The Truth which peerless Shakspeare [sic] taught
    Thro' saintly Wordsworth shone,
And from unerring Burke[17] we got,
    And th' world's idol – Gladstone.[18]

7

Oh fired at the magic name
    Of the dear Century-man,
His great life without spot or blame
    Is lesson to Time's span.

8

Blest Heaven-born Chief, how Indian tears
    Flowed at thy recent grave,
The beacon-light to unborn years,
    Sole reconciler brave!

9

How rosest thou 'bove mean convention
    To spread Truth's onward sway;
As thou spok'st, mankind stood attention,
    For justice was the way!

---

16 "Truth": the poet may refer here to progress and reason.
17 The British statesman Edmund Burke (1729–1797) famously inveighed against Warren Hastings, governor-general of Bengal, in the latter's impeachment trial, which examined corruption in the East Indian Company dealings in India.
18 William Ewart Gladstone (1809–1898): served several terms as Liberal prime minister of Great Britain (1868–1874; 1880–1885; 1886; 1892–1894). His actions in protection of Irish tenants and his support of Irish Home Rule as well as his appointment of Lord Ripon as viceroy of India in 1880 won him the support of Indians.

10

Th' oppress'd to free, old sores to heal,
    The degenerate to raise –
England's mission, – thou mad'st it real,
    To her e'erlasting praise.

11

'Twas thou indignant didst restore
    The good old policy
In India, for necessity sore,
    By irreversible decree.

12

For who could so well understand
    Britain's congenital bent,
At helm of State if thou dids't stand,
    Thro' halcyon seas she went!

13

In blind force no remedy lies
    For th' ills of human life,
'Tis a wise sympathy 'lone supplies,
    What ends all ruinous strife.

14

What Metcalfe[19] reared on Indian soil
    Was not meant for a day
Th' appointed task nothing could foil
    Fore-planned by Macaulay[20].

15

For Victoria reigns, Her words of grace
    Are treasured in our hearts,
To our fruitful hopes they give a race,
    And scope to our flow'ring parts.

---

19 Charles Metcalfe (1785–1846): colonial administrator born in Bengal. Metcalfe held several positions during the course of his career including governor of Agra, governor of Jamaica and governor of Canada. He served as acting governor-general of India from 1835–1836 during which time he repealed various restrictions on the Indian press, including the Bengal Regulations Acts of the 1820s, which instituted mandatory licensing for all newspapers.

20 Thomas Babington Macaulay (1800–1859): British politician and historian. His famous "Minute on Indian Education" (1835) influenced educational policy in India for decades to come by convincing British administrators of the need to establish English as the medium for instruction in Indian educational institutions.

16

The growing Prosperity She ordains
    On righteous rule broad-based,
It seeds of Her People's co-work contains, –
    All ignoble fears erased.

17

Hence gentle Mayo[21] staidly sowed
    Self-government's good germs,
Which grew by cares, kind Temple bestowed,
    Off from Suspicion's harms.

18

The threads continuous great Ripon[22] took,
    And wove a fabric rare;
Her old ways genial Ind forsook,
    And wrapp'd it fast and fair.

19

Oh! stay the hands that go to mar
    The work the wise designed,
For India cherisheth it dear
    Which Destiny hath signed.

20

The Gospel of self-help is thine,
    Britain! we act and con;
And carried by the tide of Time,
    With thee trusting move on.

---

21 Richard Bourke, Lord Mayo (1822–1872): Conservative Party member appointed viceroy of India in 1869. He served in this capacity until his assassination on a visit to the convict settlement in the Andaman Islands in 1872.

22 Lord Ripon (1827–1909): viceroy of India from 1880 to 1884 under then British prime minister William Gladstone. Ripon was a proponent of the Ilbert Bill (which would have allowed Indian judges to preside over cases involving Europeans) and limited self-government. He was often referred to reverently in Indian-English political discourses during the nineteenth century as a figure sympathetic to Indians and as a proponent for reform within the British Raj.

21

Thou hold'st the plough – mustn't look behind, –
    'Tis the vineyard of the Lord;
No earthly prize – thy good can find,
    But th' ultimate reward!

22

We love, we serve – our Mother-land –
    Be it our loss or gain;
Confessing the Truth taught by England,
    We sing the dear refrain.

23

This, then, is our enliv'ning faith,
    So simple and so true,
'Tis good for the state and the People, –
    To hold it none can rue.

24

By it the wheels of State run smooth,
    It supplies the needful oil,
'Tis root of all confidence, forsooth,
    It ends all vexing coil.

25

'Tis Nature's harmony with Law, –
    Accustomed India know'th;
'Tis deadly Stagnation's panacea,
    The blessed path of Growth.

26

It calm – endures Envy's pointed dart,
    In Duty buries Shame;
The glory of every Indian heart,
    It feeds the sacred flame.

27

O 'tis the Indians' burden dear,
    The weight of which we feel,
Forethought by sage, foreseen by seer,
    It bears Majesty's seal.

28

Thus just'fied we in rapture greet
    The Pandal[23] on Lucknow soil,
How vast and fair, in loyalty sweet,
    Th' emblem of our patient toil!

29

She tells kind Macdonell's[24] good will;
    Her tow'r is widely seen;
The air about her she doth fill
    With notes of "God save the Queen."

Sir Mian Muhammad Shafi

Mian Muhammad Shafi (1869–1932) was a prominent lawyer, politician, and writer who studied in England before returning to India. A member of a prominent family in Lahore, he was involved in the founding of the All-India Muslim League in 1906 and was especially active in its Punjab branch. His only other work is the political tract, *Some Important Indian Problems* (1930). *Poems* includes a dedication page of sorts which notes that it is "[p]resented to…with my best wishes" indicating that it may have been privately printed for distribution to friends. Lahore, now part of Pakistan after partition, complicates our understanding of the imagining of "India." Shafi's odes to "Delhi" and his poem "The Rise of Islam" depict the important and often conflicted roles of Islam and Muslims in the founding myth(s) of the Indian nation.

---

23 *Pandal*: usually temporary (sometimes permanent) structure, shelter, platform set up during Hindu religious rites or a ceremonial gate to welcome visitors.

24 This may refer to Arthur Anthony Macdonell (1854–1930), a noted Sanskrit scholar but most likely refers to the Liberal statesman Sir Antony Patrick Macdonnell (1844–1925), an Irish-born British civil servant. Sir Anthony served in various high administrative posts in the British Raj, including as lieutenant governor of the North-West Provinces and Oudh and member of the Council of India, until 1902 when he left to serve in Ireland.

Poems (Lahore: 1907)[25]

To a Chinar-Tree[26]

Thou glorious King of Kashmere Vale[27]
        That stands beside the winding stream
Where pine-clad hills slope down the dale –
        Beneath thy shade of heav'n I dream!

A shade so cool, of greenest green
        And sweet beyond description's pow'r,
Nowhere throughout the world is seen
        Except in thy soul-cooling bow'r.

Thy leaves, like outstretch'd human palms
        In thousands on thy branches spread,
Lavish profuse Elysian[28] charms
        As gently in thy shade I tread.

The murmurs of the sparkling rill
        That flows beneath thy widespread wings
The valley's air with music fill –
        Aye, Gabriel[29] bells of paradise rings!

And as I hear their heavenly strain
        Against thy mightly [sic] trunk reclined,
With angels this my soul is twain
        In boundless peace and love enshrined.

To live and, having lived, to die
        Here in thy soul-inspiring shade
Were bliss indeed! no grief; no sigh!
        Life's path once more in Eden[30] laid.

---

25 Mian Muhammad Shafi, *Poems* (Lahore: Mercantile Press, 1907).
26 *Chinar*: deciduous trees indigenous to the Kashmir Valley region.
27 Kashmere Vale, or the Kashmir Valley: now disputed territory between India and Pakistan. Its breathtaking scenery provided inspiration to a great many poets of the nineteenth and early twentieth centuries.
28 Elysian: blissful; beatific; glorious; from Elysium, a state or abode for the blessed dead in ideal happiness, in Greek mythology (adj. "Elysian" *OED*).
29 Gabriel: archangel who acts as a messenger of God in Judeo-Christian and Islamic religious traditions.
30 Eden: paradise in the Judeo-Christian and Islamic religions.

And now, O King of trees, farewell!
>Back must I go to Love and Home;
In mem'ry shalt thou ever dwell,
>However far from thee I roam.

(Achhbal – Kashmere. August 25th, 1905)

The Sirinagar[31] Flood and the Dal Lake[32]

Hark! Down the green hills, swift and strong,
>The torrents rush solemn and grand,
Awful indeed their martial song
>As now they lash the rocky land.

From north and south and east they fly,
>Foaming across the fertile vales;
You hear the ruined farmers cry –
>The air is filled with moans and wails.

Its thus the flood down Jhelum[33] flows,
>Whirling along with lightning speed;
Each hour in furious might it grows
>And countless streams its volume feed.

It now descends with might and main,
>A foaming mass so broad and deep,
Upon Srinagar's charming plain
>With one gigantic, roaring sweep.

Down fall the banks, the *bands* are crush'd,
>There's naught the angry flood may stand;
Awe-struck the souls, hearts throb are hush'd,
>With terror shakes the strongest hand!

---

31 Sirinagar, or Srinagar: now the capital of Jammu-Kashmir and located in the center of the Kashmir Valley. It was often used as a tourist destination for British officials during the nineteenth and early twentieth centuries.
32 Dal Lake: located just outside Srinigar in Kashmir. Although widely noted for its beauty, floods are nonetheless a source of concern in this area.
33 Jhelum: river that begins in the current-day state of Jammu and Kashmir, the Indian-administered portion of the Kashmir region, in the Vale of Kashmir and courses into modern-day Pakistan. It is the westernmost of the five rivers in the Punjab.

The golf-links and the polo-ground[34]
    Are changed into an inland lake!
Where horses ran now boats abound
    Racing, for precious is there stake.

Ah! Loud and long the cries for aid
    That from those lonely mansions come,
A grey-beard here and there a maid
    Left stranded in their island-home.

To house-boats or the hills some fly
    Safe from the furious water's reach,
A few things saved, the rest passed by;
    Some crowed upon the highest beach.

And lo! begirt by lofty hills
    Amidst this scene of wails and sighs
A fairy-land of sparkling rills
    Of sweet and peaceful hamlets lies!

The *Pari Mahal*[35] upon the slope
    In ruins now; the *Royal Spring*[36]
Whose water is as sweet as Hope
    When to Her soft embrace we cling;

---

34 The "golf-links and the polo-ground": reference to the use of this area as a vacation resort by British imperial officials.
35 Pari Mahal: built in the mid-seventeenth century on the ruins of a Buddhist monastery in Srinagar. Used as a school of astrology, it was commissioned by Emperor Shah Jahan's eldest son ("Pari Mahal" *ArchNet*).
36 Royal Spring, or Cheshma Shahi: built under Emperor Shah Jahan by the Mughal governor Ali Mardan Khan in 1632–3. It is known for the digestive properties of its water ("Royal Spring" *ArchNet*).

Bright relics of the *Mughal*[37] reign
  Those *Baghs Nishat*[38] and *Shalimar*[39]
That rouse in fancy's dream a chain
  Of mem'ries ancient as *Chinar*;[40]

This pearl of gardens *Bagh-i-Nasim*[41]
  Beneath whose soul-awakening shade
Of Love and Home, sweet Home I dream,
  My heart with deep, deep feelings sway'd:

And *Dal* lake[42] set amidst these pearls,
  Brilliant, serene as summer sky,
Untouched by river's pools and whirls,
  Where Nature smiling meets the eye.

Yes, in this earthly paradise,
  Beyond the reach of Jhelum's raid,
Beside *Nasim* our house-boat lies,
  Our tent is pitched beneath its shade.

The roaring floods beyond the hills
  While here a soft repose prevails;
In safety here the rustic tills,
  The farmer there his crops bewails!

---

37 The Mughal Empire of the subcontinent was founded in 1526 with the defeat of the Delhi Sultanate by Babur (a descendent of Timur). It was greatly expanded by Akbar in the late sixteenth century and by Aurangzeb in the late seventeenth century. After the latter's death in 1707, a series of "weak" rulers led to a decline in the fortunes of the Empire until its end in 1857 as a result of the Indian Uprising (or "Sepoy Mutiny"). The last Mughal emperor, Bahadur Shah Zafar, was deposed by the British and sent into exile in Burma.

38 The Bagh's Nishat, or Nishat Bagh (the Garden of Delight): famous for its magnificence and located on the eastern side of Dal Lake, it is thought to be the work of Asaf Khan, Nur Jahan's elder brother. Nur Jahan was one of the wives of Shah Jahan's father, Jahangir ("Nishat Bagh" *ArchNet*).

39 Shalimar Gardens: thought to be the most beautiful of the three gardens in Kashmir. It was laid out by Shah Jahan's father, the emperor Jahangir, in 1619 when founding the city of Srinagar ("Shalimar Gardens" *ArchNet*).

40 *Chinar*: deciduous trees indigenous to the Kashmir Valley region.

41 Bagh-i-Nasim, or Nasim Bagh (Garden of Breezes): located on the western side of Dal Lake and considered one of the earliest Mughal gardens in Kashmir. The garden was commissioned by Akbar in the late sixteenth century ("Nasim Bagh" *ArchNet*).

42 Dal Lake: located just outside Srinigar in Kashmir. Although the lake is noted for its beauty, floods are nonetheless a source of concern in this area.

Ah! passing strange are Nature's ways
    And deeds sublime our souls but feel
In wonder lost and sing His lays
    Whose boundless might these hills reveal.

(*Nasim Bagh*, Srinagar, September, 1905)

On Entering the Kashmere Valley[43]

Hail! Hail! ye Kashmere Vale and hills and skies!
Once more with joy I breathe your fragrant air:
How blissful to regale these longing eyes
With Nature's charms so passing sweet and rare
In thousands sprinkled by a bounteous Hand
All over the fertile plains and mountain-slopes
And silver-lakes of this your fairy-land —
Aye, charms that fill my thirsting soul with hopes,
Bright hopes of that sweet life of purest glee
When souls shall mingle with that Soul Sublime
From which they sprung — unchained, unfettered, free,
In world beyond the bounds of space and time.
A life of peace and love and bliss divine
Will then, O Kashmere Vale, indeed be mine!

(Written in the tonga[44] while proceeding
from Baramula to Srinagar — 14th August 1905.)

On the Occasion of Queen Victoria's Diamond Jubilee[45]

Victoria, Thou of boundless sea the Queen,
How many nations prosper 'neath Thy sway!
How many distant lands and peoples lean
Upon Thy arm and smile as flowers in May!

---

43 Kashmere, or Kashmir, Valley is now disputed territory between India and Pakistan. Its breathtaking scenery provided inspiration to a great many poets of the nineteenth and early twentieth centuries.
44 *Tonga*: light, small, two-wheeled carriage or cart (n. "tonga" OED).
45 The Diamond Jubilee celebrated Queen Victoria's sixtieth year as monarch in 1897. Festivities were staged all over the British Empire, including India. Numerous Indian poets wrote odes, in English as well as the other languages of the subcontinent, in honor of the Queen and her rule to mark the occasion.

Each dawn but sees millions of souls arise
Deep-stirred with joy and gratitude profound;
Each eve but sees the foolish and the wise
Content alike – for peace's gifts abound
Where e'er Thy rule extends. Bright shines the light
Of culture that all o'er Thy kingdom great
Ten thousand blessing sheds. Each day and night
Thy envied subjects thank their kindly Fate
That Thou – O mother Queen, adorns the throne –
The peerless, best, the noblest ever known!

9th June 1897.

To Delhi

Imperial Delhi! Thou of towns the Queen!
The seat of Empires past description grand!
To dream, to fancy thee as thou hast been
In years gone by! To wake the sleeping Past
And ask that goddess to uplift Her hand
And place before our wondering wistful eyes
The silent secrets of these tott'ring walls,
The blotted pages of Her book unfold
And to our awe-struck minds reveal at last
The annals of these time-worn Forts and Hall
And sacred Tombs of marble, wherein lies
The earthly mould of many a warrior bold
And crowned Head and Holy Saint! Ah me,
My saddened soul, O Delhi, mourns for thee!

(Written while visiting the tombs of *Humayoon* and *Nizamuddin Aulya* at Delhi on the morning of 29th August 1896.)[46]

---

46 Humayoon, or Humayun: second Mughal emperor who ruled from 1530–1540 and 1555–1556. Considered a weak and ineffectual ruler, he was deposed by Sher Khan and his son, Islam Shah, during the intervening years of 1540–1555 until Humayun was finally able to recapture the throne. Nizamuddin Aulya (1236–1325): Sufi saint. The tombs of both men are located in eastern Delhi.

The Rise and Fall of Islam
(Written for the 9th Mahomedan Educational Conference
held at Aligarh, December 1893)[47]

Wake Muse of mine! The awful spell
That bound so long my waking soul
And its inspired powers as well
Is broke at last! The glorious goal
Where Thou, in Thy Elysian[48] seat,
Art slumbering still, is now revealed!
The light of dawn, radiant and bright,
Has fill'd my heart with deep delight
And shown me things ere now concealed,
Arise! I stand beside Thy feet!

A theme awaits Thee, dearest friend,
Meet for the music of Thy lyre;
A theme of Moslem hearts the pride,
The precious gem that Patriots hold
Dearer than aught on earth beside;
That makes the poorest brain so bold
And sets the poet's soul on fire;
The hardest rocks beneath which bend –
A Nation's tale of weal and woe,
Another such the worlds not know.

In Arab-land, barren and drear,
Where winds blew eh! how hot and sear,
Where fertile vales to eyes unknown
And all was one vast stretch of sand,
Where spring-flowers were but seldom grown,
And hills in nakedness seemed grand;
Whose people, ignorant and wild,
No sovereign own'd, obeyed no laws,
In bloodsheds, wars their days beguiled
With weapons sharp as eagle's claws,
Was born a child who, when a man,

---

47 Founded by Sir Syed Ahmad Khan in 1886 (shortly following the founding of the Indian National Congress), the All India Muhammedan Educational Conference promoted a modern liberal education for all Muslims. The conference met annually and although it remained neutral on Indian National Congress politics, the Muslim League grew out of this organization.
48 Elysian: of or pertaining to Elysium, the state or abode of the blessed after death in Greek mythology; a state of perfect happiness (n. "Elysium" *OED*).

Founded a faith nobler than all
The world had seen in days gone-by –
A Prophet, whose soul-stirring call
Rang loud through deserts, mountains dry
And towns, from Aden's sea-girt-rocks
To Sinai's broad and sacred slopes!
First one, then few, and then in flocks
The stray sheep to the Shepherd came;
And hopeless minds were filled with hopes.

Where people lowly bow'd before
Habel, Yaghoos, Manat and Lat,[49]
Now loud the call to prayers rang,
Safely, at last, attained the shore
Arabia's storm-struck, wave-toss'd craft
What joyful song the crew now sang!
The warring tribes, the fighting men,
Were bound by Union's iron-tie,
Stronger than Vulcan's[50] chains again,
And God of feuds was feign to fly.

The light of knowledge, pure and bright,
Dispelled of ignorance the gloom,
It shower'd its blessings left and right
Its heavenly bud now reached its bloom.
Both soul and mind the nectar drank
Deep from the fountain of Islam;
From Biscay's[51] shore to Ganges' bank
From Russia's plains eastward to Anam[52]
Our Prophet's Faith like lightning spread
On every clime the light it shed.

The long-lost Grecian lore revived,
Egyptian Arts brought back to life,
The rose of culture true beshrived
Of all its thorns, fighting and strife
From chaos changed into an Art,

---

49 The goddesses al-Lāt, Manāt and al-Uzzā were three of the most venerated deities worshipped in Mecca, where temples were consecrated to them before the spread of Islam during the seventh century. Hubal and Yaghūth were gods also worshipped in pre-Islamic Mecca. All were considered false idols in the teachings of the prophet Muhammad.
50 Vulcan: god of fire in Roman mythology.
51 Biscay: province of the Basque Country.
52 Anam, or Annam: central region of Vietnam.

The seeds of civilization sown
That spread its fragrance far and wide,
The flower of Science now full-blown
And many a gift of God beside,
Dearer than ought to human heart,

Would to the world have been unknown
But for Islam. Europe, to-day
The tutor of our fallen race,
But yesterday, did she not own
Us as her masters? Yes, our May
Is gone, and we are face to face
With our December! Ah me! the past,
The glorious past! Must we but mourn
Its greatness? Fortune's withering blast
Has struck the tree and down it borne?

Mourn, did I say? Yes, mourn and weep,
Ye children of those mighty men
Who drank of Nature's fountain deep,
Who feared now waves, nor lion's den,
But onward marched in joy and glee!
Long have ye slumber'd. Yea, too long:
Arise! Awake! Look round and see
Weak nations grown in knowledge strong:
Yourselves alone lagging behind
In this fleet race of all mankind!

Of all the Europe's mighty Powers
Your God has blest you with the best,
Its blessings fall like summer's showers
Bringing us culture, peace and rest.
Thank God, ye Moslems of this land
For, lo! again the tide has turned;
The ebb is stayed! Bright looms the star
That watches on your God-lov'd band;
Long has its twinkling lamp now burned
For you to see the goal afar!

To lead you God has sent a soul
Whose love for you knoweth no bound;
A pilot knowing every shoal,
Quicksand and reef, whose judgment sound
And watchful eye will lead your craft

Safely through storms and calms alike,
Though fearful gales beset the mast
And mighty waves the hull may strike;
Straight to the harbour he will steer
Without a shadow of doubt or fear.

His boundless zeal, untiring strength
And efforts great have won for you
Boons priceless that could ne'er be gained
By scores of faithful hearts and true
In twice as many years. Ordained
By Heaven, through India's breadth and length
The foremost of his race he stands,
A people's boast, a nation's pride,
The leader of the Moslem bands
That have begun the onward stride!

The sacred bricks of this grand Hall,
The Boarding-house, the College-rooms
And this great Conference, each and all,
For ever the National heirlooms,
Priceless and lov'd, shall waft your name,
Sir Syed,[53] through the coming days
Whate'er our Nation might befall.
Immortal, lo! shall be your frame,
Never-waning, but in numerous ways,
Be ever more the joy of all!

Hearken, O Lord, this humble prayer
That from our inmost hearts we breathe,
From ill-health and from every care
This loved hoary-head Thou sheathe!
To lead the followers of his Sire,
Of Moslem hearts to be the guide,
To keep ablaze the national fire
May him no harm or pain betide!
O! God on high, this Conference bless,
Give thou its aims complete success.

                Dated 27th December 1894.

---

53 Sir Syed Ahmad Khan (1817–1898): founder of the All India Mahommedan Educational Conference and Aligarh Muslim University. Suspicious of the Indian National Congress and nationalist movements in general, he supported the British Raj and encouraged other Muslims to do so as well.

To India!

Hail India! Hail! my native land!
With tears of joy are dim these eyes
To see once more thy loved strand,
To gaze again on these dear skies!

Long have I wandered far from thee
In fairy realms and distant climes
Away across the wide, wide sea –
Not sad yet longing many a time.

Yes, longing for that home of old
Where child and boy in bliss I grew,
By loving parents spoilt and bold
That naught of fear and care I knew.

Ah! as I see thy shores arise
Above the ocean's heaving breast
Methinks, I hear the wee bird's cries
That on our eave was oft a guest!

Dear land of mine, with a beating heart
Now joyful on thy soil I tread!
Of nature's crops and fruits of art
May God the best throughout thee spread.

(On landing at Bombay on the evening of
August 8th, 1892.)

"To my mother"
(Written in a home-sick mood)

O mother dear! though far from thee,
    In London's motley crowds I rove,
Yet oft in fancy's dreams I view
    The by-gone, joyful scenes of love!

Though boundless seas between us roll,
    Even now thy loving arms I feel
Around my neck entwined to soothe
    The gloomy thoughts that over me steal.

Those lips that oft affection's kiss
    Impressed upon my heated brow
Sweet words of comfort seem to breathe:
    I hear their strains of solace now.

"Cheer, cheer, my son," they seem to say.
    "These painful days will soon be over
Not for the day when thou wilt see
    Once more dear Home's beloved bower.

"Thy mother's constant, endless love,
    Unfathomed as the ocean deep,
Shall watch thee, near, as now from far,
    Through daily work and nightly sleep!"

I hear these words, O mother dear,
    They bring me strength and comfort great
With patience will I bear my ills,
    And, trusting, leave the rest to Fate!

                (December 1889)

Tej Shankar Kochak [a "Georgian Brahmin"]

Kochak's claim to be a Georgian Brahmin, or a Brahmin under the reign of King George V, emperor of India, both asserts his caste status as well as his loyalty to the British Empire. Biographical information on Kochak has been difficult to obtain but the "Introduction" to his long poem provides insight into his perceived role as cultural emissary between Indians and their British rulers. Kochak writes:

> The very first thing that will strike to a European reader will be, "An English poem and by an Indian!" Yes; but it is Indian poetry. Now, what is poetry? It is in the highest form, the most truthful image of the soul of an author, and, through him, that of his times and community. Rhyme and meter are things of secondary consideration, and language serves only as an instrument with which he produces this image for others.
>
> To day, if there is any language, which can be called, in any sense, the *Lingua Franca* of India, it is English; though it is a foreign tongue, yet it is now the common language of the cultured classes, therefore the author uses English as the medium through which to convey his ideas to the world.

He goes on to note:

> Whatever be said to be their prejudice, by interested persons, educated Indians can not be ungrateful or unmindful of the blessings that have followed in the train of the

British rule in India. In the opinion of some persons it may be a mistake to educate the Indians, and it may be desirable to keep them in blissful ignorance; but there is no gainsaying the fact that it is they, and they only, whose active and *intelligent* faith is that "in the strength of the British rule is India's security, and in its maintenance her prosperity."

Only the first half of canto I, the invocation, is reprinted below.

Oriental Welcome to Their Most Gracious Majesties the King-Emperor and the Queen-Empress (Cawnpore: 1911)[54]

Canto I.

Invocation.

Wake up! wake up! too long hath slept
    In bowers wild, and rude, unkept;
For long, Himalayan[55] height ascended not,
    Nor flight to Heaven did attempt thy thought.
Thy lyre, thrown aside, hath lain
    Covered with moss, nor did enchain
The soul to happy slavery,
    With tones of sweetest witchery.

Muse! How long will sleep on Earth?
    Wake up! wake up! Has given birth,
The Time, the one, that will enhance
    A million-fold to thee due worth.

Did never chance for thee arise
    For so much honour, such a prize,
Twice Ram[56] did leave, and Chand[57] did go,
    And Akbar[58] left, to thee, thy woe.

---

54 Tej Shankar Kochak, *Oriental Welcome to Their Most Gracious Majesties the King-Emperor and the Queen-Empress* (Cawnpore: T. S. Kochak, 1911).
55 [Poet's Note: Himalayan; the Himalayas are the Olympia of an Indian poet.]
56 [Poet's Note: Ram; Raja Ram Chandra, the king-incarnate of the Hindus.] The mythical prince Rama, eventual ruler of the kingdom of Ayodhya, in the modern-day state of Uttar Pradesh, is the hero of the ancient Hindu epic, the *Ramayana*.
57 [Poet's Note: Chand; the poet-laureate of the court of Prithiraj, the last Hindu emperor of India.] Chand Bardai, regarded as the first major poet in Hindi, composed the *Prithviraj Raso* during the late twelfth century. Authorship of the poem is a source of some controversy.
58 [Poet's Note: Akbar; the Great Mughal, the famous emperor of India.] Akbar (1542–1605): considered one of the great leaders of the Mughal Empire, Akbar ruled from 1556 until his death. He expanded the reach of the Empire over the subcontinent to include almost all of northern India,

I bring for thee few English string.
    Put on thy lyre do but sing;
Once more, Heavenly hand of thine
    Sweep the cords, with theme sublime.

She stirs! the prayer not in vain!
    She throws aside the sloth, that lain
So long, on her ecstatic mind,
    She looks around, and different find:
The scene is changed, and there stands
    A mighty camp, her view commands.
A bustle, round she hears:
    She rubs her eyes, and fears:
A dream! a dream! But only dream,
    A vision all around her seem.
She looks around, and wildly frown;
    Where gone her robe, and where the crown.
The lyre neglected, there is laid;
    No youth attends, nor fairy maid;
She seeks, but does, in ken, not find
    Her loving Sura,[59] nor Kali[60] hind,
Nor Tulsi[61] shows her pious face;
    Her all about bewild'ring maze!
She looks, and out the bow'r stands,
    A swain in form, with folded hands.
"O youth! Who thou? What is thy want?"
    In voice sonorous Muse enchant.
Fearing, trembling, crouching, creeping low,
    He bends his head, and throws a lowly bow.

---

reformed the central administration system and instituted a more efficient tax-collection process. His tolerance and sympathy towards other Alternately, with other critics, religions, illustrated in part by including a number of Hindus in the imperial bureaucracy and allowing Hindu territories within the Empire a measure of autonomy, ensured the loyalty of many non-Muslims.

59 [Poet's Note: Sura; Sura Dass, one of the sweetest Hindu poets, the author of the well-known Divine love songs. It is said that in his youth he was a man of a roving nature, once being entangled in a love affair, he got himself blinded; this penance proved a turning point in his life. He received the Light, and turned into the best poet of his time, and that of the time to come.] Suradas (1483?–1563?): thought to have born in Braj (in the modern-day state of Uttar Pradesh) and was a *bhakti* (devotional poet) known for his lyrics addressed to the Hindu god, Krishna.

60 [Poet's Note: Kali; Kali Dass, the famous dramatist of Ind; by birth he was a cowboy or a shepherd.] Kalidas: classical Sanskrit writer who is thought to have lived during the fifth century under the Gupta dynasty. His works include the long lyric poems, *Meghaduta* and *Ritu-samhara*, as well as two epic poems and three plays.

61 [Poet's Note: Tulsi; Tulsi Dass, the author of the Hindi version of the Ramayana, the Bible of India.] The *bhakti* (devotional) poet Tulsidas (1543?–1623) is thought to have been born in Rajpur (in the modern-day state of Uttar Pradesh). His most famous work, *Ramacharitmanas*, is an epic poem addressed to the Hindu god Rama.

"Goddess of Earth! and Muse of Heaven!
    Deign to take this humble Brahmin
To Christian court of King Emperor,
    With gems from thine celestial treasure.
To Rishis[62] race, I do belong,
    Who first on Earth inspired song;
Them first, thou had thy favours shown;
    In thine celestial light had grown,
They, fit vassals of thy domain,
    Attendants worthy of thy train.
Yet nobler task, they never found
    Though epics long they did unwound –
Than one, invoke I thee this hour,
    And pray to thee to leave thy bow'r;
Fill me with thine Heavenly fire,
    To welcome Indies' Mighty Sire."

Lo! Muse smiles, looks up benign;
    Now beats my heart, for hopes for mine
Are 'bout to be fully realize':
    Her joyful glance give all I prize.
I swoon, and loose my conscious power,
    My soul ascends, and rises higher,
Himalayan heights, in clouds 'tis lost;
    A ling'ring look below it cast –
Lest reel my head, and down me fall –
    As raised, so Muse support thy thrall.

My bosom swells, and songs full throated
    Crowd upon my brain,
Enchanting scenes, and tunes full suited
    Enter close in train.

[63]In Bombay they, though, do prepare
    Papier Mache, children's scene.
At Delhi grandly camps in air,
    Schemes in India never been;

Some worldly men, of worldly race,
    Prepare for King a hunt,
And hope to please him by a chase,
    In woods with roar and grunt.

---

62 [Poet's Note: Rishi; a generic name in the Vedic Period for the Brahmins who received inspiration from God.]
63 [Poet's Note: The usual bragging of an Indian poet.]

For me – since thy protection taken,
    Thy light, who turns, to sail, his beacon,
On shoreless mane of storied Time,
    Bedecked with isles of happy clime, –
Where every haven is gate to Heaven,
    And kings are gods on earth there e'en –
 Not me, to welcome thus is meet,
    Not me, who stands so near thy seat.
O! ope' the portals of my soul,
    And light effulgent, out it roll,
Elysium's choicest blooming rose,
    Strew the path, where'er King goes.
Let me impress on endless time,
    For all the ages, all the clime:
"On Her, the King a look hath thrown,"
    "To Zenith Height, Her Luck hath grown."
Let me proclaim to end – King's fa'our –
    Of human ken, through subtle air,
With notes of sweet commotion,
    All done by England's only Sun.

                […]

Sushila Harkishen Lal

No biographical information is available on this author, whose *Stray Thoughts* seems to be her only published work. This collection includes a series of short poems: most poems consist of one stanza, rendered on one page although occasionally a poem is carried over several stanzas/pages. Printed on thick paper, this well-made little volume is dedicated "to my parents."

Stray Thoughts (Lahore: 1918)[64]

Dreams

I.

The strong bright Indian sun was shining
On the mighty roaring river,
And the sweetest streamlet flowing,
Flowing on for ever.

---

64 Sushila Harkishen Lal, *Stray Thoughts* (Lahore: n. p., 1918).

II.

Oh! it was a lovely scene,
As ever heart of man did dream.
Clearer than the clearest mirror,
Bathed in sunlight.

III.

Clothed in silver,
Was that mighty roaring river;
Heart of dreamer, cease to dream,
Look yet at this wondrous stream.

IV.

If ye dream of Paradise,
Then, fair dreamer dream no more,
For Paradise is very near,
Earthly Heaven is only here.

V.

Fairest land with lovely flowers,
Greenest grass and shady trees,
Bluest skies and rippling streams,
These, dear dreamer are you dreams.

VI.

Shining in bright sunlight,
All are here within thy sight.
Lovely lands may soon be lost,
Lose them not at any cost.

VII.

Why do ye then pause to think?
Soon decide and see this land,
Years will come and time will go.
The end will come before you know.

South

South India encompasses the Madras presidency and its various outlying districts including the modern-day states of Tamil Nadu, Andhra Pradesh, Kerala and Karnataka. Madras (now Chennai), where most of the poetry reprinted here was published, was known as the center of the Theosophical Society (and the home of the Theosophist Annie Besant) and was particularly vocal in its admiration for Lord Ripon, viceroy of India. During the nineteenth century, it also became the home of numerous institutions such as the Madras Christian College founded in 1837 by Scottish missionaries and the *Hindu*, an English-language newspaper founded by Madrassi social reformer G. Subramania Iyer and others as a weekly in 1878 (it was transformed into a daily in 1889). Both institutions survive to this day. Many of the poets reprinted here, including Harindranath Chattopadhyay (brother of Sarojini Naidu) and Nizamat Jung were from Hyderabad, a city shaped by its Mughal history. The Nizams, hereditary Muslim princes, ruled Hyderabad on behalf of the Mughal emperors and were allowed to retain nominal control of the city under the British Empire after the decisive fall of the Mughal Empire in 1857. The Nizams, particularly Mahbub Ali Khan, were known as patrons of the arts. Both Hyderabad and Madras were especially rich in English-language poetic education and production.

R. Sivasankara Pandiya

Pandiya (1853–1899) founded the Hindu Tract Society in 1887 and the Hindu Theological College in Madras in 1889. He also published *The Duties of the Natives of India to their Rulers and their country: a Public Lecture* (1888) as part of the Indian National Congress Series and various works intended for students, many of which expounded upon Hindu maxims. The long title poem of the collection *The Empress of India* (1888) details the benefits of British rule and loyalty to Queen Victoria, who was proclaimed empress of India at the Delhi Durbar in 1877. Pandiya notes that this English-language poem is a translation of a poem originally composed by him in Telugu. His English "translation" was first published in 1876 (possibly in a periodical or as a pamphlet) and later included in this longer collection. Reprints of reviews of this poem from both the British and Indian press are also included in the collection. It seems from these reviews that British reviewers praised the poem for its sentiments of loyalty to Empire although, ironically, Pandiya also spends much time glorifying an ancient Indian past, a supposedly golden age of culture, *before* British rule.

The Empress of India and Other Poems (Madras: 1888)[1]

Empress of India and Indian Poets

Though thou, our Empress good, art led aright
By ori'nt beams and beacons new and bright,
Though lustrous lords, with well-weigh'd measures rule
Our classic lands, still, as a vermicule[2]
Eats up the roots of mighty trees that fall
Prostrate on earth, a prey to th' axeman's gall,
So sullies all thy reign an only stain
That thou alone cans't well efface afmain.
Hence, Mother Queen, this truth with kindness hear
That native bards need a rich right royal cheer;
They pine away, like forest blooms, in grief,
Remote to wealth or health or ev'n relief;
Now, strange! no native monarch deigns to guard
This fancy's brood from mis'ries, fell and hard;
Unlike those worthy emperors of old,
Who valu'd poets wise above all gold,
And cheer'd minds with riches rasi'd and list;
They prided in their friendship, love, and grace,
Right trusting that the poets heav'nly race
Alone is skill'd to propagate across
Wide oceans, lands their glory's gloss,
Which 'lone will live beyond this mortal clay,
Untost by time or place, like the solar ray.
Thus, see, Manu, that Founder great of man,[3]
Whose Code divine now our great Hindustan,
Though once the world it sway'd, with firmness sways,
From time out of mind, admir'd by ev'ry race,
Did honour poesy by bidding Bhrugu[4]
Expound his laws, so pure and just and true.
Thus India rul'd that true and dut'ful Ram
Whose fame, by Valmiki write, the Ramayanam[5]

---

1 R. Sivasankara Pandiya, *The Empress of India and Other Poems*, 2nd ed. (Madras: Tawker Sadananda, 1888).
2 Vermicule: small worm or worm-like creature; a maggot or grub (n. "vermicule" *OED*).
3 Manu: in some strands of Hinduism, the first king, or founder, of the race.
4 Bhrugu, or Bhrigu: one of the great sages of ancient India and said to have compiled the tenets of predictive astrology.
5 Valmiki: poet-sage who is usually thought to have authored the "original," authoritative version of the Hindu epic, the *Ramayana* around 300 BCE. He also appears as a character within the narrative of the *Ramayana* itself. The hero Rama was thought to be an ideal ruler: wise, just and kind.

Extends unceasing to Setu's[6] sacred shoals
From high Himalayan peaks that mock the poles.
Right worthy justice, peace, and plenty decked
His reign, which neither foes nor carpers specked;
So bountiful Yudhistra's[7] noble name
Sage Vyasa's Bharat[8] fair adorns with fame;
Thus daring Vikramadit's[9] wondrous deeds,
Unnumber'd verses praise in all Ind'an meads
Thus the learned Bhoja Raj,[10] the patron renown'd
Of Kalidas[11] whose well-made elys'an sound
Soars higher than ev'n Avon's famous swan,[12]
Sway'd India's sceptre, lov'd by ev'ry man.
Those noble guardians of the po'tic child
Are seen no more, but, their memoires, great and mild,
Lie treasur'd firm in many a grateful heart;
Then, Empress new, shouldst not thou shew the part
Which India's anc'ent Chakravarty's[13] grac'd,
That India's Sixteen mighty kings embrac'd.
Look, India's worthy sage thus truly said,
"What for, should poets seek a crowned head."
Why far, thy noble Scot with frankness spake: –
"Let kinds and councils make, again unmake
Unnuber'd, harsh, and bulky laws and codes,
Let only poets true their people's odes,

---

6 Ram Setu, or Rama's Bridge: chain of limestone shoals that indicates a former land connection between what is now the southern coast of India and Sri Lanka. In the ancient Hindu epic, the *Ramayana*, the bridge is built at Rama's command in order to allow him to cross to Sri Lanka to rescue his wife Sita from the demon-king Ravana.

7 Yudhistra, or Yudhithira: eldest son of King Pandu and the leader of the heroic Pandavas in the Kurukshetra War depicted in the ancient Hindu epic, the *Mahabharata*.

8 The sage Vyasa (who, as a historical figure, may have lived around 1500 BCE) is credited with arranging the *Vedas*, the ancient Hindu Sanskrit scriptures revealed by the gods and predating the composition of the Hindu epics. Authorship of the authoritative Sanskrit *Mahabharata* is traditionally attributed to Vyasa, who as a character within the epic conveys the narrative of the epic to the god Ganesha, who acts as transcriber.

9 Vikramadit, or Vikramaditya: legendary king of Ujjain. He is regarded as an ideal ruler and the first great Hindu king who acted as patron to the "nine gems" (some of the most well-regarded writers) of Sanksrit literature.

10 Bhoja Raj (943–1022), or Bhoja-raja: ruler of Dhara in the current-day state of Madhya Pradesh. Bhoja Raj was a remarkably prolific Sanskrit scholar who wrote on topics such as ethics, religion and philosophy.

11 Very little is known about the classical Sanskrit writer Kalidas, who is thought to have lived during the fifth century under the Gupta dynasty. His works include the long lyric poems, *Meghaduta* and *Ritu-samhara*, as well as two epic poems and three plays.

12 "Avon's famous swan": Shakespeare, whose birthplace was Stratford-upon-Avon.

13 *Chakravarty*: king of kings, or an emperor in Sanskrit.

With spirit and life, with zeal and force, compose,
And, then, who wins the white unfaded rose,
Who bears the palm, with lovely laurels crown'd,
Let judges high decide with thoughts profound"
Of the seven memorials of man on earth,
Behold, none causes truer joy and mirth,
None stands with firmer hold the baneful time,
Than poesy, that art divine, sublime,
Which joys celestial and true imparts
To its votaries of firm and spotless hearts.
Of the seven ornaments of royal courts
Except good poets, see, all serve for sports.
Hence, Queen of that island pure, which noble Alfred grac'd,[14]
Which Shakespeare's silver lines with world-wide glory lac'd?
And Empress of this land which nobler Rama sway'd,
Which Valmiki's golden lays with boundless fame array'd?
If titles, long and round, and ribbons, blue and bright,
Are to be more than empty sounds and tinsels light,
Extend to poets poor of Ind thy patronage,
With a truly royal heart and hand them encourage,
That they may write in letters firm, on mem'ry's page,
"That Queen Victoria's sway in Ind is a golden age."

The University of Madras[15]
(To commemorate the celebration of its twenty-seventh Anniversary)

Lord Canning great, our Viceroy wise and bold,
In Eighteen Fifty Seven's famous year,[16]
Vouchsaf'd with kindness to our city dear
Every great boon that knowledge gives; behold!
And like a cygnet[17] that doth soon unfold
New feathers, take pure milk, quit water clear,
Doth our University, in its career,
Progress, well watch'd by patrons young and old.
Right gladly here without distinctions base

---

14 "Alfred grac'd": this reference seems to be to the poet Alfred, Lord Tennyson, who died in 1892.
15 The University of Madras was founded by Royal Charter in 1857; universities also were founded in Bombay and Calcutta of the same year.
16 Charles Canning (1812–1862): governor-general of India during the 1857 Indian Uprising (termed the "Sepoy Mutiny" by the British during the nineteenth century) and thus at the time of the university's founding.
17 Cygnet: young swan (n. "cygnet" OED).

Of sex or creed or hue, all taste, and lo!
Securely still, the fruits of knowledge sweet.
Propell'd by Harris, drawn by Duff apace,[18]
E'er onward this Minerva's car doth go
Rightly: may God it grant new blessings meet.

Krupabai Satthianadhan

Krupabai Satthianadhan (1862–1894), who died tragically at a young age from tuberculosis, is often considered the first Indian woman novelist in English. Born to a family of Christian converts, she was the first wife of the Christian educator Samuel Satthianadhan, whose second wife, Kamala Satthianadhan, was founder and editor of *The Indian Ladies' Magazine*, a Madras-based periodical. Krupabai Satthianadhan's two novels, *Kamala: A Story of Hindu Life* (1894) and *Saguna: A Story of Native Christian Life* (1895), are remarkable for their construction of Indian female heroines caught between different cultures (Indian and English, Hindu, and Christian, "traditional" and "modern"). In a "Memoir" published with the latter novel, Mrs. H. B. Grigg writes: "Unlike Toru Dutt of Bengal, who has been called her prototype, the authoress of Kamala lived to see her literary efforts recognized... Her writings seem even better known to English than to Indian readers, some of them having been reviewed in flattering terms in the leading English Journals." These writings include essays on the promotion of female education and some poetry, which were collected and published posthumously as *Miscellaneous Writings of Krupabai Satthianadhan* (1896).

Miscellaneous Writings of Krupabai Satthianadhan (Madras: 1896)[19]

Recollections of Childhood

Sweet sad strain!
Sing to me again,
Song of my land
On this foreign strand. –
What mem'ries dost awake
Of hill, wood and lake,
Of a sweet happy home
Far from where I roam!

---

18 George Francis Robert Harris (1810–1872): Liberal politician who acted as governor of Madras from 1854–1859. Alexander Duff (1806–1878): Scottish missionary and educator in India who played a part in establishing the University of Calcutta.

19 Krupabai Satthianadhan, *The Miscellaneous Writings of Krupabai Satthianadhan* (Madras: Srinivasa Varadachari, 1896).

Of sister, brother dear,
Now no longer near;
A mother's sweet smiles;
Childhood's simple wiles;
Of mirthful pleasure,
Joys' full measure;
When all the world was fair
With spirits light as air,
We carolled many a glee
Under the spreading tree;
Dreamt happy dreams,
That like sunny gleams
E'en now around me play
And cheer my weary way.
Oft my days they brighten,
Shadow and gloom lighten,
With vistas bright of deeds
Not meant for our baser needs.
Dreams of greatness
Chastened loveliness
Seen through the haze
Of sweet innocent days!
What transformations wrought,
What wonders seem fraught,
In the visions of childhood
Roaming free midst stream and wood!

Sweet sad strain!
Command those dreams again;
Once more let me be a child
In nature's innocence wild,
Making moments bright
With dreams of heavenly light.
Through the mist of years,
A heart full of tears,
My playmates I see again
Who long in the grave have lain.
Some o'er seas drear and dark,
Fearless steer their bark,
Or in foreign lands they roam
Far, far from home.
O, what longings vain
Fill my heart with pain!
Cease, sad strain!
We shall all meet again
In one happy home at last
When parting and tears are past.

Social Intercourse between Europeans and Natives

It was an English company fair
    That sat o'er the green,
In the balmy evening air,
    Enjoying the tropic scene.

A dark-browed Indian girl was brought,
    Here by a swarthy lad,
Modest her mien and wonder-fraught,
    Her downcast eyes so sad.

Alarm'd then the ladies grew,
    And their skirts around them drew,
Asking each of other what it means.
    "Social intercourse! I ween,"

A fair one promptly replied.
    And 'Oh!' was exclaimed all around;
And each with indifference vied
    To show her her proper ground.

Then bewildered a seat she takes,
    The last that she can find;
With inward trembling the hand she shakes
    Of her hostess kind.

Then ominous whispers ran,
    Which faintly around were heard;
And many a comment behind the fan,
    In each other's ear was poured.

One, bolder, the girl now questioned straight
    As to her family and name;
The august assemblage her answer wait,
    But answer none did she frame.

To move her lips so sore afraid,
    Sat the damsel awed:
While the swift whispers of 'Bashful' and 'Illbred,'
    From dainty lips now flowed.

Some a slight sneer surpressed [sic]
    And seemed unconcerned;
And some by the farce resistless oppressed,
    Their heads in haste they turned.

Thus for a weary hour and more,
    She sat bedecked a statue bright;
The *sweet* intercourse at last was o'er,
    And with it a memorable sight.

M.V. Venkatasubba Aiyar

It has been difficult to find any additional information on this author although it can be inferred from the dedication in this volume of poetry that he was an "ardent admirer and friend" of T. Ramakrishna Pillai, author of *Tales of Ind* (sections of which are published in the "Abroad" section). Indeed, many of Aiyar's poems seem to be influenced by the work of Ramakrishna. One long poem, "The Falcon, or Love's Triumph" is set in "Krishnapore," signifying a generic South Indian village, and featuring a hero and heroine named after an iconic couple in Hinduism, Krishna, and Radha (a parallel to Ramakrishna's naming of the hero and heroine of one of his poems, Rama and Seeta).

Ventures in Verse (Madras: 1899)[20]

To the Land of My Birth
Prefatory poem

Belovéd Land! though barren,[21] you appear
The one bright spot in all the world's expanse
Whose contemplation doth my joys enhance,
Or with a soothing power my gloom doth clear!
Where'er my lot is cast, Hope still sustains
My drooping heart and makes me contemplate
With joy that, though a plaything of my fate
To slave for it and meekly bear my pains,
A time shall come when I shall seek your strand
To rest my wearied limbs, from labour freed
And from the baneful influence of greed;
For are you not my own, my native land
Teeming with sweet remembrance of the days
Now past, on which with wistful glance I gaze?

---

20 M.V. Venkatasubba Aiyar, *Ventures in Verse* (Madras: Srinivasa Varadhachari, 1899).
21 Aiyar may be referring to the drought-induced famine of 1876–1879, which affected the Deccan region or to a metaphorical "barren[ness]."

Sonnets, I. Faith

All earthly power by time and space is bound!
Nations once mighty are to-day as weak
As others which, now strong, had once been meek.
And when to further conquest nought is found
The mighty victor heaves a sigh profound!
But when the time comes and his race is run,
His weakest foe, his lands, would overrun,
And mighty grown would drag him to the ground!
But who so mighty as, of Faith, could trace
The power when rightly followed, and reveal
How sweet the joy he, at his heart, would feel
Unless upon him comes the heavenly grace?
Such is the Faith that doth sustain and cheer
Our drooping heart and chase away our fear!

Ravana's Doom
An Episode from the Ramayana[22]

"With sacrifice before the morn
To free us from our state forlorn
To gods divine we made our vow
On us their mighty help bestow.
With each returning day, the sighs
Of widows and the orphans' cries,
That pierce our hearts with anguish, find
No response in their heavenly mind!
What wonder, then, that men should lose
Their faith when gods their help refuse?
We are too feeble to withstand
The havoc of the tyrant's hand!
He knows our weakness and derides
The fear that hides our heavenly guides!
Not one he spares, from Prince to page,
And saint and Brahman and the sage!

---

22 Ravan: mythical ruler of Lanka, or modern-day Sri Lanka, and great antagonist of Prince Rama in the ancient Hindu epic, the *Ramayana*. Following Ravana's abduction of Rama's wife Sita, Rama wages war against Ravana to rescue his wife. Ravana was reconfigured as an interestingly tragic hero by some Indian-English poets such as Michael Madhusudhan Dutt although Aiyar is unsympathetic to him here. Aiyar's focus in this poem is Ravana's former life as King Padmasura, ruler of the rakshasas, *before* his reincarnation as King Ravana, ruler of the rakshasas. Ravana's defeat by Rama in the *Ramayana* is caused by the former's actions as Padmasura in a prior life in this telling.

So, should ere long the gods decline
To help us with their might divine,
Then surely we shall raise the pyre
And light it with our sacred fire,
And in the leaping flames shall we
For all our woes a finish see!"

So spake a hermit, far renowned
For purity and knowledge sound,
As in a forest, dark and drear,
Far from the object of their fear,
The sages in a conclave meet
To find the means that would defeat
The Rakshas[23] in his wild career,
Whose very name inspires a fear
Far greater than the thoughts of Hell
In such as joy in actions fell!
And Ravana, in pride of might,
In cruelties had sought delight;
For who was there would dare to meet
His army and their strength defeat,
And make him think his cause forlorn
Who feared not one of woman born?
The simple Siva,[24] long ago,
Pleased with his penance, did bestow
A gift[25] that did his life secure
From gods divine and angels pure!

While by his cruelties oppressed
The sages thus their plaints addressed,
The gods divine in Council State
Are met together and debate
How they could best relieve the land
Of Ravan and his cruel band.
They knew his might and dared not fight
Lest in their fall he take delight;
For mighty though they were, they knew
With Siva's gift he mightier grew.
The people on their help rely
And for the death of Ravan cry.

---

23 *Rakshas*, or *rakshasas*: demons who inhabit the forests in Hindu mythology.
24 Siva, or Shiva: one of the major Hindu deities and often represented as one aspect of the Trimurti, which also included Vishnu and Brahma. Shiva is able to destroy and thus transform.
25 [Poet's Note: The boon that he will not meet his death at the hands of gods, &c.; in fact, from all except man.] This boon is the reason Rama, a manifestation of the god Vishnu, is able to defeat Ravana.

But ere they should this weakness see
And from their blind allegiance flee,
The Rakshas should be crushed – and how
But with the help of God above?

So they to Brahma[26] went and told
The evils wrought by Ravan bold.
They said: "Oh Lord! at thy behest
We bear his wrongs, calm though opprest.
Sky, earth and hell, all share the same
And tremble at his very name:
The Lord of Day restrains his glow,
The Wind dare not with fierceness blow,
The Ocean at his dread command
Its foamy waters brings to stand!
Oh Brahma! Lend us, then, Thy aid,
And slay this fiend! We are afraid!"

They ceased. "One only course have we,"
He said, "of him to make you free.
The giant proud, in utter scorn,
Cared not for foes of woman born!
Secure from others he shall find
His death in one of human kind.
And well you know how Vishnu laid
The Husband[27] of the Mountain Maid[28]
In obligations great, when He,
Fell Padma's[29] penance pleased to see,
Gave him a gift[30] of deadly might,
A token of his great delight.
How Siva, flying from this foe,
To Vishnu sent a cry for aid;
Nor how, He, like a handsome Maid,
Before the Rakshas stood – a sight
To move e'en hermits to delight!

---

26 [Poet's Note: The Creator.] Brahma is one of the major Hindu deities and is one aspect of the Trimurti, which also included Vishnu and Shiva.
27 [Poet's Note: Siva]
28 [Poet's Note: Parvati, Siva's spouse and daughter of Mount Himalayas.]
29 Padma, or King Padmasura, ruler of the rakshasas, was bringing trouble to the Devas, or minor divinities, who collectively beseeched the god Vishnu for aide.
30 [Poet's Note: The gift was that any one on whose head Padmasura laid his right hand will be consumed by fire. Padmasura wanted to try if the gift was effective on Siva himself, but was frustrated as described further on!]

How Padma, at her sly command,
In act of praying, laid his hand
Upon his head, when soon he gained
A knowledge of the gift obtained!
For straight the fingers touched his head
By fire consumed he fell down dead!
You know these. Then I need not say
In Him alone your chances lay."

While with such soothing words he cheered
Their drooping hearts, in time appeared
Lord Vishnu with his counsel wise,
Some plan to free them, to devise.
Conch, discus and the mighty mace
He bore; and when his godly face
And arms with armlets of bright gold
These lesser gods did but behold,
One universal shout they raised
And trutfully [sic] His glories praised.
He was their only hope, they knew,
Whom with a grateful heart and true
They hailed – as does a farmer greet
The showers, his wistful eyes, that meet!
He listened to their tale of woe
And promised safety from the foe.
Then joined they of that heavenly throng
Their voices in a choral song
That Madhu's[31] Victor once again
A success o'er the foe obtain!

Meanwhile the hermits, in despair,
The all-consuming fire prepare,
And in a body seek relief
For all their woes and for their grief!
The sacred flames impatient roar
Before the rites are well-nigh o'er!
And one by one the hermits near
The sacred pyre without a fear.
But ere they take the fatal leap,
Ere they the fruits of rashness reap,
From midst their ranks in accents clear
These hope-inspiring words they hear:

---

31 [Poet's Note: Madhu was a Rakshasa whom Vishnu killed on one occasion.] *Rakshasas*: demons in Hindu mythology.

"Oh brethren! tarry yet, I pray,
Nor cast your precious lives away!
The Lord, in pity for your fear,
Of Ravan fierce the earth will clear!
And for this purpose will be born
Of woman and the worlds adorn!
Ayodhya's King, too much of late,
Renounced the world disconsolate
That in his closing days he sees
No winsome lad his heart to please,
And save him from that hell which none
Can shun that dies without a son!
The very name[32] doth teach us clear
Without it what we have to fear!
And Vishnu, to relieve his grief
And to the people bring relief,
To Royal Dusruth[33] will be born,
And thus revive his hopes forlorn
Of safety from the dreaded hell,
And, as of womanborn will quell
The might of Ravan and his band
And from their grasp release the land!
And under him the land shall groan
With plenty; his great renown
From far and near shall draw away
The wisest to his gentle sway!
And merit, might in itself,
Shall scorn the might of power or pelf!
In merit rich the weaker still
Will find a bulwark in his will!
The strong shall under him be taught
To love and aid the weaker lot!
Such peace shall reign that men will say
Those days had never passed away!
His life so great, so good his aim,
That Nature too shall loud proclaim:
'Here *was* a man! Where shall we find
Another of his noble mind?'"

---

32 [Poet's Note: Puthran, meaning son, is a Sanskrit word meaning one who saves (the father) from the hell called "Puth." There is a belief among us that those who die without a son will be hurled down into this hell.]
33 Dusruth, or King Dasharatha: Rama's father.

>The sages hear them and rejoice
>That still for them in store are joys
>Untainted with the thoughts of fear
>That aught will mar their faith sincere.
>The raging fire they need no more
>But for some sacred rites as yore!
>They hear and to their homes repair
>Where was till then nought but despair!
>Indra[34] that did this news convey
>From where the Lord of Heaven held sway
>Returned home with a lighter heart
>That in this deed he had a part!
>So also is a noble mind
>To work some good to human kind!

M. Dinakara

Dinakara's poetry takes as its subject the Boer War. In many ways, Dinakara's poetry expresses jingoistic sentiments similar to those found in the poetry of Alfred Austin and Kipling (although the latter evinces a rather more complicated relationship to imperialist expansion, "the white man's burden," and India). Dinakara dedicates his volume "To the British Army of all Arms, and to the brave Colonials who forgot not the Mother Country in her day of trial; in profound admiration." His rhetorical positioning echoed that of many Indians at the time; even Gandhi was a public supporter of British troops during the Boer War and lent his services to the war effort through the Red Cross. Yet Dinakara's hawkish sentiments are never interrogated. As he writes in his "Prologue: The British Soldier, and his Destiny": "All the modern dire agencies to kill, were by the Boers, brought to bear upon the British, in the battle of Elandslaagte; and what was more, they had all the advantage of position… From start to finish, the assault was nothing more than a struggle to live: to get through the gusts of withering fire; and at the throats that pumped them… the scene depicted by eye-witnesses, as the assaulters struggled over the last half mile of sloping glacis, were all but decimated, – is most appalling, and harrowing…" Dinakara goes on to claim that the determination and self-sacrifice of the British soldier against advances in modern weaponry, will prevail: "So in spite of achievements which Man has achieved, or will achieve, in implements of warfare, we fall back on mother Nature's endowments of Mind, and Constitution, as the primary, and essential factors, to decide the issue of a war, be the weapons ever so deadly… And what a strong Moral incentive to self-sacrifice ever stands by the Christian soldier, – whether he plod through the miasmatic exhalations

---

34 [Poet's Note: The chief of the minor gods – the god of rain.] Indra: god of thunder and rain. In the *Vedas*, the religious scriptures predating the Hindu epics, Indra is described as the ruler of the gods but was later supplanted in importance by the Trimurti (which is composed of the gods Brahma, Vishnu and Shiva).

of the West African forest, to prevent that other human sacrifice of savagery, or he sit fast as at Ladysmith, amid devastating shells; or he charge in the face of the leaden sleet as at Elanslaagte or at Colenso – in that perfect Example of the World's Great Martyr: – Christ!"

A Ballad of the Boer War, Written for the Day of the *Coronation* of Their Most Gracious Majesties the King Emperor Edward VII and Queen Alexandra in Celebration of the Prowess of the British Army (Ramnad: 1902)[35]

The Gathering

Around the world, the girdling Call,
Electric sped the dire alarm;
From far, and near, from cot, and hall,
Come sons from Arctic climes, and warm.

Soon the Legionary of England,[36]
Marshalled o'er the Ocean's face;
Gathering thick as bees a-thousand –
Freedom's champions, by God's grace!

Six thousand miles, o'er Ocean's track,
Flowed swift the stream of Army Corps;
In freighted Might, the world doth lack,
The like to show in past-day lores.

Proudly waving her blazonry,
From the transports' serried heights;
Loured the steely Bulwarks by,
That guard her home, and o'er-sea rights.

---

35 M. Dinakara, *A Ballad of the Boer War, Written for the Day of the "Coronation" of Their Most Gracious Majesties the King Emperor Edward VII and Queen Alexandra in Celebration of the Prowess of the British Army* (Ramnad: Lakshmi Vilas, 1902).

36 "Legionary of England": most likely refers to the soldiers recruited from all over the Empire, including the British Raj.

From where the ancient flood had given,
A past-day World, as England's fee;[37]
And Tasman's Land by Pluto riven,[38] –
Her White Sons came with will, and gree.[39]

From Kiwi Land,[40] and Beaver Land,[41]
As true, and staunch, as steel can be;
To fight for Queen, and Mother-land,
Her White Sons came with will, and gree.

From where the Sacred Gunga flows;
Where palmy Lunka[42] gems the sea;
From where the luscious ruby grows; – [43]
Her White Sons came, with will, and gree.

And fast from North, South, East, and West,
O'er a realm, where all the Seasons home;
But not the Sun, which now'th no rest
Her sons came o'er the sea's white foam.

How Great Britain was Regenerated and Became 'Greater Britain'

Read here the same old lesson writ,
Great Homer in his Iliad read;
Of how the gods who ruling sit,
Reclaim the Fit tho' way-ward led:

Of ways, which wean a race from Sloth –
A Sloth that dulls Life's better state
To cope with World's progressive growth,
Compels it to degenerate.

---

37 [Poet's Note: Australia]
38 Abel Tasman (1603–1659): Dutch explorer who "discovered" and named this island Van Dieman's Land after the governor-general of the Dutch East Indies (the island is now known as Tasmania). Pluto: god of the underworld in Roman mythology. Tasmania contributed a number of troops for the fight against the Boers in the Second Boer War.
39 Gree: goodwill or pre-eminence or victory in battle (n. "gree" *OED*).
40 [Poet's Note: New Zealand]
41 [Poet's Note: Canada]
42 Lunka, or Lanka: Sri Lanka.
43 [Poet's Note: Burma]

To England, Trial's day hath brought
The knell of purblind Sophistry;
Of Rules of war in office wrought,
That make machines of soldiery:

Of falt'ring Faith[44]; egregious Creed,
That stayed when Honour called to smite;[45]
Of Fear, that preached a canting rede[46]
Then quibbled, and baulked in doing right.[47]

Tho' hind'ring forces, Life beset
To wrest its worth, and destined meed;
But, God discerns in whom is met
The utmost scope the world to lead.

In time, He sends War's chast'ning fires,
And in the van Humility;
When *lo*, the slumb'ring fire aspires,
And bursts into activity.

---

44 [Poet's Note: 'Of faltering Faith' – "When the revolution broke out, (in 1880) Mr. Gladstone had declared in the strongest language that the annexation could not be revoked and that the Queen's authority must be vindicated. When the Boers began to be successful and Mr. Gladstone found himself face to face with a difficult and expensive war, he capitulated abjectly...In the minds of the Englishmen in South Africa that surrender left a bitterness and contempt of the Imperial Government which have hardly yet been effaced. Its outcome has been feverish unrest in South Africa for eighteen years, culminating in a long and desperate struggle for supremacy, between the Transvaal and the Imperial Government." – The Times History of the War in South Africa.] William Ewart Gladstone (1809–1898): served several terms as Liberal prime minister of Great Britain (1868–1874; 1880–1885; 1886; 1892–1894).

45 [Poet's Note: "Egregious Creed that stayed…" – …Since then, up till the last war, England has held herself aloof, in spite of the repeated appeals of the Uitlanders to her, to right their wrongs; and although the terms of the Pretoria, and London Conventions were again and again deliberately violated by President Kruger.]

46 Rede: counsel or advice given; or a counsel, decision, or resolve taken by one or more persons (n. "rede" *OED*).

47 [Poet's Note: "Of fear that preached a canting rede…" – …The Pretoria Convention, and afterwards the London Convention, did not fulfil this policy of "magnanimity"; but gave to the State of Transvaal a status among the World's Goverments, that finds no parallel in the World's History. But the fact remained that the independence of the Transvaal was made to depend upon the observance by its Government of the terms set forth in the Pretoria, and London, Conventions. It is a matter for wonder that Kruger's violation of the terms of the war earlier than she did, on the Uitlander wrongs and many another wrong of political concern to England.]

Then, England's finest force did tell:
Humility was grimly worn;
Each loss the more resolve did swell,
To nothing save to reach the bourn.

What tho' the Muse, who oft had hymned.
Of English arms, in laurels wreathed;
Now veiled her theme, in words that seemed,
The moaning dirge by Sorrow breathed.

What tho' the tale of War loud wailed: –
'Penn Symon's dead: Natal, be-set:
Dundee, tho' won, is lost' – none quailed:[48]
But stern Resolve, sate sterner yet.

And fraught with stern contrasting force,
The lesson came, tho' late to shield;
But England with a steady resource,
First learned, then won on the battle-field.

Look back on England's days now gone
When clouds her face o'er-cast;
Some Nelson, – Clive, – a Wellington,[49]
Has writ her glorious past.

So now – as in the days of old,
And hushing a father's sobs,
The man who wins, came marching bold
The matchless gallant "Bobs."[50]

With blood of heroes sacrificed,
Was England re-baptized by Fame,
As 'Greater Britain'; which symbolized,
A federated Nation's name.[51]

---

48 Major-General Sir William Penn Symons (1843–1899): served in India before taking charge of the forces in Natal. He died at the battle of Dundee. The British counted this battle as a victory but it resulted in heavy losses on both sides and ultimately did not stop the Boer invasion of northern Natal and British retreat to Ladysmith.

49 Admiral Horatio Nelson (1758–1805): served during the Napoleonic wars. Major-General Robert Clive (1725–1774): instrumental in establishing the East India Company's rule. Duke of Wellington (1769–1852): famous commander whose victory in the Battle of Waterloo against Napoleon was made legendary.

50 "Bobs": perhaps a nickname for Robert Clive.

51 Dinakara seems to refer to the formation of the Kingdom of Great Britain as a result of the Acts of Union 1707 between England and Scotland. This Kingdom lasted until the Act of Union (1801), which created the United Kingdom of Great Britain and Ireland.

This time, once more, when Britain rose,
At Heaven's command, from out the sea;
Her second Chart, which awed her foes,
Read: "Thy sons shall be true to thee
O'er Greater Britain shalt thou reign;
Nor lands, nor hearts be closed to thee"
In this that first,[52] the plea doth gain:
Why, "Britons never slaves will be."

A Tribute to the Gallant Boers, Who Fought, and Fell, for their Country

Never was seen in world's embattled fields,
Such old-day folk, with all that Science yields
In arms; with wit to use, and ways in war,
Of suiting means to end, as Nature's are.

The martyrs of a dawning Change, – they gave
In blood the pledge, and passed into the grave;
Their Greatness lives; their Lesson them survives:
A wiser World, new ways, and means derives.

Ye recluses from a World that flaunts its mode!
Ye embers of a type that is no more!
Ye peasant warriors! O'er Ye light lie the load,
Of native earth ensanguined by your gore!

Chilkur C. S. Narsimha Row

Rao also published *The Song of Indiana on the Royal Visit* (1906) and *Snehalata (The Martyr and the Heroine of Bengal)* (1915). Although *The Poetical Works of Chilkur C. S. Nar Simha Row* (1911) indicates that this volume is the first of two or even several, volume two never seems to have been published. The poems below, reprinted from this 1911 volume, take an expansive view of India. The volume is dedicated to Swinburne, Rao's "master sea-muse."

---

52 [Poet's Note: The first Charter, *Vide* the song "Rule Britannia"]

The Poetical Works of Chilkur C. S. Nar Simha Row (Ellore: 1911)[53]

The Greatest Need of India
(Argument)

Having had an opportunity of attending a lecture delivered by one Mr. Musa Bhai of Ceylon[54] on "The greatest need of India," which he described as "The Spirit of Christianity," I was indeed inspired with yet loftier motives and views, and, indeed with ideas different from those cherished by him as to the "Greatest need" which my India of the present day is panting for and which as suggested to my mind found extempore expression in the following lines of my song. The learned reader will be requested to go through my ideas over and over again, as a true and worthy son of India. If my views and ideas appeal to the minds of my countrymen, and rivet their sympathy, I shall deem myself amply rewarded at the hand of Man and God.

I.

'Tis not the Dominions rich and vast,
'Tis not the heads of jewels best,
'Tis not the trick of trades or Arts,
'Tis not the legal liers [sic] and touts,
　　That India greatly needs.

II.

'Tis not even the honours of State,
The gilded shams wherewith to prate,
To wag their tails like spaniels do
With the crumb of bread that's their due
　　That India greatly needs.

III.

'Tis not even those that puppet dance
To the makebates, and their evil pranks,
'Tis not those that blow hot and cold,
Allow themselves so cheaply sold,
　　That India greatly needs.

53　Chilkur C. S. Narsimha Row, *The Poetical Works of Chilkur C. S. Nar Simha Row*, vol. 1 (Ellore: M.V. Press, 1911).
54　A Christian convert, Musa Bhai of Ceylon (modern-day Sri Lanka) was a "major" in the Salvation Army and a frequent proselytizer of Christianity.

IV.

'Tis not those that wear without
A pretty, gaudy, tiger's coat,
And wear within a sheepish heart,
At moments of Duty stand apart,
    That India greatly needs.

V.

'Tis not those that honey their lip,
But their bosoms in venom dip,
Those Mammon-mongers rank with pelf
And parasites doting on their self,
    That India greatly needs.

VI.

Those that heedless of cheers or jeers,
Their health and wealth, all earthly fears,
That sacrifice their blood and all,
And staunch to th' Country's call
    That India greatly needs.

VII.

A nation one in head and heart,
Ready to do, or dare, depart,
To fields of gore or mounts of ice
Mindless of the kindred ties,
    That India greatly needs.

VIII.

Those that true to Man and God
Bear the bell, and th' evangelic rod,
A crusade 'gainst the lawless rights
Heedless dash, and meadless fight,
    That India greatly needs.

IX.

Caste or Colour or Creed or Land,
Gold or Glory cannot disband,
The common tie that welded us.
'Tis men and women of such ideals
    That India greatly needs.

X.

Plain, practical, righteous men,
Continent men, contented men,
Able to lead, and wise to correct,
The light that leads to th' goal direct
    Are the greatest needs of India.

Madras or Rome, where's thy home?

A thousand combs of sweet honey,
A million heaps of hard money,
Are none the sweeter than th' thoughts of my native land
Which once more make me young when I touch its sand,
    Leap with joy when I breathe its air,
    I feel as proud as a lion in its lair.
Whence does this joy and pride so glorious come!
Wherein lies that charm of our native home?

    'Tis not in sweetly dribbling brooks,
    'Tis not in saintly, friendly folks,
'Tis not in honours State or field-glory,
'Tis not in meadows green, or hills hoary,
    'Tis not in men 'tis not in beasts,
    'Tis not in sumptuous feasts
Abides the secret love of nativity,
But in duty chaste or filial Duty.

    Who can claim a land as his own,
    Or reap the seeds that he's sown?
Man is a hired, temporary being
A bubble himself, a dream of his living!
    Nature is same wher'er we go,
    We 'lone change so wise we grow!
Anaxagoras[55] showed his finger to the skies
To say that he, e'en as a crow that flies
    From sea to sea and pole to pole,
    A citizen of the natural whole.

---

55 Anaxagoras (born c. 500–480 BCE): Greek philosopher who forwarded then controversial theories on the cosmos.

Born as I am in eastern lands,
    I may die perchance in western strands,
Glorious or inglorious 'tis all the same!
Where's my native home and whither I came?
    Birth at Madras and death at Rome!
    Here no less than in my native home,
I own everything to my heart's content.
By law of Nature wherever I am sent,
    There is all in all and that's my home,
    'Tis all the same for me, Madras or Rome!

Vande Mataram
(An acrostic)

Vestal were thy days of yore,
Amorous with their sacred lore.
Naughty grew the nations round,
Doughty champions licked thy ground.
Earth oped aloft its gates of gold,
Mammon-mongers slipt their hold.
Art and Science in rapid strides
Trained thy youth, and now he rides
Aloft, upright, content, and strong.
Ride on Mother! thy torch ere long,
A promise bright reveal all round,
Mills and loom of harmoneous [sic] sound!

The grand old man of India [56]
(Argument)

On my return from Bombay, I was struck with the historical and religious place of Mahabalewar[57] whither I proceeded and stopped there for a couple of days noting in a reverie of wonder all that is sublime and beautiful in that locality. Especially was I pleased with the glories of the great Emporium, and during my peregrinations in the City the one object of my admiration was the simple but noble Ketvady lane[58] and the small house of Mr. Dadabhoy Naorojee shining therein like a Star on the Firmament. My joy knew no bounds at the sight. Having read and heard a good deal about him and his work in India and for India in the Parliament of London, I thought I could well pay my tribute to him by singing to his glory in the following manner.

> Like fireflies seem the yonder gleaming orbs,
>   And gorges wide from far like narrow vales,
> The Souls of great men are how poor in garb,
>   And charm our little hearts with their wondrous tales.
>
> Behold! how small's th' home in Ketvady,
>   A nest, a span in length and an inch in breadth
> Where, a black bird gray with sallow bearded lips
>   Still chants the woes of the races of his earth.
>
> O how those chants like magic thrill my soul,
>   And sting me join the *wealing* chorus fast!
> Wherefore are they in such profusion come,
>   And cloud my aching breast, and leave me 'ghast?

---

56 The "grand old man of India" was the popular title bestowed upon Dadabhoy Naorojee (1825–1917), or Dadabhai Naoroji, a Parsi and one of the most respected leaders of the Indian nationalist movement. After teaching at Elphinstone College in Bombay for several years, he moved to England in 1855 to become a partner in the first Indian company in London. In London, he advocated for India through organizations such as the London India Society and was elected Liberal MP for Finsbury Central in northern London in 1892. He served as president of the Indian National Congress three times in 1886, 1893 and 1906 and famously critiqued Britain for its "drain of wealth" from India in his monograph *Poverty and Un-British Rule in India*.

57 Mahabalewar, or Mahabaleshwar: city in what is the modern-day state of Maharashtra. As a forested hill station in the Western Ghats, it was used by the British colonists as a summer resort. It has some religious significance for Hindus as the site of an ancient temple.

58 Ketvady, or Ketwady, Lane: street in Bombay.

Are they the paeans from Sasoor Hardwar gates[59]
    In honour of one who bore her on to the West,
Or anthems loud from various wharfs of Ind
    On one who lived and loved her people best?

Lo! a noise I hear as of an angel's voice,
    A Zephyr I feel as straight from Zenith high;
With tears of joy tickling my palsied cheeks
    I stared ensnared at the nest, and drew a sigh.

O blessed Ketvady! whose is this nest
    So simple, yet pleasant, happy, and best?
What modest bird this smallest cell abode
    By which many a Soul saluting strode?

Lo! a voice as soft as air I hear from high-
    "This house if of Dadabhoy Naorojee."
Wherewith my mind like lotus oped into bloom,
    And doubts like vapours dwindled into a gloom.

I shrugged my arms, and oped my vacant eyes,
    Surveyed the house from basement to the crest,
And found a single stair on simple rafts
    As if to mock the lofty spires abreast.

To mock? yea, an ignoble thought methinks!
    It is an ornament precious and best,
Whose lustres grand like aurora have shed
    Immortal sheen from th' East to th' far off West.

What Soul is it that spent its vital powers
Away from the sweets of home, and ties of blood,
    And lent his wits for his Country's sole cause,
    And sponged the tears India has often shed?

And who despite the crosses of his life
    Resigned him out and out for Duty's sake,
And led the high and low of his native land
    Whose rights of home and State were once at stake?

---

59 In Sanskrit, Hardwar means gateway to Hari, or god. The city of Haridwar, located in Uttarakhand, India, is one of four cities along the sacred Ganges River and is a famous pilgrimage site for Hindus.

Who is that living Soul with sedate will and heart
>   On missions grand commissioned by his clan,
Has sailed to foreign strands to fight their cause,
>   There proved him more than a match for man to man?

And who by dint of pen and speech has earned
>   The vestal love of th' East, no less of the West;
In whom an ideal being Finsbury[60] found,
>   And voted him to the House as its member blest?

Who is that grand old man of Ind who still
>   With sparkling eye decried his mother's throes,
And brought them home to the Lords gleaning from sills,
>   Like roosting owls from Windsor Castle[61] brows?

Or who is that "Uncrowned King of the East"
>   Still ruling proud the hearts of his fellow man,
And facts and figures tipped at fingers' ends
>   As bulwark stood in the House with India van?

Who is that busy bee with sober head
>   Sits in Anerley[62] park digesting deep
Books blue[63] and green of motley themes of Earth
>   Still smiling soft but ne'er wont to sleep?

Or sits in th' National Liberal Club[64]
>   With colleagues noble mooting out themes
Of India, and her vows, and promises made,
>   Chastising Britannia's lawless schemes?

Or say who is that Wilberforce[65] of Ind
>   Whose claims were thrice declaimed at last reclaimed,
As just and true as sister's vestal cry,
>   And won his day as "Black man" tho' nicknamed?

---

60 Finsbury: district in central London.
61 Windsor Castle: the royal palace and residence.
62 Anerley: located in south London.
63 Blue books: reports produced by Parliament.
64 National Liberal Club: founded in 1882 by William Ewart Gladstone for members of the Liberal Party. Dadabhai Naoroji was a member of the NLC.
65 William Wilberforce (1759–1833): British statesmen who took a leading role in the movement to abolish the slave trade.

He is the man, the grand old man of Ind,
    And this his home in Bombay, Ketvady,
Below the arbours green o'erhung its brow
    You find a head in roses wreathed and glee!

Is this the man that often thrilled the House
    With floods of Love and Light India has shed
Upon his hoary head, and sanguine heart,
    And with his opinions all his party led?

    One who by Statecraft made the prouder West
    To feel and heal the sores of th' blesséd East,
For him a name, for his land Britannia's love
    Who gained and that but all in th' sweat of his brow?
That is the man I want and him I seek,
    In this Ketvady lane beside Girgaum,[66]
The mart of many a grandee proud and fair,
    For young and old to pass a thoroughfare.
Naorojee! in glee I've stared at thy home
As a Plebion[67] at the lofty spires of Rome,
And learning thou 'rt safe on Britain's shore,
I prayed my Gods on thee long life to pour.
        Long live Naorojee great
        In health and light and State;
        And love of his native Isle
        May ever his heart beguile;
        Till East and West are one
        And greet the rising Sun!

India
(Brooding on the steps of the Taj)[68]

Now soar aloft my lofty Soul
    To regions high and sing,
Of Him that wields from pole to pole
    From high to th' tiny thing!

---

66 Girgaum: area in south Bombay, at the foot of the Malabar Hills.
67 "Plebion": Row seems to be referring to a plebian or common citizen in ancient Rome.
68 Taj Mahal: mausoleum complex in Agra commissioned by the Mughal emperor Shah Jahan (1592–1666) to commemorate his favorite wife, Arjumand Banu Begum, who died in 1631 ("Taj Mahal" *ArchNet*).

Of Ind so grand in world's epoch,
    And played a lofty part,
The seat of wondrous Art and Science
    That baffled human heart;

Of rivers of blood so glorious shed,
    And rocks of sabred bones,
Of battles fought, and treaties passed,
    I sing in lofty tones.

Attend ye lovers of damask lores
    To India's grander mart,
And ferret out the sacred ores
    That Crown the Indian Art!

The jewel rich that crowned the head
    From mine own mint is lent,
The blood in Chillianwala[69] shed
    Still breathes my chivalrous scent.

The mosaic art of "Mosque of pearls"
    Still breathes in waxing pride,
The daintiest wares of th' East unfurls
    On land and main, world-wide,

With Greece and Rome, the lights of th' world
    Her greatness still competes!
The Black Hole with its murky walls
    Still gapes its ghastly gates.

The brawny ribs that lay beneath
    Are sabres sharp and stout
That glitter in their Crimson sheath
    And fringe the bloody moat.

No hotter wars, no bloodier deeds
    No better blood is shed,
Than on th' Kurukshetra[70] meads –
    One Brine of Bharat[71] blood!

---

69 Chillianwala: town now located in the Punjab province of Pakistan and famous for the battle fought there between the residents and the British during the Second Anglo–Sikh War in 1849. Although both sides claimed victory, the British were forced to retreat.

70 Kurukshetra: located in what is the modern-day state of Haryana in India and is the famous site where the battle recounted in the ancient Hindu epic, the *Mahabharata*, between the Pandavas and the Kauravas was fought.

71 Bharat: India.

The Sikhs and Rajputs[72] are my sons
    The sinews of my land,
They bore the brunt, and still their scions
    Their birth-right proud command.

I wear my heart upon my sleeve,
    And ope my gates to all,
By pride of race, and blood, and land
    My sons to me enthral;

And lift me up on land and main
    By dint of love unscathed,
My head and heart I hold unstained
    With mine own laurels wreathed.

I bake my bread in mine own hearth.
    My sons will drink my health,
My daughters sweet then rove my earth,
    And unearth all my wealth.

My sons and daughters are my wealth,
    I hail me in their pride,
My bread and wine lie in their health,
    Myself then glorious ride

O'er alien powers that rend my peace,
    And mar my sweet repose;
And teach them that might is not right,
    And death my day can't close.

Hark to the thrilling Vedic[73] hymns
    Chanted by the wise of yore;
Grovelling roll in serene sounds
    Appealing to the core.

The blood-red crystals of the war
    Like orbs on welkin high,
Still shine on Kurukshetra plain,
    And blear the naked eye.

---

72 The Sikhs are an ethnic-social-religious group founded by the teachings of Guru Nanak in the Punjab region during the early sixteenth century. The Sikhs are known for their skills as warriors. The Rajputs are members of the warrior caste in northern and central India, for example in the modern-day state of Rajasthan, and were recruited and celebrated by the British East India Company and later Empire for their military prowess.

73 *Vedas*: ancient Hindu Sanskrit scriptures revealed by the gods and predating the composition of the Hindu epics.

The lofty strains of Ramayan[74]
        Still breathe a living life,
And wisdom teach the vile and wise
        As to how to brave the strife.

I see my sons arrayed in arms,
        And in the "cloth of gold"
Hurraying of my splendour past,
        My palmy days of old.

I hear the bubbling flow of blood
        In every sacred vein,
In festive measures beating high
        They march in solemn train.

Survey thy land, my bless'ed sons,
        My past and promise read,
And glean therefrom what's great and good,
        And sow the sacred seed.

My land! for weal or woe am born,
        And brought up in thy lap,
To revel in thy glorious past,
        From the lofty crest to the cape.

I claim thee as my all, my own,
        I shrug at thy rising Star;
I sing of scenes that crown my head,
        Thy valour and thy war.

Thy mosque of pearls as white as snow
        Unveil a new Sunrise,
And in her crystal domes vibrate
        The vespers[75] of the Wise.

My mother land! why dost thou weep
        O'er th' mirrored slabs of the tomb?
Thy sons are great, thy daughters good,
        The cream of thy jewelled womb.

Thy famous wars, and glorious arts
        Still green on pages shine;
Thy glorious past shall come again
        Thy sons shall rule thy line.

---

74 Ramayan: the ancient Hindu epic, the *Ramayana*.
75 Vespers: evening prayer or devotions, or evening song (n. "vespers" *OED*).

Rise up my Soul! and lend thy hand
        To thy hoary mother, chaste;
She lies prostrate on th' jaspered[76] Tomb,
        Her sons clinging to her waist.

Lift her veil, but what is there?
        A sword in hide and seek,
Peeping thro' the sombre blaze,
        A flower of crimson streak.

Touch her breast, and what is there?
        The emerald jewel of Peace,
The ruby streaks of blood-red wars
        She waged beyond the Seas.

Touch her, and retouch her thro',
        A mien of burnished gold;
And in her breast you find anon
        The chivalrous blood of old.

My mother land! at thy hoary shrine
        Thy sons in clusters loom,
To seek thy prop, and bear thy hand,
        To dare or else to doom.

Put off thy mask, and gaze around
        At thy Bharat sons on knees,
And lend them life, and hope afresh
        To live and die in peace.

All Earth is dark, and Heavens red,
        The sword is dazzling high,
And yet sedate and calm you feel
        Unbudged like th' orbs of the Sky.

Dost thou not see the sombre blaze
        Of blood-red streaks afar.
And glean the bright from darker spots
        That gird thy waxing Star?

From thy lofty throne of Bharat land
        Begirt by milk-white sheets,
Dost thou not see thy dauntless sons
        Quivering like swords in sheaths?

---

76 Jasper: opaque form of quartz.

And too not see thy daughters sweet
        Throw off their *purda*[77] blind,
And dash to th' front like flames of fire
        Their sons escort behind?

Thy national flag that fluttered high
        'S no longer a peaceful flag,
Beware the times are out of joint,
        Thy flag is now a 'red rag'.

Fear not, nathless; stand staunch, hold fast
        To thy wonted lotus seat,
Whence 'skance at the rueful scene,
        Thy sons in bloody heat.

What dost thou see? one murky mess
        Of ghastly pools of blood
And parched pasture grounds bedewed
        With crests of th' glorious dead.

Clear the mote that blear thy eye,
        Brandish thy arms of fire,
And brush thy cheeks of th' tears of blood,
        And calm thy vengeful ire.

Thy sons are free with their purse and heart
        To Crown thee as their Queen,
And consecrate thy name for ever
        'Mid paeans of glorious sheen.

Thy sons with sacred writs in hand
        Array the Ganga[78] shore,
And vociferate in solemn strains
        Thy chivalrous deeds of yore.

Thy daughters too, the pride of thy land,
        Romantic songs outpour,
Of the greatness of thy noble sons
        That rent thy righteous core.

---

77 *Purdah*: practice of covering or veiling women so as to prevent them from being seen by male strangers. It can also refer to the physical seclusion of women.
78 The Ganges River runs for over 1,500 miles from the Himalayas to the Bay of Bengal.

A Bard by thee inspired to sing
    The crosses of thy life,
Under the benign British flag,
    And share thy thankless strife.

My sacred sister Britain too
    Still loves to lap thee up,
And lend her heart and Soul to thee,
    Her stronghold and her prop.

Many a tempest-torn rag
    Is streaming red afar,
But care not these bootless red rags
    That blink behind thy Star.

Thy Star is high in its hallowed sheen,
    Britannia by thy side;
Thy life be green, thy buds be bright
    Shedding zephyrs world-wide.

Thy Art is safe, thy Science secure,
    Thy sons have mastered both,
Britannia loves to see you aloft,
    And hails at thy palmy Youth.

Thy sons their own arena tread,
    And breathe thine own free airs,
And find their promise and their past
    In thine own peerless fairs.

The lark that soars aloft in glee
    Thy boundless bounties know,
And warbling thro' the verdant grove
    The black-bird hails thy glow.

The sages wise that deck thy heights
    Thy glorious birth-right chime,
And pray for th' length of thy sister's reign
    Over thy jewelled clime.

The blesse'd day when the palm and pine
    Shall meet in concord sweet,
And waft right wholesome balmy gales
    Is not far off to greet.

The day when th' blesséd black and white
    Their racial tints shall drop,
And sing with an even heart and head,
    And each to each shall prop.

My Mother! lend me half thy light
    To brave my earthly strife,
A quart of thy love forsooth doth give
    A bracing blood and life.

Thy sons are panting at thy shrine
    Desperate and thread-bare,
Their hands uplifted to the skies
    Dauntless to do or dare.

My Mother! in thy verdant womb
    Thy valiant sons refuge!
Lions rampant at thy beck and call
    To dash into thy deluge.

Thy sons like beacons on the rocks
    Direct thy stormy course,
O, sail on thy vestal white wings,
    And with thy pluck and force.

Britannia too with her purse and heart
    To bear you up prepared;
The glorious Writ that wed us both
    Thy shattered ribs repaired.

O Magna Charta![79] India's hope,
    Britannia's sacred Writ!
Drop off the rust that crust thy head
    That thou mays't strongly knit

In heart and Soul, and unison best,
    And a promise bright all round
Ere long in iridescent streaks reveal,
    Thy sister's vestal sound!

---

[79] The Magna Carta (1215) was an English legal charter requiring King John of England to guarantee some rights to a limited group of men, thereby limiting his own power as sovereign. It is considered a key document in the British "constitution."

C. Lakshminarayana Aiyer

There is no biographical information on this poet, who seems to have authored only this collection of verse, but his poetry indicates some interest in celebrating those in positions of power, both Indian and British.

Poems (Tinnevelly: 1914)[80]

To the Lord Bhupalaswami, Srivaikuntam[81]

Sir, – What glorious, gorgeous form is Thine! Agape,
All stand in mute surprise. Oh Good!
The hydra-headed Snake[82] with broadened hood
Doth spread a bed of Peace. Thy wrath escape.
E'en the scoffing sceptics praise Thy shape!
Oh! Thou who lie outstretched with worlds abide
Thy consort Queens sit smiling by Thy side.
Thou great Primeval Cause with budding naval tape
Whence all Creation fair sprang forth in sight.
Oh! Thou Resplendent Light! Illume my mind;
Pray guide me on aright through alleys blind.
I yearn, I pant for thee. So let me light;
Oh! Perennial Fount of love to pious man!
Shouldst Thou not bless? Thy mercy who can scan?

To His Gracious Majesty George V Emperor of India[83]

Lo! How the smiling morn of New Year
Begins its stately march to greet Thee! King!
What songs of joy and gratitude we sing!
Oh! Thou! Our God in flesh on earth to cheer!
How deep was touched the chord of races here
By Thee on twelfth December Elev'n! How glows

---

80 C. Lakshminarayana Aiyer, *Poems* (Tinnevelly, India: Nurul Islam Press, 1914).
81 Srivaikuntam, or Srivaikundam, Temple: located in the modern-day state of Tamil Nadu.
82 "The hyrdra-headed Snake," or Shesha Naga: bed upon which the Hindu god Vishnu lays.
83 King George V (1865–1936): crowned in 1910 after the death of his father, King Edward VII. He was the only English sovereign to be present at a Durbar, in this case the Delhi Durbar of December 1911 where he was crowned with the Imperial Crown of India, created for this occasion.

Our national life that stopped its ebb and flows.
Oh! Thou has drawn our hearts to Thee so near.
Thou Saviour of Ind! Thou friend of struggling hearts!
Thy words of hope are held as Scriptures true;
We live anew with faith on Royal Charts;
Give Loyalty Thy Grace, let Folly rue.
Well may Thy flag of Peace float far and long.
May thou and noble Queen live long and strong.

Coronation Song[84]

Lift up the flags; suspend thy task awhile;
Rejoice the immortal day of cheer and smile.
String well the lute and pour the strain along
And thrill us with soft Coronation songs.
Come here, my friends, our loyalty display
To o'r Gracious Emp'ror George this festive day
The orient Sun and Moon in eternal round,
All Sires and Songs their grateful concert sound.
All modest maids come round their merry dance.
E'en Birds of air with warbling choir advance.
Now Statesman, Judges, Lawyers high and great,
Now fling to winds your party strife and hate,
And share the nation's ecstasy and pride,
At o'r Emp'ror George crowed loyally by o'r side.

The New Year, 1912[85]

I.

Ring out the old, ring in the new with cheer.
The painful Past is gone; Lo' mark New Year
Begins with verdant wreaths on o'r portals hung,
With mirth and music thro' our country rung.
Our Emp'ror George hath granted many a boon
With noble grace on twelfth December noon.
Right well is Grief's sobbing plaint decreed.

---

84 [Poet's Note: Read at the Durbar meeting held on at the Coronation Reading room, Srivaikuntam on 12-12-1911.] Srivaikuntam, or Srivaikundam: located in the modern-day state of Tamil Nadu.
85 [Poet's Note: Read at a public meeting held at the Munsiff's Court premises in January 12.]

Dead-weight of Partition is Bengal freed.[86]
Indeed a worthy step's assured by our King
His deathless fame from pole to pole may ring.
His grant of fifty lakhs to us tho' small
Confirms his pledge of sympathy to us all.[87]
The words of o'r King are words of law and love;
His acts and thoughts are all like streams from above.

II.

Ring out the old, ring in the new, forsooth.
The year of Twelve looks fair as hopes of youth
The voice of Truth, the force of Prayer deep
Have had their just reward, which they should keep.
Unkind is he who views with cynic turn
Reformed Councils of Lord of Bannockburn.[88]
And Progress plods but slow and surely on,
As soon from seed to blade, from ear to corn.
Now Royal blessings fell in plenteous showers
That o'r land may teem with foliage, fruits and flowers.
No more our Ind shall have her brow of care;
No more our youth be kept from Learning fair;
No more our goal still mock our wistful eye;
No more shall Pride tread on our rights to sigh.

III.

Right out the old, ring in the new with prayer
By which more things are wrought than by despair.
May our lovely land of Ind be bright in health
E'er with emerald fields and Nature's wealth
May Tax be light and settled permanent.[89]

---

86 The region of Bengal was partitioned into east and west in 1905 by then viceroy of India, Lord Curzon. The imperial government argued that partition would allow for greater ease in administration but many Indians believed its actual purpose was to create divisiveness and foment communal tensions between Hindus and Muslims. Partition officially ended in 1911 but created lasting divisions.

87 The relatively small sum of fifty lakhs (about £300,000) was promised to promote education; more generous grants were pledged for the future.

88 Aiyer may be referring to the Battle of Bannockburn led by Robert the Bruce in 1314. This battle was a victory in the Wars of Scottish Independence (1296–1328) insofar as it led to various council reforms and independence over a decade later.

89 The imperial taxation and revenue collection system, especially in rural areas, was notoriously crushing and exacerbated periods of drought-famine on the subcontinent. The unilateral transfer of resources from India to Britain, termed the "drain of wealth" by the Indian nationalist Dadabhai Naoroji, who detailed this process in *Poverty and Un-British Rule in India* (1876), was explored by a number of other Indian economic historians as well including Romesh Chunder Dutt in his *Economic History of India under Early British Rule* (1901) and *Economic History of India in the Victorian Age* (1903) and Mahadev Govind Ranade in his *Essay on Indian Economics* (1898).

> May knowledge free be giv'n. May Folly mend.
> May Ind of beauty, valour, virtue, truth
> Realise her new-born consciousness, forsooth.
> May Law, its worth and Love, its due maintain
> May Local councils, grow in substance, reign.[90]
> May Pax Britannica continue strong;
> May clannish views and class Ego pass off ere long
> May God vouchsafe His choicest blessings sure
> To o'r gracious King and noble Queen and pure.

P. Seshadri

Pundi Seshadri (1887–1942), a professor of English at Benares University, was active in educational reform and published several collections of poetry including *Bilhana* (1914), *Sonnets* (1914), *Champak Leaves* (1915), and *Vanished Hours* (1925) as well as a number of lectures on literature. Billed as Head of the Department of English, Benares Hindu University in a series of lectures published in 1928, Seshadri notes in his essay, "Anglo-Indian Poetry":

> The subject of Anglo-Indian poetry is of interest to students of English literature, at least in this country, as it refers to a new line of development and to a special contribution which may come to some distinction in the future… To the future chronicler of the achievements of English literature the region to be dwelt with, will not be Great Britain and Ireland merely, as in the past, but all the great empire…
>
> At the end of this brief survey of the poetic achievements of the Indian and the Englishman in this country, it is necessary to draw attention to another possible source of contribution to Anglo-Indian poetry in the future – from poets in the British Isles themselves. Without any attempt at belittling the perennial poetic interest of Britain, at least for her own children, it may be ventured that their muse must soon seek additional material in parts of the British Empire which still have an air of romance for them. The colonies and India with its baffling mysteries for the foreigner, must serve as "fresh woods and pastures new" for the English poet of this century… If one may indulge in prophecy in such matters, it could be said that some of the richest treasures of English literature in the twentieth century are likely to be associated with the aspects of life and scenery in parts of Greater Britain, and

---

90 The Indian Councils Act of 1909, also known as the Morley-Minto Reforms Act, introduced reforms, embodied in the Indian Councils Act (1909), to allow the admission of Indians into various administrative and legislative councils. While some Indian moderates welcomed these reforms, which were introduced to placate Indians angry over the 1905 partitioning of Bengal, most nationalists, including many members of the Indian National Congress, viewed it as overly cautious. Some Hindus also resented the act's provision for a separate electorate for Muslims.

India as the representative of a civilization much more ancient and mysterious than that of the colonies, will claim a large share of such attention… Almost all aspects of the country are likely to appear transformed in a halo of poetic glory at the hands of English poets.

But the poetic interpretation of India, its life and civilization, could be most effectively discharged only by the Indian as he is the son of the land and he lives, moves, and has his being in her, unlike the foreigner, or even the European in India, for whom she is only a temporary home. The Anglo-Indian poet praises the scenery and life of the land with material reservations. He always longs for the surroundings of his own foreign home, in obedience to a very laudable instinct of patriotism.[91]

Thus, for Seshadri, although it is desirable for the English and Anglo-Indians to employ India as a subject of their poetry, only Indians can truly write Indian poetry. Reprinted below are *Bilhana*, a long Orientalist poem, and selections from later collections of verse.

Bilhana: An Indian Romance, Adapted from Sanskrit (Madras: 1914)[92]

Bilhana[93]

The tardy grace of fabled Gods of yore
I scorn to seek; the mighty Triad[94] hold
No meed to lure my Muse. The dreamy Lord
Who rules the lofty world of sacred writ
Has charms for starving saints that haunt the woods
And praying, steep their days in rigid rites.
Benignant Vishnu's power wafts the world
On wings of peace and fortune, laves her shores
In milk and honey – aye, but fails to draw
My willing homage. Siva's dreaded ire
Entombed fair Kāmadev,[95] it blew to dust
His soul-enthralling form, – and let that Lord
Of Death command his dismal train of ghosts
And shapeless creatures groping in the gloom

---

91 P. Seshadri, *Anglo-Indian Poetry* (Benares: Indian Bookshop, 1928).
92 P. Seshadri, *Bilhana: An Indian Romance, Adapted from Sanskrit* (Madras: Srinivasa Varadachari, 1914).
93 Seshadri begins the preface to this volume by noting: "The Italian proverb, *Traduttori, traditori*, brands all translators as traitors, and I have taken care to avoid giving a literal version of the Sanskrit romance of Bilhana on which this poem is based. I have aimed only at a free adaptation of the story, though I have thought it necessary to preserve some of the Oriental ways of expression and have occasionally even given a faithful translation."
94 "the mighty Triad": the Trimurthi of the major Hindu gods Shiva, Vishnu and Brahma.
95 Kamadev: Hindu god of love, sometimes believed to be an avatar of Vishnu. He is said to have been burned to ashes by Shiva's third eye after disturbing Shiva's meditation.

Of sable night. The Muse now speeds in joy
To other realms: of Love that drinks its fill
Of sustenance, the instant hungering hearts
Awake to Light; of Beauty's magic spell
That claims obeisance low from all mankind;
She sings of souls ethereal whose hearts
Blossom to love and all its ecstasy;
Upbear their life fragile, through hail and storm,
Whelmed in by wicked mortals; then, the stress
Is o'er, their petals ope again to breathe
The heaven on earth.
      Beyond the golden mount
Of Heavenly Mêru, the abode of Gods,[96]
In Northern Ind, there spread the spacious clime
Of fair Panchāla.[97] Wisdom never knew
A sweeter home; the Arts bedecked her brow
In matchless splendour; Virtue shed her grace
On every son and daughter drawing breath
Within her bounds. The Roof and Crown of earth
She shone in deathless fame. A queenly city rose
Within the realm and held her sovereign sway
O'er all the mighty land; her very name
Bespoke her glory – was she not the Home
Of Lakshmi,[98] of the deity lotus-born
Whose lovely smile could rain the marveled wealth
Of empires, sweeten life with countless gifts
Of happiness? A gracious monarch held
The sceptre, Madan, bold in war, a prince
Of matchless fame who worshipped as his own
The worlds of Song and Art. Blessed was his queen,
The partner in his toils of state and joys
Of life, Mandāra, fair, sweet, and pure;
A spotless lily, she adorned her lord
In guileless passion; robed in light divine
She sanctified her home. Their wedded life
Of felicity found its highest wealth
In Yāamini Thilaka, the lovely child,
With whom her parent's wish was ever law,
A paragon of beauty, sweet beyond
All human praise. She blossomed into youth,
The fairest flower that grew on earth; her speech

---

96 Mount Meru, or Sumeru: abode of Brahma and the lesser divinities. It is sometimes thought to be historically located in Kashmir. It is also a part of Buddhist cosmology.
97 Panchala: ancient historical kingdom of northern India that was divided into separate regions. It also figures in the ancient Hindu epic, the *Mahabharata*.
98 Lakshmi: Hindu goddess of wealth and prosperity.

Was rapturous song and like the gentle swan's
Her gait; her eyes of wondrous lustre, bright
Like those of fleet gazelles that roam the woods;
Her queenly bust bespoke a noble maid
Of mighty lineage; the lips of rose
Enclosed a pretty mouth which often oped
In dimpled laughter, gay and free. The face
Shone like the full-orbed moon, and curls that waved
In gentle motion coyly bent anon
To kiss its grace.
                The father's anxious care
Was now the proper fashioning of her mind;
Her soul had flowed in sweetest harmony
To music's million charms and felt the thrill
Of every note and strain, had known the art
In all its mystery, till man or book
Could bring no higher dower. But the world
Of Poesy, of verbal witchery
In trope and figure, Drama's play of soul,
And all the virtue of the written page –
Her vision had not swept the magic shore.
The monarch drew his minister to his side
And spake the purpose: "Yamini's heavenly form
Would tempt a saint – a shame that such a thought
Should touch her father's mind – but oh, how true!
Which favoured son of learning in this realm
Shall hold in honest trust the virgin soul
And fill her mind with largesses I seek?
Which vision rest upon her lovely face
And yet have mind to hunt the crabbèd page
And care to win its lore? Which heart of flint
Shall keep unmoved and free when brought anear
Her mystic spell?" The grey-haired lord that served
His master's will in loyal faith and sought
His plaudits in the world, as highest gifts
That lay within the sphere of man – he gave
His ready counsel: "Are Panchāla's homes
Bereft of lettered men that would await
Their loyal master's need with zest, discharge
The task in dread obedience? 'Tis done
My lord, to-morrow's eve the palace hall
Shall boast of all the galaxy of men
With lore, that tread this spacious city; seers
Of splendid vision, Brahmin saints who hold
Within the hollow of a sunken palm
The wisdom of a thousand ages, minds
Replete with every thought inscribed upon

The scroll of knowledge." Forth, the mandate flew
For men of light to gather in their force
And wait the royal pleasure. Evening spread
Her sable wings and Madan sat in state,
To hail the great assembly, know its gifts,
And choose the best to hold the office. Each
Advanced his claim: – A subtle reasoner
Was one, that could in hundred ways pursue
A single thought and split a single thought
In hundred fragments. All the wealth of Speech
A second beat to shapeless form, to Roots
And Letters, traced their life from hour to hour.
The sacred tomes that chronicle the deeds
Of countless gods, a third had made his own.
There was the scholar who could solve with ease
The deepest mysteries of Soul and God;
The master of the Vêdas,[99] with each sound
In proper accent, holding in his brain
Their myriad lines; he could outpour the words
From first to last, and then if need there rise
From last to first; of Brahmin ritual,
Of holy worship in its varied forms
And minute parts, a priest lay honest claim
To perfect knowledge; wrangling schools of thought
Had there their skilful fencers in debate.
The Brahmins ceased their speech and Madan spake
Like one, that wandering on a distant way
Looks down a well for crystal waters pure
To slake his thirst and finds a barren bed
Of rock: "Does not this wide assembly count
The blessed race of poets, lyric souls
Who could enrich my lovely daughter's mind
With Song and Art? Has Nature ceased to breathe
Her fire in man, have all the glorious joys
Of earth proved vain to ope his sleeping eyes
To Beauty, bear his soul on fancy's flight
To worlds of endless felicity? Alas,
That men pursuing dull Philosophy
Should miss in thoughtless ignorance the sweets
Of life?" The Brahmins bent their hoary heads
And said in plaintive notes: "the world of song
Is not of ascetics, whose only care
Is service of their Heavenly Lord, penance

---

99 *Vedas*: ancient Hindu Sanskrit scriptures revealed by the gods and predating the composition of the Hindu epics.

And fasting in His glory; nor of minds
That ever toiling sound the inmost depths
Of knowledge. Poesy wooes [sic] the young, the minds
Imbued with taste, the gifted souls awake
In over-flowing love and open wonder
To all the finest pulses on the chords
Of God's Creation. From our paths she flies
Even as buxom maidens loathe to wed
The feeble grey-haired dolts in whom the glow
Of manhood has been chilled; or else as we
The priestly class flare down our scorn
Upon the lowest caste of men, whose touch
Is curst pollution."
                    "And belike you know
At least as darkness knows the light it strives
In vain to reach, the person that could serve
My need," the monarch spoke and answer came,
Not from the hoary scholars in the front
Intent upon their priestly lore, but far behind
From youths that only hoped for fame in time,
New pilgrims from the shrines of Knowledge fresh
From offered incense at the altar, minds
Not yet oblivious to joys of life;
"We know a noble bard whose soul is song,
Bilhan, divinely fair in form and mind,
Monarch of poets, dreaming in his sphere
Of golden fancies, first among his line
Of craftsmen. Spring is sweetest in the year;
The jasmine in the world of flowers; flight
Is speediest and aim the most devoid
Of fault in arrows blooming on the crown
Of Kama's quiver;[100] fragrance draws its breath
In finest essence from the musk; the gift
Of speech is blazoned forth in matchless form
When called to pour its rays of scorching light
On error prest with reason's show; a man's life
Is happiest and most envied in youth;
His heart most nobly blessed with woman's love;
With equal truth be it assured, the world
Of poesy knows no name of greater might
Than Bilhan's. When the royal mandate sped
For lettered men, perchance the youthful bard
Was lost in raptures of a song, or mused
Alone upon some scene of loveliness

---

100 "Kama's quiver": arrow of the Hindu god of love, Kamadeva.

That hides her witching face beyond the bounds
Of this our bustling city." Sore now sighed
Madan, as one that failed to stretch his arms
When hoards of treasure lay unclaimed. He waved
The scholars home and sent the speedy word
That Bilhana was welcome at the court;
The king himself desired the felicity
Of talk and friendly greetings with the bard.
With dawn the sovereign was upon his throne;
He sat in eager wait, and Bilhan came
Like the Preceptor of the Gods that turns
His sacred feet towards the heavenly court
Of Indra,[101] passing through the lofty gates
Of gold. The sentinels had once refused
Entrance, when as an unknown youth he sought
The royal presence and were stung by words
Of bitter sarcasm but they now beheld
In awe the poet come, an honoured guest
To court. With grace and kindness beamed the king,
And fain would know the story of the bard
Who looked an angel in a world of men.
Bilhan had spent his years of toil in the halls
Which royal benevolence had upreared
To Knowledge in the stately capital;
And ere he fared his homeward way again,
He lingered o'er the beauties of the place,
The thousand sights which filled his heart with joy
And wonder; felt in every pulse the glow
Of life and gave it leave to have its turn.
With rapture Madan scanned his form and saw
In every limb the God of Song. He gave
His glowing praise to all the priceless wealth
His gifted mind treasured in simple ease;
The royal coffers flowed as ne'r they flow'd
To honour men. A thousand gifts bestow'd
The king; a mansion now was Bilhan's own;
All worldly riches thus to wealth of mind
Were join'd. In secret council sat the king
And sought his trusted minister's aid: "Was there
Ever such marvel of a man; in form
Like Kāma himself; versed in arts of song
Like Guru, lord of every spoken word
In Heaven. But oh! this care now clouds my mind:

---

101 Indra: god of thunder and rain in Hinduism. In the *Vedas*, the religious scriptures predating the Hindu epics, he is described as the ruler of the gods but was later supplanted in importance by the Trimurti (which is composed of the gods Brahma, Vishnu and Shiva).

Which maid could face his charms with steelèd heart
And keep her soul untouched by thoughts of love?
Which father bring such loveliness divine
So near his daughter's view, if speedy love
And union were not his wanton aim?
The valued wisdom of his mind has found
No sober habitation, but a form
Of tempting beauty, meant to rouse in hearts
Of even holiest fire, delicious thoughts
Of sweet amour and wanton dalliance;
And like a blossom of the Kalpaka[102]
Which lures a myriad bees in buzzing search
Of honied essence, oh! his form would draw
The hearts of women in enraptured love,
And bear them on the wings of ecstasy;
It is no trifling folly to lay bare
The guileless fancies of a virgin soul
To all this poet's witching world. Alas,
But it is not like losing untold wealth
To miss his aid in fashioning the mind
Of one who is to us the very crown
Of earthly felicity? Thy subtle wit
Was ever known to grasp in faultless reach
The gravest problems of my home and state;
A deep and ceaseless stream, no eyes have caught
It dry; and who will doubt, it knows a way
To take us even through this stress, to keep
The precious prize without the haunting fear
Of gloomy spectres flitting on the stage
Of distant time." He spoke, and sat enwrapped
In solemn thought. A thousand schemes now flashed
Upon the minister's mind; with close-knit brows
He scanned them all and his countenance was bright
And sad by turns, as pathways oped and closed
Before his vision; till at last he gave
His words of deep import in reasoned steps:
" 'Tis clear the beauties must not blaze to flame;
They must be held in leash, apart, though near;
Unmeet it is for servile watchman eyes
To keep a zealous guard on them. Perchance
Even a silken screen fragile may serve
To partition their worlds, if wisely drawn
And kept in place by sense of fear, or else,
Better – by pious vows. 'Tis here, – I have it whole!
You know they mystic rites the princess pays

---

102 *Kalpaka*: tree that grants boons.

To Sūrya,[103] chief of heavenly orbs, the God
Whose worship hath a cult among our priests;
'Tis known at morn her fervent prayers rise
To hail the sun; each eve a thousand lights
She sets ablaze in honour of his power;
They shed their dazzling radiance upon
The city from our castled walls. Three years
Her penance lasts, begun when Vasant[104] beamed
His smile of flowers on earth this year.
On curious vows she hath resolved – no man
Devoid of light shall cross her path, before
Her sacred duties reach their fulfilment.
The hapless soul in whom the ray of heaven
Is quenched – the very sight is now to her
Pollution's touch. The city roads have oft
Been cleared of sightless men by beat of drum,
When forth her jewelled palanquin of pearl
Sallied in state beyond the palace gates
For worship at the shrine. You see the star
That glows within this maze: – A lie and all
Is done. Proclaim to her that Bilhana,
The greatest bard a royal father's care
Could seek for enriching her mind, has lost
His sight beyond all hope; a screen shall stand
Between them at their lessons; and her vow
Shall hold without a break. And as for him,
Another lie shall keep his mind in dread
Of rudeness to the veil: – The Princess fear
A dismal streak of loathsome leprosy
Is slowly spreading on her face, and hence
Desires some privacy; a near view
At least she likes to guard against." The king
Gave heed with rapt attention, lost in joy
Of prospects gained and poured a flood of praise
Upon the trusted and omniscient lord
Whose craft unravelled every tangled knot
With ease, or bound with iron strength the threads
Of deep-laid plans. The mandate shaped with care
Now reached the poet's home. The princess learnt
Her father's will and longed with glowing heart
For unknown worlds to open on her mind
At Bilhan's bidding. Madan spake in pride
About his schemes of wisdom to his queen,

---

103 Surya: chief solar deity in Hinduism; the word may refer to the sun or the sun god.
104 *Vasant*, or *Vasanth*: spring.

Who smiled her gentle smile and sweetly asked
If years of faithful love had proved in vain
To place *her* precious child beyond the pale
Of morbid suspicion? Was there the need
For all the lies two hoary heads evolved
In secret counsel? Was a daughter born
Of queen Mandāra proper aim for thoughts
Of doubt? Her virtue was a coat of mail,
Of stronger power than laws of kings or guiles
Of grey-haired ministers. The calm rebuke
Was lost in Madan's speech: "The old, perchance
Have oft displayed a flesh-consuming care
In ordering their lives – but better far
Than reckless faith of youth that leads the world
To peril's brink. The walls are there upreared
Against our mortal foe; if there be none
To-day, they serve to-morrow; if none at all,
It is because their terror holds." He sought
The Brahmin priests who knew the subtle flow
Of stars. They read the mystic scroll and scanned
Their baffling path to catch the lucky hour
To start the poet's work. The moment came,
And prayers rose for Brahma's spotless spouse,
Saraswati[105] who rules the world of speech.
The mighty bard who sang the glorious deeds
And triumphs of that ancient Solar prince
Who bridged the raging waves to reach his love
And crush the wicked foe whose guilty soul
Had wrought her pain, his muse was next invoked;
It was a day of festive joy for all;
The royal presents flowed with lavish hand;
And blessings poured on lovely Yāmini
For ever-growing wisdom. Bilhana
Now sought the palace walls each day, as noon
Mellowed to early eve and gently roused
His fount of song and wonders of the mind,
To feed the thirsting soul of Yāmini,
Till shades of gathering darkness saw him home
To muse in fondness on the joyous work
His favoured days had found for him. The hours
Were fraught for her with deep import;
She grasped with lightning speed the varied lore
That Bilhana revealed from day to day –
Till her preceptor wondered ere a year

---

105 Saraswati: Hindu goddess of learning and knowledge.

Had passed, what newer worlds his mind could draw
For her. She knew the quintessence of song
And all the forms in which the poets decked
The muse; the monuments of mind which bards
Had fashioned for the world were hers. The science
Of wealth and polity acclaimed by all
The wise as harbinger of felicity
For men had become hers, and now there passed
Before her vision plays designed for Love
That flashed their spotless bliss across the stage;
The crystal purity of laws of song
She learnt to feel at every turn; the art
Of love as bodied forth in books, her mind
Beheld in joy – the princess passed the bard
In all such wisdom and his gifts of lore
Outgrew in fruit when planted in her mind.
A train of golden fancies filled her mind
Till glowing with the joy she longer for them
In life. Her dreams now kept her company
All day and night; and lounging on her bed
Of ivory, behind the silken wall,
She mused on all the happy loves whose course
Was chronicled in books of song. Her ears
Were wide awake for sound of sweet footsteps
That brought the lyric soul whose presence chimed
With entrance into realms of untold bliss –
For did not Bilhan speak of wondrous things
Each day, of joyous tales of love that bathed
Her heart in heavenly radiance? He drew
Her sighs for one that languished on the hills
For touch of her he loved and sought to reach
Her through a cloud that swam across the skies;
The tale of woe was not in vain. And now
It was a maid that lived her life beneath
The shelter of a sage's forest home,
In virgin freedom, till she found a royal heart
That flowed to her in love. But oh, the ring
Which was their symbol of communion
She lost; her princely lover knew her not;
A nameless stranger at the palace gates,
She strove in vain to wake the memories
Of old, and flash them on the monarch's mind,
Till voices from the heavens declared her true.
And now the tale is changed – another came
To Kāma's grace with sweet and sudden steps;
She sought her downy bed in peace one night
And woke to find a prince had been with her;

The princess drew the hero of her dream
And royal embassies that sped from state
To state, approached the lover and their hearts
Were joined in holy wedlock's union.
There was again that princess pure in faith
Who sought a hermit's presence very day;
Her tender arms upbore a golden plate
Of daily offerings of flower and fruit;
She prayed and coyly asked a boon, to wed
A warrior of mighty prowess; lo!
The hermit dropped his guise, the happy prince
 She had long loved, now grasped her in his arms
It was a dismal void for Yamini,
When Bilhan turned his homeward way at fall
Of night. The stars that flowered in the skies
And even the dazzling glory of their queen
Her vision left in chill obscurity,
And tossing on her sleepless bed she longed
For love to cheer her life. When would its light
Illume her days? A lover pour his tale
Of passion in her ears, or seek a cloud
Trailing across the heavens to speed his words?
Some king of matchless greatness care to seek
Her hand? In patience would she bear
The cruel curses of a Fatal Ring,
If the same bliss were hers at start and end.
Perchance some prince that hailed from unknown lands
Was flying on his wingèd magic horse
That very night, towards her storied hall,
To light upon the marble floor and turn
His wondering eyes to her. Was there anear
To her an unknown lover? The thoughts were vain,
The leaden moments weighed upon her heart
And caused it ceaseless pain. Two years had passed,
They formed a music strain to Bilhan's soul
And roused its sweetest harmonies. Far more
Than in the worlds of song was there in her
Felicity supreme. It was a night
In *Sarath*[106] time; resplendent shone the moon
And as he poured his learned talk, the bard
Beheld in sudden joy the jewelled orb
That shimmered through the window's gilded bars
And calmly rose to view. His soul now burst
In rapturous praise of the effulgent moon.
He spoke his words – it was the wont for them

---

106 *Sarath*: autumn.

To draw a song for lovely Yamini,
To draw her lyric sweetness: "Queen of light,
Touching the eastern skies with rosy bloom,
You strike with anguish parted lovers; thrill
The seas with joy; the lotus drops its head;
The lily bares its hidden wealth; the heavens
Reveal a world of spacious breadth enrobed
In silver hues; and lovely Kama speeds
In pride, upon his thousand victories.
Sovereign star, the poet's fancy oft
Hath seen mysterious forms in dusky spots
That tinge your heart. – It is a spreading tree,
The bard hath said, or else, a hare or deer;
But oh, it is the void creation's lord
Hath caused by robbing you of nectar lodged
Within your breast, to sweeten his love's lips.
Vishnu reclining on the swelling sea
Is there; behold the starry spray, the wide
Expansive blue, that buoys Him on his bed;
What tales have poets woven round the spot!
It is the mole of luck; the muddy crust
Enwashed by ocean waves, the frisking deer;
The shadow of the earth; the sapphire piece
That Indra loves to wear; but as I see,
The mass of darkness swallowed by the moon.
The gate for Kama's passage to the earth
On mission of enthralling man, she rains
The sweet affliction on the lover's heart.
Is she a white petalled lotus flower
That springs in stately beauty in a pond
Of deep blue waters? Eve's bejewelled ball
That bounds in sport towards the aerial vault
At dusk? The magic stone on which the darts
Of Kāma win their poignant, smiting edge?
It was on such a night that Krishna[107] sought
The scented grove on Jamna's banks, to meet
His love, who stole from home and lay in wait
For sweet embrace. On such a night again,
Did Usha[108] feel her princely lover's touch
When all within the palace lay in silence hushed.

---

107 Krishna: reincarnation, or avatar, of the god Vishnu. He is often depicted playing his flute and frolicking with the *gopis* (female cowherds), especially his love, Radha.
108 Usha: goddess of the dawn in Hinduism.

Maiden of lotus eyes, behold, the moon
Hath cast her lovely mantle on the earth
In witching splendour. Will you close your life
To all this beauty,?" asked the bard, his brows
Glowing with poetic fire. His passion roused
Yamini, her whole being rushed to meet
The singer's heart. Could blindness ever view
The moon with thrilling rapture, sing her praise
In moving language? Has such wonder been
In all this world, and whence this happening?
The myth is all my father's crafty tale –
The veil shall vanish at my anxious touch,
Despite my sacred vow; it cannot be
The Gods will frown upon this act of mine;
His lofty soul is proof to al the world
Of sin, and with good Bilhan must be heaven.
Her lily arm withdrew the silken screen
And lo, there was the handsome bard who looked
Upon her form with eyes of wondrous lustre
And saw her beauty flash like lightning's glow.
"Was this the angel wickedness belied,"
Each thought of other. As she sweetly bent
Adown to hide her blushes, Bilhan strained
Her slender figure in his arms and felt
A wakening rapture claim her all his own.
His being rushed to press her rose-bud lips –
It was a happiness beyond all dreams;
The gates of bliss now poured their wealth of light
Upon the lovers drowned in sacred rites
Of Love. And now to them the world was naught,
Receding like a murmuring wave, to seek
A distant shore, beyond all human ken.
Their lives had found the highest heaven on earth;
The golden dreams of sweet romance now stood
Revealed in crystal shape; and thence their days
Were such that song of hallowed fire could draw
Its vital, moving breath from them, and blaze
To glorious form. "Now doth my soul of song
Awake to find the sordid world enrobed
In joy divine," the poet exclaimed each hour.
The lovers closed their minds to yawning gulfs
That royal wrath may ope beneath their feet;
They kissed the blossoming flower unaware
Of thorns that lurk, or bees that hide their sting
Within its perfumed walls of tender touch;
Basking on sunny banks of spring, the storm
That lowered on the distant skies to break

Its fury on their heads escaped the view;
The secret tale of love now slowly wound
Its way towards the monarch's ears through maids
That quailed in fear to see their virgin charge
Bespoiled, touched in sin by alien hands;
And like a wounded lion, the father rose
In blinding wrath: "The wicked souls shall die
And rid themselves of sin in burning Hell,"
He gasped in ire, and summoned forth the child
That was his pride, and now had wrought the taint
Upon his house. And like a tender dove
That cowers at the dreaded kite's approach,
She sought the monarch's presence, head bent down
In sorrow for her lord, whose very life
Now lay exposed to royal wrath. These words
The father spoke in shame and bitter anguish:
"Was it that thou hadst not a kingly sire
to call an assemblage of princely youths
Of noble lineage, valorous in war
And famed for form, to bestow thee for wife
On him that met your choice in eye and mind,
That though hast sought the ragged bed
Of Brahman rhymesters, basely sprung in life,
Unmindful of the blood that gave you breath.
The seeds of grovelling impurity
Thy hands have sown and they will grow in time
To make my house a shame to all the world."
"All blame is thine my lord," she gently said,
"If bringing souls to untold bliss is blame;"
You brought us near, we saw and only loved;
I met the noblest soul on earth, my being
Rushed forth to him in furious, hungering love
And all was happiness." In rage he cried,
"No more this sweetening of coarsest wrong;
Thy wicked prattling only flaunts thy sin
To greater infamy, the blazing flame
Will shed its lurid light to farther ends.
A father's instinct saves thy tainted life
To leave it lingering in long penance,
But he that lured thy guileless heart to vice
Shall expiate his secret villainy
Within the jaws of death."
                              'Tis I my Lord,
That was the temptress, all thy royal vengeance
Should aim its dart at me, the root and cause
Of all this ill to noble Bilhana

Who owns me now, my very senses all;
With him, my fateful tale now ends on earth."
"Shall little urchins preach to hoary lords
Their kingly duties? Raise their voice against
Their mandates? Ere the mellowed sun shall seek
His golden couch this night, the hangman stops
The villain's sinful breath."
                              "The shades of night,"
She murmured as he passed, "will plunge me deep
In Death and leave you childless on your throne,
To dispense justice like an Iron King
And shackle hearts in written laws of priests
And fools." The bitter words unheeded fell,
The hapless maiden languished on her couch,
Aware of nothing save her cursed fate
Which snapped the chain of bliss on earth for ever.
Mandàra sued, her husband's grace and sought
To calm his anger; their own tale of love
Bore not the severe mould of wedlock's law,
Or plaudits of their parents. Was she not
A petty chieftain's daughter raised to share
A mighty throne, because his youthful eyes
Avowed her fair? Let birds that sang the hymn
Of marriage on that lovely morn in spring,
When with the freedom of a rushing flood
They met, within the lonely champak[109] bower
Upon the margin of the lotus lake
To become man and wife, – let them declare
The truth. Which father blessed the union?
Which greedy priest drawled out his sacredness
In mystic murmurs praying gods to bear
Witness? Had not his constant pleadings wrung
His father's slow consent, their stolen bliss
Confirmed by late approval? And shall they now
Deny such gentle pardoning in turn,
To her, their only child? "The world will go
To nameless ruin, if statesmen ever heed
A woman's siren tongue" – he roared in scorn
And sternly bade her in.
                         As evening flapped
Its dusky wings for spreading flight, they led
The poet ruthlessly to death in chains
Of hardest steel. Beyond the city's bounds,

---

109 *Champak*: evergreen tree with fragrant orange-yellow flowers.

Anear a shrine to Kali's[110] dreaded power
The grim assembly stood in speechless awe;
The hangman wore a saddened look this time,
Though oft the lurid sun had seen him ply
His hireling sword with quick-deciding strength,
Felling the brawniest to grovelling earth.
The hapless lover mused in pain, and saw
In trembling fear, the gloomy scowl of Death,
The fiendish monster that had raised his hand
Of iron might to snatch his cup of bliss;
But brightened oft at cheerful thought of her,
The stainless angel of his heart. "My soul
Knows naught of sorrow's touch, illumed with light
Of holiest love," he said, when shaking heads
Would rudely fathom such a secret joy.
Ere death soon plunged him down to abysses
Of speechless agony, or what perchance
Was worse, to darkening oblivion
And empty nothingness, his dreamy eyes
Would range in raptures o'er the fleeting past
And catch its lingering joy. In rushing speed
Now flowed delicious memories; he quaffed
Again their nectared sweetness, poring o'er
His foredoomed tale of love. "I have enshrined
Within the golden temple of my heart
The Goddess of the lotus eyes. Her form
Of heavenly mould now sweetly floats upon
My vision, beaming beauty as she wakes
From sleep. Like long-lost knowledge speeding back
In sudden swelling flight, she fills my mind
With bliss intoxicant. The full-orbed moon
Swims not in greater glory up the heavens
Than she within my sight; her radiant youth
Is dower which goddesses may like to own
And love. Her luscious lips I seek again
Like hungry bee that buzzing darts on flowers
For honey. I have e'er adored her love
As life's most sacred gift, beyond compare
With even all the learning of the world.
Behold her beauteous face in fresher form,
With sweet averted look when gently vexed,

---

110 Kali: Hindu goddess often depicted as having a terrible appearance with dark-skinned, long, matted hair and sporting on her body the heads and limbs of those she has slain. She is the goddess of instability, disorder and death. Particularly popular in Bengal, she is usually depicted independently or as Shiva's consort. She is closely associated with the tantric tradition.

Her ruffled spirits calming then to joy.
My head is pillowed even at this hour
Upon her bosom's tenderness; the hands
Are locked in sweet embrace, or linger round
The golden girdle worked in stone and pearl
That greedily clasps her waist, enfolding close
Her wayward robes of foam-spun silk; or play
In childish freedom with her raven curls
Of glossy smoothness – such a life of bliss
Be mine all waking moments, and my soul
Be unaware of even highest worlds
Of Heaven, if this were not my share."
The hardened minister was there to guard
The hangman's work, to bring the king's commands
To painful fruition. Compassion's tear
Had ne'er bedimmed his eyes, but why was it
A could now sat upon them and his heart
Was quickening forth to pulses new? He loathed
To speed the murder, for his soul was now
A flood of pity rushing forth to drown
The helpless bard in kindliness? Was there
A muffled voice that whispered low to him –
He was the distant cause of all that tale
Of tragic love. The sin of rending hearts
Apart will brand his crafty, wrinkled brow
With infamy, if from that tangled maze
His crooked wisdom caused, the painless way
Remained unfound? When passions calmed to peace
Will Madan fail, to scan his share of guilt
And scorn his boasted craft which had declared
The end was safe? And was it statesmanship
To blight a daughter's happiness with fate
Of tainted widowhood? How could he bear
The lover's cry of anguish – Hark! he speaks
Again, his silver voice now breaks the calm
Of evening – "The dying moments come
And I shall never sight or groan to see
My form dissolved to primal elements –
The dreadful end most close on all. But God,
This be the only prayer on my lips,
That ever after leaving mortal worlds,
This body mine, be dedicate to serving her:
As air my fortune be to fan her face,
As water fill the envied lotus tanks
That shall be hallowed by her touch; as light
Illume her habitation and as earth

But feel her gentle tread." He stops and forth
The tears swell from all the gathered crowd;
The minister sternly bids the hangman stop
His cruel task, exclaiming "I will be
A ragged beggar trudging in the streets
Than hold my office after such a wrong,
And proffer council to my king." Post-haste
He sought his master's presence, where the queen
Was pouring forth her anguish for the child,
Imploring pardon. Pain had thawed his ire
To pity. Calmly rooted to his throne
He pilloried his judgment, wondering
If it were wisdom's way, to cause a world
Of misery where might be perfect bliss –
To see his daughter wane away to death,
His loving queen with her and himself lose
All joy in life, immured in living death.
Shall not his kingly power stem the tide,
And save his happy home? The minister rushed
To tell his tale of how the dead was stopped
And Madan joyed the way was open still,
To change the gloom to radiant light. The lord
Could swear no sin of wanton youth was there,
But love of holiest purity, and waxed
With warmth for quick repeal of what had passed
His lips. No need was there for further doubt
Or thought. The speech gave sinew to his will
And brought the monarch's mind to action's point.
Messengers flew with tidings to the poet;
Relieved of torture sprang the queen and sought
Her daughter's side with sustenance to feed
Her drooping soul; and from her death-like swoon
The princess rose to second life, when laid
Upon her mother's lap, the news was breathed
Within her ears; and as her eyes beheld
Her lover's palanquin now sway its course
Towards the palace-gates, she darted down
To meet her lord and all was endless joy,
And blessedness. Past all the stormy seas,
They found a haven lit with perfect bliss.

Sonnets (Madras: 1914)[111]

Toru Dutt
(On Reading the "Ancient Ballads and Legends of Hindustan")

With loving rapture have I heard her lyre,
    The simple music of its noble song,
    The sweet and tender notes that bear along
Her Fancy's flight, to realms that bards aspire.
The lays of ancient deeds with hope inspire
    The heart that sorely needs reviving life,
    When called to face the deadly, trying strife
Of Duty's stern command with man's desire.
She set her gaze on Life while she had breath
    And sang with fervour all its woes and joys;
    The gifted Muse of Song had scarce revealed
Her loveliness – when ah! the tyrant, Death,
    Stifled with ruthless hands the lyric voice,
    And plucked the blooming bud from Poesy's field.

The Marquis of Ripon[112]

A teeming nation lowly bend in sorrow
    And shed their heart-felt tears; for him that loved
    Their land as long as human breath allowed,
And shared their civic struggle, day and morrow,
First flashed the light of Freedom's radiant glow.
    The angel-voice that ever calmed their fears,
    The head with all the wisdom of the years,
The guiding hand of Love – who did not bow
To them in revered worship? Who shall fight
    The battle – now this soul has sought its peace –
    Or lead triumphant, workers merged in grief
That mourn their trusted leader, noble chief;
    And who shall waft across the distant seas,
The vision of the coming day of Light?

---

111 P. Seshadri, *Sonnets* (Madras: Srinivasa Varadachari, 1914).
112 Lord Ripon (1827–1909): viceroy of India from 1880 to 1884 under then British prime minister William Gladstone. Ripon was a proponent of the Ilbert Bill (which would have allowed Indian judges to preside over cases involving Europeans) and limited self-government. He was often referred to reverently in Indian-English political discourses during the nineteenth century as a figure sympathetic to Indians and as a proponent for reform within the British Raj.

Victoria
(1908)

Good Queen of mighty England's royal line,
        Of all the honoured sovereigns of fame
        In whate'er age or clime, what hallowed name
Can claim our loving worship more than thine?
Over that glorious day when thou didst sign
        With warmest heart our happiness and peace
        And send the ray of hope across the seas,
We now rejoice – we see thy greatness shine.
The days of bitter feuds have passed away,
        Chaos transformed by aid of Britain's arm,
        To ever-growing progress, void of strife:
May all thy sons devoutly walk thy way
        Of sympathy and love, in calm or storm,
        And guide our fallen land to renewed life.

Romesh Chunder Dutt

Death's dismal chilling waves have closed around
        A hero's life; a statesman, scholar, sage
        Has ceased his toil – has vanished from his age
And clime. But all behind, the shores resound
His praise – a son the ancient fathers found
        To speak their classic lore, to deck its page
        With wonders new; a warrior in his rage
Chafing at wrongs; a patriot encrowned
And dowered with his nation's love. His soul
        Was throbbing for the millions in their sorrow
            Sweating in want and misery forlorn;
And wrought each hour to cheer their weary roll,
        And speed them near the promised golden morrow –
        A beacon light to children yet unborn.

Champak Leaves[113] (Madras: 1919, originally published 1915)[114]

The Sacrifice[115]

    Begirt with foes the town of Chittore lay
        In blank despair; each hour Lakumsi saw
        His soldiers die in heaps, the enemy draw
    Nearer the walls and deemed the royal sway
    Would pass to Moslem hands at last. One day,
        In broken sleep his eyes beheld in awe
        The city's guardian spirit, whose world was law
    To Chittore's kings and trembling heard her say:
    "Twelve princes of the royal line may save
        The sceptre of your house from other hands
            With sacrifice of life." To sate her hungry soul,
    His valiant sons came forth and paid the toll
        With joy. And when the twelfth was left, he gave
        His own, to let him rule his spacious lands.

Jahangir and the Little Children[116]

    One day, through crowded streets of fair Lahore
        Royal Jahangir passed in pomp; from far
        And near, the surging people poured; minar
    And mosque and towering arch and column bore
    The gayest signs of festival. He wore
        A kindly, smiling look and beamed his grace
        Upon the humble crowd; along the city's ways,
    Thus passed the cavalcade. When lo! the roar

---

113 *Champak*: evergreen tree with fragrant orange-yellow flowers.
114 P. Seshadri, *Champak Leaves* (Madras: Ganesh & Co., 1919).
115 [Poet's Note: The Sacrifice: – The episode is from Tod's *Rajasthan*.] James Tod's *Annals and antiquities of Rajast'han, or the central and western Rajpoot states of India* was first published in two volumes between 1829 and 1832 and was reprinted in Madras in 1873, Calcutta in 1884 and London in 1914. The work, which purports to describe the geography of Rajasthan and sketch out a history of the Rajput clans and their customs, spends most of its time recounting major historical events surrounding the clans and their rule. The work captured the imagination of Indians at the time in its romantic portrayal of Rajasthan, and by extension, India.
116 [Poet's Note: Jahangir and the Little Children: – The incident is mentioned by the Italian traveler, Manucci, in his *Storia de Mogor*.] Jahangir (1569–1627): Mughal emperor who was the successor to his father, Akbar, and largely continued the former's policies in imperial administration.

And din suddenly ceased. The king got down
    His stately tusker, joining on the ground
        A knot of little ones absorbed in play,
            And loud exclaimed, "he wished he were as gay
    His life were such a simple, stainless round
Of joy, without the weighty cares of crown!"

Widowed

It was a day of joyous festival
    For wedded girls. In richest garments clad
    Wives offered worship at the temple, glad
Fortune had set her lovely coronal
Upon their brows and pleasures marital
    Sweetened their lives. They sang and danced and had
    Their fill of mirth. But one was sorely sad
And would not mingle in that carnival.
Her wedded life had closed in bitter gloom
    Ev'n ere her arms had oped for close embrace
        Of love. And thus forlorn and widowed in her youth
    She stood in agony of speechless ruth,
    A luckless woman cast upon life's ways
To pine away beneath a dreadful doom.

Queen Tissarakshita's Jealousy[117]

Asoka's loving queen was wroth in mind
    And deep distressed to see her royal spouse
    Had wrapped himself all day and night in vows
Of pious worship; sorely grieved to find

---

117 [Poet's Note: Queen Tissarakshita's Jealousy: – This is the subject of a painting by Abanindranath Tagore, C. I. E. of Calcutta. The Bodhi is the *ficus religiosa*, pipal or poplar-leaved fig-tree. Its sacredness to the Buddhist consist in the fact that the new gospel dawned upon Buddha's mind when sitting in contemplation under a tree of that species. Asoka was King of Magadha from B. C. 260–220.] Emperor Asoka (300–232 BCE) extended the reach of the Maurya Empire across the subcontinent. After converting to Buddhism in 260 BCE, he applied Buddhist principles to administering this vast empire and renounced violence. He is regarded in later historical accounts as a great ruler (wise, just and honorable) and credited with spreading Buddhism across the subcontinent. According to legend, Asoka's wife, Tissarakshita, grew jealous of her husband's devotion to the Bodhi tree and destroyed it.

He sat for hours in contemplation, blind
    To all the world. A bodhi's[118] tender boughs
    Absorbed his care and kept their loves
Apart and fondling whispers, sweet and kind,
Had ceased to be. She nursed her silent grief;
    Resolved, a tree, though sacred, shall not mar
A woman's happiness, – and sought relief
One night, by rooting out the Bodhi-tree,
    Saying, the claims of Love were greater far
Than those of God and Immortality.

Lali and Majnun[119]

They met once more, somewhere, in desert sands
    Majnun, who when his youthful love was crossed
Had fled distraught and passed through many lands
    Goaded by bitter agony, his passions tossed
Upon a restless ocean – till his fever'd soul
    Reposed in madness that obscured his mind:
And Laili who had paid her heavy toll
    Of sorrow too, now roaming forth to find
Her Majnun, whom she could not wed in youth,
    Enforced to marry one who now was dead,
She came in all her speechless pain and ruth
    And he by flitting, vacant visions led;
The long-lost light one moment lit his face
The next, he mumbling sought his desert ways.

---

118 Buddha achieved enlightenment under the shade of a *bo*, or *bodhi*, tree, a large and sacred fig tree located in Bodh Gaya in the modern-day state of Bihar in northern India.

119 [Poet's Note: Laili and Majnun: – No love-story has formed the subject of so much literary inspiration in the East especially in Persia and Arabia as the fortunes of Laili and Majnun. The name *Majnun* itself signifies "furious, frantic, or mad," the hero's real name being Kais. See Atkinson's English translation of the version of the story by Nizami. The sonnet was suggested by a striking painting of the scene by one of the artists of the new Bengal School of Indian Painting, Mr. Hakim Khan.] The Bengal School of painting, an avant-garde movement closely associated with the nationalist movement, flourished during the early twentieth century.

Indumathi's Death[120]

Imperial Aja, born of Raghu's race
      Was keeping with his spouse a holiday;
The lovers played in sun-kissed garden-ways
      And shaded bowers in bloom; the fountain-spray
Blew gently n their cheeks and on the air
      There rose the sound of music soft and sweet
From birds; the Queen, she seemed surpassing air
      That day; with admiration, at her feet
Aja reclined in love and pride – when lo!
      A wreath of flowers descended from the sky
And plunged him in a world of bitter woe;
      The garland smote her neck – he saw her die.
Does Fortune envy mortal happiness,
And ever love to see us in distress?

A Sister's Wail[121]
(Fiji)

I

Decoyed by soulless hirelings have I found
      Exile on Fiji's remote strand. My days
Are passed in speechless sorrow, in a round
      Of bitter toil, through dark and dreary ways
Of endless pain. My wistful, aching eyes
      Are ever cast across this cruel main
Which grimly mocks my grief – the monster lies
      Between me and my home, and all in vain,
I long for glimpses of my native land.
      I ask and ask, "Shall I be never free,

---

120 [Poet's Note: Indumathi's Death: – This is one of the numerous episodes found in the *Raghuvamsa* of Kalidasa. The lamentation of Aja on the death of Indumathi is one of the most well-known classics of Sanskrit Literature.] Very little is known about the classical Sanskrit writer Kalidas, who is thought to have lived during the fifth century under the Gupta dynasty. His works include the long lyric poems, *Meghaduta* and *Ritu-samhara*, as well as two epic poems and three plays.

121 [Poet's Note: A Sister's Wail, I and II: – The two Sonnets refer to the evils of the system of Indian Indentured Labour in Fiji, which roused considerable attention to the country in 1916 and 1917 and led to its abolition by Government.] Over 60,000 indentured laborers came to Fiji between 1879 and 1916. The great majority were from northern India. See Vijay Mishra, *Literature of the Indian Diaspora: Theorizing the Diasporic Imaginary* (London: Routledge, 2007) for a remarkably nuanced account of Indian diasporic literature from Fiji and the Caribbean, in particular.

And shall no gentle brother's helping hand
   Be stretched to me across this dreadful sea?"
   The swiftly swelling tears bedim my eyes
   And I am left to pine away in sighs.

II

It was a dream that came to me last night;
   I saw my little village home once more,
Nestled amidst the trees on Ganges' shore:
There was the cow-herd in the crimson light
Of summer evening, singing gay and bright,
   Driving his cattle home; the temple door
   Had oped for worship and the breezes bore
Sweet incense from the shrine; my ravish'd sight
Beheld once more, the hoary peepul tree[122]
   Sheltering out cot; the earthen lamp was there
   As I myself was wont to light at eve:
But then, I work to deepest misery
   To make my moanings to the heartless air –
   A luckless wretch, I hope for no reprieve.

The Exile[123]

That classic land of bulbul and the rose
   Thrust forth thy fathers to this Eastern clime
   In distant ages past. The waves of Time
Have touched a thousand shores since then and woes
And joys have had their turn. But now she knows
   The bitter truth – it was a thoughtless crime
   That must for e'er her vaunted fame begrime
With dirt and slime and cheer her heartless foes.
That day a world of treasures did she lose,
   Children, the noblest mother should be proud
   To own; but costliest of all wast thou
A maiden born for homage of the muse –
   For poesy's rare possession, woo'd and lov'd
     With kisses raining on thy cheeks and brow.

---

122 The *peepul*, or *peepal*: fig tree, thought to be sacred (n. "peepal" *OED*).
123 [Poet's Note: The Exile: – The reference is to the exile of the ancestors of the modern Parsis from Persia.] Parsis: Indian followers of the Iranian prophet Zoroaster. Parsis are said to have descended from Persian Zoroastrians who immigrated to India to escape religious persecution. The exact date of emigration is unknown (though it is usually placed at sometime before the tenth century).

The Rani of Ganore[124]

At last, the long-fought Moslem victor came
      Within the castle-wall and claimed her hand
      By right of conquest – more than all the land
He prized her loveliness whose bruited fame
Had drawn his passion's greed. And as the game
      Of war was lost, despite her soldier-band
      Who fought with valour under her command,
Devoid of help she stood, subdued and tame: –
Feigning assent, she made the nuptial bed
      Upon the terrace for her bitter foe
          And in the banquet made him drink a bowl
          Of poison – When with pain he 'gan to scowl,
      And writhe, she plunged into the stream below
And lay upon its waters, floating dead.

Anakarli[125]

      The Hall of Mirrors blazed with lamps one night
          When royal Akbar[126] sat in crowded state
          And held his court; with wine and song elate
      Revelled the courtiers and it was a sight
      To set the youthful heart aglow with light
          And love. Prince Selim cast his longing eye
          On fair Anarkarli and heaved a sigh
      That spoke his love-struck heart, and beaming bright,

---

124 [Poet's Note: The Sacrifice: – The episode is from Tod's *Rajasthan*.] James Tod's *Annals and antiquities of Rajast'han, or the central and western Rajpoot states of India* was first published in two volumes between 1829 and 1832 and was reprinted in Madras in 1873, Calcutta in 1884 and London in 1914. The work, which purports to describe the geography of Rajasthan and sketch out a history of the Rajput clans and their customs, spends most of its time recounting major historical events surrounding the clans and their rule. The work captured the imagination of Indians at the time in its romantic portrayal of Rajasthan, and by extension, India.

125 [Poet's Note: Anarkali: – The visitor to Lahore to-day may see the tomb of Anarkali.] According to legend, Anarkali was a beautiful slave girl from Lahore who was buried alive upon the orders of the Mughal emperor Akbar for her illicit relationship with his eldest son, who would later be known as Emperor Jahangir.

126 Akbar (1542–1605): considered one of the great leaders of the Mughal Empire, Akbar ruled from 1556 until his death. He expanded the reach of the Empire over the subcontinent to include almost all of northern India, reformed the central administration system and instituted a more efficient the tax-collection process. His tolerance and sympathy towards other religions, illustrated in part by his inclusion of a number of Hindus in the imperial bureaucracy and allowing Hindu territories within the Empire a measure of autonomy, ensured the loyalty of many non-Muslims.

> She smiled on him. But then the tell-tale glass
>   Betrayed their secret love and Akbar bade
> In wrath that she should die. The luckless lass
>   Perished, but Selim kept her story sad
> In mind, all life, and when he graced the throne
> He reared to her a monument in stone.

Ardeshir Framji Khabardar

Ardeshir Framji Khabardar (1881–1953) was a Parsi from the modern-day state of Gujarat. He wrote verse in Gujarati as well as English-language tracts on Zoroastrianism, including *New light on the Gathas of holy Zarathushtra* (1949) and *Zarathushtra, the First Prophet of the World: 101 Sonnets* (1950), which examines the life and teachings of the Parsi prophet. *The Silken Tassel* (1918; reissued 1928) is his only English-language volume of poetry. James H. Cousins writes in his "Introduction" to this collection that he has difficulty defining Khabardar as an English poet:

> I am told that Mr. Khabardar is a popular poet in his mother-tongue, Gujerati, and I can well believe it on the assumption that poet's wealth of ideas and metrical power is capable of spending itself through more than one language. In Mr. Khabardar's case it obviously should be so. He has lived and listened closely to Keats and Francis Thompson and other masters of lyrical English, and he has made their speech and method so fully his own – in these English poems of his – that it is only on the rarest occasion that a close reader comes on an accent which discloses the foreign lip. If his technical mastery is so strong in a foreign language, his expression in his mother-tongue must indeed be excellent as I am told it is. This gives on the feeling that, however fluently and sweetly he may sing in English of the joy of human love and Divine vision, one is still, in his English poems, only the threshold of his genius. My introduction of Mr. Khabardar is, therefore, somewhat complicated. I cannot introduce him as an Indian poet, for he is not here singing in an Indian language, and if he was, I should unfortunately be none the wiser. I cannot introduce him as an English poet, because he is not one. But I CAN introduce him – as himself; as one who sings in this book melodiously and with fullness of that level of human life which is the common experience of all humanity, and (which is his special excellence) of that higher level of spiritual realization which is familiar to Indian experience, and which may the sooner find utterance in English poetry by being voiced in the orient in songs such as these.

Khabardar's poems to India, reprinted below, capture the sentiments of many nationalists of the time.

The Silken Tassel (Madras: 1918)[127]

An Indian Funeral Song

What are your smiles of the golden morn,
And what are your pearly tears?
What are your strifes for a hope forlorn,
And what are your swords and spears?
What is the hollow delight that assures you
A transient bliss that nothing secures you? –
All are the charms of the *Māyā*[128] that lures you
To an ever-receding gleam:
    Rām bolo, bhai Rām,
    Rām bolo, bhai Rām,
The world is all but a dream!

What are your marble towers and halls,
And what are your gardens and flowers?
What are your gem-deck'd turbans and shawls
And what are your kingly powers?
What is your strength when the earth will shake you?
What are your knowledge and wealth that make you?
For *Yama*[129] is waiting to call and take you
From these glories that seem:
    Rām bolo, bhai Rām,
    Rām bolo, bhai Rām,[130]
The world is all but a dream!

To India

Eternal cradle of the muses fair!
Thou jewell'd throne of wisdom true, divine!
Whose pomp and wealth of many a holy shrine
Did Indra[131] and his gods come down to share;

---

127 Ardeshir Framji Khabardar, *The Silken Tassel* (Madras: Theosophical Publishing House, 1918).
128 [Poet's Note: Illusion which causes one to regard the Supreme Spirit and the Universe as two distinct realities (in the Vedanta Philosophy).]
129 [Poet's Note: The God of Death, Pluto.]
130 [Poet's Note: A cry used by the Hindus while carrying the dead body to the burning ground, meaning "Brothers, take the name of God!"]
131 Indra: god of thunder and rain. In the *Vedas*, the religious scriptures predating the Hindu epics, he is described as the ruler of the gods but was later supplanted in importance by the Trimurti (which is composed of the gods Brahma, Vishnu, and Shiva).

Whose mighty heart has nursed with kindness rare
A score of nations whom it calls now "mine";
Whose freedom of the soul doth far outshine
It blood-fed countertype of keen despair.

India! thy soil is still that cherish'd home!
Ten thousand years have gone, and still thou *art*!
No fetters can enchain thy Spirit clear

And mighty Voice under this vast blue dome:
Truth on thy Tongue, and God within thy Heart,
Speak, Mother, speak! and all the world shall hear!

The Patriot

The fire that burns within a patriot's heart
No ocean can extinguish; and its flame,
Though rising from an earth of lowly name,
Lights up the highest heavens, and strikes athwart

Its truth-unfolding wing in every part.
The one exultant, pure, unconquerable claim
Of Love and Freedom nerves his high-soul'd frame
And keeps him so, for needeth he no art.

No sword can cut his soul that stands supreme;
No force, no guile can turn him from his path;
No glittering gold, no breastwear glories shine

For him; his Country's good his inner dream;
Her greatness doth his outer Vision line,
And rises up to God beyond his death!

Rabindranath Tagore

Rabindranath Tagore (1861–1941), a nationalist, social reformer, and artist, was educated in England and India. Tagore, who wrote in both his native Bengali as well as in English, was awarded the Nobel Prize in literature in 1913. His written work spans a variety of genres including poetry, novels, essays, dairies, autobiographies, and dramas. Although too numerous to list in full, his body of work includes poetic collections *Gitanjali* (1910), *The Gardener* (1913), *Fruit-Gathering* (1916) and *The Fugitive* (1921); plays *Raja* (1910), *Dakghar* (1912), *Muktadhara* (1922) and *Raktakaravi* (1926); and novels *Gora* (1910), *Ghare-Baire* (1916), and *Yogayog* (1929). Tagore's English "translations" of his Bengali verse are not direct renditions but creative interpretations which stand as original works in and of themselves. Tagore has left a rich collection of drawings and paintings as well as numerous musical compositions, including the Indian national anthem *Jana Gana Mana*. As a testament to his unparalleled range and vision, Tagore holds a revered place in the national imaginary as a national poet. The poem reprinted below was printed on a single piece of poster-board, in what seems to be Tagore's own handwriting.

The Gift of the Poet Laureate of India to National Education Week, 1918 (Adyar: 1918)[132]

The lamp is trimmed,
Comrades, bring your own fire to light it.
For the call comes again to you to join the star pilgrims
    crossing the dark to the shrine of sunrise.
The day was when you went forth in your glad adventure of light
    and the star of hope thrilled in the sky and kissed your banner.
But as the dusk deepened you fell behind in the march
    and slept with your lights gone out
  while your dreams grew discordant
    like the ominous cries of night birds.
Yet though it is dark, and the wind in the forest
    is like the wails of lost souls
has not the breath of that prayer already touched your foreheads
    which comes from the past echoing from age to age
    "Lead me to Light from the dark,
      from death to Everlasting Life?"
Sleepers, arise from your stupor of dim desolation
    and know once more that you are children of Light.

---

132 Rabindranath Tagore, *The Gift of the Poet Laureate of India to National Education Week, 1918* (Adyar: S. P. N. E., 1918).

Harindranath Chattopadhyay

The younger brother of the much more famous poet Sarojini Naidu, Chattopadhyay (1898–1990) was a poet, playwright, actor, and politician. He was a member of the Lok Sabha in the 1950s and appeared in a number of films beginning in the 1960s. His other works include *Perfume of Earth* (1922) and *Poems and Plays* (1927). As a poet he is often compared to his sister and found lacking by many critics. Yet he had several admirers nonetheless: a July 1924 review of his verse collections *Ancient Wings* (1923) and *Grey Clouds and White Showers* (1924) in the *Theosophist Magazine* claims that his poetry stands in contrast to the West for being "full of the most sublime philosophy, knowing the great truths of Karma, Reincarnation, the Unity of Humanity and the Immanence of God, etc. This knowledge differentiates his poetry in a marked degree from most other poetry. Moreover his sublime thoughts have also a good technique in which to express themselves."[133] He was briefly married to Kamaladevi Chattopadhyay, who founded the All-India Women's Conference. James H. Cousins writes in his "Foreword" to Chattopadhyay's first volume of poems, *The Feast of Youth*:

> I have written in my book, *The Renaissance of India*, of the problem presented by the poetry of Harindranath Chattopadhyay in its exquisite and most desirable impartation of oriental vision and magic to poetry in the English language, and in its consequent menace to India's literary and national future in the possible drawing away of other young poets from their true instrument of expression, their mother-tongue...
>
> We plan out our political systems, we expound our schemes of education, we talk of the vernacular as the safeguard of national spirit (with the examples before us of Ireland preserving and uttering her soul through centuries of foreign speech, and Wales in her own ancient tongue swearing away her soul to the foreigner, examples which do not make us change our opinion as to the national necessity of vernacular expression). Then comes some individual bearing the sacred fire of genius, and its white flame makes our apparently shining "dome of many-coloured glass" look like variations of the primal darkness. We are forced to recognize that our plans and arguments are only props to weakness, stimuli to derivativeness, signs of disease through which humanity is slowly progressing towards health. They are certainly not evidences of activity of the free spirit, which shows itself through individual genius rising above the level of a race or an age, and uttering itself in any tongue it pleases to use.

The Colored Garden (1919), dedicated to his sister Suhashini Devi, is a book of poems for young children and includes a number of patriotic poems, illustrating the way Indian nationalist rhetoric and feeling may have been inculcated in children.

---

133 A. L. M., "Reviews," *Theosophist Magazine*, July 1924, 544.

The Feast of Youth (Madras: 1918)[134]

The Hour of Rest

The village sleeps with all its huts...
The tired day must die;
The dazzling knife of sunset cuts
The throbbing heart of sky,
That bleeds itself to death and shuts
Earth's beauty from its eye.

The flower of rest is blossoming
On earth and hill and stream...
The homing birds, at sunset sing
A song of shade and gleam...
The West is like a parrot-wing
Tinged with a peacock-dream!

I gaze athwart the lonely wold
And commune with the flowers...
Whose little, lovely lives are sold
To sunshine and to showers...
And in their coloured breasts they hold
The secrets of the hours!

I watch the faintly-dreaming hill,
The sky's dim-silvern line...
And feel that I have drunk my fill
Of clear, renascent wine
Drawn from the rich grape of God's will
Half-human, half-divine!

There is a sweetness in the world
That I have sometimes felt,
And oft in fragrant petals curl'd
His fragrance I have smelt...
And in sad notes of birds, unfurl'd
The kindness He hath dealt!

---

[134] Harindranath Chattopadhyay, *The Feast of Youth* (Madras: Theosophical Publishing House, 1918).

Sufi Worship[135]

Sometimes, O Love! Thou art revealed
To me, and sometimes art concealed
Somewhere. This strange Unity
Flowers in Thee and only Thee!
Love! Thou sayest to me, "I
Build my home in earth and sky…
In the hue of the new-blown rose
See! My hidden beauty glows.
I am born in every note
Showering from the bulbul's throat…
My pulsating dreams rejoice
In each tender maiden's voice.
I dwell in every starry spark,
And laugh alike in light and dark."
And yet, sayest Thou, "Behind the screen
I breathe alone, unknown, unseen!"
How oft, O Lover! Thou dost bless
Our hearts with Thy pure loveliness…
And yet, Thou whisperest, "Alone
I smile behind the screen unknown!"
How long, O hidden Lover mine,
Shall I seek Thee in mosque and shrine?
Dost Thou not hear me call to Thee?
If Thou dost hear, O answer me!
Give o'er this war of Thee and Me!
And thro' clear eyes of wisdom see,
In Love, what difference can there be
'Twixt Me and Thee?

The Coloured Garden (Madras: 1919)[136]

The Coloured Country

There's a Coloured Country
Rich with ancient fame,
What! has no one told you
India is her name?

---

135 Sufism is a sect of Islam known for its focus on the mystical and spiritual aspects of religious practice and belief, including a joyous and complete surrender to the divine.
136 Harindranath Chattopadhyay, *The Coloured Garden* (Madras: Society for the Promotion of National Education, 1919).

There the bright sun rises
Beautifully dressed
In the East, and slowly
Sets in the West.

In that Coloured Country
I have built my home,
Never will I wander
Never will I roam…
For my country gives me
Water, air and fire;
O my Country gives me
All I desire.

My own Coloured Country,
I shall serve you well,
Ring for you my lifetime
Like a crystal bell…
Till your sleeping children
Hear its sound and wake…
I shall fight when needed
For your sweet sake.

That Coloured Country
I shall spread my wing
Flying full of freedom
Like a happy king.
I shall live for India
And for her I'll die!
Though it isn't easy
Yet I shall try!

Pride

India's name is running
In my blood like flame.
All my body tingles
When I hear her name.
India's heart is holy
And her mind is great…
I feel so proud and happy
To share an Indian's fate!

India's song is ringing
In me clear and strong,
All my body dances
When I hear her song.
India's lips are sacred
All her notes ring true...
I am so glad to think that
You are an Indian too!

India's lamp is burning
In me warm and bright.
I become a temple
When I see her light...
India's life is noble!
I go mad with joy
When I chant to India
"I'm an Indian boy!"

A Sad Thing

A little Indian boy was born in England,
He built his childhood up on English toys...
So, when he came with mother down to India
He felt too proud to mix with Indian boys...

He wouldn't care to talk to Indian children
Who are so sweet and gentle, pure and young...
Poor boy was proud because he spoke in English...
But tell me, did he know his mother-tongue?

Aurobindo Ghose

Aurobindo Ghose (1872–1950) was brother of the poet Manmohan Ghose and a famous nationalist, yogi and poet. Born in Calcutta and educated in England for many years, he returned to India in 1893 to work for the Maharaja of Baroda where he published his earliest poems. He also worked as a professor of English and vice-principal at Baroda College and as principal of National College in Calcutta. As a radical nationalist politician, he was vociferous in his critiques both of British imperialism and the Indian National Congress, which he felt was too moderate and too accommodating to imperial rule. Although Ghose was gradually turning towards spirituality, it was not until 1910, after a series of encounters with the British imperial government (including being placed on trial for a bombing), that he completely abandoned politics for spirituality. He journeyed to Pondicherry where he established an ashram. Sri Aurobindo, as he came to be known, published consistently in the second half of his life including spiritual tracts such as *Essays on the Gita* (1922) and *The Life Divine* (1939–40) and his most well-regarded poetic work, *Savitri: A Legend and a Symbol* (1950). The early poems reprinted below allow readers a glimpse of a younger Ghose, whose *Baji Prabhou*, based on a legendary historical war, can be read as a call to arms for service and self-sacrifice to nationalist ideals.

Baji Prabhou, a poem (Pondicherry: 1922, originally published 1909)[137]

Baji Prabhou[138]

A noon of Deccan with its tyrant glare
Oppressed the earth; the hills stood deep in haze,
And sweltering athirst the fields glared up
Longing for water in the courses parched
Of streams long dead. Nature and man alike,
Imprisoned by a bronze and brilliant sky,
Sought an escape from that wide trance of heat.
Nor on rare herdsman only or patient hind
Tilling the earth or tending sleeplessly
The well-eared grain that burden fell. It hung
Upon the Mogul horsemen as they rode
With lances at the charge, the surf of steel
About them and behind, as they recoiled
Or circled, where the footmen ran and fired,
And fired again and ran; "For now at last,"
They deemed, "the war is over, now at last
The panther of the hills is beaten back
Right to his lair, the rebel crew to death
Is hunted, and an end is made at last."
Therefore they stayed not for the choking dust,
The slaying heat, the thirst of wounds and fight,

---

137 Aurobindo Ghose, *Baji Prabhou, a poem* (Pondicherry: Arya Office, 1922). The title page of this edition notes that the poem was "Originally published in Karma Yogin, 1909. Revised and reprinted."

138 Baji Prabhou (16??–1660), or Baji Prabhu Deshpande: lieutenant under Shivaji, founder of the Maratha empire. Ghose's poem recounts Baji Prabhou's heroic self-sacrifice to secure the safe passage of Shivaji from a siege at the fort of Panhalgarh in the modern-day state of Maharashtra. As the Mughal Empire was in decline, the Maratha Empire was in ascendancy. Shivaji was the Marathas' first great ruler. The Marathas conducted a number of raids and waged a number of battles against the Rajputs, who retaliated by staging counter-attacks.

The stumbling stark fatigue, but onward pressed
With glowing eyes. Far otherwise the foe,
Panting and sore oppressed and racked with thirst
And blinded with the blazing earth who reeled
Backward to Raigurh,[139] moistening with their blood
Their mother, and felt their own beloved hills
A nightmare hell of death and heat, the sky
A mute and smiling witness of their dire
Anguish, – abandoned now of God and man,
Who for their country and their race had striven, –
In vain, it seemed. At morning when the sun
Was yet below the verge, the Bhonsle[140] sprang
At a strong mountain fortress, hoping so
To clutch the whole wide land into his grasp;
But from the North and East the Moguls poured,
Swords numberless and hooves that shook the hills
And barking of a hundred guns. These bore
The hero backward. Silently with set
And quiet faces grim drew fighting back
The strong Mahrattas to their hills; only
Their rear sometimes with shouted slogan leaped
At the pursuer's throat, or on some rise
Or covered vantage stayed the Mogul flood
A moment. Ever foremost where men fought,
Was Baji Prabhou seen, like a wild wave
Of onset or a cliff against the surge.
At last they reached a tiger-throated gorge
Upon the way to Raigurh. Narrowing there
The hills draw close, and their forbidding cliffs
Threaten the prone incline. The Bhonsle paused,
His fiery glance travelled in one swift gyre
Hill, gorge and valley and with speed returned
Mightily like an eagle on the wing
To a dark youth beside him, Malsure[141]
The younger, with his bright and burning eyes,
Who wordless rode quivering, as on the leash;
His fierce heart hungered for the rear, where Death
Was singing mid the laughter of the swords.
"Ride, Suryaji," the Chieftain cried, his look
Inward, intent, "and swiftly from the rear

---

139 Raigurh, or Raigarh: city in the eastern part of the modern-day state of Chhattisgarhi, located in central India. It was formerly the capital of the Raigarh princely state.
140 Shivaji belonged to the Bhonsle, or Bhosle, a prominent Maratha clan. The Bhonsle dynasty ruled at Nagpur, in the modern-day state of Maharashtra.
141 Malsure, or Tanaji Malusare: renowned warrior in Shivaji's army.

Summon the Prabhou." Turning at the word
Suryaji's hooves sped down the rock-strewn slope
Into the trenchant valley's depth. Swiftly,
Though burdened with a nation's fate, the ridge
They reached, where in stern silence fought and fell,
Their iron hearts broken with desperate toil,
The Southron[142] rear, and to the Prabhou gave
The summons of the Chief; "Ride, Baji, ride,
The Bhonsle name thee, Baji." And Baji spoke
No word, but stormed with loose and streaming rein
To the high frowning gorge and silent stood
Before the leader. "Baji, more than once
In battle thou hast stood, a living shield,
Between me and the foe. But more to day,
O Baji, save than any single life, –
Thy nation's destiny. Thou seest this gorge
Narrow and fell and gleaming like the throat
Of some huge tiger, with its rocky fangs
Agrin for food: and though the lower slope
Descends too gently, yet with roots and stones
It is hampered, and the higher prone descent
Impregnably forbids assault; too steep
The sides for any to ascend and shoot
From vantage. Here might lion-hearted men,
Though few, delay a host. Baji, I speed
To Raigurh and in two brief hours return.
Say with what force thy iron heart can hold
The passage till I come. Thou seest our strength,
How it has melted like the Afghan's ice
Into a pool of blood." And while he paused
Who had been chosen, spoke an iron man
With iron brows who rode behind the Chief,
Tanaji Malsure, that living sword:
"Not for this little purpose was there need
To call the Prabhou from his toil. Enough,
Give me five hundred men; I hold the pass
Till thy return." But Shivaji kept still
His great and tranquil look upon the face
Of Baji Prabhou. Then, all black with wrath,
Wrinkling his fierce hard eyes, the Malsure;
"What ponders then the hero? Such a man
Of men, he needs not like us petty swords

---

142 Southron: belonging to or dwelling in the south of Britain; southern; *esp.* English as distinguished from Scottish (adj. "southron" *OED*).

A force behind him, but alone will hold
All Rajasthan and Agra and Cabool
From rise to set." And Baji answered him:
"Tanaji Malsure, not in this living net
Of flesh and nerve, nor in the flickering mind
Is a man's manhood seated. God within
Rules us, who in the Brahmin and the dog
Can, if He will, show equal godhead. Not
By men is mightiness achieved; Baji
Or Malsure is but a name, a robe,
And covers One alone. We but employ
Bhavani's[143] strength, who in an arm of flesh
Is mighty as in the thunder and the storm.
I ask for fifty swords." And Malsure;
"Well, Baji; I will build thee such a pyre
As man had never yet, when we return;
For all the Deccan brightening shall cry out,
"Baji the Prabhou burns!" And with a smile
The Prabhou answered; "Me thou shalt not burn
For this five feet or more of bone and flesh,
Whether pure flame or jackals of the hills
Be fattened with its rags, may well concern
Others, not Baji Prabhou." And the Chief
With a high calmness in his shining look,
"We part, O friend, but meet again we must,
When from our tasks released we both shall run
Like children to our Mother's clasp." He took
From his wide brow the princely turban sown
With aigrette[144] diamond-crowned and on the head
Of Baji set the gleaming sign, then clasped
His friend and, followed by the streaming host
That gathered from the rear, to farther hills
Rode clattering. By the Mogul van approached
Baji and his Mahrattas sole remained
Watched of the mountains in the silent gorge.

Small respite had the slender band who held
Fate constant with that brittle hoop of steel;
For like the crest of an arriving wave
The Moslem van appeared, though slow and tired,

---

143 Bhavani: avatar of the Hindu goddess Parvati. She was considered the family deity of Shivaji, who is said to have received his sword from her.
144 Aigrette: tuft of feathers, such as that seen on the aigrette, or egret; also, a spray of gems, or similar ornament worn on the head (n. "aigrette" *OED*).

Yet resolute to break such barrier faint,
And forced themselves to run: – nor long availed;
For with a single cry the muskets spoke,
Once and again and always, as they neared,
And, like a wave arrested, for a while
The assailants paused and like a wave collapsed
Spent backward in a cloud of broken spray,
Retreating. Yielded up the dangerous gorge
Saw only on the gnarled and stumbling rise
The dead and wounded heaped. But from the rear
The main tremendous onset of the North
Came in a dark and undulating surge
Regardless of the check, – a mingled mass,
Pathan and Mogul and the Rajput clans,
All clamorous with the brazen throats of war
And spitting smoke and fire. The bullets rang
Upon the rocks, but in their place unhurt,
Sheltered by tree and rock, the silent grim
Defenders waited, till on root and stone
The confident high-voiced triumphant surge
Began to break, to stumble, then to pause,
Confusion in its narrowed front. At once
The muskets clamoured out, the bullets sped,
Deadly though few; again and yet again,
And some of the impetuous faltered back
And some in wrath pressed on; and while they swayed
Poised between flight and onset, blast on blast
The volleyed death invisible hailed in
Upon uncertain ranks. The leaders fell,
The forward by the bullets chosen out,
Prone or supine or leaning like sick men
O'er trees and rocks, distressed the whole advance
With prohibition by the silent slain.
So the great onset failed. And now withdrawn
The generals consulted, and at last
In slow and ordered ranks the foot came on,
An iron resolution in their tread,
Hushed and deliberate. Far in the van,
Tall and large-limbed, a formidable array,
The Pathan[145] infantry; a chosen force,

---

145 Pathans or Pashtuns: Pashto-speaking people from parts of modern-day southeast Afghanistan and northwest Pakistan. Many Pashtuns migrated to other parts of the subcontinent, including Gujurat, Rajasthan, and Punjab, to serve as soldiers under the Mughal Empire, especially in patrolling the North-West Frontier.

Lower in crest, strong-framed, the Rajputs[146] marched;
The chivalry of Agra[147] led the rear.
Then Baji first broke the silence, "Lo, the surge!
That was but spray of death we first repelled.
Chosen of Shivaji, Bhavani's swords,
For you the gods prepare. We die indeed,
But let us die with the high-voiced assent
Of Heaven to our country's claim enforced
To freedom." As he spoke, the Mogul lines
Entered the menacing wide-throated gorge,
Carefully walking, but not long that care
Endured, for where they entered, there they fell.
Others came behind in silence stern advanced.
They came, they died; still on the previous dead
New dead fell thickening. Yet by paces slow
The lines advanced with labour infinite
And merciless expense of valiant men.
For even as the slopes were filled and held,
Still the velocity and lethal range
Increased of the Mahratta bullets, dead
Rather than living held the conquered slope, –
The living who, half-broken, paused. Abridged,
Yet wide, the interval opposed advance.
Daunting those resolute natures; eyes once bold
With gloomy hesitation reckoned up
The dread equivalent in human lives
Of cubits and of yards, and hardly hoped
One could survive the endless unacquired
Country between. But from the Southron wall
The muskets did not hesitate, but urged
Refusal stern; the bullets did not pause,
Nor calculate expense. Active they thronged
Humming like bees and stung strong lives to death
Making a holiday of carnage. Then
The heads that planned pushed swiftly to the front

---

146 Rajpoots or Rajputs: thought to be mostly members of the Kshetriya, or warrior, caste but their status varied widely. These landowning, patrilineal clans ruled central and northern India from around the tenth century, when they began to gain political power, until the collapse of the Mughal empire, with which they made settlements, at the end of the eighteenth century. After independence in 1947, the Rajput states were merged to form the state of Rajasthan. Known as soldiers, the Rajputs were celebrated for their military prowess and heavily recruited by the British East India Company and later the British Empire. They are often depicted in highly romanticized terms in Orientalist literature.

147 Agra: city in the present-day state of Uttar Pradesh. Intimately tied to the history of the Mughal Empire, Agra is the site of the Taj Mahal.

The centre yet unhurt, where Rajasthan,
Playmate of death, had sent her hero sons,
They with a rapid royal reckless pace
Came striding to the intervening ground,
Nor answered uselessly the bullets thick
Nor paused to judge, but o'er the increasing dead
Leaping and striding, shouting, sword in hand,
Rushed onward with immortal courage high
In mortal forms, and held the lower slope.
But now the higher incline, short but steep,
Baffled their speed, and as they clambered up,
Compact and fiery, like rapid breath
Of Agra's hot simoom,[148] the sheeted flame
Belched bullets. Down they fell with huge collapse,
And, rolling, with their shock drove back the few
Who still attempted. Banned advance, retreat
Threatening disgrace and slaughter, for a while
Like a bound sacrifice the Rajputs stood
Diminishing each moment. Then a lord
High-crested of the Rathore clan[149] stood out
From the perplexed assailants, with his sword
Beckoning the thousands on against the few.
And him the bullets could not touch; he stood
Defended for a moment by his lease
Not yet exhausted. And a mighty shout
Rose from behind, and in a violent flood
The Rajputs flung themselves on the incline
Like clambering lions. Many hands received
The dead as they descended, flinging back
Those mournful obstacles, and with a rush
The lead surmounted and on level ground
Stood sword in hand; yet only for a while, –
For grim and straight the slogan of the south
Leaped with the fifty swords to thrust them back,
Baji the Prabhou leading. Thrice they came,
Three times prevailed, three times the Southron charge
Repelled them; till at last the Rathore lord,
As one appointed, led the advancing death,
Nor waited to assure his desperate hold,
But hurled himself on Baji; those behind
Bore forward those in front. From right and left

---

148 Simoom: hot, dry, suffocating sand-wind which sweeps across the African and Asiatic deserts at intervals during the spring and summer (n. "simoom" *OED*).
149 The Rathore are a Rajput clan.

Mahratta muskets rang their music out
And withered the attack that, still dissolved,
Still formed again from the insistent rear
And would not end. So was the fatal gorge
Filled with the clamour of the close-locked fight.
Sword rang on sword, the slogan shout, the cry
Of guns, the hiss of bullets filled the air,
And murderous strife heaped up the scanty space,
Rajput and strong Mahratta breathing hard
In desperate battle. But far off the hosts
Of Agra stood arrested, confident,
Waiting the end. Far otherwise it came
Than they expected. For, as in the front
The Rathore stood on the disputed verge
And ever threw fresh strength into the scale
With that inspiring gesture, Baji came
Towards him singling out the lofty crest,
The princely form: and, as the waves divide
Before a driving keel, the battle so
Before him parted, till he neared, he slew.
Avoiding sword, avoiding lifted arm
The blade surprised the Rajput's throat, and down
As falls an upright poplar, with his hands
Outspread, dying, he clutched Mahratta ground.
Loud rose the slogan as he fell. Amazed,
The eager hosts of Agra saw reel back
The Rajput battle, desperate victory
Turned suddenly into entire defeat,
Not headlong, but with strong discouragement,
Sullen, convinced, rejecting the emprise.
As they retired, the brilliant Pathan van
Assumed the attempt. "Exhaust," the generals cried,
"Exhaust the stubborn mountaineers; for now
Fatigued with difficult effort and success
They hardly stand, weary, unstrung, inert.
Scatter this fringe, and we march on and seize
Raigurh and Shivaji." Meanwhile, they too
Not idle, covered by the rocks and trees,
Straining for vantage, pausing on each ledge,
Seizing each bush, each jutting promontory,
Some iron muscles, climbing, of the south
Lurked on the gorge's gloomy walls unseen.
On came the Pathans running rapidly,
But as the nearmost left the rocky curve
Where lurked the ambush, loud from stone and tree
The silence spoke, sideways, in front, behind
Death clamoured; and tall figures strewed the ground

Like trees in a cyclone. Appalled the rest
Broke this way and broke that, and some cried, "On!"
Some shouted "Back!" for those who led, fell fast.
So the advance dissolved, divided, – the more
In haste towards the plains, greeted with death
Even while they ran; but others forward, full
Of panic courage, drove towards the foe
They could not reach, – so hot a blast and fell
Stayed their unsteady valour, their retreat
So swift and obstinate a question galled,
Few through the hail survived. With gloom their chiefs
Beheld the rout and drawing back their hosts
In dubious council met, whether to leave
That gorge of slaughter unredeemed or yet
Demand the price of so immense a loss.

But to the Prabhou came with anxious eyes
The Captain of the band. "Baji," he cried,
"The bullets fail; all the great store we had
Of shot and powder by unsparing use
Is spent, is ended." And Baji Prabhou turned.
One look he cast upon the fallen men
Discernible by their attire, and saw
His ranks not greatly thinned, one look below
Upon the hundreds strewing thick the gorge,
And grimly smiled; then where the sun in fire
Descending stooped, towards the vesper verge
He gazed and cried; "Make iron of your souls.
Yet if Bhavani wills, strength and the sword
Can stay our nation's future from o'erthrow
Till victory with Shivaji's return."
And so they waited without word or sound,
And over them the silent afternoon
Waited; the hush terrestrial was profound.
Except the mountains and the fallen men
No sight, no voice, no movement was abroad,
Only a few black-wined slow-circling birds
That wandered in the sky, only the wind
That now arose and almost noiselessly
Questioned the silence of the wooded sides,
Only the occasional groan that marked the pang
By some departing spirit on its frame
Inflicted. And from time to time the gaze
Of Baji sought the ever-sinking sun.
Men fixed their eyes on him and in his firm
Expression lived. So the slow minutes passed.

But when the sun dipped very low, a stir
Was felt far off, and all men grasped their swords
Tighter and put a strain upon their hearts.
Resolved at last the stream of Mughal war
Came once more pouring, not the broken rout
Of Pathans, not discouraged Rajput swords,
But Agra's chivalry glancing with gold
And scimitars inlaid and coloured robes.
Swiftly they came expecting the assault
Fire-winged of bullets and the lethal rain,
But silence met them and to their intent
So ominous it seemed, a while they paused,
Fearing some ruse, though for much death prepared,
Yet careful of prevention. Reassured,
Onward with a high shout they charged the slope.
No bullet sped, no musket spoke; unhurt
They crossed the open space, unhurt they climbed
The rise; but even as their hands surprised
The shrubs that fringed the vantage, swords unseen
Hacked at their fingers, through the bushes thrust
Lances from warriors unexposed bore through
Their bosoms. From behind the nearest lines
Pressed on to share their fate and still the sea
Of men bore onward till with violent strain
They reached the perilous crest; there for a while
A slaughter grim went on and all the verge
Was heaped and walled and thickly fortified
With splendid bodies. But as they were piled,
The raging hosts behind tore down their dead
And mounted, till at last the force prevailed
Of obstinate numbers and upon a crest
Swarming with foemen fought against desperate odds
The Southron few. Small was the space for fight,
And meeting strength with skill and force with the soul
The strong and agile keepers of the hills
Prevailed against the city-dwelling hosts,
With covert and the swiftly stabbing blades
O'erpowering all the feints of Agra's schools.
So fought they for a while; then suddenly
Upon the Prabhou all the Goddess came.
Loud like a lion hungry on the hills
He shouted, and his stature seemed to increase
Striding upon the foe. Rapid his sword
Like lightning playing with a cloud made void
The crest before him, on his either side
The swordsmen of the South with swift assault

Preventing the reply, till like a bank
Of some wild river the assault collapsed
Over the stumbling edge and down the rise,
And once again the desperate moment passed.
The relics of the murderous strife remained,
Corpses and jewels, broidery and gold.
But not for this would they accept defeat.
Once more they came and almost held. Then wrath
Rose in the Prabhou and he raised himself
In soul to make an end; but even then
A stillness fell upon his mood and all
That god-like impulse faded from his heart,
And passing out of him a mighty form
Stood visible, Titanic, scarlet-clad,
Dark as a thundercloud, with streaming hair
Obscuring heaven, and in her sovran[150] grasp
The sword, the flower, the boon, the bleeding head, –
Bhavani. Then she vanished; the daylight
Was ordinary in a common world.
And Baji knew the goddess formidable
Who watches over India till the end.
Even then a sword found out his shoulder, sharp
A Mogul lance ran grinding through his arm.
Fiercely around him gathered in a knot
The mountaineers; but Baji, with a groan,
"Moro Deshpande, to the other side
Hasten of the black gorge and bring me word.
Rides any from the West, or canst thou hear
The Raigarh trumpets blow? I know my hour
Is ended; let me know my work is done."
He spoke and shouted high the slogan loud.
Desperate, he laboured in his human strength
To push the Mogul from the gorge's end
With slow compulsion. By his side fell fast
Mahratta and Mogul and on his limbs
The swords drank blood, a single redness grew
His body, yet he fought. Then at his side
Ghastly with wounds and in his fiery eyes
Death and rejoicing a dire figure stood,
Moro Deshpande. "Baji, I have seen
The Raigarh lances; Baji, I have heard
The trumpets." Conquering with his cry the din
He spoke, then dead upon a Mogul corpse
Fell prone. And Baji with a gruesome hand
Wiping the blood from his fierce staring eyes

---

150 Sovran: sovereign.

Saw round him only fifteen men erect
Of all his fifty. But in front, behind,
On either side the Mogul held the gorge.
Groaning, once more the grim Mahratta turned
And like a bull with lowered horns that runs,
Charged the exultant foe behind. With him
The desperate survivors hacking ran,
And as a knife cuts instantly its way
Through water, so the yielding Mogul wall
Was cleft and closed behind. Eight men alone
Stood in the gorge's narrow end, not one
Unwounded. There where hardly three abreast
Have room to stand, they faced again the foe
And from this latest hold Baji beheld
Mounting the farther incline, rank on rank,
A mass of horsemen; galloped far in front
Some forty horse, and on a turbaned head
Bright in the glory of the sinking sun
A jewelled aigrette blazed. And Baji looked
Over the wide and yawning field of space
And seemed to see a fort upon a ridge,
Raigarh; then turned and sought again the war.
So for a few minutes desperately they strove.
Man after man of the Mahrattas fell
Till only three were left. Then suddenly
Baji stood still and sank upon the ground.
Quenched was the fiery gaze, nerveless the arm:
Baji lay dead in the unconquered gorge.
But ere he fell, upon the rocks behind
The horsehooves rang and, as the latest left
Of the two hundred died, the bullets thronged
Through the too narrow mouth and hurled those down
Who entered. Clamorous, exultant blared
The Southron trumpets, but with stricken hearts
The swords of Agra back recoiled; fatal
Upon their serried unprotected mass
In hundreds from the verge the bullets rained,
And in a quick disordered stream, appalled,
The Mogul rout began. Sure-footed, swift
The hostile strength pursued, Suryaji first
Shouting aloud and singing to the hills
A song of Ramdas[151] as he smote and slew.
But Shivaji by Baji's empty frame

---

151 Ramdas (1608–1682): Marathi saint and mystic, who is known for his religious poetry and as the guru of Shivaji.

Stood silent and his gaze was motionless
Upon the dead. Tanaji Malsure
Stood by him and observed the breathless corpse,
Then slowly said, "Thirty and three the gates
By which thou enterest heaven, thou fortunate soul,
Thou valiant heart. So when my hour arrives,
May I too clasp my death, saving the land
Or winning some great fortress for my lord."
But Shivaji beside the dead beheld
A dim and mighty cloud that held a sword
And in its other hand, where once the head
Depended bleeding, raised the turban bright
From Baji's brows, still glittering with its gems,
And placed it on the chief's. But as it rose
Blood-stained with the heroic sacrifice,
Round the aigrette he saw a golden crown.

Nizamat Jung

Jung (1871–1955) was born in Hyderabad and educated in England at Trinity College, Cambridge and the Inner Temple. After returning to India, he acted as under-secretary in the Legislative Department and later as home secretary. Jung served as chief justice of the High Court of Hyderabad (1910–1918) before his appointment to the Nizam of Hyderabad's Executive Council. A member of the Nizam's royal family, Jung was also knighted by the British Empire for his public service. R. C. Fraser writes in the foreword to *Sonnets by the Nawab Nizmat Jung Bahadur* (1913):

> The following Sonnet Sequence, – written during rare intervals of leisure in a busy and strenuous life, – was privately printed in Madras early in 1914, without any intention of publication on the part of the author. He has, however, now consented to allow it to be given to a wider audience; and we anticipate in many directions a welcome for this small but significant volume by the writer of "India to England," one of the most popular and often-quoted lyrics evoked by the Great War.

Jung also published *Love's Withered Wreath* (1914) and *Sonnets and Other Poems* (1914). Shortly before his death, Jung's poems were collected and published in a volume edited by Zahir Ahmed in 1954. The poems reprinted here, although drawn from this volume, appeared in print in periodicals and poetic collections well before 1920.

Poems (Hyderabad: 1954)[152]

Ode
The Awakening of the East

From East to West the orb of Day
Through boundless aether wheels his flight;
And then relumes with quiv'ring ray
The shadow-haunted realm of Night
And lo! the brightest gems adorn
The brow of fresh-awakened Morn.
She wears once more a pure and roseate glow,
And the fairest flowers that blow
Her bosom deck and on her lap are strewn.
And, from her lofty, glist'ring throne,
Her hand, with sovereign bounty scatters round
Fair Nature's precious gifts upon the smiling ground.

So in the past thy light divine
From East to West, O Heavenly Wisdom! sped,
And as Night flees before sunshine,
So from man's heart the shades of darkness fled.
First in the East Religion rose,
That dared the gates of Heaven unclose;
First in the East heav'n-eyed Philosophy
Taught the Soul how to be free
From earthly trammels which the senses bind
About her wings when, unconfined,
She fain would take her daring upward flight
And soar in cloudless realms of Empyrean light.

Westward they moved with radiant mien,
Hopeful, steadfast and serene;
Night and Chaos passed away
And proudly rose the new-born Day.
Then Law and Justice and the gentle Arts
That Peace to noble life imparts,
Ruled in those glens where Superstition trod,
And hailed the new-found light that owned an unknown God!

---

152 Nizamat Jung, *Poems*, ed. Zahir Ahmed (Hyderabad: Sir Nizamat Jung Memorial Library, Madina Mansion, 1954).

And Nations rose and States were planned
And gorgeous Cities built, and far and wide
Fair Europe over sea and land
Unfurled the banner of her power and pride;
And o'er dark regions, once unknown,
The glimm'ring light of Faith was thrown:
The hungry savage left his quiv'ring prey –
Learnt to tremble and obey
All lost, the while, in dream of bygone days,
The East looked on with heedless gaze
Upon her youthful rival's growing power,
And dreaming, still looked on – and lost the precious hour.

Awake! arise! With throbbing breath
And wistful eyes she views the path before;
Sighs for the past – and from the West
Seeks to relearn her long-forgotten lore.
Behold! from Neptune's sunset strand
The generous West her guiding hand
Doth o'er the far-resounding waves extend,
As a sister, as a friend,
To share with her the gifts herself hath won
From earth and heaven while the sun
Through labour-crowded centuries hath rolled –
Rich gifts, more precious far than India's gems and gold.

A fairer dawn with brighter ray –
Herald of a glorious day –
O'er the far horizon's rim
Dissolves the ling'ring shadows dim.
Behold what gorgeous-winged visions rise
And sail athwart the sapphire skies!
What glowing forms, the godlike semblance wear,
What heav'n-aspiring strains float on the sunlit air!

Voice of the past that silently
Has stirred within my country's bosom long,
Voice of the future, proud and free
In one loud strain their blended notes prolong
Come forth ye wise and good and brave
From out the cradle and the grave!
The spell is broke, and from the fading gloom
Of the dark and silent tomb
Bursts forth, arrayed in all the light of thought,
Each soul that deathless work hath wrought;
Leaps from the cradle too a fearless band
To hail the mighty dead – the guardians of the land.

'Tis theirs, the song; 'tis theirs, the light
That fills the air with triumph, gilds the sky.
It swells more proudly, burns more bright
And pure, Britannia, 'neath thy favouring eye.
Britannia! Thou by Heaven's decree
The Foster-mother of the free,
Thou deemed, in every age and every clime,
Nurse of patriot hopes sublime,
Nurse of high thought and deeds of high emprise,
Nurse of the brave, the just, the wise,
Smile on their sunrise songs, for they are thine,
Who bidst the Past revive, the Future's glories shine.

Shall fainter grow that melody,
Lost in long futurity?
Fading slow, those visions gay
In the far distance die away?
Ah, no! that music fails not though mine ear
Its distant warbling fail to hear;
Those visions fade not though my failing sight
See not their lights ahead, that burn for ever bright.

The Imperial Coronation at Delhi[153]

Once more yon ancient gates, unbar;
    Undo once more the mould'ring chains that bind!
Hark, o'er the Western waves afar
    What joyous strains come floating on the wind!
Queen of the East! no longer mourn
    Thy broken sword, thy laurels torn,
Thy sceptre vanished, and the gem
    That once adorned thy diadem.
See'st thou? The clouds of ages roll away
    And brightly shines the rising day.
Long-faded scenes for which thy heart did yearn,
    From out the Past arise and to thine eyes return.

---

153 [Editor's Note: Written in 1911 at the time of the Delhi Durbar. The poem had the good fortune to be read before Their Majesties King George and Queen Mary soon after their Silver Jubilee. – Ed] The 1911 Delhi Durbar, while only one of several mass assemblies used to demonstrate loyalty and inspire awe among colonial subjects, was the only one to be attended by the British sovereign.

No longer mourn o'er crumbling piles,
    That there the Mighty Moghul[154] once bore away –
Those spots were lingering Glory smiles,
    And spectral Grandeur clothed in ruin gray.
Behold! Upon thy monarchs' throne
    Sits one whose heart is all thine own.
Let him a nobler seat obtain –
    Take him into thy heart to reign!
A King – a man who neither pomp nor power
    Doth value, nor the glitt'ring shower
Of gold and gems the gorgeous Orient brings
    To scatter at the feet of her barbaric kings.

'Twas with fierce-eyed War's alarms,
    And with Conquest's gory arms
That the Macedonian came;
    Ghazni sent her plundering horde,
And proud Persia's bloody Lord[155]
    Came with famine, slaughter, flame.
But *he* brings love and liberty and peace.
    Where'er he moves, and these his state attend.
They bid fell Discord her loud clamour cease,
    Learn to revere the master in the friend.
Soft mercy and calm justice wait
    Upon each act of sovereign power;
And wisdom from her ancient tower
    Bids truth hold high her searching light
All shades of evil to abate
    And guide his steps aright,
Who brings him with Britannia's faith and love
    Vowed before man below, and vowed 'fore God above.
When, by the dire decree of Fate,
    A feeble prey to warring whirlwinds given,
Her rudder lost, thy Ship of State
    O'er dangerous shoals and treacherous rocks was driven,

---

154 The last few centuries of Delhi's history have been intimately linked to the history of the Mughal Empire and the history of the British Empire. The Mughal Empire of the subcontinent was founded in 1526 with the defeat of the Delhi Sultanate by Babur (a descendent of Timur) and ended in 1857 as a result of the Indian Uprising (or "Sepoy Mutiny") when the last Mughal emperor, Bahadur Shah Zafar, who "ruled" from Delhi's Red Fort, was deposed by the British and sent into exile in Burma. The British announced that the capital of the British Raj would be shifted from Calcutta to Delhi at the Delhi Durbar of 1911, held to commemorate the coronation of King George V and Queen Mary as emperor and empress of India.

155 [Editor's Note: Nadir Shah] Nadir Shah (1688–1747) won a series of battles against the Afghans and eventually became Shah of Iran in 1736. He invaded Mughal India, including Delhi and Lahore and was known for his brilliant but methods of conquest and rule.

'Twas then upon the Ocean wave
    Appeared the Ocean-Queen – to save.
She took from Neptune's trembling hand
    The Trident, sceptre of command;[156]
She charmed the winds, she hushed the waters' roar,
    And steered thy battered bark ashore.
Swift at her frown the storm-clouds overhead
    Did shake their sable wings and, lightly scattered, fled.
Britannia's faith, Britannia's power
    Wide o'er the world victorious arms attest;
But Heaven bestows a nobler dower,
    By all the Graces and the Muses blest.
Of these immortal thoughts are born,
    And beauteous arts that life adorn,
Aspiring hopes that ills defy,
    That raise, ennoble, sanctify.
Land of high thought![157] still shall thine ancient use
    A younger sister's hand refuse?
Awake, arise! and burst the bands of sleep;
    Feel thy dead bosom throb, and learn to smile and weep!

See yonder streak of roseate light,
    Where gray Dawn and dusky Night
O'er the dim horizon meet.
    There the shadows of the Past
With the Present mingling fast,
    The rising Morn of Future greet.
The light of Knowledge spreads and Science gains
    Victorious sway o'er fairy realms unknown
And with triumphant skill man's mind obtains
    From Nature's heart the secrets she doth own.
When Virtue quelling passion's strife,
    Has power to guide the chastened heart,
Then will the brood of Vice depart,
    And Hope's dim eyes serenely shine.
Then will man deem his earthly life
    A spark of Life Divine;
Then Honour, Faith and Freedom, hand in hand,
    Rule o'er the earth redeemed – warders of sea and land!

Look down from your high seats of bliss,
    O Kings that once your country's sceptre swayed!
From starry spheres look down on this
    Enchanted ground where once your footsteps strayed

---

156 Neptune: god of the sea in Roman mythology; often depicted wielding a trident.
157 [Editor's Note: India]

But yesterday each haunted spot
    Yearned for the voice that answered not;
To-day the very echoes ring
    With hopeful greetings from the King.
Behold, where yonder battlements extend
    What gorgeous scenes from heaven descend!
The Past reborn! 'Tis Akbar's[158] voice sublime
    Rolls forth from golden clouds and fills the vaults of Time.

"All hearts that truth and justice own,
    All hearts that monarchs' merits seeks to scan,
Behold yon seat – an Empire's throne;
    Yon man – the Guardian of the rights of man!
By Fate and wisdom's magic art
    His throne rests on the human heart;
Upheld, not by the hand of power,
    Nor for a fleeting, dubious hour,
But for all time by glorious heritage
    Of noble deeds from age to age,
Of pure unselfish thoughts whose currents run,
    A bright unsullied stream, from noble sire to son.

Power may sink, and grandeur wane;
    Yet will noble deeds remain
Through eternity.
    When life's glitt'ring shows depart,
Generous love that swayed the heart
    Will still life's deathless record be.
All-hail O King! within whose generous breast
    Long-gathered rays of quenchless virtue shine,
We yield to thee the power we once possesst,
    To thee the sceptre of the heart resign.

Bold in thy virtue, walk the earth
    Life's noblest mission to fulfil:
Exalt the good, subdue the ill
    Until regenerate nations own
A second and a higher birth,
    And blessings erst unknown.
Thus, spreading hope and joy and peace around
    Move on thy destined course, with nations' blessings crowned!"

---

158 Akbar (1542–1605): considered one of the great leaders of the Mughal Empire, Akbar ruled from 1556 until his death. He expanded the reach of the empire over the subcontinent to include almost all of northern India, reformed the central administration system and instituted a more efficient the tax-collection process. His tolerance and sympathy towards other religions, illustrated in part by his inclusion of a number of Hindus in the imperial bureaucracy and allowing Hindu territories within the Empire a measure of autonomy, ensured the loyalty of many non-Muslims.

India to England, 1914[159]

O England! in thine hour of need,
      When Faith's reward, and Valour's meed
         Is death or glory;
When Fate indites, with biting brand
Clasped in each warrior's stiff'ning hand,
         A Nation's story;

Though weak our hands, which fain would clasp
The warrior's sword with warrior's grasp
         On Victory's field;
Yet turn, O mighty Mother! turn
Unto the thousand hearts that burn
         To be thy shield.

Thine equal justice, mercy, grace,
Have made a distant alien race
         A part of thee.
'Twas thine to bid their souls rejoice,
When first they heard the living voice
         Of Liberty.

Unmindful of their ancient name –
Their fathers' honour, glory, fame –
         And sunk in strife
Thou foundst them whom thy touch hath made
Men, and to whom thy breath conveyed
         A nobler life.

They, whom thy love hath guarded long,
They, whom thy care hath rendered strong
         In long and faith –
Their heart-strings round thy heart entwine;
They are, they ever will be thine,
         In life – in death!

---

159 [Editor's Note: Published in the *London Times* on the day of the landing of the Indian troops at Marseilles, October 1914.] Thousands of Indian troops served in the British Imperial Army during World War I; Indian troops fought in every major conflict during the war.

On the admission of Indians to the British Army[160]

Be ours the pride to do and dare
When England offers to our hand,
Even as a sacred trust to bear,
The sword that guards our native land!

That sword was ours when ours the power
And pride of sinewy hand and heart.
That sword we lost in evil hour –
Even with our manhood's nobler part.

Now England brings it, and the blade
Is brighter than it wont to be,
And England's fostering care has made
The hand that takes it firm and free.

'Tis hers, as with a mother's care,
To guard our nation's second youth;
The wrongs of ages to repair,
Rekindling Honour, Freedom, Truth.

'Tis ours with grateful hearts to own
The glorious guerdon she has brought.
Compelling fortune to atone
A hundred evils that were wrought.

We'll take it, wear it, nobly serve
With deeds the land from which we've sprung;
Serve her with might of blood and nerve –
Not with the valour of the tongue!

Who talks of rights as hire or fee;
Who'll take, and with a beggar's hand
All heedless of the infamy,
A bribe to guard his native land?

Who can love's sacred call withstand,
Or pause, by factious counsels led?
He, recreant, owns that in his land
Love, faith and chivalry are dead.

---

160 Indian soldiers, or sepoys, were used on the subcontinent in regional skirmishes and battles and to maintain "order." Recruited on an unprecedented scale into the British war effort at the start of World War I, the Indian Army suffered thousands of casualties.

If such there be, O let him hide
His shame from Honour's scornful eye!
Such hearts as his shall never bide
Where blood runs warm and hearts beat high

Not his the place where patriots throng,
Of nobler blood and prouder name;
Not his to swell his country's song
With far-heard echoes of its fame.

In Memoriam
The Late Nizam Mir Mahbub Ali Khan[161]

A radiant soul eclipsed awhile with care,
Soared back again unto the realm of light,
And left behind a day that seemed like night.
Himself of higher destiny aware,
All heaven and earth it was his lot to share;
A king in pomp, at heart an eremite,
His silent spirit soared from height to height
In search of good in realms of purer air.

He ruled by love, his sceptre of command
Was but a symbol of his heart of love,
By which the allegiance of all hearts he won.
A heart of pity and an open hand –
These were the blessings dowered from above
As his true kingdom ere his day was done.

---

161 [Editor's Note: Died in September, 1911.] The Nizam, the Mughal ruler Mir Mahboob Ali Khan (1869–1911), was the nominal ruler of the princely city of Hyderabad and was himself a poet.

Abroad

Abroad designates that region beyond the subcontinent, in the imperial "center" of Great Britain, London, but also Cambridge (where Roby Datta's *Echoes from East and West* was published) and Oxford (where Manmohan Ghose's *Songs of Love and Death* was published). Sustained mass immigration to Britain did not begin until after World War II, with the need for a new labor force to replace that lost during the war. However, a number of South Asians travelled between the subcontinent and Great Britain for education, work and emigration during the nineteenth century as well.[1] Dadabhai Naoroji, the first Indian member of Parliament in Britain and known as the "Grand Old Man of India," was an early example of settlement in London. Some of the poets included in this section, such as Manmohan Ghose, ruminate on the status of the colonial migrant and exile. Publication in England signified the acceptance of an author into English literary institutions and so was highly coveted and prized. Some of the poets included in this section, such as Toru Dutt, Sarojini Naidu, and Rabindranath Tagore, are among the most well-known or highly regarded Indian poets writing in English during the long nineteenth century. The section also includes lesser-known figures such as Hariprasad Gour and Dwijendra Lal Roy, who have been consigned to relative obscurity.

Govin Chunder Dutt, et al.

This beautifully bound, gilt-covered volume is a communal effort by the talented and famous Dutt family of Bengal, including Govin Chunder Dutt (father of Toru Dutt), Greece Chunder Dutt, Omesh Chunder Dutt and Hur Chunder Dutt. Govin Chunder Dutt, who seems to have written the preface to this collection, had by this time converted his wife and children to Christianity. The preface notes that the authors included in this collection "venture on the publication, not because they think their verses good, but in the hope that their book will be regarded, in some respects, as a curiosity" written by "foreigners, natives of India, of different ages, and in different walks of life, yet of one family, in whom the ties of blood relationship have been drawn closer by the holy bond of Christian brotherhood." Although individual poems within the collection lack authorial attribution, authorship of some poems can be provisionally ascribed since, for example, many of Greece Dutt's poems were also later published in his separately authored volumes. The poetry included here imagines India through its landscape and scenery.

---

1 See Antoinette Burton, *At the Heart of the Empire: Indians and the Colonial Encounter in Late-Victorian Britain* (Berkeley: University of California Press, 1998) and Rozina Visram, *Ayahs, Lascars, and Princes: Indians in Britain, 1700–1947* (London: Pluto Press, 1986).

The Dutt Family Album (London: 1870)[2]

Home

No picture from the master hand
    Of Gainsborough[3] or Cuyp may vie
With that which at my soul's command
    Appears before mine inward eye
In foreign climes when doomed to roam -
Its scene my own dear native home.

What though no cloud-like hills uprear
    Their serried heights sublime afar!
What though the ocean be not near,
    With wave and wind in constant war!
Nor rock nor sea could add a grace,
So perfect seems the hallowed place.

Casuarinas in solemn range
    At distance look like verdant hills,
And winds draw from them music strange,
    Such as the tide makes when it fills
Some shingle-strown and land-girt bay
From men and cities far away.

And round, as far as eye can reach
    What vivid piles of foliage green!
Mango and shaddock,[4] plum and peach,
    And palms like pillars tall between:
An emerald sea surrounds the nest,
A sea for ever charmed in rest.

What roses bloom on the lawn!
    What warblers on the bamboo boughs,
Lithe and elastic, swing at dawn,
    And pour their orisons and vows!
What dew upon the greensward lies!
How lovingly look down the skies!

---

2 Govin Chunder Dutt, et al., *The Dutt Family Album* (London: Longmans, Green & Co., 1870).
3 Sir Thomas Gainsborough (1727–1788): English landscape and portrait painter. Aelbert Cuyp: Dutch landscape painter.
4 Shaddock: pomelo, a type of citrus fruit.

And at high noon when every tree
    Stands brooding on its round of shade,
And cattle to the shelter flee
    And there, in groups recumbent laid,
Gaze ruminant — what deep repose
Lies on the landscape as it glows!

But most at evening's gentle hour
    The reign of Peace is clearly read, —
In the blue mists which hail her their power,
    Pavilions rich and banners spread, —
While 'mid the hush is heard the tone
    Of night's sweet minstrel — hers alone.

As star by star leaps out above,
    As twilight deepens into night,
As round me cluster those I love,
    And eye meets eye in glances bright,
I feel that earth itself may be
Lit up with heaven's own radiancy.

Lines
(Written while on a Visit to Kalighat[5])

They know full well that God hath said
    Thou shalt not bend in fear
To stock, nor stone, nor carvèd thing,
Nor ever to their altars bring
    The first fruits of the year.

Still grim Idolatry with pomp,
    O'er India's realm doth reign;
For still its fell and baneful power
Is owned in palace, hut, and bower,
    In city, town, and plain.

---

5 Kalighat, Calcutta: location of the famous Kali Temple, which attracted numerous pilgrims. This poem views the worship of the Hindu goddess Kali, who is often depicted with a terrible appearance, as barbaric and opposed to the worship of a singular Christian God. The Khalighat region is also known as the birthplace of a new and populist art form, Khalighat paintings, during the nineteenth century.

Where'er we turn we see them rise,
    Those temples huge and grand,
To hideous idols consecrate:
Alas for man's degraded state!
    Oh, woe to this fair land!

But most they fear that goddess dread,
    Reeking with blood and wine,
And prince and peasant trembling bring
Their rich or humble offering
    To her ensanguined shrine.

The farmer, ere he sallies forth
    To reap his waving field,
The diver, ere he goes to brave
The dangers of the treacherous wave,
    To her homage yield.

The traveller, by his guide despoiled,
    Belated and betrayed,
As night with darkness brings despair
And unknown sounds are in the air,
    In awe invokes her aid.

Her dreaded name is shouted high
    Where deepens most the fray,
It nerves the warrior's wearied hand
To wield anew the flashing brand,
    And join the wild mêlée.

Great God, tho' *all* may not have heard,
    Still *many* know Thy name,
And tho' Thy bounties they receive,
Yet recklessly Thy path they leave,
    And glory in their shame.

Woe, woe to this devoted land,
    Woe to this erring race,
That thus the evil way they choose,
And with hard wilful hearts refuse
    Thy proffered Love and Grace.

But Thou art merciful, O Lord,
    And Thou alone canst save:
Oh, let the day-spring clear arise,
Oh, open Thou their blinded eyes,
    Send freedom to the slave.

Vizagapatam[6]

Down went the anchor and the ship stood fast,
    Rocking upon the billows, while around
Wheeled the white sea-birds, rising with the blast,
    Or skimming lightly o'er the depth's profound,
White, oh! how white, beneath the morning ray,
Like fitful snowflakes 'mid the ocean-spray.

The hills down-sloping to the ocean's edge
    With verdure smooth were covered to their tops;
Clumps of tall trees o'ershadowed many a ledge,
    And coffee-plants displayed their berry crops;
And spanning all like God's embracing love,
Sublime and stainless, hung the sky above.

Villas and houses gleamed from many a peak,
    Or peeped through trees that hid them from the sight,
Like shamefast maidens beautiful and meek;
    And temples rose with banners streaming bright
And burnished spires; and humble peasant huts
Circled by slender palms and betel-nuts.[7]

And some abodes to memory might bring home
    That vision of the poet's fancy born,
His 'magic casements opening on the foam
    Of perilous seas, in faëry lands forlorn.'
These close but high, – might almost feel the shock
Of the wild surges breaking on the rock.

Oh, what a sight of varied loveliness!
    What hills! what skies! what piles of foliage green!
Is there a spot which Nature deigns to bless
    With such profusion as this woodland scene?
The fairest flowerets here perennial glow!
The freshest breezes here for ever blow!

---

6 Vizagapatam: second largest city in the modern-day state of Andra Pradesh in southern India and a major port city. Praised for its beauty, Vizagapatam was part of the Madras presidency during the nineteenth century.
7 Betel-nuts: areca nuts. These palm-tree nuts are often chewed and used in *paan*.

Thought uncontrolled erratic ever flies,
        And he that writes mused idly, – Can this be
Our long-lost, not forgotten Paradise?
        When lo! he started from his trance to see,
Where o'er the hills the devious footpath led,
A long and sad procession bear the dead.

Madras

Indifferent passages in this life, not less
        Than great events that colour all its stream,
Oft find a niche in memory's recess,
        And are invested with ethereal gleam.
Vivid and bright they sometimes rise to bless,
        At others seem 'a dream within a dream,'
Yet fading never; – wherefore should this be?
Our natures are to us a mystery.

Can I forget, till Time's scythe lays me low,
        The sea-view at Madras? The rope-tied crafts
That produce bring for freight, or fruit for show,
        The singly-managed catamaran[8] rafts
Wild plunging in the waves where'er they go,
        And the tall vessels which the sea-breeze wafts
From every clime that at their anchors strain,
Impatient till they sweep the seas again.

Can I forget our landing on the pier,
        The ramble through the straggling curious town,
In the hot April sunlight clear,
        By huts and palaces; now sitting down
On wayside benches, where the banyans[9] rear
        Their natural tents and cast their shadows brown;
And strolling now beneath the open skies
With smiling lips and ever-wondering eyes?

---

8 *Catamarans*: multi-hulled boats used by fishing communities in the region.
9 *Banyans*: trees known to grow to an immense size. Their roots can grow into thick trunks that are difficult to distinguish from the main trunk.

Can I forget the pleasant People's Park;[10]
    The savage tigers crouching in their den;
The wild hyenas in their prison dark,
    Low growling; the buffaloes in the fen;
The monkeys sporting as in Noah's ark,
    And all besides? Returning seaward, then,
The glorious ocean we beheld once more,
And all the bustle of the crowded shore.

Can I forget, though these be common things,
    And scarcely worthy to be writ at all,
The sands, the open boat, the flitting wings
    Of sea-birds white, the helmsman's cheery call,
The rower's chant that in my ear still rings,
    And, fairly out, the blue waves' rise and fall,
As steadily we held upon our way
Through rainbow showers of sprinkled ocean spray?

Or can I ever in my life forget,
    As we approached the ship's tall frowning side,
How wildly plunged our boat! Her pennants set,
    The ship rocked high above the rocking tide,
Like a trump-rousèd war-horse on the fret:
    Close, close we came, and then were parted wide,
A perilous work to board her; all in vain
The boat approaches, drifting far again.

Less anxious for myself, with what delight
    I saw my young companion boldly spring
Up the frail ladder o'er the billows white,
    And like a bird that folds its venturous wing
Gain safe the deck, I following as I might.
    Was it a shade of matters time would bring?
The ship Christ's own, on this world's boisterous sea
Where one would first be safe? Ah, woe is me!

---

10 People's Park: located in Madras, this park housed a zoo, which opened there in 1855.

Toru Dutt

Although Toru Dutt (1856–1877) died of consumption at the extremely young age of twenty-one, her literary output is remarkably prolific and varied. Her first published works were critical essays on the nineteenth-century poets, Henry Derozio (an Anglo-Portuguese poet born in India) and Leconte de Lisle (a Creole born in Mauritius), published in *Bengal Magazine*. Critics have often linked Toru Dutt's interest in transnational and interracial figures (both real and constructed) to her family's conversion to Christianity when she was four years old and to her time spent abroad in France, England, and Italy with her family from 1869 to 1873. An unfinished gothic novel *Bianca, or, The Young Spanish Maiden* was reprinted in its entirety only recently. This first edition is billed by the Prachi Prakashan Press (2001) as "the first novel by an Indian woman." A completed novel in French, *Le Journal de Mademoiselle d'Arvers*, takes the form of the diary of a young French girl. Published posthumously by the Paris firm Librairie Académique in 1879, this edition includes a preface by the French writer, Clarisse Bader (1840–1902). The first work for which Dutt gained international recognition was *A Sheaf Gleaned in French Fields* (1876) a series of translations from the French that she completed with her sister Aru. Her most well-known work, *Ancient Ballads and Legends of Hindustan* (1882), includes the now famous preface by English man of letters Edmund Gosse, who introduced Dutt to an English audience.

Ancient Ballads and Legends of Hindustan (London: 1882)[11]

Savitri[12]

Part I.

Savitri was the only child
    Of Madra's[13] wise and mighty king;
Stern warriors, when they saw her, smiled,
    As mountains smile to see the spring.
Fair as a lotus when the moon
    Kisses its opening petals red,

---

11 Toru Dutt, *Ancient Ballads and Legends of Hindustan* (London: K. Paul, Trench & Co., 1882).
12 The legend of Savitri narrates the tale of a childless king who performs sacrifices to the goddess Savitri to be granted the boon of a child. He is eventually blessed with a daughter, Savitri (named after the goddess), who grows up beautiful and beloved. It is here that Toru Dutt's poem begins.
13 Madra: located in what is now northwestern India.

After sweet showers in sultry June!
    With happier heart, and lighter tread,
Chance strangers, having met her, past,
    And often would they turn the head
A lingering second look to cast,
    And bless the vision ere it fled.

What was her own peculiar charm?
    The soft black eyes, the raven hair,
The curving neck, the rounded arm,
    All these are common everywhere.
Her charm was this — upon her face
    Childlike and innocent and fair,
No man with thought impure or base
    Could ever look; — the glory there,
The sweet simplicity and grace,
    Abashed the boldest; but the good
God's purity there loved to trace,
    Mirrored in dawning womanhood.

In those far-off primeval days
    Fair India's daughters were not pent
In closed zenanas.[14] On her ways
    Savitri at her pleasure went
Whither she chose, — and hour by hour
    With young companions of her age,
She roamed the woods for fruit or flower,
    Or loitered in some hermitage,
For to the Munis[15] gray and old
    Her presence was as sunshine glad,
They taught her wonders manifold
    And gave her of the best they had.

Her father let her have her way
    In all things, whether high or low;
He feared no harm; he knew no ill
    Could touch a nature pure as snow.
Long childless, as a priceless boon
    He had obtained this child at last

---

14 *Zenanas*: the separate quarters reserved for women usually in upper-class/caste Muslim and Hindu homes. Nineteenth-century national discourses often represented the ancient Indian woman as an ideal figure of womanhood: educated, morally firm, spiritually pure, duteous, self-sacrificing, and (in Dutt's rendering, at least), free to "roam."

15 *Muni*: holy man; sage; an ascetic or hermit (n. "muni" OED).

By prayers, made morning, night, and noon
    With many a vigil, many a fast;
Would Shiva[16] his own gift recall,
    Or mar its perfect beauty ever? –
No, he had faith, – he gave her all
    She wished, and feared and doubted never.

And so she wandered where she pleased
    In boyish freedom. Happy time!
No small vexations ever teased,
    Nor crushing sorrows dimmed her prime.
One care alone, her father felt –
    Where should he find a fitting mate
For one so pure? – His thoughts long dwelt
    On this as with his queen he sate.
"Ah, whom, dear wife, should we select?"
    "Leave it to God," she answering cried,
"Savitri, may herself elect
    Some day, her future lord and guide."

Months passed, and lo, one summer morn
    As to the hermitage she went
Through smiling fields of waving corn,
    She saw some youths on sport intent,
Sons of hermits, and their peers,
    And one among them tall and lithe,
Royal in port, – on whom the years
    Consenting, shed a grace so blithe,
So frank and noble, that the eye
    Was loth to quit that sun-browned face;
She looked and looked – then gave a sigh,
    And slackened suddenly her pace.

What was the meaning – was it love?
    Love at first sight, as poets sing,
Is then no fiction? Heaven above
    Is witness, that the heart its king
Finds often like a lightning flash;
    We play, – we jest, – we have no care, –
When hark a step, – there comes no crash, –
    But life, or silent slow despair.

---

16 Shiva: one of the major Hindu deities often represented as one aspect of the Trimurti, which also included Vishnu and Brahma. Shiva is able to destroy and thus transform. In this telling, Shiva grants the king the boon of his daughter, Savitri, in return for the king's prayers.

Their eyes just met, – Savitri past
        Into the friendly Muni's hut,
Her heart-rose opened had at last –
        Opened no flower can ever shut.

In converse with the gray-haired sage
        She learnt the story of the youth,
His name and place and parentage –
        Of royal race he was in truth.
Satyavan was he hight,[17] – his sire
        Dyoumatsen had been Salva's king,
But old and blind, opponents dire
        Had gathered round him in a ring
And snatched the sceptre from his hand;
        Now, – with his queen and only son
He lived a hermit in the land,
        And gentler hermit was there none.

With many tears was said and heard
        The story, – and with praise sincere
Of Prince Satyavan; every word
        Sent up a flush on cheek and ear,
Unnoticed. Hark! The bells remind
        'Tis time to go, – she went away,
Leaving her virgin heart behind,
        And richer for the loss. A ray
Shot down from heaven, appeared to tinge
        All objects with supernal light,
The thatches had a rainbow fringe,
        The cornfields looked more green and bright.

Savitri's first care was to tell
        Her mother all her feelings new;
The queen her own fears to dispel
        To the king's private chamber flew.
"Now what is it, my gentle queen,
        That makes thee hurry in this wise?"
She told him, smiles and tears between
        All she had heard; the king with sighs
Sadly replied: – "I fear me much!
        Whence is his race and what his creed?
Not knowing aught, can we in such
        A matter delicate, proceed?"

---

17 Hight: to be called, designated, or named (v. "hight" *OED*).

As if the king's doubts to allay,
    Came Narad Muni[18] to the place
A few days after. Old and gray,
    All loved to see the gossip's face,
Great Brahma's son, — adored of men,
    Long absent, doubly welcome he
Unto the monarch, hoping then
    By his assistance, clear to see.
No god in heaven, nor king on earth,
    But Narad knew his history, —
The sun's, the moon's, the planets' birth
    Was not to him a mystery.

"Now welcome, welcome, dear old friend,
    All hail, and welcome once again!"
The greeting had not reached its end,
    When glided like a music-strain
Savitri's presence through the room. —
    "And who is this bright creature, say,
Whose radiance lights the chamber's gloom —
    Is she an Aspara[19] or fay?"
"No son thy servant hath, alas!
    This is my one, — my only child;" —
"And married?" — "No." — "The seasons pass,
    Make haste, O king," — he said, and smiled.

"That is the very theme, O sage,
    In which thy wisdom ripe I need;
Seen hath she at the hermitage
    A youth to whom in very deed
Her heart inclines." — "And who is he?"
    "My daughter, tell his name and race,
Speak as to men who best love thee."
    She turned to them her modest face,
And answered quietly and clear. —
    "Ah, no! ah, no! — It cannot be —
Choose out another husband, dear," —
    The Muni cried, — "or woe is me!"

---

18 Narad Muni, or Narada: divine sage and son of the Hindu god, Brahma. Narada is able to pass through the various worlds and is characterized as a gossip. He is often depicted carrying a musical instrument.
19 *Aspara*: celestial nymph or maiden.

"And why should I? When I have given
      My heart away, though but in thought,
Can I take back? Forbid it, Heaven!
      It were a deadly sin, I wot.
And why should I? I know no crime
      In him or his." – "Believe me, child,
My reasons shall be clear in time,
      I speak not like a madman wild;
Trust me in this." – "I cannot break
      A plighted faith, – I cannot bear
A wounded conscience." – "Oh, forsake
      This fancy, hence may spring despair." –

"It may not be." – The father heard
      By turns the speakers, and in doubt
Thus interposed a gentle word, –
      "Friend should to friend his mind speak out,
Is he not worthy? tell us." – "Nay,
      All worthiness is in Satyavan,
And no one can my praise gainsay:
      Of solar race – more god than man!
Great Soorasen,[20] his ancestor,
      And Dyoumatsen his father blind
Are known to fame: I can aver
      No kings have been so good and kind."

"Then where, O Muni, is the bar?
      If wealth be gone, and kingdom lost,
His merit still remains a star,
      Nor melts his lineage like the frost.
For riches, worldly power, or rank
      I care not, – I would have my son
Pure, wise, and brave, – the Fates I thank
      I see no hindrance, no, not one."
"Since thou insistest [sic], King, to hear
      The fatal truth, – I tell you, – I,
Upon this day as rounds the year
      The young prince Satyavan shall die."

---

20 King Soorasen, or Surasena: ancient founder and ruler of a kingdom in North India, which had its capital in Madhura or Mathura.

This was enough. The monarch knew
    The future was no sealèd book
To Brahma's son. A clammy dew
    Spread on his brow, – he gently took
Savitri's palm in his, and said:
    "No child can give away her hand,
A pledge is nought unsanctionèd;
    And here, if right I understand,
There was no pledge at all, – a thought,
    A shadow, – barely crossed the mind –
Unblamed, it may be clean forgot,
    Before the gods it cannot bind.

And think upon the dreadful curse
    Of widowhood; the vigils, fasts,
And penances; no life is worse
    Than hopeless life, – the while it lasts.
Day follows day in one long round,
    Monotonous and bland and drear;
Less painful were it to be bound
    On some bleak rock, for aye to hear –
Without one chance of getting free –
    The ocean's melancholy voice!
Mine be the sin, – if sin there be,
    But thou must make a different choice."[21]

In the meek grace of virginhood
    Unblanched her cheek, undimmed her eye,
Savitri, like a statue, stood,
    Somewhat austere was her reply.
"Once, and once only, all submit
    To Destiny, – 'tis God's command;
Once, and once only, so 'tis writ,
    Shall woman pledge her faith and hand;
Once, and once only, can a sire
    Unto his well-loved daughter say
In presence of the witness, Fire,
    I give thee to this man away.

---

21 Upper-caste Brahmin women in certain regions such as Bengal were considered social outcasts once they became widows. They were forced to wear white, abstain from all bodily ornamentation and severely restrict their diet.

Once, and once only, have I given
      My heart and faith — 'tis past recall;
With conscience none have ever striven,
      And none may strive, without a fall.
Not the less solemn was my vow
      Because unheard, and oh! the sin
Will not be less, if I should now
      Deny the feeling felt within.
Unwedded to my dying day
      I must, my father dear, remain;
'Tis well, if so thou will'st, but say
      Can man balk Fate, or break its chain?

If Fate so rules, that I should feel
      The miseries of a widow's life,
Can man's device the doom repeal?
      Unequal seems to be a strife,
Between Humanity and Fate;
      None have on earth what they desire;
Death comes to all or soon or late;
      And peace is but a wandering fire;
Expediency leads wild astray;
      The Right must be our guiding star;
Duty our watchword, come what may;
      Judge for me, friends, — as wiser far."

She said, and meekly looked to both.
      The father, though he patient heard,
To give the sanction still seemed loth,
      But Narad Muni took the word.
"Bless thee, my child! 'Tis not for us
      To question the Almighty will,
Though cloud on cloud loom ominous,
      In gentle rain they may distil."
At this, the monarch — "Be it so!
      I sanction what my friend approves;
All praise to Him, whom praise we owe;
      My child shall wed the youth she loves."

Part II.

Great joy in Madra. Blow the shell
      The marriage over to declare!
And now to forest-shades where dwell
      The hermits, wend the wedded pair.
The doors of every house are hung
      With gay festoons of leaves and flowers;

And blazing banners broad are flung,
        And trumpets blown from castle towers!
Slow the procession makes its ground
        Along the crowded city street:
And blessings in a storm of sound
        At every step the couple greet.

Past all the houses, past the wall,
        Past gardens gay, and hedgerows trim,
Past fields, where sinuous brooklets small
        With molten silver to the brim
Glance in the sun's expiring light,
        Past frowning hills, past pastures wild,
At last arises on the sight,
        Foliage on foliage densely piled,
The woods primeval, where reside
        The holy hermits; – henceforth here
Must live the fair and gentle bride:
        But this thought brought with it no fear.

Fear! With her husband by her still?
        Or weariness! Where all was new?
Hark! What a welcome from the hill!
        There gathered are a hermits few.
Screaming the peacocks upward soar;
        Wondering the timid wild deer gaze;
And from Briarean fig-trees hoar[22]
        Look down the monkeys in amaze
As the procession moves along;
        And now behold, the bridegroom's sire
With joy comes forth amid the throng; –
        What reverence his looks inspire!

Blind! With his partner by his side!
        For them it was a hallowed time!
Warmly they greet the modest bride
        With her dark eyes and front sublime!
One grief they feel. – Shall she
        Who dwelt in palace before
Dwell in their huts beneath the tree?
        Would not their hard life press her sore; –

---

22 "Briarean fig-tree hoar": an old, thorny, fig-tree shrub (n. "briar" and adj. "hoar" OED).

The manual labour, and the want
    Of comforts that her rank became,
Valkala[23] robes, meals poor and scant,
    All undermine the fragile frame?

To see the bride, the hermit's wives
    And daughters gathered to the huts,
Women of pure and saintly lives!
    And there beneath the betel-nuts
Tall trees like pillars, they admire
    Her beauty, and congratulate
The parents, that their hearts' desire
    Had thus accorded them by Fate,
And Satyavan their son had found
    In exile lone, a fitting mate:
And gossips add, — goods signs abound;
    Prosperity shall on her wait.

Good signs in features, limbs, and eyes,
    That old experience can discern
Good signs on earth and in the skies,
    That it could read at every turn.
And now with rice and gold, all bless
    The bride and bridegroom, — and they go
Happy in others' happiness,
    Each to her home, beneath the glow
Of the late risen moon that lines
    With silver all the ghost-like trees,
Sals, tamarisks[24] and South-Sea pines,
    And palms whose plumes wave in the breeze.

False was the fear the parents felt,
    Savitri liked her new life much;
Though in a lowly home she dwelt
    Her conduct as a wife was such
As to illumine all the place;
    She sickened not, nor sighed, nor pined;
But with simplicity and grace
    Discharged each household duty kind.

---

23 *Valkala*: tree bark.
24 *Sals*: tall trees native to South Asia and often used for timber. *Tamarisks*: small ornamental tree or shrub with slender branches and pink or white flowers generally found in drier regions in Eurasia and Africa.

Strong in all manual work — and strong
    To comfort, cherish, help, and pray,
The hours past peacefully along
    And rippling bright, day followed day.

At morn Satyavan to the wood
    Early repaired and gathered flowers
And fruits, in its wild solitude,
    And fuel, — till advancing hours
Apprised him that his frugal meal
    Awaited him. Ah, happy time!
Savitri, who with fervid zeal
    Had said her orisons sublime,
And fed the Brahmins[25] and the birds,
    Now ministered. Arcadian[26] love,
With tender smiles and honeyed words,
    All bliss of earth thou art above!

And yet there was a spectre grim,
    A skeleton in Savitri's heart,
Looming in shadow, somewhat dim,
    But which would never thence depart.
It was that fatal, fatal speech
    Of Narad Muni. As the days
Slipt smoothly past, each after each,
    In private she more fervent prays.
But there is none to share her fears,
    For how could she communicate
The sad cause of her hidden tears?
    The doom approached, the fatal date.

No help from man. Well, be it so!
    No sympathy, — it matters not!
God can avert the heavy blow!
    He answers worship. Thus she thought.
And so, her prayers, by day and night,
    Like incense rose unto the throne;
Nor did she vow neglect or rite
    The Veds[27] enjoin or helpful own.

---

25 "[F]ed the Brahmins": Refers to the practice of feeding Brahmin priests or mendicants (religious beggars thought to be holy).
26 Arcadian: utopian; pastoral; from the ancient Greek.
27 *Veds*, or *Vedas*: the ancient Hindu Sanskrit scriptures revealed by the gods and predating the composition of the Hindu epics.

Upon the fourteenth of the moon,
>   As nearer came the time of dread,
In Joystee, that is May or June,
>   She vowed her vows and Bramins [sic] fed,

And now she counted e'en the hours,
>   As to Eternity they past;
O'er head the dark cloud darker lowers,
>   The year is rounding full at last.
To-day, – to-day, – with doleful sound
>   The word seem'd in her ear to ring!
O breaking heart, – thy pain profound
>   Thy husband knows not, nor the king,
Exiled and blind, nor yet the queen;
>   But One knows in His place above.
To-day, – to-day, – it will be seen
>   Which shall be victor, Death or Love!

Incessant in her prayers from morn,
>   The noon is safely tided – then
A gleam of faint, faint hope is born,
>   But the heart fluttered like a wren
That sees the shadow of the hawk
>   Sail on, – and trembles in affright,
Lest a downrushing swoop should mock
>   Its fortune, and o'erwhelm it quite.
The afternoon has come and gone
>   And brought not change; – should she rejoice?
The gentle evening's shades come on,
>   When hark! – She hears her husband's voice!

"The twilight is most beautiful!
>   Mother, to gather fruit I go
And fuel, – for the air is cool
>   Expect me in an hour or so."
"The night, my child, draws on apace,"
>   The mother's voice was heard to say,
"The forest paths are hard to trace
>   In darkness, – till the morrow stay."
"Not hard for me, who can discern
>   The forest-paths in any hour,
Blindfold I could with ease return,
>   And day has not yet lost its power."

"He goes then," thought Savitri, "thus
    With unseen bands Fate draws us on
Unto the place appointed us;
    We feel no outward force — anon
We go to marriage or to death
    At a determined time and place;
We are her playthings; with her breath
    She blows us where she lists in space.
What is my duty? It is clear
    My husband I must follow; so,
While he collects his forest gear
    Let me permission get to go."

His sire she seeks, — the blind old king,
    And asks from him permission straight.
"My daughter, night with ebon wing
    Hovers above; the hour is late.
My son is active, brave, and strong,
    Conversant with the woods, he knows
Each path; methinks it would be wrong
    For thee to venture where he goes,
Weak and defenceless as thou art,
    At such a time. If thou wert near
Thou might'st embarrass him, dear heart,
    Alone, he would not have a fear."

So spake the hermit-monarch blind,
    His wife too, entering in, exprest
The self-same thoughts in words as kind,
    And begged Savitri hard, to rest.
"Thy recent fasts and vigils, child,
    Make thee unfit to undertake
This journey to the forest wild."
    But nothing could her purpose shake.
She urged the nature of her vows,
    Required her now the rites were done
To follow where her loving spouse
    Might e'en a chance of danger run.

"Go then, my child — we give thee leave,
    But with thy husband quick return,
Before the flickering shades of eve
    Deepen to night, and planets burn,
And forest-paths become obscure,
    Lit only by their doubtful rays.

The gods, who guard all women pure,
    Bless thee and kept thee in thy ways,
And safely bring thee and thy lord!"
    On this she left and swiftly ran
Where with his saw in lieu of sword,
    And basket, plodded Satyavan.

Oh, lovely are the woods at dawn,
    And lovely in the sultry noon,
But loveliest, when the sun withdrawn
    The twilight and a crescent moon
Change all asperities of shape,
    And tone all colours softly down,
With a blue veil of silvered crape!
    Lo! By that hill which palm-trees crown,
Down the deep glade with perfume rife
    From buds that to the dews expand,
The husband and the faithful wife
    Pass to dense jungle, – hand in hand.

Satyavan bears beside his saw
    A forked stick to pluck the fruit,
His wife, the basket lined with straw;
    He talks, but she is almost mute,
And very pale. The minutes pass;
    The basket has no further space,
Now on the fruits they flowers amass
    That with their red flush all the place
While twilight lingers; then for wood
    He saws the branches of the trees,
The noise, heard in the solitude,
    Grates on its soft, low harmonies.

And all the while one dreadful thought
    Haunted Savitri's anxious mind,
Which would have fain its stress forgot;
    It came as chainless as the wind,
Oft and again: thus on the spot
    Marked with his heart-blood oft comes back
The murdered man, to see the clot!
    Death's final blow, – the fatal wrack
Of every hope, whence will it fall?
    For fall, by Narad's words, it must;
Persistent rising to appall
    This thought its horrid presence thrust.

Sudden the noise is hushed, – a pause!
    Satyavan lets the weapon drop –
Too well Savitri knows the cause,
    He feels not well, the work must stop.
A pain is in his head, – a pain
    As if he felt the cobra's fangs,
He tries to look around, – in vain
    A mist before his vision hangs;
The trees whirl dizzily around
    In a fantastic fashion wild;
His throat and chest seem iron-bound,
    He staggers, like a sleepy child.

"My head, my head! – Savitri, dear,
    This pain is frightful. Let me lie
Here on the turf." Her voice was clear
    And very calm was her reply,
As if her heart had banished fear;
    "Lean, love, thy head upon my breast,"
And as she helped him, added – "here,
    So shalt thou better breathe and rest."
    "Ah me, this pain, – 'tis getting dark,
    I see no more, – can this be death?
What means this, gods? – Savitri, mark,
    My hands wax cold, and fails my breath."

"It may be but a swoon." "Ah! no –
    Arrows are piercing through my heart, –
Farewell my love! for I must go,
    This, this is death." He gave one start
And then lay quiet on her lap,
    Insensible to sight and sound,
Breathing his last...The branches flap
    And fireflies glimmer all around;
His head upon her breast; his frame
    Part on her lap, part on the ground,
Thus lies he. Hours pass. Still the same,
    The pair look statues, magic-bound.

Part III.

Death in his palace holds his court,
    His messengers move to and fro,
Each of his mission makes report,
    And takes the royal orders, – Lo,
Some slow before his throne appear
    And humbly in the Presence kneel:

"Why hath the Prince not been brought here?
    The hour is past; nor is appeal
Allowed against foregone decree;
    There is the mandate with the seal!
How comes it ye return to me
    Without him? Shame upon your zeal!"

"O King, whom all men fear, – he lies
    Deep in the dark Medhya[28] wood,
We fled from thence in wild surprise,
    And left him in that solitude.
We dared not touch him, for there sits,
    Beside him, lighting all the place,
A woman fair, whose brow permits
    In its austerity of grace
And purity, – no creatures foul
    As we seemed, by her loveliness,
Or soul of evil, ghost or ghoul,
    To venture close, and far, far less

To stretch a hand, and bear the dead;
    We left her leaning on her hand,
Thoughtful; no tear-drop had she shed,
    But looked the goddess of the land,
With her meek air of mild command." –
    "Then on this errand I must go
Myself, and bear my dreaded brand,
    This duty unto Fate I owe;
I know the merits of the prince,
    But merit saves not from the doom
Common to man; his death long since
    Was destined in his beauty's bloom."

Part IV.

As still Savitri sat beside
    Her husband, dying, – dying fast
She saw a stranger slowly glide
    Beneath the boughs that shrunk aghast.
Upon his head he wore a crown
    That shimmered in the doubtful light;
His vestament[29] scarlet reached low down,
    His waist, a golden girdle dight.

---

28 Medhya wood: forests of Madhya.
29 Vestament, or vestment: garment or article of clothing, especially an outer garment such as a robe worn by a king on a ceremonial occasion (n. "vestament" OED).

His skin was dark as bronze; his face
    Irradiate, and yet severe;
His eyes had much of love and grace,
    But glowed so bright, they filled with fear.

A string was in the stranger's hand
    Noosed at its end. Her terrors now
Savitri scarcely could command.
    Upon the sod beneath a bough,
She gently laid her husband's head,
    And in obeisance bent her brow.
"No mortal form is thine," – she said,
    "Beseech thee say what god art thou?
And what can be thine errand here?"
    "Savitri, for thy prayers, thy faith,
Thy frequent vows, thy fasts severe,
    I answer, – list, – my name is Death.

And I am come myself to take
    Thy husband from this earth away,
And he shall cross the doleful lake
    In my own charge, and let me say
To few such honours I accord,
    But his pure life and thine require
No less from me." The dreadful sword
    Like lightning glanced one moment dire;
And then the inner man was tied,
    The soul no bigger than the thumb,
To be borne onwards by his side: –
    Savitri all the while stood dumb.

But when the god moved slowly on
    To gain his own dominion dim,
Leaving the body there – anon
    Savitri meekly followed him,
Hoping against all hope; he turned
    And looked surprised. "Go back, my child!"
Pale, pale the stars above them burned,
    More weird the scene had grown and wild;
"It is not for the living – hear!
    To follow where the dead must go,
Thy duty lies before thee clear,
    What thou shouldst do, the Shasters[30] show.

---

30 *Shasters*, or *shastras*: Hindu treatises on the scriptures or independent treatises; they can also refer to codes of conduct.

The funeral rites that they ordain
        And sacrifices must take up
Thy first sad moments; not in vain
        Is held to thee this bitter cup;
Its lessons thou shalt learn in time!
        All that thou *canst* do, thou hast done
For thy dear lord. Thy love sublime
        My deepest sympathy hath won.
Return, for thou hast come as far
        As living creature may. Adieu!
Let duty be thy guiding star,
        As ever. To thyself be true!"

"Where'er my husband dear is led,
        Or journeys of his own free will,
I too must go, though darkness spread
        Across my path, portending ill,
'Tis thus my duty I have read!
        If I am wrong, oh! with me bear;
But do not bid me backward tread
        My way forlorn, – for I can dare
All things but that; ah! pity me,
        A woman frail, too sorely tried!
And let me, let me follow thee,
        O gracious god, – whate'er betide.

By all things sacred, I entreat,
        By Penitence that purifies,
By prompt Obedience, full, complete,
        To spiritual masters, in the eyes
Of gods so precious, by the love
        I bear my husband, by the faith
That looks from earth to heaven above,
        And by thy own great name O Death,
And all thy kindness, bid me not
        To leave thee, and to go my way,
But let me follow as I ought
        Thy steps and his, as best I may.

I know that in this transient world
        All is delusion, – nothing true;
I know its shows are mists unfurled
        To please and vanish. To renew
Its bubble joys, be magic bound
        In *Maya's*[31] network frail and fair,

---

31 *Maya*: illusion.

Is not my aim! The gladsome sound
    Of husband, brother, friend, is air
To such as know that all must die,
    And that at last the time must come,
When eye shall speak no more to eye
    And Love cry, – Lo, this is my sum.

I know in such a world as this
    No one can gain his heart's desire,
Or pass the years in perfect bliss;
    Like gold we must be tried by fire;
And each shall suffer as he acts
    And thinks, – his own sad burden bear;
No friends can help, – his sins are facts
    That nothing can annul or square,
And he must bear their consequence.
    Can I my husband save by rites?
An, no, – that were a vain pretence,
    Justice eternal strict requites.

He for his deeds shall get his due
    As I for mine: thus here each soul
Is its own friend if it pursue
    The right, and run straight for the goal;
But its own worst and direst foe
    If it choose evil, and in tracks
Forbidden, for its pleasure go.
    Who knows not this, true wisdom lacks,
Virtue should be the aim and end
    Of every life, all else is vain,
Duty should be its dearest friend
    If higher life, it would attain."

"So sweet thy words ring on mine ear,
    Gentle Savitri, that I fain
Would give some sign to make it clear
    Thou hast not prayed to me in vain.
Satyavan's life I may not grant,
    Nor take before its term thy life,
But I am not all adamant,
    I feel for thee, thou faithful wife!
Ask thou aught else, and let it be
    Some good thing for thyself or thine,
And I shall give it, child, to thee,
    If any power on earth be mine."

"Well be it so. My husband's sire,
    Hath lost his sight and fair domain,
Give to his eyes their former fire,
    And place him on his throne again."
"It shall be done. Go back, my child,
    The hour wears late, the wind feels cold,
The path becomes more weird and wild,
    Thy feet are torn, there's blood, behold!
Thou feelest faint from weariness,
    Oh try to follow me no more;
Go home, and with thy presence bless
    Those who thine absence there deplore."

"No weariness, O Death, I feel,
    And how should I, when by the side
Of Satyavan? In woe and weal
    To be a helpmate swears the bride.
This is my place; by solemn oath
    Wherever thou conductest him
I too must go, to keep my troth;
    And if the eye at times should brim,
'Tis human weakness, give me strength
    My work appointed to fulfil,
That I may gain the crown at length
    The gods give those who do their will.

The power of goodness is so great
    We pray to feel its influence
For ever on us. It is late,
    And the strange landscape awes my sense;
But I would fain with thee go on,
    And hear thy voice so true and kind;
The false lights that on objects shone
    Have vanished, and no longer blind.
Thanks to thy simple presence. Now
    I feel a fresher air around,
And see the glory of that brow
    With flashing rubies fitly crowned.

Men call thee Yama[32] — conqueror,
    Because it is against their will
They follow thee, — and they abhor
    The Truth which thou wouldst aye instil.

---

32 Yama: the god of death in Hinduism. This is the first time the "stranger" is named in the poem.

If they thy nature knew aright,
    O god, all other gods above!
And that thou conquerest in the fight
    By patience, kindness, mercy, love,
And not by devastating wrath,
    They would not shrink in childlike fright
To see thy shadow on their path,
    But hail thee as sick souls the light."

"Thy words, Savitri, greet mine ear
    As sweet as founts that murmur low
To one who in the deserts drear
    With parchèd tongue moves faint and slow,
Because thy talk is heart-sincere,
    Without hypocrisy or guile;
Demand another boon, my dear,
    But not of those forbad erewhile,
And I shall grant it, ere we part:
    Lo, the stars pale, – the way is long,
Receive thy boon, and homewards start,
    For ah, poor child, thou art not strong."

"Another boon! My sire the king
    Beside myself hath children none,
Oh grant that from his stock may spring
    A hundred boughs." "It shall be done.
He shall be blest with many a son
    Who his old palace shall rejoice."
"Each heart-wish from thy goodness won,
    If I am still allowed a choice,
I fain thy voice would ever hear,
    Reluctant am I still to part,
The way seems short when thou art near
    And Satyavan, my heart's dear heart.

Of all the pleasures given on earth
    The company of the good is best,
For weariness has never birth
    In such a commerce sweet and blest;
The sun runs on its wonted course,
    The earth its plenteous treasure yields,
All for their sake, and by the force
    Their prayer united ever wields.
Oh let me, let me ever dwell
    Amidst the good, where'er it be,
Whether in lowly hermit-cell
    Or in some spot beyond the sea.

The favours man accords to men
        Are never fruitless, from them rise
A thousand acts beyond our ken
        That float like incense to the skies;
For benefits can ne'er efface,
        They multiply and widely spread,
And honour follows on their trace.
        Sharp penances, and vigils dread,
Austerities, and wasting fasts,
        Create an empire, and the blest
Long as this spiritual empire lasts
        Become the saviours of the rest."

"O thou endowed with every grace
        And every virtue, – thou whose soul
Appears upon thy lovely face,
        May the great gods who all control
Send thee their peace. I too would give
        One favour more before I go;
Ask something for thyself, and live
        Happy, and dear to all below,
Till summoned to the bliss above.
        Savitri ask, and ask unblamed." –
She took the clue, felt Death was Love,
        For no exceptions now he named.

And boldly said, – "Thou knowest Lord,
        The inmost hearts and thoughts of all!
There is no need to utter word,
        Upon thy mercy sole, I call.
If speech be needful to obtain
        Thy grace, – oh hear a wife forlorn,
Let my Satyavan live again
        And children unto us be born,
Wise, brave, and valiant." "From thy stock
        A hundred families shall spring
As lasting as the solid rock,
        Each son of thine shall be a king."

As thus he spoke, he loosed the knot
        The soul of Satyavan that bound,
And promised further that their lot
        In pleasant places should be found
Thenceforth, and that they both should live
        Four centuries, to which the name
Of fair Savitri, men would give, –

And then he vanished in a flame.
"Adieu, great god!" She took the soul,
    No bigger than the human thumb,
And running swift, soon reached her goal,
    Where lay the body stark and dumb.

She lifted it with eager hands
    And as before, when he expired,
She placed the head upon the bands
    That bound her breast which hope new fired,
And which alternate rose and fell;
    Then placed his soul upon his heart
Whence like a bee it found its cell,
    And lo, he woke with sudden start!
His breath came low at first, then deep,
    With an unquiet look he gazed,
As one awaking from a sleep
    Wholly bewildered and amazed.

Part V.

As consciousness came slowly back
    He recognized his loving wife –
"Who was it, Love, through regions black
    Where hardly seemed a sign of life
Carried me bound? Methinks I view
    The dark face yet – a noble face,
He had a robe of scarlet hue,
    And ruby crown; far, far through space
He bore me, on and on, but now," –
    "Thou hast been sleeping, but the man
With glory on his kingly brow,
    Is gone, thou seest, Satyavan!

O my belovèd, – thou art free!
    Sleep which had bound thee fast, hath left
Thine eyelids. Try thyself to be!
    For late of every sense bereft
Thou seemedst in a rigid trace;
    And if thou canst my love, arise,
Regard the night, the dark expanse
    Spread out before us, and the skies."
Supported by her, looked he long
    Upon the landscape dim outspread,
And like some old remembered song
    The past came back, – a tangled thread.

"I had a pain, as if an asp
      Gnawed in my brain, and there I lay
Silent, for oh! I could but gasp,
      Till some one came that bore away
My spirit into lands unknown:
      Thou, dear, who watchedst beside me, – say
Was it a dream from elfland blown,
      Or very truth, – my doubts to stay."
"O Love, look round, – how strange and dread
      The shadows of the high trees fall,
Homeward our path now let us tread,
      To-morrow I shall tell thee all.

Arise! Be strong! Gird up thy loins!
      Think of our parents, dearest friend!
The solemn darkness haste enjoins,
      Not likely is it soon to end.
Hark! Jackals still at distance howl,
      The day, long, long will not appear,
Lo, wild fierce eyes through bushes scowl,
      Summon thy courage, lest I fear.
Was that the tiger's sullen growl?
      What means this rush of many feet?
Can creatures wild so near us prowl?
      Rise up, and hasten homewards, sweet!"

He rose, but could not find the track,
      And then, too well, Savitri knew
His wonted force had not come back.
      She made a fire, and from the dew
Essayed to shelter him. At last
      He nearly was himself again, –
Then vividly rose all the past
      And with the past, new fear and pain.
"What anguish must my parents feel
      Who wait for me the livelong hours!
Their sore wound let us haste to heal
      Before it festers, past our powers:

For broken-hearted, they may die!
      Oh hasten dear, – now I am strong,
No more I suffer, let us fly,
      Ah me! each minute seems so long.
They told me once, they could not live
      Without men, in their feeble age,
Their food and water I must give

                    And help them in the last sad stage
Of earthly life, and that Beyond
                    In which a son can help by rites.
Oh what a love is theirs – how fond!
                    Whom now Despair, perhaps, benights.

Infirm herself, my mother dear
                    Now guides, methinks, the tottering feet
Of my blind father, for they hear
                    And hasten eagerly to meet
Our fancied steps. O faithful wife
                    Let us on wings fly back again,
Upon their safety hangs my life!"
                    He tried his feelings to restrain,
But like some river swelling high
                    They swept their barriers weak and vain,
Sudden there burst a fearful cry,
                    Then followed tears, – like autumn rain.

Hush! Hark, a sweet voice rises clear!
                    A voice of earnestness intense,
"If I have worshipped Thee in fear
                    And duly paid with reverence
The solemn sacrifices, – hear!
                    Send consolation, and thy peace
Eternal, to our parents dear,
                    That their anxieties may cease.
Oh, ever hath I loved Thy truth
                    Therefore on Thee I dare to call,
Help us, this night, and them, for sooth
                    Without thy help, we perish all."

She took in hers Satyavan's hand,
                    She gently wiped his falling tears,
"This weakness, Love, I understand!
                    Courage!" She smiled away his fears.
"Now we shall go, for thou art strong."
                    She helped him rise up by her side
And led him like a child along,
                    He, wistfully the basket eyed
Laden with fruit and flowers. "Not now,
                    To-morrow we shall fetch it hence."
And so, she hung it on a bough,
                    "I'll bear thy saw for our defence."

In one fair hand the saw she took,
    The other with a charming grace
She twined around him, and her look
    She turnèd upwards to his face.
Thus aiding him she felt anew
    His bosom beat against her own —
More firm his step, more clear his view,
    More self-possessed his words and tone
Became, as swift the minutes past,
    And now the pathway he discerns,
And 'neath the trees, they hurry fast,
    For Hope's fair light before them burns.

Under the faint beams of the stars
    How beautiful appeared the flowers
Light scarlet, flecked with golden bars
    Of the palâsas,[33] in the bowers
That Nature there herself had made
    Without the aid of man. At times
Trees on their path cast densest shade,
    And nightingales sang mystic rhymes
Their fears and sorrows to assuage.
    Where two paths met, the north they chose,
As leading to the hermitage,
    And soon before them, dim it rose.

Here let us end. For all may guess
    The blind old king received his sight,
And ruled again with gentleness
    The country that was his by right;
And that Savitri's royal sire
    Was blest with many sons, – a race
Whom poets praised for martial fire,
    And every peaceful gift and grace.
As for Savitri, to this day
    Her name is named, when couples wed,
And to the bride the parents say,
    Be thou like her, in heart and head.

---

33 *Palasas*: large trees bearing large red blossoms.

Sîta[34]

Three happy children in a darkened room!
What do they gaze on with wide-open eyes?
A dense, dense forest, where no sunbeam pries,
And in its centre a cleared spot. – There bloom
Gigantic flowers on creepers that embrace
Tall trees; there, in a quiet lucid lake
The white swans glide; there, "whirring from the brake,"
The peacock springs; there, herds of wild deer race;
There, patches gleam with yellow waving grain;
There, blue smoke from strange altars rises light,
There, dwells in peace, the poet-anchorite.
But who is this fair lady? Not in vain
She weeps, – for lo! at every tear she sheds
Tears from three pairs of young eyes fall amain,
And bowed in sorrow are the three young heads.
It is an old, old story, and the lay
Which has evoked sad Sîta from the past
Is by a mother sung.... 'Tis hushed at last
And melts the picture from their sight away,
Yet shall they dream of it until the day!
When shall those children by their mother's side
Gather, ah me! as erst at eventide?

---

34 Sita: the heroine of the ancient Hindu epic, the *Ramayana*; wife of Prince Rama. In the *Ramayana*, Sita is abducted while alone in the forest by the demon Ravana, who falls in love with Sita's beauty. Rama wages battle against Ravana to rescue Sita. During the nineteenth century, Sita was often cast as displaying the desirable feminine traits of modesty, virtue, and loyalty and was thus used as a representation of the ideal Hindu wife.

Hamid Ali Khan

As is evident in his poetry, Hamid Ali Khan was an astute, if occasionally bitter, chronicler of London life in the late nineteenth century. This volume was published first in 1884 and a second edition was issued in 1885. He also published *The Bulwark of India* (1885), which was mainly concerned with the late nineteenth-century obsession with promoting friendly "social intercourse" between the British and "natives." Khan also wrote frequently for periodicals.

A Farewell to London: The Story of the Slave and the Nose-Ring (London: 1885, 2nd ed.)[35]

A Farewell to London

My studies now are o'er, my task is done,
My object gained, the Bar's degree is won;
Now I must part from thee, dear London Town,
Honoured with wig, something 'twixt white and brown,
With long, loose, flowing robe, here termed a gown;
Full-fledged, indeed, but briefless barrister.
The Bar is glutted, and luck sinister.
To bear the name, in sooth an honour great!
While as for practice, I'll leave that to Fate;
Now with this hollow style so dearly earned,
I'll hie to that home for which I've yearned;
To my dear India — land of simple joys,
Where no exotic taste the heart alloys!
Fount of politeness and humility;
Mother of grace and of civility!
So then, farewell! A long farewell to thee,
Dear London, which I hope once more to see.
Adieu! ye verdant parks, ye shady bowers,
Ye stately buildings, and ye lofty towers;
Here, all the Arts their choicest works display,
There, Wealth and Fashion make the landscape gay.
Ye bless'd retreats, ye lovely walks, adieu!
Where Nature's charms appear in varied hue.
There, with arched necks, and graceful prancing, show

---

35 Hamid Ali Khan, *A Farewell to London: The Story of the Slave and the Nose-Ring*, 2nd ed. (London: W. Whiteley, 1885).

The fiery steeds or palfreys in the Row.[36]
Here natty beaus steel, with admiring eyes,
A glance at fairest belles beneath the skies,
Sweet maids whose charms o'erpower the coldest heart,
To stay is deadly, deadlier still to part.
Bright, sunny face, crowed with jetty hair!
Well might one dream, that night and day were there.
Others with tresses like the yellow gold,
In magic meshes many a heart enfold.
Here, trees bedecked with leafy honours rise,
There, silvery lakes delight the wandering eyes;
Where happy children sail their mimic boats,
One wrecked and lost, while one in safety floats.
This little game which these young children play,
The ups and downs of life may well portray.

* * * * * *

The levees and receptions now are o'er;
Parties and dances are for me no more,
And those soft voices, which the very air
With their sweet thrilling tones delights to bear.
Debates, societies, and clubs farewell,
Which gloom and *ennui* can so oft dispel.
Oh! land of liberty, the exile's home,
Whose sway exceeds the rule of ancient Rome;
Farewell to thee, a long and warm farewell!
How happy they who in thee ever dwell;
Where light of freedom guides the ruling power,
And sheds its radiance on the darkest hour;
And where from every class the voice is heard,
Nor ever scorned the humblest peasant's word.

* * * * * *

Farewell, ye palaces of pomp and pride,
Which seem to say not want can e'er abide
In this fair London; yet we know there dwells
Grim hunger in dark, foul, and cheerless cells;
Virtue and plenty on the surface lie,
Beneath are vice, crime, want, and misery.

---

36 [Poet's Note: "Rotten Row," corrupted from *Route du Roi*, or, the King's Walk, the fashionable London drive in Hyde Park.]

Can one who mingled with the giddy throng.
And strayed the Royal palaces among,
And saw those wondrous things which Art has wrought
Sculptures and paintings with all beauty fraught,
And heard the heated Senate in debate,
Framing the laws for this far spreading State,
And viewed the triumphs Art and Science show,
Which bid the mind with joy and wonder glow;
And listened to the preacher's loud harangue,
And the sweet hymns the white-robed children sang —
Oh! could he then, amid such scenes as these,
Think that, behind, reigned misery and disease;
That cruel hunger prowls amid the streets,
And death so oft its easy victim meets?
Come here, ye rich, who nought but comfort know,
And learn to ponder on these scenes of woe.
Could strangers deem that in so fair a State,
Where youth is taught all crime and vice to hate;
That bane of health, destroyer of the mind,
Chief cause of misery, its way could find?
Used to excess, intoxicating drinks —
When folly floats and higher reason sinks —
A fatal spell cast with their evil hand,
And leave a foul stain on this joyous land.
Secretly here the good, the evil, hides,
For vice, alas, with virtue still resides.
'Tis true, weak mortals strive, but strive in vain,
In transient life the highest end to gain.
The soul exclaims, whene'er the world we scan,
How great is God! How weak is sinful man!
But stay, enough! Suffice it man to know
Wise Providence directs our fate below.
And now, dear partners of my sojourn here,
While to my native shore my way I steer,
The fond remembrance to my bosom clings,
Of happy hours that flew on rapid wings.
Accept then, heartfelt thanks, though weak the rhyme,
For show'ring joys on your Bekhabar's[37] time.

---

37 [Poet's Note: Our poets invariably insert their *noms de plumes* in the closing couplet of their compositions. I have taken the liberty of following the rule here. Bekhabar means careless — indifferent.]

The Slave and the Nose-Ring

Among the countless customs quaint,
    Observed by us for long
In India, reigns the one which forms
    The subject of my song.

Our Indian women, rich and poor,
    Of ev'ry caste and creed,
Throughout our vast and famous land,
    The shining nose-ring need.[38]

At tender age, the nostril's pierced —
    The nostril on the right;
They bear the pain, to gain the ring —
    Indeed, a glittering sight.

The relatives and friends appear
    In best apparel clad;
They greet the maids and parents too;
    And ev'ry heart is glad.

The luscious sweets are handed round,
    Nor absent friends forgot;
No sordid thoughts exclude the poor,
    Or those of humble lot.[39]

It has two pearls, this ring of gold,
    One tiny end is bent;
The other has a little hole,
    Through which that end is sent.

And when 'tis worn it thus assumes
    A perfect oval grace;
And from the nostril as it hangs,
    It seems to suit the face.

The rings with pearls are fitly due
    To married girls alone;
Whereas the little pearl-less ones
    'Tis only maidens own.

---

38 [Poet's Note: I say "need," since it expresses an obligation, which as a matter of fact exists.]
39 [Poet's Note: This brief account of the observance of the ceremony applies to the Mussulmans of India, and not to the Hindoos. It is worthy of notice that the Muhammedan ladies have borrowed the custom of wearing the nose-ring, in common with a good many others, from their Hindoo sisters.]

And further yet, when husband dies
    And leaves behind his wife,
No longer must she wear the ring,
    Or jewels all her life.[40]

I.

There lived a certain wealthy man,
    In a small Indian town;
A man whose fervent faith, withal,
    Added to his renown.

II.

Amid the comforts wealth can give,
    No cares he knew in life,
But passed his joyful, happy days,
    With his dear, loving wife.

III.

The lord of many a faithful slave,
    And countless servants too;
While for his pretty wife there were,
    Handmaidens not a few.

IV.

Among his slaves of sterner sex,
    Shone forth a handsome youth,
Who well deserved the highest praise
    For his great love of truth.

V.

He license had within to go,
    Beyond the curtained screen,[41]
Which hides those charms that never may
    By eye of man be seen.

---

40 [Poet's Note: Though a second marriage is lawful, it is seldom, if ever, contracted. If, however, the widow should marry again, she, in that case, becomes re-entitled to her nose-ring and other jewellery.]

41 [Poet's Note: As is well known, our ladies are not allowed to go out-of-doors. From their earliest years, they are restricted to that portion of the house exclusively set apart for their use. This custom is rigidly observed among the Muhammedans of India. The relatives mentioned in the following verse nearly exhaust the list of those who are permitted, by their religion, to enter within the precincts sacred to the "fair sex." The females of the poorer classes, who are obliged to pursue their daily avocations abroad are particular to veil their faces in the thoroughfares.]

VI.

Except by father, brother, son,
    Or other kinsman near,
As uncle, cousin, nephew, too,
    And sure the husband dear.

VII.

It chanced the lady of my tale,
    Would lave her face one day;
First, from her nose, as was her wont,
    She took the ring away.

VIII.

Just then, there came the truthful slave,
    By household matters led,
He saw her nose without the ring,
    And thought her husband dead.

IX.

With bitter sorrow overwhelmed,
    As pale as death he stood,
And down his pallid cheek there rolled,
    Of tears a swelling flood.

X.

"Why weepest though," the lady spake,
    "O slave why dost thou cry?
Tell me the cause, my truthful slave,
    O tell the reason why?"

XI.

"What dire affliction," thus he cried,
    "Must we, alas, deplore!
My heart is fraught with grief to think
    Your husband is no more."

XII.

With ev'ry sign of frantic woe,
    That lady, young and fair,
Did beat her head, and strike her feet,
    And tear her jetty hair.[42]

XIII.

Away this foolish, simple slave,
    To tell his master ran,
Of news that well might strike a chord
    In heart of ev'ry man.

XIV.

Within his lofty, spacious room,
    He soon his master found,
In some profound reflection lost,
    With many a book around.

XV.

Straightaway he broke the mournful news,
    With many a bitter cry,
And shed a stream of tears of blood,
    And drew a choking sigh.

XVI.

No sooner heard than, like the deer
    When struck by hunter's dart,
To where the ladies dwelt alone,
    He made a sudden start.

XVII.

His prostrate wife he quickly raised,
    And gently placed her head
On knees that shook, because his wife
    Had thought that he was dead.

---

42 [Poet's Note: I have here most literally translated the original, for the facts mentioned in the two latter lines comprise a custom common with us. When the news of the death of her husband is announced to the wife, she strikes her 'head and feet' and tears her hair. In these exhibitions of grief she is joined not only by her own very near relatives, but also by those of her husband. I have called the hair "jetty," as Indian ladies have almost invariably black hair.]

XVIII.

With gentle voice he called on her,
    And then sprang forth a flood
Of tears, which down his pallid cheeks
    Ran like a stream of blood.

XIX.

"Methinks my heart has ceased to beat,
    Outrun the sand of life,
And thou, alone, art left to weep;
    A widow, dearest wife."

XX.

No longer could the wife restrain
    The tears that swiftly rolled;
Loud wept the slaves, loud wept the maids,
    Loud wept both young and old.

XXI.

The friends and neighbours gathered fast,
    Where men alone may go;[43]
Forthwith he came and met them all,
    And told his tale of woe.

XXII.

As soon as this sad news they heard,
    Sore, sore were they distressed;
And one and all with much ado,
    Their sympathy expressed.

XXIII.

Among his friends there was a sage,
    For wisdom vast renowned,
For sparkling wit, and matchless mind,
    And eke for judgment sound.

XXIV.

These wise and soothing words he spake,
    In gentle tone and clear;
His face looked pale, his heart was full,
    And in his eye a tear.

---

43 [Poet's Note: *Vide* Note, p. 30.] Please see footnote 41 on page 333.

XXV.

"Alive thou art, methinks, my child,
    Say then, how can it be
That thou art lost to us for aye,
    Thy wife, a widow she?"

XXVI.

Their hearts received the joyful words,
    Uprose the deafening shout
Through all the crowd, from man to man,
    Went loud applause about.

XXVII.

When ceased the cheer, and calm restored,
    The husband soft began,
" 'Tis true, 'tis true, I know full well,
    O wise, O wisest man."

XXVIII.

" 'Tis true, 'tis true," quoth he again,
    "But humbly I reply;
My slave I must, perforce believe,
    For he ne'er speaks a lie.

XXIX.

"Never escaped a word that was
    Not true from my true slave;
So faithful, honest, guileless, frank,
    And just and bold and brave.

XXX.

"We cannot, then, belie the slave;
    We must find out the truth
That lies beneath this mystic tale —
    This puzzling tale, in sooth."

XXXI.

Then spake again the wisest man,
    And thus addressed the throng,
"I see a way from out the maze —
    The maze we've trod so long."

XXXII.

Intent they gave their eager ears,
    While patiently they stood,
To hear the words of hoary sage,
    So noble and so good.

XXXIII.

"The wisest course to you I point,
    Now let us ask the slave –
The why and wherefore of his tale –
    Our slave so true and brave."

XXXIV.

The wondering throng approved full well
    The wise, suggestive word,
And raised a long and deafening cheer,
    That far and wide was heard.

XXXV.

"I saw her nose without the ring,
    When last I her descried,
And she a widow stood revealed:"
    So spake the slave, and sighed.

XXXVI.

"True were his words," the master cried,
    "True," said the worthy sage;
"The slave spake truth," the echo ran
    Through all of ev'ry age.

XXXVII.

The husband ran to tell the tale
    To his dear, pretty wife;
Who, when she heard, to heaven prayed
    "May God prolong your life."[44]

---

44 [Poet's Note: This is a common Eastern expression, generally employed to the young. The wife's justification for the use of the phrase consists in her relationship.]

XXXVIII.

Loud shouts of joy then rent the air,
    And shook the gathered throng,
Who, while they parted, sang the strain,
    "May God your life prolong."

And thence was scattered far and wide,
    In every thorp and town,
From house to house, from man to man,
    The truthful slave's renown.

Henceforth this faithful slave obtained
    The nick-name "Honest Truth";
A man who never falsehood used,
    But shunned it from his youth.

Through all the glorious land of Ind,
    Where e'er this tale is told;
Of husband, wife, and ring, and slave,
    It gladdens young and old.

Dejen L. Roy

Dejen L. Roy (1864–1913), or Dvijendralala Roy, was a Bengali poet, playwright, composer, and nationalist who studied in Calcutta and England. Although as a young man Roy often wrote in English, he would later became famous for his Bengali-language patriotic and Hindu devotional songs. His other English-language collection of poetry, as noted in advertisements for *The Lyrics of Ind*, was *Aryan Melodies*. Roy dedicates *The Lyrics of Ind* to the Orientalist poet Edwin Arnold "as a token of sincere respect, love, and admiration." He writes in his author's "Preface":

> My principal object in the composition of the following verses has been to harmonise English and Indian poetries as they ought to be. Both are beautiful; but whilst the one is visionary and sensuous, the other is vigorous and chaste; whilst one dreams, the other soars; whereas the one makes a poetry of Religion, the other makes a religion of Poetry. If it has pleased God to unite England and India in the strong ties of wedded interests, and in the still stronger, more sacred, and indissoluble bond of mutual love and gratitude, it is the aim of the author to establish a marriage and an intellectual commerce between their poetries as well.

The Lyrics of Ind (London: 1886)[45]

The Land of the Sun

There's a land rank and blazing with beauty,
Where a radiance perpetual shines,
Where Love's angels sleep pillowed in Terror,
And round Grandeur frail Loveliness twines —

Where soft murmurs the love-dreaming brooklet,
In her sleep, as the *kokilas* sing;[46]
Bloom the odorous *bakul* and *jati*,[47]
As the sun wakes the zephyr in Spring —

Where green Autumn floods Earth with a verdure,
Makes the sky reel with moonlight above,
And bright Summer fills Eve's fleecy sun-clouds
With the glittering visions of love —

In the arms of the slumbering valleys
The young moonbeams enamoured repose,
And the loveliest stars faint, entangled
In the mazes of *champak*[48] and rose —

Whom the Year woos with tears, smiles, and whispers,
Whom the Seasons with rare treasures greet;
Where Dawn blushes with fragrance and music,
And the sunset is glorious and sweet.

Here, too, fierce is the sun in his splendour,
The snakes coil in their cavernous home;
Here, 'midst wilderness lightless and shoreless,
Its imperial denizens roam.

Here, too, rings the wild songs of the tempest,
Through the deserts and forests untrod,
Flock black clouds over clouds nursed in darkness,
And wild howls the chained thunder of God.

---

45 Dejen L. Roy, *The Lyrics of Ind* (London: Trübner & Co., 1886).
46 *Kokila*, also known as the *kokil*, *coil*, *koil*, *koel*, *koyal*, or *kokila*: bird famed for its melodious calls; often termed the Indian cuckoo.
47 *Bakul*: white, star-shaped, sweet-smelling flower, which grows on evergreen trees native to the subcontinent. *Jati*: strong-smelling jasmine flower.
48 *Champak*: evergreen tree with fragrant orange-yellow flowers.

In her breast surge the mightiest rivers;
At her feet foams the wildest of seas;
By her watches the monarch of mountains;
O'er her sweet beams the bluest of skies.

There too Poetry glows in the sunlight,
Beauty sings and sweet Voices dance;
There a heavenly, glorious transport
Melts away into dream and romance.

O my land! can I cease to adore thee,
Though to gloom and to misery hurled?
O dear Bharat![49] my beautiful maiden,
O sweet Ind once the queen of the world.

And though wrecked is thy pride and thy glory,
Of it nothing remains but the name;
Yet a beauty and sunshine still lingers,
And yet gleams through the mist of thy shame.

The Island[50]

Sweet isle of the noble, the brave, and the free,
     And crowned with a beauty divine!
Thou smilest; what spirit soft whispers to thee?
     What madness, what transport is thine?
Though born in the mist and caressed by the gloom,
Yet thine are the rainbow-hued flowers that bloom
In the woodlands; wild songs in thy valley and glen;
Thy daughters are angels, and gods are thy men.

Thou, parent of Science of luminous birth!
     Sweet friend of the heavenly Art!
Kind nurse of a Poetry matchless on earth!
     To gild and ennoble the heart: –
Thou bold as an eagle and meek as a dove,
The strength of a Titan curbed, tempered by love,
The flag of thy wisdom and prowess, unfurled,
Emancipate Bondage, illumine the world.

---

49 Bharat: India.
50 The Island: England.

Sweet isle of fair mountains and valleys and streams,
    The nightingale, lily, and rose!
One arm ever cradling and nursing thy dreams,
    The other repulsing thy foes:
Brave isle! foreign strands from thy continents pour
Their harvests, pearls orient unto thy shore;
Thou sendest thy glorious light to each clime,
Dispel their wild chaos,- thy mission sublime.

Greece Chunder Dutt

A member of the famous Dutt family, Greece Chunder Dutt, brother to Govin Chunder Dutt and uncle to Toru Dutt, was an accomplished poet in his own right. His first single-author volume of poetry, *Cherry Stones* (1881), was followed by *Cherry Blossoms* (1887). (Poems from *Cherry Stones* are included in the "East" section.) Many of the sonnets and "Miscellaneous Pieces" published in *Cherry Blossoms* were also published in *Cherry Stones* although Dutt also includes a number of newer poems in this second collection. One poem in particular, "In the Bush," is a fascinating and unusual piece that seems to take as its subject the experience of the Indian migrant in South Africa.

Cherry Blossoms (London: 1887)[51]

The Soonderbuns[52]

In the wild district where the Ganges pours
Its lavish waters by a hundred mouths
Into the bosom of the sounding sea,
Are plains, like prairies, of enormous length,
Adorned with ancient trees of stately growth, –
And shady coverts of white tasselled cane,
In which, defended from the noonday heat,
The mighty monarchs of the waste repose, –
And shallow pools where wild fowl pluck in sport,
The fragrant spathes[53] of blossoms rich that deck,

---

51 Greece Chunder Dutt, *Cherry Blossoms* (London: T. Fisher Unwin, 1887).
52 Soonderbuns, or Sunderbans: jungle forest that lies at the bottom of the Ganges and is spread across what is now Bangladesh and West Bengal, India. It is home to a complex ecosystem of mangrove forests, tidal waterways, small islands, the Bengal tiger and numerous other animals including crocodiles and deer.
53 Spathe: large bract enveloping a flower cluster (n. "spathe" OED).

The hardy creepers that delight in swamps, –
And leagues of woodlands sparsely scattered o'er
With mat-fenced villages, – and seaward slopes,
As smooth and verdant as a billiard board,
O'er which unnumbered troops of nimble deer
Range undisturbed, – and fens whose sluggish streams
With mazy error twist ten thousand ways, –
And dreary moors where naught the stillness breaks
Except the eagle's scream, the bittern's boom,
Or yet the sullen tiger's hoarse "ragum."
Although no hills diversify its face,
Or swelling uplands crowned with hamlets white,
Or babbling rills with banks of splintered rock,
Or foaming water-breaks o'er which the ash
Inclines its graceful arms, or brooklets keen,
With beds of gravel like new minted gold
The chosen play ground of the lusty trout,
Or winding dells that half unwillingly
Reveal the gabled roofs of dairy farms,
Or vast cathedrals with elm-guarded spires,
Or modest manses amid bright parterres,[54]
Or high-walled orchards, where on mossy trees
Defended safely from the jay with nets
The black-heart darkens in the genial sun, –
Yet has this delta an inherent grace,
An unsophisticated loveliness,
And rustic glory not to be surpassed.

Its dented coast line to the stranger yields,
On his first journey to Bengal by sea,
A sight as beautiful as that which greets
The sailor in the Channel, when he makes
The shores of England near the isle of Wight,
For when half hopefully and half afraid,
He scans with stedfast gaze the goal at last,
Delightful slopes green to the water's edge,
And lofty trees, that viewed from ocean seem
Arranged to screen the windows of a pile,
(The castled dwelling of some might earl,)
From the rude ferry of the wild sea blast
Enchant his soul, and as the ship draws near
The herds of antlered deer that haunt the coast

---

[54] Parterre: level space in a garden occupied by an ornamental arrangement of flowerbeds (n. "parterre" OED).

Rivet his fancy, and still fan the dream
The waste before him is a mighty park:
And if perchance his eyes one moment miss,
The gentle uplands and the white chalk cliffs,
That loss at once the graceful palm atones,
With its rich tuft of leaves like drooping plumes,
And clusters strange of green and golden nuts.

Landwards the sylvan solitude affords
To him who slowly follows in a boat,
The lazy mazes of its tidal streams
In shrewd November, that delicious draught
Of genuine pleasure, that rewards the toil
Of keen explorers in the favored parts
Of Brazil or Australia or the Cape:
Whether he glide by clearances where yet
The rifted roots of giant trunks attest
The squatter's toil, or watch at morn the smoke
Curl upwards from the leaf-fed forest fire, –
Or mooring fast his cumbrous vessel chase
In a light skiff, on some lagoon immense,
The countless swarms of wild ducks that infest
The land-locked inlets edged with graceful reeds, –
Or by a rustic weir[55] of mats and stakes
Assist the fisher, and with lusty arm
Drag up his net, that oft has fish enough
To fill a barrel, – or in jungle deep,
Where not one single sign of man appears,
(Not e'en a rude built trap of unbarked logs
Of knotted soondri[56], ponderous as lead,
Among the thickets on the river's brink,)
At shut of eve, while on the cabin roof
His haunch of fen deer smokes "mid charcoal gleams,"
Prepare to anchor for the night his craft.

---

55 Weir: barrier or dam to restrain water, especially one placed across a river or canal; a fence or enclosure of stakes made in the river for taking and preserving fish (n. "weir" *OED*).
56 Soondri, or sundari: trees that give the Sunderbans its name.

The Neem Tree[57]

The withered Neem that stands forlorn,
Beside the house where I was born,
    Is dearer to my heart,
Than every tree that wins from air,
Fresh leaves to clothe its branches bare,
    When frosty days depart.

With more than e'en a wizard's might,
It dissipates the cheerless night,
    That clings around the past,
And paints old scenes with lustrous hues,
As pure as those that frozen dews,
    Or pendant crystals cast.

Beneath its forks grotesque and rude,
My youthful sisters rendezvoused,
    With laughter-lightened eyes,
And seemed, while waved their airy swing,
Like doves that tried with fearless wing,
    To penetrate the skies.

It saw my mother as a bride,
Come home to bless the old fireside,
    With soul imbued with love,
And witnessed too the mournful day,
In which her spirit passed away,
    To join the blest above.

When timid peasants quaked for fear
Of harm, to herds that pastured near,
    As soon as twilight died,
And scarce a furlong from the door,
In careless freedom staked the boar,
    O'er heath and marsh wide.

It cheered my grandsire's infancy,
And flung about him playfully,
    Its wealth of berries bright,
Whene'er the gentle south-west breeze,
(Meek rover of the woods and seas,)
    Brushed by on pinions light.

---

57 *Neem*: tree native to South Asia; known for its fragrant flowers.

In the Bush[58]

After a journey of three weary days
Across a dreary tract of heated sand
And barren pebbles that severely tried
The strength and patience of both man and ox,
I came at sunset to an oasis,
Set like a jewel in the tawny waste.
It seemed about five acres in extent,
And held a tranquil tarn[59] of azure hue
Fed by a tiny tributary spring
Of purest lustre but exhausted strength;
And overshadowed at one point by palms,
And old homeras[60] of dimensions vast,
That safely harboured in full throated ease,
A placid colony of timid doves.

Behind the spring were huge misshapen blocks
Which the fierce ardour of volcanic fire
Had rudely pushed up in some bypast age,
And here and there the date-palm's slender shaft
Reared high in air its graceful crown that bore
Attractive clusters of nutritious fruit,
But an entangled mat of cactus stems,
Gigantic ferns and lemon-grass, commixed,
With bearded burrs arrayed in scented down,
Obscured the soil wherever there was space
Unoccupied by water, rocks, or trees.

It was a savage but romantic spot,
A desert paradise, by which with joy
I could have lived a hunter's life for years,
And sought for antelopes that haunt at morn,
The silent sand-hills of the thirsty waste,

---

58 The setting for this poem seems to be the African bush, more specifically the Transvaal where a number of Indian emigrants settled.
59 Tarn: small mountain lake with no significant tributaries (n. "tarn" *OED*).
60 Homera: variety of pepper, or capsicum, plant that can grow over two feet tall; produces long yellow fruit that turns red as it ripens.

Or with devoted zeal discharged at eve
The humbler duties of my chosen sphere,
Like a lone emigrant amid the wilds
Of favored Natal, or Van Dieman's land.[61]

All nature seemed at work around the pool
What time the waggons came: the kingfisher
Surveyed its shallows with malignant eyes,
The lively swallow chased its wrathful gnats,
The honey-bee regardless of the hour
Explored its coverts cool, and while the frog
Croaked from its weeds to flout the solemn owl
On ruthless thoughts intent, a single pair
Of scarlet-crested, long-legged, moor-hens sought
Their frugal supper on its margin dank,
And probed its scanty sedge with busy bills.

By pity urged, the instant I arrived,
I led the cattle to the water's brink,
And when the fever of their thirst was quelled,
I cut the tangled thorns, and neatly built
For their behoof with unremitted toil,
A small but well-fenced kraâl[62], where presently,
In perfect safety from all chance of harm,
The docile beasts in ordered ranks commenced
To munch their rations with keen appetite:
I kindled next with careful hand the fire
Beneath the cloudless canopy of heaven,
And as the peaceful smoke curled lightly o'er
The white-roofed waggons drawn up side by side,
And the rich smell of aromatic herbs
Rose from the stew-pot on the ruddy blaze,
I stretched my carpet on the level sand,
And lit my pipe to charm fatigue away.

---

61 Natal: region in South Africa. The Natal was a British colony from 1843 until 1910 when it was combined with other regions. Van Dieman's Land: the island of Tasmania, now part of Australia. The island was colonized by the British during the early nineteenth century and used as a penal colony. See James Boyce, *Van Dieman's Land* (Melbourne: Black Inc., 2008) for an excellent history of the island.
62 *Kraâl*: enclosure for livestock.

The Taj Mahal[63]

1.

Tax not the prince with pride,
  Or foolish greed of Praise
That with the mushroom's growth
  Develops and decays,
Who built by Duty urged,
  With taste and pious care,
Above his buried Love,
  This cenotaph[64] so fair, —

2.

This triumph grand of Art,
  This dream in marble pure,
That shall unharmed by Time,
  For ages yet endure,
And witness give to all,
  How well she played her part,
As consort and as friend
  To him who owned her heart,

3.

How constant was her soul,
  That feared no adverse shock,
But seemed a structure firm,
  Let deeply in the rock,
How noble were her aims,
  How holy and how high,
Like minarets sublime,
  That strive to pierce the sky;

---

63 The famous Taj Mahal in Agra was erected by Mughul emperor Shah Jahan (1592–1666) to commemorate his favorite wife, Mumtaz.
64 Cenotaph: monument erected in honor of a person or group whose remains are elsewhere (n. "cenotaph" *OED*).

4.

'Tis known a mighty queen,
    Blest servant of the cross,
Felt humbled and subdued
    When (mindful of her loss,
And of his tender love,
    With whom her youth was spent,)
At Frogmore[65] she upreared,
    A stately monument.

On the Day of Lord Ripon's Departure from Calcutta[66]
Ezek., Chap xxxvii. 1–14

Long ages past the prophet saw,
A sight that filled his soul with awe,
    When by his Maker led,
He gained amid the mountains drear,
With humble heart and faith sincere,
    The valley of the Dead.

For all around were human bones,
As sinewless and dry as stones
    That strew the deserts brown,
Discovered by the earthquakes shock,
From some stupendous wall of rock,
    And flung in fragments down.

But soon his awe was changed to hope,
When prompted by his Guide he spoke,
    Such magic words of might,
That bone joined bone and quickly grew,
(Breathed o'er by summoned winds that blew,)
    A host prepared for fight.

---

65 Frogmore: estates located south of Windsor Castle in England; sometimes used by the Royal Family during the nineteenth century.
66 Lord Ripon (1827–1909): viceroy of India from 1880 to 1884 under then British prime minister William Gladstone. Ripon was a proponent of the Ilbert Bill (which would have allowed Indian judges to preside over cases involving Europeans) and limited self-government. He was often referred to reverently in Indian-English political discourses during the nineteenth century as a figure sympathetic to Indians and as a proponent for reform within the British Raj.

We also see the relic dread,
Of peoples who once boldly led
    The march of cultured thought,
Encumber earth, like leaves that lie,
When surly winter rules the sky
    In woods and wastes unsought.

Relics so withered and so bare,
That even hopeful in despair,
    To find in them a trace,
Of undeveloped germs that strive
To renovate − restore − revive,
    What evil years deface.

But gentle winds sigh soft above,
And testify that God is Love,
    Albeit in whispers small,
And if the words were asked to-day,
Can these bones live? our hearts would say,
    Thou knowest, Lord, who knowest all.

Sita[67]

I.

For vest of vair,
Oh lady fair,
Bark mantles robe thee now,
Rudrakhis[68] brown
Replace the crown
That bound thy queenly brow.

---

[67] Sita: heroine of the ancient Hindu epic, the *Ramayana*; wife of Prince Rama. In the *Ramayana*, Sita is abducted while alone in the forest by the demon Ravana, who falls in love with Sita's beauty. Rama wages battle against Ravana to rescue Sita. During the nineteenth century, Sita was often cast as displaying the desirable feminine traits of modesty, virtue, and loyalty and was thus used as a representation of the ideal Hindu wife.

[68] *Rudrakhis* or *rudrakshis*: large trees. However, the word usually refers to the brown seeds it produces and which are used as Hindu prayer beads.

2.

For walks ere dawn,
O'er clean swept lawn,
Thy feet thread waste to bring,
When noon's fierce eye,
Burns earth and sky,
The pitcher from the spring.

3.

Thy fingers white,
That touched so light,
The lute at fall of day,
With pain at eve,
Green rushes weave,
Beneath the taper's ray.

4.

Yet chase all fear,
Is He not near
To shield, to help, to bless,
Whose love faints not
Who ne'er forgot
The righteous in distress.

T. (Pillai) Ramakrishna

While the first edition of *Tales of Ind, and Other Poems* by the Madras-based writer T. (Pillai) Ramakrishna (1855–1920), published in 1886 in Madras, was dedicated to Tennyson, the second edition, published in 1896 in London, includes an ode to Tennyson. In his role as poet laureate of Britain, and by extension, the British Empire, Tennyson served as an occasionally contested model for Indians writing English-language poetry. Indeed, in reprinted reviews of *Tales of Ind* that accompany the second edition, Ramakrishna's poems are often compared to Tennyson's *Idylls* in their atmospheric descriptions. Ramakrishna also published novels, including the romances *Padmini, An Indian Romance* (1903) and *The Dive for Death, an Indian Romance* (1911); an ethnographic study of a "typical" South Indian village, *Life in an Indian Village* (1891); and a travel narrative entitled *My Visit to the West* (1915), which includes an introduction by Grant Duff. The Indian-English poet, M. V. Venkatasubba Iyer [Aiyer], also from Madras, dedicates his volume *Ventures in Verse* (1899) to Ramakrishna. (Poetry from Iyer's volume is included in the "South" section of the anthology.) Ramakrishna's poem, "Seeta and Rama – *a Tale of the Indian Famine* ," is set in a supposedly prototypical South Indian village during the actual drought-induced famine of 1876–1879, which affected the Deccan region.

Tales of Ind, and Other Poems (London: 1896, 2nd ed.)[69]

Lord Tennyson

A Poet of my native land has said —
The life the good and virtuous lead on earth
Is like the black-eyed maiden of the East,
Who paints the lids to look more bright and fair.
The eyes may smart and water, but withal
She loves to please them that behold her face.
E'en so, my Master, thine own life has been.
Thy songs have pleased the world, thy thoughts divine
Have purified, likewise ennobled man.
And what are they, those songs and thoughts divine,
But sad experience of thy life, dipt deep
In thine own tears, and traced on nature's page?
To please and teach the world for two dear ones
You mourned — a friend in youth, a son in age.
'Tis said the life that gives one moment's joy
To one lone mortal is not lived in vain;
But lives like thine God grants as shining lights
That we in darkness Him aright may see.
Nay more, such lives the more by ills beset
Do shine the more and better teach His ways.
Alas! thou'rt gone that were so kind to one
Obscure — a stranger in a distant land.
Accept from him this wreath uncouth of words
Which do but half express the grief he feels.

Seeta and Rama[70]
A Tale of the Indian Famine

It was by far the loveliest scene in Ind: —
A deep sunk lonely vale, 'tween verdant hills
That, in eternal friendship, seemed to hold
Communion with the changing skies above;
Dark shady groves the haunts of shepherd boys
And wearied peasants in the midday noon;

---

69 T. (Pillai) Ramakrishna, *Tales of Ind, and other poems*, 2nd ed. (London: T. Fisher Unwin, 1896).
70 Ramakrishna self-consciously uses the names of the hero and heroine of the epic, the *Ramayana*, to name his own hero and heroine.

A lake that shone in lustre clear and bright
Like a pure Indian diamond set amidst
Green emeralds, where every morn, with songs
Of parted lovers that tempted blooming maids
With pitchers on their heads to stay and hear
Those songs, the busy villagers of the vale
Their green fields watered that gave them sure hopes
Of future plenty and of future joys.
Oh, how uncertain man's sure hopes and joys!
In this enchanted hollow that was scooped –
For so it seemed – by God's own mighty hand,
Where Nature shower'd her richest gifts to make
Another paradise, stood Krishnapore[71]
With her two score and seven huts reared by
The patient labour of her simple men.

In this blest hamlet one there was that owned
Its richest lands: beloved by all its men,
Their friend in times of need, their guide in life,
Partaker of their joys and woes as well,
The arbiter of all their petty strifes.
By him his friend the village master lived
That at his door a group of children taught;
A man he was well versed in ancient lore;
And oft at night, when ended was their toil,
The villagers with souls enraptured heard him
In fiery accents speak of Krishna's[72] deeds
And Rama's[73] warlike skill, and wondered that
He knew so well the deities they adored.
One only daughter this schoolmaster had,
And Seeta was her name, the prettiest maid
In all the village, nursed by the fond cares
Of her indulgent sire, and loved with all
The tender feelings that pure love inspires
By the rich villager's only son, the heir
Of all his father's wealth; the best at school,
The boldest of the village youths at play,
And the delight of all those that saw him;
And these seemed such a fitting pair that oft
The secret whisper round the village ran

---

71 The rather generic name of Krishnapore is used to signify a typical South Indian village.
72 Krishna: avatar of the god Vishnu. Krishna figured prominently in the ancient Hindu epic, the *Mahabharata*, in which he helped the Pandavas ultimately attain victory in their war against the Kauravas.
73 Rama: hero of the Hindu epic the *Ramayana*. Seeta, or Sita: Rama's wife.

That Seeta was to wed the rich man's son.
Thus, in this Eden, its blest inmates lived
And passed their days, the villagers at the fields,
Their busy women at the blazing hearths,
The village master at this cottage door,
And Rama and fair Seeta in true love.

Hither a monster came, that slowly sucked
The vigour, the very life of Krishnapore.
The brilliant lustre of the diamond lake,
The emerald greenness of the waving fields,
The shady groves and pleasant cottage grounds,
And all the beauties of the happy vale
Soon vanished imperceptibly, as if
Some consuming furnace underneath
Had baked the earth and rendered it all bare,
Until its inmates wandered desolate,
With hollow cheeks, sunk eyes, and haggard faces,
Like walking skeletons pasted o'er with skin.
No more would blooming girls with pitchers laden
Repair to the clear lake while curling smoke
Rose from their cottage roofs; no more at morn
Would Rama be the first at school to see
His Seeta deck her father's house with flowers;
No more at eve the village master pour
From Hindu lore the mighty deeds of gods
To the delighted ears of simple men;
For these have left their lands and their dear homes.
And Seeta with her father left her cot,
And cast behind, with a deep, heavy sigh,
One ling'ring look upon that vale where she
Was born and fondly nursed, – where glided on
Her days in pleasure and pure innocence, –
Where Rama lived and loved her tenderly.
Her father died of hunger on the way,
And the lone creature wandered in the streets
Of towns from door to door, and vainly begged
For food, till some, deep moved by the sad tales
Of the lone straggler, safely lodged her in
A famine camp, where, heavy laden with
A double sorrow (for her lover too,
She thought, had died), her tedious life she spent.
And days and weeks and months thus rolled away,
Until at last her love for the dead youth
Mysterious waned, and, like a shallow lamp,
Burnt in her breast with nothing to feed it.

One day the news went through the famine shed
That a lean youth, plucked from the very arms
Of cruel death, was tenderly nursed there;
And all its inmates hurried to the scene.
Poor Seeta saw the youth, and that sad sight
She ne'er forgot; the youth was in her mind
Too firmly rooted to be rooted out,
Who ev'ry day in strength and beauty grew, till he
Appeared the fairest youth in all the camp.
First pity for the youth, then love for him
Mysterious came to her, until at last
The flick'ring flame shone sudden in her breast.
"This stranger I must wed, for him I love,
I know not how; that pleasant face is like
The face of him I dearly loved; I see
Appearing ev'ry day upon that face,
As if by magic wrought, those beauties that
Were seated on dead Rama's face." Thus mused
This maiden of the camp, and the fair youth
Thus kindled in her breast the hidden flame
Of love and fed it ever with new strength,
Which shone again in all its purity.

As the moon whose effulgence hidden lies
When dimmed by clouds, suddenly blazes forth
And in her wonted beauty shines again
What time she darts into the cloudless vault,
So shone again in lovely Seeta's breast
The lamp of love by clouds of sorrow dimmed.
The smothered passion suddenly blazed forth
In brighter lustre, and to her returned
With double force, as when the flaming fire
Is smothered when more fuel is on it thrown,
And straightaway flames and gives a brighter light.

At last the monster left the land, the camp
Was broke, its inmates left it for their homes.
England, would that one of thy sons were there
To hear what words, what blessings now burst from
Their inward hearts for nursing them when they
From all estranged had poured into thine arms!
Poor Seeta hastened to the youth she loved,
And to him with a gladdened heart thus spake: –
Her rosy lips, just oped to speak, were like
A half-blown rosebud bloss'ming all at once;

Such magic was wrought on her ere she spake:
"King stranger, whither goest thou? I am
A lonely maiden, and friends I have none;
And thee alone I trust as my safe guide
to Krishnapore."

      "Dear maid! thy sorrows cease;
My way now lies through Krishnapore: fear not,
I shall restore thee to thy home and friends;
Trust me as your safe guide and dearest friend."
She, overjoyed, recounted to the youth
Her tale – how she, her father's only hope
And pride, reluctant left their native vale
And cottage home; how he died on the way,
And she, a lonely creature, wandered in
The streets from door to door and begged for food;
How she was taken to the famine camp;
How he, with hollow cheeks and sunken eyes,
Was brought one day and there nursed tenderly;
And how in beauty ev'ry day he grew
Until like her dead Rama he appeared.
The village youth, unable any more
Now to suppress him, suddenly exclaimed,
"Look here, whose name is on this arm tattooed?"
"O Rama, Krishna, Govinda,[74] and all
Ye Gods that I adore, ye have blest me;
This is the happiest moment in my life,
And this the happiest spot in all the earth,
For now my long-lost Rama I have found."
So saying, she intently gazed on him.

As a rich mine pours forth its hidden wealth
To the delight of those that day and night
Court eagerly its treasures them t'enrich;
So from this lovely pair's deep mine of feelings,
What honeyed words escaped now through their lips
To their intense joy, better far than all
The treasures any ample mine bestows!
With sweet talk they beguiled their tedious way;
The verdant hills sublime rose to the view;
The broad lake glittered diamond-like again;
And wreathing smoke curled from the cottage roofs;
The lovely vale became the lovely vale

---

74 Govinda: another name for Krishna, in his role as cowherd. Rama, Krishna and Govinda are all considered avatars of the Hindu god, Lord Vishnu.

Again, and all the long forgotten scenes
In quick succession flowed before them both;
And never was a happier marriage seen
In all that happy vale of Krishnapore.

Manmohan Ghose

Manmohan Ghose (1869–1924) was the brother of another famous poet, Aurobindo Ghose. (Aurobindo Ghose's poetry is included in the "West" section of the anthology.) Educated in England (1879–1894), Manmohan Ghose returned to India where he worked as a professor of English at Patna College and at Presidency College, Calcutta. His earliest poetry was published in *Primavera, Poems by Four Authors* (1890), a pamphlet of verse which also included poems by fellow Oxford classmates Laurence Binyon, Arthur S. Cripps and Stephen Phillips. Ghose's later, single-authored, collections include *Love Songs and Elegies* (1898) and the posthumously published *Songs of Love and Death* (1926), which features a memoir by Laurence Binyon (included in the Appendix section of this anthology). Having spent his formative years in England, Ghose's poetry reflects his sense of living as an exile in India.

Love Songs and Elegies (London: 1898)[75]

The Exile

Sleep, sweet sleep, O not so soon forsake me,
    Nor in desolation leave complete
The lost exile! Wherefore dost thou wake me,
    Or what sound is that, so far and sweet?

Sundered here, than sad oblivion deeper,
    What articulate thing remembers me?
Me, the abandoned, world-forgotten sleeper
    In this rain-beat cavern by the sea.

Ceased it is, that rain! From out my prison
    Gaze I, sad with unrefreshing sleep;
Through the parted hills as in a vision
    Wild and gray appears the troubled deep.

---

75 Manmohan Ghose, *Love Songs and Elegies* (London: Elkin Mathews, 1898).

Wherefore, heart forlorn, that mountains bury,
    Lean'st thou to the world so wistful yet,
Though forgotten, for some fragmentary
    Sweetness listening? Utterly forgot!

What melodious life of blast and moor,
    Or what forest fluctuating grand,
Calls me? Hush, thou melancholy wooer!
    I have known, alas! a lovelier land.

Frustrate, wild for all thy gold endeavour,
    Autumn, dost thou shake thy relics free?
There are leaves that fade and yet for ever
    Cling unfalling. Hush, and let me be!

In the caverns of oblivion fortunate
    Let me lie, an alien even to fate;
Sleep unwounded of them, those importunate
    Murmurs – murmurs that commiserate.

Is it some caught rumour of the city,
    London, through the night, immense, apart?
Peace! thou whisperer of perfidious pity:
    There a million faces, not one heart.

Me no more the beauteous world shall witness
    Here beside the sea's remorseless beat,
Obdurate, hard to every human sweetness!
    I with the disdainful silence treat.

Only when the storm-pent moon outsealing,
    Gazes down compassionately bright,
Then I quiver for a moment, feeling
    Something almost human in that light.

Once again, and tenderer, closer falling,
    To my thought, what tones, familiar, dear?
O, what voices, by my own name calling,
    To me? On my arm I rise to hear.

Charmed I listen, and that sound comes sweeter
    On my heart than angel melodies.
Sleep and exile fade, grow incompleter,
    In that music. Home is in mine eyes.

Heavenlier now it fall o'er heath and hollow,
      Slow retires, a mitigated roar;
All impassioned I uprise and follow,
      Lost in dreams, towards the voiceful shore.

Lost in dreams I follow; and a vision
      And a trance doth all my heart surprise:
O what happy sights are these arisen?
      Well my soul remembers paradise!

Lovely as of old, loved mountains hover,
      Valleys that with vast regret I see;
Edens sweet, my heart would fain recover: —
      Yet far sweeter inexpressibly,

All the heaven of dim beloved faces
      I have wept to see, swims undefined;
Hand that I have held, my hand embraces;
      And I gaze with rushing tears half blind.

Is it you indeed, afflicted shadows,
      Is it you from that tremendous sphere,
Come again to visit the sweet meadows,
      Apparitions from a home severe?

Ah, disdain me not, nor these bright regions,
      Solemn musers in that dread abode!
One poor land you loved of all earth's legions:
      See, it is our own familiar sod.

Clasp me to you, calm these burning wishes!
      My delight reprove not yet awhile.
Each cold cheek I'll cover with sad kisses;
      Cheeks too conscious of the grave to smile.

But what is it, ere my heart rejoices,
      Comes upon me with that moan of hate?
Hark! a sound between the wind's vext voices;
      The wild tide that turns in haughty state.

"Stay, unlocking arms, break not asunder."
      Mad I cry, the mad blasts answer me.
Bursting harshly near, deep comes in thunder,
      Surge on surge, the loud disdainful sea.

Whelmed in that great world of sound I hearken,
    Wakeful, solitary, hushed in fear.
All too real, the endless waters darken;
    Giant space, my sight can hardly bear.

Was't for this that thou, remorseless breaker,
    In my cavern whispering murmuring bliss
Drew'st in dreams my spirit, to forsake her
    Here 'mid thunders and immensities?

Deafened, mocked with desolate sprays, all banished,
    Laughing foe, yet will I baffle thee:
Here with faces of farewell they vanished.
    Here beside the tinged, mysterious sea!

Whither fled ye, my swift thoughts outleaping,
    Spirits? But now a form companionless
Stood amidst you, passionately weeping,
    Thronged with soft and mournful presences.

O 'mid sprays abandoned they perceive me.
    For a moment pause they, each turned Shade,
Ere they plunge into the tempest, leave me,
    Me on alien shores for ever sad.

Turn back at my cry, sweet phantoms! linger
    For me: see, I reach across this verge:
Lean out of the winds one pitying finger;
    Snatch me from the insane unpitying surge.

From deaf waters that with ireful gestures
    Bar me, and vociferating sweep,
To your sorrowful belovèd vestures
    Over the spurned breakers will I leap.

In your bosom like a stormblast bear me
    On to that sweet land my spirit craves
From shores insupportable, O tear me!
    With a cry I rush into the waves.

But the haughty breakers, mountain after
    Mountain, listen, come convulsed with foam.
Back they fling me with derisive laughter,
    Shouting, "Exile, back unto thy home!"

Gasping, buffeted with foam stupendous,
      Eyes and mouth full of the alien wave,
From those cruel, glittering seas tremendous,
      Desperate, as a man out of his grave,

Back I struggle; and beat senseless, reeling,
      To some last impossible deity
Hands in agony I stretch appealing
      Upwards. Infinite sky, and infinite sea!

In despair I look up wide and wistful
      Through the tears that blind me, through the spray,
Even to that dim limit, heaving tristful;
      Lo, a single sail-speck far away!

Whence art thou, angelic apparition;
      Whither, like a hope across me thrown,
Hastening? What the land, and what the mission?
      Surely that I weep for, that alone?

Heaven be in thy sails, O unknown vessel,
      Till those heavenly shores grow into view.
See! my spirit, with no storm to wrestle,
      Follows, goes on wind wings thither too.

For long miles into the heart of morning,
      Miles and miles, far over lands and seas,
Past enchanted regions of forewarning,
      Dawns at last the land that dims all these.

Go, like lightning: be the imaginary
      Wings to bliss that exiles weary for.
Here, O hard compulsion, must I tarry.
      Hie thee, hie thee, sweet ambassador!

Hasten, though the immeasurable distance
      Break my heart, imploring, forced to stay;
Not a surge, and not a blast's resistance!
      Quiet be the waters of thy way.

Mine alone be all this deaf commotion.
      Let the breakers lash me with their scorn
O'er the unfooted, vast, relentless ocean
      I would still remember, though I mourn.

Songs of Love and Death (Oxford: 1926)[76]

London

Farewell, sweetest country; out of my heart, you roses,
    Wayside roses, nodding, the slow traveller to keep.
Too long have I drowsed alone in the meadows deep,
    Too long alone endured the silence Nature espouses.
Oh, the rush, the rapture of life! throngs, lights, houses,
    This is London. I wake as a sentinel from sleep.

Stunned, with the fresh thunder, the harsh delightful noises,
    I move entranced on the thronging pavement. How sweet,
To eyes sated with green, the dusty brick-walled street!
    And the lone spirit, of self so weary, how it rejoices
To be lost in others, bathed in the tones of human voices,
    And feel hurried along the happy tread of feet.

And a sense of vast sympathy my heart almost crazes,
    The warmth of kindred hearts in thousands beating with mine.
Each fresh face, each figure, my spirit drinks like wine, –
    Thousands endlessly passing. Violets, daisies,
What is your charm to the passionate charm of faces,
    This ravishing reality, this earthliness divine?

O murmur of men more sweet than all the wood's caresses,
    How sweet only to be an unknown leaf that sings
In the forest of life! Cease, Nature, thy whisperings.
    Can I talk with leaves, or fall in love with breezes?
Beautiful boughs, your shade not a human pang appeases.
    This is London. I lie, and twine in the roots of things.

Home-Thoughts

While I recall you o'er deep parting seas,
Lonelier have grown these cliffs, this English grass.
Haunt of my heart, dear faces, let me pass
To that far south, till presence bring me peace.

---

76 Manmohan Ghose, *Songs of Love and Death* (Oxford: Basil H. Blackwell, 1926).

Unsatisfied with those dead memories,
I muse, and mould from each sweet day that was
An image of the future; but, alas!
What hunger can oblivious hope appease?

My soul may travel to you, but the sea
Sternly puts back the pilgrim feet of life
With the harsh warning of necessity; —
That oft-taught truth my sighs would fain unlearn,
How idle is human passion! Yet its strife
Is duty, and our hearts are made to yearn.

Song of Britannia

Muse, who art quick to fire
    At the least noble thing,
And frankest praise to bring
Upon the quivering lyre,
Why art thou slow to sing
    Now, when the world beclouds
    With battle such as shrouds
    Earth in a mist of tears?
For want of heart belike,
    While thunder sings afar,
    And even the bravest fears.
Seek'st thou a theme for song,
    No fear can ever wrong,
    No tears can tarnish — strike,
    And sing Britannia.

Britannia the fair,
    Whom oceans girdle round
    With hill and valley crowned
And purest wash of air
    From her Atlantic bound,
What heaths so fresh as hers
With blossom? And how stirs
    The soft wind in her pines!
Earth's fairest isle, 'tis said,
    Where all things lovely are;
    Yet beauty there not mines

Strength, for no cliff is there,
No headland calmly fair
But fringed with wild spray wed
    To shout Britannia.

Britannia the strong,
    Whom God designed should queen
    The ocean plain serene,
Though threatning [sic] foes bethrong,
    Whose fate shall not be long,
    While round her, every deck
    Bristling with cannon, speck
The seas her angry fleet.
    Not earth to dominate,
Nor to embroil with war,
Tower they: 'tis to keep sweet
    The world's dear peace, they bulk
        So with their silent hulk
    In all eyes power, elate
To speak Britannia.

Britannia the free,
    Of soil so virtuous, such
    No foot of slave can touch
But walks at liberty;
    The staff she is, the crutch
By whom weak lands arise,
Who, nourished in her eyes,
    Grow and shake off the sloth
Of old anarchic power.
    Two richly tokens are
    Of her boon influences both.
What man of Ind or Nile
That sees his fat fields smile,
But his lips burst aflower
    To praise Britannia?

Britannia the sage,
    With her own history wise!
    The stars were her allies
To write that ample page.
    'Twas her adventurous eyes
The vantage saw, whence she
To this wide regency
    Through acts adventurous won;

And if from strife and jar
  She keep, the secret learn
  From her mild brow alone
How not the world to daunt
Or power imperial flaunt;
  She makes the queen'd earth yearn
To serve Britannia.

Britannia the good,
  With her own heart at school,
  Whom flatterer cannot fool
Nor rebels sour, at flood
  Her own strength taught to rule.
Hers are the mighty hands
Which o'er a hundred lands
  Weave good from dawn to grey;
Like fond words from afar
  Her are the wingèd sails
  O'er ocean, words are they
Which in a moment bring
  Her brood beneath her wing;
  And none so small that fails
To knit Britannia.

Britannia wide flung
  Over the globe, its half
  Her children, whether graff
Or scion mother-sprung
  Sons, now to be her staff
When her path glooms, though Rhine,
Danube, and Elbe combine,
  Of these, O idlest dream!
To reave her. Hers they are,
  Roused ardent in her right
  From Ganges utmost stream
Far as Canadian firs
And bush Australian; hers
  Joined now in Hell's despite
To help Britannia.

Britannia, the heart
  And brain, which bulwarks power,
  See at the crucial hour
How well she bears her part!
  From fields how peaceful flower
In millions, arms and men,

Which now she pours again
      To those old battle fields,
France, Flanders; makes her star
      Of glory, that she shields
The weak, confronts the strong.
Brute force let us others sing;
      She shows in everything
      To her it shall belong
      To be − Britannia.

On the Centenary of the Presidency College[77]

A hundred years! The very phrase
      Unsepultures the million'd dead;
Three generations in that space,
      Ghosts of the past, have breathed and fled.
Time shakes his hour-glass, and we slide,
      We running humans sands, away;
Vain, individual atoms, − glide
      From name and memory. But the play
Of his chance-reaping scythe stops here:
Our frail race flowers upon its bier,
Man, feeble man, who from his dark
      Gets no more, can no more endear
To the stern harvester his year,
Than soaring eagle feels a spark
      Of the eternal burn in him. Some ark
That may survive the flood of things
      He fashions; not for what so flies
      His brief self, but that children's eyes
May see, and children's children, builds
      In the void future. There on wings
Indignant Immortality
      Lends him, in that abysm of time,
      Where no sure certainty can climb,
He fledges his sheer hope; where sings
      Some torrent his lone fancy gilds

---

77 Presidency College, formerly Hindu College, was founded in 1817 in Calcutta by Raja Rammohun Roy, the early nineteenth-century Hindu social reformer and other like-minded men such as Scottish David Hare. In June 1855, the name of the college was changed from Hindu College to Presidency College and the college was opened to all members of the community.

In mists, the everlasting snows
Above him, nests his brave repose,
    High-eyried in posterity.
So thought, so toil'd, so built the men
    Our founders whom to-day we laud,
Commemorate; from now to then
    Over a hundred years applaud.
To the true-hearted Britons praise!
    Those three! From law and church who rose
And shop, this lasting fane to raise
    For the lov'd Muses, verse and prose,
Thought, science, numbers: to enshrine
Fair Learning's self, the lamp divine
    In God's hand for mortality
To see by. Gulf of "mine" and "thine,"
Though come from o'er the bitter brine,
    They knew not; no dividing sea
In race, pride, alien ancestry,
    That with such cold estranging wave
Makes severance of us; through our blood
Howls against human brotherhood;
    Than towering Himalaya more
Parts land from land; as in a grave
    Buries mankind's growth, to congeal
In icy barrier: which with ease
They leap'd. Nor could caste, custom freeze
    Their fiery souls, those two, our brave,
Our native founders, who both bore
The name, and the large heart of kings.
    To them, while all the patriot springs
To our lips, let the heart's thanks peal.
For they saw, those far-sighting five,
    Or, dim-divining, surely felt
    Shakespeare in Kalidasa[78] thrive
    In Bhababhuti[79] Milton melt.
Through creed, race, colour they saw kin,
    The bleeding ransom Calvary's tree[80]

---

78 Kalidas: classical Sanskrit writer who is thought to have lived during the fifth century under the Gupta dynasty. His works include the long lyric poems, *Meghaduta* and *Ritu-samhara*, as well as two epic poems and three plays.

79 Bhababuti, or Bhavabuti: late seventh-/early eighth-century Sanskrit poet and dramatist who authored the plays *Mahavir-charit* and *Uttara-Rama-charit*, based on the story of the Hindu god, Rama.

80 Calvary: proper name of the place where Christ was crucified; can also refer to a life-size, outdoor representation of the crucifixion (n. "Calvary" *OED*).

Shed for us, and what under this
    Tathagata's thought-agony
Dropped in the dreaming bo-leaf shade
At Gaya.[81] And as, never to fade,
    What they in man's adoring soul
    Hope, rapture, worship built, they made,
Those Heavenly Founders, one and whole
    Like some cathedral's vault to roll,
Or God's blue, o'er humanity
    For all to breathe in; so divined
Ours, building earthlier, that mind,
    Like soul (that catholic lesson) is
    For all men; spreads like empire free
    This glorious fabric she uprears,
    Britannia. Under the third George
    When she pent Europe's splendid scourge
        In Helena, they, rapt to see,
    Prophets, the large imperial bliss
        To be now, when earth's peace is spilt
        By a worse madman, rose and built
This structure of a hundred years.[82]

Romesh Chunder Dutt

This Bengali poet, novelist, historian, economist and civil servant was a widely respected figure in late nineteenth-century India. A member of the famous Dutt family of Calcutta, which included his cousin Toru Dutt, Romesh Chunder Dutt (1848–1909) published works in a variety of genres in both his native Bengali and in English: a travelogue entitled *Three Years in Europe* (1872); political and economic treatises such as *Bengal Peasantry* (1875), *England and India* (1897), *A History of Civilization in Ancient India, based on Sanscrit Literature* (1893), *Famines and Land Assessments in India* (1900), *Economic History of India (1757–1857)* (1902, 1904); four historical novels entitled *Banga Bijeta*, *Madhabi Kankan*, *Rajput Jiban Sandhya*, and *Maharastra Prabhat*; two social novels entitled *Samaj* (1885) and *Sangsar* (1893); and books of original poetry and poetic translations including *Lays of Ancient India: Selections from Indian Poetry Rendered into English Verse* (1894) and *Reminiscences of a Workman's Life* (1896). He famously

---

81 Tathagata: appellation used by the historical Buddha when referring to himself. Buddha achieved enlightenment under the shade of a *bo* tree. *Bo*, or *Bodhi* tree: large and sacred fig tree located in Bodh Gaya in the modern-day state of Bihar in northern India.

82 Ghose seems to credit (or blame) the mad king George III (1738–1820) for the expansion of British imperial interests and the defeat and exile of Napoleon Bonaparte on St. Helena in 1815.

published two English-language "translations" of the authoritative Sanskrit versions of the Hindu epics, the *Maha-Bharata: Epic of the Bharatas, Condensed into English Verse* (1898) and the *Ramayana: the Epic of Rama, Prince of India, Condensed into English Verse* (1899). (The "Translator's Epilogue" to his rendering of the *Mahabharata* is included in the Appendix.) Like many later twentieth-century nationalists, Dutt was a product of imperial rule; but he was also a supporter of rising nationalist movements at the end of the nineteenth century as evidenced in works critical of British imperial policy. Educated in Calcutta as well as at University College and the Middle Temple, London, Dutt worked as an Indian Civil Service officer from 1871 to 1897. He returned to University College, London, to act as lecturer in Indian history from 1898 to 1904. In the brief excerpt included below, Rama's sons narrate to their father the ancient Hindu epic, the *Ramayana*, in a fascinating moment of meta-commentary on literary creation and circulation within the epic itself.

Ramayana: the Epic of Rama, Prince of India, Condensed into English Verse (London: 1899)[83]

Recital of the Ramayana[84]

When the silent night was ended, and their pure ablutions done,
Joyous went the minstrel brothers, and their lofty lay begun,

Rama to the hermit minstrels lent a monarch's willing ear,
Blended with the simple music dulcet was the lay to hear,

And so sweet the chanted accents, Rama's inmost soul was stirred,
With his royal guests and courtiers still the deathless lay he heard!

Heralds versed in old *Puranas*,[85] Brahmans skilled in pious rite,
Minstrels deep in lore of music, poets fired by heavenly might,

---

83　Romesh Chunder Dutt, trans., *Ramayana: the Epic of Rama, Prince of India, Condensed into English Verse* (London: J. M. Dent and Co., 1899).
84　The *Ramayana*, one of the Hindu epics, was subject to numerous retellings during the nineteenth century. See Dutt, trans., *Ramayana: the Epic of Rama, Prince of India*, 171. Dutt explains in the introduction to Book XII that "[t]he real Epic ends with Rama's happy return to Ayodhya. An *Uttara-Kanda* or Supplement is added, describing the fate of Sita, and giving the poem a sad ending." Banished to the forest by the poem's hero Rama, his wife Sita is offered "asylum in the hermitage of Valmiki, the reputed author of this Epic," and there gives birth to Rama's twin sons. At a sacrifice held by Rama many years later, Rama's sons recite the epic to their father, who then realizes his sons' identities.
85　*Puranas*: Sanskrit literary verse texts; the time of their composition is generally thought to date after that of the ancient Hindu epics, the *Ramayana* and *Mahabharata*. Dutt seems to refer here to religious texts more generally.

Watchers of the constellations, min'sters of the festive day,
Men of science and of logic, bards who sang the ancient lay,

Painters skilled and merry dancers who the festive joy prolong,
Hushed and silent in their wonder listed to the wondrous song!

And as poured the flood of music through the bright and live-long day,
Eyes and ears and hearts insatiate drank the nectar of the lay,

And the eager people whispered: "See the boys, how like our king
As two drops of limpid water from the parent bubble spring!

Were the boys no hermit-children, in the hermit's garments clad,
We would deem them Rama's image, – Rama as a youthful lad!"

Twenty cantos of the Epic thus the youthful minstrels sung,
And the voice of stringèd music through the Epic rolled along,

Out spake Rama in his wonder: "Scarce I know who these may be,
Eighteen thousand golden pieces be the children-minstrels' fee!"

"Not so," answered thus the children, "we in darksome forests dwell,
Gold and silver, bounteous monarch, forest life beseem not well!"

"Noble children!" uttered Rama, "dear to me the words you say,
Tell me who composed this Epic, – Father of this deathless Lay?"

"Saint Valmiki,"[86] *spake the minstrels, "framed the great immortal song*
Four and twenty thousand verses to this noble Lay belong,

Untold tales of deathless virtue sanctify his sacred line,
And five hundred glorious cantos in this glorious Epic shine,

In six Books of mighty splendour was the poet's task begun,
With a seventh Book, supplemental is the poet's labour done,

All thy matchless deeds, O monarch, in this Lay will brighter shine,
List to us from first to ending if thy royal heart incline!"

"Be it so," thus Rama answered, but the hours of day were o'er,
And Valmiki's youthful pupils to their cottage came once more.

---

86 Valmiki: poet-sage who is usually thought to have authored the "original," authoritative version of the Hindu epic, the *Ramayana* around 300 BCE. He also appears as a character within the narrative of the *Ramayana* itself.

Rama with his guests and courtiers slowly left the royal hall,
Eager was his heart to listen, eager were the monarchs all,

And the voice of song and music thus was lifted day to day,
And from day to day they listened to Valmiki's deathless Lay!

Hary Sing Gour

Harisingh Gour (1870–1949?) was a barrister, educator, social reformer, and poet. Educated in England at Cambridge and a member of the Inner Temple, London, Gour returned to India where he was active in Indian politics and social reform. He wrote a number of legal tracts including the famous *The Law of Transfer in British India* (1902), *The Penal Law of India* (1909), *The Hindu Code, being a codified statement of Hindu Law with Commentary thereon* (1919), and *The Future Constitution of India* (1930), a series of lectures delivered at Nagpur University. He founded the University of Saugar, later renamed Dr. Harisingh Gour University, in 1946. He dedicates this early collection of poetry to a British political figure well-regarded in India, Viceroy Ripon.

Stepping Westward and Other Poems (London: 1890)[87]

Stepping Westward, or Emigrants to the West

It is the queen of beauties joyous spring,
Sweet summer nears; and now the greenwood glades
Look 'tired in festal trim, soft crystal gems
Of loveliest hue bestud enchanting scene
And turn the land into an Eden fair,
Where smiling dew-tipp'd pastures sacred lie
Secure to reflexion. The snowdrop low,
Of light harbinger, opes its chaliced cup;
Chaste daisy blooms, and e'er-young ivy twines
Her tender threads around the hoary oak,
The virgin maid unites in sisterhood
Her russet limbs till deck'd the 'broidered shade
Presents a nook poetic — envied quiet,
Calm meditation's sacred set: Age, Care,
Pain, Sorrow, life's grim tyrants as their names
Here hermit-like they seemed all winsome kind,

---

[87] Hari Sing Gour, *Stepping Westward and Other Poems* (London: Simpkin, Marshall and Co., 1890).

Embosomed in the loveliness of spring.
That wild report like dreams of sickened brains
Appeared a fancy-fabric wild romance,
For here the cooling shady leafy bowers
Charmed down the troubled spirits into peace,
And like the ray of beaming morning Sun,
Shot forth a graceful gentle courtesy.
        And as I looked beyond the sunlit lawns,
I saw the margin of the vasty deep
Expanding limitless: the silvery moon,
As if, ere half her zone was crossed, had chose
To light upon this orb — moonlike it seemed.
And on its surface rode a vessel high,
Which seem'd like verdant bank amidst the waste,
And massive chains still rattled as they waved
Unyielding protest, high a mighty flag,
Emblazoned in the radiance of the Sun,
Crownèd the stern. While pendant from aloft
Gave signal to the watchers from afar
A ship is westward bound; the sea-gull rose
And hovered around the mizzen-mast,[88]
Quavering forth some carol wild, and broke
The silence of the sea.

                I saw apace
The phantom-circle[89] lit with sudden gale,
Like silver blade sharp brandished in the Sun,
Or like some warrior steel-shod starting forth
With playing sunbeams on his shield and casque,[90]
To stir up havoc like the angry sea.
I stood and watched proud Triton[91] wax and wane;
The year was calm, yet in her stillness rose
The sea-waves, lashing loud their rugged shore;
Secure, I loved the music: stood at ease,
And watched the steamer toiling in the flood,
As toiled the sturdy seaman on her board,
As toils the silver-breasted swan with stream
Coursing contrariwise; but soon the Eve

---

88 Mizen-mast: after-most mast of a three-masted ship (n. "mizen-mast" OED).
89 [Poet's Note: Standing on the sea-shore and looking away in the distance towards it, the horizon at first appears like a "phantom-circle" — but this is often seen illuminated by the high waves produced by the wind at spring-time.]
90 Casque: piece of armor to cover the head; a helmet (n. "casque" OED).
91 Triton: messenger of the sea and the son of Poseidon, god of the sea, in Greek mythology.

Approaching, shed her pearly train and sowed,
The land with slumberous dews. The emigrants
Some British zealots, workwrights, sons of plough,
But most the luckless race of sad Erin,[92]
Together stood on the quay, and bade farewells.

    It was a solemn hour — a solemn scene,
O! Who would paint? When feeling hearts rough-hewn
Forgot the lusty vigour of their youth,
Sobbed, sighed in silence; some were quite alone,
And sat meditative, piping thoughts away;
Yet some whom wealth and worldly pomp had bred,
They from astern[93] applied their optic tube
To hook in nature and the phantom zone
Within their vision; heedless of life's trials,
Begirt by Love, they stood, and viewed with scorn,
As neared the matron sorrowful distraught,
Fixing her blank and feeling piercing gaze
Upon the furrowed visage of her lord
Careworn and wasted, yet affecting glee,
A double-dyed[94] pain heart-deep. He soothes her,
Subdues the stormy tumult of her soul,
Gives Hope, the only proxy in his place,
And pressing warm his angel's tender arm,
Bids her a long adieu!

                  And mingling forth,
Now with this voice of love, there rose aloft
A sailor's lay, which filled with tuneless mirth
The arches of an ancient battlement
In ruin, still struck by jocund tune it seem'd,
Roused 'turn reproof amain; the eddied stream
Beat on its foot, but still it proudly stood
And shed the shadow of its turret-tops
Upon the bark below — herself a hold
For serving best defence to human kind,
Where pilgrim-fathers of a future race,
The heralds of a golden dawn in mist,
Invisible through film of distance, doubt,

---

92 "race of sad Erin": the Irish.
93 "from astern": rear of the ship (adv. "astern" *OED*).
94 [Poet's Note: The pain is called 'double-dyed' because, in addition to the pain which the man naturally feels on this occasion, he has to bear a pain equally as great by trying to *suppress* his present feelings, out of regard to his beloved ones present before him.]

Sought rest: to sight it was confusion all,
Like new-born earth on second night, methought
I read in love-dazed eyes, the starlets sheen
Full life-crate, and eke the thronging heap,
Of soul-sick bones which stalked the pavement still,
All Spirit-like, were seed of better race
The dusky grain pot-coop'd, which crushed and sown,
Ere long the autumn's genial ray hath spent,
Will yield a golden harvest next time,
Till Nature smile: This is a nobler race,
The rolling time hath cleared the dross and left
The shining virtues in their native light,
Till Freedom, Reason, and a love of kind,
And joy in nature, filial courtesy,
Full Truth shall shine. Then this uncertain ark
Is blest, unseen, unnotic'd though it stands;
No Doric pageant, minstrel-led, nor priests,
Nor arches green, and glowing triumph wreaths;
The harp which struck a gladdening note to all,
And citizens shouting God-speed as they rode,
And fathers bearded, saviours of their race,
To crown the parting souls with benison
Much-loved and courted then, now passed with age,
E'en as the world. Yet our's is not the loss
For what we've lost in grace, we've gained in strength,
And World progresses as progresses all.
So still in silence and midst solemn scene
I stood and watched one humbled son of woe,
Who was the only bud of fading spring,
For by his side aged sire stood,
That had no eyes, and limbs had crossed his will,
Yet, still supported by a tender arm
He stood, like battered tower ivy-twined,
And greedy of the parting sight for good
He fed his famished soul with mortal flame;
He felt, and pressed most gently his dry arm
Upon the shrunken shoulder of his son
Never again![95] –

                But close beside this scene
There sat the siren-goddess trimming Hope
(By Reason friendless tost, and torn from Truth,
For Hope besides is angel wakeful Love

---

95 [Poet's Note: Upon visiting the cottage of this old farmer, about a couple of months after this time, I was informed that he had died a few days ago. Man dies, affections live: "E'en in our ashes glow to their wonted fires!"]

And feeds the feeble Duty with her balm,
Which lost the World is blank, the Sun a sink,)
Arrayed in rosy fragrance like the morn,
And busy recked the chances of good gain
From off their bondsmen[96] priced and bought for aye.
O slavery! What better is thy name,
And thou the blushless thing of Humanity,
Exporting freemen like a sack of coal.
Thus musing o'er the passing race of man,
Some blithe, some calm, but most of all distressed,
Methought this ship a fragment of the world,
Where Present was the goddess o'er To-be.
But yet the whole proclaim'd the counter truth,
As tolled the bells a loud farewell to all,
And weighed the ship her anchor from the sea,
And soon the orient orb of sprightly day
Approach'd the purpled West and quiv'ring disc
Of the great light, beyond far numb, dead lands
Went down, and left but mellow fume of light,
As faint as fragrance pervading the west.
One said, 'She goes,' but still the steamer stay'd,
And ling'ring on the wharf, aboard Love star'd,
And interchanged the kisses ever oft,
The happy home recalling evermore;
And thus, the youthful visions of the past,
All distance-sweetened, fancy-chased he sees: —
The piping shepherd by his native woods
Or ploughman turning forth his madrigal,
Or hears the gleaning reapers' rustic notes
And sits himself beside the flowing rill,
And in the sombre darkness of the Eve
He plights his troth to some bright village maid
The lode-star of his essay to the West.

    Fair Hope rejoic'd and waved her purified wing,
He sees the morrow's Sun now overcast,
But still in distance reads his cheery beams,
Ringing out all the chill of Penury,
Restoring all the peace which Plenty brings.

---

96 [Poet's Note: It is a custom by no means now extinct, to hire labourers by 'terms,' and then emigrate them to foreign countries. Last year no less than twelve hundred persons were thus emigrated from a single sea-port. The life of these wretches is one of great privation and suffering, and the capitalist is often exact to his bond, even to the pound of flesh.]

O Hope! fair goddess born of morning light,
How with thy soul thou guides Destiny,
How Phoenix-like when life's last embers burn
Thou breath'st the soul again into new life!

    The ship now sailed, and darkness drew apace,
But by the slanting moonbeams' silver light
Love chased the sight which ever shunn'd the shore
And in the distance winged her fairy flight
Approaching lands beside the starry Zone
Where like a Glory changed to star it seem'd;
One said 'She goes': lo 'neath the circling marge
Another, 'Howso she lords it o'er the Deep,
And shines like sacred star of Bethlehem
Bringing salvation to the human race.'
Thus musing, in the mist the crowd dispersed.
Then I, climbing the crown of the high cliff
Hard-by, sea-laved, the basement of the hold[97]
Time-spoiled and shapeless, 'dust to dust' return'd
Descried the faintest glimpse as in a dream,
And wished the parting ship remembered seen,
Deep-felt farewell. And then methinks I heard
A self-same chord re-echo through the hills,
And in a voice prophetic thus proclaim: –
The old world reeling to the winds shall fall,
And mighty mountains nod their haughty heads
But God's one plan and purpose still prevail,
For fro ranks ashes oft, sweet violets spring,
And nations raised out of such homely seeds;
Then thou the cradle of angelic race
Emigrants to brighter lands more Peace, farewell!

---

97 [Poet's Note: c.f. lines 82 *ante et seq.* [in ruin, still struck by jocund tune it seem'd…?]]

Sarojini Naidu

Sarojini Naidu (1879–1949) published three collections of poetry: *The Golden Threshold* (1905) and *The Bird of Time: Songs of Life, Death and the Spring* (1912) and *The Broken Wing: Songs of Love, Death & Destiny, 1915–1916* (1917). Known as the "Nightingale of India" for her poetry and oratory, Naidu's poetic production coexisted with her political efforts for Indian independence and for various women's issues, including women's suffrage. Acclaimed early in life as a poetic genius, she was awarded a scholarship to study at King's College, London and Girton College, Cambridge. Naidu acted as the first female Indian president of the Indian National Congress in 1925 and the appointed governor of the United Provinces, now Uttar Pradesh, in 1947. "The Gift of India" was not only included in her last collection of poems but also delivered orally at a meeting of the Hyderabad Ladies' War Relief Association in December 1915 and is included in her collected speeches.

The Golden Threshold (London: 1905)[98]

To India

O young through all thy immemorial years![99]
Rise, Mother, rise, regenerate from thy gloom,
And, like a bride high-mated with the spheres,
Beget new glories from thine ageless womb!

The nations that in fettered darkness weep
Crave thee to lead them where great mornings break…
Mother, O Mother, wherefore dost thou sleep?
Arise and answer for thy children's sake!

Thy Future calls thee with a manifold sound
To crescent honours, splendours, victories vast;
Waken, O slumbering Mother and be crowned,
Who once wert empress of the sovereign Past.

---

98 Sarojini Naidu, *The Golden Threshold* (London: Heinemann, 1905).
99 This trope of India awakening from a deep slumber was a common one in poetry of the period. India was characterized as a Mother and Indians as her children, whose duty it was to protect and care for her.

Nightfall in the City of Hyderabad

See how the speckled sky burns like a pigeon's throat,
Jewelled with embers of opal and peridote.

See the white river that flashes and scintillates,
Curved like a tusk from the mouth of the city-gates.

Hark, from the minaret, how the *muezzin's* call
Floats like a battle-flag over the city wall.

From the trellised balconies, languid and luminous
Faces gleam, veiled in a splendour voluminous.

Leisurely elephants wind through the winding lanes,
Swinging their silver bells hung from their silver chains.

Round the high Char Minar sounds of gay cavalcades
Blend with the music of cymbals and serenades.

Over the city bridge Night comes majestical,
Borne like a queen to a sumptuous festival.

Ode to H. H. The Nizam of Hyderabad
(Presented at the Ramzan Durbar)[100]

Deign, Prince, my tribute to receive,
This lyric offering to your name,
Who round your jewelled sceptre bind
The lilies of a poet's fame;
Beneath whose sway concordant dwell
The peoples whom your laws embrace,
In brotherhood of diverse creeds,
And harmony of diverse race:

The votaries of the Prophet's faith,
Of whom you are the crown and chief;
And they, who bear on Vedic brows
Their mystic symbols of belief;

---

100 Nizam of Hyderabad: Mughal ruler Mir Mahboob Ali Khan (1869–1911). The Nizam was the nominal ruler of the princely city of Hyderabad and was known as a poet in his own right.

And they, who worshiping the sun,
Fled o'er the old Iranian sea;
And they, who bow to Him who trod
The midnight waves of Galilee.[101]

Sweet, sumptuous fables of Baghdad
The splendours of your court recall,
The torches of a *Thousand Nights*
Blaze through a single festival;
And Saki-singers down the streets,
Pour for us, in a stream divine,
From goblets of your love-*ghazals*
The rapture of your Sufi wine.

Prince, where your radiant cities smile,
Grim hills their sombre vigils keep,
Your ancient forests hoard and hold
The legends of their centuried sleep;
Your birds of peace white-pinioned float
O'er ruined fort and storied plain,
Your faithful stewards sleepless guard
The harvests of your gold and grain.

God give you joy, God give you grace
To shield the truth and smite the wrong,
To honour Virtue, Valour, Worth.
To cherish faith and foster song.
So may the lustre of your days
Outshine the deeds Firdusi[102] sung,
Your name within a nation's prayer,
Your music on a nation's tongue.

---

101 Sea of Galilee: largest freshwater lake in what is now Israel; significant in the Judeo-Christian and Islamic traditions.
102 The Persian poet Firdusi (c. 940–1020 AD) is the composer of the *Book of Kings* (*Shah Nameh*), an epic account of Persian "national" history presented to his patron, the sultan Mahmud.

The Broken Wing: Songs of Love, Death & Destiny, 1915–1916 (London: 1917)[103]

Awake![104]

Waken, O mother! thy children implore thee,
Who kneel in thy presence to serve and adore thee!
The night is aflush with a dream of the morrow,
Why still dost thou sleep in thy bondage of sorrow?
Awaken and sever the woes that enthral us,
And hallow our hands for the triumphs that call us!

Are we not thine, O Belov'd, to inherit
The manifold pride and power of thy spirit?
Ne'er shall we fail thee, forsake thee or falter,
Whose hearts are thy home and thy shield and thine altar.
Lo! we would thrill the high stars with thy story,
And set thee again in the forefront of glory.

Hindus: Mother! the flowers of our worship have crowned thee!

Parsis: Mother! the flame of our hope shall surround thee!

Mussulmans: Mother! the sword of our love shall defend thee!

Christians: Mother! the song of our faith shall attend thee!

All Creeds: Shall not our dauntless devotion avail thee?
Hearken! O queen and O goddess, we hail thee!

---

103 Sarojini Naidu, *The Broken Wing: Songs of Love, Death & Destiny, 1915–1916* (London: W. Heinemann, 1917).
104 [Poet's Note: Recited at the Indian National Congress, 1915.]

The Gift of India[105]

Is there aught you need that my hands withhold,
Rich gifts of raiment or grain or gold?
Lo! I have flung to the East and West
Priceless treasures torn from my breast,
And yielded the sons of my stricken womb
To the drum beats of duty, the sabres of doom.

Gathered like pearls in their alien graves
Silent they sleep by the Persian waves,
Scattered like shells on Egyptian sands,
They lie with pale brows and brave, broken hands,
They are strewn like blossoms mown down by chance
On the blood-brown meadows of Flanders and France.

Can ye measure the grief of the tears I weep
Or compass the woe of the watch I keep?
Or the pride that thrills thro' my heart's despair,
And the hope that comforts the anguish of prayer?
And the far sad and glorious vision I see
Of the torn red banners of Victory?

When the terror and tumult of hate shall cease
And life be refashioned on anvils of peace,
And your love shall offer memorial thanks
To the comrades who fought in your dauntless ranks,
And you honour the deeds of the deathless ones
Remember the blood of thy martyred sons!

Roby Datta

Roby Datta (1883–1917) published numerous poetic collections including *Poems, Pictures, and Songs* (1915), *Stories in Blank Verse, to which is added an epic fragment* (1915), and *Echoes from East and West, to which are added stray notes of mine own* (1909), which includes a substantial number of translations of other poets' works into English. His fluency in European languages, including French and German; ancient languages, including Sanskrit, Greek,

---

105 See Sumit Sarkar, *Modern India: 1885–1947*, 2nd ed. (London: Macmillan, 1989), 169. Indian soldiers were conscripted in great numbers to fight for the British Army during various battles in World War I, resulting in an expansion of the Indian Army to 1.2 million soldiers and thousands of casualties.

and Latin; and Indian languages, including Bengali and Hindi illustrate his remarkable command of several linguistic and poetic traditions. Datta's decision to arrange the poems' included in *Echoes from East and West* not by region but rather by a rough "chronology" places the works of the subcontinent (or the "Orient") in intimate dialogue with works from Europe, thereby marking them as aesthetically and historically equivalent. Included below are a few of Datta's translations as well as some of Datta's "original" poetry. Datta's discussion of meter and rhythm in rendering the Sanskrit epics into English echoes that of Romesh Chunder Dutt (see the Appendix). For example, Datta comments in his note to the poem, "The Lay of the Lord (From the so-called Vyasa), Book I. The Sadness of Arjun," of Krishna's speech to Arjuna, included in the *Mahabharata*: "It has been translated again and again into most of the European languages, and in India, it is read a thousand times more than the *Vedas* themselves, for which there is more national than religious veneration. The metre of the present version is that of Tennyson's "Locksley Hall." Like Dutt over fifteen years earlier, Datta also settles on the trochaic octameter as the most appropriate and approximate translation into English from the "original." The section in *Echoes from East and West* entitled "Stray notes of mine own" includes original poetry by Datta himself, two of which, "On Tibet" and "To Britain," are reprinted below.

Echoes from East and West (Cambridge: 1909)[106]

The Grief of Ravan[107]
(From Michael M. S. Dutt)

So at the Lord of Lanka's[108] hest the messenger began –
But ere the word was on his lips, his lips grew pale and wan.

Then for a while, like one amazed, his eye around he cast;
And o'er his cheek, as he would speak, a sudden colour past.

The colour past from cheek to eye; he knew not how he spake:
"Sir King, Virbahu's[109] gone to sleep, O never more to wake!"

---

106 Roby Datta, *Echoes from East and West, to which are added stray notes of mine own* (Cambridge: Galloway and Porter, 1909).
107 [Poet's Note: Michael Dutt's conception of Fate throughout his great epic of "The Slaughter of Meghanad," from which this extract is taken, is more Greek than Indian. With regard to the metre of the version, it was quite unconsciously that I used that of Chapman's "Homer."] Ravan was the great antagonist of Prince Rama in the ancient Hindu epic, the *Ramayana*. He abducts Rama's wife Sita; Rama then wages war against Ravana to rescue his wife.
108 Ravana: ruler of Lanka, or modern-day Sri Lanka (known as Ceylon under British rule).
109 Virbahu: son of Ravana. One of Ravana's other sons, Meghnad, would become the subject of Michael Madhusudan Dutt's great Bengali epic, *Meghanadavadha kavya* (1861). Like Milton's depiction of Satan, Dutt's depiction of Ravana and his family is seductively sympathetic.

To whom said Ravan sore at heart, his face with sorrow white:
"This tale of thine is like unto a vision seen at night.

"My son, whose might kept Gods in dread, hath beggar Rama slain?
Hath Fate, then, fell'd the stubborn oak with but a flower-chain?

"Alas, my darling! thou art gone so early! — woe is me!
Thro' what great sin of mine have I made thee mine arms to flee?

"O Fate Almighty, dost thou will to see me thus undone?
Give me mine own; where hast thou kept my loved and loving son?

"My race, O cruel Fate, is fast decaying day by day!
Or why did Kumbhakarna,[110] too, so early pass away?

"As stout wood-cutters in a wood first cut off one by one
The boughs, and last against the tree their mighty axes run,

'So will my foemen in their wrath first lop off all my kin,
And, lastly, felling down myself, my golden island win.

O Surpanakha![111] in what hour did first thine eye behold
Yon cruel crawling human snake in Dandak's[112] woods of old?

"Me wretched! in what hour again, to set my house on fire,
Brought I yon fairy fiery nymph from Panchavati[113] dire?

"O who shall keep the honour now of this far-honoured line?
My hopes are gone; ere long, I see, a downfall will be mine.

"I wish I were within a wood, from man and sin apart,
Where, lone and tranquil, I could soothe the burning of my heart.

---

110 Kumbhakarna: Ravana's brother; cursed to sleep for months and awoken with great difficulty by Ravana for battle. Kumbhakarna is often depicted as criticizing the actions Ravana took that led to battle with Rama.
111 Surpanakha: female rakshasa, or demon, who becomes enamored of Rama's beauty after encountering him in the forest. Rama, married to Sita, turns down her advances but somewhat unkindly suggests that she approach his younger brother, Lakshama. The latter, insulted by her, humiliates Surpanakha, who reacts by attacking Sita. The angry Lakshmana mutilates Surpanakha by slicing off her nose. In retaliation, she praises Sita's beauty to Ravana while at his court and goads him into kidnapping Rama's wife.
112 Dandak: forest located in east-central India.
113 Panchavati: forest where Rama, Sita and Lakshmana lived during Rama's period of exile; where Lakshmana mutilates Surpanakha.

'My life is barren as a waste — no joy therein can grow;
For, he for whom I die is dead; I wish I could be so."

So saying, Ravan once again: "Good envoy, briefly tell
How sweet Virbahu bore himself, how he in battle fell."

Then spake the messenger in grief: "The task is all too hard,
For, how can I unfold his feats, who am no cunning bard?

"The Demon-host did ne'er before see such a leader brave;
Tho' mild at home, yet in the field he bore a figure grave.

"His battle-cry did shake, my lord, the heart of ev'ry foe;
His bow he bent, his shafts he sent, and laid whole legions low.

"His arrows flash'd and flash'd; their blaze, reflected in the sky,
Did make a sunbow when the cloud of dust had risen high.

"Upon his shoulders clang'd his shield, his brand was in his hand,
No fear had he of Rama's arms, nor of his Monkey-band.[114]

"His skill he show'd in bending bow, in wielding sword and shield,
Death-blows he dealt on ev'ry side, and dyed the battle-field."

The messenger stopt short in grief, for he could speak no more;
The Lord of Lanka wail'd and wept, deep-wounded in the core.

Then to his courtiers Ravan said: "Come, from the house-top high
Look we upon Virbahu's death and soothe our eager eye."

The King did mount his palace-top, his courtiers all behind;
He let his veering glance alight on whatso he could find.

On all sides round the island shone with golden-crested towers
Inlaid like brooches in the heart of groves besprent with flowers.

And here upon the grassy green, above a silver fount,
Thin thread on thread of stealing mist did many a palm surmount.

And here a lovely pleasure-lake, and here a splendid shrine,
And here a gaily-gilded shop in fine array did shine.

---

114 Rama was aided in battle by the monkey god Hanuman, a devotee of Rama and member of the Vanara, a race of monkey-warriors who live in the forests. Hanuman is sent by Rama to locate Sita.

For, all the wealth of all the world, exhaustless and untold,
Was hoarded up, O Lanka fair, at thy bright feet of gold.

He saw the rampart, long and strong, of Lanka's mothertown,
And on the rampart stairs the guards all hurrying up and down.

The Lion-portals all were closed; and here within the doors,
He saw, fully ready and awake, a countless Demon-force.

And there without the town he saw a locust horde of men,
That hung and hover'd line on line as far as he could ken.

Then to another scene he turn'd, his courtiers at his back;
It was the field of battle, and he felt his bosom crack.

In grief he cried: "O fallen friends, on you the jackals feed!
They grin and grapple o'er your hearts and make your bodies bleed!

"The vultures pounce upon your flesh — I cannot bear it more!
The war-dogs and the war-hawks, too, will they thus suck your gore?"

There, in the midst of friends laid low, he found Virbahu dead;
He lookt but once, then shut his eyes, and broken-hearted, said:

"The bed whereon, my darling son, Virbahu, thou hast lain,
Is glorious; for, in fighting for thy country thou was slain.

"Thy bed is glorious: yet my heart doth not for glory care:
What booteth glory unto me, if thou art lost for e'er?

"This world, O Fate, is but the field of all thy sports below;
Why art thou pleased with having see a mortal suffer woe?"

So saying, Ravan in his woe his eyes to seaward cast,
Beheld the bridge by Rama built,[115] and slowly spake at last:

"O Sea! how fine a necklace thou on thy fine neck dost wear! —
Yet fie! no necklace, 'tis a chain! — so rude dost thou appear?

---

115 To cross the ocean from the mainland to Lanka, Rama requests the Vanara, the monkey-warriors, to build him a bridge. This bridge has been geographically identified as a chain of shoals now known as Adam's Bridge.

"So rude to such a golden isle, that decks thy sable breast
Like myriad-lightning'd Koustubh-gem[116] upon young Madhav's[117] chest?

"Throw off that chain! Throw off that chain! why with the bridge thus bound?
This isle is waste; in waters vast let all our foes be drown'd."

Then from the golden palace-top he came down with his men
And 'mid the courtiers in the court did mount his throne again.

Pale, as, nay paler than, a cloud, Chitrangada[118] came there;
A creeping plant bereft of bloom, half-wither'd and half-bare.

She wore no trinkets in her grief; a simple dress she wore;
She lookt to Ravan, beat her breast, her golden ringlets tore.

For, stung at heart as with a dart, she could not ope her tongue
Like stork what time a snake, her nest approaching, eats her young.

The Lord of Lanka saw her face, he saw her face and wept,
The courtiers wept, the gateman too, of one so dear bereft.

And for a while a silence reign'd, an evil silence, there;
No nose did breathe, no lips did move, so sad the mourners were.

Then spake the Queen: "A gem serene kind Fate bestow'd on me;
With thee I kept it: where is it? I ask it back of thee.

"Thou art a king, thy duty is the poor man's all to save;
And I am poor; return me now the gem to thee I gave."

"And thou," said Ravan, "thou, my dear, wilt also vex me so?
O add not fuel to the fire, my heart is full of woe.

"This Lanka, nurse of heroes once, hath now no warrior great;
My realm is left all hero-reft at thy son's woful [sic] fate.

"At one child's death, my dearest Queen, thou art so pale with grief;
While at a thousand children's death my mind hath no relief.

---

116 Koustubh or Kaustubh: auspicious jewel worn by Vishnu, one of the gods of the Hindu Trimurti, around his neck.
117 Madhav: another name for Lord Krishna, who is an avatar of the Hindu god, Vishnu.
118 Chitrangada seems to be a wife of Ravan and mother of his son Virbahu in Dutt's telling of this tale.

"This Lanka will decay, I see in fancy's eye, my Queen;
My men fall day by day before the foeman's arrow keen.

"Then weep not, fair Chitrangada, for neither tears nor sighs
Can change the fixt decree of Fate or bid the dead arise."

The Fair Martyrs[119]
(From a Bengali Song)

Blaze, blaze thy last and brightest,
    Thou fiendly-friendly pyre:
The chaste will cast their bodies
    Upon thy mouth of fire.
Blaze, blaze, and in a moment
    Our burnings will be o'er;
O Chitor, crown of Princeland,
    Farewell for evermore!

List, list, ye sons of Islam,
    The ever-blazing pain
Ye raise within our bosoms
    Will never go in vain.
Ye Moslems iron-hearted,
    Ye may not hear our cry;
That Judge Whose ear is open
    Will listen from on high.

Look, look how all the women,
    To shun undying shame,
Resign their dying bodies
    Unto the jaws of flame.

---

119 [Poet's Note: This refers to one of the saddest chapters of Indian history, when Hindus and Muhammadans were constantly at war; consult Todd's [sic] "Rajasthan."] James Tod's *Annals and antiquities of Rajast'han, or the central and western Rajpoot states of India* was first published in two volumes between 1829 and 1832 and was reprinted in Madras in 1873, Calcutta in 1884 and London in 1914. The work, which purports to describe the geography of Rajasthan and sketch out a history of the Rajput clans and their customs, spends most of its time recounting major historical events surrounding the clans and their rule. The work captured the imagination of Indians at the time in its romantic portrayal of Rajasthan. A series of battles were waged during the fourteenth and sixteenth centuries by the Rajpoots of Chittor against the invading Mughal forces, who were finally successful in capturing Chittor fort in 1568. To avoid capture by the enemy, the royal women sacrificed themselves in rituals of mass self-immolation as their men rode to war and possible death, in an act known as *jauhar*.

Come, sisters, come, O maidens,
    Take leave here the earth,
Be true unto the nation
    To which we owe our birth.

Let us, ere all our feelings
    Are thaw'd away by death,
Let us, ere we are ashes,
    Breathe out one last long breath;
For, ne'er shall bard of Chitor
    In after ages say
We chose the gloss of pleasure
    And flung the gem away.

Blaze, blaze thy last and brightest,
    Thou fiendly-friendly pyre:
The chaste will cast their bodies
    Upon thy mouth of fire.
Look, look, ye heartless Moslems,
    Look how we shun disgrace –
We will be burnt to ashes,
    Yet never stain our race.

Come, sisters, come, O maidens,
    Why do we make delay?
O wear the crown of glory
    By throwing life away.
Look, look with eyes wide open,
    Thou earth, thou moon, thou sky;
Write, write in starry letters,
    Ye gods that dwell on high.

The Sworn Hero[120]
(From Roby Tagore)

'Tis for thee, O mother mine,
    My limbs I throw away;
'Tis for thee, O mother mine,
    My life adown I lay.

---

120 [Poet's Note: There is a pathetic tone about this patriotism.]

'Tis thy wrong, O mother mine,
    My tears from eyes will wring;
'This thy song, O mother mine,
    My lyre will ever sing.

Tho' this arm be weak and frail,
    Yet it will do thy deed;
Tho' this sword with rust be stain'd,
    Yet it will have thee freed.
Tho' this lyre contain no fire,
    No power, welladay! −
What know I? − one son of thine
    May wake to hear its lay!

Piyadasi[121]
(From Asoka)

Thus the royal Piyadasi,
Of the holy gods belovèd,
Of the gods and of the learned,
And of all the Bhikhus[122] holy, −
To his many subject nations,
To the peoples whom he loveth,
Speaketh in this edict boldly:

"Hear, O hear, ye subject nations;
Hear, ye peoples whom I care for,
Care for with a sire's affection,
And a teacher's watchful tending:
Hear what I have carved on pillar.
Carved for guidance of the govern'd
Under monks of royal sending.

---

121 [Poet's Note: Asoka was the first great Emperor of Northern India. He sent Buddhist missionaries to all parts of his empire and even to Ceylon. Most of his edicts were inscribed on pillars or in caves in different parts of the country. These inscriptions led Cunningham, Grierson, and Bühler to investigate the origin of the several scripts of India. The original of this poem is in prose.] Piyadasi, or Priyadashi, was the signature attached to edicts in the form of thirty-three inscriptions on pillars, boulders, and cave walls that are dispersed throughout modern-day India, Pakistan and Nepal. These edits were inscribed by missionaries sent out by Asoka, who is also believed to have authored the edicts. Emperor Asoka (300−232 BCE) extended the reach of the Maurya Empire across the subcontinent. After converting to Buddhism in 260 BCE, he applied Buddhist principles to administering this vast empire and renounced violence. He is regarded in later historical accounts as a great ruler (wise, just and honorable) and credited with spreading Buddhism across the subcontinent.

122 *Bhikhu*: male Buddhist monk.

"Public highways in mine empire
By the mango-trees are shaded;
Wells and inns, refreshing, cheering,
Calm the drouthy[123] and the weary; —
But no inn or well or highway
Hath been made by me before this
For refreshing bosoms dreary!

"Therefore shall the monks of mission,
Famed for rectitude and piety,
Famed for all the varied virtues
That 'neath heaven should adorn all, —
Unto ev'ry sect of people,
Bahman, Saman, or Niggantha,[124]
Show the path of peace eternal.

Would ye know that path of piety,
Know that path of glory genuine?
Seek O seek Religion truly,
Which is neither rite nor blindness,
Which is not a heap of dogmas,
Nor a mass of sacrifices,
But an inward love and kindness.

"Are there such as spread religion
By the iron rod of harshness,
By employ of means tyrannic?
Such is not King Piyadasi, —
Who doth look for inspiration,
And the wakening of the bosom,
Not a show of piety glossy."

On Tibet[125]

Deep in the bosom dark of mystery,
Housed in the gleam of days that are no more
And dreams that like her Himalayas soar
To height incredible — methinks I see
The land of mystic faith and llamas hoar!

---

123 Drouthy: thirsty; the condition of being dry (adj. "drouthy" *OED*).
124 Bahmans and Samans: sects of Iranians. Nigganthas: sect of Jains.
125 This is an original poem by Datta.

A glamour thro' the creeping sunset steals,
Weird Tibet, o'er thy snow-encircled brow;
A glamour from the Occident, that now,
Silent, pursues thy gloom-engirdled heels,
Mother of fossil modes and customs thou!

Though mighty miracle of centuries,
To us, the dwellers in the setting sun,
Perpetual dream-land, child of sunrise dun,
Who "teasest out of thought" man's memories,
Grim in thy glory, till thy race be run!

Land of the faith by pensive Buddha's rear'd, –
Where thought is stable, prayers are roll'd by wheels,
Faith moves with a dull motion as she feels
Her way thro' gloom of births, – where Fate is fear'd,
God is unknown, and man in darkness reels!

To Britain
(A quadruple virelay)[126]

To Britain, Queen of all the Seas,
    Whose Alfred first did show her might,
    Whose Nelson, strong and bold of sprite,
Did waft her fame from breeze to breeze,

The land where Caedmon saw the light,
    Where Chaucer shaped his harmonies.
    Whose Shakespeare fathom'd all that is,
Whose Milton rose to starry height,

To her whose light shall e'er increase,
    Whose might in countless foeman's spite
    From land to land shall spread aright,
Whose right to rule shall ne'er decrease,

---

126 This is an original poem by Datta. *Virelay*: medieval French verse form that developed from the common dance song of the period. Short lines are arranged in stanzas with only two rhymes, the end rhyme of one stanza being the chief rhyme of the next stanza. It was used mainly during the late sixteenth century and during the nineteenth century (n. "virelay" *OED*).

> To her who ever shall be bright,
> > I, prone to perish, offer these
> > Decaying, dying melodies,
> I, rushing into endless night.

Hasan Shahid Suhrawardy

Hasan Shahid Suhrawardy (1890–1965) was a poet, art critic, and diplomat. Educated at Presidency College, Calcutta and at Oxford, Suhrawardy settled in Russia, where he taught literature to university students. After the 1919 Bolshevik Revolution, Suhrawardy left Russia and eventually resettled in India for research and teaching. He was the older brother of Husein Shahid Suhrawardy, who acted as the chief minister of Bengal in 1946 and, after partition in 1947, as law minister for Pakistan and prime minister of Pakistan (1956–1957). *Faded Leaves* seems to be Hasan Shahid Suhrawardy's first major published work although he would soon publish prolifically in other fields, including translations of works from the Russian and Chinese, as well as art and literary criticism.

> Faded Leaves, a collection of poems (London: 1910)[127]
>
> ## *Dedication*
>
> > Mother, though endless miles in greyness stretch,
> > And 'twixt us rolls the vast unconstant sea,
> > When this poor heart is breaking with its grief,
> > My tend'rest love-thoughts ever are of thee.
>
> > Grief at the distance from thee, the sad scene
> > When we last parted burns into my brain,
> > Each dear, remembered look and word arise
> > To add a keenness to the edge of pain.
>
> > When sunk in England's gathering twilight gloom,
> > I sit and think about the dear, dear East,
> > Thy Being invests with radiance every dream,
> > A part of all in life and Nature best.

---

[127] Hasan Shahid Suhrawardy, *Faded Leaves, a collection of poems* (London: J. M. Baxter & Co., 1910).

These songs, the tremblings of a restless heart,
That long has lost its prime, though young in years,
With deepest love that bridges lands and seas,
Mother, to thee I dedicate with tears.

The Indian Maid's Lament

Come to me, beloved, through the darkening gloom,
The starts are glittering, and the clear-cut Moon
Shoots frigid arrows; Night, lovely Night,
With her myriad eyes sleeps heavy on flowers,
The darkness is od'rous; Come to me now,
As I sit a white streak with outstretched arms
As e'er beneath the skies waiting for you.
Thus vainly have I yearned through long, long years,
Kept up with hopes and with those sweetest thoughts,
That thronging come to my mind roseate,
And leave my throbbing heart more desolate.
Was it but yesterday I dreamt of you?
I see you every night, as restlessly
I lie awake with blood-shot eyes, weeping.
I saw you standing 'gainst a glittering hill,
A silver star shone like a maiden's kiss,
And the Autumn sunset deepened in your cheeks.
Ah me! Your lovely eyes of liquid fire
Were clouded, and a pallor as of death
O'erspread your features, as you stood so sad,
Sunk in your thoughts, mute, ruminating.
My dearest, what a crowd of aching pangs
Did petal by petal sere my bleeding heart;
I looked at you through mist of gathering tears,
And longed for days that never can return.
Come to me, beloved! Even as you stay
My poor lone heart is breaking; the bulbuls
Sleep in radiant darkness on the bloss'ming boughs
Hushed. The ruby rose withers on the stalk.
Come to me, but for a while, and hold me close,
And let me taste your fever-kisses red
On my lips, and brows, and neck; but once again
Feel your presence, as I lean against you
With pent-up thoughts in a rich, rich silence.
Come, by beloved, come.

Swinburne[128]

Swing low your censers for a full-blown Rose,
Cut through the cheeks, the while his purple breath
Enriched the love-lit air, here sleeps in death,
His honey lips with blood on them fast-froze.
His fragrance, fresh as life, hung like a wreath
Of golden mist among the mountain heights,
A radiance purer than the rainbow-lights,
With heavenlier hues, within their folds that sheathe
Eternal splendour and eternal glow.
His soul, gauze-textured, moved amongst the stars,
Shared in their hush aureoled in their woe,
His voice, fire-food for gods, a heart unbars,
Red with its pains, and joys, and hopes high-kist,
The heart of England's Master-Melodist.

Rabindranath Tagore

Rabindranath Tagore (1861–1941), was a nationalist, social reformer, and artist, educated in England and India. Tagore, who wrote in both his native Bengali as well as in English, was awarded the Nobel Prize in literature in 1913. His written work spans a variety of genres including poetry, novels, essays, dairies, autobiographies, and dramas. Although too numerous to list in full, his body of work includes poetic collections *Gitanjali* (1910), *The Gardener* (1913), *Fruit-Gathering* (1916) and *The Fugitive* (1921); plays *Raja* (1910), *Dakghar* (1912), *Muktadhara* (1922) and *Raktakaravi* (1926); and novels *Gora* (1910), *Ghare-Baire* (1916) and *Yogayog* (1929). Tagore's English "translations" of his Bengali verse are not direct renditions but creative interpretations which stand as original works in and of themselves. Tagore has left a rich collection of drawings and paintings as well as numerous musical compositions, including the Indian national anthem *Jana Gana Mana*. As a testament to his unparalleled range and vision, Tagore holds a revered place in the Indian imaginary as a national poet. Reprinted below are selections from two early English-language collections "translated" (or, more accurately, adapted) from the Bengali by the author: *The Gardener* (1913) and *Fruit-Gathering* (1916).

---

128 Swinburne was frequently made the subject of odes by Indian-English poets.

Gardener, trans. by author (London: 1913)[129]

17

The yellow bird sings in their tree and makes my heart dance with gladness.
We both live in the same village, and that is our one piece of joy.
Her pair of pet lambs come to graze in the shade of our garden trees.
If they stray into our barley field, I take them up in my arms.
The name of our village is Khanjanā, and Anjanā they call our river.
My name is known to all the village, and her name is Ranjanā.

Only one field lies between us.
Bees that have hived in our grove go to seek honey in theirs.
Flowers launched from their landing-stairs come floating by the stream where we bathe.
Baskets of dried *kusm*[130] flowers come from their fields to our market.
The name of our village is Khanjanā, and Anjanā they call our river.
My name is known to all the village, and her name is Ranjanā.

The lane that winds to their house is fragrant in the spring with mango flowers.
When their linseed is ripe for harvest the hemp is in bloom in our field.
The stars that smile on their cottage send us the same twinkling look.
The rain that floods their tank makes glad our *kadam*[131] forest.
The name of our village is Khanjanā, and Anjanā they call our river.
My name is known to all the village, and her name is Ranjanā.

Fruit-Gathering, trans. by author (London: 1916)[132]

XIX

Sudās, the gardener, plucked from his tank the last lotus left by the ravage of winter and went to sell it to the king at the palace gate.

There he met a traveller who said to him, "Ask your price for the last lotus, – I shall offer it to Lord Buddha."

Sudās said, "If you pay one golden *māshā*[133] it will be yours."

The traveller paid it.

---

129 Rabindranath Tagore, *The Gardener*, trans. by author (London: Macmillan, 1913).
130 *Kusm*: flower.
131 *Kadam*: tree indigenous to West Bengal, Asssam and neighboring regions.
132 Rabindranath Tagore, *Fruit-Gathering*, trans. by author (London: Macmillan, 1916).
133 *Masha*: unit of currency under the Mughal Empire.

At that moment the king came out and he wished to buy the flower, for he was on his way to see Lord Buddha, and he thought, "It would be a fine thing to lay at his feet the lotus that bloomed in winter."

When the gardener said he had been offered a golden *māshā* the king offered him ten, but the traveller doubled the price.

The gardener, being greedy, imagined a greater gain from him for whose sake they were bidding. He bowed and said, "I cannot sell this lotus."

In the hushed shade of the mango grove beyond the city wall Sudās stood before Lord Buddha, on whose lips sat the silence of love and whose eyes beamed peace like the morning star of the dew-washed autumn.

Sudās looked in his face and put the lotus at his feet and bowed his head to the dust.

Buddha smiled and asked, "What is your wish, my son?"

Sudās looked in his face and put the lotus at his feet and bowed his head to the dust.

Buddha smiled and asked, "What is your wish, my son?"

Sudās cried, "The least touch of your feet."

LV

Tulsidas, the poet,[134] was wandering, deep in thought, by the Ganges, in that lonely spot where they burn their dead.

He found a woman sitting at the feet of the corpse of her dead husband, gaily dressed as for a wedding.

She rose as she saw him, bowed to him, and said, "Permit me, Master, with your blessing, to follow my husband to heaven."

"Why such hurry, my daughter?" asked Tulsidas. "Is not this earth also His who made heaven?"

"For heaven I do not long," said the woman. "I want my husband."

Tulsidas smiled and said to her, "Go back to your home, my child. Before the month is over you will find your husband."

The woman went back with glad hope. Tulsidas came to her every day and gave her high thoughts to think, till her heart was filled to the brim with divine love.

When the month was scarcely over, her neighbours came to her, asking, "Woman, have you found your husband?"

The widow smiled and said, "I have."

Eagerly they asked, "Where is he?"

"In my heart is my lord, one with me," said the woman.

---

134 The *bhakti* (devotional) poet Tulsidas (1543?–1623) is thought to have been born in Rajpur (in modern-day state of Uttar Pradesh). His most famous work, *Ramacharitmanas*, is an epic poem addressed to the Hindu god Rama.

LXIV[135]

The sun had set on the western margin of the river among the tangle of the forest.

The hermit boys had brought the cattle home, and sat round the fire to listen to the master, Guatama,[136] when a strange boy came, and greeted him with fruits and flowers, and, bowing low at his feet, spoke in a bird-like voice – "Lord, I have come to thee to be taken into the path of the supreme Truth.

"My name is Satyakāma."

"Blessings be on thy head," said the master.

"Of what clan art thou, my child? It is only fitting for a Brahmin to aspire to the highest wisdom."

"Master," answered the boy, "I know not of what clan I am. I shall go and ask my mother."

Thus saying, Satyakāma took leave, and wading across the shallow stream, came back to his mother's hut, which stood at the end of the sandy waste at the edge of the sleeping village.

The lamp burnt dimly in the room, and the mother stood at the door in the dark waiting for her son's return.

She clasped him to her bosom, kissed him on his hair, and asked him of his errand to the master.

"What is the name of my father, dear mother?" asked the boy.

"It is only fitting for a Brahmin to aspire to the highest wisdom, said Lord Guatama to me."

The woman lowered her eyes, and spoke in a whisper.

"In my youth I was poor and had many masters. Thou didst come to thy mother Jabālā's arms, who had no husband."

The early rays of the sun glistened on the tree-tops of the forest hermitage.

The students, with their tangled hair still wet with their morning bath, sat under the ancient tree, before the master.

There came Satyakāma.

He bowed low at the feet of the sage, and stood silent.

"Tell me," the great teacher asked him, "of what clan art thou?"

"My lord," he answered, "I know it not. My mother said when I asked her, 'I had served many masters in my youth, and thou hadst come to thy mother Jabālā's arms, who had no husband.'"

There rose a murmur like the angry hum of bees disturbed in their hive; and the students muttered at the shameless insolence of that outcast.

Master Guatama rose from his seat, stretched out his arms, took the boy to his bosom, and said, "Best of all Brahmins art thou, my child. Thou hast the noblest heritage of truth."

---

135 This poem is a telling of a tale from the *Chandogya Upanishad*, dating from the Vedic period.
136 Guatama: a great historical sage (not to be confused with Siddhartha Gautama, or the Buddha).

Peshoton Sorabji Goolbai Dubash

Dubash was a lecturer, poet and homeopath. His other books include *Dreaming: a Philosophic and Scientific Treatise* (1916), *Romance of Souls: a Philosophic Romance in Verse* (1918) and the interestingly titled *Can a prostitute go to heaven and other essays* (1945). In the preface to *Rationalistic*, he includes a letter to his "Dear Reader," claiming his "impartial[ity]" towards all religions on the subcontinent (especially his own Parsi religion):"The injurious points in the religion and the race of my birth are as vehemently exposed as those of others, because these verses are not composed with the aim to amuse. To amuse is noble, to instruct more noble, and to elevate is most noble." He notes of his last poem:"The same is the attitude in my poem "Britannia and Mother Hind." It is only for the narrow-minded patriots to overlook the faults of their own countries. It does not matter to me whether the English rule Hind or the Indians rule it. The object is that the Indians should be happy and Hindoostan should advance." This almost utilitarian philosophy towards government – that it should mean the maximum happiness for the most people on the subcontinent – effectively sidesteps the contentious opposition between support of the British Raj and participation in Indian nationalist movements. "Britannia and Mother Hind" is, as Dubash claims, a critique of both British imperial policy in India as well as of Indians themselves.

Rationalistic and Other Poems (London: 1917)[137]

Britannia and Mother Hind[138]
(A Dialogue)

Britannia:
Now come to me my sister Mother Hind,
And let us have a plain and open talk,
So that I understand Thy children all
Of Hindoostan, if facts thou wouldst explain.
    Mother Hind:
With intuition I feel thy call sincere;
O prosperous Britannia, I am here.
    Britannia:
Thy sons of India in war have done so well,

---

[137] Peshoton Sorabji Goolbai Dubash, *Rationalistic and Other Poems* (London: British Bardic Brotherhood, 1917).

[138] Mother Hind: Mother India. "Hind" was commonly used in the nineteenth century to designate India. Dubash also uses the term "Hindi" (now used to designate the language) to refer to the inhabitants of Hind, or India. He does not seem to limit the term to Hindus since Dubash himself was a Parsi.

Not only with wealth and sympathy quite true,
But willingly have shed their Aryan blood,
And dauntlessly have fought the ruthless foe.
And so, I wish to give the due reward.
  Mother Hind:
I've not the slightest doubt about thy aim,
And so will solve all thy difficulties.
  Britannia:
The foremost things I like to know is this:
Is any superiority by colour expressed?
Can thy dark children be equal to the white?
  Mother Hind:
At first 'tween them so difference wide appears.
But slow gradation Thou canst easy find
From Polar white to black of negroid kind.
My Hindi children though not milky white,
Yet not are Indians all so black as night.
As we can see the blue and red differ
But spectrum shows a continuous blend of light
From violet deep right down to crimson bright,
And a spread of peaceful green just is the mean.
And just the same the Hindi colour of wheat,
Perhaps though the golden mean has no conceit.
But even at those not 'tween these two extremes
That one who looks with scorn is wrong, it seems.
Because between two cats of black and white
Thou finds no special trait of good or ill.
Thou shows no scorn for colour in the beast,
But in fellow-beings of West and sunburn East.
No prophet out of Asia was ever born.
As Europe's prophet was dark, dark men don't scorn.
And here thy painters of past and modern days
A want of imagination thus betrayed.
A sheet of white self-adulation
Perchance so much confines their small vision
That nothing but all white they could perceive
And painted Christ and all his followers
European white though they were all quite burnt
By Palestine's and Syria's scorching sun.
  Britannia:
It never struck to me that there's a string
Unbroken from complexion white to black
And the Hindi colour forms the modest mean.
'Tis vain to have the colour prejudice.
But are not they inferior in mental gifts?
  Mother Hind:
When this is seen materialistically

> I grant that this is a mournful present face...
> No modern strides of science in Hind are made.
> But this can be perhaps quite well explained
> Thus, that no chance to them is given yet.
> Still, when, they will get some opportunity
> My children's some success I guarantee.
> For, know that the marconigraph was first
> Conceived by a Bengali professor Boss.[139]
> Again will shine the sons of men who built
> The Goombaz Gol of Bijapore,[140] the Taj
> Mahal of Agra, Amritshar's Golden shrine,[141]
> And scores of gorgeous temples and stately mosques.
> How can one think that Chandragupta's race[142]
> And whose of the kind of glorious Akbar Great[143]
> With a sprinkling of Cyrus the Great's Irânian breed[144]
> Shall not again some day their metal show,
> Though now in history's strange cyclic turn
> Are slumbering in matter's progress fast?
>   Britannia:
> These races surely have great mental gifts
> In which are born such architects of fame
> And glorious monarchs of immortal names.
> Pray tell with various heathen faiths so vile
> Can they profess to have spiritual ight,
> And can a moral standard good maintain?
>   Mother Hind:
> O pardon me, Britannia sister mine,
> The Indians have a great spiritual shine:

---

139 Marconigraph: the Marconi wireless telegraph. Although the Italian scientist Guglielmo Marconi is credited with inventing the wireless telegraph in the late nineteenth century, Professor Jagdish Chandra Bose of Presidency College in Calcutta gave a public demonstration of wireless communication during the same period. There was a great deal of dispute at the time regarding who should be credited with the invention.

140 Gol Bumbaz in Bijapur: mausoleum of Muhammad Adil Shah (1627–1656); located in the modern-day state of Karnataka.

141 Golden Temple of Amritsar: Sikh temple built during the sixteenth century and located in the Punjab region.

142 Chandragupta Maurya (321–297 BCE): founder of the Maurya Empire, which encompassed a large swath of the subcontinent.

143 Akbar (1542–1605): considered one of the great leaders of the Mughal Empire, Akbar ruled from 1556 until his death. He expanded the reach of the empire over the subcontinent to include almost all of northern India, reformed the central administration system and instituted a more efficient the tax-collection process. His tolerance and sympathy towards other religions, illustrated in part by his inclusion of a number of Hindus in the imperial bureaucracy and allowing Hindu territories within the Empire a measure of autonomy, ensured the loyalty of many non-Muslims.

144 Cyrus the Great (c. 590–529 BCE): founder of the Persian Empire. Cyrus established the rule of the Achaemenian dynasty and may have been a follower of Zoroastrianism.

Which none who knows and is just can e'er deny.
And this in Eastern women is by far the higher.[145]
Thou must remember that spiritual light
By births of prophets on Asia shines quite bright.
No prophet out of Asia was ever born;
As Europe's prophet was dark, dark me don't scorn.
    Britannia:
If this is so, why are Thy daughters kept
Behind the purdah? Tell, what social life
Have they, deprived of freedom and thus confined
In the "harem" of the luxurious life?
    Mother Hind:
Again I must Thy pardon beg to tell
The greatest fault of children Thine is this:
No wish, no search, no thirst have they to find
The truthful facts and knowledge of divers kinds
About the people of any foreign land;
And yet will hastily wrong notions form.
The purdah[146] by no means is universal there,
And only the Musleem[147] women suffer thus,
And event they are now removing it.
In those invasion days of Abdali[148]
And Timur,[149] when the men behaved so ill
As the Germans do to the Belgian women now.[150]
In ancient days of foreign raids and rule,
To just protect the women this was done.
And also this was why confinement came.
The Hindoo women of the modern times
Are free, though not quite as in the glorious days
Of Vikram, Vanraj and of Shalivan.[151]

---

145 See Partha Chatterjee, *The Nation and its Fragments: Colonial and Postcolonial Histories* (Princeton: Princeton University Press, 1993). A common claim of Indian nationalists and Indians in general was that Indians, and especially Indian women, were spiritually superior to the materialist West.

146 *Purdah*: practice of covering or veiling women so as to prevent them from being seen by male strangers. It can also refer to the physical seclusion of women.

147 Musleem: Muslim.

148 Abdali, or Ahmad Shah Durrani (1722?–1773): founder of the Durrani Empire, which extended over the Punjab region, Kashmir, and Sindh.

149 Timur, known as Tamerlane in the West (1336–1405): Turkish conqueror of West, Central and South Asia, including Delhi, and founder of the Timurid empire.

150 "Germans do to the Belgian women now": reference to reports during World War I of German soldiers raping Belgian women.

151 Vikram or Vikramaditya: ruled Avanti in the first century CE. Vanraj, or Vanraja: ruled Gujurat during the eighth century CE. Shalivan, or Shalivahan: ruled Pratisthana in the first century CE. All three figures were legendary rulers of India associated with the Jain religion.

The Parsee women are quite free like Thine,
They have their sports and concerts and even clubs.
And what "hareem" means children Thine don't know.
It means no more than women's "private" place.
If 'tis luxurious, it only shows
The good regards for the mothers and the wives.
Though, sometimes the men quite wicked selfish are,
Still that proves not the "hareem" a place of vice.
The Musilmans may rare have many wives,
But make no secret of their practice wrong.
But others practice polygamy much
In secret, which is worse if th' other is bad.
Say, does the social life of women mean
To do a-shopping half the day or whole,
And keep on buying things of fashions new?
Or led by selfish freedom's notions strange;
To earn, and oft, without a cause but pride,
And make deficiencies by ways not good,
Instead attend her own and husband's house?
To be so much engrossed in pleasures light,
To hate the noble duties of motherhood?
The women of Hind in quiet their duties do
As daughters, wives and Nature's mothers true.
These quiet homely daughters have shone
In days of past in strenuous times of need
With a splendour rivalling Thy daughters' deeds.
These daughters of Mirabais[152] of pious hearts,
Of Chandbibies[153] of great heroic parts,
Of Noor-Jahans[154] of governmental arts,
Who have from purdah and confinement rose
To zeniths of fame, so often when they chose,
Will sure a brilliant lustre on India cast
When chance be given to their gifts so vast.
    Britannia:
To me it is a source of joy to know

---

152 Mirabai (1498–1547): Hindu mystical singer and devotee of the Hindu god, Lord Krishna. Born into a Rajput noble family, she is considered one of the foremost artists of the *bhakti* (devotional) movement. Over two hundred poems (or *bhajans*) have been attributed to her though there are hundreds more that are often thought to come from her pen.

153 Chand Bibi (1550–1599): female Muslim ruler who acted at different times as regent of Bijapur and regent of Ahmednagar, which she defended against the Mughal army of Emperor Akbar.

154 Noor Jahan, or Nur Jahan, (1577–1645): empress of the Mughal dynasty and the favorite wife of Emperor Jahangir. She consolidated her family's power in court and took a leading role in politics, administration, and economics.

That daughters Thine have such a latent glow,
And wish that those illustrious days are nigh
When British brilliancy may reach the sky.
Yet tell, why do Thy sons seditious sigh,
What does this imply, and why they always cry?
      Mother Hind:
First know, the size of Hindoostan so wide
Compares with Europe but for Russian side.
Now put together all Europeans' acts
Seditious against own king and mother lands
In just one year. And take again those acts
Of discontent of sons of Hindoostan.
And Thou wouldst find the Hindi number dwindling
Away into comparative obscurity.
The papers thine in ignorance magnify
The slight occasional acts of clamour just
To ask for more of what they well deserve.
Just as a growing son of a family,
When fit, from parents wants more liberty
Without the wish to drive the parents out,
So, India's sons as they advance by steps,
They ask for freedom more, and more redress.
And not like Thy sons take steps desperate
As to behead their own King Royal Charles.[155]
How oft in history thy sons have rose
Against their Royal governmental rule
At the slightest trespass over freedom theirs?
How oft in Europe all seditious acts
Are done and kings are killed by native men.
Have Indians done one act so drastic yet?
Not once in fact and rare in lying tales
Of mutiny[156] to get importance false.
That peaceful country lies so far fro Thee
That thou believes the falsehood told to Thee.
And little troubles so well exaggerated
By some to make of mole-hills, mountains great.
By natures are the Indians peaceful quite;
If they complain there is some reason right.
      Britannia:
But what are those sad grievances Thou spoke?

---

155 King Charles I (1600–1649) was beheaded after the second civil war in England.
156 This may refer to the 1857 "Sepoy Mutiny," a rebellion now commonly seen as the first Indian war of independence, or to any number of smaller uprisings during the past century. Dubash seems to claim that reports about and fear generated by the mutiny is exaggerated for effect by the British.

There must be something burning where is smoke.
      Mother Hind:
The first of all that much disgusts my sons
Is the insulting way of missionaries.
They stop a man of any post or creed
At any place and any time and ask
If he is Christian. If the man is not,
He tells him that he is not saved at all.
Without regards of feelings of the man
He runs low down the other's faith and God,
And forces on the man's unwilling ears
All sorts of nonsense and mad rigmarole,
The only genius of the missionaries all,
That can surpass their ignorance so great
Of virtues of th' oriental noble faiths.
Thy children think that wonderful work is done
By them, and pay the sums of money large.
But these are used for ease and comfort all
Of missionaries first, then some ignorant
Child or some roughian lost is made to say
That he is come to the Lord and the rites are done.
No sensible man of any faith think worth
His while to change his creed (perhaps quite rare).
No man of good position or good birth
Has listened to their blasphemy without disgust,
And be induced to take their creed because
Of the allurement of good positions got
On the strength of having called himself a Christian.
Those thus allured the Christian faith to take
Do so for profit's and not for prophet's sake.
But this is not so bad as when a child
That does not understand is oft seduced
To leave it's father's roof, and oft'ner pressed
To take the step in such infernal haste,
So that it's parents know of it too late.
And thus so many families in tears
Are left by stealthy mean conversion forced
Upon a simple child or even on
A grown-up helpful son supporting them,
Who leaves them helpless under wrong advice.
Say, why not follow Salvation Army's ways,
To help the needy and leave to them to take
The faith, if liked, and no conditions make
To help, and no one's heart regardless ache?
Instead of taking pride in numbers false
Of large conversions, children Thine should try

To make true Christians of those already born
In pious Jesus's humane faith of love.
For, all the energy of the Christian folds
Is needed to re-Christian those of Christian wolds.
  Britannia:
Then after these religious grievances
Against the missionaries, but not against
The ways of the Salvation Army there,
Please tell, what next disturbs their peaceful minds?
  Mother Hind:
Thou knowest well that the most of England's food
Is got from India. So all efforts should
Be made to well encourage agriculture
In Hindoostan. Instead of that, the work
Is made so difficult and profitless
By high taxations in geometric progression
That many people th' occupation leave.
Is any thing done to promote in India
The agriculture of scientific
Right kind amongst the proper Hindi men?
Then 'gain, if my sons of Hindoostan desire
To buy a piece of land quite freehold there
In his own motherland, he mostly can't;
But he can buy some freehold land in England
And in many countries but his own.
The agriculture was quite better then
When ruled the good Feerogsha of Taglakh[157] line
And Sidhhraj Jay Singh of Gujrati[158] shine.
  Britannia:
I grant, it looks quite strange that sons of Hind
Cannot purchase a piece of their own land,
But can do so in foreign countries all.
Yet there must be, I'm sure, some reason good
For my just children to behave so crude.
Now let us pass on to the trouble next.
  Mother Hind:
The next is one that needs quite urgent thought:
It is the question of free education.
Is it not time that learning should be spread
Quite wide all over Hind for Britain's aid

---

157 Feerogsha of Taglakh or Firoze Tughluq, (1309–1388): member of the Muslim Tughluq dynasty; presided as Sultan of Delhi from 1351 until his death, which marked the beginning of a slow decline of that dynasty.

158 Sidhhraj Jay Singh, or Siddhraj Jaisingh: twelfth-century ruler of Gujarat.

In the achievements of worldly progress wide,
So that, Great Britain and Hind shine side by side?
The subjects of Akbar and Ashoka Great[159]
Were learned better than of present date.
'Tis education, education good
The greatest cure of India's sorry mood.
Why not to Indians give free education?
The greatest and most promising of all
The Indian ports, most suitable a place
As a centre of education, Karachi,[160]
Should be presented with our Princess Mary's
University with a Royal Charter soon.[161]
    Britannia:
I always thought that children mine had brought
In Hindoostan all learning and the rest,
And that before the advent of British rule
There were no intellectual claims or life;
But now I find my old impressions wrong.
    Mother Hind:
And this was so because, as yet one does
Not find the history of Hind that's writ
In English, which is a truthful history
Of Hind, by an impartial man of facts.
    Britannia:
Yet these do not appear such great complaints.
Hast thou some serious grievances to tell.
    Mother Hind:
If Thou art anxious and thus wish'st to know,
I am quite ready here to tell Thee all.
This time is opportune for it, because,

---

159 Emperor Asoka (300–232 BCE): extended the reach of the Maurya empire across the subcontinent. After converting to Buddhism in 260 BCE, he applied Buddhist principles to administering this vast empire and renounced violence. He is regarded in later historical accounts as a great ruler (wise, just, and honorable) and credited with spreading Buddhism across the subcontinent. Akbar (1542–1605): considered one of the great leaders of the Mughal Empire, Akbar ruled from 1556 until his death. He expanded the reach of the empire over the subcontinent to include almost all of northern India, reformed the central administration system and instituted a more efficient the tax-collection process. His tolerance and sympathy towards other religions, illustrated in part by his inclusion of a number of Hindus in the imperial bureaucracy and allowing Hindu territories within the empire a measure of autonomy, ensured the loyalty of many non-Muslims.
160 Karachi: one of the largest cities in modern-day Pakistan.
161 Princess Mary: daughter of King George V and Queen Mary, who were also emperor and empress of the British Empire. Royal Charters were necessary to establish incorporated universities in the territories ruled by the British Empire. In these lines, Dubash calls for the issuing of a Royal Charter to establish a university, named after Princess Mary, in Karachi.

If Thou will know my children's greatest needs,
From now will Thou begin to sow the seeds
Of which the rewarding fruits be timely ripe
To give to them and thus the troubles wipe
At th' end of war, when all will as, their due
And all will get, but India out of view.
      Britannia:
No, no, Thou must no say such vexing things.
My sons have always been and will be just.
      Mother Hind:
Why wait till th' end of war? Right in midst
Of it, there been flag-days for foreign lands,
For their colonies, and even horses,
And yet a flag-day for India has not come
Though many my sons have tried quite hard for it.
Pray tell, is it Christianity that thy
White nurses most refuse to tend my sons,
That get so wounded for the white people's sake?
Pray tell why separation allowance
Is not given to Indian soldiers' wives?
      Britannia:
These ills of war will end with th' end of war.
Tell me of serious ills that should be cured,
At th' end of war. My sister, rest assured
That if my sons so just will know of all,
They'll try to settle grievances great and small.
      Mother Hind:
Then list, 'tis very difficult for Indians
To earn the livelihood at home in Hind.
For all the good posts in the Government
Are mostly filled by English natives Thine.[162]
The same is the case wherever th' influence
Of colour goes, the white get a better chance,
Though often less deserving than the dark.
The white are paid such princely salaries
For some soft job, and soon they can retire.
But my poor children in the motherland
Are paid so niggardly that they must toil
All through the life, except for Royal service.
And when they starve in their paternal clime
They chance their luck in countries of Europe.
But alas, slight chance they stand in foreign lands

---

162 This was a common source of grievance for Indians who perceived difficulties advancing within the imperial bureaucracy, which depended a great deal upon Indian labor. Indeed, many of the poets included in this anthology worked for the imperial bureaucracy in some form.

Thus scorched by sun 'gainst native people white:
In Transvaal positively treated ill;
Australia to enter not allowed;
In Canada but little luck is theirs.[163]
If not in foreign climes, and not in British
Colonies, and not in own motherland,
Have they got a chance to prosper very well?
    Britannia:
In colonies they must not go and vie,
For they bring labour down so very cheap.
    Mother Hind:
And will the white give work to the dark if he
Does not do it much cheaper than the white?
If chance quite fair be given in Hindoostan,
Then children mine wish not to go abroad.
    Britannia:
But why should they all strive the service to get,
And not commercial, industrial
And other undertakings try themselves?
    Mother Hind:
As far as they can do they try, but mind,
There even such difficulties are brought
That oft the poor man has to give way again.
Hear, if Hindi man of moderate means
May wish to start a steamship line his own,
The English people find so many faults
In everything, and that, he is in fact
So harassed by th' inspecting non-darkmen
That he must give the idea up, unless,
So very rich he be to hold his own.
    Britannia:
As yet Thou hast not said a word about
The home-rule question. What hast Thou to say?
    Mother Hind:
That there are men quite capable to rule
Is a fact without the slightest doubt whatever.
But the people to be ruled are not as yet
Of such a condition as to render it

---

163 The diaspora of Indians throughout Great Britain, Africa, Southeast Asia, the Caribbean, Europe, the United States, Canada, and Australia has followed migration patterns based on labor, education and legal restrictions. Large-scale diaspora can be said to have begun in the early nineteenth century when indentured labor was used to replace plantation labor lost by the British abolition of slavery. See Vijay Mishra, *The Literature of the Indian Diaspora: Theorizing the Diasporic Imaginary* (London: Routledge, 2007) for a nuanced discussion of the literature produced by this diaspora.

Quite possible. For, the inhabitants
Of Hind are not of one kind or simple creed.
A constant harmful disagreement ill
Of "creedly" jealousy there will be between
The different communities which may
Perhaps create confusion serious bad.
When every year all hearts in fear abide
That Musleem religious "hoollar" shall take place,
And blood shall smear each non-Muslim's face.
If even a trifling annual cricket match
Oft leads to words and quarrels and childish fights
Between th' opposing these communities,
How shall they unite to act for mutual rule?
First let them learn to kill distinctions these,
And banish mad religious bigotry,
Which is the greatest fault of Muslims yet.
But Hindoos also are not better much
They rush not to fight, yet they within their hearts
A sense of great superiority maintain,
And will not condescend to dine with the rest.
And what are Parsees, but a group of men
Who think so much of their own self as take
It bad to convert a willing one to their faith,
Or marry people of other communities?
How can the Muslims and the Hindoos expect
Themselves to rule themselves if they as yet
In twentieth century have not uplifted
Their women, the wives and mothers of the future race?
The women who with the least opportunities
In the past have earned immortal names of fame.
But why the women? E'en all men are not
As yet quite educated, and believe
In superstitious mad beliefs of all
The harmful kinds and by distinctions doomed
Into a chaos of differences of faiths.
No home-rule till all men and most women
Are educated enough to help such a rule,
And all distinctions of faith are rooted out.
O, Hindoos, though you are to animals kind,
Yet for young widows you no pity find,
And treat them cruelly or like beasts in grind.
O, Muslims, the salvation of your race
Lies in uplifting women of modern days.
O, Parsees, though solid education should take,
Try commerce, arts, but service and show forsake.
O, Christians, through creed as Europeans don't feign.

Of India, you true Indians still remain.
O, Jews of Hind, for Indians you must stand,
Take Indians as brothers and Hind as motherland:
The ancient land where Hebrew blood is not shed.
O, Indians all, unite, unite, unite;
Let union be your watchword firm and right.
    Britannia:
So now, if Thou dost think that children mine
Have done some good, tell that to children Thine.
    Mother Hind:
O, most of them know it well, though some don't,
And I shall tell them where they argue wrong.
For example, they maintain that these divers
Innovations that are brought in Hindoostan
Would sure have come in Hind with the lapse of time.
Yet they forget that there are things, perhaps
As yet would have been bad if natives Thine
Had not improved. For, now, the women can
Quite freely move about with the dread
Of being kidnapped by some Muslim king,
Or stolen by some Hindoo highwayman.
If time did this, then why it has not done
The same in Afghanistan, Baluchistan,
And Persia. What have their true natives done
Yet to protect the women of diff'rent creeds?
And then again the things that the Government
Neglected, what the Hindoos and the Muslims
Yet done for them? Just take th' example again
Of women. Have they of themselves advanced
Their women by good education, say?
Are more than twenty-five per cent literate
Of Muslim women, thirty-five per cent
Of Hindoo women, though, full ninety-five
Per cent of Parsee women literate are?
And these are various things if left to time
Would not as yet have entered Hindoostan.
For these my prudent sons Thy native thank,
Though ask more rights deserved to be given them.
    Britannia:
Quite pleased I am to know that sons of Thine
So prudently can see some good in mine.
And Thou who can impartial think so well,
What steps to take, what rights to give should tell.
    Mother Hind:
Thou first must care to see that the men Thou sends
As Viceroys are not a vice nor given as a curse,

But "rays" from which delightful sway can sweep
The deeds of an unwise one making Indians weep.
For once a "Vice-boy"[164] made a wicked rule
That Indians should not get a pay of more
Than four pounds a month in Governmental posts,
And the well-paid positions only for
Th' Europeans kept. White foreigners rather than
Dark Britishers be better paid and helped.
O, send to Hind some Viceroys with some heart
To feel and brains to think in righteous ways.
The next, advance the agriculture much
By low taxations, and by proper works
Of irrigation from the rivers huge.
Then stop this nuisance of these missionaries mad,
And madder still the colour distinction sad.
Give Indians an equal chance in Governmental
Positions, also in commerce and the rest.
This, this is the sorest and the worst request.
Give Indians a treatment human in Transvaal,
And treat them well in Canada and Australia.
Then give free education to all in Hind,
A princely university in Sindh.[165]
No more should this important question great
Be neglected to make Hind up-to-date.
'Tis education, education good
The greatest cure of India's sorry mood.
Proclaim the eldest Princess as that of Hind.[166]
Let Hind in Parliament be shown by eight,
Two Parsees, Hindoos two and Muslims two,
One Jew, and one of Christian faith from hind,[167]
So that Thy sons in England can command
The first-rate Indian information true.
    Britannia:
To me all wants Thou named quite simple look;

---

164 "Vice-boy" seems to be a derogatory term for viceroy, the head of British administration in the Indian empire. Dubash seems to refer here to Lord Chelmsford, Frederic John Napier Thesiger, who acted as viceroy from 1916–1921.
165 Sindh: located in modern-day southeastern Pakistan.
166 Dubash advocated strongly for conferring the title of "Princess of Hindoostan" on the eldest British royal princess throughout his volume of poetry. Indeed, he includes a poem entitled "The Princess of Hindoostan (A 'Bashet)" which begins: "O, give us the Princess Royal. India's is the claim, – / The Princess of Hindoostan henceforward be her name. For just as the eldest Prince is given to men o' Wales, / So India for such a recognition now bewails."
167 Dubash seems to call for Indian representation in the British parliament, a rather bold extension of the calls of other Indian politicians for limited self-government and representation in the governance of India.

>   Surprised I am that they were given not
>   Ere long without being asked for, as they are just.
>   Mother Hind:
>   So will Thy sons in England be surprised,
>   But this is so because our Press is gagged.
>   So, you know not in England the haps of Hind.
>   Britannia:
>   Let us now hope that Indians' needs at once
>   Shall answered be, so that, th' Empire British
>   Be stronger and consolidated well.
>   Of grievances there be not the slightest smell.
>   BEGUN.

Śrî Ânanda Āchārya

Śrî Ânanda Āchārya (1881–1945) was born in Bengal to a prosperous Brahmin family. As a young man, he turned to spirituality. He left India in 1912 for a tour of Europe, where he promoted his beliefs for several years in England before eventually settling in Norway. Āchārya's poetry, including that from his later collections such as *Arctic Swallows* (1926) and *Girirani* (1926), reflects his self-identification as a spiritual leader. His vision of India in the following poem is one which promotes a conviction in India's supposedly innate spirituality.

Snow-birds (London: 1919)[168]

LXXXII. Ode on the Rishis, the Dārsanikas, and the Sannyāsins of India[169]

They have lit the this lamp of worship on the altar of our human heart,
To illumine paths for all mankind through the endless night of time unborn.
The ancient peace of heaven-crown'd hills those guardians of the hallowed flame have borne.
To every home where unsophisticated love of man for man still dwells enshrined;
Full of fragrance of the dark-dispelling dawn and silent eve, their message do the mystic seas proclaim,
From dreams of shadows to awaken nations and turn their hearts unto the God within.
The lives of lesser beings ebb and flow, their self-appointed destiny to fulfil;
The Rishis' souls, like never-setting suns, on all that lives shed peace and truth and loving benediction

---

168 Śrî Ânanda Āchārya, *Snow-birds* (London: Macmillan & Co., 1919).
169 *Rishis*: divinely inspired sages. *Dārsanikas*: seers, the enlightened. *Sannyasins*: mendicants or ascetics.

Over the threshold of Becoming they have seen the advent and the going-forth of Life,
The Why, the Whence and Whither have they known of souls ensheathed in vestments of decay;
But wisely are these things unutterable unuttered still. Each whispers unto each:
"Nay, let the heaven and earth upholding pillars be concealed – from curious gaze for ever be concealed!"
To move the world they live, the world forgetting – the world renouncing to redeem the world;
Starlike they dwell, each pilgrim guiding who sunward climbs the hill; waiting, foreknowing, with patience strong as faith, till all existences, all lives, all beings, the highest and the lowest, attain their joyous freedom, peace perpetual, made one with Bliss Supreme – Brahman, The True.

Appendices

Indian Poets on their Poetry

"Preface" by Behramji Merwanji Malabari, from *The Indian Muse in English Garb* (Bombay: 1876)[1]

Preface

The writer of these lines commenced the study of English, about eleven years ago, under very trying circumstances – want of means and of clever, conscientious teachers. With the latter difficulty, he struggled on for about two years and a half; and then with almost a self-acquired knowledge of the elements, joined the Surat Mission School, under the superintendence of the late Rev. William Dixon, a very worthy gentleman from Belfast, and a scholar of brilliant promise.[2] It was here, that some time after, the author began to attract notice by his predilection for English literature. Though he belonged to a lower class, special arrangements were made for him to join his seniors, whenever a lecture on Shakespeare was expected; and as a return for the concession he was required to explain the more difficult lines to those who could not follow the lecturer. It was very flattering, indeed, to an Indian of fourteen summers, to interpret lines of the Myriad-minded to men double his age; but he suspects his pupils spared the poor boy any very searching tests; or that, perhaps Heaven had spared those gentlemen the inconvenience of a critical or appreciative taste.

After a course of two years and six months here, the author was found qualified to present himself at the University Entrance Examination. And here ceased all the systematic education of which he can boast. His pride too was effectually humbled at this stage. Three times he failed at the Examination; and scraped through it the fourth time by the barest chance. The reason, though not too far to seek, need not be disclosed here, as it hardly interests the readers.

In his own way, however, the author was not idle all this while. He has devoured, he believes, more poetry in one year than he could digest in five. Many of the British poets, Shakespeare, Byron, Shelley, Burns, Wordsworth, Keats and Campbell in particular, have long become his household gods. He worships them with a strong, passionate heart-homage, and derives the chief happiness of life from them. Such a taste could not long remain without its effects. At eighteen he felt an irresistible desire to make verses. Acting upon the impulse, he multiplied lines upon lines, till in 1872, they grew to nearly five thousand. These lines

---

1 Behramji Merwanji Malabari, *The Indian Muse in English Garb* (Bombay: "Reporters" Press by Merwanjee Nowrojee Daboo, 1876).
2 Reverend William Dixon (d. 1871): served as headmaster of the Surat Mission School in the modern-day state of Gujarat.

were much liked by several competent judges, among the earliest of them, the Hon. Sorabji Shapurji Bengali, Rev. J. V. S. Taylor, Messer. Mansukhram Suryaram, Ranchhodbhai Udairam, and last but most, by the late Dr. Wilson;[3] and mainly through the exertions of this good and great man, two successive editions were taken in a short time. This book was written in a pure Gujaráti, Gujaráti racy of the soil – a feat attempted by few and achieved by fewer Parsis. The Doctor was charmed with its success; and in a moment of generous pride, asked the author why he could not present H. R. H. the Prince of Wales,[4] on the happy occasion of his visit to Bombay, with a few English verses. The idea took, and in a few weeks about six hundred lines were submitted to Dr. Wilson, who spoke very kindly of them, and held out high hopes of seeing them accepted by the illustrious Visitor.

Time wore on; and the Bombayites at last set their anxious eyes on their future Emperor. But in the midst of the general rejoicings that followed, not a few hearts were overcast with deep anxiety. Dr. Wilson, their venerated friend, was relapsing into a state of exhaustion, from which he had but lately rallied. In a few days, Bombay lost its oldest and best friend – Dr. Wilson died, and with him died the author's hopes of winning the smiles of Royalty! He however remained loyal to his friend's advice, and respectfully applied to the Prince, for permission to present the verses to him. But H. R. H. 'regretted that he was unable to break through the rule he had made of never giving any special permission for the dedication to him, of works, with the authors of which he was not personally acquainted.' Poor ill-starred verses! The timid offspring of a hopeful muse! To be thus treated by him for whom they were so joyously hastened into existence! But the author took heart of grace; and set about thinking what was the next best thing to do. He heard that Miss Carpenter, the zealous advocate of female education in India was then in Bombay. To apply to her for permission, and to obtain it readily, was the work of a few hours. Such is the history of 'The Indian Muse' and its Indian author. It is more than nine months since then, and the lines have, during the interval, grown almost threefold. The merit of the work is as modest as its scope is limited. It can claim little more than a passing interest. This much, the author flatters himself, he can count upon from his own countrymen: in what light the Englishman takes it, he cannot tell. To an observant mind it can not be a secret that English, which bids fair, at no distant date, to become a world language, has so far identified herself with our dearest interests, that we not only speak and write through her medium: we have grown almost to thinking in English. Persian and Sanskrit are studied for pleasure or for fame; but the one is too light and the other too heavy for this utilitarian age.

It is English that is becoming the current language of India – the soft insinuating English – rich in her song and her science and her philosophy – the mother and moulder of the divinest human thoughts! We resort to her not only from the selfish political point of view, but from the social and intellectual point. We have schools and colleges enough to rear the rising generation of all Asia; and week by week, the English have been sending us the freshest 'thought-crystals' of the West, in the form of books and reviews and pamphlets. Surely, then, it is no fault of ours if we turn these blessings to some account! It is in this

---

3 Sorabji Shapurji Bengali (1831–1893): active social reformer who published a number of Gujarati periodicals. Reverend J. V. S. Taylor (d. 1881): English missionary in Gujarat. Mansukhram Suryaram (1840–1907) and Ranchhodbahi Udairam: Gujarati-language playwrights. Horace Hayman Wilson (1786–1860): English Orientalist scholar.
4 H. R. H.: His Royal Highness.

spirit that the author would have his verses viewed by the Englishman: everything else he would leave to his candour.

While the lines were in the compositor's hands, the author was advised to avoid all obscurity attending the metrical compositions of a foreigner. He has, therefore, scattered a few explanatory and other notes here and there, very hastily jotted, for which he craves the reader's indulgence. Though aware of the necessity of an Englishman to examine the proof-sheets, the author has even that satisfaction denied him. Perhaps it is for the best; for the reader will thus be able to see the lines in their beauties and their blemishes.

The author owes one more apology to his readers. For reasons, which it were an insult to them to offer here, he had to be his own scribe and proof-reader. It can be easily imagined how glibly the sheets were run over, and how in consequence, some errors in spelling, overlooked…

"Prefaces" and "Appendix" by Hamid Ali Khan, from *A Farewell to London: The Story of the Slave and the Nose-Ring* (London: 1885, 2nd ed.)[5]

Preface to the First Edition

To my friends and acquaintances, for whose entertainment the following "prosaic rhymes" have been strung together in such "admired disorder," I owe a word of apology. Heaven forbid that I should be so presumptuous and "wicked" as to put forth my hand to corrupt the purity of English verse. I only hope that my friends will not infer from the fact of my presenting them with these verses – if such they may be called – in printed form, that I attach the slightest merit to them, or that I think have successfully steered clear of the formidable rocks and shoals, which shipwreck many a novice sailing over the sea of poetry. In fact, I had no intention at first of having these lines put in type; and am only prevailed upon to do so on the ground that my friends will have greater facility in perusal, and that the verses themselves will have a better chance of remaining with them as a memento of my feelings. Except among my numerous friends, I do not desire to circulate them. Should they, however, fall into the hands of any reader who is a stranger to me, I hope that they will receive generous and courteous treatment. The gentle reader will, I feel sure, pardon one who, like myself, has been led by a certain amount of capacity for composing in his own mother tongue, to wish his friends good-bye in English "rhyming prose." I can fancy one who reads these lines indulging in a smile and not a frown.

[…]

Though it be somewhat out of place, I cannot conclude without expressing my heartfelt and deep gratitude for the kindness, courtesy, and hospitality I have received from English friends during my sojourn in this, to me, strange land.

---

5   Hamid Ali Khan, *A Farewell to London: The Story of the Slave and the Nose-Ring*, 2nd ed. (London: W. Whiteley, 1885).

On my return, I shall carry home with me many lively recollections, and a deep and inexpressible sense of gratitude towards those with whom I have come in contact, and of respect and honour for the English race in general, infinitely exceeding that which I felt when I first landed in England.

Preface to the Second Edition

The liberal reception accorded to the First Edition of my "Farewell to London" has far exceeded my most sanguine expectations. Though fully conscious of the kindly sentiments and profound regards my friends entertain towards me, I must frankly admit that I had no adequate notion of the extent of my popularity before the publication of the poem. The only return I can make for this act of kindness, this unmistakable token of their appreciation of my cordial and friendly feelings, is, to adopt for a moment the ideas of a Persian poet with some qualification, the assurance that my esteem and affection and gratitude have increased in proportion, and shall continue to grow, as time will wear on, so long as I breathe. Meanwhile I take this opportunity of expressing my satisfaction at the circumstance, brought to my notice, that a few readers with whom I have not the pleasure and honour of a personal acquaintance, but into whose hands my poem fell, have notified their approbation of my maiden and (I must add, without assuming an air of humility,) worthless production.

In these circumstances I may be pardoned for my desire, which I hope will meet with indulgence, of leaving behind me with my friends a revised, and, so far as versification is concerned, an improved edition of my "Farewell," instead of the one bristling with all sorts of mistakes and errors. And here it must be candidly acknowledged that for these unfortunate faults and blunders I, and I alone, am responsible. I make this voluntary confession, lest my friends who were kind enough to give me some assistance, and whose names I have mentioned in my preface to the First Edition, may be held my accessories, if I may be permitted to indulge for a moment in legal phraseology, in a crime in which I did not seek the help of an accomplice, and which I committed with absolute impunity, receiving from some lenient judges, in place of punishment, an acquittal which coincided with the verdict of the public in possession of the evidence adverse to a criminal like myself, who was the recipient of unexpected congratulations and eulogies. To drop the metaphor, it is not my intention to impose upon my friends and acquaintances the unpleasant task of comparing the old with the new edition, and of discovering the improvements I have effected in the latter. I, therefore, approach them with something new for their amusement. I have added an Indian story, for the particulars of which I am indebted to a friend. At the moment of hearing the tale, I conceived the idea of clothing it in an English poetic garb, and in order to ascertain whether, and how far, it would be interesting to my English readers, I narrated it before more than one English friend. Without a single exception the experiment proved successful; and extremely satisfied with the result, I earnestly set to work. To my great discouragement, at first I found that I had been mistaken in my estimate of the ticklish difficulties that obstructed my way to the rendering of the story. With perseverance and patience I broke down, one by one, the strong barriers which "lifted their awful form," and I succeeded, I think, after repeated failures, in my attempts at rescuing the description of the custom of wearing the nose-ring from all manner of technicality. I believe that the reader, destitute of any previous knowledge of what may be termed "the wearing a hole in the nose," will be able to understand it, as given by me, without the least exertion of his faculties, and thus to relish the whole anecdote which is, as is evident, dependent for its very existence, to say nothing of its diversion and humour, upon that immemorial, reigning, queer, and (I cannot help adding) absurd custom. Nevertheless, the truth must be told. I can by no means persuade myself to believe that my somewhat difficult task has been performed in a manner worthy of the important nature of the original. If I have unconsciously offended again English idiom, or used an inappropriate word, or inaccurate expression, or written an intolerably bad line – for these and similar shortcomings I trust to the generosity and forgiveness of my English readers. If I have failed, here and there, to give such literal translation as my Indian readers, familiar with the tale, might have desired, I confidently appeal to their courtesy and forbearance.

And here let me express a hope that some of my young and rising countrymen, resident in India or England, who may have an extensive command over the English tongue, a wide and lofty range of knowledge, a clear and keen perception, a soul burning with poetic fire, and an imagination soaring "above the Aonian Mount" will not laugh, with scorn, at my humble, slight, and poor toils in the field of poetry, when they bear in mind that my position is fraught with all those disadvantages and obstacles, and perils, that impede the path of one who leads the way.

I deeply regret to add that owing to pressure of work, and absence of books of reference, my intention of enlarging my essays on the poetry of the Urdoo language, published in the *Journal of the National Indian Association*, in the course of the year 1883, into a book, with a short account of the lives of our leading poets, yet remains an unaccomplished fact. Time and circumstances permitting, I hope to be able to execute that important and laborious task on my return to India.

I deem it necessary to state that the word "slave," which so frequently occurs in the tale is not to be taken in its popular sense. A great deal of misconception exists as regards the term as it is employed in England, and its interpretation in our country. It is rather unfortunate that the English tongue does not supply us with a word which may signify our exact meaning. We understand by "slave" the one whom we are bound to afford the necessaries of life – to feed him and clothe him – to provide for his marriage, to emancipate him, when he chooses, to take every possible care of him, to treat him with kindness, which often ripens into affection, and in a word, to regard him, at all events in a certain sense, as part and parcel of the family. And, perhaps, the sense of our duty is keener, if the slave belong to the weaker sex. Our slaves, in their turn, are warmly attached to us, the first and foremost to sacrifice their lives, in moments of peril, to save ours, and even to die for the protection of our property – these are some of the innumerable and elevated qualities of our bondsmen, which reflect not a little credit upon them, and serve to prove the kind and generous character of the treatment they, as a rule, receive at our hands. I do not purpose to write an essay upon our mode of dealing with them. Such an account would not only be foreign to the purpose, but entirely useless, at all events, on this occasion; as slavery does not *now* exist in India. I have, however, considered it proper to make the foregoing remarks in order to give – as I have said above – a correct and accurate idea of the meaning in which I have used the word "slave."

[…]

Appendix

The following is taken from my "Indian Poetry," which appeared in the course of the year 1883, in the *Journal of the National Indian Association*.[6] Explaining as it does, the character and construction of a Persian form of verse, which is also employed in the *Urdoo* language, and called *Mokhammas* or *Tazmeen*, I reproduce it, with such modifications and alterations as seem called for by the present occasion. The Persian verse is a stanza consisting of five lines, as its first name indicates. The last two lines are generally borrowed from some poet; and the preceding three are prefixed to them by another. All the five lines, or the first four only, rhyme together according as the borrowed couplet is, or is not, a rhyming couplet. The third is phrased *Misra agirha*, and may be expressed in English as a "connecting line;" as this it is, that unites the two foregoing with the two following (borrowed) lines. They are all chained together by one link of meaning. I need not go deeper into the details of the verse, as it might probably lead to confusion and perplexity. Suffice it to say that the repetition of a certain rhyme, in one and the same stanza, is not sanctioned by competent authorities. The couplet given below in italics has been extracted from Pope's "Rape of the Lock," Canto II., and with three lines of mine prefixed serves as an instance of the form of composition we are considering.

It runs as follows: –

> Parted for ever, to enjoy no more
> Her sweet companionship – what anguish sore!
> I mind me in those happy days of yore,
> *On her white breast a sparkling cross she wore,*
> *Which Jews might kiss and Infidels adore.*

It is hardly necessary to note that the foregoing couplet of Pope's being a rhyming one, the above verse has a monorhyme throughout; whereas in the following stanzas the first four lines only rhyme, as each set of couplets borrowed from Goldsmith's ballad "The Hermit," is a non-rhyming one –

> Oh! Monarch of the this lovely vale,
> Most noble, with long vigils pale;
> Save, leave me not to mourn and wail,
> *Turn, gentle hermit of the dale*
> *And guide my lonely way;*
> To where yon fountain tells the tale
> Of things untold with which each gale,
> Sweet, soft, and mystic floods the dale,
> *To where yon taper cheers the vale*
> *Wish hospitable ray.*

Let me pause to explain that where the sense of the first two lines runs into the succeeding two, as is the case in these lines of Goldsmith's, it is somewhat hard to separate the four lines and yet to connect them by a thread of meaning and signification. The following is best with the difficulty just mentioned: –

> Erst was I in abundance bred,
> Nought lacked I then of goodlihead;

---

6 Khan's essay appeared in two successive issues (May 1883 and June 1883).

> But ah! those happy days are fled,
> *For here forlorn and lost I tread,*
> *With fainting steps and slow.*
> Where desert-regions lone and dread,
> Whence e'en the beasts for fear are fled,
> Where the sun strikes the wand'rer dead.
> *Where wilds immeasurably spread,*
> *Seem lenth'ning as I go.*

Far lower down in the same piece, Goldsmith's lines are thus "tazmeened": –

> Full many a year I've wander'd, bound
> To seek if love be on earth's round,
> At last the world gave back the sound,
> *On earth unseen, or only found*
> *To warm the turtle's nest.*

> Heiress to villages and farms,
> At home I lived, nor knew alarms,
> My father kept me from all harms;
> *To win me from his tender arms,*
> *Unnumber'd suitors came.*

"Translator's Epilogue" by Romesh Chunder Dutt, from *Maha-Bharata: Epic of the Bharatas, Condensed into English Verse* (London: 1898) [7]

Translator's Epilogue

Ancient India, like ancient Greece, boasts of two great Epics. One of them, the *Maha-bharata*, relates to a great war in which all the warlike races of Northern India took a share, and may therefore be compared to the Iliad. The other, the *Ramayana*, relates mainly to the adventures of its hero, banished from his country and wandering for long years in the wildernesses of Southern India, and may therefore be compared to the Odyssey. It is the first of these two Epics, the Iliad of Ancient India, which is the subject of tile foregoing pages.

The great war which is the subject of this Epic is believed to have been fought in the thirteenth or fourteenth century before Christ. For generations and centuries after the war its main incidents must have been sung by bards and minstrels in the courts of Northern India. The war thus became the centre of a cycle of legends, songs, and poems in ancient India, even as Charlemagne and Arthur became the centres of legends in mediæval Europe. And then, probably under the direction of some enlightened king, the vast mass of legends and poetry, accumulated during centuries, was cast in a narrative form and formed the Epic of the Great Bharata nation, and therefore called the *Maha-bharata*. The real facts of

---

7 Romesh Chunder Dutt, *Maha-Bharata: Epic of the Bharatas, Condensed into English Verse*, 2nd ed. (London: J. M. Dent and Co., 1899).

the war had been obliterated by age, legendary heroes had become the principal actors, and, as is invariably the case in India, the thread of a high moral purpose, of the triumph of virtue and the subjugation of vice, was woven into the fabric of the great Epic.

We should have been thankful if this Epic, as it was thus originally put together some centuries before the Christian era, had been preserved to us. But this was not to be. The Epic became so popular that it went on growing with the growth of centuries. Every generation of poets had something to add; every distant nation in Northern India was anxious to interpolate some account of its deeds in the old record of the international war; every preacher of a new creed desired to have in the old Epic some sanction for the new truths he inculcated. Passages from legal and moral codes were incorporated in the work which appealed to the nation much more effectively than dry codes; and rules about the different castes and about the different stages of the human life were included for the same purpose. All the floating mass of tales, traditions, legends, and myths, for which ancient India was famous, found a shelter under the expanding wings of this wonderful Epic; and as Krishna-worship became the prevailing religion of India after the decay of Buddhism, the old Epic caught the complexion of the times, and Krishna-cult is its dominating religious idea in its present shape.[8] It is thus that the work went on growing for a thousand years after it was first compiled and put together in the form of an Epic; until the crystal rill of the Epic itself was all but lost in an unending morass of religious and didactic episodes, legends, tales, and traditions.

When the mischief had been done, and the Epic had nearly assumed its present proportions, a few centuries after Christ according to the late Dr. Bühler,[9] an attempt was made to prevent the further expansion of the work. The contents of the Epic were described in some prefatory verses, and the number of couplets in each Book was stated. The total number of couplets, according to this metrical preface, is about eighty-five thousand. But the limit so fixed has been exceeded in still later centuries; further additions and interpolations have been made; and the Epic as printed and published in Calcutta in this century contains over ninety thousand couplets, excluding the Supplement about the Race of Hari.[10]

The modern reader will now understand the reason why this great Epic – the greatest work of imagination that Asia has produced – has never yet been put before the European reader in a readable form. A poem of ninety thousand couplets, about seven times the size of the Iliad and the Odyssey put together, is more than what the average reader can stand; and the heterogeneous nature of its contents does not add to the interest of the work. If the religious works of Hooker and Jeremy Taylor, the philosophy of Hobbes and Locke, the commentaries of Blackstone and the ballads of Percy, together with the

---

8 Lord Krishna: avatar of the Hindu god Vishnu. Krishna figures as a central character in the *Mahabharata*, particularly in the *Bhagavad Gita*, the philosophical treatise structured in the form of a dialogue between Krishna and Arjuna on the nature of duty and included as part of the *Mahabharata*.
9 Johann Georg Bühler (1837–1898): German-born Orientalist scholar.
10 The Race of Hari, or *Harivamsa*, describes the creation of the universe; details the life and adventures of the Hindu god, Lord Krishna, a prominent character in the "main" narrative of the *Mahabharata*; and ends with a description of future ages. This text of over 16,000 couplets was seen as a supplement to the authoritative Sanskrit *Mahabharata*.

tractarian writings of Newman, Keble, and Pusey,[11] were all thrown into blank verse and incorporated with the *Paradise Lost*, the reader would scarcely be much to blame if he failed to appreciate that delectable compound. A complete translation of the *Maha-bharata* therefore into English verse is neither possible nor desirable, but portions of it have now and then been placed before English readers by distinguished writers. Dean Milman's graceful rendering of the story of Nala and Damayanti[12] is still read and appreciated by a select circle of readers; and Sir Edwin Arnold's beautiful translation of the concluding books of the Epic is familiar to a larger circle of Englishmen.[13] A complete translation of the Epic into English prose has also been published in India, and is useful to Sanscrit scholars for the purpose of reference.

But although the old Epic had thus been spoilt by unlimited expansion, yet nevertheless the leading incidents and characters of the real Epic are still discernible, uninjured by the mass of foreign substance in which they are embedded – even like those immortal marble figures which have been recovered from the ruins of an ancient world, and now beautify the museums of modern Europe. For years past I have thought that it was perhaps not impossible to exhume this buried Epic from the superincumbent mass of episodical matter, and to restore it to the modern world. For years past I have felt a longing to undertake this work, but the task was by no means an easy one. Leaving out all episodical matter, the leading narrative of the Epic forms about one-fourth of the work; and a complete translation even of this leading story would be unreadable, both from its length and its prolixness. On the other hand, to condense the story into shorter limits would be, not to make a translation, but virtually to write a new poem; and that was not what I desired to undertake, nor what I was competent to perform.

There seemed to me only one way out of this difficulty. The main incidents of the Epic are narrated in the original work in passages which are neither diffuse nor unduly prolix,

---

11   Richard Hooker (1554–1600) and Jeremy Taylor (1613–1667): Anglican clergymen and theologians. Thomas Hobbes (1588–1679): English political philosopher and author of *Leviathan*. John Locke (1632–1704): English political philosopher and an influential Enlightenment thinker known for his *An Essay Concerning Human Understanding*. Sir William Blackstone (1723–1780): English jurist, judge, educator, and legal commentator known for his *Commentaries on the Laws of England*. Thomas Percy (1729–1811): English clergyman and editor of *Reliques of Ancient English Poetry*, a collection of ballads and popular songs. John Henry Newman (1801–1890): clergyman in the Church of England and a leader in the Oxford Movement (also known as the Tractarian Movement) before converting to Roman Catholicism and eventually being appointed Cardinal. John Keble (1792–1866): English clergyman, a leader in the Oxford Movement and a poet. Edward Pusey (1800–1882): English clergyman and leader in the Oxford Movement.

12   Henry Hart Milman (1791–1868): dramatist and historian, known for his monograph *History of the Jews* (1829) and his annotation of Edward Gibbon's *The History of the Decline and Fall of the Roman Empire* (1838). An ecclesiastic, he was appointed the Dean of St. Paul's in 1849. Milman's *Nala and Damayanti and other poems* (1835) includes a translation of the love story of Nala and Damayanti, which appears as a digression within the authoritative Sanskrit telling of the *Mahabharata*.

13   Sir Edwin Arnold (1832–1904): English journalist and poet. His works include *The Light of Asia* (1879), an epic poem about the life and philosophy of the Buddha; *Pearls of the Faith* (1883) on Islam; and *The Light of the World* (1891) on Christianity. His translation of the *Bhagavad Gita*, a philosophical tract included within the authoritative Sanskrit telling of the *Mahabharata*, was published in 1885.

and which are interspersed in the leading narrative of the Epic, as that narrative itself is interspersed in the midst of more lengthy episodes. The more carefully I examined the arrangement, the more clearly it appeared to me that these main incidents of the Epic would bear a full and unabridged translation into English verse; and that these translations, linked together by short connecting notes, would virtually present the entire story of the Epic to the modern reader in a form and within limits which might be acceptable. It would be, no doubt, a condensed version of the original Epic, but the condensation would be effected, not by the translator telling a short story in his own language, but by linking together those passages of the original which describe the main and striking incidents, and thus telling the main story as told in the original work. The advantage of this arrangement is that, in the passages presented to the reader, it is the poet who speaks to him, not the translator. Though vast portions of the original are skipped over, those which are presented are the portions which narrate the main incidents of the Epic, and they describe those incidents as told by the poet himself.

This is the plan I have generally adopted in the present work. Except in the three books which describe the actual war (Books viii., ix., and x.), the other nine books of this translation are complete translations of selected passages of the original work. I have not attempted to condense these passages nor to expand them; I have endeavoured to put them before the English reader as they have been told by the poet in Sanscrit. Occasionally, but rarely, a few redundant couplets have been left out, or a long list of proper names or obscure allusions has been shortened; and in one place only, at the beginning of the Fifth Book, I have added twelve couplets of my own to explain the circumstances under which the story of Savitri[14] is told. Generally, therefore, the translation may be accepted as an unabridged, though necessarily a free translation of the passages describing the main incidents of the Epic.

From this method I have been compelled to depart, much against my wish, in the three books describing the actual war. No translation of an Epic relating to a great war can be acceptable which does not narrate the main events of the war. The war of the *Maha-bharata* was a series of eighteen battles, fought on eighteen consecutive days, and I felt it necessary to present the reader with an account of each day's work. In order to do so, I have been compelled to condense, and not merely to translate selected passages. For the transactions of the war, unlike the other incidents of the Epic, have been narrated in the original with almost inconceivable prolixity and endless repetition; and the process of condensation in these three books has therefore been severe and thorough. But, nevertheless, even in these books I have endeavoured to preserve the character and the spirit of the original. Not only are the incidents narrated in the same order as in the original, but they are told in the style of the poet as far as possible. Even the similes and metaphors and figures of speech are all or mostly adopted from the original; the translator has not ventured either to adopt his own distinct style of narration, or to improve on the style of the original with his own decorations.

Such is the scheme I have adopted in presenting an Epic of ninety thousand Sanscrit couplets in about two thousand English couplets.

---

14 The tale of Savitri, who was cast as an ancient model of ideal Indian womanhood during the nineteenth century by Indian nationalists, is included as a digression within the authoritative Sanskrit telling of the epic poem, the *Mahabharata*.

The excellent and deservedly popular prose translation of the Odyssey of Homer by Messrs. Butcher and Lang[15] often led me to think that perhaps a prose translation of these selected passages from the *Maha-bharata* might be more acceptable to the modern reader. But a more serious consideration of the question dispelled that idea. Homer has an interest for the European reader which the *Maha-bharata* cannot lay claim to; as the father of European poetry he has a claim on the veneration of modern Europe which an Indian poet can never pretend to. To thousands of European readers Homer is familiar in the original, to hundreds of thousands he is known in various translations in various modern languages. What Homer actually wrote, a numerous class of students in Europe wish to know; and a literal prose translation therefore is welcome, after the great Epic has been so often translated in verse. The case is very different with the *Maha-bharata*, practically unknown to European readers. And the translators of Homer themselves gracefully acknowledge, "We have tried to transfer, not all the truth about the poem, but the historical truth into English. In this process Homer must lose at least half his charm, his bright and equable speed, the musical current of that narrative, which, like the river of Egypt, flows from an undiscoverable source, and mirrors the temples and the palaces of unforgotten gods and kings. Without the music of verse, only a half truth about Homer can be told."

Another earnest worker of the present day, who is endeavouring to interpret to modern Englishmen the thoughts and sentiments and poetry of their Anglo-Saxon ancestors, has emphatically declared that "of all possible translations of poetry, a merely prose translation is the most inaccurate." "Prose," says Mr. Stopford Brooke, further on, "no more represents poetry than architecture does music. Translations of poetry are never much good, but at least they should always endeavour to have the musical movement of poetry, and to obey the laws of the verse they translate."[16]

This appears to me to be a very sound maxim. And one of my greatest difficulties in the task I have undertaken has been to try and preserve something of the "musical movement" of the sonorous Sanscrit poetry in the English translation. Much of tile Sanscrit Epic is written in the well-known *Sloka* metre of sixteen syllables in each line,[17] and I endeavoured to choose some English metre which is familiar to the English ear, and which would reproduce to some extent the rhythm, the majesty, and the long and measured sweep of the Sanscrit verse. It was necessary to adopt such a metre in order to transfer something of the truth about the *Maha-bharata* into English, for without such reproduction or imitation of the musical movement of the original very much less than a half truth is told. My kind friend Mr. Edmund Russell,[18] impelled by that enthusiasm for Indian poetry and Indian art which is a part of him, rendered me valuable help and assistance in this matter, and I gratefully acknowledge the benefit I have derived from his advice and suggestions. After considerable trouble and anxiety, and after rendering several books in different English

---

15   S. H. Butcher and A. Lang, trans., *The Odyssey of Homer, done into English Prose by S. H. Butcher and A. Lang* (London: Macmillan and Co. Ltd, 1887).
16   Stopford Brooke, *The History of Early English Literature, being the history of English poetry from its beginnings to the ascension of King Alfred*, 2 vols (London: Macmillan, 1892), ix. Stopford Brooke (1832–1916): clergyman, literary critic, and poet.
17   *Sloka*: Sanskrit meter composed of four feet, each of which must have eight syllables, with two feet, or sixteen syllables, in each line. Couplets are marked by a caesura so that each line typically falls into two four-syllable halves.
18   Edmund Russell: American actor and enthusiastic connoisseur of Indian theater and poetry.

metres, I felt convinced that the one finally adopted was a nearer approach to the Sanscrit *Sloka* than any other familiar English metre known to me.

I have recited a verse in this English metre and a *Sloka* in presence of listeners who have a better ear for music than myself, and they have marked the close resemblance. I quote a few lines from the Sanscrit showing varieties of the *Sloka* metre, and comparing them with the scheme of the English metre selected.

> Ēshă Kūntīshŭtāh srīmān | ēshă mādhyămā Pāndāvāh
> Ēshă pūtrō Măhēndrāsyă | Kŭrūnām ēshă rākshĭtā
> — Maha-bharata, i. 5357.

> Yēt Ĭ doŭbt nŏt thrōugh the āgĕs | ōne ĭncrēasĭng pūrpŏse rūns
> Ănd the thōughts ŏf mēn ăre wīdenĕd | wīth the prōcĕss ōf thĕ sūns
> — Locksley Hall.

> Mālānchă sămŭpādāyă | kānchănīm sămălāmkrĭtām
> Ăvătīrnā tătō rāngăm | Drāupădī Bhărătārshăbhaă
> — Maha-bharata, i. 6974.

> Vīsiŏns ŏf the dāys dĕpārtĕd | shădŏwy phāntŏms fīlled my brāin;
> Thōse who līve ĭn hĭstŏry ōnly | sēemed to wālk the eārth ăgāin
> — Belfry of Bruges.

> Ăsūryăm ĭvă sūryēnā | nīrvātăm ĭvă vāyŭnā
> Bhāsĭtām hlādĭtānchāivă | Krīshnēnēdām sădō hĭ năh
> — Maha-bharata, ii. 1334.

> Quāint ōld tōwn ŏf toīl ănd trāffĭc | quāint ōld tōwn ŏf ārt ănd sōng,
> Mēmoriĕs hāunt thy pōintĕd gāblĕs, | līke the rōōks that roūnd thee thrōng.
> — Nüremberg.

> Hā Pāndō hā măhārājā | kvāsĭ kīm sămŭpēkshăsē
> Pūtrān vĭvāsyătāh sādhūn | ărĭbhīr dyūtănīrjĭtān
> — Maha-bharata, ii. 2610.

> Ĭn hĕr eār hĕ whīspĕrs gāily, | Ĭf my heārt by sīgns căn tēll,
> Māidĕn Ī hăve wātched thĕe dāily, | Ănd I thīnk thŏu lŏv'st mĕ wēll
> — Lord of Burleigh.

It would be too much to assume that even with the help of this similarity in metres, I have been able to transfer into my English that sweep and majesty of verse which is the charm of Sanscrit, and which often sustains and elevates the simplest narration and the plainest ideas. Without the support of those sustaining wings, my poor narration must often plod through the dust; and I can only ask for the indulgence of the reader, which every translator of poetry from a foreign language can with reason ask, if the story as told in the translation is sometimes but a plain, simple, and homely narrative. For any artistic decoration I have neither the inclination nor the necessary qualification. The crisp and ornate style, the quaint expression, the chiselled word, the new-coined phrase, in which modern English poetry is rich, would scarcely suit the translation of an old Epic whose predominating characteristic is its simple and easy flow of narrative. Indeed, the *Maha-bharata* would lose that unadorned simplicity which is its first and foremost feature if the translator ventured to decorate it with the art of the modern day, even if he had been qualified to do so.

For if there is one characteristic feature which distinguishes the *Maha-bharata* (as well as the other Indian Epic, the *Ramayana*) from all later Sanscrit literature, it is the grand simplicity of its narrative, which contrasts with the artificial graces of later Sanscrit poetry. The poetry of Kalidasa,[19] for instance, is ornate and beautiful, and almost scintillates with similes in every verse; the poetry of the *Maha-bharata* is plain and unpolished, and scarcely stoops to a simile or a figure of speech unless the simile comes naturally to the poet. The great deeds of godlike kings sometimes suggest to the poet the mighty deeds of gods; the rushing of warriors suggests the rushing of angry elephants in the echoing jungle; the flight of whistling arrows suggests the flight of sea-birds; the sound and movement of surging crowds suggest the heaving of billows; the erect attitude of a warrior suggests a tall cliff; the beauty of a maiden suggests the soft beauty of the blue lotus. When such comparisons come naturally to the poet, he accepts them and notes them down, but he never seems to go in quest of them, he is never anxious to beautify and decorate. He seems to trust entirely to his grand narrative, to his heroic characters, to his stirring incidents, to hold millions of listeners in perpetual thrall. The majestic and sonorous Sanscrit metre is at his command, and even this he uses, carelessly, and with frequent slips, known as *arsha* to later grammarians. The poet certainly seeks for no art to decorate his tale, he trusts to the lofty chronicle of bygone heroes to enchain the listening mankind.

And what heroes! In the delineation of character the *Maha-bharata* is far above anything which we find in later Sanscrit poetry. Indeed, with much that is fresh and sweet and lovely in later Sanscrit poetry, there is little or no portraiture of character. All heroes are cast much in the same heroic mould; all love-sick heroines suffer in silence and burn with fever, all fools are shrewd and impudent by turns, all knaves are heartless and cruel and suffer in the end. There is not much to distinguish between one warrior and another, between one tender woman and her sister. In the *Maha-bharata* we find just the reverse; each hero has a distinct individuality, a character of his own, clearly discernible from that of other heroes. No work of the imagination that could be named, always excepting the Iliad, is so rich and so true as the *Maha-bharata* in the portraiture of the human character, – not in torment and suffering as in Dante, not under overwhelming passions as in Shakespeare, – but human character in its calm dignity of strength and repose, like those immortal figures in marble which the ancients turned out, and which modern sculptors have vainly sought to reproduce. The old Kuru monarch Dhrita-rashtra, sightless and feeble, but majestic in his ancient grandeur; the noble grandsire Bhishma, "death's subduer" and unconquerable in war; the doughty Drona, venerable priest and vengeful warrior; and the proud and peerless archer Karna – have each a distinct character of his own which can not be mistaken for a moment. The good and royal Yudhishthir, (I omit the final *a* in some long names which occur frequently), the "tiger-waisted" Bhima, and the "helmet-wearing" Arjun are the Agamemnon, the Ajax, and the Achilles of the Indian Epic. The proud and unyielding Duryodhan, and the fierce and

---

19 Kalidas: classical Sanskrit writer who is thought to have lived during the fifth century under the Gupta dynasty. His works include the long lyric poems, *Meghaduta* and *Ritu-samhara*, as well as two epic poems and three plays.

fiery Duhsasan stand out foremost among the wrathful sons of the feeble old Kuru monarch. And Krishna possesses a character higher than that of Ulysses; unmatched in human wisdom, ever striving for righteousness and peace, he is thorough and unrelenting in war when war has begun. And the women of the Indian Epic possess characters as marked as those of the men. The stately and majestic queen Gandhari, the loving and doting mother Pritha, the proud and scornful Draupadi nursing her wrath till her wrongs are fearfully revenged, and the bright and brilliant and sunny Subhadra, – these are distinct images pencilled by the hand of a true master in the realm of creative imagination.

And if the characters of the *Maha-bharata* impress themselves on the reader, the incidents of the Epic are no less striking. Every scene on the shifting stage is a perfect and impressive picture. The tournament of the princes in which Arjun and Karna – the Achilles and Hector of the Indian Epic – first met and each marked the other for his foe; the gorgeous bridal of Draupadi; the equally gorgeous coronation of Yudhishthir and the death of the proud and boisterous Sisupala; the fatal game of dice and the scornful wrath of Draupadi against her insulters; the calm beauty of the forest life of the Pandavs; the cattle-lifting in Matsyaland in which the gallant Arjun threw off his disguise and stood forth as warrior and conqueror; and the Homeric speeches of the warriors in the council of war on the eve of the great contest, – each scene of this venerable old Epic impresses itself on the mind of the hushed and astonished reader. Then follows the war of eighteen days. The first few days are more or less uneventful, and have been condensed in this translation often into a few couplets; but the interest of the reader increases as he approaches the final battle and fall of the grand old fighter Bhishma. Then follows the stirring story of the death of Arjun's gallant boy, and Arjun's fierce revenge, and the death of the priest and warrior, doughty Drona. Last comes the crowning event of the Epic, the final contest between Arjun and Karna, the heroes of the Epic, and the war ends in a midnight slaughter and the death of Duryodhan. The rest of the story is told in this translation in two books describing the funerals of the deceased warriors, and Yudhishthir's horse-sacrifice.

"The poems of Homer," says Mr. Gladstone,[20] "differ from all other known poetry in this, that they constitute in themselves an encyclopædia of life and knowledge; at a time when knowledge, indeed, such as lies beyond the bounds of actual experience, was extremely limited, and when life was singularly fresh, vivid, and expansive." This remark applies with even greater force to the *Maha-bharata*; it is an encyclopædia of the life and knowledge of Ancient India. And it discloses to us an ancient and forgotten world, a proud and noble civilisation which has passed away. Northern India was then parcelled among warlike races living side by side under their warlike kings, speaking the same language, performing the same religious rites and ceremonies, rejoicing in a common literature, rivalling each other in their schools of philosophy and learning as in the arts of peace and civilisation, and forming a confederation of Hindu nations unknown to and unknowing the outside world. What this confederation of nations has done for the cause of human knowledge and human civilisation is a matter of history. Their inquiries into the hidden truths of religion, embalmed in the

---

20 William Ewart Gladstone, *Studies on Homer and the Homeric Age*, 3 vols (Oxford: Oxford University Press, 1858). William Ewart Gladstone (1809–1898): served several terms as Liberal prime minister of Great Britain (1868–1874; 1880–1885; 1886; 1892–1894). His protection of Irish tenants and his support of Irish Home Rule as well as his appointment of Lord Ripon as viceroy of India in 1880 won him the support of Indians. He was also known as a great orator.

ancient *Upanishads*, have never been excelled within the last three thousand years.[21] Their inquiries into philosophy, preserved in the *Sankhya* and the *Vedanta* systems,[22] were the first systems of true philosophy which the world produced. And their great works of imagination, the *Maha-bharata* and the *Ramayana*, will be placed without hesitation by the side of Homer by critics who survey the world's literatures from a lofty standpoint, and judge impartially of the wares turned out by the hand of man in all parts of the globe. It is scarcely necessary to add that the discoveries of the ancient Hindus in science, and specially in mathematics, are the heritage of the modern world; and that the lofty religion of Buddha, proclaimed in India five centuries before Christ, is now the religion of a third of the human race.

For the rest, the people of modern India know how to appreciate their ancient heritage. It is not an exaggeration to state that the two hundred millions of Hindus of the present day cherish in their hearts the story of their ancient Epics. The Hindu scarcely lives, man or woman, high or low, educated or ignorant, whose earliest recollections do not cling round the story and the characters of the great Epics. The almost illiterate oil-manufacturer or confectioner of Bengal spells out some modern translation of the Maha-bharata to while away his leisure hour. The tall and stalwart peasantry of the North-West know of the five Pandav brothers, and of their friend the righteous Krishna. The people of Bombay and Madras cherish with equal ardour the story of the righteous war. And even the traditions and tales interspersed in the Epic, and which spoil the work as an Epic, have themselves a charm and an attraction; and the morals inculcated in these tales sink into the hearts of a naturally religious people, and form the basis of their moral education. Mothers in India know no better theme for imparting wisdom and instruction to their daughters, and elderly men know no richer storehouse for narrating tales to children, than these stories preserved in the Epics. No work in Europe, not Homer in Greece or Virgil in Italy, not Shakespeare or Milton in English-speaking lands, is the *national* property of the nations to the same extent as the Epics of India are of the Hindus. No single work except the Bible has such influence in affording moral instruction in Christian lands as the *Maha-bharata* and the *Ramayana* in India. They have been the cherished heritage of the Hindus for three thousand years; they are to the present day interwoven with the thoughts and beliefs and moral ideas of a nation numbering two hundred millions.

"Preface" by Avadh Behari Lall, from *Behar, and other poems* (Calcutta: 1898)[23]

Preface

[…]

It is necessary for me to say a few words in justification of the fact why I, a Native of India, fully knowing that the English language is already rich with the works of its own native poets, should insist on making compositions in – which, I hope, are at least not encroachments upon – the English language, which is to me at best a foreign tongue?

---

21 *Upanishads*: ancient Hindu religious texts.
22 Sankhya and the Vedanta: two schools of classical Indian philosophy.
23 Avadh Behari Lall, *Behar, and other poems* (Calcutta: Avadh Behari Lall, 1898).

It is this language which has enabled and still enables the Rulers and the Ruled of this vast Country, a Continent in itself, to understand and appreciate each other and appreciate each other and to spread good-will between them; it is this language by which the heterogeneous races of India, having separate dialects of their own, communicate with one another; it is this language, this vehicle of thought, in which the state-education is imparted to us and which has thus laid open to us the vast unexplored treasures of the Literatures and Sciences of the West; and moreover, it is this language in which I have received my scholastic training (though my education is indeed imperfect) and which cannot but be, after my native speech, the best medium for me to express my thoughts to others, especially to those already conversant with this alien tongue of mine.

Besides England, the United States of America, and the Australasian Colonies, where English is the mother-tongue of the present inhabitants, there are now many other countries on the surface of the globe, India among the number, where this foreign tongue of mine passes current – a tongue that has thus ceased to be the monopoly of the Anglo-Saxon race. What harm then, if some of the natives of such other countries, such non-English residents of the Earth, while using the English prose freely in their daily talks and ordinary communications, should dare write English verses also? It would be a bold attempt no doubt, beset with so many obstacles that success would be, at first sight, ordinarily almost despaired of, but the difficulties are such that *true* poets can, with comparative ease, readily surmount. There was a day when the English of the "Yankee" was an object of almost universal contempt with the true-born Briton, but the writings of Irving and Longfellow and many more have long since not only removed his somewhat natural prejudices, but have also evoked merited applause from his jealous countrymen; and so if a Native of India does dare write English verses (provided, of curse, that they really be worth the name), no Englishman should be now ashamed to own them as if they had been composed by one of his own race. There are already among the Natives of this country, some persons whose command over the English language – the English prose, of curse [sic], whether spoken or written – is great – greater than that of even many Englishmen here – and true English critics are sympathizingly glad to own this fact. But, Oh! there exists in some quarters a tendency to despise every English composition of a Native of India, on no other ground than this – that it is un-English in its origin; though at the same time (be it said to the glory of the English race) there are a great number of Englishmen here and abroad who judging unbiasedly, without race-prejudice, are ready to acknowledge any qualifications they may find in the English books composed by the Natives of India, pointing out, if they so chose, the defects in each case. The age – the century – is, I believe, advanced enough for not accepting the eccentric individual opinions of a few uncompromising English critics, as the universal judgment of an upright nation. One thing is certain, *viz.*, that I have attempted, successfully or unsuccessfully English versification, and, be whatever it may, I am resolved to make in future more essays at writing English poems, having a firm faith in my *true* English critics that they will do justice to my humble and sincere aspirations – criticising severely my productions for their short-comings, commending unjealously the merits, if any, which they may find in them, suggesting plainly methods further improvements, shewing unreservedly the true ways to English Poetry, and encouraging me unhesitatingly in every case. I must, however, request one favour of all, *viz.*, that they should examine my verses from a *literary* point of view only; for a Poem is not to be confounded with a complete or comprehensive Philosophical, Religious, or Scientific treatise; Dryden's *Hind and Panther* is still admired as a great religious argumentative poem, though its reasonings are sometimes not much sound.

Trusting that I have presented to my gentle Readers something to beguile an infinitesimally small portion of their leisures, I would now beg to take leave of them; and I have every ray of hope that my critics – whether English or Native – forgiving my faults, will encourage me to appear before them again another time, specially when my labours in the field of Poetry are, from indifferent health and other causes, 'few and far between.'

"Preface" by Roby Datta, from *Echoes from East and West* (Cambridge: 1909)[24]

Preface

The aim of the "Echoes from East and West" is to produce on an English gramophone some of the finest records of Indo-European songs. It is to wake up at a grind the "music of the moon" that slept "in the plain eggs" of that "nightingale enveloped in the mist of ages," the primitive Aryan of Mid-Asia, whose natural and adopted off-spring are scattered over five continents. It is to bring together the voices of some of the Indic, Persic, Hellenic, Italic, Romance, and Teutonic makers of melodies, so that the only notable nestlings here silent are those that chirped through Celtic and Slavonic tongues. It is also to show that a true song floats above race and age and land and may be heard by all. Thanks to the strenuous devotion of eminent scholars, the Muses of Comparative Philology and Comparative Mythology have in recent years lightened up the path of the seeker of poetry and prosody. I should, therefore, invite some far abler man, some future Aryan Palgrave, some soul athirst for Beauty and hungered for Truth, to roam farther and farther afield through literatures and come back with fresher and fresher songs for real lovers of poetry in all English-speaking lands. In the meantime I hope that the public would kindly receive this humble collection of many years, which I have made as representative as possible within the narrow range of my quest. Naturally enough, I have given the greatest prominence to the earlier part as well as the Northern section of English literature, as it is highly interesting to see the beginnings of modern English literature, which is second to no other in the whole history of the world. Again, the selections from other European literatures have been made in proportion to the interest they may excite in us for their direct or indirect bearing on the poetry of this country. Lastly, I have given some prominence to Indic literatures, because of the present intimate connexion between England, which has absorbed the best part of Greek, Italic, Romance, and Teutonic literatures, and India, which has preserved for us the earliest monuments of Aryan culture. I may add that I have ended the volume with "Stray Notes of Mine Own," as they show some of my predilections. Of these poems the one that I care for most is the Sonnet on Milton's "Paradise Lost."

As regards the arrangement of the selected pieces, a few words need be said. I have not thought it fit to present them in the order of the languages, which would give the book

---

24 Roby Datta, *Echoes from East and West* (Cambridge: Galloway and Porter, 1909).

a formidable appearance and would not make the poems really effective. I have, therefore, given them in their chronological order of composition, which, I trust, would be found to be also their psychological and poetically effective order. This order, I need hardly say, was not the order in which I learnt the languages. A few verses, however, taken from my translation of Kalidasa's "Sakuntala and her Keepsake,"[25] have been interspersed through the volume. Again, as regards the method of rendering, I may say that all the pieces down to "To the Muse" exhibit what I call the process of version, that is, rendering the sense of the original in my own manner and in a metrical form something like that of the original; while all the rest show what I call the process of translation, that is, rendering the original in the order of its words and in its exactly equivalent metrical form as far as it is in keeping with the true genius of the English language. In a few cases the process of translation has been more or less that of modernization. The essential thing in these processes, which I have always tried to keep in view, is to fall into the inspiration of the original poet before attempting a rendering. Next, with regard to the prosody, I may say that most of the poems are in recognized English or Anglicised metrical forms, but there are a few poems written in Hexameters, Elegiacs, Alliterative Verse, Assonant Verse, and Unrimed Verse. In translating Classical Lyrical metres, I have given the same number of syllables and the same pauses as the original with an English disposition of accents, with the exception of "The Calm of Nature" from Alcman[26] and "The Crab and the Snake" from a Greek skolion,[27] where I have tried to replace the quantity of the original by the accent in English, as I have done in the case of the Hexameters and Elegiacs. One piece entitled "Baby and Nurse" has been rendered in hexameters, although the original is in a metre full of short syllables. I have introduced rime in translating Classical Sanskrit Quatrains and Pali Quatrains and Sestets, in order to lay stress on the fact that there is a deep rhythmic pause at the end of the second and fourth quarters of the quatrain or the second, fourth and sixth sections of the sestet, and that the uneven quarters or sections are pitched against each other; but I have not applied this principle in translating Vedic triplets, quatrains, quintuplets and sestets, because there the rhythm and sense seem to me almost confined to each line. Lastly, with regard to foreign names, they are to be pronounced under the English laws of accent, with the exception of a few classical names; and I my add that in accordance with Elizabethan practice, names of Greek god and goddesses have been given in their more familiar and more easily pronounced Latin forms – only we should not confound Greek and Roman mythology.

It should be remarked that the main features of the book are variety and diversity from the voint [sic] of view of language, matter, manner, and metre. Poems have been brought together sometimes for comparison, sometimes for contrast, sometimes for showing evolution of thought, overflow of ideas and sentiments from country to country, and so on. To enhance the interest of the reader, I have introduced a few philosophical poems from the East, and a few devotional poems from both East and West. Whatever the opening or a part of a great poem has been given in these pages, it is implied that some knowledge

---

25 Kalidas: classical Sanskrit writer who is thought to have lived during the fifth century under the Gupta dynasty. His works include the long lyric poems, *Meghaduta* and *Ritu-samhara*, as well as two epic poems and three plays.
26 Alcman: ancient Greek poet.
27 *Skolion*: song sung by guests at a banquet in ancient Greece (n. "skolion" *OED*).

of the whole will always be found edifying, because of the side-lights thrown on racial characteristics, which are more or less insular, and on human sentiments, which are bound to be universal. In fact, Life in its insular intensity, and in its universal extensity, and – to go a step further – in its eternal protensity, is the highest goal of study in Art. It is this three-sided Life which Homer and Shakespeare saw mostly, but of which a good deal remains a sealed book to us mortals.

[…]

Cambridge. 28th September, 1908.

British Poets/Critics on Indian Poets

"Introductory Memoir" by Edmund Gosse for Toru Dutt's *Ancient Ballads and Legends of Hindustan* (London: 1882)[28]

Introductory Memoir

If Toru Dutt were alive, she would still be younger than any recognized European writer, and yet her fame, which is already considerable, has been entirely posthumous. Within the brief space of four years which now divides us from the date of her decease, her genius has been revealed to the world under many phases, and has been recognized throughout France and England. Her name, at least, is no longer unfamiliar in the ear of any well-read man or woman. But at the hour of her death she had published but one book, and that book had found but two reviewers in Europe. One of these, M. André Theuriet, the well-known poet and novelist, gave the "Sheaf gleaned in French Fields" adequate praise in the "Revue des Deux Mondes;" but the other, the writer of the present notice, has a melancholy satisfaction in having been a little earlier still in sounding the only note of welcome which reached the dying poetess from England. It was while Professor W. Minto was editor of the "Examiner,"[29] that one day in August, 1876, in the very heart of the dead season for books, I happened to be in the office of that newspaper, and was upbraiding the whole body of publishers for issuing no books worth reviewing. At that moment the postman brought in a thin and sallow packet with a wonderful Indian postmark on it, and containing a most unattractive orange pamphlet of verse, printed at Bhowanipore, and entitled "A Sheaf gleaned in French Fields, by Toru Dutt." This shabby little book of some two hundred pages, without preface or introduction, seemed specially destined by its particular providence to find its way hastily into the waste-paper basket. I remember that Mr. Minto thrust it into my unwilling hands, and said "There! see whether you can't

---

28 Edmund Gosse, "Introductory Memoir," in Toru Dutt, *Ancient Ballads and Legends of Hindustan* (London: K. Paul, Trench & Co., 1882).
29 William Minto (1845–1893): editor of the weekly English periodical, the *Examiner*, during the 1870s.

make something of that." A hopeless volume it seemed, with its queer type, published at Bhowanipore, printed at the Saptahiksambad Press! But when at last I took it out of my pocket, what was my surprise and almost rapture to open at such verse as this: —

> Still barred thy doors! Thy far east glows,
>   The morning wind blows fresh and free
> Should not the hour that wakes the rose
>   Awaken also thee?
>
> All look for thee, Love, Light, and Song,
>   Light in the sky deep red above,
> Song, in the lark of pinions strong,
>   And in my heart, true Love.
>
> Apart we miss our nature's goal,
>   Why strive to cheat our destinies?
> Was not my love made for thy soul?
>   Thy beauty for mine eyes?
>   No longer sleep,
>   Oh, listen now!
>   I wait and weep,
>   But where art thou?

When poetry is as good as this it does not much matter whether Rouveyre prints it upon Whatman paper, or whether it steals to light in blurred type from some press in Bhowanipore.

Toru Dutt was the youngest of the three children of a high-caste Hindu couple in Bengal. Her father, who survives them all, the Baboo Govin Chunder Dutt, is himself distinguished among his countrymen for the width of his views and the vigour of his intelligence. His only son, Abju, died in 1865, at the age of fourteen, and left his two younger sisters to console their parents. Aru, the elder daughter, born in 1854, was eighteen months senior to Toru, the subject of this memoir, who was born in Calcutta on the 4th of March, 1856. With the exception of one year's visit to Bombay, the childhood of these girls was spent in Calcutta, at their father's garden-house. In a poem now printed for the first time, Toru refers to the scene of her earliest memories, the circling wilderness of foliage, the shining tank with the round leaves of the lilies, the murmuring dusk under the vast branches of the central casuarina-tree. Here, in a mystical retirement more irksome to an European in fancy than to an Oriental in reality, the brain of this wonderful child was moulded. She was pure Hindu, full of the typical qualities of her race and blood, and, as the present volume shows us for the first time, preserving to the last her appreciation of the poetic side of her ancient religion, though faith itself in Vishnu and Siva had been cast aside with childish things and been replaced by a purer faith. Her mother fed her imagination with the old songs and legends of their people, stories which it was the last labour of her life to weave into English verse; but it would seem that the marvellous faculties of Toru's mind still slumbered, when, in her thirteenth year, her father decided to take his daughters to Europe to learn English and French. To the end of her days Toru was a better French than English scholar. She loved France best, she knew its literature best, she wrote its language with more perfect elegance. The Dutts arrived in Europe at the close of 1869, and the girls went to school, for the first and last time, at a French pension.

They did not remain there very many months; their father took them to Italy and England with him, and finally they attended for a short time, but with great zeal and application, the lectures for women at Cambridge. In November, 1873, they went back again to Bengal, and the four remaining years of Toru's life were spent in the old garden-house at Calcutta, in a feverish dream of intellectual effort and imaginative production. When we consider what she achieved in these forty-five months of seclusion, it is impossible to wonder that the frail and hectic body succumbed under so excessive a strain.

She brought with her from Europe a store of knowledge that would have sufficed to make an English or French girl seem learned, but which in her case was simply miraculous. Immediately on her return she began to study Sanskrit with the same intense application which she gave to all her work, and mastering the language with extraordinary swiftness, she plunged into its mysterious literature. But she was born to write, and despairing of an audience in her own language, she began to adopt ours as a medium for her thought. Her first essay, published when she was eighteen, was a monograph, in the "Bengal Magazine," on Leconte de Lisle, a writer with whom she had a sympathy which is very easy to comprehend.[30] The austere poet of "La Mort de Valmiki" was, obviously, a figure to whom the poet of "Sindhu" must needs be attracted on approaching European literature. This study, which was illustrated by translations into English verse, was followed by another on Joséphin Soulary,[31] in whom she saw more than her maturer judgment might have justified. There is something very interesting and now, alas! still more pathetic in these sturdy and workmanlike essays in unaided criticism. Still more solitary her work became, in July, 1874, when her only sister, Aru, died, at the age of twenty. She seems to have been no less amiable than her sister, and if gifted with less originality and a less forcible ambition, to have been finely accomplished. Both sisters were well-trained musicians, with full contralto voices, and Aru had a faculty for design which promised well. The romance of "Mlle. D'Arvers" was originally projected for Aru to illustrate, but no page of this book did Aru ever see.

In 1876, as we have said, appeared that obscure first volume at Bhowanipore. The "Sheaf gleaned in French Fields" is certainly the most imperfect of Toru's writings, but it is not the least interesting. It is a wonderful mixture of strength and weakness, of genius overriding great obstacles and of talent succumbing to ignorance and inexperience. That it should have been performed at all is so extraordinary that we forget to be surprised at its inequality. The English verse is sometimes exquisite; at other times the rules of our prosody are absolutely ignored, and it is obvious that the Hindu poetess was chanting to herself a music that is discord in an English ear. The notes are no less curious, and to a stranger no less bewildering. Nothing could be more naïve than the writer's ignorance at some points, or more startling than her learning at others. On the whole, the attainment of the book was simply astounding. It consisted of a selection of translations from nearly one hundred French poets, chosen by the poetess herself on a principle of her own which gradually dawned upon the careful reader. She eschewed the Classicist writers as though they had never existed. For her André Chenier was the next name in chronological order after

---

30 Dutt published critical essays on the nineteenth-century poets, Henry Louis Vivian Derozio (an Anglo-Portuguese poet born in India) and Leconte de Lisle (a Creole born in Mauritius), in the Indian-English Calcutta-based periodical *Bengal Magazine*.
31 Joséphin Soulary (1815–1891): French poet.

Du Bartas.[32] Occasionally she showed a profundity of research that would have done no discredit to Mr. Saintsbury[33] or "le doux Assellineau." She was ready to pronounce an opinion on Napol le Pyrénéan or to detect a plagiarism in Baudelaire. But she thought that Alexander Smith was still alive, and she was curiously vague about the career of Saint Beuve. This inequality of equipment was a thing inevitable to her isolation, and hardly worth recording, except to show how laborious her mind was, and how quick to make the best of small resources.

We have already seen that the "Sheaf gleaned in French Fields" attracted the very minimum of attention in England. In France it was talked about a little more. M. Garcin de Tassy, the famous Orientalist,[34] who scarcely survived Toru by twelve months, spoke of it to Mlle. Clarisse Bader, author of a somewhat remarkable book on the position of women in ancient Indian society.[35] Almost simultaneously this volume fell into the hands of Toru, and she was moved to translate it into English, for the use of Hindus less instructed than herself. In January, 1877, she accordingly wrote to Mlle. Bader requesting her authorization, and received a prompt and kind reply. On the 18th of March Toru wrote again to this, her solitary correspondent in the world of European literature, and her letter, which has been preserved, shows that she had already descended into the valley of the shadow of death: –

> Ma constitution n'est pas forte; j'ai contracté une toux opiniâtre, il y a plus de deux ans, qui ne me quitte point. Cependant j'espère mettre la main à l'œuvre bientôt. Je ne peux dire, mademoiselle, combien votre affection, – car vous les aimez, votre livre et votre lettre en témoignent assez, – pour mes compatriotes et mon pays me touche; et je suis fière de pouvoir le dire que les héroïnes de nos grandes épopées sont dignes de tout honneur et de tout amour. Y a-ti-il d'héroïnes plus touchante, plus aimable que Sîta? Je ne le crois pas. *Quand j'entends ma mère chanter, le soir, les vieux chants de notre pays, je pleure presque toujours.* La plainte de Sîta, quand, bannie pour la séconde fois, elle erre dans la vaste forêt, seule, le désespoir et l'effroi dans l'âme, est si pathétique qu'il n'y a personne, je crois, qui puisse l'entendre sans verser des larmes. Je vous envois sous ce pli deux petites traductions du Sanscrit, cette belle langue antique. Malheureusement j'ai été obligée de faire cesser mes traductions de Sanscrit, il y a six mois. Ma santé ne me permet pas de les continuer.

These simple and pathetic words, in which the dying poetess pours out her heart to the one friend she had, and that one gained too late, seem as touching and as beautiful as any strain of Marceline Valmore's immortal verse. In English poetry I do not remember anything that exactly parallels their resigned melancholy. Before the month of March was over, Toru had taken to her bed. Unable to write, she continued to read, strewing her

---

32 André Chenier (1762–1794) and Guillaume de Salluste Du Bartas (1544–1590): French poets.
33 George Saintsbury was (1845–1933): English literary critic who wrote a number of studies of French and English literature, including the famous three-volume *A History of English Prosody from the Twelfth Century to the Present Day*.
34 Garcin de Tassey, or Tassy, (1794–1878): French Orientalist scholar.
35 Clarisse Bader (1840–1902): French scholar and author of *Women in Ancient India: Moral and Literary Studies*, an Orientalist examination of the representation of women in ancient Hindu texts. Bader and Toru Dutt were frequent correspondents.

sick-room with the latest European books, and entering with interest into the questions raised by the Société Asiatique of Paris in its printed Transactions. On the 30th of July she wrote her last letter to Mlle. Clarisse Bader, and a month later, on the 30th of August, 1877, at the age of twenty-one years, six months, and twenty-six days, she breathed her last in her father's house in Maniktollah Street, Calcutta.

In the first distraction of grief it seemed as though her unequalled promise had been entirely blighted, and as though she would be remembered only by her single book. But as her father examined her papers, one completed work after another revealed itself. First a selection from the sonnets of the Comte de Grammont, translated into English, turned up, and was printed in a Calcutta magazine; then some fragments of an English story, which were printed in another Calcutta magazine. Much more important, however, than any of these was a complete romance, written in French, being the identical story for which her sister Aru had proposed to make the illustrations. In the meantime Toru was no sooner dead than she began to be famous. In May, 1878, there appeared a second edition of the "Sheaf gleaned in French Fields," with a touching sketch of her death, by her father; and in 1879 was published, under the editorial care of Mlle. Clarisse Bader, the romance of "Le Journal de Mlle. D'Arvers," forming a handsome volume of 259 pages. This book, begun, as it appears, before the family returned from Europe, and finished nobody knows when, is an attempt to describe scenes from modern French society, but it is less interesting as an experiment of the fancy, than as a revelation of the mind of a young Hindu woman of genius. The story is simple, clearly told, and interesting; the studies of character have nothing French about them, but they are full of vigour and originality. The description of the hero is most characteristically Indian: –

> Il est beau en effet. Sa taille est haute, mais quelques-uns la trouveraient mince, sa chevelure noire est bouclée et tombe jusqu'à la nuque; ses yeux noirs sont profonds et bien fendus, le front est noble; la lèvre supérieure, couverte par une moustache naissante et noire, est parfaitement modelée; son menton a quelque chose de sévère; son teint est d'un blanc presque féminin, ce qui dénote sa haute naissance.

In this description we seem to recognize some Surya or Soma of Hindu mythology,[36] and the final touch, meaningless as applied to an European, reminds us that in India whiteness of skin has always been a sign of aristocratic birth, from the days when it originally distinguished the conquering Aryas from the indigenous race of the Dasyous.[37]

As a literary composition "Mlle. D'Arvers" deserves high commendation. It deals with the ungovernable passion of two brothers for one placid and beautiful girl, a passion which leads to fratricide and madness. That it is a very melancholy and tragical story is obvious from this brief sketch of its contents, but it is remarkable for coherence and self-restraint no less than for vigour of treatment. Toru Dutt never sinks to melodrama

---

36 Surya: Hindu god of the sun. Soma: sometimes referred to as the Hindu god of the moon (and equated with Chandra) as well as a plant from which a potent drink for the gods is brewed.

37 In this highly racialized categorization, Aryas were thought to be Indo-European races which migrated into northern India thousands of years ago. Dasyous were aboriginals who were often portrayed as demons. This dichotomy was reinforced by British Orientalist scholarship and imperial discourse during the nineteenth century.

in the course of her extraordinary tale, and the wonder is that she is not more often fantastic and unreal.

But we believe that the original English poems, which we present to the public for the first time to-day, will be ultimately found to constitute Toru's chief legacy to posterity. These ballads form the last and most matured of her writings, and were left so far fragmentary at her death that the fourth and fifth in her projected series of nine were not to be discovered in any form among her papers. It is probable that she had not even commenced them. Her father, therefore, to give a certain continuity to the series, has filled up these blanks with two stories from the "Vishnupurana," which originally appeared respectively in the "Calcutta Review" and in the "Bengal Magazine." These are interesting, but a little rude in form, and they have not the same peculiar value as the rhymed octo-syllabic ballads. In these last we see Toru no longer attempting vainly, though heroically, to compete with European literature on its own ground, but turning to the legends of her own race and country for inspiration. No modern Oriental has given us so strange an insight into the conscience of the Asiatic as is presented in the stories of "Prehlad" and of "Savitri," or so quaint a piece of religious fancy as the ballad of "Jogadhya Uma." The poetess seems in these verses to be chanting to herself those songs of her mother's race to which she always turned with tears of pleasure. They breathe a Vedic solemnity and simplicity of temper, and are singularly devoid of that littleness and frivolity which seem, if we may judge by a slight experience, to be the bane of modern India.

As to the merely technical character of these poems, it may be suggested that in spite of much in them that is rough and inchoate, they show that Toru was advancing in her mastery of English verse. Such a stanza as this, selected out of many no less skilful, could hardly be recognized as the work of one by whom the language was a late acquirement: –

> What glorious trees! The sombre saul,
>   On which the eye delights to rest, –
> The betel-nut, a pillar tall,
>   With feathery branches for a crest, –
> The light-leaved tamarind spreading wide, –
>   The pale faint-scented bitter neem,
> The seemul, gorgeous as a bride,
>   With flowers that have the ruby's gleam.

In other passages, of course, the text reads like a translation from some stirring ballad, and we feel that it gives but a faint and discordant echo of the music welling in Toru's brain. For it must frankly be confessed that in the brief May-day of her existence she had not time to master our language as Blanco White did, or as Chamisso mastered German.[38] To the end of her days, fluent and graceful as she was, she was not entirely conversant with English, especially with the colloquial turns of modern speech. Often a very fine thought is spoiled for hypercritical ears by the queer turn of expression which she has innocently given to it.

---

38 Joseph Blanco White (1775–1841): Spanish theologian and poet who lived the second part of his life in England, where he became an Anglican cleric. Adelbert von Chamisso (1781–1838): French-born naturalist and poet who lived most of his life in Prussia after his family fled the French Revolution.

These faults are found to a much smaller degree in her miscellaneous poems. Her sonnets, here printed for the first time, seem to me to be of great beauty, and her longer piece entitled "Our Casuarina Tree," needs no apology for its rich and mellifluous numbers.

It is difficult to exaggerate when we try to estimate what we have lost in the premature death of Toru Dutt. Literature has no honours which need have been beyond the grasp of a girl who at the age of twenty-one, and in languages separated from her own by so deep a chasm, had produced so much of lasting worth. And her courage and fortitude were worthy of her intelligence. Among "last words" of celebrated people, that which her father has recorded, "It is only the physical pain that makes me cry," is not the least remarkable, or the least significant of strong character. It was to a native of our island, and to one ten years senior to Toru, to whom it was said, in words more appropriate, surely, to her than to Oldham,

> Thy generous fruits, though gathered ere their prime,
> Still showed a quickness, and maturing time
> But mellows what we write to the dull sweets of Rime.[39]

That mellow sweetness was all that Toru lacked to perfect her as an English poet, and of no other Oriental who has ever lived can the same be said. When the history of the literature of our country comes to be written, there is sure to be a page in it dedicated to this fragile exotic blossom of song.

"Introduction" by Arthur Symons for Sarojini Naidu's *The Golden Threshold* (London: 1905)[40]

Introduction

It is at my persuasion that these poems are now published. The earliest of them were read to me in London in 1896, when the writer was seventeen; the later ones were sent to me from India in 1904, when she was twenty-five; and they belong, I think, almost wholly to those two periods. As they seemed to me to have an individual beauty of their own, I thought they ought to be published. The writer hesitated. "Your letter made me very proud and very sad," she wrote. "Is it possible that I have written verses that are 'filled with beauty,' and is it possible that you really think them worthy of being given to the world? You know how high my ideal of Art is; and to me my poor casual little poems seem to be less than beautiful – I mean with that final enduring beauty that I desire." And, in another letter, she writes: "I am not a poet really. I have the vision and the desire, but not the voice. If I could write just one poem full of beauty and the spirit of greatness, I should be exultantly silent for ever; but I sing just as the birds do, and my songs are as ephemeral." It is for this bird-like quality of song, it seems to me, that they are to be valued. They hint,

---

39 Gosse quotes from the poem "To the Memory of Mr. Oldham" by John Dryden to commemorate the death of the English poet John Oldham.
40 Arthur Symons, "Introduction," in Sarojini Naidu, *The Golden Threshold* (London: Heinemann, 1905).

in a sort of delicately evasive way, at a rare temperament, the temperament of a woman of the East, finding expression through a Western language and under partly Western influences. They do not express the whole of that temperament; but they express, I think, its essence; and there is an Eastern magic in them.

Sarojini Chattopâdhyây was born at Hyderabad on February 13, 1879. Her father, Dr. Aghorenath Chattopâdhyây, is descended from the ancient family of Chattorajes of Bhramangram, who were noted throughout Eastern Bengal as patrons of Sanskrit learning, and for their practice of Yoga. He took his degree of Doctor of Science at the University of Edinburgh in 1877, and afterwards studied brilliantly at Bonn. On his return to India he founded the Nizam College at Hyderabad, and has since laboured incessantly, and at great personal sacrifice, in the cause of education.

Sarojini was the eldest of a large family, all of whom were taught English at an early age. "I," she writes, "was stubborn and refused to speak it. So one day when I was nine years old my father punished me – the only time I was ever punished – by shutting me in a room alone for a whole day. I came out of it a full-blown linguist. I have never spoken any other language to him, or to my mother, who always speaks to me in Hindustani. I don't think I had any special hankering to write poetry as a little child, though I was of a very fanciful and dreamy nature. My training under my father's eye was of a sternly scientific character. He was determined that I should be a great mathematician or a scientist, but the poetic instinct, which I inherited from him and also from my mother (who wrote some lovely Bengali lyrics in her youth) proved stronger. One day, when I was eleven, I was sighing over a sum in algebra: it *wouldn't* come right; but instead a whole poem came to me suddenly. I wrote it down.

"From that day my 'poetic career' began. At thirteen I wrote a long poem à la 'Lady of the Lake' – 1300 lines in six days. At thirteen I wrote a drama of 2000 lines, a full-fledged passionate thing that I began on the spur of the moment without forethought, just to spite my doctor who said I was very ill and must not touch a book. My health broke down permanently about this time, and my regular studies being stopped I read voraciously. I suppose the greater part of my reading was done between fourteen and sixteen. I wrote a novel, I wrote fat volumes of journals; I took myself very seriously in those days."

Before she was fifteen the great struggle of her life began. Dr. Govindurajulu Naidu, now her husband, is, though of an old and honourable family, not a Brahmin. The difference of caste roused an equal opposition, not only on the side of her family, but of his; and in 1895 she was sent to England, against her will, with a special scholarship from the Nizam. She remained in England, with an interval of travel in Italy, till 1898, studying first at King's College, London, then, till her health again broke down, at Girton. She returned to Hyderabad in September 1898, and in the December of that year, to the scandal of all India, broke through the bonds of caste, and married Dr. Naidu. "Do you know I have some very beautiful poems floating in the air," she wrote to me in 1904; "and if the gods are kind I shall cast my soul like a net and capture them, this year. If the gods are kind – and grant me a little measure of health. It is all I need to make my life perfect, for the very 'Spirit of Delight' that Shelley wrote of dwells in my little home; it is full of the music of birds in the garden and children in the long arched verandah." There are songs about the children in this book; they are called the Lord of Battles, the Sun of Victory, the Lotus-born, and the Jewel of Delight.

"My ancestors for thousands of years," I find written in one of her letters, "have been lovers of the forest and mountain caves, great dreamers, great scholars, great ascetics. My father is a dreamer himself, a great dreamer, a great man whose life has been a magnificent failure. I suppose in the whole of India there are few men whose learning is greater than his, and I don't think there are many men more beloved. He has a great white beard and the profile of Homer, and a laugh that brings the roof down. He has wasted all his money on two great objects: to help others, and on alchemy. He holds huge courts every day in his garden of all the learned men of all religions – Rajahs and beggars and saints and downright villains all delightfully mixed up, and all treated as one. And then his alchemy! Oh dear, night and day the experiments are going on, and every man who brings a new prescription is welcome as a brother. But this alchemy is, you know, only the material counterpart of a poet's craving for Beauty, the eternal Beauty. 'The makers of gold and the makers of verse,' they are the twin creators that sway the world's secret desire for mystery; and what in my father is the genius of curiosity – the very essence of all scientific genius – in me is the desire for beauty. Do you remember Pater's phrase about Leonardo da Vinci, 'curiosity and the desire of beauty'?"

It was the desire of beauty that made her a poet; her "nerves of delight" were always quivering at the contact of beauty. To those who knew her in England, all the life of the tiny figure seemed to concentrate itself in the eyes; they turned towards beauty as the sunflower turns towards the sun, opening wider and wider until one saw nothing but the eyes. She was dressed always in clinging dresses of Eastern silk, and as she was so small, and her long black hair hung straight down her back, you might have taken her for a child. She spoke little, and in a low voice, like gentle music; and she seemed, wherever she was, to be alone.

Through that soul I seemed to touch and take hold upon the East. And first there was the wisdom of the East. I have never known any one who seemed to exist on such "large draughts of intellectual day" as this child of seventeen, to whom one could tell all one's personal troubles and agitations, as to a wise old woman. In the East, maturity comes early; and this child had already lived through all a woman's life. But there was something else, something hardly personal, something which belonged to a consciousness older than the Christian, which I realised, wondered at, and admired, in her passionate tranquillity of mind, before which everything mean and trivial and temporary caught fire and burnt away in smoke. Her body was never without suffering, or her heart without conflict; but neither the body's weakness nor the heart's violence could disturb that fixed contemplation, as of Buddha on his lotus-throne.

And along with this wisdom, as of age or of the age of a race, there was what I can hardly call less than an agony of sensation. Pain or pleasure transported her, and the whole of pain or pleasure might be held in a flower's cup or the imagined frown of a friend. It was never found in those things which to others seemed things of importance. At the age of twelve she passed the Matriculation of the Madras University, and awoke to find herself famous throughout India. "Honestly," she said to me, "I was not pleased; such things did not appeal to me." But here, in a letter from Hyderabad, bidding one "share a March morning" with her, there is, at the mere contact of the sun, this outburst: "Come and share my exquisite March morning with me: this sumptuous blaze of gold and sapphire sky; these scarlet lilies that adorn the sunshine; the voluptuous scents of neem and champak and serisha[41] that beat upon the languid air with their implacable sweetness; the thousand little gold and blue

---

41 *Neem*: tree native to South Asia and known for its fragrant flowers. *Champak*: evergreen tree with fragrant orange-yellow flowers. *Serisha*, or *sirisha*: evergreen shrub with small dark green leaves and small white flowers.

and silver breasted birds bursting with the shrill ecstasy of life in nesting time. All is hot and fierce and passionate, ardent and unashamed in its exulting and importunate desire for life and love. And, do you know that the scarlet lilies are woven petal by petal from my heart's blood, these little quivering birds are my soul made incarnate music, these heavy perfumes are my emotions dissolved into aerial essence, this flaming blue and gold sky is the 'very me,' that part of me that incessantly and insolently, yes, and a little deliberately, triumphs over that other part – a thing of nerves and tissues that suffers and cries out, and that must die to-morrow perhaps, or twenty years hence."

Then there was her humour, which was part of her strange wisdom, and was always awake and on the watch. In all her letters, written in exquisite English prose, but with an ardent imagery and a vehement sincerity of emotion which make them, like the poems, indeed almost more directly, un-English, Oriental, there was always this intellectual, critical sense of humour, which could laugh at one's own enthusiasm as frankly as that enthusiasm had been set down. And partly the humour, like the delicate reserve of her manner, was a mask or a shelter. "I have taught myself," she writes to me from India, "to be commonplace and like everybody else superficially. Every one thinks I am so nice and cheerful, so 'brave,' all the banal things that are so comfortable to be. My mother knows me only as 'such a tranquil child, but so strong-willed.' A tranquil child!" And she writes again, with deeper significance: "I too have learnt the subtle philosophy of living from moment to moment. Yes, it is a subtle philosophy, though it appears merely an epicurean doctrine: 'Eat, drink, and be merry, for to-morrow we die.' I have gone through so many yesterdays when I strove with Death that I have realised to its full the wisdom of that sentence; and it is to me not merely a figure of speech, but a literal fact. Any to-morrow I might die. It is scarcely two months since I came back from the grave: is it worth while to be anything but radiantly glad? Of all things that life or perhaps my temperament has given me I prize the gift of laughter as beyond price."

Her desire, always, was to be "a wild free thing of the air like the birds, with a song in my heart." A spirit of too much fire in too frail a body, it was rarely that her desire was fully granted. But in Italy she found what she could not find in England, and from Italy her letters are radiant. "This Italy is made of gold," she writes from Florence, "the gold of dawn and daylight, the gold of the stars, and, now dancing in weird enchanting rhythms through this magic month of May, the gold of fireflies in the perfumed darkness – 'aerial gold.' I long to catch the subtle music of their fairy dances and make a poem with a rhythm like the quick irregular wild flash of their sudden movements. Would it not be wonderful? One black night I stood in a garden with fireflies in my hair like darting restless stars caught in a mesh of darkness. It gave me a strange sensation, as if I were not human at all, but an elfin spirit. I wonder why these little things move me so deeply? It is because I have a most 'unbalanced intellect,' I suppose." Then, looking out on Florence, she cries, "God! how beautiful it is, and how glad I am that I am alive to-day!" And she tells me that she is drinking in the beauty like wine, "wine, golden and scented, and shining, fit for the gods; and the gods have drunk it, the dead gods of Etruria, two thousand years ago. Did I say dead? No, for the gods are immortal, and one might still find them loitering in some solitary dell on the grey hillsides of Fiesole. Have I seen them? Yes, looking with dreaming eyes, I have found them sitting under the olives, in their grave, strong, antique beauty – Etruscan gods!"

In Italy she watches the faces of the monks, and at one moment longs to attain to their peace by renunciation, longs for Nirvana; "then, when one comes out again into the hot sunshine that warms one's blood, and sees the eager hurrying faces of men and women in the street, dramatic faces over which the disturbing experiences of life have passed and left their symbols, one's heart thrills up into one's throat. No, no, no, a thousand times no! how can one deliberately renounce this coloured, unquiet, fiery human life of the earth?" And, all the time, her subtle criticism is alert, and this woman of the East marvels at the women of the West, "the beautiful worldly women of the West," whom she sees walking in the Cascine, "taking the air so consciously attractive in their brilliant toilettes, in the brilliant coquetry of their manner!" She finds them "a little incomprehensible," "profound artists in all the subtle intricacies of fascination," and asks if these "incalculable frivolities and vanities and coquetries and caprices" are, to us, an essential part of their charm? And she watches them with amusement as they flutter about her, petting her as if she were a nice child, a child or a toy, not dreaming that she is saying to herself sorrowfully: "How utterly empty their lives must be of all spiritual beauty *if* they are nothing more than they appear to be."

She sat in our midst, and judged us, and few knew what was passing behind that face "like an awakening soul," to use one of her own epithets. Her eyes were like deep pools, and you seemed to fall through them into depths below depths.

"Introductory Memoir" by Laurence Binyon for Manmohan Ghose's *Songs of Love and Death* (Oxford: 1926)[42]

Introductory Memoir

> Mislike me not for my complexion,
> The shadowed livery of the burnished sun!

These words, spoken as if from some spontaneous compulsion in a voice low and thrilled that itself seemed to glow, caused all the class of school-boys to turn their heads. At the back of the room, behind the rest, sat a young Indian with thick hair falling about his forehead, and dark lustrous eyes. It was he who had startled us with his impassioned tones. Where had he come from? How had he mysteriously joined us? Perhaps I deceive myself, but to my memory this was my first sight of Manmohan Ghose – an unaccountable apparition from an unknown hemisphere. The legendary East seemed suddenly to have projected a fragment of itself into our little world of everyday things and humdrum studies, disturbing it with colour, mystery, romance. No doubt I should not have been moved as I was had not the new-comer spoken the rich lines in a voice that betrayed the capacity to be intoxicated by poetry: and of such capacity I had found no trace in my classmates. I felt immediate sympathy, and besides anyone foreign who brought a breath from a world outside the world of habit ever attracted me.

[…]

Manmohan Ghose and I made friends, and by degrees disclosed to each other our secret ambitions. We had long walks and talks together, discussing everything in heaven and earth, after the manner of youth, but especially poetry and the poets. My home was indifferent to the arts, my school fellows also, so far as I knew them: and it was a great delight to expand

---

42 Laurence Binyon, "Introductory Memoir," in Manmohan Ghose, *Songs of Love and Death* (Oxford: Basil H. Blackwell, 1926).

in these talks on the subjects I cared for most. We had enough difference of taste to salt our conversation with arguments and dispute. At that time I was in the stage of an ardent worship of Browning, but I think he never shared this enthusiasm.

He lived in lodgings with two brothers, but what his actual circumstances were when he came to England, and how he came to be at S. Paul's, I do not think I ever inquired. As to the School, the High Master, a notable and formidable personality famous for his prescience in judging a boy's future capabilities, would at times, for his own reasons, insert a promising pupil into one of the upper forms without notice, and in the middle of the term: hence my unconsciousness of having ever set eyes on Manmohan Ghose till all our heads were turned to the strange new-comer on that particular morning is not so improbable as it may seem. But of Ghose's background I knew scarcely anything. His enthusiasm for literature sufficed my curiosity. He was well read in the English poets, better tread than I in the Elizabethans and the older lyrists. But what struck me most was his enthusiastic appreciation of Greek poetry, not so much the books prescribed in the school as those which he had sought out on his own account. Theocritus, Meleager, above all Simonides, were his special favourites. I had imagined that an Oriental's taste must of necessity be for the luxuriant and ornate, and was surprised that he should feel so strong an attraction to the limpid and severe. Yet many of us are attracted to arts and literatures remote from our own traditions and just because of qualities in them which these have not. Why should not an Indian feel a parallel attraction? Manmohan Ghose never forgot the Greeks, and to the end his delight was in European literature and European art.

[...]

In the summer term of 1890 Mr. Blackwell published a little volume bound in brown paper for which Selwyn Image had made an exquisite design. It was called *Primavera*, and was the joint production of Stephen Philips, Manmohan Ghose, Arthur Cripps, of Trinity, and myself. It was received with the indulgence often accorded to such youthful efforts, and was soon in a second edition.

Addington Symonds reviewed us kindly and, at length, in the *Academy*. Oscar Wilde in the *Pall Mall Gazette* was no less favourable, and had particular praise for the "young Indian of brilliant scholarship and high literary attainment who gives some culture to Christ Chruch." Mr. Ghose, he said, ought some day to make a name in our literature. Not long after this, I think, Ghose went down to live in London. As we were at different colleges, and were not of the same year, I had seen much less of him at Oxford than at school, and now for some time he was largely lost to view, for my home was in the country. We exchanged poems and criticisms, and on visits to London I met him in company with artists and men of letters, whom he had come to know through Lionel Johnson, Ernest Dowson, and others of our contemporaries. At one time he thought of seeking a post of some kind in England, but nothing came of such projects. Not all his time was spent in London; he knew something of the more beautiful parts of England and of Wales, and cherished the memory of them. Yet he could not forget that he was an exile.

> Heaven be in thy sails, O unknown vessel,
>   Till those heavenly shores grow into view,
> See my spirit, with no storm to wrestle,
>   Follows, goes on wind-wings thither too.

> For long miles into the heart of morning,
>   Miles and miles, far over land and seas,
> Past enchanted regions of forewarning,
>   Dawns at last the land that dims all these.

So he cried in a poem written in these last years before leaving England for ever. Alas! it was not long before he was to feel that his spirit had exchanged one exile for another. During the last year of this period, being now settled in London, I saw him frequently. He was unoccupied, I think, except for verse-making, and would drift into my room at odd hours, and stay talking till late into the night.

The ship which in the autumn of 1894 bore Manmohan Ghose down the Thames estuary and the Channel on his journey home was named, I recall, *Patroclus*. It seems traditional with ship-builders to christen their grimy-funnelled iron monsters with such legendary names. But in this case there seemed something symbolic in the attachment of a name, breathing of bright Hellas and the Tale of Troy, to the efficient product of a practical civilization made with the sole thought of use and comfort. There went gliding the big liner, a prodigious piece of throbbing mechanism, the modern West's achievement and pride; painted on her bows was a relic of old poetry and lettered tradition, just as our restless civilization still carries with it, hoarded in a few brains, cherished in a few imaginations, the heritage of Greece, no more to the multitude than a painted name with the dimmest of associations; and on board was an Indian poet, to whom the Iliad and the name of Achilles' friend meant more perhaps than to any of his English co-voyagers; a young Indian returning to an unknown home, for whom the English cliffs and the roar of London and the whole hurried stream of western life were inextricably to be mingled in memory with the glory of the classics of Europe.

"I arrived on October 25th, and have since been staying at a beautiful country place called Baidyanath, in my grandfather's house, all among the mountains and green sugarcane fields and shallow rivers. My own people I found charming and cultivated folk, and spent an extremely pleasant time among them. This, I think very fortunate indeed – to find at once friends, and that of one's own blood, so congenial and interesting as soon as I landed."

Such was Manmohan's first happy impression, on his return to his own country. The one drawback he lamented was that he had forgotten his own tongue, Bengali, and had to learn it afresh. But I imagine that all his life he thought in English. He soon obtained a post as Professor of English Literature at Patna College. It was dull, fatiguing, ill-paid work. His consolation was in the country and the climate…

[…]

Sharp indeed was the contrast between this strange land which was yet his own, and the western country of his memories, still so recent. England had given him much, and to the best she had to give a singularly receptive spirit had responded with delight. Her poetry glorified England for this stranger from the East. Was her last gift to be the cruel gift of estrangement from his people? No doubt with passing years he grew to be more at home in Indian life: he made it one of his objects: but for long there were frequent moments of keen repining.

Yet after all he was Indian in his nature. His verse follows the forms and traditions of English poetry, but his temperament and attitude were Eastern. Physically he responded joyfully to the congenial ardour of the Indian climate. What a glorious pleasure the sun, and the heat of the sun! He revelled in the floods of sunlight, the luxuriant leafiness. The country itself was full of charm and romance; he loved the primeval simplicity of the people and their life. Only he remained outside it. Mentally, he was torn in two. I often urged him to take a theme from Indian legend; and he attempted a poem on Savitri[43] among other Indian subjects. But it would not shape itself. He felt the need to Europeanise the atmosphere in some sort and then the essence evaporated. Thus he hovered between two hemispheres, not wholly belonging to either.

In one respect, in his acceptance of tradition, he was certainly more Oriental than Western. I had given him at parting Bullen's Lyrics from the Elizabethan Song books,[44] and he found in these, and in Campion especially, an unceasing delight. "How we have sacrificed form and expression in our devotion for modern thought and for contemporary subject matter, and the idea that a poet should have something new to say! How did people first come to have this idea? The Elizabethans don't seem to trouble themselves much about having a new poetical mission. What old and timeworn subjects they chose, seeming evidently to care for nothing except for rhythm and expression, on which they spend the whole power of their art."

Love Songs and Elegies by Manmohan Ghose appeared in 1898 in Mr. Elkin Mathew's Shilling Garland. This little book was all that he was to publish except some occasional poems in magazines…

[…]

Poetry and his children – two daughters – were his consolation [following the death of his wife]. He continued to write, though he never cared to publish. Apart from his fellows, knowing little of the currents of contemporary literature, with no help from friendly criticism, he wrote verse which sometimes showed little signs of his isolation, in being out of touch with the most exacting standards. A tendency to become obscure from grammatical inversion, to indulge in a certain prolixity, occasional failure to cope with elaborate rhyme-structure – but he would set himself tasks in intricate and dissyllabic rhyming which would have daunted most English poets – these blemishes might easily have disappeared in revision which he did not live to make. The devotion of his love for his wife, the desolation of his loss, inspired the groups of poems called "Immortal Eve" and "Orphic Mysteries" containing the finest and most original of his lyrics.

[…]

Would Manmohan Ghose have achieved more if he had been a purely Indian poet – if his father, with a whole-hearted faith in western culture, had not transplanted

---

43 The tale of Savitri, who was cast as an ancient model of ideal Indian womanhood during the nineteenth century by Indian nationalists, is included as a digression within the authoritative Sanskrit telling of the epic poem, the *Mahabharata*.
44 A. H. Bullen, ed., *Lyrics from the Song-Books of the Elizabethan Age* (London: John C. Nimmo, 1887).

him to England at the tender age of seven, so that all his most impressionable years were spent in a foreign country? Perhaps; for on his return to India he wrote English verse in surroundings from which they drew no natural nourishment, and his isolation hampered him. He began a drama on the story of Nala and Damayanti,[45] which was never finished; but otherwise his poems were little concerned with India. They are full of English imagery, of the trees and flowers of England. Circumstances had prevented him from being like Rabindra Nath Tagore, an interpreter to the West of Indian thought and life. But at least he was an eloquent interpreter of the West to India. He admired the Bengali language, but it seemed to him lacking in a certain quality which he found in English. No Indian had ever before used our tongue with so poetic a touch, and he would coin a phrase, turn a noun into a verb with the freedom, often the felicity, of our own poets. But he remains Indian. I do not think that an Indian reader would feel him as a foreign poet, for all his western tastes and allusions. Yet to us he is a voice among the great company of English singers; somewhat apart and solitary, with a difference in his note, but not an echo. I hope that fate, so malignant to him in his life-time, may not pursue him after death with the hasty and cheap criticism that his verse is neither Indian nor English, and so dismiss it. On the contrary, it is both Indian and English; that is its interest. We English, ready enough to adorn with haloes of romance any country not our own that is sufficiently far off, are apt to feel embarrassed and incredulous if a like tribute is offered to our own land. But why this coyness? We are vain of our efficiency in business and administration, and parade it before the Eastern world. Is it not something for pride also that England could be to this Indian a nursing-mother of imagination and the dear home of the Muses? Yet with English people I fancy that the Orientalism of a Flecker or a Lafcadio Hearn[46] finds much readier sympathy than the romantic admiration of England that inspired Manmohan Ghose. I remember that I myself was quite annoyed with him for persisting in choosing a Greek legend, Perseus, for the subject of a long poem rather than an Indian one. How unreasonable this was! I should not have been annoyed with myself for wanting to write a poem on Savitri or Nala and Damayanti. Let us become acquainted with the riches of India's tradition by all means, but let us make exchange of our own best also, and regard with sympathy the effort of one like Ghose, for whom England was above all the country of immortal poets. Oscar Wilde wrote of his early poems: "His verses show how quick and subtle are the intellectual sympathies of the Oriental mind, and suggest how close is the bond of union that may some day bind India to us by other methods than those of commerce and military strength!" Was this a fond aspiration? Not so fond as the delusions of those who think only in terms of politics and business.

[...]

---

45 The tale of Nala and Damayanti and their love story is included as a digression within the authoritative Sanskrit telling of the epic poem, the *Mahabharata*.
46 James Elroy Flecker (1884–1915): poet and playwright known for his works on the Middle East and the Mediterranean. Lafcadio Hearn (1850–1904): Greek-born scholar who lived the last part of his life in Japan, which served as the subject of a number of his cultural and literary studies.

"Introduction" by W. B. Yeats for Rabindranath Tagore's *Gitanjali* (London: 1912)[47]

Introduction

I.

A few days ago I said to a distinguished Bengali doctor of medicine, "I know no German, yet if a translation of a German poet had moved me, I would go to the British Museum and find books in English that would tell me something of his life, and of the history of his thought. But though these prose translations from Rabindranath Tagore have stirred my blood as nothing has for years, I shall not know anything of his life, and of the movements of thought that have made them possible, if some Indian traveller will not tell me." It seemed to him natural that I should be moved, for he said, "I read Rabindranath every day, to read one line of his is to forget all the troubles of the world." I said, "An Englishman living in London in the reign of Richard the Second had he been shown translations from Petrarch or from Dante, would have found no books to answer his questions, but would have questioned some Florentine banker or Lombard merchant as I question you. For all I know, so abundant and simple is this poetry, the new Renaissance has been born in your country and I shall never know of it except by hearsay." He answered, "We have other poets, but none that are his equal; we call this the epoch of Rabindranath. No poet seems to me as famous in Europe as he is among us. He is as great in music as in poetry, and his songs are sung from the west of India into Burmah wherever Bengali is spoken. He was already famous at nineteen when he wrote his first novel; and plays, written when he was but little older, are still played in Calcutta. I so much admire the completeness of his life; when he was very young he wrote much of natural objects, he would sit all day in his garden; from his twenty-fifth year or so to his thirty-fifth perhaps, when he had a great sorrow, he wrote the most beautiful love poetry in our language"; and then he said with deep emotion, "Words can never express what I owed at seventeen to his love poetry. After that his art grew deeper, it became religious and philosophical; all the aspirations of mankind are in his hymns. He is the first among our saints who has not refused to live, but has spoken out of Life itself, and that is why we give him our love." I may have changed his well-chosen words in my memory but not his thought. "A little while ago he was to read divine service in one of our churches – we of the Brahma Samaj[48] use your word 'church' in English – it was the largest in Calcutta and not only was it crowded, but the streets were all but impassable because of the people."

Other Indians came to see me and their reverence for this man sounded strange in our world, where we hide great and little things under the same veil of obvious comedy and half-serious depreciation. When we were making the cathedrals had we a like reverence for our great men? "Every morning at three – I know, for I have seen it," one said

---

47 W. B. Yeats, "Introduction," in Rabindranath Tagore, *Gitanjali*, trans. by author (London: Macmillan, 1912).
48 Brahmo Samaj: Hindu reform movement that promoted monotheism. It was founded by Ram Mohun Roy in 1828 in Calcutta and many members of the movement, including the Tagore family, participated in a variety of social reform movements during the nineteenth century.

to me, "he sits immovable in contemplation, and for two hours does not awake from his reverie upon the nature of God. His father, the Maha Rishi,[49] would sometimes sit there all through the next day; once, upon a river, he fell into contemplation because of the beauty of the landscape, and the rowers waited for eight hours before they could continue their journey." He then told me of Mr. Tagore's family and how for generations great men have come out of its cradles. "Today," he said, "there are Gogonendranath and Abanindranath Tagore, who are artists; and Dwijendranath, Rabindranath's brother, who is a great philosopher. The squirrels come from the boughs and climb on to his knees and the birds alight upon his hands." I notice in these men's thought a sense of visible beauty and meaning as though they held that doctrine of Nietzsche that we must not believe in the moral or intellectual beauty which does not sooner or later impress itself upon physical things. I said, "In the East you know how to keep a family illustrious. The other day the curator of a museum pointed out to me a little dark-skinned man who was arranging their Chinese prints and said, 'That is the hereditary connoisseur of the Mikado,[50] he is the fourteenth of his family to hold the post.'" He answered, "When Rabindranath was a boy he had all round him in his home literature and music." I thought of the abundance, of the simplicity of the poems, and said, "In your country is there much propagandist writing, much criticism? We have to do so much, especially in my own country, that our minds gradually cease to be creative, and yet we cannot help it. If our life was not a continual warfare, we would not have taste, we would not know what is good, we would not find hearers and readers. Four-fifths of our energy is spent in the quarrel with bad taste, whether in our own minds or in the minds of others." "I understand," he replied, "we too have our propagandist writing. In the villages they recite long mythological poems adapted from the Sanscrit in the Middle Ages, and they often insert passages telling the people that they must do their duties."

II.

I have carried the manuscript of these translations about with me for days, reading it in railway trains, or on the top of omnibuses and in restaurants, and I have often had to close it lest some stranger would see how much it moved me. These lyrics – which are in the original, my Indians tell me, full of subtlety of rhythm, of untranslatable delicacies of colour, of metrical invention – display in their thought a world I have dreamed of all my life long. The work of a supreme culture, they yet appear as much the growth of the common soil as the grass and the rushes. A tradition, where poetry and religion are the same thing, has passed through the centuries, gathering from learned and unlearned metaphor and emotion, and carried back again to the multitude the thought of the scholar and of the noble. If the civilization of Bengal remains unbroken, if that common mind which – as one divines – runs through all, is not, as with us, broken into a dozen minds that know nothing of each other, something even of what is most subtle in these verses will have come, in a few generations, to the beggar on the roads. When there was but one mind in England, Chaucer wrote his *Troilus and Cressida*, and thought he

---

49 *Maha Rishi*, or *maharishi*: Hindu sage or holy man or a popular spiritual leader (n. "maharishi" *OED*).
50 Mikado: European term for the emperor of Japan.

had written to be read, or to be read out – for our time was coming on apace – he was sung by minstrels for a while. Rabindranath Tagore, like Chaucer's forerunners, writes music for his words, and one understands at every moment that he is so abundant, so spontaneous, so daring in his passion, so full of surprise, because he is doing something which has never seemed strange, unnatural, or in need of defence. These verses will not lie in little well-printed books upon ladies' tables, who turn the pages with indolent hands that they may sigh over a life without meaning, which is yet all they can know of life, or be carried by students at the university to be laid aside when the work of life begins, but, as the generations pass, travellers will hum them on the highway and men rowing upon the rivers. Lovers, while they await one another, shall find, in murmuring them, this love of God a magic gulf wherein their own more bitter passion may bathe and renew its youth. At every moment the heart of this poet flows outward to these without derogation or condescension, for it has known that they will understand; and it has filled itself with the circumstance of their lives. The traveller in the red-brown clothes that he wears that dust may not show upon him, the girl searching in her bed for the petals fallen from the wreath of her royal lover, the servant or the bride awaiting the master's home-coming in the empty house, are images of the heart turning to God. Flowers and rivers, the blowing of conch shells, the heavy rain of the Indian July, or the moods of that heart in union or in separation; and a man sitting in a boat upon a river playing upon a lute, like one of those figures full of mysterious meaning in a Chinese picture, is God Himself. A whole people, a whole civilization, immeasurably strange to us, seems to have been taken up into this imagination; and yet we are not moved because of its strangeness, but because we have met our own image, as though we had walked in Rossetti's willow wood, or heard, perhaps for the first time in literature, our voice as in a dream.

Since the Renaissance the writing of European saints – however familiar their metaphor and the general structure of their thought – has ceased to hold our attention. We know that we must at last forsake the world, and we are accustomed in moments of weariness or exaltation to consider a voluntary forsaking; but how can we, who have read so much poetry, seen so many paintings, listened to so much music, where the cry of the flesh and the cry of the soul seem one, forsake it harshly and rudely? What have we in common with St. Bernard covering his eyes that they may not dwell upon the beauty of the lakes of Switzerland, or with the violent rhetoric of the Book of Revelation? We would, if we might, find, as in this book, words full of courtesy. "I have got my leave. Bid me farewell, my brothers! I bow to you all and take my departure. Here I give back the keys of my door – and I give up all claims to my house. I only ask for last kind words from you. We were neighbours for long, but I received more than I could give. Now the day has dawned and the lamp that lit my dark corner is out. A summons has come and I am ready for my journey." And it is our own mood, when it is furthest from à Kempis or John of the Cross,[51] that cries, "And because I love this life, I know I shall love death as well." Yet it is not only in our thoughts of the parting that this book fathoms all. We had not known that we loved God, hardly it may be that we believed in Him; yet looking backward upon our life we discover, in our exploration of the pathways of woods, in

---

51 Thomas à Kempis (1380–1471): German Catholic monk and author of *Imitation of Christ*. St. John of the Cross (1542–1591): Spanish Carmelite friar, mystic, and saint.

our delight in the lonely places of hills, in that mysterious claim that we have made, unavailingly on the woman that we have loved, the emotion that created this insidious sweetness. "Entering my heart unbidden even as one of the common crowd, unknown to me, my king, thou didst press the signet of eternity upon many a fleeting moment." This is no longer the sanctity of the cell and of the scourge; being but a lifting up, as it were, into a greater intensity of the mood of the painter, painting the dust and the sunlight, and we go for a like voice to St. Francis and to William Blake who have seemed so alien in our violent history.

III.

We write long books where no page perhaps has any quality to make writing a pleasure, being confident in some general design, just as we fight and make money and fill our heads with politics – all dull things in the doing – while Mr. Tagore, like the Indian civilization itself, has been content to discover the soul and surrender himself to its spontaneity. He often seems to contrast life with that of those who have lived more after our fashion, and have more seeming weight in the world, and always humbly as though he were only sure his way is best for him: "Men going home glance at me and smile and fill me with shame. I sit like a beggar maid, drawing my skirt over my face, and when they ask me, what it is I want, I drop my eyes and answer them not." At another time, remembering how his life had once a different shape, he will say, "Many an hour I have spent in the strife of the good and the evil, but now it is the pleasure of my playmate of the empty days to draw my heart on to him; and I know not why this sudden call to what useless inconsequence." An innocence, a simplicity that one does not find elsewhere in literature makes the birds and the leaves seem as near to him as they are near to children, and the changes of the seasons great events as before our thoughts had arisen between them and us. At times I wonder if he has it from the literature of Bengal or from religion, and at other times, remembering the birds alighting on his brother's hands, I find pleasure in thinking it hereditary, a mystery that was growing through the centuries like the courtesy of a Tristan or a Pelanore. Indeed, when he is speaking of children, so much a part of himself this quality seems, one is not certain that he is not also speaking of the saints, "They build their houses with sand and they play with empty shells. With withered leaves they weave their boats and smilingly float them on the vast deep. Children have their play on the seashore of worlds. They know not how to swim, they know not how to cast nets. Pearl fishers dive for pearls, merchants sail in their ships, while children gather pebbles and scatter them again. They seek not for hidden treasures, they know not how to cast nets."

"Preface," "Introduction" and poems from *A Garland of Ceylon Verse, 1837–1897* (Columbo: 1897),[52] edited and with an introduction and notes by Isaac Tambyah[53]

Prefatory: Purely Personal

In the preparation of this book there has been less difficulty in the task of selection than in that of collection. My success in the work of getting together a number of local poems from which to select matter for the one hundred and thirty-two pages here presented to the reader is very largely due to the liberal assistance rendered me by Mr. Aelian Ondaatje, Law-Student, Colombo, (also of "Hawthorn Villa," Bambalapitiya). I cannot help regretting, however, that I have been unable to come across more verses of English poetry. As regards the selection I take upon myself the entire responsibility; gratefully though I acknowledge the very kind and ungrudging help I have received, in the choice and arrangement of the pieces, from a friend who shrinks from the luxury of having to blush at finding his name in print.

I should be sorry to see it argued, from the avowal of my not having been successful in securing an exhaustive collection of Ceylon verse, that the pieces which appear in the present collection have found admission there through any lack of editorial severity. On the contrary, I fear one or two writers of verse will not be overgushing in their thanks to me for the exercise of discretion which, I trust, I shall not be the only person to make use of in the interests of literary elegance.

In cases where it was possible for me to communicate with living writers I had done so, and I am thankful to them for their ready help in supplying me with materials. The absence of copyright law in this country, however much it is to be regretted, has been very beneficial to me in the collecting of poems from sundry local magazines, books, and newspapers as easily as from private scrap-books. Those who fancy that in taking over their verses, from any printed source whatever, I have infringed any right will, I hope, amply forgive me, and allow me to plead in my defence the year of Jubilee,[54] and the circumstance of their poetry appearing in a memorial book of this memorable year. Those who choose to affect serious displeasure, however, are reminded that the face of the preparation of the book was duly announced in all detail, months before this date, and the period of demurrers is past.

[...]

---

52 Ceylon was declared a Crown Colony and placed under direct administration of the Colonial Office in 1802. Ceylon won its independence from Britain in 1948 and officially changed its name to Sri Lanka in 1972. Reprinted here are poems by "native" Sri Lankans.

53 Isaac Tambyah, ed., *A Garland of Ceylon Verse, 1837–1897* (Colombo: Ceylon Printing Works, 1897). The collection, as noted by the introduction, features verse by both "native" Ceylonese as well as British residents and colonists. Many of the verses mention "Ind," which seems to indicate that these writers conceptualized themselves as part of the British Raj even if they were not administratively included within the Raj. Reprinted here are poems by three Ceylonese poets.

54 Queen Victoria's Golden Jubilee in 1887 celebrated her fiftieth year of rule and was marked by elaborately staged celebrations in Great Britain and its colonies. British and Indian-English poets wrote numerous odes to the queen-empress and on the Jubilee.

Introduction

This collection of Ceylon Verse is published as a literary memento of the record reign in English history and in commemoration of the year of the Royal Diamond Jubilee.[55] The several expressions of loyalty which are given the first place in this anthology, but half suggest the purpose of the book, for it is in a deeper sense that we have meant it to be a Ceylon literary souvenir of that historical fact and the year of its celebration. It is as a shewing forth, a grateful shewing forth, of not the least part of what England has achieved among the people of Ceylon, particularly during the last sixty years.

Those that appreciate what a potent factor in moulding and maintaining loyalty in the English-speaking world is the Queen's English, of which one of Ceylon's sons beautifully exclaims:

> Her speech – O store of priceless worth!
> Echoes from pole to pole;
> Yes! hearts that glow not as they should
> For all your martial pride,
> With love and wonder are subdued
> At Milton's, Shakespeare's side! (p. 12)

will readily concede that the progress made by a people in that speech is no equivocal sign of advancement. That her children are able to sing in sincere imitation of the songs of the Great Motherland of the Empire – sing steeped in English thought and English diction – is a fact upon which England may well smile with maternal satisfaction, gladdened in spirit. Hence the thought in the prefatory ode:

> Sea-strong is sea girded England,
> Sea-strong the throne and the sceptre,
> And far as the foam froths her shadow is flung
> And queen of the waves in songs she is sung,
> But stronger the tie of her conquering tongue: –

and the thought is carried further and completed in the last two lines of the stanza where the above occur.

This purpose of the book is carried out in the harmonious distribution of the compositions of the natives of Ceylon, who form more than half the number of writers, throughout the book interspersing them with the productions of some of the most gifted and respected Europeans in the island. Such an arrangement has been considered sufficient for the purposes of honest and unprejudiced comparison, in preference to any other plan of grouping, especially one that might suggest fanciful contrasts.

[...]

---

55 The Royal Diamond Jubilee was celebrated in June 1897 to mark the sixtieth year of Queen Victoria's reign. A number of celebrations were held both in Great Britain as well as in the various British colonies and "native" poets wrote odes in English as well as in the vernaculars to mark the occasion.

...Should this *Garland of Ceylon Verse*, the first book of its kind in Ceylon be the means of awakening serious interest in the English poetry of Ceylon, of rousing dormant energies into literary activity and of prompting high and lofty efforts of creation as of criticism, the editor would have cause to be more than thankful. So contented in the hope he leaves to other and abler hands the production of fuller and more exhaustive collections – let other hands cull other flowers, and other fingers weave another Garland!

An Appeal

"Tu regere imperio populos, Romane, memento;
Hae tibi erunt artes, pacisque inponere morem,
Parcere subjectis, et debellare suerbos." – Vergil.

Poet and Statesman, patriot hearts
    That love old England's might,
Why trust ye but in warlike arts
    To keep her honour bright?
Why trust alone in swords and guns,
    And fleets of matchless power?
Who doubts the valour of her sons
    In England's darkest hour?

Her banners wave o'er all the earth,
    Myriads her laws control;
Her speech – O store of priceless worth!
    Echoes from pole to pole.
Yes! hearts that glow not as they should
    For all your martial pride,
With love and wonder are subdued
    At Milton's, Shakespeare's side.

Herald of Freedom! Where her voice
    Breathes, let the air be free.
Whate'er she gives – this her first choice
    The gift of Liberty!
To raise the fallen, not oppress;
    To train, not crush, the shoot
That raised from generous seed may bless
    The giver with rich fruit.

Or, Time her glorious work may mar,
    Her realms to nought be hurl'd,
When the great storm that broods afar
    Bursts on a frenzied world.

>   Will she abandon, in her need,
>   Her own from sea to sea?
>   Or proudly watch them fight and bleed
>   Beside her, loyally?

1890.   Bel.

Kaiser-i-Hind[56]

>   Kaisar-i-Hind! in name and power!
>   'Twas but today, with noiseless tread,
>   The great White Bear from out the North[57]
>   Approached thy distant empire. In that hour
>   A million gleaming swords leaped forth
>   Flashing defiance. Fat the tidings spread.
>   And from thine universal Empire rose, O Queen,
>   A swelling flood of pure devotion, loyal love,
>   Like the impetuous flood of Indus old,
>   That breaks his puny barriers, vainly bold,
>   And rolls resistless to the sea,
>   So our long-waiting hearts have leaped to prove
>   Ev'n to the death our loyalty,
>   Till German, Frank, and Muscovite had seen
>   Thine Indian Empire owns but thee,
>   Kaiser-i-Hind!
>
>   From those eternal Walls of Snow,[58]
>   Unto the incense-breathing hills
>   Of sweet Ceylon;
>   From where the sacred streams[59] of Ganges flow,
>   To where the branching Indus fills
>   Her plains thus fertile; from Nepaul[60];
>   From pleasant Kashmir's happy vales;
>   From Rajputana's rocky steeps; – there fails

---

56 Kaiser-i-Hind: emperor of India.
57 "White Bear from out the North": Russia, which was engaged in the "Great Game" with Great Britain for control of Central Asia during the nineteenth century.
58 [Editor's Note: Eternal walls of snow. – The snow clad Himalayas.]
59 [Editor's Note: Sacred streams. – The Ganges and its tributaries are sacred to the Sivites. It is a meritorious act to throw the ashes of the creamed dead into the Ganges. The sacred town of Benares is on the Ganges.]
60 Nepaul: Nepal.

No sign of glad allegiance. All
    Breathe the same stedfast spirit. Thou hast won
Our hearts' true love, O Empress-Mother, noble Queen!
    And on this day,
This proud, Imperial day, on which we see
Thy long-desired Jubilee,[61] –
    O earnestly we pray
That the same god, Who shelters us and thee,
The One True God, Whose shining face appears
Above the midst of struggling creeds; Who hears
Alike our various prayers; – that He
May make most glad thy Jubilee!
May keep thee safe from every shade of ill,
May with His own right hand sustain thee still;
Give thee long, happy years of earthly life
I reserve thy realms from foreign foe and civil strife,
Call thee unto His Kingdom at the last.

1887.   Bel.

Sunset in Ceylon[62]

Motionless masses of cloud
    Eastern mountains encumber
Heavy and indolent bowed,
    Purple curtained in slumber.
As ground in the glacier's track,
    Where ice as a land enfolded,
Shaped as a sheep's broad back
    Rocks are modelled and moulded
So, fashioned by sun and by wind,
    Born of a day that decreases,
High over them floats light-lined
    A field of feathery fleeces.
Beyond to the Southward gleams
    The tranquil, tropical glory,
Hardly imagined in dreams,
    Not to be uttered in story,
Unsung by a liver mouth,
    By lyric or lay unacquainted,

---

61 Queen Victoria's Golden Jubilee in 1887.
62 Ceylon: Sri Lanka.

The splendid sheen of the south,
    Ineffable, not to be painted,
To be mixed with the soul by the sight –
    This kingdom of colour and gladness,
This marvel of glorious light,
    A dole to the earth for its sadness.
And shafts of delicate green
    Pure as the depths of a fountain,
Or as in the dawn far-seen
    The dew-clad heights of a mountain,
Green that changes to gold,
    Softly, silently changing,
With courses of colour untold,
    Westward wreathing and ranging.

[…]

1892.   Hippograf.

Rondeau

By Kandy Lake[63]

Oh placid lake! I, standing nigh,
Scarce can preserve an undimmed eye,
    So deep thy beauty. On thy marge
    The bamboo shyly bends. At large,
Unchecked, the gracile herons fly
Swift skimming o'er thy mimic sky
Of blue intense. Bright cloudlets lie
    Athwart the bows of yon brown lurking barge,
    Oh placid Lake!

Thy hills around keep ward on high,
Meseems they say, "On us rely
"O turquoise rare – our sacred charge;
    "We shall present a stubborn targe
    "And all thy jealous foes defy,
    Oh placid Lake!"

1896.   J.H.S.

---

63 Kandy Lake: man-made lake commissioned by the Sinhalese king during the early nineteenth century and located in the city of Kandy in what is modern-day central Sri Lanka.

Bibliography

Primary Sources and Anthologies

Āchārya, Śrî Ânanda. *Snow-birds*. London: Macmillan & Co., 1919.
Aiyar, M.V. Venkatasubba. *Ventures in Verse*. Madras: Srinivasa Varadhachari, 1899.
Aiyer, C. Lakshminarayana. *Poems*. Tinnevelly, India: Nurul Islam Press, 1914.
Aiyer, C. S. Ramamritam. *Sudha veera Charitram: A Biographical Epic on Dewan Bahadur R. Ragoonatha Rao, The Grand Old Man of Southern India*. Kumbakonam, India: Aryan Press, 1907.
Ali, Ahmed, ed. *The Golden Tradition: An Anthology of Urdu Poetry*. New York: Columbia University Press, 1973.
Bhushan, V. N., ed. *The Peacock Lute: Anthology of Poems in English by Indian Writers*. Bombay: Padma Publications, 1945.
Binyon, Laurence, Stephen Philips, Arthur S. Cripps and Manmohan Ghose. *Primavera*. London: B. H. Blackwell, 1890.
Bose, Bipin Bihari. *Congress Songs and Ballads*. Lucknow, India: Sukh Sambad Press, 1901.
Bose, Charu Chandra. *A Voice from Bengal: Welcome Address to Their Majesties Landed in India*. Calcutta: The Herald Printing Works, 1912.
Chattopadhyay, Harindranath. *The Feast of Youth*. Madras: Theosophical Publishing House, 1918.
———. *The Coloured Garden*. Madras: Society for the Promotion of National Education, 1919.
Dastur, Jamasp Phiroza. *The Temple of Justice [a poem in praise of justice]*. Bombay: J. P. Dastur, 1916.
Datta, Michael Madhusudan. *The Slaying of Meghanada, A Ramayana from Colonial Bengal*, trans. Clinton B. Seely. Oxford: Oxford University Press, 2004.
Datta, Roby. *Echoes from East and West, to which are added stray notes of mine own*. Cambridge: Galloway and Porter, 1909.
Derozio, Henry Louis Vivian. *Poems*. Calcutta: H. L.V. Derozio, 1827.
———. *The Fakeer of Jungheera, A Metrical Tale, and Other Poems*. Calcutta: S. Smith & Co., 1828.
———. *Derozio, Poet of India: The Definitive Edition*, ed. Rosinka Chaudhuri. New Delhi: Oxford University Press, 2008.
De Souza, Eunice., ed. *Early Indian Poetry in English, an Anthology: 1829–1947*. New Delhi: Oxford University Press, 2005.
Dey, Lala Prasanna Kumar. *Indian Bouquet*. Calcutta: n. p., 1906.
Dinakara, M. *A Ballad of the Boer War, Written for the Day of the Coronation of Their Most Gracious Majesties the King Emperor Edward VII and Queen Alexandra in Celebration of the Prowess of the British Army*. Ramnad: Lakshmi Vilas, 1902.
Dubash, Peshoton Sorabji Goolbai. *Rationalistic and Other Poems*. London: British Bardic Brotherhood, 1917.
Dunn, Theodore Douglas, ed. *India in Song: Eastern Themes in English Verse by British and Indian Poets*. Bombay: Humphrey Milford, 1918.
Dutt, Babu S. C. [Shoshee Chunder]. *Last Moments of Pratapa*. Lahore: Arorbans Press, 1893.
Dutt, Gooroo Churn. *School Hours, or Poems Composed at School*. Calcutta: Gooroo Churn Dutt, 1839.
———. *The Loyal Hours, Being a Couple of Poems to Welcome Their Royal Highnesses the Prince of Wales and the Duke of Edinburgh…* Calcutta: Gooroo Churn Dutt, 1876.
Dutt, Govin Chunder, et al. *The Dutt Family Album*. London: Longmans, Green, & Co., 1870.
Dutt, Greece Chunder. *Cherry Stones*. Calcutta: P. S. D'Rozario, 1879.
———. *Cherry Blossoms*. London: T. Fisher Unwin, 1887.
Dutt, Michael Madhusudan. *The Captive Ladie: A Fragment of an Indian Tale*. Madras: M. M. Dutt, 1849.
Dutt, Ramkinoo. *Songs with Native Tunes of Different Sorts and Dances*. Calcutta: Babu Ramkinoo Dutt, 1864.

———.·*Manipure Tragedy*. Chittagong: Chandrasekhar Press, 1893.
Dutt, Romesh Chunder. *Lays of Ancient India: Selections from Indian Poetry Rendered into English Verse*. London: Kegan Paul, Trench, Trübner, & Co., 1894.
———. *Reminiscences of a Workman's Life*. Calcutta: Elm Press, 1896.
———, trans. *Ramayana: the Epic of Rama, Prince of India, Condensed into English Verse*. London: J. M. Dent and Co., 1899.
———, trans. *Maha-Bharata: Epic of the Bharatas, Condensed into English Verse*. 1898. Allahabad, India: Kitabistan, 1944.
Dutt, Shoshee Chunder. *Miscellaneous Verses*. Calcutta: S. C. Dutt, 1848.
———. *A Vision of Sumeru, and Other Poems*. Calcutta: Thacker, Spink, 1878.
Dutt, Toru. *A Sheaf Gleaned in French Fields*. London: C. K. Paul & Co., 1880.
———. *Ancient Ballads and Legends of Hindustan*, introduced by Edmund Gosse. London: K. Paul, Trench & Co., 1882.
———. *Collected Prose and Poetry of Toru Dutt*, ed. Chandani Lokuge. New Delhi: Oxford University Press, 2006.
Ghose, Aurobindo. *Songs to Myrtilla and other poems*. Baroda: Laxmi Villa Printing Press, 1895.
———. *Baji Prabhou, a poem*. Pondicherry: Arya Office, 1922.
Ghose, Manmohan. *Love-Songs and Elegies*. London: Elkin, 1898.
———. *Songs of Love and Death*. Oxford: Basil H. Blackwell, 1926.
Gibson, Mary Ellis, ed. *Anglophone Poetry in Colonial India, 1780–1913: A Critical Anthology*. Athens, OH: Ohio University Press, 2011.
Gokak, V. K., ed. *The Golden Treasury of Indo-Anglian Poetry 1828–1965*. New Delhi: Sahitya Akademi, 1970.
Goodwin, Gwendoline, ed. *Anthology of Modern Indian Poetry*. London: John Murray, 1927.
Gour, Hari Sing. *Stepping Westward and Other Poems*. London: Simpkin, Marshall and Co., 1890.
Hussain, A. S. H. *Loyal Leaves*. Calcutta: S. M. Hossain, 1911.
———. *The Voice of Islam and other poems*. Calcutta: B. M. Dutt, 1914.
Jung, Nizamat. *Poems*, ed. Zahir Ahmed. Hyderabad: Sir Nizamat Jung Memorial Library, Madina Mansion, 1954.
Kabraji, Fredoon, ed. *This Strange Adventure: An anthology of poems in English by Indians*. London: New India Pub. Co., 1946.
Khan, Hamid Ali. *A Farewell to London: The Story of the Slave and the Nose-Ring*, 2nd ed. London: W. Whiteley, 1885.
Khabardar, Ardeshir Framji. *The Silken Tassel*. Madras: Theosophical Publishing House, 1918.
Kochak, Tej Shankar. *Oriental Welcome to Their Most Gracious Majesties the King-Emperor and the Queen-Empress*. Cawnpore: T. S. Kochak, 1911.
Kunte, Madhavarava M. *The Risi: A Poem Explaining the Daily Life and Manners of the Risi as Described in the Rig-Veda-Sanhitâ*. Poona, India: M. M. Kunte, 1890.
Lal, P. ed. *Modern Indian Poetry in English: An Anthology and a Credo*. Calcutta: Writer's Workshop, 1969.
Lal, Sushila Harkishen. *Stray Thoughts*. Lahore: n. p., 1918.
Lall, Avadh Behari. *The Irish Home Rule Bill, a poetical pamphlet*. Calcutta: I. C. Bose & Co., 1893.
———. *An Elegy on the Late Right Hon'ble William Ewart Gladstone, M. P.* Calcutta: Avadh Behari Lall, 1898.
———. *Behar, and other poems*. Calcutta: Avadh Behari Lall, 1898.
Malabari, Behramji Merwanji. *The Indian Muse in English Garb*. Bombay: "Reporters" Press by Merwanjee Nowrojee Daboo, 1876.
Mangiah, J. *Indian National Odes with an Apology of Poesy*. Madras: Ananda Steam Press, 1906.
———.·*To Gurukul*. Madras: Addison & Co., 1911.
Naidu, C. R. Doraswami. *Heart Buds, poems*. Ahmedabad: C. R. Doraswami Naidu, 1914.
Naidu, Sarojini. *The Golden Threshold*, introduced by Arthur Symons. London: Heinemann, 1905.

———. *The Bird of Time: Songs of Life, Death and the Spring*, introduced by Edmund Gosse. London: W. Heinemann, 1912.
———. *The Broken Wing: Songs of Love, Death & Destiny, 1915–1916*. London: W. Heinemann, 1917.
———. *Sarojini Naidu: Selected letters, 1890s to 1940s*, ed. Makarand Paranjpe. New Delhi: Kali for Women, 1996.
Pai, Nagesh Wishwanath. *The Angel of Misfortune: A Fairy Tale*. Bombay: W. N. Mulgaokar & Co., 1903.
Pandiya, R. Sivasankara. *The Empress of India and Other Poems*, 2nd ed. Madras: Tawker Sadananda, 1888.
Paranjape, Makarand, ed. *Indian Poetry in English*. Madras: Macmillan India, 1993.
Paymaster, Rustam B. *Navroziana, or The Dawn of a New Era: Being Poems on Mr. Dadabhai Naoroji and Other Friends of India, with "The Voice of the East on the Great War"*, foreword by Sir Narayen G. Chandavarkar. Bombay: R. B. Paymaster, 1917.
Ramakrishna, T. *Life in an Indian Village*, introduced by Sir M. E. Grant Duff. London: T. Fisher Unwin, 1891.
———. *Tales of Ind, and other poems*, 2nd ed. London: T. Fisher Unwin, 1896.
———. *My Visit to the West*, introduced by Sir Andrew H. L. Fraser. London: T. Fisher Unwin, 1915.
Ramanujan, C. R. *The Ode on White Lotus Day.—An ode written in honour of the anniversary of the death of Madame Blavatsky, the founder of the Theosophical Society*. Nagpur: C. R. Ramanujan, 1910.
Row, Chilkur C. S. Narsimha. *The Poetical Works of Chilkur C. S. Nar Simha Row*. Cocanada, India: Chilkur C. S. Narsimha Rao, 1911.
Roy, Dejen L. *The Lyrics of Ind*. London: Trübner & Co., 1886.
Saklatvala, S. D. *An Appeal for Peaces, some verses*. Bombay: Times Press, 1910.
Satthianadhan, Krupabai. *The Miscellaneous Writings of Krupabai Satthianadhan*. Madras: Srinivasa Varadachari, 1896.
Seshadri, P. *Bilhana: An Indian Romance Adapted from Sanskrit*. Madras: Srinivasa Varadachari, 1914.
———. *Sonnets*. Madras: Srinivasa Varadachari, 1914.
———. *Champak Leaves*. Madras: Ganesh & Co., 1919.
———. *Anglo-Indian Poetry*. Benares: Indian Bookshop, 1928.
Shafi, Mian Muhammad. *Poems*. Lahore: Mercantile Press, 1907.
Sharma, Ram. *The Last Day: A Poem*. Calcutta: Indian Echo Press, 1886.
———. *The Poetical Works of Ram Sharma*, ed. Debendra Chandra Mullick. Calcutta: P. N. Mallick, 1919.
Suhrawardy, Hasan Shahid. *Faded Leaves, a collection of poems*. London: J. M. Baxter & Co., 1910.
Tagore, Joteendro Mohun. *Flights of Fancy in Prose and Verse*. Calcutta: Rajah Comm., 1881.
Tagore, Rabindranath. *The Gardener*, trans. by author. London: Macmillan, 1913.
———. *Fruit-Gathering*, trans. by author. London: Macmillan, 1916.
Tagore, Sourindro Mohun Tagore. *English Verses Set to Hindu Music In Honor of His Royal Highness The Prince of Wales*. Calcutta: Presidency Press, 1875.
Thadani, Nanikram Vasanmal. *Krishna's Flute, and other poems*. London: Longmans, Green & Co., 1916.
———. *The Triumph of Delhi and Other Poems*. Calcutta: Rai M. C. Sarkar Bahadur, 1916.
Vesuvala, Cowasji Nowrosji. *Courting the Muse: being a Collection of Poems*. Bombay: Gopal Narayen, 1879.
Williams, H. M, ed. *Indo-Anglian Literature, 1800–1979: A Survey*. Bombay: Orient Longman, 1976.

Secondary Sources

Alexander, Meena, "Outcaste Power: Ritual Displacement and Virile Maternity in Indian Women Writers." *Journal of Commonwealth Literature* 24.1 (1989): 12–29.
Anand, Mulk Raj. *The Golden Breath: Studies in Five Poets of the New India*. London: John Murray, 1933.
Arora, Anupama. "The Nightingale's Wanderings: Sarojini Naidu in North America." *Journal of Commonwealth Literature* 44.3 (September 2009): 87–105.
Bhattacharya, Sabyasachi. *Vande Mataram: The Biography of a Song*. New Delhi: Penguin Books, 2003.

Bhushan, V. N. *The Moving Finger: Anthology of Essays in Literary and Aesthetic Criticism by Indian Writers.* Bombay: Padma Publications, 1945.
Boehmer, Elleke. "East is East and South is South: The Cases of Sarojini Naidu and Arundhati Roy." *Women: A Cultural Review* 11.1–2 (Spring–Summer 2000): 61–70.
Capwell, Charles. "Sourindro Mohun Tagore and the National Anthem Project." *Ethnomusicology* 31.3 (Autumn 1987): 407–30.
Chaudhuri, Rosinka. *Gentlemen Poets in Colonial Bengal: Emergent Nationalism and the Orientalist Project.* Calcutta: Seagull Books, 2002.
Das, Harihar. *Life and Letters of Toru Dutt.* Oxford: Oxford University Press, 1921.
Dharwadker, Vinay. "English in India and Indian Literature in English: The Early History, 1579–1834." *Comparative Literature Studies* 39.2 (2002): 93–119.
Gibson, Mary Ellis. *Indian Angles: English Verse in Colonial India from Jones to Tagore.* Athens, OH: Ohio University Press, 2011.
Gidumal, Dayaram. *The Life and Life-Work of Behramji M. Malabari.* Bombay: Education Society's Press, 1888.
Gopal, Priyamvada Gopal. *The Indian English Novel: Nation, History, and Narration.* Oxford: Oxford University Press, 2009.
Iyengar, K. R. Srinivasa. *Indo-Anglian Literature.* Bombay: P. E. N. Books, 1943.
———. *The Indian Contribution to English Literature.* Bombay: Karnatak Publishing House, 1945.
———. *Indian Writing in English*, 3rd ed. New Delhi: Sterling Publishers Pvt. Ltd, 1983.
Jha, Amaranatha. 'Introductory Memoir," in Toru Dutt, *Ancient Ballads and Legends of Hindustan.* Allahabad, India: Kitabistan, 1969.
Joshi, Priya. *In Another Country: Colonialism, Culture, and the English Novel in India.* New York: Columbia University Press, 2002.
Kaul, Suvir. *Poems of Nation, Anthems of Empire: English Verse in the Long Eighteenth Century.* Charlottesville: University Press of Virginia, 2000.
Khilnani, Sunil. *The Idea of India.* London: Hamish Hamilton Ltd, 1997.
King, Bruce. *Modern Indian Poetry in English*, rev. ed. New Delhi: Oxford University Press, 2001.
Knippling, Alpana Sharma. "'Sharp contrasts of all colors': The Legacy of Toru Dutt," in *Going Global: The Transnational Reception of Third World Women Writers*, ed. Amal Amireh and Lisa Suhair Majaj. New York: Garland Publishing Co., 2000.
———. "In-Between Modernity: Toru Dutt (1856–1877) from a Postcolonial Perspective," in *Women's Experience of Modernity, 1875–1945: New Voices, New Views*, ed. Ann L. Ardis and Leslie W. Lewis. Baltimore: Johns Hopkins University Press, 2003.
Krishnaswamy, N. and Lalitha Krishnaswamy, *The Story of English in India.* New Delhi: Foundation Books Pvt. Ltd, 2006.
Lootens, Tricia. "Alien Homelands: Rudyard Kipling, Toru Dutt, and the Poetry of Empire," in *The Fin-de-Siècle Poem: English Literary Culture and the 1890s*, ed. Joseph Bristow. Athens, OH: Ohio University Press, 2005.
———. "Bengal, Britain, France: The Locations and Translations of Toru Dutt." *Victorian Literature and Culture* 34 (2006): 573–90.
Mehrotra, Arvind Krishna, ed. *A History of Indian Literature in English.* London: Hurst and Company, 2003.
Mishra, L. N. *The Poetry of Sarojini Naidu.* Delhi: B. R. Publishing Corporation, 1995.
Mufti, Aamir R. "Towards a Lyric History of India." *boundary 2* 31.2 (2004): 245–74.
Mukherjee, Meenakshi. *The Twice Born Fiction: Themes and Techniques of the Indian Novel in English.* New Delhi: Heinemann, 1971.
———. "Hearing her Own Voice: Defective Acoustics in Colonial India," in *Women's Poetry, Late Romantic to Late Victorian: Gender and Genre, 1830–1900*, ed. Isobel Armstrong and Virginia Blain. New York: St. Martin's Press, 1999.

---. *The Perishable Empire: Essays on Indian Writing in English*. New Delhi: Oxford University Press, 2000.

---. "Gender and Conversion: Personal Narratives of Two Nineteenth-Century Indian Women," in *Indian Feminisms*, ed. Jasbir Jain and Avadhesh Kumar Singh. New Delhi: Creative Books, 2001.

Nair, K. R. Ramachandran. *Three Indo-Anglian Poets*. New Delhi: Sterling Publishers Private Limited, 1987.

Phillips, Natalie A. "Claiming Her Own Context(s): Strategic Singularity in the Poetry of Toru Dutt." *Nineteenth-Century Gender Studies* 3.3 (Winter 2007).

Rajyalakshmi, P. V. *The Lyric Spring (A Study of the Poetry of Sarojini Naidu)*. New Delhi: Abhinav Publications, 1977.

Ramazani, Jahan. *The Hybrid Muse: Postcolonial Poetry in English*. Chicago: University of Chicago Press, 2001.

Reddy, Sheshalatha. "The Cosmopolitan Nationalism of Sarojini Naidu, Nightingale of India." *Victorian Literature and Culture* 38.2 (September 2010): 571–89.

Rege, Josna E. *Colonial Karma: Self, Action, and Nation in the Indian English Novel*. New York: Palgrave Macmillan, 2004.

Reynolds, Matthew. *Realms of Verse 1830–1870: English Poetry in a Time of Nation-Building*. Oxford: Oxford University Press, 2001.

Roy, Parama. *Indian Traffic: Identities in Question in Colonial and Postcolonial India*. Berkeley: University of California Press, 1998.

Said, Edward. *Orientalism*. New York: Vintage Books, 1979.

---. *Culture and Imperialism*. New York: Vintage Books, 1994.

Sen, Prabodhchandra. *India's National Anthem*. Calcutta: Visva-Bharati, 1972.

Sengupta, Padmini. *Sarojini Naidu: A Biography*. New York: Asia Publishing House, 1966.

Singh, Bhupal. *A Survey of Anglo-Indian Fiction*. London: Oxford University Press, 1934.

Srivastava, Neelam. "Anthologizing the Nation: Literature Anthologies and the Idea of India." *Journal of Postcolonial Writing* 46.2 (2010): 151–63.

---. "'Pidgin English or Pigeon English?' Babus and Babuisms in Colonial and Postcolonial Fiction." *Journal of Postcolonial Writing* 43.1 (2007): 55–64.

Tharu, Susie. "Tracing Savitri's Pedigree: Victorian Racism and the Image of Women in Indo-Anglian Literature," in *Recasting Women: Essays in Colonial History*, ed. Kumkum Sangari and Sudesh Vaid. New Delhi: Kali for Women, 1989.

Trumpener, Katie. *Bardic Nationalism: The Romantic Novel and the British Empire*. Princeton: Princeton University Press, 1997.

Vanita, Ruth. "Gandhi's Tiger: Multilingual Elites, the Battle for Minds, and English Romantic Literature in Colonial India." *Postcolonial Studies* 5.1 (2002): 95–112.

Viswanathan, Gauri. *Masks of Conquest: Literary Study and British Rule in India*. New York: Columbia University Press, 1989.

Index of Titles

XXVII. Sonnet (The Nepali Peasant) 10
XXX. Sonnet (Near Goa) 11
XLVII. Sonnet (1858) 12
LIV. Sonnet (Sacoontala) 12
LXXXII. Ode on the Rishis, the Dārsanikas, and the Sannyāsins of India 412
Address to the Ganges 2
A Farewell to London 329
Anakarli 262
An Appeal for Peace, some verses [excerpts] 137
An Epistle to the Right Hon'ble Alfred Lord Tennyson, Poet-Laureate, England 24
An Indian Funeral Song 264
An Old Indian Melody 76
A Protest 102
A Sad Thing 271
A Sister's Wail 260
A Tribute to the Gallant Boers, Who Fought, and Fell, for their Country 217
Autumn-Night in a Bengal Rice-Field 32
Awake! 380
Baji Prabhou 272
Bande Mataram 90
Bilhana 237
Britannia and Mother Hind 398
Charles Stewart Parnell 132
Coronation Song 234
Dadabhai Naoroji 158
Dedication 392
Dreams 196
Empress of India and Indian Poets 200
Foreword 142
Fruit-Gathering [excerpts] 395
Gardener [excerpts] 395
Home [I stand upon the airy deck,] 28
Home [No picture from the master hand] 296
Home-Thoughts 362
How Great Britain was Regenerated and Became 'Greater Britain' 214
India 225
India to Britain 89
India to England, 1914 291
India's Vindication of Lord Ripon and her Farewell 80
Indumathi's Death 260
In Memoriam 293
In the Bush 346

Jahangir and the Little Children 257
Last Moments of Pratapa 168
Lines on India 29
Lines on Ireland [Sweet Erin! on thy emerald hills] 30
Lines on Ireland [After six hundred years did Fate intend] 132
Lines (Written while on a Visit to Kalighat) 297
London 362
Lord Hardinge 160
Lord Tennyson 352
Madras 300
Madras or Rome, where's thy home? 220
Moonlight on the River 17
"Mother and Mother-Country are more estimable than Heaven itself" 173
Mr. Dadabhai Naoroji, An Ode of Welcome 153
Mr. Dadabhai Naoroji, On His 79th Birthday 155
My Native Land 6
Nightfall in the City of Hyderabad 378
O Coil, Coil 131
Ode for her Imperial Majesty Queen Victoria's Golden Jubilee 42
Ode on the Meeting of the Congress at Allahabad on the 26th December 1888 85
Ode, The Awakening of the East 285
Ode to H. H. The Nizam of Hyderabad 378
On Entering the Kashmere Valley 185
On the admission of Indians to the British Army 292
On the Centenary of the Presidency College 366
On the Day of Lord Ripon's Departure from Calcutta 349
On the Occasion of Queen Victoria's Diamond Jubilee 185
On Tibet 390
Oriental Welcome to Their Most Gracious Majesties the King-Emperor and the Queen-Empress [excerpts] 193
Piyadasi 389
Pride 270
Queen Tissarakshita's Jealousy 258

Ravana's Doom 207
Recital of the Ramayana 369
Recollections of Childhood 203
Romesh Chunder Dutt 256
Saraswati with the Lotus 136
Savitri 302
Seeta and Rama, A Tale of the Indian Famine 352
Sita [Three happy children in a darkened room!] 328
Sita [For vest of vair,] 350
Social Intercourse between Europeans and Natives 205
Song 15
Song of Britannia 363
Song of the Indian Conservative 75
Sonnet: Bombay Harbour 130
Sonnets, I. Faith 207
Sonnets—India 9
Sonnet to India 17
Sonnet to the Kokil 14
Stepping Westward, or Emigrants to the West 371
Sufi Worship 269
Svami Vivekananda at Chicago 40
Swinburne 394
The Anglo-Indian War-Cry, or Bluster in Excelsis 78
The British Character 101
The Coloured Country 269
The Congress-man's Confession 175
The Dewallee, or The Feast of Light 16
"The dream of my youth" H. R. H. the Prince of Wales 94
The Exile [It is the sunny April, –] 27
The Exile [That classic land of bulbul and the rose] 261
The Exile [Sleep, sweet sleep, O not so soon forsake me,] 357
The Fair Martyrs 387
The Gathering 213
The Gift of India 381
The Gift of the Poet Laureate of India to National Education Week, 1918 266
The grand old man of India 222
The Greatest Need of India 218
The Grief of Ravan 382
The Hindu Widow's Lament 18
The Hour of Rest 268
The Imperial Coronation at Delhi 287

The Indian Maid's Lament 393
The Irish Home Rule Bill, a poetical pamphlet 19
The Island 341
The Land of the Sun 340
The Late Hon. Mr. G. K. Gokhale, C. I. E. 159
The Marquis of Ripon 255
The Neem Tree 345
The New Year, 1912 234
The Parsi New Year's Day 166
The Patriot 265
The Rajpootnee's Song 13
The Rani of Ganore 262
The Rise and Fall of Islam 187
The Sacrifice 257
The Secret of a Successful Rule 165
The Sirinagar Flood and the Dal Lake 182
The Slave and the Nose-Ring 332
The Song of the Tirhoot Planters 77
The Soonderbuns 342
The Stages of a Hindu Female Life 95
The Sworn Hero 388
The Taj Mahal 348
The Taj Mahal – Agra 148
The Temple of Justice 150
The Triumph of Delhi 62
The University of Madras 202
The Voice of Islam 47
Time of Famine 100
To a Chinar-Tree 181
To Britain 391
To Delhi 186
To His Gracious Majesty George V Emperor of India 233
To India [Eternal cradle of the muses fair!] 264
To India [O young through all thy immemorial years!] 377
To India! [Hail India! Hail! my native land!] 191
To Indian Patriots 89
To K. V. M., A Vision – Young India 148
"To my mother" 191
Toru Dutt 255
To the Land of My Birth 206
To the Lord Bhupalaswami, Srivaikuntam 233
To the Missionaries of Faith 98
To the Motherland 144

True Indian Opinion, or Native Croakers 105
Vande Mataram 221
Victoria 256
Vizagapatam 299

War 39
Welcome Address to Their Majesties landed in India 61
Widowed 258

Index of Authors

Āchārya, Śrî Ânanda 412
Aiyar, M.V. Venkatasubba 206
Aiyer, C. Lakshminarayana 233
Binyon, Laurence 443
Bose, Bipin Bihari 172
Bose, Charu Chandra 60
Chattopadhyay, Harindranath 267
Dastur, Jamasp Phiroze 150
Datta, Roby 381–2, 431
Dey, Lala Prasanna Kumar 39
Dinakara, M. 212–13
Dubash, Peshoton Sarobji Goolbai 398
Dutt, Babu S. C.: *see* Dutt, Shoshee Chunder
Dutt, Govin Chunder et al. 295
Dutt, Greece Chunder 10, 342
Dutt, Romesh Chunder 26–7, 368–9, 421
Dutt, Shoshee Chunder 1, 167
Dutt, Toru 302
Ghose, Aurobindo 130, 271–2
Ghose, Manmohan 357
Gosse, Edmund 433
Gour, Hary Singh 371
Hussain, A. S. H. 41–2
Jung, Nizamat 284
Khabardar, Ardeshir Framji 263
Khan, Hamid Ali 329, 417

Kochak, Tej Shankar [a "Georgian Brahmin"] 192–3
Lal, Sushila Harkishen 196
Lall, Avadh Behari 19, 429
Malabari, Behramji Merwanji 93, 415
Naidu, C. R. Doraswami 141
Naidu, Sarojini 377
Pandiya, R. Sivasankara 199
Paymaster, Rustam B. 153
Ramakrishna, T. (Pillai) 351
Row, Chilkur C. S. Narsimha 217
Roy, Dejen L. 339
Saklatvala, S. D. 136–7
Satthianadhan, Krupabai 203
Seshadri, P. 236–7
Shafi, Sir Mian Muhammad 180
Sharma, Ram 74
Suhrawardy, Hasan Shahid 392
Symons, Arthur 439
Tagore, Joteendro Mohun 13
Tagore, Rabindranath 266, 394
Tambyah, Isaac 452
Thadani, Nanikram Vasanmal 62
Vesuvala, Cowasji Nowrosji 104
Yeats, W. B. 448

www.ingramcontent.com/pod-product-compliance
Lightning Source LLC
Chambersburg PA
CBHW030103010526
44116CB00005B/70